NOTES

ON THE

NEW TESTAMENT

EXPLANATORY AND PRACTICAL

BY

ALBERT BARNES

ENLARGED TYPE EDITION

EDITED BY

ROBERT FREW, D.D.

WITH NUMEROUS ADDITIONAL NOTES AND A SERIES OF ENGRAVINGS

II. CORINTHIANS AND GALATIANS

BAKER BOOK HOUSE
GRAND RAPIDS 6, MICHIGAN
1949

Photo-Lithoprint Reproduction
EDWARDS BROTHERS, INC.
Lithoprinters
ANN ARBOR, MICHIGAN, U.S.A.
1949

INTRODUCTION.

§ 1. *The Design of the Second Epistle to the Corinthians.*

In the Introduction to the first Epistle to the Corinthians, the situation and character of the city of Corinth, the history of the church there, and the design which Paul had in view in writing to them at first, have been fully stated. In order to a full understanding of the design of this epistle, those facts should be borne in distinct remembrance, and the reader is referred to the statement there made as material to a correct understanding of this epistle. It was shown there that an important part of Paul's design at that time was to reprove the irregularities which existed in the church at Corinth. This he had done with great fidelity. He had not only answered the inquiries which they proposed to him, but he had gone with great particularity into an examination of the gross disorders of which he had learned by some members of the family of Chloe. A large part of the epistle, therefore, was the language of severe reproof. Paul felt its necessity; and he had employed that language with unwavering fidelity to his Master.

Yet it was natural that he should feel great solicitude in regard to the reception of that letter, and to its influence in accomplishing what he wished. That letter had been sent from Ephesus, where Paul proposed to remain until after the succeeding Pentecost (1 Cor. xvi. 8); evidently hoping by that time to hear from them, and to learn what had been the manner of the reception of his epistle. He proposed then to go to Macedonia, and from that place to go again to Corinth (1 Cor. xvi. 5—7); but he was evidently desirous to learn in what manner his first epistle had been received, and what was its effect, before he visited them. He sent Timothy and Erastus before him to Macedonia and Achaia (Acts xix. 22; 1 Cor. xvi. 10), intending that they should visit Corinth, and commissioned Timothy to regulate the disordered affairs in the church there. It would appear also that he sent Titus to the church there in order to observe the effect which his epistle would produce, and to return and report to him, 2 Cor. ii. 13; vii. 6—16. Evidently Paul felt much solicitude on the subject; and the manner in which they received his admonitions would do much to regulate his own future movements. An important case of discipline; his authority as an apostle; and the interests of religion in an important city, and in a church which he had himself founded, were all at stake. In this state of mind he himself left Ephesus, and went to Troas on his way to Macedonia, where it appears he had appointed Titus to meet him, and to report to him the manner in which his first epistle had been received; see Note on chap. ii. 13. Then his mind was greatly agitated and distressed because he did not meet Titus as he had expected, and in this state of mind he went forward to Macedonia. There he had a direct interview with Titus (chap. vii. 5, 6), and learned from him that his first epistle had accomplished all which he had desired, chap. vii. 7—16. The act of discipline which he had directed had been performed; the abuses had been in a great measure corrected, and the Corinthians had been brought to a state of true repentance for their former irregularities and disorders. The heart of Paul was greatly comforted by this intelligence, and by the signal success which had attended this effort to produce reform. In this state of mind he wrote to them this second letter.

Titus had spent some time in Corinth. He had had an opportunity of learning the views of the parties, and of ascertaining the true condition of the church. This epistle is designed to meet some of the prevailing views of the party which was opposed to him there, and to refute some of the prevailing slanders in regard to himself. The epistle, therefore, is occupied to a considerable extent in refuting the slanders which had been heaped upon him, and in vindicating his own character. This letter also he sent by the hands of Titus, by whom the former had been sent, and he designed doubtless that the presence of Titus should aid in accomplishing the objects which he had in view in the epistle; see 2 Cor. viii. 17, 18.

§ 2. *The Subjects treated of in this Epistle.*

It has been generally admitted that this epistle is written without much definite arrangement or plan. It treats on a variety of topics mainly as they occurred to the mind of the apostle at the time, and perhaps without having formed any definite arrangement before he commenced writing it. Those subjects are all important, and are all treated in the usual manner of Paul, and are all useful and interesting to the church at large; but we shall not find in this epistle the same systematic arrangement which is apparent in the epistle to the Romans, or which occurs in the first epistle to the Corinthians. Some of the subjects of which it treats are the following.

(1.) He mentions his own sufferings, and particularly his late trials in Asia. For deliverance from these trials, he expresses his gratitude to God; and states the design for which God called him to endure such trials to have been, that he might be better qualified to comfort others who might be afflicted in a similar manner. chap. i. 1—12.

(2.) He vindicates himself from one of the accusations which his enemies had brought against him, that he was unstable and fickle-minded. He had promised to visit them; and he had not yet fulfilled his promise. They took occasion, therefore, to say that he was unstable, and that he was afraid to visit them. He shows to them, in reply, the true reason why he had not come to them, and that his real object in not doing it, had been "to spare" them, chap. i. 13—24.

(3.) The case of the unhappy individual who had been guilty of incest, had deeply affected his mind. In the first epistle, he had treated of this case at large, and had directed that discipline should be exercised. He had felt deep solicitude in regard to the manner in which his commands on that subject should be received, and had judged it best not to visit them until he should be informed of the manner in which they had complied with his directions. Since they had obeyed him, and had inflicted discipline on him, he now exhorts them to forgive the unhappy man, and to receive him again to their fellowship, chap. ii. 1—11.

(4.) He mentions the deep solicitude which he had on this subject, and his disappointment when he came to Troas and did not meet with Titus as he had expected, and had not been informed as he hoped to have been of the manner in which his former epistle had been received, chap. ii. 12—17. In view of the manner in which they had received his former epistle, and of the success of his efforts, which he learned when he reached Macedonia, he gives thanks to God that all his efforts to promote the welfare of the church had been successful, chap. ii. 14—17.

(5.) Paul vindicates his character, and his claims to be regarded as an apostle. He assures them that he does not need letters of commendation to them, since they were fully acquainted with his character, chap. iii. 1—6. This subject leads him into an examination of the nature of the ministry and its importance, which he illustrates by showing the comparative obscurity of the Mosaic ministrations, and the greater dignity, and permanency of the gospel, chap. iii. 7—18.

(6.) In chaps. iv. v. he states the principles by which he was actuated in the ministry. He and the other apostles were greatly afflicted, and were subjected to great and peculiar trials, but they had also great and peculiar consolations. They were sustained with the hope of heaven, and with the assurance that there was a world of glory. They acted in view of that world, and had gone forth in view of it to entreat men to be reconciled to God.

(7.) Having referred in chap. v. to the nature and objects of the Christian ministry, he expatiates with great beauty on the temper with which he and his brethren, in the midst of great trials and afflictions, executed this important work; chap. vi. 1—10.

(8.) Having in this manner pursued a course of remark that was calculated to conciliate their regard, and to show his affection for them, he exhorts them (chap. vi. 11—18), to avoid those connections which would injure their piety, and which were inconsistent with the gospel which they professed to love. The connections to which he particularly referred were, improper marriages and ruinous alliances with idolaters, to which they were particularly exposed.

(9) In chap. vii. he again makes a transition to Titus, and to the joy which he had brought him in the intelligence which he gave of the manner in which the commands of Paul in the first epistle had been received, and of its happy effect on the minds of the Corinthians.

(10.) In chaps. viii. and ix. Paul refers to, and discusses the subject on which his heart was so much set—the collection for the poor and afflicted Christians in Judea. He had commenced the collection in Macedonia, and had boasted to them that the Corinthians would aid largely in that benevolent work, and he now sent Titus to complete it in Corinth.

(11.) In chap. x. he enters upon a vindication of himself, and of his apostolic authority against the accusation of his enemies; and pursues the subject through chap. xi. by a comparison of himself with others, and in chap. xii. by an argument directly in favour of his apostolic authority from the favours which God had bestowed on him, and the evidence which he had given of his having been commissioned by God. This subject he pursues also in various illustrations to the end of the epistle.

The *objects* of this epistle, therefore, and subjects discussed, are various. They are, to show his deep interest in their welfare—to express his gratitude that his former letter had been so well received, and had so effectually accomplished what he wished to accomplish—to carry forward the work of reformation among them which had been so auspiciously commenced—to vindicate his authority as an apostle from the objections which he had learned through Titus they had continued to make—to secure the collection for the poor saints in Judea, on which his heart had been so much set—and to assure them of his intention to come and visit them according to his repeated promises. The epistle is substantially of the same character as the first. It was written to a church where great dissensions and other evils prevailed; it was designed to promote a reformation; and is a model of the manner in which evils are to be corrected in a church. In connection with the first epistle, it shows the manner in which offenders in the church are to be dealt with, and the spirit and design with which the work of discipline should be entered on and pursued. Though these were local evils, yet great principles are involved here, of use to the church in all ages; and to these epistles the church must refer at all times, as an illustration of the proper manner of administering discipline, and of silencing the calumnies of enemies.

§ 3. *The time and place in which the Epistle was written.*

It is manifest that this epistle was written from Macedonia (see chap. viii. 1—14, and ix. 2), and was sent by Titus to the church at Corinth. If so, it was written probably about a year after the former epistle. Paul was on his way to Corinth, and was expecting to go there soon. He had left Ephesus, where he was when he wrote the first epistle, and had gone to Troas, and from thence to Macedonia, where he had met with Titus, and had from him learned what was the effect of his first epistle. In the overflowing of his heart with gratitude for the success of that letter, and with a desire to carry forward the work of reformation in the church, and completely to remove all the objections which had been made to his apostolic authority, and to prepare for his own welcome reception when he went there, he wrote this letter—a letter which we cannot doubt was as kindly received as the former, and which like that accomplished the objects which he had in view.

THE RUINS OF CESAREA.

CORINTH, FROM THE NORTH.

THE SECOND

EPISTLE TO THE CORINTHIANS.

CHAPTER I.

PAUL, an apostle [a] of Jesus Christ by the will of God, and Timothy *our* brother, untc the church of God which is at

a 1 & 2 Tim.1.1.

CHAPTER I.

This chapter consists of the following parts, or subjects :

1. The usual salutation and benediction in the introduction of the epistle, ver. 1. 2. This is found in all the epistles of Paul, and was at once an affectionate salutation and an appropriate expression of his interest in their welfare, and also an appropriate mode of commencing an address to them by one who claimed to be inspired and sent from God.

2. He refers to the consolation which he had had in his heavy trials, and praises God for that consolation, and declares that the reason for which he was comforted was, that he might be qualified to administer consolation to others in the same or in similar circumstances, ver. 3—7.

3. He informs them of the heavy trials which he was called to experience when he was in Ephesus, and of his merciful deliverance from those trials, ver. 8—12. He had been exposed to death, and had despaired of life, (ver. 8, 9) ; yet he had been delivered (ver. 10) ; he desired them to unite with him in thanksgiving on account of it (ver. 11) ; and in all this he had endeavoured to keep a good conscience, and *had* that testimony that he had endeavoured to maintain such a conscience toward all, and especially toward them, ver. 12.

4. He refers to the design which he had in writing the former letter to them, ver, 13. 14. He had written to them only such things as they admitted to be true and proper ; and such as he was persuaded they would always admit. They had always received his instructions favourably and kindly ; and he had always sought their welfare.

5. In this state of mind, Paul had designed to have paid them a second visit, ver. 15, 16. But he had not done it yet, and it appears that his enemies had taken occasion from this to say that he was inconstant and fickle-minded. He, therefore, takes occasion to vindicate himself, and to convince them that he was not faithless to his word and purposes, and to show them the true reason why he had not visited them, ver. 17—24. He states, therefore, that his real intentions had been to visit them (ver. 15, 16) ; that his failure to do so had not proceeded from either levity or falsehood (ver. 17) ; as they might have known from the uniform doctrine which he had taught them, in which he had inculcated the necessity of a strict adherence to promises, from the veracity of Jesus Christ his great example (ver. 18—20) ; and from the fact that God had given to him the Holy Spirit, and anointed him (ver. 21, 22); and he states, therefore, that the true reason why he had not come to them was, that he wished to spare them (ver. 23, 24) ; he was willing to remain away from them until they should have time to correct the evils which existed in their church, and prevent the necessity of severe discipline when he should come.

1. *Paul an apostle, &c.*; see Notes on Rom. i. 1, and 1 Cor. i. 1. ¶ *By the will of God.* Through, or agreeably to the will of God; Note, 1 Cor. i. 1. ¶ *And Timothy* our *brother.* Paul was accustomed to associate some other person or persons with

Corinth, with all the saints [a] which are in all Achaia:

2 Grace [b] *be* to you, and peace, from God our Father, and *from* the Lord Jesus Christ.

3 Blessed [c] *be* God, even the Father of our Lord Jesus Christ, the Father of mercies, and the God of all comfort;

a Ph.1.1 b Rom.1.7. c Ep.1.3.

him in writing his epistles. Thus in the first epistle to the Corinthians, Sosthenes was associated with him. For the reasons of this, see Note on 1 Cor. i. 1. The name of Timothy is associated with his in the epistles to the Philippians and Colossians. From the former epistle to the Corinthians (chap. xvi. 10), we learn that Paul had sent Timothy to the church at Corinth, or that he expected that he would visit them. Paul had sent him into Macedonia in company with Erastus (Acts xix. 21, 22), intending himself to follow them, and expecting that they would visit Achaia. From the passage before us, it appears that Timothy had returned from this expedition, and was now with Paul. The reason why Paul joined Timothy with him in writing this epistle may have been the following: (1.) Timothy had been recently with them, and they had become acquainted with him, and it was not only natural that he should express his friendly salutations, but his name and influence among them might serve in some degree to confirm what Paul wished to say to them; comp. Note, 1 Cor. i. 1. (2.) Paul may have wished to give as much influence as possible to Timothy. He designed that he should be his fellow-labourer; and as Timothy was much younger than himself, he doubtless expected that he would survive him, and that he would in some sense succeed him in the care of the churches. He was desirous, therefore, of securing for him all the authority which he could, and of letting it be known that he regarded him as abundantly qualified for the great work with which he was intrusted. (3.) The influence and name of Timothy might be supposed to have weight with the party in the church that had slandered Paul, by accusing him of insincerity or instability in regard to his purposed visit to them. Paul had designed to go to them directly from Ephesus, but he had changed his mind, and the testimony of Timothy might be important to prove that it was done from motives purely conscientious. Timothy was doubtless acquainted with the reasons; and his testimony might meet and rebut a part of the charges against him; see chap. i. ver. 13—16. ¶ *Unto the church of God*, &c.; see Note 1 Cor. i. 2. ¶ *With all the saints which are in all Achaia.* Achaia, in the largest sense, included the whole of Greece. Achaia proper, however, was the district or province of which Corinth was the capital. It comprehended the part of Greece lying between Thessaly and the southern part of the Peloponnesus, embracing the whole western part of the Peloponnesus. It is probable that there were not a few Christians scattered in Achaia, and not improbably some small churches that had been established by the labours of Paul or of others. From Rom. xvi. 1, we know that there was a church at Cenchrea, the eastern port of Corinth, and it is by no means improbable that there were other churches in that region. Paul doubtless designed that copies of this epistle should be circulated among them.

2. *Grace* be *to you*, &c. This is the usual Christian salutation; see Note, Rom. i. 7; 1 Cor. i. 3.

3. *Blessed* be *God.* This is the commencement properly of the epistle, and it is the language of a heart that is full of joy, and that bursts forth with gratitude in view of mercy. It may have been excited by the recollection that he had formerly written to them, and that during the interval which had elapsed between the time when the former epistle was written and when this was penned, he had been called to a most severe trial, and that from that trial he had been

4 Who comforteth us in all our tribulation, that we may be able to comfort them which are in any trouble, by the comfort

mercifully delivered. With a heart full of gratitude and joy for this merciful interposition, he commences this epistle. It is remarked by Doddridge, that eleven out of the thirteen epistles of Paul, begin with exclamations of praise, joy, and thanksgiving. Paul had been afflicted, but he had also been favoured with remarkable consolations, and it was not unnatural that he should allow himself to give expression to his joy and praise in view of all the mercies which God had conferred on him. This entire passage is one that is exceedingly valuable, as showing that there may be elevated joy in the midst of deep affliction, and as showing what is the reason why God visits his servants with trials. The phrase "blessed be God," is equivalent to "praised be God," or is an expression of thanksgiving. It is the usual formula of praise (comp. Eph. i. 3); and shows his entire confidence in God, and his joy in him, and his gratitude for his mercies. It is *one* of innumerable instances which show that it is possible and proper to bless God in view of the trials with which he visits his people, and of the consolations which he causes to abound. ¶ *The Father of our Lord Jesus Christ.* God is mentioned here in the relation of the "Father of the Lord Jesus," doubtless because it was through the Lord Jesus, and him alone, that He had imparted the consolation which he had experienced, ver. 5. Paul knew no other God than the "Father of the Lord Jesus;" he knew no other source of consolation than the gospel; he knew of no way in which God imparted comfort except through his Son. That is genuine Christian consolation which acknowledges the Lord Jesus as the medium by whom it is imparted; that is proper thanksgiving to God which is offered through the Redeemer; that only is the proper acknowledgment of God which recognises him as the "Father of the Lord Jesus." ¶ *The Father of mercies.* This is a Hebrew mode of expression, where a noun performs the place of an adjective, and the phrase is synonymous nearly with "merciful Father." The expression has however somewhat more energy and spirit than the simple phrase "merciful Father." The Hebrews used the word *father* often to denote the author, or source of any thing; and the idea in phraseology like this is, that mercy proceeds from God, that he is the source of it, and that it is his nature to impart mercy and compassion, as if he *originated* it; or was the source and fountain of it—sustaining a relation to all true consolation analogous to that which a father sustains to his offspring. God has the *paternity* of all true joy. It is one of his peculiar and glorious attributes that he thus *produces* consolation and mercy. ¶ *And the God of all comfort.* The source of all consolation. Paul delighted, as all should do, to trace *all* his comforts to God; and Paul, as all Christians have, had sufficient reason to regard God as the source of true consolation. There is no other real source of happiness but God; and he is able abundantly, and willing to impart consolation to his people.

4. *Who comforteth us.* Paul here doubtless refers primarily to himself and his fellow apostles as having been filled with comfort in their trials; to the support which the promises of God gave; to the influences of the Holy Spirit, the Comforter; and to the hopes of eternal life through the gospel of the Redeemer. ¶ *That we may be able to comfort,* &c. Paul does not say that this was the *only* design which God had in comforting them that they might be able to impart comfort to others; but he does say that this is an important and main purpose. It is an object which he seeks, that his people in their afflictions should be supported and comforted; and for this purpose he fills the hearts of his ministers with consolation; gives them personal experience of the sustaining power of grace in their trials; and enables them to

wherewith we ourselves are comforted of God.

5 For as the sufferings [a] of Christ abound in us, so our consolation also aboundeth by Christ.

6 And whether we be afflicted, *it is* for [b] your consolation and salvation, which is [1] effectual in the enduring of the same sufferings, which we also suffer; or whether we be comforted, *it is*

a Col.1.24. *b* chap.4.15. 1 Or, *wrought.*

speak of what they have felt in regard to the consolations of the gospel of the Lord Jesus. ¶ *By the comfort,* &c. By the same topics of consolation; by the same sources of joy which have sustained us. They would have experience; and by that experience they would be able to minister consolation to those who were in any manner afflicted. It is only by personal experience that we are able to impart consolation to others. Paul refers here undoubtedly to the consolations which are produced by the evidence of the pardon of sin, and of acceptance with God, and the hope of eternal life. These consolations abounded in him and his fellow apostles richly; and sustained by them he was able also to impart like consolation to others who were in similar circumstances of trial.

5. *For as the sufferings of Christ abound in us.* As we are called to experience the same sufferings which Christ endured; as we are called to suffer in his cause, and in the promotion of the same object. The sufferings which they endured were in the cause of Christ and his gospel; were endured in endeavouring to advance the same object which Christ sought to promote; and were substantially of the same nature. They arose from opposition, contempt, persecution, trial, and want, and were the same as the Lord Jesus was himself subjected to during the whole of his public life; comp. Col. i. 24. Thus Peter says (1 Pet. iv. 13) of Christians that they were "partakers of Christ's sufferings." ¶ *So our consolation also aboundeth by Christ.* By means of Christ, or through Christ, consolation is abundantly imparted to us. Paul regarded the Lord Jesus as the source of consolation, and felt that the comfort which *he* imparted, or which was imparted through him, was more than sufficient to overbalance all the trials which he endured in his cause. The comforts which he derived from Christ were those, doubtless, which arose from his presence, his supporting grace, from his love shed abroad in the heart; from the success which he gave to his gospel, and from the hope of reward which was held out to him by the Redeemer, as the result of all his sufferings. And it may be observed as an universal truth, that if we suffer in the cause of Christ, if we are persecuted, oppressed, and calumniated on his account, he will take care that our hearts shall be filled with consolation.

6. *And whether we be afflicted.* If we are afflicted; or, our affliction is for this purpose. This verse is designed to show one of the reasons of the sufferings which the apostles had endured; and it is a happy specimen of Paul's skill in his epistles. He shows that all his trials were for their welfare and would turn to their benefit. He suffered that they might be comforted; he was afflicted for their advantage. This assurance would tend to conciliate their favour, and strengthen their affection for him, as it would show them that he was disinterested. We are under the deepest obligations of gratitude to one who suffers for us; and there is nothing that will bind us more tenderly to any one than the fact that he has been subjected to great calamity and trial on our account. This is *one* of the reasons why the Christian feels so tenderly his obligation to the Lord Jesus Christ. ¶ It is *for your consolation and salvation.* It will be *useful* for your consolation; or it is endured in order to secure your comfort, and promote your salvation. Paul had suffered in Ephesus, and it

9 But we had the [1] sentence
of death in ourselves, that we
should not trust [a] in ourselves,
but in God which raiseth the
dead:
10 Who delivered [b] us from so

1 Or, *answer*. a Jer.17.5,7. b 2 Pet.2.9.

in ourselves. Marg. "answer." The word rendered "sentence" (ἀπόκριμα) means properly an answer, judicial response, or sentence; and is here synonymous with *verdict.* It means that Paul felt that he was condemned to die; that he felt as if he were under sentence of death and with no hope of acquittal; he was called to contemplate the hour of death as just before him. The words "in ourselves," mean, against ourselves; or, we expected certainly to die. This seems as if he had been condemned to die, and may either refer to some instance when the popular fury was so great that he felt it was determined he should die; or more probably to a judicial sentence that he should be cast to the wild beasts, with the certain expectation that he would be destroyed, as was always the case with those who were subjected to the execution of such a sentence. ¶ *That we should not trust in ourselves.* This is an exceedingly beautiful and important sentiment. It teaches that in the time to which Paul refers, he was in so great danger, and had so certain a prospect of death, that he could put no reliance on himself. He felt that he must die; and that human aid was vain. According to every probability he would die; and all that he could do was to cast himself on the protection of that God who had power to save him even then, if he chose, and who, if he did it, would exert power similar to that which is put forth when the dead are raised. The *effect*, therefore, of the near prospect of death was to lead him to put increased confidence in God. He felt that God only could save him; or that God only could sustain him if he should die. Perhaps also he means to say that the effect of this was to lead him to put increased confidence in God *after* his deliverance; not to trust in his own plans, or to confide in his own strength; but to feel that all that he had was entirely in the hands of God. This is a common, and a happy effect of the near prospect of death to a Christian; and it is well to contemplate the effect on such a mind as that of Paul in the near prospect of dying, and to see how instinctively then it clings to God. A true Christian in such circumstances will rush to *His* arms and feel that there he is safe. ¶ *But in God which raiseth the dead.* Intimating that a rescue in such circumstances would be like raising the dead. It is probable that on this occasion Paul was near dying; that he had given up all hope of life—perhaps, as at Lystra (Acts xiv. 19), he was supposed to be dead. He felt, therefore, that he was raised up by the immediate power of God, and regarded it as an exertion of the same power by which the dead are raised. Paul means to intimate that so far as depended on any power of his own, he was dead. He had no power to recover himself, and but for the gracious interposition of God he would have died.

10. *Who delivered us from so great a death.* From a death so terrible, and from a prospect so alarming. It is intimated here by the word which Paul uses, that the death which he apprehended was one of a character peculiarly terrific—probably a death by wild beasts; Note, ver. 8. He was near to death; he had no hope of rescue; and the manner of the death which was threatened was peculiarly frightful. Paul regarded rescue from such a death as a kind of *resurrection;* and felt that he owed his life to God *as if* he had raised him from the dead. All deliverance from imminent peril, and from dangerous sickness, whether of ourselves or our friends, should be regarded as a kind of resurrection from the dead. God could with infinite ease have taken away our breath, and it is only by his merciful interposition that we live. ¶ *And doth deliver.* Continues yet to deliver us; or preserve us—intimating perhaps that danger had continued to follow him

great a death, and doth deliver: in whom we trust that he will yet deliver *us;*

11 Ye also helping *a* together by prayer for us, that for the gift *bestowed* upon us by the

a Rom.15.30; Phil.1.19; James 5 16—18.

after the signal deliverance to which he particularly refers, and that he had continued to be in similar peril of his life. Paul was daily exposed to danger; and was constantly preserved by the good providence of God. In what manner he was rescued from the peril to which he was exposed he has no where intimated. It is implied, however, that it was by a remarkable divine interposition; but whether by miracle, or by the ordinary course of providence, he no where intimates. Whatever was the mode, however, Paul regarded *God* as the source of the deliverance, and felt that his obligations were due to him as his kind Preserver. ¶ *In whom we trust that he will yet deliver* us. That he will continue to preserve us. We hope; we are accustomed to cherish the expectation that he will continue to defend us in the perils which we shall yet encounter. Paul felt that he was still exposed to danger. Everywhere he was liable to be persecuted (comp. Note, Acts xx. 23), and everywhere he felt that his life was in peril. Yet he had been thus far preserved in a most remarkable manner; and he felt assured that God would continue to interpose in his behalf, until his great purpose in regard to him should be fully accomplished, so that at the close of life he could look to God as his Deliverer, and feel that all along his perilous journey he had been his great Protector.

11. *Ye also helping together by prayer for us.* Tindal renders this in connection with the close of the previous verse; "we trust that yet hereafter he will deliver us, by the help of your prayer for us." The word rendered "helping together," means co-operating, aiding, assisting; and the idea is, that Paul felt that his trials might be turned to good account, and give occasion for thanksgiving; and that this was to be accomplished by the aid of the prayers of his fellow Christians. He felt that the church was one, and that Christians should sympathize with one another. He evinced deep humility and tender regard for the Corinthians when he called on them to aid him by their prayers. Nothing would be better calculated to excite their tender affection and regard than thus to call on them to sympathize with him in his trials, and to pray that those trials might result in thanksgiving throughout the churches. ¶ *That for the gift* bestowed *upon us.* The sentence which occurs here is very perplexing in the original, and the construction is difficult. But the main idea is not difficult to be seen. The "gift" here referred to (τὸ χάρισμα) means doubtless the *favour* shown to him in his rescue from so imminent a peril; and he felt that this was owing to the prayers of many persons on his behalf He believed that he had been remembered in the petitions of his friends and fellow Christians, and that his deliverance was owing to their supplications. ¶ *By the means of many persons.* Probably meaning that the favour referred to had been imparted by means of the prayers of many individuals who had taken a deep interest in his welfare. But it may also imply perhaps that he had been directly assisted, and had been rescued from the impending danger by the interposition of many friends who had come to his relief. The usual interpretation is, however, that it was by the prayers of many in his behalf. ¶ *Thanks may be given by many on our behalf.* Many may be induced also to render thanks for my deliverance. The idea is, that as he had been delivered from great peril by the prayers of many persons, it was proper also that thanksgiving should be offered by as many in his behalf, or on account of his deliverance. "Mercies that have been obtained by prayer should be acknowledged by praise."—*Doddridge.* God had mercifully interposed in answer to the prayers of

means of many persons, thanks may be given by many on our behalf.

12 For our rejoicing is this, the testimony of our conscience, that in simplicity and godly sin-

his people; and it was proper that his mercy should be as extensively acknowledged. Paul was desirous that God should not be forgotten: and that those who had sought his deliverance should render praise to God: perhaps intimating here that those who had obtained mercies by prayer are prone to forget their obligation to return thanks to God for his gracious and merciful interposition.

12. *For our rejoicing is this.* The source or cause of our rejoicing. "I have a just cause of rejoicing, and it is, that I have endeavoured to live a life of simplicity and godly sincerity, and have not been actuated by the principles of worldly wisdom." The connection here is not very obvious, and it is not quite easy to trace it. Most expositors, as Doddridge, Locke, Macknight, Bloomfield, &c., suppose that he mentions the purity of his life as a reason why he had a right to expect their prayers, as he had requested in ver. 11. They would not doubt, it is supposed, that his life had been characterized by great simplicity and sincerity, and would feel, therefore, a deep interest in his welfare, and be disposed to render thanks that he had been preserved in the day of peril. But the whole context and the scope of the passage is rather to be taken into view. Paul had been exposed to death. He had no hope of life. *Then* the ground of his rejoicing, and of his confidence, was that he had lived a holy life. He had not been actuated by "fleshly wisdom," but he had been animated and guided by "the grace of God." His aim had been simple, his purpose holy, and he had the testimony of his conscience that his motives had been right, and he had, therefore, no concern about the result. A good conscience, a holy life through Jesus Christ, will enable a man always to look calmly on death. What has a Christian to fear in death? Paul had kept a good conscience towards all; but he says that he had special and peculiar joy that he had done it towards the Corinthians. This he says, because many there had accused him of fickleness, and of disregard for their interests. He declares, therefore, that even in the prospect of death he had a consciousness of rectitude towards them, and proceeds to show (ver. 13—23) that the charge against him was not well founded. I regard this passage, therefore, as designed to express the fact that Paul, in view of sudden death, had a consciousness of a life of piety, and was comforted with the reflection that he had not been actuated by the "fleshly wisdom" of the world. ¶ *The testimony of our conscience.* An approving conscience. It does not condemn me on the subject. Though others might accuse him, though his name might be calumniated, yet he had comfort in the approval which his own conscience gave to his course. Paul's conscience was enlightened, and its decisions were correct. Whatever others might charge him with, he *knew* what had been the aim and purpose of his life; and the consciousness of upright aims, and of such plans as the "grace of God" would prompt to, sustained him. An approving conscience is of inestimable value when we are calumniated;—*and when we draw near to death.* ¶ *That in simplicity* (ἐν ἁπλότητι.) Tindal renders this forcibly "without doubleness." The word means sincerity, candour, probity, plain-heartedness, Christian simplicity, frankness, integrity; see 2 Cor. xi. 3. It stands opposed to double-dealings and purposes; to deceitful appearances, and crafty plans; to mere policy, and craftiness in accomplishing an object. A man under the influence of this, is straight-forward, candid, open, frank; and he expects to accomplish his purpose by integrity and fair-dealing, and not by stratagem and cunning. Policy, craft, artful plans, and deep-laid schemes of deceit belong to the world; simplicity of aim and purpose are the true characteristics of a real Chris-

cerity, not [a] with fleshly wisdom, but by the grace of [b] God, we have had our conversation in the world, and more abundantly to you-ward.

a 1 Cor.2.4,13. *b* 1 Cor.15.10.

tian. ¶ *And godly sincerity.* Gr. "sincerity of God." This may be a Hebrew idiom, by which the superlative degree is indicated, when, in order to express the highest degree, they added the name of God, as in the phrases "mountains of God," signifying the highest mountains, or "cedars of God," denoting lofty cedars. Or it may mean such sincerity as God manifests and approves such as he, by his grace, would produce in the heart; such as the religion of the gospel is fitted to produce. The word used here, εἰλικρινεία, and rendered *sincerity*, denotes, properly, *clearness*, such as is judged of or discerned in sunshine (from εἵλη and κρίνω), and thence pureness, integrity. It is most probable that the *phrase* here denotes that sincerity which God produces and approves; and the sentiment is, that pure religion, the religion of God, produces entire sincerity in the heart. Its purposes and aims are open and manifest, *as if seen in the sunshine.* The plans of the world are obscure, deceitful, and dark, *as if in the night.* ¶ *Not with fleshly wisdom.* Not with the wisdom which is manifested by the men of this world; not by the principles of cunning, and mere policy, and expediency, which often characterize them. The phrase here stands opposed to simplicity and sincerity, to openness and straight-forwardness. And Paul means to disclaim for himself, and for his fellow-labourers, all that carnal policy which distinguishes the mere men of the world. And if Paul deemed such policy improper for him, we should deem it improper for us; if he had no plans which he wished to advance by it, we should have none; if he would not employ it in the promotion of good plans, neither should we. It has been the curse of the church and the bane of religion; and it is to this day exerting a withering and blighting influence on the church. The moment that such plans are resorted to, it is proof that the vitality of religion is gone, and any man who feels that his purposes cannot be accomplished *but* by such carnal policy, should set it down as full demonstration that his plans are wrong, and that his purpose should be abandoned. ¶ *But by the grace of God.* This phrase stands opposed, evidently, to "fleshly wisdom." It means that Paul had been influenced by such sentiments and principles as would be suggested or prompted by the influence of his grace. Locke renders it, "by the favour of God directing me." God had shown him *favour;* God had directed him; and he had kept him from the crooked and devious ways of mere worldly policy. The idea seems to be not merely that he had pursued a correct and upright course of life, but that he was indebted for this to the mere grace and favour of God, an idea which Paul omitted no opportunity of acknowledging. ¶ *We have had our conversation.* We have conducted ourselves (ἀνεστράφημεν). The word here used means literally, to turn up, to overturn; then to turn back, to return, and in the middle voice, to turn one's self around, to turn one's self to any thing, and, also, to move about in, to live in, to be conversant with, to conduct one's self. In this sense it seems to be used here; comp. Heb. x. 33; xiii. 18; 1 Tim. iii. 15; 1 Pet. i. 17. The word *conversation,* we usually apply to oral discourse, but in the Scriptures, it means *conduct,* and the sense of the passage is, that Paul had conducted himself in accordance with the principles of the grace of God, and had been influenced by that. ¶ *In the world.* Everywhere; wherever I have been. This does not mean in the world as contradistinguished from the church, but in the world at large, or wherever he had been, as contradistinguished from the church at Corinth. It had been his common and universal practice. ¶ *And more abundantly to you-ward.* Especially towards you. This was added doubt-

13 For we write none other things unto you than what ye read or acknowledge; and I trust ye shall acknowledge even to the end;

less because there had been charges against him in Corinth, that he had been crafty, cunning, deceitful, and especially that he had deceived them (see ver. 17), in not visiting them as he had promised. He affirms, therefore, that in all things he had acted in the manner to which the grace of God prompted, and that his conduct, in all respects, had been that of entire simplicity and sincerity.

13. *For we write none other things*, &c. There has been much variety in the interpretation of this passage; and much difficulty felt in determining what it means. The sense seems to me to be this. Paul had just declared that he had been actuated by pure intentions and by entire sincerity, and had in all things been influenced by the grace of God. This he had shown everywhere, but more particularly among them at Corinth. That they fully knew. In making this affirmation they had full evidence from what they had known of him in former times that such had been his course of life; and he trusted that they would be able to acknowledge the same thing to the end, and that they would never have any occasion to form a different opinion of him. It will be recollected that it is probable that some at Corinth had charged him with insincerity; and some had accused him of fickleness in having promised to come to Corinth and then changing his mind, or had charged him with never having intended to come to them. His object in this verse is to refute such slanders, and he says, therefore, that all that he affirmed in his writings about the sincerity and simplicity of his aims, were such as they *knew* from their past acquaintance with him to be true; and that they *knew* that he was a man who would keep his promises. It is an instance of a minister who was able to appeal to the people among whom he had lived and laboured in regard to the general sincerity and uprightness of his character—such an appeal as every minister *ought* to be able to make to refute all slanders; and such as he *will* be able to make successfully, if his life, like that of Paul, is such as to warrant it. Such seems to me to be the sense of the passage. Beza, however, renders it, "I write no other things than what ye read, or may understand," and so Rosenmüller, Wetstein, Macknight, and some others interpret it; and they explain it as meaning, "I write nothing secretly, nothing ambiguously, but I express myself clearly, openly, plainly, so that I may be read and understood by all." Macknight supposes that they had charged him with using ambiguous language, that he might afterwards interpret it to suit his own purpose. The objection to this is, that Paul never adverts to the obscurity or perspicuity of his own language. It was his *conduct* that was the main subject on which he was writing, and the connection seems to demand that we understand him as affirming that they had abundant evidence that what he affirmed of his simplicity of aim, and integrity of life, was true. ¶ *Than what ye read* (ἀναγινώσκετε). This word properly means to *know accurately;* to distinguish; and in the New Testament usually to know by reading. Doddridge remarks, that the word is ambiguous, and may signify either to acknowledge, to know, or to read. He regards it as here used in the sense of *knowing*. It is probably used here in the sense of knowing accurately, or surely; of *recognising* from their former acquaintance with him. They would *see* that the sentiments which he now expressed were such as accorded with his character and uniform course of life. ¶ *Or acknowledge* (ἐπιγινώσκετε). The preposition ἐπί in composition here is *intensive*, and the word denotes to know fully; to receive full knowledge of; to know well; or to recognise. It here means that they would fully recognise, or know entirely to their satisfaction, that the sentiments which he here expressed were such as accorded with his general manner of life. From

14 As also ye have acknowledged us in part, that [a] we are
your rejoicing, even as ye also
are ours in the day of the Lord
Jesus.
15 And in this confidence I

a Phil.4.1.

---

what they knew of him, they could not but admit that he had been influenced by the principles stated. ¶ *And I trust ye shall acknowledge.* I trust that my conduct will be such as to convince you always that I am actuated by such principles. I trust you will never witness any departure from them—the language of a man of settled principle, and of fixed aims and honesty of life. An honest man can always use such language respecting himself. ¶ *Even to the end.* To the end of life; always. "We trust that you will never have occasion to think dishonourably of us; or to reflect on any inconsistency in our behaviour." —*Doddridge.*

14. *As also ye have acknowledged us.* You have had occasion to admit my singleness of aim, and purity of intention and of life by your former acquaintance with me; and you have cheerfully done it. ¶ *In part* (ἀπὸ μέρους). Tindal renders this, "as ye have found us partly." The sense seems to be, "as part of you acknowledge;" meaning that *a portion* of the church was ready to concede to him the praise of consistency and uprightness, though there was a faction, or a part that denied it. ¶ *That we are your rejoicing.* That we are your joy, and your boasting. That is, you admit me to be an apostle. You regard me as your teacher, and guide. You recognise my authority, and acknowledge the benefits which you have received through me. ¶ *Even as ye also* are *ours.* Or, as you will be our rejoicing in the day when the Lord Jesus shall come to gather his people to himself. Then it will be seen that you were saved by our ministry; and then it will be an occasion of abundant and eternal thanksgiving to God that you were converted by our labours. And as you now regard it as a matter of congratulation and thanksgiving that you have such teachers as we are, so shall *we* regard it as a matter of congratulation and thanksgiving—as our chief joy—that we were the instruments of saving *such* a people. The expression implies that there was mutual confidence, mutual love, and mutual cause of rejoicing. It is well when ministers and people *have* such confidence in each other, and have occasion to regard their connection as a mutual cause of rejoicing and of καύχημα or *boasting.*

15. *And in this confidence.* In this confidence of my integrity, and that you had this favourable opinion of me, and appreciated the principles of my conduct. I did not doubt that you would receive me kindly, and would give me again the tokens of your affection and regard. In this Paul shows that however *some* of them might regard him, yet that he had no doubt tnat the majority of the church there would receive him kindly. ¶ *I was minded.* I willed (ἐβουλόμην); it was my intention. ¶ *To come unto you before.* Tindal renders this, "the other time." Paul refers doubtless to the time when he wrote his former epistle, and when it was his serious purpose, as it was his earnest wish, to visit them again; see 1 Cor. xvi. 5. In this purpose he had been disappointed, and he now proceeds to state the reasons why he had not visited them as he had purposed, and to show that it did not arise from any fickleness of mind. His purpose *had* been at first to pass through Corinth on his way to Macedonia, and to remain some time with them; see ver. 16. comp. 1 Cor. xvi. 5, 6. This purpose he had now changed; and instead of passing *through* Corinth on his way to Macedonia, he had gone *to* Macedonia by the way of Troas (chap. ii. 12); and the Corinthians having, as it would seem, become acquainted with this fact, had charged him with insincerity in the promise, or fickleness in regard to his plans. Probably it had been said by some of his enemies that he had never intended to visit them. ¶ *That ye might have a*

was minded to come unto you before, that ye might have a second [1] benefit;

16 And to pass by you into Macedonia, and to come again out of Macedonia unto you, and of you to be brought on my [a] way toward Judea.

17 When I therefore was thus minded, did I use lightness? or

1 Or, *grace*.

a Acts 21. 5.

second benefit. Marg. *grace.* The word here used (χάρις) is that which is commonly rendered *grace,* and means probably favour, kindness, good-will, beneficence; and especially favour to the undeserving. Here it is evidently used in the sense of gratification, or pleasure. And the idea is, that they had been formerly gratified and benefitted by his residence among them; he had been the means of conferring important favours on them, and he was desirous of being again with them, in order to gratify them by his presence, and that he might be the means of imparting to them other favours. Paul presumed that his presence with them would be to them a source of pleasure, and that his coming would do them good. It is the language of a man who felt assured that he enjoyed, after all, the confidence of the mass of the church there, and that they would regard his being with them as a favour. He had been with them formerly almost two years. His residence there had been pleasant to them and to him; and had been the occasion of important benefits to them. He did not doubt that it would be so again. Tindal renders this, "that ye might have had a double pleasure." It may be remarked here that several MSS. instead of χάριν, *grace,* read χαράν, *joy.*

16. *And to pass by you.* Through (δι') you; that is, through your city, or province; or to take them, as we say, in his way. His design was to pass through Corinth and Achaia on his journey. This was not the direct way from Ephesus to Macedonia. An inspection of a map (see the map of Asia Minor prefixed to the Notes on the Acts of the Apostles) will show at one view that the direct way was that which he concluded finally to take—that by Troas. Yet he had designed to go out of his way in order to make them a visit; and intended also, perhaps, to make them also a longer visit on his return. The former part of the plan he had been induced to abandon. ¶ *Into Macedonia.* A part of Greece having Thrace on the north, Thessaly south, Epirus west and the Ægean Sea east; see Note, Acts xvi. 9. ¶ *And of you to be brought on my way.* By you; see Note, 1 Cor. xvi. 6. ¶ *Toward Judea.* His object in going to Judea was to convey the collection for the poor saints which he had been at so much pains to collect throughout the churches of the Gentiles; see Notes, Rom. xv. 25, 26; comp. 1 Cor. xvi. 3, 4.

17. *When I therefore was thus minded.* When I formed this purpose; when I willed this, and expressed this intention. ¶ *Did I use lightness?* The word ἐλαφρίᾳ (from ἐλαφρός) means properly *lightness* in weight. Here it is used in reference to the mind; and in a sense similar to our word *levity,* as denoting lightness of temper or conduct; inconstancy, changeableness, or fickleness. This charge had been probably made that he had made the promise without any due consideration, or without any real purpose of performing it; or that he had made it in a trifling and thoughtless manner. By the interrogative form here, he sharply denies that it was a purpose formed in a light and trifling manner. ¶ *Do I purpose according to the flesh.* In such a manner, as may suit my own convenience and carnal interest. Do I form plans adapted only to promote my own ease and gratification, and to be abandoned when they are attended with inconvenience? The phrase "according to the flesh" here seems to mean "in such a way as to promote my own ease and gratification; in a manner such as the men of the world form; such as would be formed under the influence of earthly passions and

the things that I purpose, do I purpose according [a] to the flesh, that with me there should be yea, yea, and nay, nay?

18 But as God *is* true, our [1] word toward you was not yea [b] and nay.

19 For the Son [c] of God, Jesus

a chap.10.2. 1 Or, *preaching*. *b* Mat.5.37. *c* Mark 1.1.

desires, and to be forsaken when those plans would interfere with such gratifications." Paul denies in a positive manner that he formed *such* plans; and they should have known enough of his manner of life to be assured that that was not the nature of the schemes which he had devised? Probably no man ever lived who formed his plans of life *less* for the gratification of the flesh than Paul. ¶ *That with me there should be yea, yea, and nay, nay?* There has been a great variety in the interpretation of this passage; see Bloomfield, Crit. Dig. *in loco.* The meaning seems to be, "that there should be such inconstancy and uncertainty in my counsels and actions, that no one could depend on me, or know what they had to expect from me." Bloomfield supposes that the phrase is a proverbial one, and denotes a headstrong, self-willed spirit which will either do things, or not do them as pleases, without giving any reasons. He supposes that the *repetition* of the words "yea and nay" is designed to denote *positiveness* of assertion—such positiveness as is commonly shown by such persons, as in the phrases, "what I have written I have written," "what I have done I have done." It seems more probable, however, that the phrase is designed to denote the *ready compliance* which an inconstant and unsettled man is accustomed to make with the wishes of others; his expressing a ready assent to what they propose; falling in with their views; readily making promises; and instantly, through some whim, or caprice, or wish of others, saying "yea, nay," to the same thing; that is, changing his mind, and altering his purpose without any good reason, or in accordance with any fixed principle or settled rule of action. Paul says that this was not his character. He did not affirm a thing at one time and deny it at another; he did not promise to do a thing one moment and refuse to do it the next.

18. *But* as *God* is *true.* Tindal renders this, in accordance more literally with the Greek, "God is faithful; for our preaching unto you was not yea and nay." The phrase seems to have the form of an oath, or to be a solemn appeal to God as a witness, and to be equivalent to the expression "the Lord liveth," or "as the Lord liveth." The idea is, "God is faithful and true. He never deceives; never promises that which he does not perform. *So true* is it that I am not fickle and changing in my purposes." This idea of the faithfulness of God is the argument which Paul urges why he felt himself bound to be faithful also. That faithful God he regarded as a witness, and to that God he could appeal on the occasion. ¶ *Our word.* Marg. *preaching* (ὁ λόγος). This may refer either to his preaching, to his promises of visiting them, or his declarations to them in general on any subject. The particular subject under discussion was the promise which he had made to visit them. But he here seems to make his affirmation general, and to say universally of his promises, and his teaching, and of *all* his communications to them, whether orally or in writing, that they were not characterized by inconstancy and changeableness. It was not his character to be fickle, unsettled, and vacillating.

19. *For the Son of God.* In this verse, and the following, Paul states that he felt himself bound to maintain the strictest veracity for two reasons; the one, that Jesus Christ always evinced the strictest veracity (ver. 19); the other, God was always true to all the promises that he made (ver. 20); and as he felt himself to be the servant of the Saviour and of God, he was bound by the most sacred obligations also to maintain a character irreproachable in regard to veracity

Christ who was preached among you by us, *even* by me and Silvanus and Timotheus, was not yea and nay, but in him was yea.

20 For all the promises of God in [a] him *are* yea, and in him amen, unto the glory of God by us.

a Rom.15.8,9; Heb.13.8.

On the meaning of the phrase "Son of God," see Note, Rom. i. 4. ¶ *Jesus Christ.* It is agreed, says Bloomfield, by the best commentators, ancient and modern, that by Jesus Christ is here meant his doctrine. The sense is, that the preaching respecting Jesus Christ, did not represent him as fickle, and changeable; as unsettled, and as unfaithful; but as TRUE, consistent, and faithful. As that had been the regular and constant representation of Paul and his fellow-labourers in regard to the Master whom they served, it was to be inferred that they felt themselves bound sacredly to observe the strictest constancy and veracity. ¶ *By us,* &c. Silvanus, here mentioned, is the same person who in the Acts of the Apostles is called *Silas.* He was with Paul at Philippi, and was imprisoned there with him (Acts xvi.), and was afterwards with Paul and Timothy at Corinth when he first visited that city; Acts xviii. 5. Paul was so much attached to him, and had so much confidence in him, that he joined his name with his own in several of his epistles; 1 Thess. i. 1; 2 Thess. i. 1. ¶ *Was not yea and nay.* Our representation of him was not that he was fickle and changeable. ¶ *But in him was yea.* Was not one thing at one time, and another at another. He is the same, yesterday, to-day, and forever. All that he says is true; all the promises that he makes are firm; all his declarations are faithful. Paul may refer to the fact that the Lord Jesus when on earth was eminently characterized by TRUTH. Nothing was more striking than his veracity. He called himself "the truth," as being eminently true in all his declarations. "I am the way, and THE TRUTH, and the life;" John xiv 6; comp. Rev. iii. 7. And thus (Rev. iii. 14) he is called "the faithful and true witness." In all his life he was eminently distinguished for that. His declarations were simple truth; his narratives were simple, unvarnished, uncoloured, unexaggerated statements of what actually occurred. He never disguised the truth; never prevaricated; never had any mental reservation; never deceived; never used any word, or threw in any circumstance, that was fitted to lead the mind astray. He himself said that this was the great object which he had in view in coming into the world. "To this end was I born and for this cause came I into the world, that I should bear witness unto the truth;" John xviii. 37. As Jesus Christ was thus distinguished for simple truth, Paul felt that he was under sacred obligations to imitate him, and always to evince the same inviolable fidelity. The most deeply felt obligation on earth is that which the Christian feels to imitate the Redeemer.

20. *For all the promises of God in him.* All the promises which God has made through him. This is *another* reason why Paul felt himself bound to maintain a character of the strictest veracity. The reason was, that *God* always evinced that; and that as none of *his* promises failed, he felt himself sacredly bound to imitate him, and to adhere to all his. The promises of God which are made through Christ, relate to the pardon of sin to the penitent; the sanctification of his people; support in temptation and trial; guidance in perplexity; peace in death, and eternal glory beyond the grave. All of these are made through a Redeemer, and none of these shall fail. ¶ Are *yea.* Shall all be certainly fulfilled. There shall be no vacillation on the part of God; no fickleness; no abandoning of his gracious intention. ¶ *And in him amen.* In Rev. iii. 14, the Lord Jesus is called the "Amen." The word means true, faithful, certain. And the expression here means that all the promises which are made to men

21 Now he which stablisheth [a] us with you in Christ, and hath anointed [b] us, *is* God;

a 2 Th.2.8; 1 Pet.5.10.
b 1 John 2.20,27; Rev.3.18.

22 Who hath also sealed [c] us, and given the earnest of the Spirit [d] in our hearts.

c Ep.1.13,14; 4.30; 2Ti.2.19.
d Rom.8.9,14—16.

through a Redeemer shall be certainly fulfilled. They are promises which are confirmed and established, and which shall by no means fail. ¶ *Unto the glory of God by us.* Either by us ministers and apostles; or by us who are Christians. The latter, I think, is the meaning; and Paul means to say, that the fulfilment of all the promises which God has made to his people shall result in his glory and praise as a God of condescension and veracity. The fact that he has made such promises is an act that tends to his own glory—since it was of his mere grace that they were made; and the fulfilment of these promises in and through the church, shall also tend to produce elevated views of his fidelity and goodness.

21. *Now he which stablisheth us.* He who makes us *firm* (ὁ βεβαιῶν ἡμᾶς): that is, he who has confirmed us in the hopes of the gospel, and who gives us grace to be faithful, and firm in our promises. The *object* of this is to trace all to God, and to prevent the appearance of self-confidence, or of boasting. Paul had dwelt at length on his own fidelity and veracity. He had taken pains to prove that he was not inconstant and fickle-minded. He here says, that this was not to be traced to himself, or to any native goodness, but was all to be traced to God. It was God who had given them all confident hope in Christ; and it was God who had given him grace to adhere to his promises, and to maintain a character for veracity. The first "us," in this verse refers probably to Paul himself; the second includes also the Corinthians, as being also anointed and sealed. ¶ *And hath anointed us.* Us who are Christians. It was customary to *anoint* kings, prophets, and priests on their entering on their office as a part of the ceremony of inauguration. The word *anoint* is applied to a priest, Ex. xxviii. 41; xl. 15; to a prophet, 1 Kings xix. 16; Isa. lxi. 1; to a king, 1 Sam. x. 1; xv. 1; 2 Sam. ii. 4; 1 Kings i. 34. It is applied often to the Messiah as being set apart, or consecrated to his office as prophet, priest, and king—*i. e.* as appointed by God to the highest office ever held in the world. It is applied also to Christians as being consecrated, or set apart to the service of God by the Holy Spirit—a use of the word which is derived from the sense of *consecrating*, or setting apart to the service of God. Thus in 1 John ii. 20, it is said, "But ye have an unction from the Holy One and know all things." So in ver. 27, "But the anointing which ye have received abideth in you," &c. The anointing which was used in the consecration of prophets, priests, and kings, seems to have been designed to be emblematic of the influences of the Holy Spirit, who is often represented as *poured* upon those who are under his influence (Prov. i. 23; Isa. xliii. 4; Joel ii. 28, 29; Zech. xii. 10; Acts x. 45), in the same way as water or oil is poured out. And as Christians are everywhere represented as being under the influence of the Holy Spirit, as being those on whom the Holy Spirit is *poured*, they are represented as "anointed." They are in this manner solemnly set apart, and consecrated to the service of God. ¶ Is *God.* God has done it. All is to be traced to him. It is not by any native goodness which we have, or any inclination which we have by nature to his service. This is one of the instances which abound so much in the writings of Paul, where he delights to trace all good influences to God.

22. *Who hath also sealed us.* The word used here (from σφραγίζω) means to seal up; to close and make fast with a seal, or signet; as, *e. g.*, books, letters, &c. that they may not be read. It is also used in the sense of setting a mark on any thing, or a seal, to

23 Moreover I call God for a record upon my soul, that, to spare you, I came not as yet unto Corinth.

denote that it is genuine, authentic, confirmed, or approved, as when a deed, compact, or agreement is sealed. It is thus made sure; and is confirmed or established. Hence it is applied to *persons*, as denoting that they are approved, as in Rev. vii. 3: "Hurt not the earth, neither the sea, nor the trees, till we have sealed the servants of our God in their foreheads;" comp. Ezek. ix. 4; see Note, John vi. 27, were it is said of the Saviour, "for him hath God the Father *sealed*;" comp. John iii. 33. In a similar manner Christians are said to be sealed; to be sealed by the Holy Spirit (Eph. i. 13; iv. 30); that is, the Holy Spirit is given to them to confirm them as belonging to God. He grants them his Spirit. He renews and sanctifies them. He produces in their hearts those feelings, hopes, and desires which are an *evidence* that they are approved by God; that they are regarded as his adopted children; that their hope is genuine, and that their redemption and salvation are SURE—in the same way as a seal makes a will or an agreement sure. God grants to them his Holy Spirit as the certain pledge that they are his, and shall be approved and saved in the last day. In this there is nothing miraculous, or in the nature of direct revelation. It consists of the ordinary operations of the Spirit on the heart, producing repentance, faith, hope, joy, conformity to God, the love of prayer and praise, and the Christian virtues generally; and *these things* are the evidences that the Holy Spirit has renewed the heart, and that the Christian is sealed for the day of redemption. ¶ *And given the earnest of the Spirit.* The word here used (ἀῤῥαβὼν from the Heb. עֵרָבוֹן) means properly a pledge given to ratify a contract; a part of the price, or purchase money; a first payment; that which confirms the bargain, and which is regarded as a pledge that all the price will be paid. The word occurs in the Septuagint and Hebrew, in Gen. xxxviii. 17, 18; xxxviii. 20. In the New Testament it occurs only in this place, and in chap. v. 5, and Eph. i. 14, in each place in the same connection as applied to the Holy Spirit, and his influences on the heart. It refers to those influences as a *pledge* of the future glories which await Christians in heaven. In regard to the "earnest," or the part of a price which was paid in a contract, it may be remarked, (1.) That it was of the same *nature* as the full price, being regarded as a *part* of it; (2.) It was regarded as a pledge or assurance that the full price would be paid. So the "earnest of the Spirit," denotes that God gives to his people the influences of his Spirit: his operation on the heart as a part or pledge that all the blessings of the covenant of redemption shall be given to them. And it implies, (1.) That the comforts of the Christian here are of the same *nature* as they will be in heaven. Heaven will consist of *like* comforts; of love, and peace, and joy, and purity begun here and simply *expanded* there to complete and eternal perfection. The joys of heaven differ only in *degree*, not in *kind*, from those of the Christian on earth. That which is begun here is perfected there; and the feelings and views which the Christian has here, if expanded and carried out, would constitute heaven. (2.) These comforts, these influences of the Spirit, are a *pledge* of heaven. They are the security which God gives us that we shall be saved. If we are brought under the renewing influences of the Spirit here; if we are made meek, and humble, and prayerful by his agency; if we are made to partake of the joys which result from pardoned sin; if we are filled with the hope of heaven, it is all produced by the Holy Spirit, and is a *pledge*, or earnest of our future inheritance; —as the first sheaves of a harvest are a pledge of a harvest; or the first payment under a contract a pledge that all will be payed. God thus gives to his people the assurance that

24 Not for that we have [a] dominion over your faith, but are helpers of your joy: for by [b] faith ye stand.

a 1Cor.3 5; 1Pet.5.3. b Rom.11.20; 1Cor.15.1.

they shall be saved; and by this "pledge" makes their title to eternal life sure.

23. *Moreover, I call God for a record upon my soul.* It is well remarked by Rosenmüller, that the second chapter should have commenced here, since there is here a transition in the subject more distinct than where the second chapter is actually made to begin. Here Tindal commences the second chapter. This verse, with the subsequent statements, is designed to show them the true reason why he had changed his purpose, and had not visited them according to his first proposal. And that reason was not that he was fickle and inconstant; but it was that he apprehended that if he should go to them in their irregular and disorderly state, he would be under a necessity of resorting to harsh measures, and to a severity of discipline that would be alike painful to them and to him. Dr. Paley has shown with great plausibility, if not with moral certainty, that Paul's change of purpose about visiting them was made *before* he wrote his first epistle; that he had at first resolved to visit them, but that on subsequent reflection, he thought it would be better to try the effect of *a faithful letter to them,* admonishing them of their errors, and entreating them to exercise proper discipline themselves on the principal offender; that with this feeling he wrote his first epistle, in which he does not state to them *as yet* his change of purpose, or the reason of it; but that now after he had written that letter, and after it had had all the effect which he desired, he states the true reason why he had not visited them. It was now proper to do it; and that reason was, that he desired to spare them the severity of discipline, and had resorted to the more mild and affectionate measure of sending them a letter, and thus not making it *necessary* personally to administer discipline; see Paley's Horæ Paulinæ, on 2 Cor. Nos. iv. and v. The phrase, "I call God for a record upon my soul," is in the Greek, "I call God for a witness against my soul." It is a solemn oath, or appeal to God; and implies, that if he did not in that case declare the truth, he desired that God would be a witness *against* him, and would punish him accordingly. The *reason* why he made this solemn appeal to God was, the importance of his vindicating his own character before the church, from the charges which had been brought against him. ¶ *That to spare you.* To avoid the necessity of inflicting punishment on you; of exercising severe and painful discipline. If he went among them in the state of irregularity and disorder which prevailed there, he would feel it to be necessary to exert his authority as an apostle, and remove at once the offending members from the church. He expected to avoid the necessity of these painful acts of discipline, by sending to them a faithful and affectionate epistle, and thus inducing them to reform, and to avoid the necessity of a resort to that which would have been so trying to him and to them. It was not, then, a disregard for them, or a want of attachment to them, which had led him to change his purpose, but it was the result of tender affection. This cause of the change of his purpose, of course, he would not make known to them in his first epistle, but now that that letter had accomplished all he had desired, it was proper that they should be apprized of the reason why he had resorted to this instead of visiting them personally.

24. *Not for that we have dominion,* &c. The sense of this passage I take to be this: "The course which we have pursued has been chosen not because we wish to lord it over your faith, to control your belief, but because we desired to promote your happiness. Had the former been our object, had we wished to set up a lordship or dominion over you, we

should have come to you with our apostolical authority, and in the severity of apostolic discipline. We had power to command obedience, and to control your faith. But we chose not to do it. Our object was to promote your highest happiness. We, therefore, chose the mildest and gentlest manner possible; we did not exercise authority in discipline, we sent an affectionate and tender letter." While the apostles had the right to prescribe the articles of belief, and to propound the doctrines of God, yet they would not do even that in such a manner as to seem to "lord it over God's heritage" (οὐκ κυριεύομεν); they did not set up absolute authority, or prescribe the things to be believed in a lordly and imperative manner; nor would they make use of the severity of power to enforce what they taught. They appealed to reason; they employed persuasion; they made use of light and love to accomplish their desires. ¶ *Are helpers of your joy.* This is our main object, to promote your joy. This object we have pursued in our plans, and in order to secure this, we forbore to come to you, when, if we *did* come at that time, we should have given occasion perhaps to the charge that we sought to lord it over your faith. ¶ *For by faith ye stand;* see Note, 1 Cor. xv. 1. This seems to be a kind of proverbial expression, stating a general truth, that it was by faith that Christians were to be established or confirmed. The connection here requires us to understand this as a reason why he would not attempt to lord it over their faith; or to exercise dominion over them. That reason was, that thus far they *had* stood firm, in the main, in the faith (1 Cor. xv. 1); they had adhered to the truths of the gospel, and *in a special manner now, in yielding obedience to the commands and entreaties of Paul in the first epistle,* they had showed that they *were* in the faith, and firm in faith. It was not necessary or proper, therefore, for him to attempt to exercise lordship over their belief, but all that was needful was to help forward their joy, for they *were* firm in the faith. We may observe, (1.) That it is a part of the duty of ministers to help forward the joy of Christians. (2.) This should be the object even in administering discipline and reproof. (3.) If even Paul would not attempt to lord it over the faith of Christians, to establish a domination over their belief, how absurd and wicked is it for uninspired ministers now, for individual ministers, for conferences, conventions, presbyteries, synods, councils, or for the pope, to attempt to establish a spiritual dominion in *controlling* the faith of men. The great evils in the church have arisen from their attempting to do what Paul *would* not do; from attempting to establish a dominion which Paul never sought, and which Paul would have abhorred. Faith must be free, and religion must be free, or they cannot exist at all.

REMARKS.

In view of this chapter we may remark,

1st. God is the only true and real source of comfort in times of trial, ver. 3. It is from him that all real consolation must come, and he only can meet and sustain the soul when it is borne down with calamity. All persons are subjected to trial, and at some periods of their lives, to severe trial. Sickness is a trial; the death of a friend is a trial; the loss of property or health, disappointment, and reproach, and slander, and poverty, and want, are trials to which we are all more or less exposed. In these trials, it is natural to look to *some* source of consolation; some way in which they may be borne. Some seek consolation in philosophy, and endeavour to blunt their feelings and destroy their sensibilities, as the ancient stoics did. But "to destroy sensibility is not to produce comfort."—*Dr. Mason.* Some plunge deep into pleasures, and endeavour to drown their sorrows in the intoxicating draught; but this is not to produce *comfort* to the soul, even were it possible in such pleasures to forget their sorrows. Such were the ancient epicureans. Some seek consolation in their surviving friends, and look to them to comfort and sustain the sinking heart. But the arm of an earthly friend is feeble, when *God* lays his hand upon us. It is only the hand that smites that can heal; only the God that sends the affliction, that can bind up the broken spirit. He is the "Father of mercies," and he "the God of ALL consolation;" and in affliction there is no true comfort but in him.

(2.) This consolation in God is derived from many sources. (*a*) He is the "Father of mercies," and we may be assured, therefore, that he does nothing inconsistent with MERCY. (*b*) We may be assured that he is right—always right, and that he does nothing *but* right. We may not be able to see the *reason* of his doings, but we may have the assurance that it *is* all right, and will yet be seen to be right. (*c*) There is comfort in the fact, that our afflictions are ordered by an *intelligent* Being, by one who is all-wise, and all-knowing. They are not the result of blind chance; but they are ordered by one who is wise to *know* what *ought* to be done; and who is so just that he will do nothing wrong. There could be no consolation in the feeling that mere *chance* directed our trials; nor can there be consolation except in the feeling that a being of intelligence and goodness directs and orders all. The true comfort, therefore, is to be found in *religion*, not in atheism and philosophy.

(3.) It is possible to bless God in the midst of trials, and as the result of trial. It is possible so clearly to see his hand, and to be so fully satisfied with the wisdom and goodness of his dealings, even when we are severely afflicted, as to see that he is worthy of our highest confidence and most exalted praise, ver. 3. God may be seen, then, to be the "Father of mercies;" and he may impart, even then, a consolation which we never experience in the days of prosperity. Some of the purest and most elevated joys known upon earth, are experienced in the very midst of outward calamities, and the most sincere and elevated thanksgivings which are offered to God, are often those which are the result of sanctified afflictions. It is when we are brought out from such trials, where we have experienced the rich consolations and the sustaining power of the gospel, that we are most disposed to say with Paul, "Blessed be God;" and can most clearly see that he is the "Father of mercies." No Christian will ever have occasion to regret the trials through which God has brought him. I never knew a sincere Christian who was not finally benefitted by trials.

(4.) Christian joy is not *apathy*, it is *comfort*; ver. 4, 5. It is not insensibility to suffering; it is not stoical indifference. The Christian *feels* his sufferings as keenly as others. The Lord Jesus was *as* sensitive to suffering as any one of the human family ever was; he was as susceptible of emotion from reproach, contempt, and scorn, and he *as* keenly felt the pain of the scourge, the nails, and the cross, as any one could. But there is *positive* joy, there is true and solid comfort. There is substantial, pure, and elevated happiness. Religion does not blunt the feelings, or destroy the sensibility, but it brings in consolations which enable us to bear our pains, and to endure persecution without murmuring. In this, religion differs from all systems of philosophy. The one attempts to *blunt* and destroy our sensibilities to suffering; the other, while it makes us more delicate and tender in our feelings, gives consolation *adapted* to that delicate sensibility, and fitted to sustain the soul, *notwithstanding* the acuteness of its sufferings.

(5.) Ministers of the gospel may expect to be *peculiarly* tried and afflicted; ver. 5. So it was with Paul and his fellow-apostles; and so it has been since. They are the special objects of the hatred of sinners, as they stand in the way of the sinful pursuits and pleasures of the world; and they are, like their Master, especially hated by the enemy of souls. Besides, they are, by their office, required to minister consolation to others who are afflicted; and it is so ordered in the providence of God that they are subjected to peculiar trials often, *in order* that they may be able to impart peculiar consolations. They are to be the examples and the guides of the church of God; and God takes care that they shall be permitted to show by their example, as well as by their preaching, the supporting power of the gospel in times of trial.

(6.) If we suffer much in the cause of the Redeemer, we may also expect much consolation; ver. 5. Christ will take care that our hearts shall be filled with joy and peace. As our trials in his cause are, so shall our consolations be. If we suffer much, we shall enjoy much; if we are persecuted much, we shall have much support; if our names are cast out among men for his sake, we shall have increasing evidence that they are written in his book of life. There *are* things in the Christian religion which can be learned only in the furnace of affliction; and he who has never been afflicted on account of his attachment to Christ, is a stranger yet to *much, very much* of the fulness and beauty of that system of religion which has been appointed by the Redeemer, and to much, very much, of the beauty and power of the promises of the Bible. No man will ever understand *all* the Bible who is not *favoured* with much persecution and many trials.

(7.) We should be willing to suffer; ver. 3—5. If we are willing *to be happy*, we should also be willing to suffer. If we *desire* to be happy in religion, we should be willing to suffer. If we *expect* to be happy, we should also be willing to endure much. Trials fit us for enjoyment here, as well as for heaven hereafter.

(8.) One great design of the consolation which is imparted to Christians in the time of affliction is, that they may be able to impart consolation also to others; ver. 4, 6, 7. God designs that we should thus be mutual aids. And he comforts a pastor in his trials, that he may, by his own experience, be able to minister consolation to the people of his charge; he comforts a parent, that he may administer consolation to his children; a friend, that he may comfort a friend. He who attempts to administer consolation should be able to speak from experience: and God, therefore, afflicts and comforts all his people, that they may know how to administer consolation to those with whom they are connected.

(9.) If we have experienced peculiar consolations ourselves in times of trial, we are under obligations to seek out and comfort others who are afflicted. So Paul felt. We should feel that God has qualified us for this work; and having qualified us for it, that he calls on us to do it. The consolation which God gives in affliction is a rich treasure which we are bound to impart to others; the experience which we have of the true sources of consolation is an inestimable talent which we are to use for the promotion of his glory. No man has a talent for doing more direct good than he who can go to the afflicted, and bear testimony, from his own experience, to the goodness of God. And every man who *can* testify that God is good, and is able to support the soul in times of trial,—and what Christian cannot do it who has ever been afflicted?—should regard himself as favoured with a peculiar talent for doing good, and should rejoice in the privilege of using it to the glory of God. For there is no talent more honourable than that of being able to promote the divine glory, to comfort the afflicted, or to be able, from personal experience, to testify that God is good—always good. "The *power* of doing good, always implies an *obligation* to do it."—*Cotton Mather.*

(10.) In this chapter, we have a case of a near contemplation of death; ver. 8, 9. Paul expected soon to die. He had the sentence of death in himself. He saw no human probability of escape. He was called, therefore, calmly to look death in the face, and to contemplate it as an event certain and near. Such a condition is deeply interesting, it is *the* important crisis of life. And yet it is an event which all must soon contemplate. We all, in a short period, each one for himself, *must* look upon death as certain, and as near to us; as an event in which we are personally interested, and from which we cannot escape. Much as we may turn away from it in health, and unanxious as we may be then in regard to it, yet by no possibility can we long avert our minds from the subject. It is interesting, then, to inquire how Paul felt when he looked at death; how we *should* feel; and how we actually *shall* feel when we come to die.

(11.) A contemplation of death as near and certain, is fitted to lead us to trust in God. This was the effect in the case of Paul; ver. 9. He had learned in health to put his trust in him, and now, when the trial was apparently near, he had no where else to go, and he confided in him alone. He felt that if he was rescued, it could be only by the interposition of God; and that there was none but God who could sustain him if he should die. And what event *can* there be that is so well fitted to lead us to trust in God as death? And where else can we go in view of that dark hour? For, (*a*) We know not what death is. We have not tried it · nor do we know what grace may be necessary for us in those unknown pangs and sufferings; in that deep darkness, and that sad gloom. (*b*) Our friends *cannot* aid us then. They will, they *must*, then, give us the parting hand; and as we *enter* the shades of the dark valley, they must bid us farewell. The skill of the physician then will fail. Our worldly friends will forsake us when we come to die. They do not love to be in the room of death, and they can give us no consolation if they are there. Our pious friends cannot attend us far in the dark valley. They may pray, and commend us to God, but even they must leave us to die alone. Who but God *can* attend us? Who but he can support us then? (*c*) God only knows what is *beyond* death. How do we know the way to his bar, to his presence, to his heaven? How can we direct our own steps in that dark and unknown world? None but God our Saviour can guide us there; none else can conduct us to his abode. (*d*) None but God can *sustain* us in the pain, the anguish, the feebleness, the sinking of the powers of body and of mind in that distressing hour. He *can* uphold us then; and it is an unspeakable privilege to be permitted then, "when heart and flesh faint," to say of him, "God is the strength of" our "heart, and" our "portion for ever;" Ps. lxxiii. 26.

(12.) We should regard a restoration from dangerous sickness, and from imminent peril of death as a kind of resurrection. So Paul regarded it; ver. 9. We should remember how easy it would have been for God to have removed us; how rapidly we were tending to the grave; how certainly we should have descended there but for his interposition. We should feel, therefore, that we owe our lives to him as really and entirely as though we had been raised up from the dead; and that the same kind of power and goodness have been evinced as would have been had God given us life anew. Life is God's gift; and every instance of recovery from peril, or from dangerous illness, is as really an interposition of his mercy as though we had been raised up from the dead.

(13.) We should, in like manner, regard a restoration of our friends from dangerous sickness, or peril of any kind, as a species of resurrection from the dead. When a parent, a husband, a wife or a child has been dangerously ill, or exposed to some imminent danger, and has been recovered, we cannot but feel that the recovery is entirely owing to the interposition of God. With infinite ease he could have consigned them to the grave; and had he not mercifully interposed, they would have died. As they were originally his gift to us, so we should regard each interposition of that kind as a *new gift*, and receive the recovered and restored friend as a fresh gift from his hand.

(14.) We should feel that lives thus preserved and thus recovered from danger, belong to God. He has preserved them. In the most absolute sense they belong to him, and to him they should be consecrated. So Paul felt; and his whole life shows how entirely he regarded himself as bound to devote a life often preserved in the midst of peril, to the service of his kind Benefactor. There is no claim more absolute than that which God has on those whom he has preserved from dangerous situations, or whom he has raised up from the borders of the grave. All the strength which he has imparted, all the talent, learning, skill, which he has thus preserved, should be regarded in the most absolute sense as his, and should be honestly and entirely consecrated to him. *But* for him we should have died; and he has a right to our services and obedience which is entire, and which should be felt to be perpetual. And it may be added, that the right is not less clear and strong to the service of those whom he keeps without their being exposed to such peril, or raised up from such beds of sickness. A very few only of the interpositions of God in our behalf are seen by us. A small part of the perils to which we may be really exposed are seen. And it is no less owing to his preserving care that we are *kept in* health, and strength, and in the enjoyment of reason, than it is that we are *raised up* from dangerous sickness. Man is as much bound to devote himself to God for preserving him *from* sickness and danger, as he is for raising him up *when* he has been sick, and defending him in danger.

(15.) We have here an instance of the *principle* on which Paul acted, ver. 12. In his *aims,* and in the *manner* of accomplishing his aims, he was guided only by the principles of simplicity and sincerity, and by the grace of God. He had no sinister and worldly purpose; he had no crooked and subtle policy by which to accomplish his purposes. He sought simply the glory of God and the salvation of man; and he sought this in a manner plain, direct, honest, and straight-forward. He admitted none of the principles of worldly policy which have been so often acted on since in the church; he knew nothing of "pious frauds," which have so often disgraced the *professed* friends of the Redeemer; he admitted no form of deception and delusion, even for the promotion of objects which were great, and good, and desirable. He knew that all that *ought* to be done could be accomplished by straight-forward and simple-hearted purposes; and that a cause which depended on the carnal and crooked policy of the world was a bad cause; and that *such* policy would ultimately ruin the best of causes. How happy would it have been if these views had always prevailed in the church!

(16.) We see the value of a good conscience, ver. 12. Paul had the testimony of an enlightened conscience to the correctness and uprightness of his course of life everywhere. He felt assured that his aims had been right; and that he had endeavoured in all simplicity and sincerity to pursue a course of life which such a conscience would approve. Such a testimony, such an approving conscience is of inestimable value. It is worth more than gold, and crowns, and all that the earth can give. When like Paul we are exposed to peril, or trial, or calamity, it matters little, if we have an approving conscience. When like him we are persecuted, it matters little if we have the testimony of our own minds that we have pursued an upright and an honest course of life. When like him we look death in the face, and feel that we "have the sentence of death in ourselves," of what inestimable value then will be an approving conscience! How unspeakable the consolation if we can look back then on a life spent in conscious integrity; a life spent in endeavouring to promote the glory of God and the salvation of the world!

(17.) Every Christian should feel himself sacredly bound to maintain a character of veracity, ver. 19, 20. Christ was always true to his word; and all that God has promised shall be certainly fulfilled. And as a Christian is a professed follower of him who was 'the Amen and the true witness," he should feel himself bound by the most sacred obligations to adhere to all his promises, and to fulfil all his word. No man can do any good who is not a man of truth; and in no way can Christians more dishonour their profession, and injure the cause of the Redeemer, than by a want of character for unimpeachable veracity. If they make promises which are never fulfilled; if they state that as true which is not true; if they overload their narratives with circumstances which had no existence; if they deceive, and defraud others; and if they are so loose in their statements that no one believes them, it is impossible for them to do good in their Christian profession Every Christian *should* have—as he easily *may* have—such a character for veracity that every man shall put implicit confidence in all his promises and statements; *so* implicit that they shall deem his word as good as an oath; and his promise as certain as though it were secured by notes and bonds in the most solemn manner. The word of a Christian should *need* no strengthening by oaths and bonds; it should be such that it could really *not* be strengthened by any thing that notes and bonds could add to it.

(18.) All Christians should regard themselves as consecrated to God, ver. 21. They have been anointed, or set apart to his service. They should feel that they are as really set apart to his service as the ancient prophets, priests, and kings were to their appropriate offices by the ceremony of anointing. They belong to God, and are under every sacred and solemn obligation to live to him, and him alone.

(19.) It is an inestimable *privilege* to be a Christian, ver. 21, 22. It is regarded as a privilege to be an heir to an estate, and to have an assurance that it will be ours. But the Christian has an "earnest," a pledge that heaven is his. He is anointed of God; he is sealed for heaven. Heaven is his home; and God is giving to him daily evidence in his own experience that he will soon be admitted to its pure and blissful abodes.

(20.) The joys of the Christian on earth are of the same *nature* as the joys of heaven. These comforts are an "earnest' of the future inheritance: a *part* of that which the Christian is to enjoy forever. His joys on earth are "heaven begun;" and all that is needful to constitute *heaven* is that these joys should be expanded and perpetuated. There will be no other heaven than that which would be constituted by the expanded joys of a Christian.

(21.) No one is a Christian, no one is fitted for heaven, who has not such principles and joys as being fully expanded and developed would constitute heaven. The joys of heaven are not to be *created* for us as some new thing; they are not to be such as we have had no foretaste, no conception of; but they are to be such as will be produced of necessity by removing imperfection from the joys and feelings of the believer, and carrying them out without alloy, and without interruption, and without end. The man, therefore, who has such a character, that if fairly developed would not constitute the joys of heaven, is not a Christian. He has no evidence that he has been born again; and all his joys are fancied and delusive.

(22.) Christians should be careful not to grieve the Holy Spirit; comp. Eph. iv. 30. It is by that Spirit that they are "anointed" and "sealed," and it is by his influences that they have the earnest of their future inheritance. All good influences on their minds proceed from that Spirit; and it should be their high and constant aim not to grieve him. By no course of conduct, by no conversation, by no impure thought, should they drive that Spirit from their minds. All their peace and joy is dependent on their cherishing his sacred influences; and by all the means in their power they should strive to secure his constant agency on their souls.

CHAPTER II.

In this chapter Paul continues the discussion of the subject which had been introduced in the previous chapter. At the close of that chapter, he had stated the reasons why he had not visited the church at Corinth; see Notes on chap. i 23, 24. The main reason was, that instead of com-

CHAPTER II.

BUT I determined this with myself, that I would not come again to you in heaviness. [a]

[a] chap.1,23; 12.20,21; 13.10.

2 For if I make you sorry, who is he then that maketh me glad, but the same which is made sorry by me?

ing to them in that disordered, and irregular state, he had preferred to send them an affectionate letter. Had he come to them personally he would have felt himself called on to exercise the severity of discipline. He chose, therefore, to try what the effect would be of a faithful and kind epistle. In this chapter, he prosecutes the same subject. He states, therefore, more at length, the reason why he had not come to them, ver. 1—5. The reason was, that he resolved not to come to them, if he could avoid it, with severity; that his heart was pained even with the necessity of sending such a letter; that he wrote it with much anguish of spirit; yet that he cherished towards them the most tender love. In his former epistle (chap. v.) he had directed them to exercise discipline on the offending person in the church. This had been done according to his direction; and the offender had been suitably punished for his offence. He had been excommunicated; and it would seem that the effect on him had been to induce him to forsake his sin, and probably to put away his father's wife, and he had become a sincere penitent. Paul, therefore, in the next place (ver. 6—11), exhorts them to receive him again into fellowship with the church The punishment he says had been sufficient (ver. 6); they ought now to be kind and forgiving to him lest he should be overwhelmed with his sorrow (ver. 7); he says, that *he* had forgiven him, so far as he was concerned, and he entreated them to do the same (ver. 10); and says that they ought, by all means, to pursue such a course that Satan could get no advantage of them, ver. 11. Paul then states the disappointment which he had had at Troas in not seeing Titus, from whom he had expected to learn what was the state of the church at Corinth, and what was the reception of his letter there; but that not seeing him there, he had gone on to Macedonia, ver. 12, 13. There, it would seem, he met Titus, and learned that his letter had had all the success which he could have desired. It had been kindly received; and all that he had wished in regard to discipline had been performed, ver. 14. The hearing of this success gives him occasion to thank God for it, as one among many instances in which his efforts to advance his cause had been crowned with success. God had made him everywhere successful; and had made him triumph in Christ in every place. This fact gives him occasion (ver. 15, 16) to state the general effect of his preaching and his labours. His efforts, he says, were always acceptable to God—though he could not be ignorant that in some cases the gospel which he preached was the occasion of the aggravated condemnation of those who heard and rejected it. Yet he had the consolation of reflecting that it was by no fault of his, ver. 17. It was not because he had corrupted the word of God; it was not because he was unfaithful; it was not because he was not sincere. He had a good conscience—a conscience which assured him that he spoke in sincerity and as in the sight of God—though the unhappy effect might be that many would perish from under his ministry.

1. *But I determined this with myself.* I made up my mind on this point; I formed this resolution in regard to my course. ¶ *That I would not come again to you with heaviness.* In grief (ἐν λύπῃ). "I would not come, if I could avoid it, in circumstances which must have grieved both me and you. I would not come while there existed among you such irregularities as must have pained my heart, and as must have compelled me to resort to such acts of discipline as would be painful to you. I resolved, therefore, to endeavour to remove these evils

3 And I wrote this same unto you, lest, when I came, I should have sorrow from them of whom I ought to rejoice; having confidence in you all, that my joy is *the joy* of you all.

before I came, that when I did come, my visit might be mutually agreeable to us both. For that reason I changed my purpose about visiting you, when I heard of those disorders, and resolved to send an epistle. If *that* should be successful, then the way would be open for an agreeable visit to you." This verse, therefore, contains the statement of the principal reason why he had not come to them as he had at first proposed. It was really from no fickleness, but it was from love to them, and a desire that his visit should be mutually agreeable, comp. Notes, chap. i. 23.

2. *For if I made you sorry.* "If when I should come among you, I should be called on to inflict sorrow by punishing your offending brethren by an act of severe discipline as soon as I came, who would there be to give me comfort but those very persons whom I had affected with grief? How little prepared would they be to make me happy, and to comfort me, amidst the deep sorrow which I should have caused by an act of severe discipline. After such an act—an act that would spread sorrow through the whole church, how could I expect that comfort which I should desire to find among you. The whole church would be affected with grief; and though I might be sustained by the sound part of the church, yet my visit would be attended with painful circumstances. I resolved, therefore, to remove all cause of difficulty, if possible, before I came, that my visit might be pleasant to us all." The idea is, that there was such a sympathy between him and them; that he was so attached to them, that he could not expect to be happy unless they were happy; that though he might be conscious he was only discharging a duty, and that God would sustain him in it, yet that it would mar the pleasure of his visit, and destroy all his anticipated happiness by the general grief.

3. *And I wrote this same unto you.* The words "this same" (τοῦτο αὐτὸ) refer to what he had written to them in the former epistle, particularly to what he had written in regard to the incestuous person, requiring them to excommunicate him. Probably the expression also includes the commands in his former epistle to reform their conduct in general, and to put away the abuses and evil practices which prevailed in the church there. ¶ *Lest when I come,* &c. Lest I should be obliged if I came personally to exercise the severity of discipline, and thus to diffuse sorrow throughout the entire church. ¶ *I should have sorrow from them of whom I ought to rejoice.* Lest I should have grief in the church. Lest the conduct of the church, and the abuses which prevail in it should give me sorrow. I should be grieved with the existence of these evils; and I should be obliged to resort to measures which would be painful to me, and to the whole church. Paul sought to avoid this by persuading them before he came to exercise the discipline themselves, and to put away the evil practices which prevailed among them. ¶ *Having confidence in you all.* Having confidence that this is your general character, that whatever adds to my joy, or promotes my happiness, would give joy to you all. Paul had enemies in Corinth; he knew that there were some there whose minds were alienated from him, and who were endeavouring to do him injury. Yet he did not doubt that it was the general character of the church that they wished him well, and would desire to make him happy; that what would tend to promote his happiness would also promote theirs; and therefore, that they would be willing to do any thing that would make his visit agreeable to him when he came among them. He was, therefore, persuaded that if he wrote them an affectionate letter, they would listen to his injunctions, that thus all that was painful might be avoided when he came among them.

4. *For out of much affliction.* Pos-

4 For out of much affliction
and anguish of heart I wrote unto you with many tears; not that
ye should be grieved, but that ye
might know the love [a] which
I have more abundantly unto
you.
5 But if [b] any have caused

a chap.11.2. b Gal.5.10.

sibly Paul's enemies had charged him with being harsh and overbearing. They may have said that there was much needless severity in his letter. He here meets that, and says, that it was with much pain and many tears that he was constrained to write as he did. He was pained at their conduct, and at the necessity which existed for such an epistle. This is an eminently beautiful instance of Paul's kindness of heart, and his susceptibility to tender impressions. The evil conduct of others gives pain to a good man; and the necessity of administering reproof and discipline is often as painful to him who does it, as it is to those who are the subjects of it. ¶ *And anguish of heart.* The word rendered "anguish" (συνοχὴ) means, properly, a holding together or shutting up; and then, pressure, distress, anguish—an affliction of the heart by which one feels tightened or constrained; such a pressure as great grief causes at the heart. ¶ *I wrote unto you with many tears.* With much weeping and grief that I was constrained to write such a letter. This was an instance of Paul's great tenderness of heart—a trait of character which he uniformly evinced. With all his strength of mind, and all his courage and readiness to face danger, Paul was not ashamed to weep; and especially if he had any occasion of censuring his Christian brethren, or administering discipline; comp. Phil. iii. 88; Acts xx. 31. This is also a specimen of the manner in which Paul met the faults of his Christian brethren. It was not with bitter denunciation. It was not with sarcasm and ridicule. It was not by blazoning those faults abroad to others. It was not with the spirit of rejoicing that they had committed errors, and had been guilty of sin. It was not as if he was glad of the opportunity of administering rebuke, and took pleasure in denunciation and in the language of reproof. All this is often done by others; but Paul pursued a different course. He sent an affectionate letter to the offenders themselves; and he did it with many tears. IT WAS DONE WEEPING. Admonition would always be done right if it was done with tears. Discipline would always be right, and would be effectual, if it were administered with tears. Any man will receive an admonition kindly, if he who administers it does it weeping; and the heart of an offender will be melted, if he who attempts to reprove him comes to him with tears. How happy would it be if all who attempt to reprove should do it with Paul's spirit. How happy, if all discipline should be administered in the church in his manner. But, we may add, how seldom is this done! How few are there who feel themselves called on to reprove an offending brother, or to charge a brother with heresy or crime, that do it with tears! ¶ *Not that ye should be grieved.* It was not my object to give you pain. ¶ *But that ye might know the love, &c.* This was one of the best evidences of his great love to them which he could possibly give. It is proof of genuine friendship for another, when we faithfully and affectionately admonish him of the error of his course; it is the highest proof of affection when we do it with tears. It is cruelty to suffer a brother to remain in sin unadmonished; it is cruel to admonish him of it in a harsh, severe, and authoritative tone; but it is proof of tender attachment when we go to him with tears, and entreat him to repent and reform. No man gives higher proof of attachment to another than he who affectionately admonishes him of his sin and danger.

5. *If any have caused grief.* There is doubtless here an allusion to the incestuous person. But it is very delicately done. He does not mention him by *name*. There is not *any-*

grief, he hath not grieved me, [a] but in part: that I may not overcharge you all.

6 Sufficient to such a man *is* this [1] punishment, which *was inflicted* [b] of many.

a Gal.4.12.

1 or, *censure*. b 1Cor.5.4,5; 1Tim.5.20.

where an allusion to his name; nor is it possible now to know it. Is this not a proof that the *names* of the offending brethren in a church should not be put on the records of sessions, and churches, and presbyteries, to be handed down to posterity? Paul does not here either *expressly* refer to such a person. He makes his remark *general*, that it might be *as* tender and kind to the offending brother as possible. They would know whom he meant, but they had already punished him, as Paul supposed, enough, and *now* all that he said in regard to him was as tender as possible, and fitted, as much as possible, to conciliate his feelings and allay his grief. He did not harshly charge him with sin; he did not use any abusive or severe epithets; but he gently insinuates that he "had caused grief;" he had pained the hearts of his brethren. ¶ *He hath not grieved me, but in part*. He has not particularly offended or grieved ME. He has grieved me only in common with others, and as a part of the church of Christ. All have common cause of grief; and I have no interest in it which is not common to you all. I am but one of a great number who have felt the deepest concern on account of his conduct. ¶ *That I may not overcharge you all*. That I may not *bear hard* (ἐπιβαρῶ) on you all; that I may not accuse you all of having caused me grief. The sense is, "Grief has been produced. I, in common with the church, have been pained, and deeply pained, with the conduct of the individual referred to; and with that of his abettors and friends. But I would not charge the whole church with it; or seem to bear hard on them, or overcharge them with want of zeal for their purity, or unwillingness to remove the evil." They had shown their willingness to correct the evil by promptly removing the offender when he had directed it. The *sense* of this verse should be connected with the verse that follows; and the idea is, that they had promptly administered sufficient discipline, and that they were not now to be charged severely with having neglected it. Even while Paul said he had been pained and grieved, he had seen occasion not to bear hard on the whole church, but to be ready to commend them for their promptness in removing the cause of the offence.

6. *Sufficient to such a man*. The incestuous person that had been by Paul's direction removed from the church. The object of Paul here is to have him again restored. For that purpose he says that the punishment which they had inflicted on him was "sufficient." It was, (1.) A sufficient expresion of the evil of the offence, and of the readiness of the church to preserve itself pure; and, (2.) It was a sufficient punishment to the offender. It had accomplished all that he had desired. It had humbled him, and brought him to repentance; and doubtless led him to put away his wife; comp. Note, 1 Cor. v. 1. As that had been done, it was proper now that he should be again restored to the privileges of the church. No evil would result from such a restoration, and their duty to their penitent brother demanded it. Mr. Locke has remarked that Paul conducts this subject here with very great tenderness and delicacy. The entire passage from ver. 5 to ver. 10 relates solely to this offending brother, yet he never once mentions his *name*, nor does he mention his *crime*. He speaks of him only in the soft terms of "such a one" and "any one:" nor does he use an epithet which would be calculated to wound his feelings, or to transmit his name to posterity, or to communicate it to other churches. So that though this epistle should be read, as Paul doubtless intended, by other churches, and be transmitted to future times, yet no one would ever be acquainted with

7 So [a] that contrariwise ye ought rather to forgive *him*, and

a Gal.6.1.

the name of the individual. How different this from the temper of those who would blazon abroad the names of offenders, or make a permanent record to carry them down with dishonour to posterity? ¶ *Which* was inflicted *of many*. By the church in its collective capacity; see Note on 1 Cor. v. 4. Paul had required the church to administer this act of discipline, and they had promptly done it. It is evident that the *whole* church was concerned in the administration of the act of discipline; as the words "of many" (ἀπὸ τῶν πλειόνων) are not applicable either to a single "bishop," or a single minister, or a presbytery, or a bench of elders; nor can they be so regarded, except by a forced and unnatural construction. Paul had directed it to be done by the assembled church (1 Cor. v. 4), and this phrase shows that they had followed his instructions. Locke supposes that the phrase means, "by the majority;" Macknight renders it, "by the greater number;" Bloomfield supposes that it means that the "punishment was carried into effect by all." Doddridge paraphrases it, "by the whole body of your society." The expression proves beyond a doubt that the whole body of the society was concerned in the act of the excommunication, and that is a proper way of administering discipline. Whether it proves, however, that that is the mode which is to be observed in all instances, may admit of a doubt, as the *example* of the early churches, in a particular case, does not prove that that mode has the force of a binding rule on all.

[It cannot fairly be argued from this verse, that the "many" or the whole congregation, were *judicially* concerned in the act of excommunication; yet as their concurrence was essential, in order to carry the sentence into effect, it was "inflicted of many" in a most emphatic sense. The refusal, on the part of the members of the church, to hold intercourse with the incestuous man, *carried into effect* what the apostle had *judicially pronounced*. See the Supplementary Note on 1 Cor. v. 4.]

7. *So that contrariwise*. On the other hand: on the contrary. That is, instead of continuing the punishment. Since the punishment was sufficient, and has answered all the purpose of bearing your testimony against the offence, and of bringing him to repentance, you ought again to admit him to your communion. ¶ *Ye* ought *rather to forgive* him. Rather than continue the pain and disgrace of excommunication. It follows from this, (1.) That the proper time for restoring an offender is only when the punishment has answered the purpose for which it was designed; *i. e.* has shown the just abhorrence of the church against the sin, and has reformed the offender; and, (2.) That *when* that is done the church ought to forgive the offending brother, and admit him again to their fellowship. *When* it can be ascertained that the punishment has been effectual in reforming him, may depend somewhat on the nature of the offence. In this case, it was sufficiently shown by his putting away his wife, and by the manifestations of sorrow. So in other cases, it may be shown by a man's abandoning a course of sin, and reforming his life. If he has been unjust, by his repairing the evil; if he has been pursuing an unlawful business, by abandoning it; if he has pursued a course of vice; by his forsaking it, and by giving satisfactory evidences of sorrow and of reformation, for a period sufficiently long to show his sincerity. The *time* which will be required in each case, must depend, of course, somewhat on the nature of the offence, the previous character of the individual, the temptations to which he may be exposed, and the disgrace which he may have brought on his Christian calling. It is to be observed, also, that *then* his restoration is to be regarded as an act of *forgiveness*, a favour (χαρίσασθαι, *i. e.* χαρις, favour, grace) on the part of the church. It is not a matter of justice, or of claim on his part, for having once dishonoured his call-

comfort *him*, lest perhaps such a one should be swallowed up with overmuch sorrow.

8 Wherefore I beseech you that ye would confirm *your* love toward him.

9 For to this end also did I write, that I might know the proof

---

ing, he has forfeited his right to a good standing among Christians; but it is a matter of favour, and he should be willing to humble himself before the church, and make suitable acknowledgment for his offences. ¶ *And comfort* him. There is every reason to think that this man became a sincere penitent. If so, he must have been deeply pained at the remembrance of his sin, and the dishonour which he had brought on his profession, as well as at the consequences in which he had been involved. In this deep distress, Paul tells them that they ought to comfort him. They should receive him kindly, as God receives to his favour a penitent sinner. They should not cast out his name as evil; they should not reproach him for his sins; they should not harrow up his recollection of the offence by often referring to it; they should be willing to bury it in lasting forgetfulness, and treat him now as a brother. It is a duty of a church to treat with kindness a true penitent, and receive him to their affectionate embrace. The offence should be forgiven and forgotten. The consolations of the gospel, adapted to the condition of penitents, should be freely administered; and all should be done that can be, to make the offender, when penitent, happy and useful in the community. ¶ *Lest perhaps such a one.* Still forbearing to mention his name; still showing towards him the utmost tenderness and delicacy. ¶ *Should be swallowed up*, &c. Should be overcome with grief, and should be rendered incapable of usefulness by his excessive sorrow. This is a strong expression, denoting intensity of grief. We speak of a man's being drowned in sorrow; or overwhelmed with grief; of grief preying upon him. The figure here is probably taken from deep waters, or from a whirlpool which seems to swallow up any thing that comes within reach. Excessive grief or calamity, in the Scriptures, is often compared to such waters; see Ps. cxxiv. 2—5. "If it had not been the LORD who was on our side when men rose up against us, then they had swallowed us up quick, when their wrath was kindled against us; then the waters had overwhelmed us, the stream had gone over our soul; then the proud waters had gone over our soul;" see Ps. lxix. 1. "Save me, O God, for the waters are come into my soul." Paul apprehended that by excessive grief, the offending brother would be destroyed. His life would waste away under the effect of his excommunication and disgrace, and the remembrance of his offence would prey upon him, and sink him to the grave.

8. *Wherefore I beseech you that ye would confirm* your *love toward him.* The word here rendered confirm (κυρῶσαι) occurs in the New Testament only here and in Gal. iii. 15. It means to give authority, to establish as valid, to confirm; and here means that they should give strong expressions and assurances of their love to him; that they should pursue such a course as would leave no room for doubt in regard to it. Tindal has well rendered it, "Wherefore I exhort you that love may have strength over him." Paul referred, doubtless, here to some public act of the church by which the sentence of excommunication might be removed, and by which the offender might have a public assurance of their favour.

9. *For to this end did I write.* The apostle did not say that this was the *only* purpose of his writing, to induce them to excommunicate the offender. He does not say that he wished in an arbitrary manner to test their willingness to obey him, or to induce them to do a thing in itself wrong, in order to try their obedience. But the meaning is this: This was the main reason why he *wrote* to them, rather than to come personally among them.

of you, whether ye be obedient [a]
in all things.
10 To whom ye forgive any
thing, I *forgive* also: for if I
forgave any thing, to whom I forgave *it*, for your sakes *forgave I it*
in the [1] person of Christ.
11 Lest Satan should get an advantage of us: for we are not ignorant of his devices.

a chap. 7. 16.

1 or, *sight*.

The thing ought to have been done; the offender ought to be punished; and Paul says that he adopted the method of *writing* to them rather than of coming among them in person, in order to give them an opportunity to show whether they were disposed to be obedient. And the sense is, "You may now forgive him. He has not only been sufficiently punished, and he has not only evinced suitable penitence, but also another object which I had in view has been accomplished. I desired to see whether you were, as a church, disposed to be obedient. That object, also, has been accomplished. And now, since every thing aimed at in the case of discipline has been secured, you may forgive him, and should, without hesitation, again receive him to the bosom of the church."

10. *To whom ye forgive any thing.* The sense here is, "I have confidence in you as a Christian society and such confidence, that if you forgive an offence in one of your members, I shall approve the act, and shall also be ready to forgive." He refers, doubtless, to this particular case; but he makes his remark general. It is implied here, I think, that the Corinthians were *disposed* to forgive the offending brother; and Paul here assures them that they had his hearty assent to this, and that if they did forgive him, he was ready to join them in the act, and to forgive him also. ¶ *For if I forgave any thing.* If I *forgive* any thing; if I remit any of the punishments which have been inflicted by my authority. ¶ *For your sakes.* It is not on account of the offender alone; it is in order to promote the happiness and purity of the church. ¶ *In the person of Christ.* Locke paraphrases this, "By the authority, and in the name of Christ." Doddridge, "As in the person of Christ, and by the high authority with which he has been pleased to invest me." Tindal, "In the room of Christ." The word rendered *person* (Marg. *sight*, πρόσωπον, from πρός and ὤψ), means properly the part towards, at, and around the eye.—*Robinson.* Then it means the face, visage, countenance; then the presence, person, &c. Here it probably means, in the presence of Christ; with his eye upon me, and conscious that I am acting before him, and must give account to him. It implies, undoubtedly, that Paul acted by his authority, and felt that he was doing that which Christ would approve.

11. *Lest Satan.* The devil. The name Satan denotes an adversary, an accuser, an enemy. It is the usual proper name which is given to the devil, the great adversary of God and man. ¶ *Should get an advantage of us.* The literal translation of the Greek would be, "That we may not be defrauded by Satan." (Ἵνα μὴ πλεονεκτηθῶμεν ὑπὸ τοῦ σατανᾶ). The verb here used denotes *to have more than another;* then to gain, to take advantage of one, to defraud. And the idea is, that they should at once re-admit the penitent offender to their communion, lest if they did not do it, Satan would take advantage of it to do injury to him and them. It is a *reason* given by Paul why they should lose no time in restoring him to the church. What the advantage was which Satan might gain, Paul does not specify. It might be this: That under pretence of duty, and seeking the purity of the church, Satan would tempt them to harsh measures; to needless severity of discipline; to an unkind and unforgiving spirit; and thus, at the same time, injure the cause of religion, and ruin him who had been the subject of discipline. ¶ *For we are not ignorant of his devices.* We know his plans, his thoughts, his cunning, his skill. We are not ignorant of the great number

12 Furthermore, when [a] I came to Troas to *preach* Christ's gospel, and a [b] door was opened unto me of the Lord.

13 I had no rest [c] in my spirit, because I found not Titus my brother: but taking my leave of them I went from thence into Macedonia.

a Acts 16.8. *b* 1 Cor. 16.9. *c* chap. 7.5,6.

of stratagems which he is constantly using to injure us, and to destroy the souls of men. He is full of wiles; and Paul had had abundant occasion to be acquainted with the means which he had used to defeat his plans and to destroy the church. The church, at all times, has been subjected to the influence of those wiles, as well as individual Christians. And the church, therefore, as well as individual Christians, should be constantly on its guard against those snares. Even the best and purest efforts of the church are often perverted, as in the case of administering discipline, to the worst results; and by the imprudence and want of wisdom; by the rashness or overheated zeal; by the pretensions to great purity and love of truth; and by a harsh, severe, and censorious spirit, Satan often takes advantage of the church, and advances his own dark and mischievous designs.

12. *Furthermore.* But (δὲ). This particle is properly adversative; but frequently denotes transition, and serves to introduce *something else*, whether opposite to what precedes, or simply continuative or explanatory. Here, it is designed to *continue* or *explain* the statement before made of his deep affection for the church, and his interest in its affairs. He therefore tells them that when he came to Troas, and was favoured there with great success, and was engaged in a manner most likely of all others to interest his feelings and to give him joy, yet he was deeply distressed because he had not heard, as he expected, from them; but so deep was his anxiety that he left Troas and went into Macedonia. ¶ *When I came to Troas* This was a city of Phrygia, or Mysia, on the Hellespont, between Troy on the north, and Assos on the south; see Note on Acts xvi. 8 It was on the regular route from Ephesus to Macedonia. Paul took that route because on his journey to Macedonia he had resolved, for the reasons above stated, not to go to Corinth. ¶ *To preach Christ's gospel.* Greek. "For (εἰς) the gospel of Christ;" that is, on account of his gospel; or to promote it. Why he selected Troas, or the region of the Troad (Note, Acts xvi. 8), as the field of his labours, he does not say. It is probable that he was waiting there to hear from Corinth by Titus, and while there he resolved not to be idle, but to make known as much as possible the gospel. ¶ *And a door was opened unto me;* see Note, 1 Cor. xvi. 9. There was an opportunity of doing good, and the people were disposed to hear the gospel. This was a work in which Paul delighted to engage, and in which he usually found his highest comfort. It was of all things the most adapted to promote his happiness.

13. *I had no rest in my spirit.* I was disappointed, sad, deeply anxious. Though the work in which I was engaged was that which usually gives me my highest joy, yet such was my anxiety to learn the state of things in Corinth, and the success of my letter, and to see Titus, whom I was expecting, that I had comparatively no peace, and no comfort. ¶ *But taking my leave of them.* Though so many considerations urged me to stay; though there was such a promising field of labour, yet such was my anxiety to hear from you, that I left them. ¶ *I went from thence into Macedonia;* see Note, Acts xvi. 9. I went over where I expected to find Titus, and to learn the state of your affairs. This is one of the few instances in which Paul left an inviting field of labour, and where there was a prospect of signal success, to go to another place. It is adduced *here* to show the deep interest which he had in the church at Corinth, and his

14 Now thanks *be* unto God, [a] which always causeth us to tri-

a Rom.8.37.

---

anxiety to learn what was their condition. It shows that there *may* be cases where it is proper for ministers to leave a field of great and inviting usefulness, to go to another field and to engage in another part of the great vineyard.

14. *Now thanks* be *unto God,* &c. There seem to have been several sources of Paul's joy on this occasion. The principal was, his constant and uniform success in endeavouring to advance the interests of the kingdom of the Redeemer. But in particular he rejoiced, (1.) Because Titus had come to him there, and had removed his distress; comp. ver. 13. (2.) Because he learned from him that his efforts in regard to the church at Corinth had been successful, and that they had hearkened to his counsels in his first letter; and, (3.) Because he was favoured with signal success in Macedonia. His being compelled, therefore, to remove from Troas and to go to Macedonia had been to him ultimately the cause of great joy and consolation. These instances of success Paul regarded as occasions of gratitude to God. ¶ *Which always causeth us.* Whatever may be our efforts, and wherever we are. Whether it is in endeavouring to remove the errors and evils existing in a particular church, or whether it be in preaching the gospel in places where it has been unknown, still success crowns our efforts, and we have the constant evidence of divine approbation. This was *Paul's* consolation in the midst of his many trials; and it proves that, whatever may be the external circumstances of a minister, whether poverty, want, persecution, or distress, he will have abundant occasion to give thanks to God if his efforts as a minister are crowned with success. ¶ *To triumph in Christ.* To triumph through the aid of Christ, or in promoting the cause of Christ. Paul had no joy which was not connected with Christ, and he had no success which he did not trace to him. The word which is here rendered *triumph* (θριαμβεύοντι from θριαμβεύω) occurs in no other place in the New Testament, except in Col. ii. 15. It is there rendered "*triumphing* over them in it," that is, triumphing over the principalities and powers which he had spoiled, or plundered; and it there means that Christ led them in triumph after the manner of a conqueror. The word is here used in a causative sense—the sense of the Hebrew Hiphil conjugation. It properly refers to a triumph; or a triumphal procession. Originally the word θρίαμβος meant a hymn which was sung in honour of Bacchus; then the tumultuous and noisy procession which constituted the worship of the god of wine; and then any procession of a similar kind.—*Passow.* It was particularly applied among both the Greeks and the Romans to a public and solemn honour conferred on a victorious general on a return from a successful war in which he was allowed a magnificent entrance into the capital. In these triumphs, the victorious commander was usually preceded or attended by the spoils of war; by the most valuable and magnificent articles which he had captured; and by the princes, nobles, generals, or people whom he had subdued. The victor was drawn in a magnificent chariot, usually by two white horses. Other animals were sometimes used. "When Pompey triumphed over Africa, his chariot was drawn by elephants; that of Mark Antony by lions; that of Heliogabalus by tigers; and that of Aurelius by deer."—*Clark.* The people of Corinth were not unacquainted with the nature of a triumph. About one hundred and forty-seven years before Christ, Lucius Mummius, the Roman consul, had conquered all Achaia, and had destroyed Corinth, Thebes, and Colchis, and by order of the Roman senate was favoured with a triumph, and was surnamed *Achaicus.* Tindal renders this place, "Thanks be unto God which always giveth us the victory in Christ." Paul refers here to a victory which

umph in Christ, and maketh manifest the savour [a] of his knowledge by us in every place.

a Ca.1.3.

15 For we are unto God a sweet savour of Christ, in them [b] that are saved, and in them that perish:

b 1Cor.1.18.

he had, and a triumph with which he was favoured by the Redeemer. It was a victory over the enemies of the gospel; it was success in advancing the interests of the kingdom of Christ; and he rejoiced in that victory, and in that success, with more solid and substantial joy than a Roman victor ever felt on returning from his conquests over nations, even when attended with the richest spoils of victory, and by humbled princes and kings in chains, and when the assembled thousands shouted *Io triumphe!* ¶ *And maketh manifest.* Makes known; spreads abroad—as a pleasant fragrance is diffused through the air. ¶ *The savour* (ὀσμὴν). The smell; the fragrance. The word in the New Testament is used to denote a pleasant or fragrant odour, as of incense, or aromatics; John xii. 3; see Eph. v. 2; Phil. iv. 18. There is an allusion here doubtless to the fact that in the triumphal processions fragrant odours were diffused around; flowers, diffusing a grateful smell, were scattered in the way; and on the altars of the gods incense was burned during the procession, and sacrifices offered, and the whole city was filled with the smoke of sacrifices, and with perfumes. So Paul speaks of *knowledge* — the knowledge of Christ. In his triumphings, the knowledge of the Redeemer was diffused abroad, like the odours which were diffused in the triumphal march of the conqueror. And that odour or savour was acceptable to God—as the fragrance of aromatics and of incense was pleasant in the triumphal procession of the returning victor. The phrase "makes manifest the savour of his knowledge," therefore, means, that the knowledge of Christ was diffused everywhere by Paul, as the grateful smell of aromatics was diffused all around the triumphing warrior and victor. The effect of Paul's conquests everywhere was to diffuse the knowledge of the Saviour—and this was acceptable and pleasant to God—though there might be many who would not avail themselves of it, and would perish; see ver. 15.

15. *For we are unto God.* We who are his ministers, and who thus triumph. It is implied here that Paul felt that ministers were labouring *for* God, and felt assured that their labours would be acceptable to him. —The *object* of Paul in the statement, in this and in the following verses, is undoubtedly to meet the charges of his detractors and enemies. He says, therefore, that whatever was the result of his labours in regard to the future salvation of men; yet, that his well-meant endeavours, and labours, and self-denials in preaching the gospel, were acceptable to God. The measure of God's approbation in the case was not his *success*, but his fidelity, his zeal, his self-denial, whatever might be the reception of the gospel among those who heard it. ¶ *A sweet savour.* Like the smell of pleasant incense, or of grateful aromatics, such as were burned in the triumphal processions of returning conquerors. The meaning is, that their labours were acceptable to God; he was pleased with them, and would bestow on them the smiles and proofs of his approbation. The word here rendered "sweet savour" (εὐωδία) occurs only in this place, and in Eph. v. 2; Phil. iv. 18; and is applied to persons or things well-pleasing to God. It properly means good odour, or fragrance, and in the Septuagint it is frequently applied to the *incense* that was burnt in the public worship of God and to sacrifices in general; Gen. viii. 21; Ex. xxix. 18, 25, 41; Lev. i. 9, 13, 17; ii. 2, 9, 12; iii. 5, 16; iv. 31, &c. &c. Here it means that the services of Paul and the other ministers of religion were *as* grateful to God as sweet incense, or acceptable sacrifices. ¶ *Of Christ.* That is, we are Christ's sweet savour to God: we are that which he has ap-

pointed, and which he has devoted and consecrated to God; we are the offering, so to speak, which he is continually making to God. ¶ *In them that are saved.* In regard to them who believe the gospel through our ministry and who are saved. Our labour in carrying the gospel to them, and in bringing them to the knowledge of the truth, is acceptable to God. Their salvation is an object of his highest desire, and he is gratified with our fidelity, and with our success. This reason why their work was acceptable to God is more fully stated in the following verse, where it is said that in reference to them they were the "savour of life unto life." The word "saved" here refers to all who become Christians, and who enter heaven; and as the salvation of men is an object of such desire to God, it cannot but be that all who bear the gospel to men are engaged in an acceptable service, and that all their efforts will be pleasing to him, and approved in his sight In regard to *this* part of Paul's statement, there can be no difficulty. ¶ *And in them that perish.* In reference to them who reject the gospel, and who are finally lost.—It is implied here, (1.) That some *would* reject the gospel and perish, with whatever fidelity and self-denial the ministers of religion might labour. (2.) That though this would be the result, yet the labours of the ministers of religion would be acceptable to God. This is a fearful and awful declaration, and has been thought by many to be attended with difficulty. A few remarks may present the true sense of the passage, and remove the difficulty from it. (1.) It is not affirmed or implied here that the destruction of those who would reject the gospel, and who would perish, was *desired* by God or would be pleasing to him. This is no where affirmed or implied in the Bible. (2.) It is affirmed only that the labours of the ministers of religion in endeavouring to save them would be acceptable and pleasing to God. Their labours would be *in order* to save them, not to destroy them. *Their* desire was to bring all to heaven—and this was acceptable to God. Whatever might be the result, whether successful or not, yet God would be pleased with self-denial, and toil, and prayer that was honestly and zealously put forth to save others from death. They would be approved by God in proportion to the amount of labour, zeal, and fidelity which they evinced. (3.) It would be by no fault of faithful ministers that men would perish. Their efforts would be to save them, and those efforts would be pleasing to God. (4.) It would be by no fault of the gospel that men would perish. The regular and proper tendency of the gospel is to save, not to destroy men; as the tendency of medicine is to heal them, of food to support the body, of air to give vitality, of light to give pleasure to the eye, &c. It is provided for all, and is adapted to all. There is a sufficiency in the gospel for all men, and in its nature it is as really fitted to save one as another. Whatever may be the manner in which it is received, it is always in itself the same pure and glorious system; full of benevolence and mercy. *The bitterest enemy of the gospel cannot point to one of its provisions that is adapted or designed to make men miserable, and to destroy them.* All its provisions are adapted to salvation; all its arrangements are those of benevolence; all the powers and influences which it originates, are those which are fitted to save, not to destroy men. The gospel is what it is in itself—a pure, holy, and benevolent system, and is answerable only for effects which a pure, holy, and benevolent system is fitted to produce. To use the beautiful language of Theodoret, as quoted by Bloomfield, "We indeed bear the sweet odour of Christ's gospel to *all;* but all who participate in it do not experience its salutiferous effects. Thus to diseased eyes even the light of heaven is noxious; yet the sun does not bring the injury. And to those in a fever, honey is bitter; yet it *is sweet* nevertheless. Vultures too, it is said, fly from sweet odours of myrrh; yet myrrh is myrrh though the vultures avoid it. Thus,

16 To [a] the one *we are* the saviour of death unto death; and

a John 9.39; 1 Pet.2.7,8.

if some be saved, though others perish, the gospel retains its own virtue, and we the preachers of it remain just as we are; and the gospel retains its odorous and salutiferous properties, though some may disbelieve and abuse it, and perish." Yet, (5.) It is implied that the gospel would be the occasion of heavier condemnation to some, and that they would sink into deeper ruin in consequence of its being preached to them. This is implied in the expression in ver. 16. "to the one we are a savour of death unto death." In the explanation of this, we may observe, (*a*) That those who perish would have perished at any rate. All were under condemnation whether the gospel had come to them or not. None will perish in consequence of the gospel's having been sent to them who would not have perished had it been unknown. Men do not perish because the gospel is sent to them, but for their own sins. (*b*) It is in fact by their own fault that men reject the gospel, and that they are lost. They are voluntary in this; and, whatever is their final destiny, they are not under compulsion. The gospel compels no one against his will either to go to heaven, or to hell. (*c*) Men under the gospel sin against greater light than they do without it. They have more to answer for. It increases their responsibility. If, therefore, they reject it, and go down to eternal death, they go from higher privileges; and they go, of course, to meet a more aggravated condemnation. For condemnation will always be in exact proportion to guilt; and guilt is in proportion to abused light and privileges. (*d*) The preaching of the gospel, and the offers of life, are often the occasion of the deeper guilt of the sinner. Often he becomes enraged. He gives vent to the deep malignity of his soul. He opposes the gospel with malice and infuriated anger. His eye kindles with indignation, and his lip curls with pride and scorn. He is profane and blasphemous; and the offering of the gospel to him is the occasion of exciting deep and malignant passions against God, against the Saviour, against the ministers of religion. Against the gospel, men often manifest the same malignity and scorn which they did against the Saviour himself. Yet this is not the fault of the gospel, nor of the ministers of religion. It is the fault of sinners themselves; and while there can be no doubt that such a rejection of the gospel will produce their deeper condemnation, and that it is a savour of death unto death unto them; still the gospel is good and benevolent, and still God will be pleased with those who faithfully offer its provisions, and who urge it on the attention of men.

16. *To the one.* To those who perish. ¶ *We are the savour of death unto death.* We are the occasion of deepening their condemnation, and of sinking them lower into ruin. The expression here used means literally, "to the one class we bear a death-conveying odour leading to their death"—a savour, a smell which, under the circumstances, is destructive to life, and which leads to death. Mr. Locke renders this, "To the one my preaching is of ill savour, unacceptable and offensive, by their rejecting whereof they draw death on themselves." Grateful as their labours were to God, and acceptable as would be their efforts, whatever might be the results, yet Paul could not be ignorant that the gospel would in fact be the means of greater condemnation to many; see Notes on ver. 15. It was indeed by their own fault; yet wherever the gospel was preached, it would to many have this result. It is probable that the language here used is borrowed from similar expressions which were common among the Jews. Thus in Debarim Rabba, sec. 1, fol. 248, it is said, "As the bee brings home honey to the owner, but stings others, so it is with the words of the law." "They (the words of the law) are a savour of life to Israel, but a savour of death to the people of this world." Thus

to the other the savour of life unto life. And who [a] *is* sufficient for these things?

17 For we are not as many, which corrupt [1] the word of God: but as of sincerity, but as of God, in the sight [b] of God, speak we [2] in Christ.

a chap.3.5,6. 1 or, *deal deceitfully with*, chap.4.2. b Heb.11.27. 2 or, *of*.

in Taarieth, fol. 7, 1, "Whoever gives attention to the law on account of the law itself, to him it becomes an aromatic of life (כם החיים), but to him who does not attend to the law on account of the law itself, to him it becomes an aromatic of death (מות כם)"—the idea of which is, that as medicines skilfully applied will heal, but if unskilfully applied will aggravate a disease, so it is with the words of the law. Again, "The word of the law which proceeds out of the mouth of God is an odour of life to the Israelites, but an odour of death to the Gentiles;" see Rosenmüller, and Bloomfield. The sense of the passage is plain, that the gospel, by the wilful rejection of it, becomes the means of the increased guilt and condemnation of many of those who hear it. ¶ *And to the other.* To those who embrace it, and are saved. ¶ *The savour of life.* An odour, or fragrance producing life, or tending to life. It is a living, or life-giving savour. It is in itself grateful and pleasant. ¶ *Unto life.* Tending to life; or adapted to produce life. The word *life* here, as often elsewhere, is used to denote salvation. It is (1.) Life in opposition to the death in sin in which all are by nature; (2.) In opposition to death in the grave—as it leads to a glorious resurrection; (3.) In opposition to eternal death; to the second dying, as it leads to life and peace and joy in heaven; see the words "life" and "death" explained in the Notes on Rom. vi. 23. The gospel is "the savour of life unto life," because, (1.) It is its nature and tendency to produce life and salvation. It is adapted to that; and is designed to that end. (2.) Because it actually results in the life and salvation of those who embrace it. It is the immediate and direct cause of their salvation; of their recovery from sin; of their glorious resurrection; of their eternal life in heaven; ¶ *And who is sufficient for these things?* For the arduous and responsible work of the ministry; for a work whose influence *must* be felt either in the eternal salvation, or the eternal ruin of the soul. Who is worthy of so important a charge? Who can undertake it without trembling? Who can engage in it without feeling that he is in himself unfit for it, and that he needs constant divine grace? This is an exclamation which any one may well make in view of the responsibilities of the work of the ministry. And we may remark, (1.) If *Paul* felt this, assuredly others should feel it also. If, with all the divine assistance which he had; all the proofs of the peculiar presence of God, and all the mighty miraculous powers conferred on him, Paul had such a sense of unfitness for this great work, then a consciousness of unfitness, and a deep sense of responsibility, may well rest on all others. (2.) It was this sense of the responsibility of the ministry which contributed much to Paul's success. It was a conviction that the results of his work must be seen in the joys of heaven, or the woes of hell, that led him to look to God for aid, and to devote himself so entirely to his great work. Men will not feel much concern unless they have a deep sense of the magnitude and responsibility of their work. Men who feel as they should about the ministry will look to God for aid, and will feel that he alone can sustain them in their arduous duties.

17. *For we are nct as many.* This refers doubtless to the false teachers at Corinth; and to all who mingled human philosophy or tradition with the pure word of truth. Paul's *design* in the statement in this verse seems to be to affirm that he had such a deep sense of the responsibility of the min∙isterial office, and of its necessary influence on the eternal destiny of man, that it led him to preach the

simple gospel, the pure word of God. He did not dare to dilute it with any human mixture. He did not dare to preach philosophy, or human wisdom. He did not dare to mingle with it the crude conceptions of man. He sought to exhibit the simple truth as it was in Jesus; and so deep was his sense of the responsibility of the office, and so great was his desire on the subject, that he had been enabled to do it. and to triumph always in Christ. So that, although he was conscious that he was in himself unfit for these things, yet by the grace of God he had been able always to exhibit the simple truth, and his labours had been crowned with constant and signal success. ¶ *Which corrupt the word of God.* Margin, "deal deceitfully with." The word here used (καπηλεύοντες) occurs no where else in the New Testament, and does not occur in the Septuagint. The word is derived from κάπηλος, which signifies properly a huckster, or a *retailer of wine*, a petty chapman; a man who buys up articles for the purpose of selling them again. It also means sometimes a vintner, or an innkeeper. The proper idea is that of a small dealer and especially in wine. Such persons were notorious, as they are now, for diluting their wines with water (comp. Sept. in Isa. i. 22); and for compounding wines of other substances than the juice of the grape for purposes of gain. Wine, of all substances in trade, perhaps, affords the greatest facilities for such dishonest tricks; and accordingly the dealers in that article have generally been most distinguished for fraudulent practices and corrupt and diluted mixtures. Hence the word comes to denote to adulterate; to corrupt, &c. It is here applied to those who adulterated or corrupted the pure word of God in any way, and for any purpose. It probably has particular reference to those who did it either by Judaizing opinions, or by the mixtures of a false and deceitful philosophy. The latter mode would be likely to prevail among the subtle and philosophizing Greeks. It is in such ways that the gospel has been usually corrupted. (1.) It is done by attempting to attach a philosophical explanation to the facts of revelation, and making *the theory* as important as *the fact.* (2.) By attempting to explain away the offensive points of revelation by the aid of philosophy. (3.) By attempting to make the facts of Scripture accord with the prevalent notions of philosophy, and by applying a mode of interpretation to the Bible which would fritter away its meaning, and make it mean any thing or nothing at pleasure. In these, and in various other ways, men have corrupted the word of God; and of all the evils which Christianity has ever sustained in this world, the worst have been those which it has received from philosophy, and from those teachers who have corrupted the word of God. The fires of persecution it could meet, and still be pure; the utmost efforts of princes, and monarchs, and of Satan to destroy it, it has outlived, and has shone purely and brightly amidst all these efforts; but, when corrupted by philosophy, and by "science falsely so called," it has been dimmed in its lustre, paralyzed in its aims, and shorn of its power, and has ceased to be mighty in pulling down the strong holds of Satan's kingdom. Accordingly, the enemy of God has ceased to excite persecution, and now aims in various ways to *corrupt* the gospel by the admixture of philosophy, and of human opinions. Tindal renders this passage, "For we are not as many are which *choppe and chaunge* with the word of God"—an idea which is important and beautiful—but this is one of the few instances in which he mistook the sense of the original text. In general, the accuracy of his translation and his acquaintance with the true sense of the Greek text are very remarkable. ¶ *But as of sincerity.* Sincerely; actuated by unmingled honesty and simplicity of aim; see Note on chap. i. 12. ¶ *As of God.* As influenced by him; as under his control and direction; as having been sent by him; as acting by his command; see Note, chap. i. 12. ¶ *In the sight of God.* As if we felt that his eye was always on us. Nothing is better fitted to make a man sincere and honest, than this. ¶ *Speak we in Christ.* In the name, and in the service of Christ. We deliver our message with a deep consciousness that the eye of the all-seeing God is on us; that we can conceal nothing from him; and that we must soon give up our account to him.

REMARKS.

1. In this chapter, and in the management of the whole case to which Paul here refers, we have an instance of his *tenderness* in administering discipline. This tenderness was manifested in many ways. (1.) He did nothing to wound the feelings of the offending party. (2.) He did nothing in the way of punishment which a stern sense of duty did not demand. (3.) He did it all with many tears. He wept at the necessity of administering discipline at all. He wept over the remissness of the church. He wept over the fall of the offending brother. (4.) He did not mention even the name of the offender. He did not blazon his faults abroad; nor has he left any clue by which it can be known; nor did he take any measures which were fitted to pain, unnecessarily, the feelings of his friends. If all discipline in the church were conducted in this manner, it would probably always be effectual and successful, ver. 1—10.

2. We ought cordially to receive and forgive an offending brother, as soon as he gives evidence of repentance. We should harbour no malice against him; and if, by repentance, he has put away his sins, we should hasten to forgive him. This we should do as individuals, and as churches. God cheerfully forgives us, and receives us into favour on our repentance; and we should hail *the privilege* of treating all our offending brethren in the same manner, ver. 7, 8.

3. *Churches* should be careful that Satan should not get an advantage over them, ver. 11. In every way possible he will attempt it; and perhaps in few modes is it more often done than in administering discipline. In such a case, Satan gains an advantage over a church in the following ways. (1.) In inducing it to *neglect* discipline. This occurs often because an offender is rich, or talented, or is connected with influential families; because there is a fear of driving off such families from the church; because the individual is of elevated rank, and the church suffers him to remain in her bosom. The laws of the church, like other laws, are often like cobwebs: Great flies break through, and the smaller ones are caught. The consequence is, that Satan gains an immense advantage. Rich and influential offenders remain in the church; discipline is relaxed; the cause of Christ is scandalized; and the church at large feels the influence, and the work of God declines. (2.) Satan gains an advantage in discipline, sometimes, by too great *severity* of discipline. If he cannot induce a church to relax altogether, and to suffer offenders to remain, then he excites them to improper and needless severity. He drives them on to harsh discipline for small offences. He excites a spirit of persecution He enkindles a false zeal on account of the Shibboleth of doctrine. He excites a spirit of party, and causes the church to mistake it for zeal for truth. He excites a spirit of persecution against some of the best men in the church, on account of pretended errors in doctrine, and kindles the flames of intestine war; and breaks the church up into parties and fragments. Or he urges on the church, even in cases where discipline is proper, to needless and inappropriate severity; drives the offender from its bosom; breaks his spirit; and prevents ever-onward his usefulness, his return, and his happiness. One of the chief arts of Satan has been to cause the church in cases of discipline to use *severity* instead of *kindness;* to excite a spirit of persecution instead of love. Almost all the evils which grow out of attempts at discipline might have been prevented by a spirit of LOVE. (3.) Satan gains an advantage in cases of discipline, when the church is unwilling to re-admit to

fellowship an offending but a penitent member. His spirit is broken; his usefulness is destroyed. The world usually takes sides with him against the church, and the cause of religion bleeds.

4. *Individual Christians*, as well as churches, should be careful that Satan does not get an advantage over them, ver. 11. Among the ways in which he does this are the following: (1.) By inducing them to conform to the world. This is done under the plea that religion is not gloomy, and morose, and ascetic. Thence he often leads professors into all the gayeties, and amusements, and follies of which the world partake. Satan gains an immense advantage to his cause when this is done—for all the influence of the professed Christian is with him. (2.) By producing laxness of opinion n regard to doctrine. Christ intends that his cause shall advance by the influence of truth; and that his church shall be the witness of the truth. The cause of Satan advances by error and falsehood; and when professed Christians embrace falsehood, or are indifferent to truth, their whole influence is on the side of Satan, and his advantage is immense when they become the advocates of error. (3.) By producing among Christians despondency, melancholy, and despair. Some of the best men are often thus afflicted and thrown into darkness, as Job was; Job xxiii. 8—9. Indeed, it is commonly the best members of a church that have doubts in this manner, and that fall into temptation, and that are left to the buffetings of Satan. Your gay, and worldly, and fashionable Christians have usually no such troubles—except when they lie on a bed of death. They are not in the way of Satan. They do not oppose him, and he will not trouble them. It is your humble, praying, self-denying Christians that he dreads and hates; and it is these that he is suffered to tempt, and to make sad, and to fill with gloom and doubt. And when this is done, it is an immense advantage to his cause. It produces the impression that religion is nothing but gloom and melancholy, and the people of the world are easily led to hate and avoid it. Christians, therefore, *should be* cheerful, and benevolent, and happy—as they may be—lest Satan should get an advantage over them. (4.) By fanaticism. For when Satan finds that he can get no advantage over Christians by inducing them to do *nothing*, or to do any thing positively wrong or immoral, he drives them on with over-heated and ill-timed zeal; he makes them unreasonably strenuous for some single opinion or measure; he disposes them to oppose and persecute all who do not fall into their views, and feel as they feel. (5.) By contentions and strifes. Satan often gets an advantage in that way. No matter what the cause may be, whether it be for doctrines, or for any other cause, yet the very fact that there are contentions among the professed followers of "the Prince of peace" does injury, and gives Satan an advantage. No small part of his efforts, therefore, have been to excite contentions among Christians, an effort in which he has been, and is still, eminently successful.

5. Satan gets an advantage over sinners, and *they* should be on their guard. He does it, (1.) By producing a sense of security in their present condition; and by leading them to indifference in regard to their eternal condition. In this he is eminently successful; and when this is gained, all is gained that his cause demands. It is impossible to conceive of greater success in any thing than Satan has in producing a state of indifference to the subject of religion among men. (2.) By inducing them to *defer* attention to religion to some future time. This is an advantage, because, (*a*) It accomplishes all he wishes at present; (*b*) Because it is usually successful altogether. It is usually the same thing as resolving not to attend to religion at all. (3.) By producing false views of religion. He represents it at one time as gloomy, sad, and melancholy; at another, as so easy, that it may be obtained, whenever they please; at another, by persuading them that their sins are so

great that they cannot be forgiven. One great object of Satan is to blind the minds of sinners to the true nature of religion; and in this he is usually successful. (4.) He deludes the aged by telling them it is too late; and the young by telling them that now is the time for mirth and pleasure, and that religion may be attended to at some future period of life. (5.) He gains an advantage by plunging the sinner deeper and deeper in sin; inducing him to listen to the voice of temptation; by making him the companion of the wicked; and by deluding him with the promises of pleasure, honour, and gain in this world until it is too late, and he dies.

6. Ministers of the gospel *may* have occasion to triumph in the success of their work. Paul always met with success of some kind; always had some cause of triumph. In all his trials, he had occasion of rejoicing, and always was assured that he was pursuing that course which would lead him ultimately to triumph, ver. 14.

7. The gospel may be so preached as to be successful, ver. 14. In the hands of Paul it was successful. So it was with the other apostles. So it was with Luther, Knox, Calvin. So it was with Whitefield, Edwards, Wesley, and Payson. If ministers are not successful, it is not the fault of the gospel. It is adapted to do good, and to save men; and it *may be* so preached as to accomplish those great ends. If all ministers were as self-denying, and laborious, and prayerful as were these men, the gospel would be as successful now as it has ever been.

[There is much truth in this representation. Certainly no great revival of religion can rationally be expected when the ministers of the gospel are not self-denying, laborious, and prayerful. Yet we cannot *certainly* pronounce, that equal diligence in the use of means will in every case be attended with equal success. Allowance must be made for God's sovereignty, in dispensing his grace. Otherwise, wherever the word was preached under most favourable circumstances, as far as excellence of means is concerned, there also, we should expect, and find most success. But it has not been so in reality. Never did hearers enjoy a more favourable opportunity of conversion, than when more than the eloquence of angels fell from the lips of Jesus, and he taught the people as one having authority and not as the Scribes. Yet comparatively few, a solitary one here and there, listened to the voice of the charmer, though he charmed so wisely. Was it that he did not display the gospel in all its fulness, sufficiency, and loveliness? Was there any want of moral suasion, powerful argument, strong motive, touching appeal, in the Saviour's addresses? No! Yet immediately after the ascension of Jesus, the word of God subdued thousands on thousands, although employed by apostles only, whose ministrations, considered apart, must have been immeasurably inferior to those of Jesus. The same Jews that persisted in their unbelief, under the ministry of Christ, were disarmed of their prejudice, under the preaching of Peter! Whence the difference of efficacy? Whence the want of success, where most we should have expected to find it, and the command of it, where least we could have looked for it? One sentence solves the difficulty. "The Holy Ghost was not yet given, because that Jesus was not yet glorified."

Similar comparisons might be made between the ministrations of different individuals now. Men of the highest abilities, persevering diligence, and elevated piety, have been left to complain of comparative barrenness in the sphere which they occupied, while humbler instruments, in a field no way more promising, have been blessed with the harvest of souls. The comparison might even be made of different periods of the same ministry. All other circumstances being equal, or differing so slightly as not to affect the argument, the word spoken at one time seems to fall powerless to the ground, as the arrow on the breast of steel. No shaft hits the mark, no sinner retires like the stricken deer to bleed alone. At another time, the people are made willing in the day of power. Conviction spreads with the rapidity of contagion, and the Lord daily adds to his people such as shall be saved. Now this difference cannot be explained but by referring it to the different measures in which God is pleased to communicate his SPIRIT.]

8. Much of the work of the ministry is pleasant and delightful. It is the savour of life unto life, ver. 15, 16. There is no joy on earth of a higher and purer character than that which the ministers of the gospel have in the success of their work. There is no work more pleasant than that of imparting the consolations of religion to the sick, and the afflicted; than that of directing inquiring sinners to the

Lamb of God; no joy on earth so pure and elevated as that which a pastor has in a revival of religion. In the evidence that God accepts his labours, and that to many his message is a savour of life unto life, there is a joy which no other pursuit can furnish; a joy, even on earth, which is more than a compensation for all the toils, self-denials, and trials of the ministry.

9. In view of the *happy* and *saving* results of the work of the ministry, we see the importance of the work. Those results are to be seen in heaven. They are to enter into the eternal destiny of the righteous. They are to be seen in the felicity and holiness of those who shall be redeemed from death. The very happiness of heaven, therefore, is dependent on the fidelity and success of the ministry. This work stretches beyond the grave. It reaches into eternity. It is to be seen in heaven. Other plans and labours of men terminate at death. But the work of the ministry reaches in its results into the skies; and is to be seen ever onward in eternity. Well might the apostle ask, "Who is sufficient for these things?"

10. The ministers of the gospel will be accepted of God, if faithful, whatever may be the result of their labours; whether seen in the salvation, or the augmented condemnation of those who hear them, ver. 15. They are a sweet savour to God. Their acceptance with him depends not on the measure of their success; but on their fidelity. If men reject the gospel, and make it the occasion of their greater condemnation, the fault is not that of ministers, but is their own. If men are faithful, God accepts their efforts; and even if many reject the message and perish, still a faithful ministry will not be to blame. That such results *should* follow from their ministry, indeed, increases their responsibility, and makes their office more awful, but it will not render them less acceptable in their labours in the sight of God.

11. We are to anticipate that the ministry will be the means of the deeper condemnation of many who hear the gospel, ver. 16. The gospel is to them a savour of death unto death. We are to expect that many will reject and despise the message, and sink into deeper sin, and condemnation, and wo. We are not to be disappointed, therefore, when we see such effects follow, and when the sinner sinks into a deeper hell from under the ministry of the gospel. It always *has* been the case, and we have reason to suppose it always will be. And painful as is the fact, yet ministers must make up their minds to witness this deeply painful result of their work.

12. The ministry is a deeply and awfully responsible work, ver. 16. It is connected with the everlasting happiness, or the deep and eternal condemnation of all those who hear the gospel. Every sermon that is preached is making an impression that will never be obliterated, and producing an effect that will never terminate. Its effects will never all be seen until the day of judgment, and in the awful solemnities of the eternal world. Well might Paul ask, "Who is sufficient for these things?"

13. It is a solemn thing to *hear* the gospel. If it is solemn for a minister to dispense it, it is not less solemn to hear it. It is connected with the eternal welfare of those who hear. And thoughtless as are multitudes who hear it, yet it is deeply to affect them hereafter. If they ever embrace it, they will owe their eternal salvation to it; if they continue to neglect it, it will sink them deep and for ever in the world of wo. Every individual, therefore, who hears the gospel dispensed, no matter by whom, should remember that he is listening to God's solemn message to men; and that it will and must exert a deep influence on his eternal doom.

14. A people should pray much for a minister. Paul often entreated the churches to which he wrote to pray for him. If *Paul* needed the prayers of Christians, assuredly Christians now do. Prayer for a minister is demanded because, (1.) He has the same infirmities, conflicts, and temptations which other Christians have. (2.)

CHAPTER III.

DO we begin again to commend *a* ourselves? or need we, as some *others*, epistles *b* of commendation to you, or *letters* of commendation from you?

a chap.5.12. *b* Acts 18.27.

He has those which are *peculiar*, and which grow out of the very nature of his office; for the warfare of Satan is carried on mainly with the leaders of the army of God. (3.) He is engaged in a great and most responsible work—the greatest work ever committed to mortal man. (4.) His success will be generally in proportion as a people pray for him. The welfare of a people, therefore, is identified with their praying for their minister. He will preach better, and they will hear better, just in proportion as they pray for him. His preaching will be dull, dry, heavy; will be without unction, spirituality, and life, unless they pray for him; and their hearing will be dull, lifeless, and uninterested, unless they pray for him. No people will hear the gospel to much advantage who do not feel anxiety enough about it to pray for their minister.

15. The interview between a minister and his people in the day of judgment will be a very solemn one. Then the effect of his ministry will be seen. Then it will be known to whom it was a savour of life unto life, and to whom it was a savour of death unto death. Then the eternal destiny of all will be settled. Then the faithful minister will be attended to heaven by all to whom his ministry has been a savour of life unto life; and then he will part for ever with all whom he so often warned and entreated in vain. In distant worlds—worlds for ever separated—shall be experienced the result of his labours. O! how solemn must be the scene when *he* must give up his account for the manner in which he has preached; and *they*, for the manner in which they attended on his ministry!

16. Let all ministers, then, be careful that they do not corrupt the word of God, ver. 17. Let them preach it in simplicity and in truth. Let them not preach philosophy, or metaphysics, or their own fancy, or the tradition of men, or the teaching of the schools, but the simple truth as it is in Jesus. Let them preach as sent *by* God; as in the sight of God; as commissioned by Christ to deliver a simple, plain, pure message to mankind, whether they will hear or forbear. Their *success* will be in proportion to the simplicity and purity of the gospel which they present; their peace and joy in death and in heaven will be just as they shall have evidence then that in simplicity and sincerity they have endeavoured to present everywhere, and to all, the pure and simple gospel of Jesus Christ. As ministers, therefore, desire acceptance with God and success in the work, let them preach the pure gospel; not adulterating it with foreign admixtures; not endeavouring to change it so as to be palatable to the carnal mind; not substituting philosophy for the gospel, and not withholding any thing in the gospel because men do not love it; and let the people of God everywhere sustain the ministry by their prayers, and aid them in their work by daily commending them to the God of grace. So shall they be able to perform the solemn functions of their office to divine acceptance; and so shall ministers and people find the gospel to be "a savour of life unto life.

CHAPTER III.

THIS chapter is closely connected in its design with the preceding. Paul had said in that chapter (ver. 14), that he had always occasion to triumph in the success which he had, and that God always blessed his labours; and especially had spoken, in the close of the previous chapter (ver. 17), of his sincerity as contrasted with the conduct of some who corrupted the word of God. This *might* appear to some as if he designed to commend himself to them, or that he had said this for the purpose of securing their favour. It is probable also, that the false teachers at Corinth had been introduced there by letters of recommendation, perhaps from Judea. In reply to this, Paul intimates (ver.

1) that this was not his design; (ver. 2) that he had no need of letters of recommendation to them, since (ver. 2, 3) *they* were his commendatory epistle; they were themselves the best evidence of his zeal, fidelity, and success in his labours. He could appeal to them as the best proof that he was qualified for the apostolic office. His success among them, he says (ver. 4), was a ground of his trusting in God, an evidence of his acceptance. Yet, as if he should seem to rely on his own strength, and to boast of what he had done, he says (ver. 5) that his success was not owing to any strength which he had, or to any skill of his own, but entirely to the aid which he had received from God. It was God, he says (ver. 6), who had qualified him to preach, and had given him grace to be an able minister of the New Testament.

It is not improbable that the false teachers, being of Jewish origin, in Corinth, had commended the laws and institutions of Moses as being of superior clearness, and even as excelling the gospel of Christ. Paul takes occasion, therefore (ver. 7—11), to show that the laws and institutions of Moses were far inferior in this respect to the gospel. His was a ministration of death (ver. 7); though glorious it was to be done away (ver. 7); the ministration of the Spirit was therefore to be presumed to be far more glorious (ver. 8); the one was a ministration to condemnation, the other of righteousness (ver. 9); the one had comparatively no glory, being so much surpassed by the other (ver. 10;) and the former was to be done away, while the latter was to remain, and was therefore far more glorious, ver. 11.

This statement of the important difference between the laws of Moses and the gospel, is further illustrated by showing the *effect* which the institutions of Moses had had on the Jews themselves, ver. 12—15. That effect was to blind them. Moses had put a veil over his face (ver. 13), and the effect had been that the nation was blinded in reading the Old Testament, and had no just views of the true meaning of their own Scriptures, ver. 14, 15.

Yet, Paul says, that that veil should be taken away, ver. 16—18. It was the *intention* of God that it should be removed. When that people should turn again to the Lord, it should be taken away, ver. 16. It *was* done where the Spirit of the Lord was, ver. 17. It was done *in fact* in regard to all true Christians, ver. 18. They were permitted to behold the glory of the Lord as in a glass, and they were changed into the same image. The same subject is continued in chap. iv., where Paul illustrates *the effect* of this clear revelation of the gospel, as compared with the institutions of Moses, on the Christian ministry.

1. *Do we begin again.* This is designed evidently to meet an objection. He had been speaking of his triumph in the ministry (chap. ii. 14), and of his sincerity and honesty, as contrasted with the conduct of many who corrupted the word of God, chap. ii. 17. It might be objected that he was magnifying *himself* in these statements, and designed to commend himself in this manner to the Corinthians. To this he replies in the following verses. ¶ *To commend ourselves?* To recommend ourselves; do we speak this in our own praise, in order to obtain your favour. ¶ *Or need we, as some* others. Probably some who had brought letters of recommendation to them from Judea. The false teachers at Corinth had been originally introduced there by commendatory letters from abroad. These were letters of introduction, and were common among the Greeks, the Romans, and the Jews, as they are now. They were usually given to persons who were about to travel, as there were no inns, and as travellers were dependent on the hospitality of those among whom they travelled. ¶ *Of commendation from you.* To other churches. It is implied here by Paul, that he sought no such letter; that he travelled without them; and that he depended on his zeal, and self-denial, and success to make him known, and to give him the affections of those to whom he

2 Ye [a] are our epistle, written in our hearts, known and read of all men:

3 *Forasmuch as ye are* manifestly declared to be the epistle of Christ ministered by us, written

a 1 Cor.9.2.

ministered—a much better recommendation than mere introductory letters. Such letters were, however, sometimes given by Christians, and are by no means improper, Acts xviii. 27. Yet, they do not appear to have been sought or used by the apostles generally. They depended on their miraculous endowments, and on the attending grace of God to make them known.

2. *Ye are our epistle;* comp. 1 Cor. ix. 2. This is a most beautiful and happy turn given to the whole subject. The sense is plain. It is, that the conversion of the Corinthians, under the faithful labours of the apostle, was a better testimonial of his character and fidelity than any letters could be. To see the force of this, it must be remembered, (1.) That Corinth was an exceedingly dissolute and abandoned place (see the Introduction to the first epistle); (2.) That a large number of them had been converted, and a church organized; (3.) That their conversion, and the organization of a church in *such* a city were events that would be known abroad; and, (4.) That it had been accomplished entirely under the labour of Paul and his companions. To their knowledge of him, therefore, and to his success there, he could confidently appeal as a testimonial of his character. The *characteristics* of this commendatory epistle, he proceeds immediately to state. The general sense is, that they were the letter of recommendation which God had given to him; and that their conversion under his ministry was the public testimonial of his character which all might see and read. ¶ *Written in our hearts.* A few MSS. and versions read thus, "your hearts;" and Doddridge has adopted this reading, and supposes that it means that the change produced not only in their external conduct, but in their inward temper, was so great, that all must see that it was an unanswerable attestation to his ministry. But there is not sufficient authority for changing the text; nor is it necessary. The sense is, probably, that this letter was, as it were, written on *his* heart. It was not merely that Paul had a tender affection for them, as Clarke supposes; nor was it that he regarded them as "a copy of the letter of recommendation from Christ written in his heart," according to the fanciful conceit of Macknight; but Paul's idea seems to have been this. He is speaking of the testimonial which he had from God. That testimonial consisted in the conversion of the Corinthians. This he says was written on his heart. It was not a cold letter of introduction, but it was such as, while it left him no room to doubt that God had sent him, also affected his feelings, and was engraven on his soul. It was to him, therefore, far more valuable than any mere letter of commendation or of introduction could be. It was a direct testimonial from God to his own heart of his approbation, and of his having appointed him to the apostolic office. All the difficulty, therefore, which has been felt by commentators in this passage, may be obviated by supposing that Paul here speaks of this testimonial or epistle as addressed to *himself*, and as satisfactory to *him*. In the other characteristics which he enumerates, he speaks of it as fitted to be a letter commendatory *of* himself to others. ¶ *Known and read of all men.* Corinth was a large, splendid, and dissipated city. Their conversion, therefore, would be known afar. All men would hear of it; and their reformation, their subsequent life under the instruction of Paul, and the attestation which God had given among them to his labours, was a sufficient testimonial to the world at large, that God had called him to the apostolic office.

3. Forasmuch as ye are *manifestly declared.* You are made manifest as

not with ink, but with the Spirit of the living God; not in tables of stone, [a] but [b] in fleshly tables of the heart.

a Ex.24.12. b Jer.31.33; Eze.11.19.

the epistle of Christ; or you, being made manifest, are the epistle, &c. They had been made manifest to be such by their conversion. The sense is, it is plain, or evident, that ye are the epistle of Christ. ¶ *To be the epistle of Christ.* That which Christ has sent to be our testimonial. He has given this letter of recommendation. He has converted you by our ministry, and that is the best evidence which *we* can have that we have been sent by him, and that our labour is accepted by him. Your conversion is his work, and it is his public attestation to our fidelity in his cause. ¶ *Ministered by us.* The idea here is, that Christ had employed their ministry in accomplishing this. They were Christ's letter, but it had been prepared by the instrumentality of the apostles. It had not been prepared by him independently of their labours, but in connection with, and as the result of those labours. Christ, in writing this epistle, so to speak, has used our aid; or employed us as amanuenses. ¶ *Written not with ink.* Paul continues and varies the image in regard to this "epistle," so that he may make the testimony borne to his fidelity and success more striking and emphatic. He says, therefore, that that it was not writtten as letters of introduction are, with ink—by traces drawn on a lifeless substance, and in lines that easily fade, or that may become easily illegible, or that can be read only by a few, or that may be soon destroyed. ¶ *But with the Spirit of the living God.* In strong contrast thus with letters written with ink. By the Spirit of God moving on the heart, and producing that variety of graces which constitute so striking and so beautiful an evidence of your conversion. If written by the Spirit of the living God, it was far more valuable, and precious, and permanent than any record which could be made by ink. Every trace of the Spirit's influences on the heart was an undoubted proof that God had sent the apostles; and was a proof which they would much more sensibly and tenderly feel than they could any letter of recommendation written in ink. ¶ *Not in tables of stone.* It is generally admitted that Paul here refers to the evidences of the divine mission of Moses which was given by the law engraven on tablets of stone, comp. ver. 7. Probably those who were false teachers among the Corinthians were Jews, and had insisted much on the divine origin and permanency of the Mosaic institutions. The law had been engraven on stone by the hand of God himself; and had thus the strongest proofs of divine origin, and the divine attestation to its pure and holy nature. To this fact the friends of the law, and the advocates for the permanency of the Jewish institutions, would appeal. Paul says, on the other hand, that the testimonials of the divine favour through him were not on tablets of stone. *They* were frail, and easily broken. There was no life in them (comp. ver. 6 and 7); and valuable and important as they were, yet they could not be compared with the testimonials which God had given to those who successfully preached the gospel. ¶ *But in fleshly tables of the heart.* In truths engraven on the heart. This testimonial was of more value than an inscription on stone, because, (1.) No hand but that of God could reach the heart, and inscribe these truths there. (2.) Because it would be attended with a life-giving and living influence. It was not a mere dead letter. (3.) Because it would be permanent. Stones, even where laws were engraven by the finger of God, would moulder and decay, and the inscription made there would be destroyed. But not so with that which was made on the heart. It would live for ever. It would abide in other worlds. It would send its influence into all the relations of life; into all future scenes in this world; and that influence would be seen and

4 And such trust have we through Christ to God-ward:
5 Not that we are sufficient of *a* ourselves to think any thing, as of ourselves, but *b* our sufficiency *is* of God;

a John 15.5. *b* 1Cor.15.10; Phil.2.13.

felt in the world that shall never end. By all these considerations, therefore, the testimonials which Paul had of the divine approbation were more valuable than any mere letters of introduction, or human commendation could have been; and more valuable even than the attestation which was given to the divine mission of Moses himself.

4. *And such trust have we.* Such confidence have we that we are appointed by God, and that he accepts our work. Such evidence have we in the success of our labours; such irrefragable proof that God blesses us; that we have trust, or confidence, that we are sent by God, and are owned by him in our ministry. His confidence did not rest on letters of introduction from men, but in the evidence of the divine presence, and the divine acceptance of his work. ¶ *Through Christ.* By the agency of Christ. Paul had no success which he did not trace to him; he had no joy of which he was not the source; he had no confidence, or trust in God of which Christ was not the author; he had no hope of success in his ministry which did not depend on him. ¶ *To God-ward.* Toward God; in regard to God (πρὸς τὸν Θεόν). Our confidence relates to God. It is confidence that he has appointed us, and sent us forth; and confidence that he will still continue to own and to bless us.

5. *Not that we are sufficient of ourselves.* This is evidently designed to guard against the appearance of boasting, or of self-confidence. He had spoken of his confidence; of his triumph; of his success; of his undoubted evidence that God had sent him. He here says, that he did not mean to be understood as affirming that any of his success came from himself, or that he was able by his own strength to accomplish the great things which had been effected by his ministry. He well knew that he had no such self-sufficiency; and he would not insinuate, in the slightest manner, that he believed himself to be invested with any such power, comp. Note on John xv. 5. ¶ *To think any thing* (λογίσασθαί τι). The word here used means properly to reason, think, consider; and then to reckon, count to, or impute to any one. It is the word which is commonly rendered *impute;* see it explained more fully in the Note on Rom. iv. 5. Robinson (*Lexicon*) renders it in this place, "to reason out, to think out, to find out by thinking." Doddridge renders it, "to reckon upon any thing as from ourselves." Whitby renders it, "to reason; as if the apostle had said, We are unable by any reasoning of our own to bring men to conversion. Macknight gives a similar sense. Locke renders it, "Not as if I were sufficient of myself, to reckon upon any thing as from myself:" and explains it to mean that Paul was not sufficient of himself by any strength of natural parts to attain the knowledge of the gospel truths which he preached. The word may be rendered here, to reckon, reason, think, &c.; *but it should be confined to the immediate subject under consideration.* It does not refer to thinking in general; or to the power of thought on any, and on all subjects—however true it may be in itself—but to the preaching the gospel. And the expression may be regarded as referring to the following points, which are immediately under discussion. (1.) Paul did not feel that he was sufficient of himself to have *reasoned* or *thought out* the truths of the gospel. They were communicated by God. (2.) He had no power by reasoning to convince or convert sinners. That was all of God. (3.) He had no right to *reckon* on success by any strength of his own. All success was to be traced to God. It is, however, also true, that all our powers of thinking and reasoning are from God; and that we have no ability to think clearly, to reason calmly, closely, and correctly, unless he shall

6 Who also hath made us able [a] ministers of the New [b] Testament; not of the letter, [c] but of the spirit: for the [d] letter killeth, but [e] the spirit [1] giveth life.

a Eph 3.7; 1Ti.1.12.
b Mat.26.28; Heb.8.6—10.
c Rom.2.28.29.
d Rom.4.15; 7.9.10.
e John 6.63; Rom.8.2.
1 or, *quickeneth*

preside over our minds and give us clearness of thought. How easy is it for God to disarrange all our faculties, and produce insanity! How easy to suffer our minds to become unsettled, bewildered, and distracted with a multiplicity of thoughts! How easy to cause every thing to appear cloudy, and dark, and misty! How easy to affect our *bodies* with weakness, languor, disease, and through them to destroy all power of close and consecutive thought! No one who considers *on how many things* the power of close thinking depends, can doubt that all our sufficiency in this is from God; and that we owe to him every clear idea on the subjects of common life, and on scientific subjects, no less certainly than we do in the truths of religion, comp. the case of Bezaleel and Aholiab in common arts, Ex. xxxi. 1—6, and Job xxxii. 8.

6. *Who also hath made us able ministers,* &c. This translation does not *quite* meet the force of the original. It would seem to imply that Paul regarded himself and his fellow-labourers as men of talents, and of signal ability; and that he was inclined to boast of it. But this is not the meaning. It refers properly to his sense of the responsibility and difficulty of the work of the ministry; and to the fact that he did not esteem himself to be *sufficient* for this work in his own strength (chap. ii. 16; iii. 5); and he here says that God had made him *sufficient:* not able, talented, learned, but *sufficient* (ἱκάνωσεν ἡμᾶς); he has supplied our deficiency; he has rendered us competent, or fit;—if a word may be coined after the manner of the Greek here, "he has *sufficienced* us for this work." There is no assertion, therefore, here, that they were men of talents, or peculiar ability, but only that God had qualified them for their work, and made them by his grace sufficient to meet the toils and responsibilities of this arduous office. ¶ *Of the New Testament.* Of the new covenant (Note, Matt. xxv. 28), in contradistinction from the old covenant, which was established through Moses. They were appointed to go forth and make the provisions of that new covenant known to a dying world. ¶ *Not of the letter.* Not of the literal, or verbal meaning, in contradistinction from the Spirit; see Notes on Rom. ii. 27, 29; vii. 6. This is said, doubtless, in opposition to the Jews, and Jewish teachers. They insisted much on the letter of the law, but entered little into its real meaning. They did not seek out the true spiritual sense of the Old Testament; and hence they rested on the mere literal observance of the rites and ceremonies of religion without understanding their true nature and design. Their service, though in many respects conformed to the letter of the law, yet became cold, formal, and hypocritical; abounding in mere ceremonies, and where the heart had little to do. Hence there was little pure spiritual worship offered to God; and hence also they rejected the Messiah whom the old covenant prefigured, and was designed to set forth. ¶ *For the letter killeth,* comp. Notes on Rom. iv. 15; vii. 9, 10. The mere letter of the law of Moses. The effect of it was merely to produce condemnation; to produce a sense of guilt, and danger, and not to produce pardon, relief, and joy. The law denounced death; condemned sin in all forms; and the effect of it was to produce a sense of guilt and condemnation. ¶ *But the spirit giveth life.* The spirit, in contradistinction from the mere literal interpretation of the Scriptures. The Spirit, that is, Christ, says Locke, comp. ver. 17. The spirit here means, says Bloomfield, that new spiritual system, the gospel. The Spirit of God speaking in us, says Doddridge.

7 But if the ministration of death, written *and* engraven in stones, was glorious, so that the children of Israel could not stead-

The spirit here seems to refer to the *New* Testament, or the new dispensation in contradistinction from the old. That was characterized mainly by its strictness of law, and by its burdensome rites, and by the severe tone of its denunciation for sin. It did not in itself provide a way of pardon and peace. Law condemns; it does not speak of forgiveness. On the contrary, the gospel, a spiritual system, is designed to impart life and comfort to the soul. It speaks peace. It comes not to condemn, but to save. It discloses a way of mercy, and it invites all to partake and live. It is called "spirit," probably because its consolations are imparted and secured by the Spirit of God—the source of all true life to the soul. It is the dispensation of the Spirit; and it demands a spiritual service—a service that is free, and elevated, and tending eminently to purify the heart, and to save the soul; see Note on ver. 17.

7. *But if the ministration of death.* In the previous verses, Paul had referred incidentally to the institutions of Moses, and to the superiority of the gospel. He had said that the former were engraven on stones, but the latter on the heart (ver. 3); that the letter of the former tended to death, but the latter to life (ver. 6). This sentiment he proceeds further to illustrate, by showing in what the superior glory of the gospel consisted. The *design* of the whole is, to illustrate the nature, and to show the importance of the ministerial office; and the manner in which the duties of that office were to be performed. That the phrase "ministration of death" refers to the Mosaic institutions, the connection sufficiently indicates, ver. 13—15. The word "ministration" (διακονία) means, properly, ministry; the office of ministering in divine things. It is usually applied to the officers of the church in the New Testament, Acts i. 17, 25; Rom. xi. 13; 1 Cor. xii. 5. The word here, however, seems to refer to the whole arrangement under the Mosaic economy, by which his laws were promulgated, and perpetuated. The expression "a ministration—written and engraven on stone," is somewhat harsh; but the *sense* evidently is, the ministration of a covenant, or of laws written on stones. The word "ministration" there refers to the arrangement, office, &c. by which the knowledge of these laws was maintained; the *ministering* under a system like that of the Jewish; or, *more strictly*, the act and occasion on which Moses himself *ministered*, or promulgated that system to the Jews, and when the glory of the work was irradiated even from his countenance. And the purpose of the apostle is to show that the ministry of the gospel is more glorious than *even* the ministry of Moses, when he was admitted near to God on the holy mount; and when such a glory attended his receiving and promulgating the law. It is called the "ministration of death," because it tended to condemnation; it did not speak of pardon: it was fitted only to deepen the sense of sin, and to produce alarm and dread; see Note on ver. 6. ¶ *Written* and *engraven in stones.* The ten commandments—the substance of all the Mosaic institutes, and the principal laws of his economy—were written, or engraven on tables of stone. ¶ *Was glorious.* Was attended with magnificence and splendour. The glory here referred to, consisted in the circumstance of sublimity and grandeur in which the law of Moses was given. It was, (1.) The glory of God as he was manifested on Mount Sinai, as the Lawgiver and Ruler of the people. (2.) The glory of the attending circumstances, of thunder, fire, &c. in which God appeared. The law was given in these circumstances. Its *giving*—called here the "ministration"—was amidst such displays of the glory of God. It was, (3.) A high honour and glory for Moses to be permitted to approach so near to God; to commune with him; and to receive at his hand the law for his

fastly behold the face of Moses for [a] the glory of his countenance; which *glory* was to be done away;

a Ex. 34. 1, 29—35.

8 How shall not the ministration of the Spirit be rather glorious?

people, and for the world. These were circumstances of imposing majesty and grandeur, which, however, Paul says were eclipsed and surpassed by the ministry of the gospel. ¶ *So that the children of Israel*, &c. In Ex. xxxiv. 29, 30, it is said, that "When Moses came down from Mount Sinai with the two tables of testimony in Moses' hand, when he came down from the mount, that Moses wist not that the skin of his face shone, while He talked with him. And when Aaron and all the children of Israel saw Moses, behold, the skin of his face shone; and they were afraid to come nigh him." The word rendered "steadfastly behold" (ἀτενίσαι), means to gaze intently upon; to look steadily, or constantly, or fixedly; see Note on Acts i. 10. There was a dazzling splendour, an irradiation; a diffusion of light, such that they could not look intently and steadily upon it—as we cannot look steadily at the sun. *How* this was produced, is not known. It cannot be accounted for from natural causes, and was doubtless designed to be to the Israelites an attestation that Moses had been with God, and was commissioned by him. They would see, (1.) That it was unnatural, such as no known cause could produce; and, (2.) Not improbably they would recognise a resemblance to the manner in which God usually appeared—the glory of the Shechinah in which he so frequently manifested himself to them. It would be to them, therefore, a demonstration that Moses had been with God. ¶ *Which* glory *was to be done away*. The splendour of that scene was transitory. It did not last. It was soon destroyed (τὴν καταργουμένην). It was not adapted or designed long to continue. This does not mean, as Doddridge supposes, "soon to be abolished in death;" or, as others, "ceasing with youth;" but it means, that the shining or the splendour was transitory; it was soon to cease; it was not designed to be permanent. Neither the wonderful scenes accompanying the giving of the law on Sinai, nor the shining on the countenance of Moses, was designed to abide. The thunders of Sinai would cease to roll; the lightenings to play; the visible manifestations of the presence of God would all be gone; and the supernatural illumination of the face of Moses also would soon cease—*perhaps* as Macknight, Bloomfield, and others suppose, as a prefiguration of the abrogation of the glory of the whole system of the Levitical law. Paul certainly means to say, that the glory of Moses, and of his dispensation, was a fading glory; but that the glory of the gospel would be permanent, and increasing for ever.

8. *How shall not the ministration of the Spirit*. This is an argument from the less to the greater. Several things in it are worthy of notice. (1.) The proper contrast to the "ministration of death" (ver. 7), would have been 'ministration of life.' But Paul chose rather to call it the 'ministration of the spirit;' as the source of life; or as conferring higher dignity on the gospel than to have called it simply the ministration of life.' (2.) By the "Spirit" here is manifestly meant the Holy Spirit; and the whole phrase denotes the gospel, or the preaching of the gospel, by which eminently the Holy Spirit is imparted. (3.) It is the high honour of the gospel ministry, that it is the means by which the Holy Spirit is imparted to men. It is designed to secure the salvation of men by his agency; and it is through the ministry that the Holy Spirit is imparted, the heart renewed, and the soul saved. The work of the ministry is, therefore, the most important and honourable in which man can engage. ¶ *Be rather glorious*. (1.) Because that of Moses tended to death; this to life. (2.) Because that was engraven on stone; this is engraved on the heart. (3.) Because that was the mere giving of a law; this is con-

9 For if the ministration of condemnation *be* glory, much more doth the ministration of righteousness exceed in glory.

10 For even that which was made glorious had no glory in this respect, by reason of the glory that excelleth.

nected with the renovating influences of the Holy Spirit. (4.) Because that was soon to pass away. All the magnificence of the scene was soon to vanish. But this is to remain. Its influence and effect are to be everlasting. It is to stretch into eternity; and its main glory is to be witnessed in souls renewed and saved; and amidst the splendours of heaven. "The work of the Spirit of God on the heart of a rational being, is much more important than any dead characters which can be engraved on insensible stones."—*Doddridge.*

9. *For if the ministration of condemnation.* Of Moses in giving the law, the effect of which is to produce condemnation.—Law condemns the guilty; it does not save them. It denounces punishment; it contains no provisions of pardon. To *pardon* is to depart from the law; and must be done under the operation of another system—since a law which contains a provision for the pardon of offenders, and permits them to escape, would be a burlesque in legislation. The tendency of the Mosaic institutions, therefore, was to produce a sense of condemnation. And so it will be found by all who attempt to be justified by the law. It will tend to, and result in, their condemnation. ¶ Be *glory.* Be glorious; or be glory itself.—It was glorious as a manifestation of the holiness and justice of God; and glorious in the attending circumstances. No event in our world has been more magnificent in the circumstances of external majesty and splendour than the giving of the law on Mount Sinai. ¶ *The ministration of righteousness.* The gospel; the promulgation of the plan of mercy. It is called "the ministration of righteousness," in contradistinction from the law of Moses, which was a "ministration of condemnation." The word "righteousness," however, does not exactly express the force of the original word. That word is δικαιοσύνης, and it stands directly opposed to the word κατακρίσεως, *condemnation.* It should be rendered 'the ministration of *justification;*' the plan by which God justifies men; see Note, Rom. i. 17. The law of Moses *condemns;* the gospel is the plan by which man is *justified.* And if that which *condemns* could be glorious, much more must that be by which men can be justified, acquitted, and saved. The superior glory of the gospel, therefore, consists in the fact that it is a scheme to justify and save lost sinners. And this glory consists, (1.) In *the fact* that it can be done when all *law* condemns. (2.) In the showing forth of the divine character while it *is* done, as just, and merciful, and benevolent in doing it—blending all his great and glorious attributes together—while the law disclosed only *one* of his attributes—his justice. (3.) In the *manner* in which it is done. It is by the incarnation of the Son of God—a far more glorious manifestation of deity than was made on Mount Sinai. It is by the toils, and sufferings, and death of him who made the atonement, and by the circumstances of awful and imposing grandeur which attended his death, when the sun was darkened, and the rocks were rent—far more grand and awful scenes than occurred when the law was given. It is by the resurrection and ascension of the Redeemer—scenes far more sublime than all the external glories of Sinai when the law was given. (4.) In the *effects,* or results. The one condemns; the other justifies and saves. The effect of the one is seen in the convictions of conscience, in alarm, in a sense of guilt, in the conscious desert of condemnation, and in the apprehension of eternal punishment. The other is seen in sins forgiven; in peace of conscience; in the joy of pardon; in the hope of heaven; in comfort and triumph on the bed of death, and amidst the glories of heaven.

11 For if [a] that which is done away *was* glorious, much more that which remaineth *is* glorious.

12 Seeing then that we have such hope, we use great [1] plainness of speech:

a Rom. 5. 20, 21.

1 Or, *boldness*.

10. *For even that which was made glorious* (τὸ δεδοξασμένον). That was splendid, excellent, or glorious. This refers doubtless, to the laws and institutions of Moses, especially to the primary giving of the law. Paul does not deny that *it* had an honour and majesty such, in some respects, as the Jews claimed for it. It was glorious in the manner in which it was given; it was glorious in the purity of the law itself; and it was glorious, or splendid in the magnificent and imposing ritual in which the worship of God was celebrated. But all this was surpassed in the brighter glory of the gospel. ¶ *Had no glory.* Gr. Was not glorious, or splendid (οὐδὲ δεδόξασται). Had comparatively no glory, or splendour. Its glory was all eclipsed. It was like the splendour of the moon and stars compared with the bright light of the sun. ¶ *By reason of the glory that excelleth.* In the gospel; in the incarnation, life, sufferings, death, and resurrection of the Lord Jesus; in the pardon of sin; in the peace and joy of the believer; and in the glories of the heavenly world to which the gospel elevates dying men.

11. *For if that which is done away,* &c. The splendour that attended the giving of the law; the bright shining of the face of Moses; and the ritual institutions of his religion. It was *to be* done away. It was never designed to be permanent. Every thing in it had a transient existence, and was so designed. Yet it was attended, Paul admits, with much that was magnificent and splendid. He had, in the previous verses, stated several important differences between the law and the gospel. He here states another. The law he calls (τὸ καταργούμενον) *the* thing which was to be made to cease; to be put an end to; to be done away with; to be abolished. It had no permanency; and it was designed to have none. Its glory, therefore, great as in many respects it might be, could not be compared with that which was to be permanent —as the light of the stars fades away at the rising sun. It is implied here, that it was originally designed that the Mosaic institutions should not be permanent; that they should be mere shadows and types of better things; and that when the things which they adumbrated should appear, the shadows would vanish of course. This idea is one which prevails everywhere in the New Testament, and which the sacred writers are often at great pains to demonstrate. ¶ Was *glorious.* Gr. *By glory* (διὰ δόξης). That is, it was attended *by* glory; it was introduced by glory, it was encompassed *with* glory when it was established The idea here is, not that it was glorious *in itself*, but that it was accompanied *with* splendour and majesty. ¶ *That which remaineth.* The gospel (τὸ μένον). The thing that is to remain; that is permanent, abiding, perpetual; that has no principle of decay, and whose characteristic it is, that it is everlasting. The gospel is permanent, or abiding, (1.) Because it is designed to remain immutable through the remotest ages. It is not to be superseded by any new economy, or institution. It is *the* dispensation under which the affairs of the world are to be wound up, and under which the world is to close; see Note, 1 Cor. xv. 51. (2.) Its effects on the heart are permanent. It is complete in itself. It is not to be succeeded by any other system, and it looks to no other system in order to complete or perfect its operations on the soul. (3.) Its effects are to abide for ever. They will exist in heaven. They are to be seen in the soul that shall be recovered from sin, and that shall be glorious in the bosom of God for ever and ever. The Mosaic system—glorious as it was—shall be remembered as *introducing* the gospel; the gospel shall be remembered as directly fitting for heaven. Its most great and

glorious results shall be seen in the permanent and eternal joys of heaven. The gospel contemplates a great, permanent, and eternal good, adapted to all ages, all climes, all people, and all worlds. It is, therefore, so much more glorious than the limited, temporary, and partial good of the Mosaic system, that that may be said in comparison to have had *no* glory.

12. *Seeing then that we have such hope.* *Hope* properly is a compound emotion, made up of a *desire* for an object, and an *expectation* of obtaining it. If there is no *desire* for it; or if the object is not pleasant and agreeable, there is no hope, though there may be expectation—as in the *expectation* of the pestilence, of famine, or sickness, or death. If there is no expectation of it, but a strong desire, there is no hope, as in cases where there is a strong desire of wealth, or fame, or pleasure; or where a man is condemned for murder, and has a strong desire but no prospect of pardon; or where a man is shipwrecked, and has a strong desire, but no expectation of again seeing his family and friends. In such cases, despondency or despair are the results. It is the union of the two feelings in proper proportions which constitutes hope. There has been considerable variety of views among expositors in regard to the proper meaning of the word in this place. Mr. Locke supposes that Paul here means the honourable employment of an apostle and minister of the gospel, or the glory belonging to the ministry in the gospel; and that his calling it "hope," instead of "glory," which the connection would seem to demand, is the language of modesty. Rosenmüller understands it of the hope of the perpetual continuance of the gospel dispensation. Macknight renders it "persuasion," and explains it as meaning the full persuasion or assurance that the gospel excels the law in the manner of its introduction; its permanency, &c. A few remarks may, perhaps, make it clear. (1.) It refers primarily to Paul, and the other ministers of the gospel. It is not properly the *Christian hope* as such to which he refers, but it is that which the ministers of the gospel had. (2.) It refers to *all* that he had said before about the superiority of the gospel to the law; and it is designed to express the *result* of all that on his mind, and on the minds of his fellow-labourers. (3.) It refers to the *prospect*, confidence, persuasion, anticipation which he had as the effect of what he had just said. It is the prospect of eternal life; the clear expectation of acceptance, and the anticipation of heaven, based on the fact that this was a ministry of the Spirit (ver. 8): that it was a ministry showing the way of justification (ver. 9): and that it was never to be done away, but to abide for ever (ver. 11). On all these this strong hope was founded; and in view of these, Paul expressed himself clearly, not enigmatically; and not in types and figures, as Moses did. Every thing about the gospel was clear and plain; and this led to the confident expectation and assurance of heaven. The word *hope*, therefore, in this place will express the effect on the mind of Paul in regard to the work of the ministry, produced by the *group* of considerations which he had suggested, showing that the gospel was superior to the law; and that it was the ground of more clear and certain confidence and hope than any thing which the law could furnish. ¶ *We use.* We employ; we are accustomed to. He refers to the manner in which he preached the gospel. ¶ *Great plainness of speech.* Marg. *boldness.* We use the word "plainness" as applied to speech chiefly in two senses, (1.) To denote boldness, faithfulness, candour; in opposition to trimming, timidity, and unfaithfulness; and, (2.) To denote clearness, intelligibleness, and simplicity, in opposition to obscurity, mist, and highly-wrought and laboured forms of expression. The connection here shows that the *latter* is the sense in which the phrase here is to be understood; see ver. 13. It denotes openness, simplicity, freedom from the obscurity which arises from enigmatical and parabolical, and typical modes of speaking. This stands in opposition to figure, metaphor, and allegory—to

13 And not as Moses, *which* put a vail over his face that the

an affected and laboured concealment of the idea in the manner which was common among the Jewish doctors and heathen philosophers, where their meaning was carefully concealed from the vulgar, and from all except the *initiated*. It stands opposed also to the necessary obscurity arising from typical institutions like those of Moses. And the doctrine of the passage is, that such is the clearness and fulness of the Christian revelation, arising from the fact, that it is the *last* economy, and that it does not look to the future, that its ministers may and should use clear and intelligible language. They should not use language abounding in metaphor and allegory. They should not use unusual terms. They should not draw their words and illustrations from science. They should not use mere technical language. They should not attempt to vail or cloak their meaning. They should not seek a refined and overwrought style. They should use expressions which other men use; and express themselves as far as possible in the language of common life. What is preaching worth that is not understood? Why should a man talk at all unless he is intelligible? Who was ever more plain and simple in his words and illustrations than the Lord Jesus?

13. *And not as Moses.* Our conduct is not like that of Moses. We make no attempt to conceal any thing in regard to the nature, design, and duration of the gospel. We leave nothing designedly in mystery. ¶ Which *put a vail over his face.* That is, when he came down from Mount Sinai, and when his face shone. Ex. xxxiv. 33, "And till Moses had done speaking with them, he put a vail on his face." This vail he put off when he went to speak with God, but put on again when he delivered his commands to the people, What was the *design* of this, Moses has not himself declared. The statement which he makes in Exodus would lead us to suppose that it was on account of the exceeding brightness and dazzling splendour which shone around him, and which made it difficult to look intently upon him; and that this was in part the reason, even Paul himself seems to intimate in ver. 7. He, however, in this verse intimates that there was another design, which was that he might be, as Doddridge expresses it, "a kind of type and figure of his own dispensation." ¶ *That the children of Israel.* Mr. Locke understands this of the apostles, and supposes that it means, "We do not vail the light, so that the obscurity of what we deliver should hinder the children of Israel from seeing in the law which was to be done away, Christ who is the end of the law." But this interpretation is forced and unnatural. The phrase rendered "that" (πρὸς τὸ) evidently connects what is affirmed here with the statement about Moses; and shows that the apostle means to say that Moses put the vail on his face *in order* that the children of Israel should not be able to see to the end of his institutions. That Moses had such a design, and that the putting on of the vail was emblematic of the nature of his institutions, Paul here distinctly affirms. No one can prove that this was *not* his design; and in a land and time when types, and emblems, and allegorical modes of speech were much used, it is highly probable that Moses *meant* to intimate that the end and full purpose of his institutions were designedly concealed. ¶ *Could not stedfastly look.* Could not gaze intently upon (ἀτενίσαι); see Note on ver. 7. They could not clearly discern it; there was obscurity arising from the fact of the designed concealment. He did not *intend* that they should clearly see the full purport and design of the institutions which he established. ¶ *To the end* (εἰς τὸ τέλος). Unto the end, purpose, design, or ultimate result of the law which he established. A great many different interpretations have been proposed of this. The meaning seems to me to be this: There was a glory and splendour in that which the institutions of Moses typified, which the children of Israel were not permitted then to be-

children of Israel could not stedfastly look to the end[a] of that which is abolished:

a Ro.10.4.

14 But their minds were blinded; [a] for until this day remaineth the same vail untaken away in

a Ro.11.7,8,25.

hold. There was a splendour and lustre in the face of Moses, which they could not gaze upon, and therefore he put a vail over it to diminish its intense brightness. In like manner there was a glory and splendour in the ultimate design and scope of his institutions, in that to which they referred, which they were not then *able, i. e.* prepared to look on, and the exceeding brightness of which he of design concealed. This was done by obscure types and figures, that resembled a vail thrown over a dazzling and splendid object. The word "end," then, I suppose, does not refer to termination, or close, but to the *design, scope,* or *purpose* of the Mosaic institutions; to that which they were intended to introduce and adumbrate. THAT END was the Messiah, and the glory of his institutions; see Note on Rom. x. "Christ is the *end* of the law." And the meaning of Paul, I take to be, is, that there was a splendour and a glory in the gospel which the Mosaic institutions were designed to typify, which was so great that the children of Israel were not fully prepared to see it, and that he designedly threw over that glory the vail of obscure types and figures; as he threw over his face a vail that partially concealed its splendour. Thus interpreted there is a consistency in the entire passage, and very great beauty. Paul, in the following verses, proceeds to state that the vail to the view of the Jews of his time was not removed; that they still looked to the obscure types and institutions of the Mosaic law rather than on the glory which they were designed to adumbrate; *as if* they should choose to look on the *vail* on the face of Moses rather than on the splendour which it concealed. ¶ *Of that which is abolished.* Or rather *to be abolished,* (τοῦ καταργουμένου), whose nature, design, and intention it was that it should be abolished. It was never designed to be permanent: and Paul speaks of it here as a thing that was known and indisputable that the Mosaic institutions were designed to be abolished.

14. *But their minds were blinded.* The word here used (πωρόω) means rather to harden; to make hard like stone; and then to make dull or stupid. It is applied to the heart, in Mark vi. 52; viii. 17; to persons, in Rom. xi. 7; and to the eyes, in Job xvii. 7. Paul refers here to the fact that the understandings of the Jews were stupid, dull, and insensible, so that they did not see clearly the design and end of their own institutions. He states simply the fact; he does not refer to the cause of it. The fact that the Jews were thus stupid and dull is often affirmed in the New Testament. ¶ *For until this day,* &c. The sense of this is, that even to the time when Paul wrote, it was a characteristic of the great mass of the Jewish people, that they did not understand the true sense of their own Scriptures. They did not understand its doctrines in regard to the Messiah. A vail seems to be thrown over the Old Testament when they read it, as there was over the face of Moses, so that the glory of their own Scriptures is concealed from their view, as the glory of the face of Moses was hidden. ¶ *Of the Old Testament.* Greek, "of the old covenant." See this word "testament," or covenant, explained in the Notes on 1 Cor. xi. 25. This, I believe, is the only instance in which the Scriptures of the Jews are called the "Old Testament," or covenant, in the Bible. It was, of course, not a name which they used, or would use; but it is now with Christians the common appellation. No doubt can be entertained but that Paul uses the terms in the same manner in which we now do, and refers to all the inspired writings of the Jews. ¶ *Which* vail *is done away in Christ.* In the manifestation, or appearance of Jesus the Messiah, the vail is removed. The

the reading of the Old Testament; which *vail* is done away in Christ.
15 But even unto this day, when Moses is read, the vail is upon their heart.
16 Nevertheless, when it shall

obscurity which rested on the prophecies and types of the former dispensation is withdrawn; and as the face of Moses could have been distinctly seen if the vail on his face had been removed, so it is in regard to the true meaning of the Old Testament by the coming of the Messiah. What was obscure is now made clear; and the prophecies are so completely fulfilled in him, that his coming has removed the covering, and shed a clear light over them all. Many of the prophecies, for example, until the Messiah actually appeared, appeared obscure, and almost contradictory. Those which spoke of him, for illustration, as man and as God; as suffering, and yet reigning; as dying, and yet as ever-living; as a mighty Prince, a conqueror, and a king, and yet as a man of sorrows; as humble, and yet glorious: all seemed difficult to be reconciled until they were seen to harmonise in Jesus of Nazareth. Then they were plain, and the vail was taken away. Christ is seen to answer all the previous descriptions of him in the Old Testament; and his coming casts a clear light on all which was before obscure.

15. *But even unto this day.* To the time when Paul wrote this epistle, about thirty years after Christ was put to death. But it is still as true as it was in the time of Paul; and the character and conduct of the Jews now so entirely accords with the description which he gives of them in his time, as to show that he drew from nature, and as to constitute one of the strong incidental proofs that the account in the New Testament is true. Of no other people on earth, probably, would a description be accurate eighteen hundred years *after* it was made. ¶ *When Moses is read.* When the five books of Moses are read, as they were regularly and constantly in their synagogues; see Note on Luke iv. 16. ¶ *The vail is upon their heart.* They do not see the true meaning and beauty of their own Scriptures—a description as applicable to the Jews now as it was to those in the time of Paul.

16. *Nevertheless.* This is not always to continue. The time is coming when they shall understand their own Scriptures, and see their true beauty. ¶ *When it shall turn to the Lord.* When the Jewish people shall be converted. The word "it" here refers undoubtedly to "Israel" in ver. 13; and the sense is, that their blindness is not always to remain; there is to be a period when they shall turn to God, and shall understand his promises, and become acquainted with the true nature of their own religion. This subject the apostle has discussed at much greater length in the eleventh chapter of the epistle to the Romans; see Notes on that chapter. ¶ *The vail shall be taken away.* They shall then understand the true meaning of the prophecies, and the true nature of their own institutions. They shall see that they refer to the Lord Jesus, the incarnate Son of God, and the true Messiah. The genuine sense of their sacred oracles shall break upon their view with full and irresistible light. There may be an allusion in the *language* here to the declaration in Isa. xxv. 7, "And he will destroy in this mountain the face of the covering cast over all people, and the vail that is spread over all nations." This verse teaches, (1.) That the time will come when the Jews shall be converted to Christianity; expressed here by their turning unto the Lord, that is, the Lord Jesus; see Note, Acts i. 24. (2.) It seems to be implied that their conversion will be a conversion of *the people* at large; a conversion that shall be nearly simultaneous; a conversion *en masse.* Such a conversion we have reason to anticipate of the Jewish nation. (3.) The effect of this will be to make them acquainted with the true sense of their own Scriptures, and the light and beauty of the sayings of their own prophets. Now

turn to the Lord, the vail shall be taken away.[a]

17 Now the Lord [b] is that Spirit; and where the [c] Spirit of the Lord *is*, there *is* liberty.

18 But we all, with open face

a Is.25.7. b 1 Cor.15.45. c Rom.8.2.

they are in deep darkness on the subject; then they will see how entirely they meet and harmonise in the Lord Jesus. (4.) The true and only way of having a correct and full meaning of the Bible is by turning unto God. Love to him, and a disposition to do his will, is the best means of interpreting the Bible.

17. *Now the Lord is that Spirit.* The word "Lord" here evidently refers to the Lord Jesus; see ver. 16. It may be observed in general in regard to this word, that where it occurs in the New Testament unless the connection require us to understand it of God, it refers to the Lord Jesus. It was the common name by which he was known; see John xx. 13; xxi. 7, 12; Eph. iv. 1, 5. The *design* of Paul in this verse seems to be to account for the "liberty" which he and the other apostles had, or for the boldness, openness, and plainness (ver. 12) which they evinced in contradistinction from the Jews, who so little understood the nature of their institutions. He had said (ver. 6), that he was a minister "not of the letter, but of the Spirit;" and he had stated that the Old Testament was not understood by the Jews who adhered to the literal interpretation of the Scriptures. He here says, that the Lord Jesus was "the Spirit" to which he referred, and by which he was enabled to understand the Old Testament so as to speak plainly, and without obscurity. The sense is, that Christ was the Spirit; *i. e.* the sum, the substance of the Old Testament. The figures, types, prophecies, &c. all centered in him, and he was the end of all those institutions. If contemplated as having reference to him, it was easy to understand them. This I take to be the sentiment of the passage, though expositors have been greatly divided in regard to its meaning. Thus explained, it does not mean absolutely and abstractly that the Lord Jesus was "a Spirit," but that he was the sum, the essence, the end, and the purport of the Mosaic rites, the spirit of which Paul had spoken in ver. 6, as contradistinguished from the letter of the law. ¶ *And where the Spirit of the Lord* is, *there* is *liberty.* This is a general truth designed to illustrate the particular sentiment which he had just advanced. The word "liberty" here (ἐλευθερία) refers, I think, to freedom in speaking; the power of speaking openly, and freely, as in ver. 12. It states the general truth, that the effect of the Spirit of God was to give light and clearness of view; to remove obscurity from a subject, and to enable one to see it plainly. This would be a truth that could not be denied by the Jews, who held to the doctrine that the Spirit of God revealed truth, and it must be admitted by all. Under the influence of that Spirit, therefore, Paul says, that he was able to speak with openness, and boldness; that he had a clear view of truth, which the mass of the Jews had not; and that the system of religion which he preached was open, plain, and clear. The word "freedom," would perhaps, better convey the idea. "There is freedom from the dark and obscure views of the Jews; freedom from their prejudices, and their superstitions; freedom from the slavery and bondage of sin; the freedom of the children of God, who have clear views of him as their Father and Redeemer, and who are enabled to express those views openly and boldly to the world."

18. *But we all.* All Christians. The discussion in the chapter has related mainly to the apostles; but this declaration seems evidently to refer to all Christians, as distinguished from the Jews. ¶ *With open face,* comp. Note on 1 Cor. xiii. 12. Tindal renders this, "and now the Lord's glory appeareth in us all as in a glass." The sense is, "with unvailed face," alluding to the fact (ver. 13) that the face of

beholding as in a glass [a] the glory of the Lord, are changed into the same [b] image from [c] glory to glory *even* as [1] by the Spirit of the Lord.

a 1 Cor.13.12. *b* Rom.8.29. *c* Ps 84.7.

1 or, *of the Lord the Spirit.*

Moses was vailed, so that the children of Israel could not stedfastly look on it. In contradistinction from that, Paul says that Christians are enabled to look upon the glory of the Lord in the gospel without a vail—without any obscure intervening medium. ¶ *Beholding as in a glass.* On the word *glass,* and the sense in which it is used in the New Testament, see Note on 1 Cor. xiii. 12. The word here used (κατοπτριζόμενοι) has been very variously rendered. Macknight renders it, "we all reflecting as mirrors the glory of the Lord." Doddridge, "beholding as by a glass." Locke, "with open countenances as mirrors, reflecting the glory of the Lord." The word κατοπτρίζω occurs no where else in the New Testament. It properly means to look in a mirror; to behold as in a mirror. The mirrors of the ancients were made of burnished metal, and they reflected images with great brilliancy and distinctness. And the meaning is, that the gospel reflected the glory of the Lord; it was, so to speak, the mirror—the polished, burnished substance in which the glory of the Lord shone, and where that glory was irradiated and reflected so that it might be seen by Christians. There was no vail over it; no obscurity; nothing to break its dazzling splendour, or to prevent its meeting the eye. Christians, by looking on the gospel, could see the glorious perfections and plans of God as bright, and clear, and brilliant as they could see a light reflected from the burnished surface of the mirror. So to speak, the glorious perfections of God shone from heaven; beamed upon the gospel, and were thence reflected to the eye and the heart of the Christian, and had the effect of transforming them into the same image. This passage is one of great beauty, and is designed to set forth the gospel as being *the reflection* of the infinite glories of God to the minds and hearts of men. ¶ *The glory of the Lord.* The splendour, majesty, and holiness of God as manifested in the gospel, or of the Lord as incarnate. The idea is, that God was clearly and distinctly seen in the gospel. There was no obscurity, no vail, as in the case of Moses. In the gospel they were permitted to look on the full splendour of the divine perfections—the justice, goodness, mercy, and benevolence of God—to see him as he is with undimmed and unvailed glory. The idea is, that the perfections of God shine forth with splendour and beauty in the gospel, and that we are permitted to look on them clearly and openly. ¶ *Are changed into the same image.* It is possible that there may be an allusion here to the effect which was produced by looking into an ancient mirror. Such mirrors were made of burnished metal, and the reflection from them would be intense. If a strong light were thrown on them, the rays would be cast by reflection on the face of him who looked on the mirror, and it would be strongly illuminated. And the idea may be, that the glory of God, the splendour of the divine perfections, was thrown on the gospel, so to speak like a bright light on a polished mirror; and that that glory was reflected from the gospel on him who contemplated it, so that he appeared to be transformed into the same image. Locke renders it, "We are changed into his very image by a continued succession of glory, as it were, streaming upon us from the Lord.' The figure is one of great beauty; and the idea is, that by placing ourselves within the light of the gospel; by contemplating the glory that shines there, we become changed into the likeness of the same glory, and conformed to that which shines there with so much splendour. By contemplating the resplendent face of the blessed Redeemer, we are changed into something of the same image. It is a law of our nature that we are moulded, in our moral feelings, by the persons with whom we associate, and by the objects which we contemplate. We become insensibly assimilated to those with whom we have intercourse, and to the objects with which we are familiar. We imbibe the opinions, we copy the habits, we imitate the manners, we fall into the customs of those with whom we have daily conversation, and whom we make our companions and friends. Their sentiments insensibly become our sentiments, and their ways our ways. It is thus with the *books* with which we are familiar. We are insensibly, but certainly moulded into conformity to the opinions, maxims, and feelings which are there expressed. Our own sentiments undergo a gradual change, and we are likened to those with which in this manner we are conversant. So it is in regard to the opinions and feelings which from any cause we are in the habit of bringing before our minds. It is the way by which men become corrupted in their sentiments and feelings, in their contact with the world; it is the way in which amusements, and the company of the gay and the dissipated possess so much power; it is the way in which the young and inexperienced are beguiled and ruined; and it is the way in which Christians dim the lustre of their piety, and obscure the brightness of their religion by their contact with the gay and fashionable world.—And it is on the same great principle that Paul says that by contemplating the glory of God in the gospel, we become insensibly, but certainly conformed to the same image, and made like the Redeemer. His image will be reflected on us. We shall imbibe his sentiments, catch his feelings, and be moulded into the image of his own purity. Such is the great and wise law of our nature; and it is on this principle, and by this means, that God designs we should be *made* pure on earth, and *kept* pure in heaven for ever. ¶ *From glory to glory.* From one degree of glory to another. "The more we behold this brilliant and glorious light, the more do we reflect back its rays; that is, the more we contemplate the great truths of the Christian religion, the more do our minds become imbued with its spirit."—*Bloomfield.* This is said in contradistinction probably to Moses. The splendour on his face gradually died away. But not so with the light reflected from the gospel. It becomes deeper and brighter constantly.—This sentiment is parallel to that expressed by the psalmist; "They go from strength to strength" (Ps. lxxxiv. 7); *i. e.* they go from one degree of strength to another, or one degree of holiness to another, until they come to the full vision of God himself in heaven. The idea in the phrase before us is, that there is a continual increase of moral purity and holiness under the gospel until it results in the perfect glory of heaven. The *doctrine* is, that Christians advance in piety; and that this is done by the contemplation of the glory of God as it is revealed in the gospel. ¶ *As by the Spirit of the Lord.* Marg. "Of the Lord of the Spirit." Gr. "As from the Lord the Spirit." So Beza, Locke, Wolf, Rosenmüller, and Doddridge render it. The idea is, that it is by the Lord Jesus Christ the spirit of the law, the spirit referred to by Paul above, ver. 6, 17. It is done by the Holy Spirit procured or imparted by the Lord Jesus. This sentiment is in accordance with that which prevails everywhere in the Bible, that it is by the Holy Spirit alone that the heart is changed and purified. And the *object* of the statement here is, doubtless, to prevent the supposition that the change from "glory to glory" was produced in any sense by the *mere* contemplation of truth, or by any physical operation of such contemplation on the mind. It was by the Spirit of God alone that the heart was changed even under the gospel, and amidst the full blaze of its truth. Were it not for *his* agency, even the contemplation of the glorious truths of the gospel would be in vain, and would produce no saving effect on the human heart.

REMARKS.

1. The best of all evidences of a call to the office of the ministry is the divine blessing resting on our labours

ver. 1, 2. If sinners are converted; if souls are sanctified; if the interests of pure religion are advanced; if by humble, zealous, and self-denying efforts, a man is enabled so to preach as that the divine blessing shall rest constantly on his labours, it is among the best of all evidences that he is called of God, and is approved by him. And though it may be true, and is true, that men who are self-deceived, or are hypocrites, are sometimes the means of doing good, yet it is still true, as a general rule, that eminent, and long-continued success in the ministry is an evidence of God's acceptance, and that he has called a minister to this office. *Paul* felt this, and often appealed to it; and why may not others also?

2. A minister may appeal to the effect of the gospel among his own people as a proof that it is from God, ver. 2, 3. Nothing else would produce such effects as were produced at Corinth, but the power of God. If the wicked are reclaimed; if the intemperate and licentious are made temperate and pure; if the dishonest are made honest; and the scoffer learns to pray, under the gospel, it proves that it is from God. To such effects a minister may appeal as proof that the gospel which he preaches is from heaven. A system which will produce these effects must be true.

3. A minister should *so* live among a people as to be able to appeal to them with the utmost confidence in regard to the purity and integrity of his own character, ver. 1, 2. He should so live, and preach, and act, that he will be under no necessity of adducing testimonials from abroad in regard to his character. The effect of his gospel, and the tenor of his life, should be his best testimonial; and to that he should be able to appeal. A man who is under a necessity, constantly, or often, of defending his own character; of bolstering it up by testimonials from abroad; who is obliged to spend much of his time in defending his reputation, or who chooses to spend much of his time in defending it, has usually a character and reputation *not worth defending.* Let a man live as he ought to do, and he will, in the end, have a good reputation. Let him strive to do the will of God, and save souls, and he will have all the reputation which he *ought* to have. God will take care of his character; and will give him just as much reputation as it is desirable that he should have; see Ps. xxxvii. 5, 6.

4. The church is, as it were, an epistle sent by the Lord Jesus, to show his character and will, ver. 3. It is his representative on earth. It holds his truth. It is to imitate his example. It is to show how he lived. And it is to accomplish that which he would accomplish were he personally on earth, and present among men—as a letter is designed to accomplish some important purpose of the writer when absent. The church, therefore, *should* be such as shall appropriately express the will and desire of the Lord Jesus. It should resemble him. It should hold his truth; and it should devote itself with untiring diligence to the great purpose of advancing his designs, and spreading his gospel around the world.

5. Religion has its seat in the heart, ver. 3. It is engraven there. It is written not with ink, or engraven on stone, but it is written by the Spirit of God on the heart. That professed religion, therefore, which does not reach the heart, and which is not felt there, is false and delusive. There *is* no true religion which does not reach and affect the heart.

6. We should feel our dependence on God in all things, ver. 5. We are dependent on him, (1.) For revelation itself. Man had no power of originating the truths which constitute revelation. They are the free and pure gift of God. (2.) For success in saving souls. God only can change the heart. It is not done by human reasoning; by any power of man; by any eloquence of persuasion. It is by the power of God; and if a minister of religion meets with any success, it will be by the presence and by the power of God alone. (3.) We are dependent on him for the power of thought at all; for clearness of intel-

lect; for such a state of bodily health as to permit us to think; for bright conceptions; for ability to arrange our thoughts; for the power of expressing them clearly; for such a state of mind as shall be free from vain fancies, and vagaries, and eccentricities; and for such a state as shall mark our plans as those of common sense and prudence. On such plans much of the comfort of life depends; and on such plans depends also nearly all the success which men ever meet with in any virtuous and honourable calling. And if men *felt*, as they should do, how much they are dependent on God for the power of *clear thinking*, and for the characteristics of sound sense in their schemes, they would pray for it more than they do; and would be more grateful that such a rich blessing is so extensively conferred on men.

7. Religion has a living power, ver. 6. It is not the letter, but the spirit. It is not made up of forms and ceremonies. It does not consist in cold, external rites, however regular they may be; nor in formal prayer, or in stated seasons of devotion. All these will be dead and vain unless the heart is given to God, and to his service. If these are all, there is no religion. And if we have no better religion than that, we should at once abandon our hopes, and seek for that which does not kill, but which makes alive.

8. The office of the ministers of the gospel is glorious, and most honourable, ver. 7—9. It is *far more* honourable than was the office of Moses; and their work is far more glorious than was his. *His* consisted in giving the law on tables of stone; in the external splendour which attended its promulgation; and in introducing a system which must be soon done away. His was a ministry "of death" and of "condemnation." *Theirs* is a ministration by which the Holy Spirit is communicated to men—*through* them as channels, or organs by which the saving grace of that Spirit is imparted; it is a work by which men are made righteous, justified, and accepted; it is a work whose effects are never to fade away, but which are to live amidst the splendours of heaven.

9. The responsibility and solemnity of the work of the ministry. It was a solemn and responsible work for Moses to give the law amidst the thunders of Sinai to the children of Israel. It is *much* more solemn to be the medium by which the eternal truths of the gospel are made known to men. The one, imposing as it was, was designed to be temporary, and was soon to pass away. The other is to be eternal in its effects, and is to enter vitally and deeply into the eternal destiny of man. The one pertained to laws written on stone; the other to influences that are deeply and for ever to affect the heart. No work *can* be more solemn and responsible than that through which the Holy Spirit, with renewing and sanctifying power, is conveyed to man; that which is connected with the justification of sinners; and that which in its effects is to be permanent as the soul itself, and to endure as long as God shall exist.

10. We see the folly of attempting to be justified by the law, ver. 7, 9. It is the ministration of death and of condemnation. It speaks only to condemn. Law knows nothing of pardon. It is not given for that purpose; and no perfect law can contain within itself provisions for pardon. Besides, no one has ever complied with all the demands of the law; no one ever will. All have sinned. But if ALL the demands of the law be not complied with, it speaks only to condemn, James ii. 10. If a man in other respects has been ever so good a citizen, and yet has committed murder, he must die. So says the law. If a man has been ever so valiant, and fought ever so bravely, and yet is guilty of an act of treason, he must die. The question is not what he has been in in other respects, or what else he may, or may not have done, but has he committed *this* offence? If he has, the law knows no forgiveness; and pronounces his condemnation. If pardoned, it must be by some other system than by the regular operation of law. So with the sinner against

God. If the law is violated, it speaks only to condemn. If he is pardoned, it can be only by the gospel of Jesus Christ.

11. The danger of grieving the Holy Spirit, ver. 8. The gospel is the field of the operations of the Holy Spirit in our world. It is the ministration of the Spirit. It is the channel by which his influences descend on man. To reject that gospel is to reject Him, *and to cut off the soul from all possibility of being brought under his saving influence and power for ever.* He strives with men only in connection with the gospel; and all hope, therefore, of being brought under his saving power, is in attending *to* that gospel, and embracing its provisions. The multitudes, therefore, who are rejecting or neglecting that gospel, are throwing themselves beyond his saving influences; and placing themselves beyond the possibility of salvation.

12. We see the *guilt* of neglecting or rejecting the gospel. It is the scheme, and the only scheme for pardon, ver. 8—10. It is a far more glorious manifestation of the goodness of God than the law of Moses. It is the glorious and benevolent manifestation of God through the incarnation, the sufferings, and the death of his Son. It is the ONLY plan of pardoning mercy that has been, or that will be revealed. If men are not pardoned through that, they are not pardoned at all. If they are not saved *by* that, they must die for ever. What guilt is there, therefore, in neglecting and despising it! What folly is there in turning away from its provisions of mercy, and neglecting to secure an interest in what it provides!

13. The gospel is to spread around the world, and endure to the end of time, ver. 11. It is not like the institutions of Moses, to endure for a limited period, and then to be done away. The cloud and tempest; the thunder and lightning on Mount Sinai which attended the giving of the law, soon disappeared. The unusual and unnatural splendour on the countenance of Moses soon vanished away. All the magnificence of the Mosaic ritual also soon faded away. But not so the gospel. That abides. That is the *last* dispensation; the *permanent* economy: that under which the affairs of the world are to be brought to an end. That is to pervade all lands; to bless all people; to survive all revolutions; to outlive all the magnificence of courts, and all the splendour of mighty dynasties, and is to endure till this world shall come to an end, and live in its glorious effects for ever and ever. It is, therefore, to be the fixed principle on which all Christians are to act, that the gospel is to be permanent, and is to spread over all lands, and yet fill all nations with joy. And if so, how fervent and unceasing should be their prayers and efforts to accomplish this great and glorious result!

14. We learn from this chapter the duty of preaching in a plain, simple, intelligible manner, ver. 12. Preaching should always be characterised indeed by good sense, and ministers should show that they are not fools, and their preaching should be such as to interest thinking men—for there is no folly or nonsense in the Bible. But their preaching should not be obscure, metaphysical, enigmatical, and abstruse. It should be so simple that the unlettered may learn the plan of salvation; so plain that no one shall mistake it except by his own fault. The *hopes* of the gospel are so clear that there is no need of ambiguity or enigma; no need of abstruse metaphysical reasoning in the pulpit. Nor should there be an attempt to *appear* wise or profound, by studying a dry, abstruse, and cold style and manner. The preacher should be open, plain, simple, sincere; he should *testify* what he feels; should be able to speak as himself animated by *hope*, and to tell of a world of glory to which he is himself looking forward with unspeakable joy.

15. It is the privilege of the Christian to look on the unvailed and unclouded glory of the gospel, ver. 12, 13. He does not look at it through types and shadows. He does not contemplate it when a vail of obscurity is

drawn designedly over it. He sees it in its true beauty and splendour. The Messiah has come, and he may contemplate openly and plainly his glory, and the grandeur of his work. The Jews looked upon it in the light of *prophecy;* to us it is history. They saw it only through obscure shadows, types, and figures; we see it in open day, may survey at leisure its full beauty, and contemplate in the fulness of its splendour the gospel of the blessed God. For this we cannot be too thankful; nor can we be too anxious lest we undervalue our privileges, and abuse the mercies that we enjoy.

16. In reading the Old Testament, we see the importance of suffering the reflected light of the New Testament to be thrown upon it, in order correctly to understand it, ver. 13, 14. It is our privilege to *know* what the institutions of Moses meant; to see the *end* which he contemplated. And it is our privilege to see what they referred to, and how they prefigured the Messiah, and his gospel. In reading the Old Testament, therefore, there is no reason why we should not take with us the knowledge which we have derived from the New, respecting the character, work, and doctrines of the Messiah; and to suffer them to influence our understanding of the laws and institutions of Moses. Thus shall we treat the Bible *as a whole,* and allow one part to throw light on another—a privilege which we always concede to any book. There is no reason why Christians in reading the Old Testament should remain in the same darkness as the ancient, or the modern Jews.

17. Thus read, the Old Testament will be to us of inestimable value, ver. 14. It is of value not only as *introducing* the gospel; as furnishing predictions whose fulfilment are full demonstration of the truth of religion; as containing specimens of the sublimest and purest poetry in the world; but it is of value as embodying, though amidst many types and shadows and much obscurity, all the great doctrines of the true religion. Though to the Jews, and to the world, there is a vail cast over it; yet to the Christian there is a beauty and splendour on all its pages—for the coming of Christ has removed that vail, and the sense of those ancient writings is now fully seen. True piety will value the Old Testament, and will find there, in the sweetest poetry in the world, the expression of feelings which the religion of the Messiah only can produce; and pure and elevated thoughts which could have been originated by nothing but his anticipated coming. It is no mark of piety or of wisdom to disparage the Jewish Scriptures. But the higher the attainments in Christian feeling, the more will the writings of Moses and the prophets be loved.

18. Men may have the Bible, and may read it long, and much, and yet not understand it, ver. 15. So it was, and is with the Jews. The Scriptures were attentively read by them, and yet they did not understand them. So it is still. There is a vail on their heart, and they are blinded. So it is often now with others. Men often read the Bible and see little beauty in it. They read, and they do not understand it. The reason is, the heart is not right. There should be a correspondence of feeling between the heart and the Bible, or a congeniality of view in order to appreciate its value and its truth. No man can understand or appreciate Milton or Cowper who has not a taste like theirs. No man can understand and appreciate a poem or an essay on patriotism, who is not a lover of his country; or on chastity, who is impure; or on temperance, who is intemperate; or on virtue in general, who is a stranger to virtue in every form. And so in reading the Bible. To appreciate and understand fully the writings of David, Isaiah, Paul, or John, we must have their feelings: our hearts must glow with their love to God and the Redeemer; we must feel as they did the guilt and burden of sin; and we must rejoice as they did in the hope of deliverance, and in the prospect of heaven. Till men have these feelings, they are not to wonder that the Bible

CHAPTER IV.

THEREFORE, seeing we have this ministry, as we have received [a] mercy, we faint not;

2 But have renounced the hidden things of [1] dishonesty, not walking in craftiness, nor handling the word of God deceitfully, [b] but by manifestation of the truth commending ourselves to every man's conscience in the sight of God.

a 1 Cor. 7.25. 1 *shame*. b chap. 2.17.

is to them a dead letter, or a sealed book, and that they do not understand it, or see any beauty in its pages.

19. This chapter furnishes an argument for the fidelity and truth of the statement of Paul, ver. 15. The argument is, that his description is as applicable to the Jews now as it was in his own time—and that, therefore, it must have been drawn from nature. The same vail is on their hearts now as in his time; there is the same blindness and darkness in regard to the true meaning of their Scriptures. The language of Paul will accurately express that blindness now; and his description, therefore, is not drawn from fancy, but from fact. It is true now in regard to that singular people, and it was true in his own time; and the lapse of eighteen hundred years has only served to confirm the truth of his description in regard to the people of his own nation and time.

20. That veil is to be removed only by their turning to God, ver. 16. It is only by true conversion that the mind can be brought to a full and clear understanding of the Scriptures; and that event will yet take place in regard to the Jews. They shall yet be converted to the Messiah whom their fathers slew, and whom they have so long rejected; and when that event shall occur, they shall see the beauty of their own Scriptures, and rejoice in the promises and glorious hopes which they hold out to the view.

21. The duty of *meditating* much on the glory of the gospel, ver. 18. It is by that we are purified. It is by keeping it constantly before the mind; dwelling on it splendour; thinking of its glorious truths, that we become transformed into the same image, and made like God. If the character is formed by the objects which we contemplate, and with which we are familiar; if we are insensibly moulded in our feelings and principles by that with which we constantly associate, then we should *think* much of the truths of the gospel. We should pray much—for thus we come in contact with God and his truth. We should read the Scripture much. We should commune with the good and the pure. We should make our companions of those who most love the Lord Jesus, and most decidedly bear his image. We should think much of a pure heaven. Thus shall we be moulded, insensibly it may be, but certainly, into the image of a holy God and Saviour, and be prepared for a pure and holy heaven.

CHAPTER IV.

This chapter is intimately connected with the preceding, and is indeed merely a statement of the consequences or results of the doctrine advanced there. In that chapter, Paul had stated the clearness and plainness of the gospel as contrasted with the institutions of Moses, and particularly that the Christian ministry was a ministration more glorious than that of Moses. It was more clear. It was a ministration of justification (ver. 9), and of the Spirit (ver. 8), and was a ministration where they were permitted to look upon the unvailed and unclouded glories of God, ver. 18. In this chapter he states some of the *consequences*, or *results* of their being called to this ministry; and the design is, to magnify the office of the ministry; to show the sustaining power of the truths which they preached; the interest which the Corinthian Christians and all other Christians had in the ministry, and this to conciliate their favour; and to show what there was to comfort them in the various trials to which as ministers they were exposed. Paul states therefore in this chapter—

1. That these clear and elevated views of the gospel sustained him; kept him from fainting; preserved him from deceit and all improper acts; made him open and honest; since he had no necessity for craft and guilt, but proclaimed a system of religion which *could* be commended to every man's conscience, and be seen to be true, ver. 1, 2.

2. That if any persons were lost, it was not the fault of the gospel, ver. 3, 4. That was clear, open, plain, glorious, and might be understood; and if they were lost, it was to be traced to the malign influence of the god of this world, and not to the gospel.

3. That the great purpose of Paul and his associates was to make known this clear and glorious truth of the gospel, and that, therefore, the apostles did not preach themselves, but Christ Jesus, the revealer and source of all this glory, ver. 5, 6. Their sole object was to show forth this pure and glorious light of the gospel.

4. That it was so arranged by God's appointment and providence that all the glory of the results of the ministry should be his, ver. 7—11. He had taken especial care that they should have no cause of self-exultation or glorying in preaching the gospel; and had taken effectual means that they should be humbled, and not lifted up with pride, from the fact that they were commissioned to make known such glorious truths, and had a ministry more honourable than that of Moses. He had, therefore, committed the treasure to earthen vessels; to frail, weak, dying men, and to men in humble life (ver. 7), and he had called them to submit to constant trials of persecution, poverty, peril, and want, in order that they might be humbled, and that God might manifestly have all the glory, ver. 8—11.

5. All this was for the sake of the church, a fact which was adapted to conciliate the favour of Christians, and excite their sympathy in the sufferings of the apostles, and to lead them to honour the ministry in a proper manner, ver. 12—15. It was not for their own welfare, happiness, honour, or emolument that they endured these trials in the ministry; it was that the church might be benefited, and thus abundant praise redound to God.

6. These considerations sustained them in their trials, ver. 16—18. They *had* comfort in all their afflictions. They felt that they were doing and suffering these things for the salvation of souls, and the glory of God, (ver. 16); they had inward strength given them every day, though the outward man perished (ver. 16); they knew that the result of this would be an eternal weight of glory (ver. 17); and they were enabled to look to another and a better world; to keep the eye on heaven, and to contemplate by faith the things which were unseen and eternal, ver. 18. These things supported them; and thus upheld, they went cheerfully to their great work, and met with calmness and joy all the trials which it involved.

1. *Therefore* (Διὰ τοῦτο). On account of this. That is, because the light of the gospel is so clear; because it reveals so glorious truths, and all obscurity is taken away, and we are permitted to behold as in a mirror the glory of the Lord, chap. iii. 18. Since the glories of the gospel dispensation are so great, and its effects on the heart are so transforming and purifying. The object is, to show the *effect* of being intrusted with such a ministry, on the character of his preaching. ¶ *Seeing we have this ministry.* The gospel ministry, so much more glorious than that of Moses (chap. iii. 6); which is the ministry by which the Holy Spirit acts on the hearts of men (chap. iii. 8); which is the ministry of that system by which men are justified (chap. iii. 9); and which is the ministry of a system so pure and unclouded, chap. iii. 9—11, 18. ¶ *As we have received mercy.* Tindal renders this, "even as mercy is sure in us." The idea is, that it was by the mere mercy and favour of God, that he had been intrusted with the ministry, and the object of Paul is doubtless to prevent the *appearance* of arrogance and self-confidence by stating that it was to be traced entirely to God that he was put into the min-

istry. He doubtless had his eye on the fact that he had been a persecutor and blasphemer; and that it was by the mere favour of God that he had been converted and intrusted with the ministry, 1 Tim. i. 13. Nothing will more effectually humble a minister, and prevent his assuming any arrogant and self-confident airs, than to look over his past life; especially if his life was one of blasphemy, vice, or infidelity; and to remember that it is by the mere mercy of God that he is intrusted with the high office of an ambassador of Jesus Christ. Paul never forgot to trace his hope, his appointment to the ministerial office, and his success, to the mere grace of God. ¶ *We faint not.* This is one of the *effects* of being intrusted with such a ministry. The word here used (ἐκκακοῦμεν) means, properly, to turn out a coward; to lose one's courage; then to be faint-hearted, to faint, to despond, in view of trial, difficulty, &c—*Robinson.* Here it means, that by the mercy of God, he was not disheartened by the difficulties which he met; his faith and zeal did not flag; he was enabled to be faithful, and laborious, and his courage always kept up, and his mind was filled with cheerfulness; see Note on chap. ii. 14. He was deterred by no difficulties; embarrassed by no opposition; driven from his purpose by no persecution; and his strength did not fail under any trials. The consciousness of being intrusted with *such* a ministry animated him; and the mercy and grace of God sustained him.

2. *But have renounced* (ἀπειπάμεθα from ἀπὸ and εἶπον). The word means properly to speak out or off; to refuse or deny; to interdict or forbid. Here it means, to renounce, or disown; to spurn, or scorn with aversion. It occurs no where else in the New Testament; and the sense here is, that the apostles had such a view of the truth of religion, and the glory of the Christian scheme (chap. iii. 13—18), as to lead them to discard every thing that was disguised, and artful, and crafty; every thing like deceit and fraud. The religions of the heathen were made up mainly of trick, and were supported by deception practised on the ignorant, and on the mass of men. Paul says, that he and his fellow-labourers had such views of the truth, and glory, and holiness of the Christian scheme, as to lead them solemnly to abjure and abhor all such dishonest tricks and devices. Truth never needs such arts; and no cause will long succeed by mere trick and cunning. ¶ *The hidden things of dishonesty.* Marg. *shame.* The Greek word most commonly means shame, or disgrace. The hidden things of shame here mean disgraceful conduct; clandestine and secret arts, which were in themselves shameful and disgraceful. They denote all *underhanded* dealings; all dishonest artifices and plans, such as were common among the heathen, and such probably as the false teachers adopted in the propagation of their opinions at Corinth. The expression here does not imply that the apostles ever had any thing to do with such arts; but that they solemnly abjured and abhorred them. Religion is open, plain, straight-forward. It has no alliance with cunning, and trick, and artifice. It should be defended openly; stated clearly; and urged with steady argument. It is a work of light, and not of darkness. ¶ *Not walking in craftiness.* Not acting craftily; not behaving in a crafty manner. The word here used (πανουργία from πᾶν, *all,* ἔργον, *work, i. e.* doing every thing, or capable of doing any thing) denotes shrewdness, cunning, and craft. This was common; and this was probably practised by the false teachers in Corinth. With this Paul says he had nothing to do. He did not adopt a course of carnal wisdom and policy (Note, chap. i. 12); he did not attempt to impose upon them, or to deceive them; or to make his way by subtile and deceitful arts. True religion can never be advanced by trick and craftiness. ¶ *Nor handling the word of God deceitfully* (δολοῦντες). Not falsifying; or deceitfully corrupting or disguising the truth of God. The phrase seems to be synonymous with that used in chap. ii. 17 and rendered "corrupt the word of God;" see Note on that verse. It

properly means to falsify, adulterate, corrupt, by Jewish traditions, &c. (Robinson, Bloomfield, Doddridge, &c.); or it may mean, as in our translation, to handle in a deceitful manner; to make use of trick and art in propagating and defending it. Tindal renders it, "neither corrupt we the word of God." ¶ *But by manifestation of the truth.* By making the truth manifest; *i. e.* by a simple exhibition of the truth. By stating it just as it is, in an undisguised and open manner. Not by adulterating it with foreign mixtures; not by mingling it with philosophy, or traditions; not by blunting its edge, or concealing any thing, or explaining it away; but by an open, plain, straight-forward exhibition of it as it is in Jesus. Preaching should consist in a simple exhibition of the truth. There is no deceit in the gospel itself; and there should be none in the manner of exhibiting it. It should consist of a simple statement of things as they are. The whole design of preaching is, to make known the truth. And this is done in an effectual manner only when it is simple, open, undisguised, without craft, and without deceit. ¶ *Commending ourselves to every man's conscience.* That is, so speaking the truth that every man's conscience shall approve it *as* true; every man shall see it to be true, and to be in accordance with what he knows to be right. Conscience is that faculty of the mind which distinguishes between right and wrong, and which prompts us to choose the former and avoid the latter; John viii. 9; Note, Rom. ii. 15; 1 Cor. x. 25, 27—29; 2 Cor. i. 12. It is implied here, (1.) That a course of life, and a manner of preaching that shall be free from dishonesty, and art, and trick, will be such as the consciences of men will approve. Paul sought such a course of life as should accord with their sense of *right*, and thus serve to commend the gospel to them. (2.) That the gospel may be so preached as to be seen by men to be true; so as to be approved as right; and so that every man's conscience shall bear testimony to its truth. Men do not *love* it, but they may see that it is *true;* they may hate it, but they may see that the truth which condemns their practices is from heaven. This is an exceedingly important principle in regard to preaching, and vastly momentous in its bearing on the views which ministers should have of their own work. The gospel is reasonable. It may be seen to be true by every man to whom it is preached. And it should be the aim of every preacher *so* to preach it, as to enlist the consciences of his hearers in his favour. And it is a very material fact that *when* so preached the conscience and reason of every man *is* in its favour, and they know that it is true even when it pronounces their own condemnation, and denounces their own sins. This passage proves, therefore, the following things. (1.) That the gospel *may* be so preached as to be seen to be true by all men. Men are capable of seeing the truth, and even when they do not love it; they can perceive that it has demonstration that it is from God. It is a system so reasonable; so well established by evidence; so fortified by miracles, and the fulfilment of prophecies; so pure in its nature; so well-adapted to man; so fitted to his condition, and so well designed to make him better; and so happy in its influence on society, that men may be led to see that it is *true.* And this I take to be the case with almost all those men who habitually attend on the preaching of the gospel. Infidels do not *often* visit the sanctuary; and when they are in the habit of doing it, it is a fact that they gradually come to the conviction that the Christian religion is true. It is rare to find professed infidels in our places of worship; and the great mass of those who attend on the preaching of the gospel may be set down as *speculative* believers in the truth of Christianity. (2.) The consciences of men are on the side of truth, and the gospel may be so preached as to enlist their consciences in its favour. Conscience prompts to do right, and condemns us if we do wrong. It can never be made to approve of wrong, never to give a man peace if he does that which

3 But if our gospel be hid, it is hid to them[a] that are lost:

a 2 Th. 2.10.

4 In whom the god[a] of this world hath blinded the minds of

a John 12.31,40.

he knows to be evil. By no art or device; by no system of laws, or bad government; by no training or discipline, can it be made the advocate of sin. In all lands, at all times, and in all circumstances, it prompts a man to do what is right, and condemns him if he does wrong. It may be silenced for a time; it may be "seared as with a hot iron," and for a time be insensible, but if it speak at all, it speaks to prompt a man to do what he believes to be right, and condemns him if he does that which is wrong. The consciences of men are on the side of the gospel; and it is only their hearts which are opposed to it. Their consciences are in favour of the gospel in the following, among other respects. (*a*) They approve of it as a just, pure, holy, and reasonable system; as in accordance with what they feel to be right; as recommending that which ought to be done, and forbidding that which ought not to be done. (*b*) In its special requirements on themselves. Their consciences tell them that they *ought* to love God with all the heart; to repent of their sins; to trust in that Saviour who died for them; and to lead a life of prayer and of devotedness to the service of God; that they ought to be sincere and humble Christians, and prepare to meet God in peace. (*c*) Their consciences approve the truth that condemns them. No matter how strict it may seem to be; no matter how loud its denunciation against their sins; no matter how much the gospel may condemn their pride, avarice, sensuality, levity, dishonesty, fraud, intemperance, profaneness, blasphemy, or their neglect of their soul, yet their consciences approve of it as right, and proclaim that these things *ought* to be condemned, and ought to be abandoned. The heart may *love* them, but the conscience cannot be made to approve them. And the minister of the gospel may *always* approach his people, or an individual man, with the assurance that however much they may *love* the ways of sin, yet that he has their *consciences* in his favour, and that in urging the claims of God on them, their consciences will *always* coincide with his appeals (3.) The *way* in which a minister is to commend himself to the consciences of men, is that which was pursued by Paul. He must (*a*) Have a clear and unwavering conviction of the truth himself. On this subject he should have no doubt. He should be able to look on it as on a burnished mirror (Note, chap. iii. 18); and to see its glory as with open face. (*b*) It should be by the simple statement of the truth of the gospel. Not by preaching philosophy, or metaphysics, or the traditions of man, or the sentiments of theologians, but the simple truths of the gospel of Jesus Christ. Men may be made to see that these *are* truths, and God will take care that the reason and consciences of men shall be in their favour. (*c*) By the absence of all trick and cunning, and disguised and subtle arts. The gospel has nothing of these in itself, and it will never approve of them, nor will God bless them. A minister of Jesus should be frank, open, undisguised, and candid. He should make a sober and elevated appeal to the reason and conscience of man. The gospel is not "a cunningly-devised fable;" it has no trick in itself, and the ministers of religion should solemnly abjure all the hidden things of dishonesty. ¶ *In the sight of God.* As in the immediate presence of God. We act as if we felt that his eye was upon us; and this consideration serves to keep us from the hidden things of dishonesty, and from improper arts in spreading the true religion; see Note on chap. ii. 17.

3. *But if our gospel be hid.* Paul here calls it *his* gospel, because it was that which he preached, or the message which he bore; see Note, Rom. xvi. 25. The sense here is, "if the gospel which I preach is not understood; if its meaning is obscure or hidden; if its glory is not seen." It

them which believe not, lest the light of the glorious gospel of Christ, who is the image [a] of God, should shine unto them.

a John 1. 14, 18.

is *implied* here, that to many the beauty and glory of the gospel was not perceived. This was undeniable, notwithstanding the plainness and fulness with which its truths were made known. The *object* of Paul here is, to state that this fact was not to be traced to any want of clearness in the gospel itself, but to other causes, and thus probably to meet an objection which might be made to his argument about the clearness and fulness of the revelation in the gospel. In the language which Paul uses here, there is undoubted allusion to what he had said respecting Moses, who put a vail on his face, chap. iii. 13. He had hid, or concealed his face, as emblematic of the nature of his institutions (Note, chap. iii. 14); and here Paul says that it was not to be denied that the gospel was *vailed* also to some. But it was not from the nature of the gospel It was not because God had purposely concealed its meaning. It was not from any want of clearness in itself. It was to be traced to other causes. ¶ *It is hid to them that are lost.* On the meaning of the word here rendered "lost;" see Note, chap. ii. 15, there rendered "perish." It is hid among them who are about to perish; who are perishing (ἐν τοῖς ἀπολλυμένοις); those who deserve to perish. It is concealed only among that class who may be designated *as* the perishing, or *as* the lost. Grotius explains this, "those who deserve to perish, who foster their vices, and will not see the truth which condemns those vices." And he adds, that this might very well be, for, "however conspicuous the gospel was in itself, yet like the sun it would not be visible to the blind." The cause was not in the gospel, but in themselves. This verse teaches, therefore, (1.) That the beauty of the gospel may be hidden from many of the human family. This is a matter of simple fact. There are thousands and millions to whom it is preached who see no beauty in it, and who regard it as foolishness. (2.) That there is a class of men who may be called, even now, *the lost.* They are lost to virtue, to piety, to happiness, to hope. They deserve to perish; and they are hastening to merited ruin. This class in the time of Paul was large; and it is large now. It is composed of those to whom the gospel is hidden, or to whom it appears to be vailed, and who see no beauty in it. It is made up indeed of all the profane, polluted, and vile; but their *characteristic* feature is, that the gospel is hidden from them, and that they see no beauty and glory in it. (3.) This is not the fault of the gospel. It is not the fault of the sun when men shut their eyes and will not see it. It is not the fault of a running stream, or a bubbling fountain, if men will not drink of it, but rather choose to die of thirst. The gospel does not obscure and conceal its own glory any more than the sun does. It is in itself a clear and full revelation of God and his grace; and that glory is adapted to shed light upon the benighted minds of men.

4. *In whom.* In respect to whom; among whom; or in whose hearts. The design of this verse is *to account* for the fact that the glory of the gospel was not seen by them. It is to be traced entirely to the agency of him whom Paul here calls "the god of this world." ¶ *The god of this world.* There can be no doubt that Satan is here designated by this appellation; though some of the fathers supposed that it means the true God, and *Clarke* inclines to this opinion. In John xii. 31, he is called "the prince of this world." In Eph. ii. 2, he is called "the prince of the power of the air." And in Eph. vi. 12, the same bad influence is referred to under the names of "principalities, and powers," "the rulers of the darkness of this world," and "spiritual wickedness in high places." The name "god" is here given to him, not because he has any divine attributes, but because he actually has the homage of the men of

this world *as* their god, as the being who is really worshipped, or who has the affections of their hearts in the same way as it is given to idols. By "this world" is meant the wicked world; or the mass of men. He has dominion over the world. They obey his will; they execute his plans; they further his purposes, and they are his obedient subjects. He has subdued the world to himself, and was really adored in the place of the true God; see Note on 1 Cor. x. 20. "They sacrified to devils and not to God." Here it is meant by the declaration that Satan is the god of this world, (1.) That the world at large was under his control and direction. He secured the apostacy of man, and early brought him to follow his plans; and he has maintained his sceptre and dominion since. No more abject submission could be desired by him than has been rendered by the mass of men. (2.) The *idolatrous* world particularly is under his control, and subject to him; 1 Cor. x. 20. He is worshipped there; and the religious rites and ceremonies of the heathen are in general just such as a mighty being who hated human happiness, and who sought pollution, obscenity, wretchedness, and blood would appoint; and over all the heathen world his power is absolute. In the time of Paul all the world, except the Jews and Christians, was sunk in heathen degradation. (3.) He rules in the hearts and lives of all wicked men—and the world is full of wicked men. They obey him, and submit to his will in executing fraud, and rapine, and piracy, and murder, and adultery, and lewdness; in wars and fightings; in their amusements and pastimes; in dishonesty and falsehood. The dominion of Satan over this world has been, and is still almost universal and absolute; nor has the lapse of eighteen hundred years rendered the appellation improper as descriptive of his influence, that he is the god of this world. The world pursues his plans; yields to his temptations; neglects, or rejects the reign of God as he pleases; and submits to his sceptre, and is still full of abomination, cruelty, and pollution, as he desires it to be. ¶ *Hath blinded the minds of them which believe not.* Of all who discern no beauty in the gospel. and who reject it. It is implied here, (1.) That the minds of unbelievers are blinded; that they perceive no beauty in the gospel. This is often affirmed of those who reject the gospel, and who live in sin; see Note on chap. ii. 13; Mat. xxiii. 16, 17, 26; Luke iv. 18; John ix. 39; xii. 40; Rom. xi. 7. The sense is, that they did not *see* the spiritual beauty and glory of the plan of redemption. They act in reference to that as they would in reference to this world, if a bandage were over their eyes, and they saw not the light of the sun, the beauty of the landscape, the path in which they should go, or the countenance of a friend. All is dark, and obscure, and destitute of beauty to *them*, however much beauty may be seen in all these objects by others. (2.) That this is done by the agency of Satan; and that his dominion is secured by keeping the world in darkness. The affirmation is direct and positive, that it is by his agency that it is done. Some of the *modes* in which it is done are the following. (*a*) By a direct influence on the minds of men. I do not know why it is absurd to suppose that one intellect may, in some way unknown to us, have access to another, and have power to influence it; nor can it be proved that Satan may not have power to pervert the understanding; to derange its powers; to distract its attention; and to give in view of the mind a wholly delusive relative importance to objects. In the time of the Saviour it cannot be doubted that in the numerous cases of demoniacal possessions, Satan directly affected the minds of men; nor is there any reason to think that he has ceased to delude and destroy them (*b*) By the false philosophy which has prevailed—a large part of which seems to have been contrived as if on purpose to deceive the world, and destroy the peace and happiness of men. (*c*) By the systems of superstition and idolatry. All these seem to be under the control of one master mind. They are so well conceived and adapted to prostrate the moral powers; to fetter the intellect; to pervert the will; to make men debased, sunken, polluted, and degraded; and they so uniformly accomplish this effect, that they have all the marks of being under the control of one mighty mind, and of having been devised to accomplish his purposes over men. (*d*) By producing in the minds of men a wholly disproportionate view of the value of objects. *A very small object held before the eye will shut out the light of the sun.* A piece of money of the smallest value laid on the eye will make every thing appear dark, and prevent all the glory of midday from reaching the seat of vision. And so it is with the things of this world. They are placed directly before us, and are placed directly between us and the glory of the gospel. And the trifles of wealth and of fashion; the objects of pleasure and ambition, are made to assume an importance in view of the mind which wholly excludes the glory of the gospel, and shuts out all the realities of the eternal world. And he does it (*e*) By the blinding influence of passion and vice. Before a vicious mind all is dark and obscure. There is no beauty in truth, in chastity, or honesty, or in the fear and love of God. Vice always renders the mind blind, and the heart hard, and shrouds every thing in the moral world in midnight. And in order to blind the minds of men to the glory of the gospel, Satan has only to place splendid schemes of speculation before men; to tempt them to climb the steeps of ambition; to entice them to scenes of gayety; to secure the erection of theatres, and gambling houses, and houses of infamy and pollution; to fill the cities and towns of a land with taverns and dram-shops; and to give opportunity everywhere for the full play and unrestrained indulgence of passion; and the glory of the gospel will be as effectually *unseen* as the glory of the sun is in the darkest night. ¶ *Lest the light,* &c. This passage states the *design* for which Satan blinds the minds of men. It is because he *hates* the gospel, and wishes to prevent its influence and spread in the world Satan has always hated and opposed it, and all his arts have been employed to arrest its diffusion on earth. The word *light* here means excellence, beauty, or splendour. Light is the emblem of knowledge, purity, or innocence; and is here and elsewhere applied to the gospel, because it removes the errors, and sins, and wretchedness of men, as the light of the sun scatters the shades of night. This purpose of preventing the light of the gospel shining on men, Satan will endeavour to accomplish by all the means in his power. It is his *grand* object in this world, because it is by the gospel only that men can be saved; by that that God is glorified on earth more than by any thing else; and because, therefore, if he can prevent sinners from embracing that, he will secure their destruction, and most effectually show his hatred of God. And it is to Satan a matter of little importance what men *may be*, or *are,* provided they are NOT Christians. They may be amiable, moral, accomplished, rich, honoured, esteemed by the world, because in the possession of all these he may be equally sure of their ruin, and *because,* also, these things may contribute somewhat to turn away their minds from the gospel. Satan, therefore, will not oppose plans of gain or ambition; he will not oppose purposes of fashion and amusement; he may not oppose schemes by which we desire to rise in the world; he will not oppose the theatre, the ball-room, the dance, or the song; he will not oppose thoughtless mirth; but the moment the gospel begins to shine on the benighted mind, that moment he will make resistance, and then all his power will be concentrated. ¶ *The glorious gospel.* Gr. 'The gospel of the glory of Christ,' a Hebraism for the glorious gospel. Mr. Locke renders it, "the glorious brightness of the light of the gospel of Christ," and supposes it means the brightness, or clearness, of the doctrine wherein Christ is manifested in the gospel.— It is all light, and splendour, and

5 For we preach not ourselves, but Christ Jesus the Lord; and ourselves your servants for Jesus' sake.

---

beauty, compared with the dark systems of philosophy and heathenism. It is glorious, for it is full of splendour; makes known the glorious God; discloses a glorious plan of salvation; and conducts ignorant, weak, and degraded man to a world of light. No two words in our language are so full of rich and precious meaning, as the phrase "glorious gospel." ¶ *Who is the image of God.* Christ is called the image of God, (1.) In respect to his divine nature, his exact resemblance to God in his divine attributes and perfections; see Col. i. 15, and Heb. i. 3; and, (2.) In his moral attributes as Mediator, as showing forth the glory of the Father to men. He *resembles* God, and in him we see the divine glory and perfections embodied, and shine forth. It is from his *resemblance* to God in all respects that he is called his image; and it is through him that the divine perfections are made known to men.—It is an object of especial dislike and hatred to Satan that the glory of Christ, who is the image of God, should shine on men, and fill their hearts. Satan hates that image; he hates that men should become like God; and he hates all that has a resemblance to the great and glorious Jehovah.

5. *For we preach not ourselves.* The connection here is not very apparent, and the design of this verse has been variously understood. The connection seems to me to be this. Paul gives here a reason for what he had said in the previous parts of the epistle respecting his conduct in the ministry. He had said that his course had been open, and pure, and free from all dishonest arts and tricks, and that he had not corrupted the word of God, or resorted to any artifice to accomplish his designs; chap. ii. 17; iv. 1, 2. The *reason* of this he here says is, that he had not preached himself, or sought to advance his own interest. He regarded himself as sent to make known a Saviour; himself as bound by all means to promote his cause, and to imitate him. Other men—the false teachers, and the cunning priests of the heathen religion—sought to advance their own interest, and to perpetuate a system of delusion that would be profitable to themselves; and they therefore resorted to all arts, and stratagems, and cunning devices to perpetuate their authority, and extend their influence. But the fact that Paul and his associates went forth to make known the Lord Jesus, was a reason why they avoided all such dishonest arts and artifices. "We are merely the *ambassadors* of another. We are not *principals* in this business, and do not despatch it as a business of our own, but we transact it as the *agents* for another, *i. e.* for the Lord Jesus, and we feel ourselves bound, therefore, to do it as he would have done it himself; and as he was free from all trick, and dishonest art, we feel bound to be also." This seems to me to be the design of this passage. Ministers may be said to preach themselves in the following ways. (1.) When their preaching has a primary reference to their own interest; and when they engage in it to advance their reputation, or to secure in some way their own advantage. When they aim at exalting their authority, extending their influence, or in any way promoting their own welfare (2.) When they proclaim their own opinions and not the gospel of Christ; when they derive their doctrines from their own reasonings, and not from the Bible. (3.) When they put themselves forward; speak much of themselves; refer often to themselves; are vain of their powers of reasoning, of their eloquence, and of their learning, and seek to make these known rather than the simple truths of the gospel. In one word, when self is primary, and the gospel is secondary; when they prostitute the ministry to gain popularity; to live a life of ease; to be respected; to obtain a livelihood; to gain influence; to rule over a people; and to make the preaching of the gospel merely *an occasion* of advanc-

ing themselves in the world.—Such a plan, it is implied here, would lead to dishonest arts and devices, and to trick and stratagem to accomplish the end in view. And it is implied here, also, that to avoid all such tricks and arts the true way is not to preach ourselves, but Jesus Christ. ¶ *But Christ Jesus the Lord.* This Paul states to be the only purpose of the ministry. It is so far the sole design of the ministry that had it not been to make known the Lord Jesus, it would never have been established; and whatever other objects are secured by its appointment, and whatever other truths are to be illustrated and enforced by the ministry, yet, if this is not the primary subject, and if every other object is not made subservient to this, the design of the ministry is not secured. The word "Christ" properly means the anointed, *i. e.* the Messiah, the anointed of God for this great office (see Note, Mat. i. 1); but it is used in the New Testament as a proper name, the name that was appropriate to *Jesus.* Still it may be used with a reference to the fact of the Messiahship, and not merely as a proper name, and in this place it may mean that they preached Jesus *as* the Messiah, or the Christ, and defended his claims to that high appointment. The word "Lord" also is used to designate him (Mark xi. 3; John xx. 25); and when it stands by itself in the New Testament, it denotes the Lord Jesus (Note, Acts i. 24); but it properly denotes one who has rule or authority, or proprietorship; and it is used here not merely as a part of the appropriate title of the Saviour, but with reference to the fact that he had the supreme headship, or lordship over the church and the world. This important passage, therefore, means, that they made it their sole business to make known Jesus the Messiah, or the Christ, as the supreme head and Lord of people; *i. e.* to set forth the Messiahship and the lordship of Jesus of Nazareth, appointed to these high offices by God. To do this, or to preach Jesus Christ the Lord, implies the following things. (1.) To prove that he is the Messiah so often predicted in the Old Testament, and so long expected by the Jewish people. To do this was a very vital part of the work of the ministry in the time of the apostles, and was essential to their success in all their attempts to convert the Jews; and to do this will be no less important in all attempts to bring the Jews now or in future times to the knowledge of the truth. No man *can* be successful among them who is not able to prove that Jesus is the Messiah.—It is not indeed so vital and leading a point now in reference to those to whom the ministers of the gospel usually preach; and it is probable that the importance of this argument is by many overlooked, and that it is not urged as it should be by those who "preach Christ Jesus the Lord." It involves the whole argument for the truth of Christianity. It leads to all the demonstrations that this religion is from God; and the establishment of the proposition that Jesus is the Messiah, is one of the most direct and certain ways of proving that his religion is from heaven. For (*a*) It contains the argument from the fulfilment of the prophecies—one of the main evidences of the truth of revelation; and (*b*) It involves an examination of all the evidences that Jesus gave that he was the Messiah sent from God, and of course an examination of all the miracles that he wrought in attestation of his divine mission. The first object of a preacher, therefore, is to demonstrate that Jesus is sent from God in accordance with the predictions of the prophets. (2.) To proclaim the truths that *he taught.* To make known his sentiments, and his doctrines, and not our own. This includes, of course, all that he taught respecting God, and respecting man; all that he taught respecting his own nature, and the design of his coming; all that he taught respecting the character of the human heart, and about human obligation and duty; all that he taught respecting death, the judgment, and eternity—respecting an eternal heaven, and an eternal hell. To explain, enforce, and vindicate his doctrines, is one great design of the ministry; and were there nothing else, this would be a field sufficiently ample to employ the life; sufficiently glorious to employ the best talents of man. The minister of the gospel is to teach the sentiments and doctrines of Jesus Christ, in contradistinction from all his own sentiments, and from all the doctrines of mere philosophy. He is not to teach science, or mere morals, but he is to proclaim and defend the doctrines of the Redeemer. (3.) He is to make known *the facts* of the Saviour's life. He is to show how he lived—to hold up his example in all the trying circumstances in which he was placed. For he came to show by his life what the law required; and to show how men *should* live. And it is the office of the Christian ministry, or a part of their work in preaching "Christ Jesus the Lord," to show how he lived, and to set forth his self-denial, his meekness, his purity, his blameless life, his spirit of prayer, his submission to the divine will, his patience in suffering, his forgiveness of his enemies, his tenderness to the afflicted, the weak, and the tempted; and the manner of his death. Were *this* all, it would be enough to employ the whole of a minister's life, and to command the best talents of the world. For he was the only perfectly pure model; and his example is to be followed by all his people, and his example is designed to exert a deep and wide influence on the world. Piety flourishes just in proportion as the pure example of Jesus Christ is kept before a people; and the world is made happier and better just as that example is kept constantly in view. To the gay and the thoughtless, the ministers of the gospel are to show how serious and calm was the Redeemer; to the worldly-minded, to show how he lived above the world; to the avaricious, how benevolent he was; to the profane and licentious, how pure he was; to the tempted, how he endured temptation; to the afflicted, how patient and resigned; to the dying, how he died:—to all, to show how holy, and heavenly-minded, and prayerful, and pure he was; in order that they may be won to the same purity, and be prepared to dwell with him in his kingdom. (4.) To set forth the design of his death. To show why he came to die; and what was the great object to be effected by his sufferings and death. To exhibit, therefore, the sorrows of his life; to describe his many trials; to dwell upon his sufferings in the garden of Gethsemane, and on the cross. To show *why* he died, and what was to be the influence of his death on the destiny of man. To show *how* it makes an atonement for sin; how it reconciles God to man; how it is made efficacious in the justification and the sanctification of the sinner. And were there nothing else, *this* would be sufficient to employ all the time, and the best talents in the ministry. For the salvation of the soul depends on the proper exhibition of the design of the death of the Redeemer. There is no salvation but through his blood; and hence the nature and design of his atoning sacrifice is to be exhibited to every man, and the offers of mercy through that death to be pressed upon the attention of every sinner. (5.) To set forth the truth and the design of his resurrection. To *prove* that he rose from the dead, and that he ascended to heaven; and to show the influence of his resurrection on our hopes and destiny. The whole structure of Christianity is dependent on making out the fact that he rose; and *if* he rose, all the difficulties in the doctrine of the resurrection of the dead are removed at once, and his people will also rise. The influence of that fact, therefore, on our hopes and on our prospects for eternity, is to be shown by the ministry of the gospel; and were there nothing else, *this* would be ample to command all the time, and the best talents of the ministry. (6.) To proclaim him as "Lord." This is expressly specified in the passage before us. "For we preach Christ Jesus THE LORD;" we proclaim him *as* the Lord. That is, he is to be preached as having dominion over the conscience; as the supreme Ruler in his Church; as above all councils, and

6 For God, who commanded [a] the light to shine out of darkness,

a Gen. 1. 3.

synods, and conferences, and all human authority; as having a right to legislate for his people; a right to prescribe their mode of worship; a right to define and determine the doctrines which they shall believe. He is to be proclaimed also as ruling over all, and as exalted in his mediatorial character over all worlds, and as having all things put beneath his feet; Ps. ii. 6; Isa. ix. 6, 7; Mat. xxviii. 18; John xvii. 2; Eph. i. 20; Heb. ii. 8. ¶ *And ourselves your servants,* &c. So far as we make any mention of ourselves, it is to declare that we are your servants, and that we are bound to promote your welfare in the cause and for the sake of the Redeemer. That is, they were their servants in all things in which they could advance the interests of the Redeemer's kingdom among them. The doctrine is, that they regarded themselves as under obligation not to seek their own interest, or to build up their own reputation and cause, but to seek the welfare of the church; and promote its interests, as a servant does that of his master. They should not seek to lord it over God's heritage, and to claim supreme and independent authority. They were not masters but servants. The church at large was the master, and they were its servants. This implies the following things. (1.) That the *time* of ministers belongs to the church, and should be employed in its welfare. It is not their own; and it is not to be employed in farming, or in speculating, or in trafficking, or in idleness, or in lounging, or in unprofitable visiting, or in mere science, or in reading or making books that will not advance the interests of the church. The time of the ministry is not for ease, or ambition, or self-indulgence, but is to promote the interests of the body of Christ. So Paul felt, and so he lived. (2.) Their *talents* belong to the church. All their original talents, and all that they can acquire, should be honestly devoted to the welfare of the church of the Redeemer. (3.) Their best efforts and plans, the avails of their best thoughts and purposes, belong to the church, and should be honestly devoted to it. Their strength and vigour, and influence should be devoted to it, as the vigour, and strength, and talent, and skill of a servant belong to the master; see Ps. cxxxvii. 5, 6. The language of the ministry, as of every Christian, should be:

> I love thy church, O God,
> Her walls before thee stand,
> Dear as the apple of thine eye,
> And graven on thy hand.
>
> If e'er to bless thy sons
> My voice or hands deny,
> These hands let useful skill forsake,
> This voice in silence die.
>
> If e'er my heart forget
> Her welfare or her wo,
> Let every joy this heart forsake,
> And every grief o'erflow.
>
> For her my tears shall fall,
> For her my prayers ascend,
> To her my cares and toils be given,
> Till toils and cares shall end.

And it implies, (4.) That they are the servants of the church in time of trial, temptation, and affliction. They are to devote themselves to the comfort of the afflicted. They are to be the guide to the perplexed. They are to aid the tempted. They are to comfort those that mourn, and they are to sustain and console the dying. They are to regard themselves as the servants of the church to accomplish these great objects; and are to be willing to deny themselves, and to take up their cross, and to consecrate their time to the advancement of these great interests. And they are, in all respects, to devote their time, and talents, and influence to the welfare of the church, with as much single-mindedness as the servant is to seek the interest of his master. It was in this way eminently that Paul was favoured with the success with which God blessed him in the ministry; and so every minister will be successful, just in proportion to the single-mindedness with which he devotes himself to the

1 hath shined in our hearts, to *give* the light of the knowledge of the glory of God in the face of Jesus Christ.

1 *it is he who hath.*

work of preaching Jesus Christ THE Lord.

6. *For God, who commanded,* &c. The design of this verse seems to be, to give a reason why Paul and his fellow-apostles did not preach themselves, but Jesus Christ the Lord, ver. 5. That reason was, that their minds had been so illuminated by that God who had commanded the light to shine out of darkness, that they had discerned the glory of the divine perfections shining in and through the Redeemer, and they therefore gave themselves to the work of making him known among men. The doctrines which they preached they had not derived from men in any form. They had not been elaborated by human reasoning or science, nor had they been imparted by tradition. They had been communicated directly by the source of all light—the true God—who had shined into the hearts that were once benighted by sin. Having been thus illuminated, they had felt themselves bound to go and make known to others the truths which God had imparted to them. ¶ *Who commanded the light,* &c. Gen. i. 3. God caused it to shine by his simple command. He *said,* "let there be light, and there was light." The fact that it was produced by *his saying so* is referred to here by Paul by his use of the phrase (ὁ εἰπὼν) "Who *saying,*" or speaking the light to shine from darkness. The passage in Genesis is adduced by Longinus as a striking instance of the sublime. ¶ *Hath shined in our hearts.* Marg. "It is he who hath." This is more in accordance with the Greek, and the sense is, "The God who at the creation bade the light to shine out of darkness, is he who has shined into our hearts; or it is the same God who has illuminated us, who commanded the light to shine at the creation." *Light* is every where in the Bible the emblem of knowledge, purity, and truth; as darkness is the emblem of ignorance, error, sin, and wretchedness. See Note, John i. 4, 5. And the sense here is, that God had removed this ignorance, and poured a flood of light and truth on their minds. This passage teaches, therefore, the following important truths in regard to Christians—since it is as applicable to all Christians, as it was to the apostles. (1.) That the mind is by nature ignorant and benighted—to an extent which may be properly compared with the darkness which prevailed before God commanded the light to shine. Indeed, the darkness which prevailed before the light was formed, was a most striking emblem of the darkness which exists in the mind of man before it is enlightened by revelation, and by the Holy Spirit. For (*a*) In all minds by nature there is deep ignorance of God, of his law, and his requirements; and (*b*) This is often greatly deepened by the course of life which men lead; by their education; or by their indulgence in sin, and by their plans of life; and especially by the indulgence of evil passions. The tendency of man if left to himself is to plunge into deeper darkness, and to involve his mind more entirely in the obscurity of moral midnight. "Light is come into the world, and men loved darkness rather than light, because their deeds were evil," John iii. 19. (2.) This verse teaches the fact, that the minds of Christians are illuminated. They are enabled to see things as they are. This fact is often taught in the Scriptures; see 1 John ii. 20; 1 Cor. ii. 12—15. They have different views of things from their fellow-men, and different from what they once had. They perceive a beauty in religion which others do not see, and a glory in truth, and in the Saviour, and in the promises of the gospel, which they did not see before they were converted. This does not mean (*a*) That they are superior in their powers of understanding to other men—for the reverse is often the fact; nor (*b*) That the effect of religion is at once to enlarge their

own intellectual powers, and make them different from what they were before in this respect. But it means that they have clear and consistent views; they look at things as they are; they perceive a beauty in religion and in the service of God which they did not before. They see a beauty in the Bible, and in the doctrines of the Bible, which they did not before, and which sinners do not see. The temperate man will see a beauty in temperance, and in an argument for temperance, which the drunkard will not; the benevolent man will see a beauty in benevolence which the churl will not: and so of honesty, truth, and chastity. And especially will a man who is *reformed* from intemperance, impurity, dishonesty, and avarice, see a beauty in a virtuous life which he did not before see. There is indeed no *immediate* and *direct* enlargement of the intellect; but there is an effect on the heart which produces an appropriate and indirect effect on the understanding. It is at the same time true, that the practice of virtue, that a pure heart, and that the cultivation of piety all tend to regulate, strengthen, and expand the intellect, as the ways of vice and the indulgence of evil passions and propensities tend to enfeeble, paralyze, darken, and ruin the understanding; so that, other things being equal, the man of most decided virtue, and most calm and elevated piety, will be the man of the clearest and best regulated mind. His powers will be the most assiduously, carefully, and conscientiously cultivated, and he will feel himself bound to make the most of them.—The influence of piety in giving light to the mind is often strikingly manifested among unlettered and ignorant Christians. It often happens, as a matter of fact, that they have by far clearer, and more just and elevated views of truth than men of the most mighty intellects, and most highly cultivated by science and adorned with learning, but who have no piety; and a practical acquaintance with their own hearts, and a practical experience of the power of religion in the days of temptation and trial is a better enlightener of the mind on the subject of religion than all the learning of the schools. (3.) This verse teaches, that it is the *same God* who enlightens the mind of the Christian that commanded the light at first to shine. He is the source of all light. He formed the light in the natural world; he gives all light and truth on all subjects to the understanding; and he imparts all correct views of truth to the heart. Light is not originated by man; and man on the subject of religion no more creates the light which beams upon his benighted mind than he created the light of the sun when it first shed its beams over the darkened earth. "All truth is from the sempiternal source of light divine;" and it is no more the work of man to enlighten the mind, and dissipate the darkness from the soul of a benighted sinner, than it was of man to scatter the darkness that brooded over the creation, or than he can now turn the shades of midnight to noonday. All this work lies beyond the proper province of man; and is all to be traced to the agency of God—the great fountain of light. (4.) It is taught here that it is the *same power* that gives light to the mind of the Christian which at first commanded the light to shine out of darkness. It requires the exertion of the same Omnipotence; and the change is often *as* remarkable, and surprising.—Nothing can be conceived to be more grand than the first creation of light—when by one word the whole solar system was in a blaze. And nothing in the moral world is more grand than when by a word God commands the light to beam on the soul of a benighted sinner. Night is at once changed to day; and all things are seen in a blaze of glory. The works of God appear different; the word of God appears different; and a new aspect of beauty is diffused over all things.—If it be asked IN WHAT WAY God thus imparts light to the mind, we may reply, (1.) By his written and preached word. All spiritual and saving light to the minds of men has come through his revealed truth. Nor does the Spirit of God now give or reveal any light to the mind which is not to be found in the word of God.

and which is not imparted through that medium. (2.) God makes use of his providential dealings to give light to the minds of men. They are then, by sickness, disappointment, and pain, made to see the folly and vanity of the things of this world, and to see the necessity of a better portion. (3.) It is done especially and mainly by the influences of the Holy Spirit. It is directly by his agency that the heart becomes affected, and the mind enlightened. It is his province in the world to prepare the heart to receive the truth; to dispose the mind to attend to it: to remove the obstructions which existed to its clear perception; to enable the mind clearly to see the beauty of truth, and of the plan of salvation through a Redeemer. And whatever may be the means which may be used, it is still true that it is only by the Spirit of God that men are ever brought to see the truth clearly and brightly. The same Spirit that inspired the prophets and apostles also illuminates the minds of men now, removes the darkness from their minds, and enables them clearly to discover the truth as it is in Jesus. See Notes, 1 Cor. ii. 10–15. ¶ *To give the light of the knowledge of the glory of God.* This shows the *object*, or the *effect* of enlightening the mind. It is that Christians may behold the divine glory. The meaning is, that it is for the purpose of enlightening and instructing them *concerning* the knowledge of the glory of God.—*Bloomfield.* Doddridge renders it, "the lustre of the knowledge of God's glory." Tindal, "to give the light of the knowledge of the glorious God.' The sense is, that the purpose of his shining into their hearts was to give light (πρὸς φωτισμὸν) *i. e.* unto the enlightening; and the purpose of that light was to acquaint them with the knowledge of the divine glory. ¶ *In the face of Jesus Christ.* That is, that they might obtain the knowledge of the divine glory as it shines in the face of Jesus Christ; or as it is reflected on the face, or the person of the Redeemer.—There is undoubted allusion here to what is said of Moses (chap. iii. 13) when the divine glory was reflected on his face, and produced such a splendour and magnificence that the children of Israel could not steadfastly look upon it. The sense here is, that in the face or the person of Jesus Christ the glory of God shone clearly, and the divinity appeared without a vail. The divine perfections, as it were, illuminated him, as the face of Moses was illuminated; or they shone forth through him, and were seen in him. The word rendered "face" here (προσώπον) may mean either face or person; see Note, chap. ii. 10. The sense is not materially affected which ever translation is preferred. It is, that the divine perfections shone in and through the Redeemer. This refers doubtless to the following truths. (1.) That the glory of the divine *nature* is seen in him, since he is "the brightness of his glory, and the express image of his person." Heb. i. 3. And it is in and through him that the glory of the divine perfections are made known, (2.) That the glory of the divine *attributes* are made known through him, since it is through him that the work of creation was accomplished (John i. 3, Col. i. 16); and it is by him that the mercy and goodness of God have been manifested to men. (3.) That the glory of the divine *moral character* is seen through him, since when on earth he manifested the embodied divine perfections; he showed what God is when incarnate; he lived as became the incarnate God—he was as pure and holy in human nature as God is in the heavens. And there is not, that we know of, one of the divine attributes or perfections which has not at some period, or in some form, been evinced by Jesus Christ. If it be the prerogative of God to be eternal, he was eternal; Isa. ix. 6; Rev. i. 8, 18. If it be the prerogative of God to be the creator, he was also the creator (John i. 3); if to be omniscient, he was omniscient (Matt. xi. 27; Luke x. 22); if to be omnipresent, he is omnipresent (Matt. xviii. 20); if to be almighty, he was almighty (Isa. ix. 6); if to raise the dead, to give life, he did it (John v.

7 But we have this treasure in earthen vessels, that the ex-

21; xii. 43, 44; if to still waves and tempests, he did it (Mark iv. 39); if to be full of benevolence, to be perfectly holy, to be without a moral stain or spot, then all this is found in Jesus Christ. And as the wax bears the perfect image of the seal—perfect not only in the outline, and in the general resemblance, but in the filling up—in all the lines, and features, and letters on the seal, so it is with the Redeemer. There is not one of the divine perfections which has not the counterpart in him, and if the glory of the divine character is seen at all, it will be seen in and through him.

7. *But we have this treasure.* The treasure of the gospel; the rich and invaluable truths which they were called to preach to others. The word "treasure" is applied to those truths on account of their inestimable worth. Paul in the previous verses had spoken of the gospel, the knowledge of Jesus Christ, as full of glory, and infinitely precious. This rich blessing had been committed to him and his fellow-labourers, to dispense it to others, and to diffuse it abroad. His purpose in this and the following verses is, to show that it had been so intrusted to them as to secure all the glory of its propagation to God, and so also as to show its unspeakable value. For this purpose, he not only affirms that it is a treasure, but says that it had been so entrusted to them as to show the power of God in its propagation; that it had showed its value in sustaining them in their many trials; and *they* had showed their sense of its worth by being willing to endure all kinds of trial in order to make it everywhere known, ver. 8—11. The expression here is similar to that which the Saviour uses when he calls the gospel "the pearl of great price," Matt. xiii. 46. ¶ *In earthen vessels.* This refers to the apostles and ministers of religion, as weak and feeble; as having bodies decaying and dying; as fragile, and liable to various accidents, and as being altogether unworthy to hold a treasure so invaluable; as if valuable diamonds and gold were placed in vessels of earth of coarse composition, easily broken, and liable to decay. The word *vessel* (σκεῦος) means properly any utensil or instrument; and is applied usually to utensils of household furniture, or hollow vessels for containing things, Luke viii. 16; John xix. 29. It is applied to the human body, as made of clay, and therefore frail and feeble, with reference to its *containing* any thing, as, *e.g.*, treasure; compare Note on Rom. ix. 22, 23. The word rendered earthen, (ὀστρακίνοις) means that which is made of shells (from ὄστρακινον), and then burnt clay, probably because vessels were at first made of burnt shells. It is fitted well to represent the human body; frail, fragile, and easily reduced again to dust. The purpose of Paul here is, to show that it was by no excellency of his nature that the gospel was originated; it was in virtue of no vigour and strength which he possessed that it was propagated; but that it had been, of design, committed by God to weak, decaying, and crumbling instruments, in order that it might *be seen* that it was by the power of God that such instruments were sustained in the trials to which they were exposed, and in order that it might be manifest to all that it was not originated and diffused by the power of those to whom it was intrusted. The idea is, that they were altogether insufficient of their own strength to accomplish what was accomplished by the gospel. Paul uses a metaphor similar to this in 2 Tim. ii. 20 ¶ *That the excellency of the power.* An elegant expression, denoting the exceeding great power. The great power referred to here was that which was manifested in connection with the labours of the apostles—the power of healing the sick, raising the dead, and casting out devils; the power of bearing persecution and trial, and the power of carrying the gospel over sea and land, in the midst of danger, and in spite of all the opposition which men could make, whether as individuals or as combined; and especially the power of converting the hearts of sin-

cellency [a] of the power may be of God, and not of us.
8 *We are* troubled [b] on every side, yet not distressed: *we are* perplexed, but not [1] in despair;

a 1Co.2.5. b chap.7.5. 1 or, *not altogether without help or means.*

ners, of humbling the proud, and leading the guilty to the knowledge of God, and the hope of heaven. The idea is, that all this was manifestly beyond human strength; and that God had of design chosen weak and feeble instruments *in order* that it might be everywhere seen that it was done not by human power but by his own. The instrumentality employed was altogether *disproportionate* in its nature to the effect produced. ¶ *May be of God.* May evidently appear to be of God; that it may be manifest to all that it is God's power and not ours. It was one great purpose of God that this should be kept clearly in view. And it is still done. God takes care that this shall be apparent. For, (1.) It is *always* true, whoever is employed, and however great may be the talents, learning, or zeal of those who preach, that it is by the power of God that men are converted. Such a work cannot be accomplished by man. It is not by might or by strength; and between the conversion of a proud, haughty, and abandoned sinner, and the power of him who is made the instrument, there is such a manifest disproportion, that it is evident it is the work of God. The conversion of the human heart is not to be accomplished by man. (2.) Ministers are frail, imperfect, and sinful, as they were in the time of Paul. When the imperfections of ministers are considered; when their frequent errors, and their not unfrequent moral obliquities are contemplated; when it is remembered how far many of them live from what they ought to do, and how few of them live in any considerable degree as becometh the followers of the Redeemer, it is wonderful that God blesses their labour as he does; and the matter of amazement is not that *no more* are converted under their ministry, but it is that *so many* are converted, or that *any* are converted; and it is manifest that it is the mere power of God. (3.) He often makes use of the most feeble, and unlearned, and weak of his servants to accomplish the greatest effects. It is not splendid talents, or profound learning, or distinguished eloquence, that is always or even commonly most successful. Often the ministry of such is entirely barren; while some humble and obscure man shall have constant success, and revivals shall attend him wherever he goes. It is the man of faith, and prayer, and self-denial, that is blessed; and the purpose of God in the ministry, as in every thing else, is to "*stain the pride of all human glory,*" and to show that he is all in all.

8. We are *troubled.* We the apostles. Paul here refers to some of the *trials* to which he and his fellow-labourers were subjected in making known the gospel. The *design* for which he does it seems to be to show them, (1.) What they endured in preaching the truth; (2.) To show the sustaining power of that gospel in the midst of afflictions; and, (3.) To conciliate their favour, or to remind them that they had endured these things on their account, ver. 12—15. Perhaps one leading design was to recover the affections of those of the Corinthians whose heart had been alienated from him, by showing them how much he had endured on their account. For this purpose he freely opens his heart to them, and tenderly represents the many and grievous pressures and hardships to which love to souls, and theirs among the rest, had exposed him.—*Doddridge.* The whole passage is one of the most pathetic and beautiful to be found in the New Testament. The word rendered troubled (θλιβόμενοι, from θλίβω) may have reference to *wrestling*, or to the contests in the Grecian games. It properly means, to press, to press together; then to press as in a crowd where there is a throng (Mark iii. 9); then to compress together (Matt. vii. 14); and then to oppress, or compress with evils, to distress, to afflict, 2

9 Persecuted, but not forsaken; cast down, but not destroyed;

10 Always bearing [a] about in the body the dying of the Lord Je-

[a] Ga. 6. 17.

Thess. i. 6; 2 Cor. i. 6. Here it may mean, that he was encompassed with trials, or placed in the midst of them so that they pressed upon him as persons do in a crowd, or, possibly, as a man was close pressed by an adversary in the games. He refers to the fact that he was called to endure a great number of trials and afflictions. Some of those trials he refers to in chap. vii. 5. "When we were come into Macedonia, our flesh had no rest, but we were troubled on every side; without were fightings, within were fears." ¶ *On every side.* In every respect. In every way. We are subjected to all kinds of trial and affliction. ¶ *Yet not distressed.* This by no means expresses the force of the original; nor is it possible perhaps to express it in a translation. Tindal renders it, "yet we are not without our shift." The Greek word here used (στενοχωρούμενοι) has a relation to the word which is rendered "troubled." It properly means to crowd into a narrow place; to straiten as to room; to be so straitened as not to be able to turn one's self. And the idea is, that though he was close pressed by persecutions and trials, yet he was not so hemmed in that he had no way to turn himself; his trials did not wholly prevent motion and action. He was not *so* closely pressed as a man would be who was so straitened that he could not move his body, or stir hand or foot. He had still resources; he was permitted to move; the energy of his piety, and the vigour of his soul could not be entirely cramped and impeded by the trials which encompassed him. The Syriac renders it, "In all things we are pressed, but are not suffocated." The idea is, he was not wholly discouraged, and disheartened, and overcome. He had resources in his piety which enabled him to bear up under these trials, and still to engage in the work of preaching the gospel. ¶ We are *perplexed* (ἀπορούμενοι). This word (from ἄπορος, without resource, which is derived from α, priv., and πόρος, way, or exit) means to be without resource; to know not what to do; to hesitate; to be in doubt and anxiety, as a traveller is, who is ignorant of the way, or who has not the means of prosecuting his journey. It means here, that they were often brought into circumstances of great embarrassment, where they hardly knew what to do, or what course to take. They were surrounded by foes; they were in want; they were in circumstances which they had not anticipated, and which greatly perplexed them. ¶ *But not in despair.* In the margin, "not altogether without help or means." Tindal renders this, "We are in poverty, but not utterly without somewhat." In the word here used, (ἐξαπορούμενοι) the preposition is intensive or emphatic, and means *utterly, quite.* The word means to be utterly without resource; to despair altogether; and the idea of Paul here is, that they were not left *entirely* without resource. Their wants were provided for; their embarrassments were removed; their grounds of perplexity were taken away; and unexpected strength and resources were imparted to them. When they did not know what to do; when all resources seemed to fail them, in some unexpected manner they would be relieved and saved from absolute despair. How often does this occur in the lives of all Christians! And how certain is it, that in all such cases God will interpose by his grace, and aid his people, and save them from absolute despair.

9. *Persecuted.* Often persecuted, persecuted in all places. The "Acts of the Apostles" show how true this was. ¶ *But not forsaken.* Not deserted; nor left by God Though persecuted by men, yet they experienced the fulfilment of the divine promise that he would never leave nor forsake them. God always interposed to aid them; always saved them from the power of their enemies; always sustained them in the time of persecution. It is still true. His people

sus, that [a] the life also of Jesus might be made manifest in our body.

11 For we which live are [b] alway delivered unto death for Jesus' sake, that the life also of Jesus

a 2 Ti. 2. 11, 12.

b 1 Cor. 15. 31, 49.

have been often persecuted. Yet God has often interposed to save them from the hands of their enemies; and where he has not saved them from their hands, and preserved their lives, yet he has never left them, but has sustained, upheld, and comforted them even in the dreadful agonies of death. ¶ *Cast down.* Thrown down by our enemies, perhaps in allusion to the contests of wrestlers, or of gladiators. ¶ *But not destroyed.* Not killed. They rose again; they recovered their strength; they were prepared for new conflicts. They surmounted every difficulty, and were ready to engage in new strifes, and to meet new trials and persecutions.

10. *Always bearing about in the body.* The expression here used is designed to show the great perils to which Paul was exposed. And the idea is, that he had on his body the marks, the stripes and marks of punishment and persecution, which showed that he was exposed to the same violent death which the Lord Jesus himself endured; comp. Gal. vi. 17: "I bear in my body the marks of the Lord Jesus." It is a strong energetic mode of expression, to denote the severity of the trials to which he was exposed, and the meaning is, that his body bore the marks of his being exposed to the same treatment as the Lord Jesus was; and evidence that he was probably yet to die in a similar manner under the hands of persecutors; comp. Col. i. 24. ¶ *The dying of the Lord Jesus.* The death; the violent death. A death similar to that of the Lord Jesus. The idea is, that he was always exposed to death, and always suffering in a manner that was equivalent to dying. The expression is parallel to what he says in 1 Cor. xv. 31. "I die daily;" and in 2 Cor. xi. 23, where he says, "in deaths oft." It does not mean that he bore about *literally* the dying of the Lord Jesus, but that he was exposed to a similar death, and had marks on his person which showed that he was always exposed to the same violent death. This did not occur once only, or at distant intervals, but it occurred constantly, and wherever he was it was still true that he was exposed to violence, and liable to suffer in the same manner that the Lord Jesus did. ¶ *That the life also of Jesus,* &c. This passage has received a considerable variety of interpretation. Grotius renders it, "such a life as was that of Christ, immortal, blessed, heavenly." Locke, "That also the life of Jesus, risen from the dead, may be made manifest by the energy that accompanies my preaching in this frail body." Clarke supposes that it means, that he might be able in this manner to show that Christ was risen from the dead. But perhaps, Paul does not refer to one single thing in the life of the Lord Jesus, but means that he did this in order that in all things the same life, the same kind of living which characterized the Lord Jesus might be manifested in him; or that he resembled him in his sufferings and trials, in order that in all things he might have the same life in his body. Perhaps, therefore, it may include the following things as objects at which the apostle aimed. (1.) A desire that his *life* might resemble that of the Lord Jesus. That there might be the same self-denial; the same readiness to suffer; the same patience in trials; the same meekness, gentleness, zeal, ardour, love to God, and love to men evinced in his body which was in that of the Lord Jesus. Thus understood, it means that he placed the Lord Jesus before him as the model of his life, and deemed it an object to be attained even by great self-denial and sufferings to be conformed to him. (2.) A desire to attain to the same life in the resurrection which the Lord Jesus had attained to. A desire to be made like him, and that in his body which bore about the dying of the Lord Jesus, he might again

might be made manifest in our mortal flesh.

12 So then [a] death worketh in us, but life in you.

a chap. 13. 9.

live after death as the Lord Jesus did. Thus understood, it implies an earnest wish to attain to the resurrection of the dead, and accords with what he says in Phil. iii. 8—11, which may perhaps be considered as Paul's own commentary on this passage, which has been so variously, and so little understood by expositors. "Yea, doubtless, and I count all things but loss, for the excellency of the knowledge of Jesus Christ my Lord; for whom I have suffered the loss of all things, and do count them but dung that I may win Christ. That I may know him, and the power of his resurrection, and the fellowship of his sufferings, being made conformable unto his death; if by any means I might attain unto the resurrection of the dead;" comp. Col. i. 24. It intimates Paul's earnest desire and longing to be made like Christ in the resurrection (comp. Phil. iii. 21); his longing to rise again in the last day (comp. Acts xxvi. 7); his sense of the importance of the doctrine of the resurrection and his readiness to suffer any thing if he might at last attain to the resurrection of the just, and be ready to enter with the Redeemer into a world of glory. The attainment of this is the high object before the Christian, and to be made like the Redeemer in heaven, to have a body like his, is the grand purpose for which they should live; and sustained by this hope they should be willing to endure any trials, and meet any sufferings, if they may come to that same "life" and blessedness above.

11. *For we which live.* Those of us, the apostles and ministers of the Redeemer who still survive. James the brother of John had been put to death (Acts xii. 2); and it is probable also that some other of the apostles had been also. This verse is merely explanatory of the previous verse. ¶ *Are alway delivered unto death.* Exposed constantly to death. This shows what is meant in ver. 10, by bearing about in the body the dying of the Lord Jesus; see Note on 1 Cor. xv. 31. ¶ *In our mortal flesh.* In our body. In our life on earth; and in our glorified body in heaven; see Note on ver. 10.

12. *So then death worketh in us* We are exposed to death. The preaching of the gospel exposes us to trials which may be regarded as death working in us. Death has an energy over us (ἐνεργεῖται, is at work, is active, or operates); it is constantly employed in inflicting pains on us, and subjecting us to privation and trials. This is a strong and emphatic mode of saying that they were always exposed to death. We are called to serve and glorify the Redeemer, as it were, by repeated deaths and by constantly dying. ¶ *But life in you.* You live as the effect of our being constantly exposed to death. You reap the advantage of all our exposure to trials, and of all our sufferings. You are comparatively safe; are freed from this exposure to death; and will receive eternal life as the fruit of our toils, and exposures. Life here may refer either to exemption from danger and death; or it may refer to the life of religion; the hopes of piety; the prospect of eternal salvation. To me it seems most probable that Paul means to use it in the latter sense, and that he designs to say that while *he* was exposed to death and called to endure constant trial, the effect would be that *they* would obtain, in consequence of his sufferings, the blessedness of eternal life; comp. ver. 15. Thus understood, this passage means, that the sufferings and self-denials of the apostles were for the good of others, and would result in their benefit and salvation; and the design of Paul here is to remind them of his sufferings in their behalf, in order to conciliate their favour and bind them more closely to him by the remembrance of his sufferings on their account.

13. *We having the same spirit of faith.* The same spirit that is ex-

13 We having the same [a] spirit
of faith, according as it is written, [b] I believed, and therefore
have I spoken; we also believe,
and therefore speak;
14 Knowing [c] that he which

a 2 Pe.1.1. b Ps.116.10. c chap.5.1—4.

pressed in the quotation which he is about to make; the same faith which the psalmist had. We have the very spirit of faith which is expressed by David. The sense is, we have the same spirit of faith which he had who said, "I believed," &c. The phrase, "spirit of faith," means substantially the same as faith itself; a believing sense or impression of the truth. ¶ *According as it is written.* This passage is found in Ps. cxvi. 10. When the psalmist uttered the words, he was greatly afflicted; see ver. 3, 6—8. In these circumstances, he prayed to God, and expressed confidence in him, and placed all his reliance on him. In his affliction he spoke to God; he spoke of his confidence in him; he proclaimed his reliance on him; and his having spoken in this manner was the result of his belief, or of his putting confidence in God. Paul, in quoting this, does not mean to say that the psalmist had any reference to the preaching of the gospel; nor does he mean to say that his circumstances were in all respects like those of the psalmist. The circumstances resembled each other only in these respects, (1.) That Paul, like the psalmist, was in circumstances of trial and affliction; and, (2.) That the language which both used was that which was prompted by faith—faith, which led them to give utterance to the sentiments of their hearts; the psalmist to utter his confidence in God, and the hopes by which he was sustained, and Paul to utter *his* belief in the glorious truths of the gospel; to speak of a risen Saviour, and to show forth the consolations which were thus set before men in the gospel. The sentiments of both were the language of faith. Both, in afflictions, uttered the language of faith; and Paul uses here, as he often does, the language of the Old Testament, as *exactly* expressing his feelings, and the principles by which he was actuated. ¶ *We also believe,* &c. We believe in the truths of the gospel; we believe in God, in the Saviour, in the atonement, in the resurrection, &c. The sentiment is, that they had a firm confidence in these things, and that, as the result of that confidence they boldly delivered their sentiments. It prompted them to give utterance to their feelings. "Out of the abundance of the heart," said the Saviour, "the mouth speaketh," Matt. xii. 34. No man should attempt to preach the gospel who has not a firm belief of its truths; and he who *does* believe its truths will be prompted to make them known to his fellow-men. All successful preaching is the result of a firm and settled conviction of the truth of the gospel; and when such a conviction exists, it is natural to give utterance to the belief, and such an expression will be attended with happy influences on the minds of other men: see Note on Acts iv. 20.

14. *Knowing.* Being fully confident; having the most entire assurance. It was the assured hope of the resurrection which sustained them in all their trials. This expression denotes the full and unwavering belief, in the minds of the apostles, that the doctrines which they preached were true. They *knew* that they were revealed from heaven, and that all the promises of God would be fulfilled. ¶ *Shall raise up us also.* All Christians. In the hope of the resurrection they were ready to meet trials, and even to die. Sustained by this assurance, the apostles went forth amidst persecutions and opposition, for they knew that their trials would soon end, and that they would be raised up in the morning of the resurrection, to a world of eternal glory. ¶ *By Jesus.* By the power or the agency of Jesus. Christ will raise up the dead from their graves, John v. 25—29. ¶ *And shall present* us

raised up the Lord Jesus, shall
raise up us also by Jesus, and
shall present *us* with you.
15 For [a] all things *are* for your
sakes, that the abundant grace
[b] might, through the thanksgiving
of many, redound to the glory of
God.
16 For which cause [c] we faint
not; but though our outward

a 1 Co.3.21,22. b chap.8.19. c 1 Co.15.58.

with you. Will present us before the throne of glory with exceeding joy and honour. He will present us to God as those who have been redeemed by his blood. He will present us in the courts of heaven, before the throne of the eternal Father, as his ransomed people; as recovered from the ruins of the fall; as saved by the merits of his blood. They shall not only be raised up from the dead; but they shall be publicly and solemnly *presented* to God as his, as recovered to his service, and as having a title in the covenant of grace to the blessedness of heaven.

15. *For all things are for your sakes.* All these things; these glorious hopes, and truths, and prospects; these self-denials of the apostles, and these provisions of the plan of mercy. ¶ *For your sakes.* On your account. They are designed to promote your salvation. They are not primarily for the welfare of those who engage in these toils and self-denials; but the whole arrangement and execution of the plan of salvation, and all the self-denial evinced by those who are engaged in making that plan known, are in order that you might be benefitted. One object of Paul in this statement, doubtless, is, to conciliate their favour, and remove the objections which had been made to him by a faction in the church at Corinth. ¶ *That the abundant grace.* Grace abounding, or overflowing. The rich mercy of God that should be manifested by these means. It is *implied* here, that grace *would* abound by means of these labours and self-denials of the apostles. The grace referred to here is that which would be conferred on them in consequence of these labours. ¶ *Through the thanksgiving of many.* That many may have occasion of gratitude to God; that by these labours more persons may be led to praise him. It was an object with Paul so to labour that as many as possible might be led to praise God, and have occasion to thank him to all eternity. ¶ *Redound to the glory of God.* That God may have augmented praise; that his glory in the salvation of men may abound. The sentiment of the passage is, that it would be for the glory of God that as many as possible should be brought to give praise and thanksgivings to him; and that, therefore, Paul endeavoured to make as many converts as possible. He denied himself; he welcomed toil; he encountered enemies; he subjected himself to dangers; and he sought by all means possible to bring as many as could be brought to praise God. The word "redound" (περισσεύσῃ) here means abound, or be abundant; and the sense is, *that the overflowing grace thus evinced in the salvation of many would so abound as to promote the glory of God.*

16. *For which cause.* With such an object in view, and sustained by such elevated purposes and desires. The sense is, that the purpose of trying to save as many as possible would make toil easy, privations welcome, and would be so accompanied by the grace of God, as to gird the soul with strength, and fill it with abundant consolations. ¶ *We faint not.* For an explanation of the word here used, see Note on ver. 1. We are not exhausted, desponding, or disheartened. We are sustained, encouraged, emboldened by having such an object in view. ¶ *But though our outward man perish.* By outward man, Paul evidently means the body. By using the phrases, "the outward man," and the "inward man," he shows that he believed that man was made up of two parts, body and soul. He was no materialist. He has described two parts as constituting man, so distinct,

man perish, yet the inward [a] *man* is renewed day by day.

a Ro.7.22.

17 For [b] our light affliction, which is but for a moment,

b Rom.8.18,34.

that while the one perishes, the other is renewed; while the one is enfeebled, the other is strengthened; while the one grows old and decays, the other renews its youth and is invigorated. Of course, the soul is not dependent on the body for its vigour and strength, since it expands while the body decays; and of course the soul may exist independently of the body, and in a separate state. ¶ *Perish*. Grows old; becomes weak and feeble; loses its vigour and elasticity under the many trials which we endure, and under the infirmities of advancing years. It is a characteristic of the "outer man," that it thus perishes. Great as may be its vigour, yet it must decay and die. It cannot long bear up under the trials of life, and the wear and tear of constant action, but must soon sink to the grave. ¶ *Yet the inward* man. The soul; the undecaying, the immortal part. ¶ *Is renewed*. Is renovated, strengthened, invigorated. His powers of mind expanded; his courage became bolder; he had clearer views of truth; he had more faith in God. As he drew nearer to the grave and to heaven, his soul was more raised above the world, and he was more filled with the joys and triumphs of the gospel. The understanding and the heart did not sympathize with the suffering and decaying body; but, while that became feeble, the soul acquired new strength, and was fitting for its flight to the eternal world. This verse is an ample refutation of the doctrine of the materialist, and proves that there is in man something that is distinct from decaying and dying matter, and that there is a principle which may gain augmented strength and power, while the body dies; comp. Note, Rom. vii. 22. ¶ *Day by day*. Constantly. There was a daily and constant increase of inward vigour. God imparted to him constant strength in his trials, and sustained him with the hopes of heaven, as the body was decaying, and tending to the grave. The sentiment of this verse is, that in an effort to do good, and to promote the salvation of man, the soul will be sustained in trials, and will be comforted and invigorated even when the body is weary, grows old, decays, and dies. It is the testimony of Paul respecting his own experience; and it is a fact which has been experienced by thousands in their efforts to do good, and to save the souls of men from death.

17. *For our light affliction*. This verse, with the following, is designed to show further the sources of consolation and support which Paul and his fellow-labourers had in their many trials. Bloomfield remarks on this passage, that "in energy and beauty of expression, it is little inferior to any in Demosthenes himself, to whom, indeed, and to Thucydides in his orations, the style of the apostle, when it rises to the oratorical, bears no slight resemblance." The passage abounds with intensive and emphatic expressions, and manifests that the mind of the writer was labouring to convey ideas which language, even after all the energy of expression which he could command, would very imperfectly communicate. The trials which Paul endured, to many persons would have seemed to be any thing else but light. They consisted of want, and danger, and contempt, and stoning, and toil, and weariness, and the scorn of the world, and constant exposure to death by land or by sea; see ver. 7—10, comp. chap. xi. 23—27. Yet these trials, though continued through many years, and constituting, as it were, his very life, he speaks of as the lightest conceivable thing when compared with that eternal glory which awaited him. He strives to get an expression as emphatic as possible, to show that in his estimation they were not worthy to be named in comparison with the eternal weight of glory. It is not sufficient to say that the affliction was "light" or was a mere trifle; but he

worketh for us a far more exceeding *and* eternal weight of glory;

says that it was to endure but for a moment. Though trials had followed him ever since he began to make known the Redeemer, and though he had the firmest expectation that they would follow him to the end of life and everywhere (Acts xx. 23), yet all this was a *momentary trifle* compared with the eternal glory before him. The word rendered "light" (ἐλαφρὸν) means that which is easy to bear, and is usually applied to a burden; see Mat. xi. 30, comp. 2 Cor. i. 17. ¶ *Which is but for a moment.* The Greek word here used (παραυτίκα) occurs no where else in the New Testament. It is an adverb, from αὐτίκα, αὐτός, and means properly, *at this very instant; immediately.* Here it seems to qualify the word "light," and to be used in the sense of momentary, transient. Bloomfield renders it, "for the at present lightness of our affliction." Doddridge, "for this momentary lightness of our affliction, which passes off so fast, and leaves so little impression that it may be called levity itself." The apostle evidently wished to express two ideas in as emphatic a manner as possible; first, that the affliction was *light*, and, secondly, that it was transient, momentary, and soon passing away. His object is to *contrast* this with the glory that awaited him, as being *heavy*, and as being also *eternal*, ¶ *Worketh for us;* see Note, ver. 12. Will produce, will result in. The effect of these afflictions is to produce eternal glory. This they do, (1.) By their tendency to wean us from the world; (2.) To purify the heart, by enabling us to break off from the sins on account of which God afflicts us; (3.) By disposing us to look to God for consolation and support in our trials; (4.) By inducing us to contemplate the glories of the heavenly world, and thus winning us to seek heaven as our home, and, (5.) Because God has graciously promised to reward his people in heaven as the result of their bearing trials in this life. It is by affliction that he purifies them (Isa. xlviii. 10); and by trial that he takes their affections from the objects of time and sense, and gives them a relish for the enjoyments which result from the prospect of perfect and eternal glory. ¶ *A far more exceeding* (καθ' ὑπερβολὴν εἰς ὑπερβολὴν). There is not to be found any where a more energetic expression than this. The word (ὑπερβολή,) here used (whence our word *hyperbole*) means properly a throwing, casting, or throwing beyond. In the New Testament it means excess, excellence, eminence; see ver. 7. "The *excellency* of the power." The phrase καθ' ὑπερβολὴν means exceedingly, supereminently, Rom. vii. 13; 1 Cor. xii. 31; 2 Cor. i. 8; Gal. i. 13. This expression would have been by itself intensive in a high degree. But this was not sufficient to express Paul's sense of the glory which was laid up for Christians. It was not enough for him to use the ordinary highest expression for the superlative to denote the value of the object in his eye. He therefore coins an expression, and adds εἰς ὑπερβολὴν. It is not merely eminent; but it is eminent *unto* eminence; excess *unto* excess; a hyperbole *unto* hyperbole—one hyperbole heaped on another· and the expression means that it is "exceeding exceedingly" glorious; glorious in the highest possible degree, —*Robinson.* Mr. Slade renders it, "infinitely exceeding." The expression is the Hebrew form of denoting the highest superlative; and it means that all hyperboles fail of expressing that eternal glory which remains for the just. It is infinite and boundless. You may pass from one degree to another; from one sublime height to another; but still an infinity remains beyond. Nothing can describe the uppermost height of that glory; nothing can express its infinitude. ¶ *Eternal.* This stands in contrast with the affliction that is for a moment (παραυτίκα). The one is momentary, transient; so short, even in the longest life, that it may be said to be an instant; the other has no limits to its duration. It is literally everlasting. ¶ *Weight* (βάρος). This

18 While we look not at the things which are seen, but at the

stands opposed to the (ἐλαφρὸν) *light* affliction. That was so light that it was a trifle. It was easily borne. It was like the most light and airy objects, which constitute no burden. It is not even here called *a burden*, or said to be heavy in any degree. This is so heavy as to be *a burden*. Grotius thinks that the image is taken from gold or silver articles, that are solid and heavy, compared with those that are mixed or plated. But why may it not refer to the insignia of glory and honour; a robe heavy with gold, or a diadem or crown, heavy with gold or diamonds: glory so rich, so profuse as to be heavy? The affliction was light; but the crown, the robe, the adornings in the glorious world were not trifles, or baubles, but solid, substantial, weighty. We apply the word weighty now to that which is valuable and important, compared with that which is of no value, probably because the precious metals and jewels are heavy; and it is by them that we usually estimate the value of objects. ¶ *Of glory* (δόξης). The Hebrew word כבוד denotes weight as well as glory. And perhaps Paul had that use of the word in his eye in this strong expression. It refers here to the splendour, magnificence, honour, and happiness of the eternal world.—In this exceedingly interesting passage, which is worthy of the deepest study of Christians, Paul has set in most beautiful and emphatic contrast the trials of this life and the glories of heaven. It may be profitable to contemplate at a single glance the view which he had of them, that they may be brought distinctly before the mind.

THE ONE IS

1. AFFLICTION, θλῖψις.
2. *Light*, ἐλαφρόν.
3. For a moment, παραυτίκα

THE OTHER IS, by contrast,

(1.) GLORY, δόξη.
(2.) Weight, βάρος.
(3.) Eternal, αἰώνιον.
(4.) Eminent, or excellent, καθ' ὑπερβολήν.
(5.) Infinitely excellent, eminent in the highest degree, εἰς ὑπερβολήν.

So the *account* stands in the view of Paul; and with this *balance* in favour of the eternal glory, he regarded afflictions as mere trifles, and made it the grand purpose of his life to gain the glory of the heavens. What wise man, looking at the account, would not do likewise?

18. *While we look*, &c. Or, rather, we not looking at the things which are seen. The design of this is, to show in what way the afflictions which they endured became in their view light and momentary. It was by looking to the glories of the future world, and thus turning away the attention from the trials and sorrows of this life. If we look directly at our trials; if the mind is fixed wholly on them, and we think of nothing else, they often appear heavy and long. Even comparatively light and brief sufferings will appear to be exceedingly difficult to bear. But if we can turn away the mind from them and contemplate future glory; if we can compare them with eternal blessedness, and feel that they will introduce us to perfect and everlasting happiness, they will appear to be transitory, and will be easily borne. And Paul here has stated the true secret of bearing trials with patience. It is to look at the things which are unseen. To anticipate the glories of the heavenly world. To fix the eye on the eternal happiness which is beyond the grave; and to reflect how short these trials *are*, compared with the eternal glories of heaven; and how short they will *seem* to be when we are there. ¶ *The things which are seen.* The things here below; the things of this life—poverty, want, care, persecution, trial, &c. ¶ *The things which are not seen.* The glories of heaven, comp. Heb. xi. 1. ¶ *The things which are seen are temporal.* This refers particularly to the things which they *suffered*. But

things which are not [a] seen: for the things which are seen *are* temporal; but the things which are not seen *are* eternal.

a Heb.11.1.

it is *as* true of all things here below. Wealth, pleasure, fame, the three idols which the people of this world adore, are all to endure but for a little time. They will all soon vanish away. So it is with pain, and sorrow, and tears. All that we enjoy, and all that we suffer here, must soon vanish and disappear. The most splendid palace will decay; the most costly pile will moulder to dust; the most magnificent city will fall to ruins; the most exquisite earthly pleasures will soon come to an end; and the most extended possessions can be enjoyed but a little time. So the acutest pain will soon be over; the most lingering disease will soon cease; the evils of the deepest poverty, want, and suffering will soon be passed. There is nothing on which the eye can fix, nothing that the heart can desire here, which will not soon fade away; or, if it survives, it is temporary in regard to us. We must soon leave it to others; and *if* enjoyed, it will be enjoyed while *our bodies* are slumbering in the grave, and *our souls* engaged in the deep solemnities of eternity. How foolish then to make these our portion, and to fix our affections supremely on the things of this life? How foolish also to be very deeply affected by the trials of this life, which at the furthest CAN be endured but a little longer before *we* shall be for ever beyond their reach! ¶ *The things which are not seen* are *eternal.* Every thing which pertains to that state beyond the grave. (1.) God is eternal; not to leave us as our earthly friends do. (2.) The Saviour is eternal—to be our everlasting friend. (3.) The companions and friends there are eternal. The angels who are to be our associates, and the spirits of the just with whom we shall live, are to exist for ever. The angels never die; and the pious dead shall die no more. There shall be then no separation, no death-bed, no grave, no sad vacancy and loss caused by the removal of a much-loved friend. (4.) The joys of heaven are eternal. There shall be no interruption; no night; no cessation; no end. Heaven and all its joys shall be everlasting; and he who enters there shall have the assurance that those joys shall endure and increase while eternal ages shall roll away. (5.) It may be added, also, that the woes of hell shall be eternal. They are now among the things which to us "are not seen;" and they, as well as the joys of heaven, shall have no end. Sorrow there shall never cease; the soul shall there never die; the body that shall be raised up "to the resurrection of damnation" shall never again expire.—And when all these things are contemplated, well might Paul say of the things of this life—the sorrows, trials, privations, and persecutions which he endured, that they were "light," and were "for a moment." How soon will they pass away; how soon shall we all be engaged amidst the unchanging and eternal realities of the things which are not seen!

REMARKS.

1. Ministers of the gospel have no cause to faint or to be discouraged, ver. 1. Whatever may be the reception of their message, and whatever the trials to which they may be subjected, yet there are abundant sources of consolation and support in the gospel which they preach. They have the consciousness that they preach a system of truth; that they are proclaiming that which God has revealed; and, if they are faithful, that they have his smiles and approbation. Even, therefore, if men reject, and despise their message, and if they are called to endure many privations and trials, they should not faint. It is enough for them that they proclaim the truth which God loves, and that they meet with his approbation and smiles. Trials will come in the ministry as every where else, but there are also peculiar consolations. There

may be much opposition and resistance to the message, but we should not faint or be discouraged. We should do our duty, and commit the result to God.

2. The gospel should be embraced by those to whom it comes, ver. 2. If it has their reason and conscience in its favour, then they should embrace it without delay. They are under the most sacred obligation to receive it, and to become decided Christians. Every man is bound, and may be urged to pursue, that course which his conscience approves; and the gospel may thus be pressed on the attention of all to whom it comes.

3. If men wish peace of conscience, they should embrace the gospel, ver. 2. They can never find it elsewhere. No man's *conscience* is at peace from the fact that he does not repent, and love God and obey the gospel. His *heart* may love sin; but his conscience cannot approve it. That is at peace only in doing the work of God; and that can find self-approbation only when it submits to him, and embraces the gospel of his Son. Then the conscience is at ease. *No man ever yet had a troubled conscience from the fact that he had embraced the gospel, and was an humble and decided Christian.* Thousands and millions have had a troubled conscience from the fact that they have neglected it. No man on a death-bed ever had a troubled conscience because he embraced religion too early in life. Thousands and millions have been troubled when they came to die, because they neglected it so long, or rejected it altogether. No man when death approaches has a troubled conscience because he has lived *too much* devoted to God the Saviour, and been too active as a Christian. But O how many have been troubled then because they have been worldly-minded, and selfish, and vain, and proud? The conscience gives peace just in proportion as we serve God faithfully; nor can all the art of man or Satan give peace to one conscience in the ways of sin, and in the neglect of the soul.

4. Ministers should preach the truth—the simple truth—and nothing but the truth, ver. 2. They should make use of no false art, no deception, no trick, no disguise. They should be open, sincere, plain, pure in all their preaching, and in their manner of life. Such was the course of the Saviour; such the course of Paul; and such a course only will God approve and bless.

5. This is a deluded world, ver. 4. It is blinded and deceived by him who is here called the "god of this world." Satan rules in the hearts of men; and he rules by deceiving them, and in order to deceive them. Every thing which operates to prevent men from embracing the gospel has a tendency to blind the mind. The man who is seeking wealth as his only portion, is blinded and deceived in regard to its value. The man who is pursuing the objects of ambition as his main portion, is deceived in regard to the true value of things. And he, or she, who pursues pleasure as the main business of life, is deceived in regard to the proper value of objects. It is impossible to conceive of a world more deluded than this. We can conceive of a world more sinful, and more miserable, and such is hell; but there is no delusion and deception there. Things are seen as they are; and no one is deceived in regard to his character or prospects there. But here, every impenitent man is deceived and blinded. He is deceived about his own character; about the relative value of objects; about his prospects for eternity; about death, the judgment, heaven, hell. On none of these points has he any right apprehension; and on none is it possible for any human power to break the deep delusion, and to penetrate the darkness of his mind.

6. Men are in danger, ver. 4. They are under deep delusion, and they tread unconcerned near to ruin. They walk in darkness—blinded by the god of this world, and are very near a precipice, and nothing will rouse them from their condition. It is like children gathering flowers near a deep gulf, when the pursuit of *one* more flower may carry them too far, and

they will fall to rise no more. The delusion rests on every unsanctified mind; and it needs to remain but a little longer, and the soul will be lost. That danger deepens every day and every hour. If it is continued but a little longer it will be broken in upon by the sad realities of death, judgment, and hell. But then it will be too late. The soul will be lost—*deluded* in the world of probation; *sensible* of the truth only in the world of despair.

7. Satan will practise every device and art possible to prevent the gospel from shining upon the hearts of men. That light is painful and hateful to his eyes, and he will do all that can be done to prevent its being diffused. Every art which long-tried ingenuity and skill can devise, will be resorted to; every power which he can put forth will be exerted. If he can blind the minds of men, he will do it. If men *can* be hoodwinked, and gulled, it will be done. If error can be made to spread, and be embraced—error smooth, plausible, cunning—it will be diffused. Ministers will be raised up to preach it; and the press will be employed to accomplish it. If sinners can be deceived, and made to remain at ease in their sins, by novels and seductive poetry; by books false in sentiments, and perverse in morals, the press will be made to groan under the works of fiction. If theatres are necessary to cheat and beguile men, they will be reared; and the song, and the dance, the ball, and the splendid party will alike contribute to divert the attention from the cross of Christ, the worth of the soul, and the importance of a preparation to die. No art has been spared, or will be spared to deceive men; and the world is full of the devices of Satan to hoodwink and blind the perishing, and lead them down to hell.

8. Yet, Satan is not alone to blame for this. He does all he can, and he has consummate skill and art. Yet, let not the deluded sinner take comfort to himself because Satan is the tempter, and because he is deluded. The bitterness of death is not made sweet to a young man because he has been deluded by the arts of the veteran in temptation; and the fires of hell will not burn any the less fiercely because the sinner suffered himself to be deluded, and chose to go there through the ball-room or the theatre. The sinner is, after all, *voluntary* in his delusions. He does, or he might, know the truth. He goes voluntarily to the place of amusement; voluntarily forms the plans of gain and ambition which deceive and ruin the soul; goes voluntarily to the theatre, and to the haunts of vice; and *chooses* this course in the face of many warnings, and remonstrances. Who is to blame if he is lost! Who but himself?

9. Sinners should be entreated to rouse from this delusive and false security. They are now blinded, and deceived. Life is too short and too uncertain to be playing such a game as the sinner does. There are too many realities here to make it proper to pass life amidst deceptions and delusions. Sin is real, and danger is real, and death is real, and eternity is real; and man should rouse from his delusions, and look upon things as they are. Soon he will be on a bed of death, and then he will look over the follies of his life. Soon he will be at the judgment bar, and from that high and awful place look on the past and the future, and see things as they are. But, alas! it will be too late then to repair the errors of a life; and amidst the realities of those scenes, all that he may be able to do, will be to sigh unavailingly that he suffered himself to be deluded, deceived, and destroyed in the only world of probation, by the trifles and baubles which the great deceiver placed before him to beguile him of heaven, and to lead him down to hell!

10. The great purpose of the ministry is to make known in any and every way the Lord Jesus Christ, ver. 5. To this, the ministers of the gospel are to devote themselves. It is not to cultivate farms; to engage in traffic; to shine in the social circle; to be distinguished for learning; to become fine scholars; to be profoundly versed in science; or to be distinguished as authors, that they are

set apart; but it is in every way possible to make known the Lord Jesus Christ. Whatever other men do, or not do; however the world may choose to be employed, their work is simple and plain, and it is not to cease or be intermitted till death shall close their toils. Neither by the love of ease, of wealth, or pleasure are they to turn aside from their work, or to forsake the vocation to which God has called them.

11. We see the responsibility of the ministry, ver. 5. On the ministry devolves the work of making the Saviour known to a dying world. If they will not do it, the world will remain in ignorance of the Redeemer and will perish. *If there is one soul to whom they might make known the Saviour, and to whom they do not make him known, that soul will perish, and the responsibility will rest on the minister of the Lord Jesus.* And, O! how great is this responsibility! And who is sufficient for these things?

12. Ministers of the gospel should submit to any self-denial in order that they may do good. Their Master did; and Paul and the other apostles did. It is sufficient for the disciple that he be as the master; and the ministers of the gospel should regard themselves as set apart to a work of self-denial, and called to a life of toil, like their Lord. Their rest is in heaven, and not on the earth. Their days of leisure and repose are to be found in the skies when their work is done, and not in a world perishing in sin.

13. The ministry is a glorious work, ver. 5. What higher honour is there on earth than to make known a Redeemer? What pleasure more exquisite can there be than to speak of pardon to the guilty? What greater comfort than to go to the afflicted and bind up their hearts; to pour the balm of peace into the wounded spirit, and to sustain and cheer the dying? The ministry has its own consolations amidst all its trials; its own honour amidst the contempt and scorn with which it is often viewed by the world.

14. The situation of man would have been dreadful and awful had it not been for the light which is imparted by revelation, and by the Holy Spirit, ver. 6. Man would have ever remained like the dark night before God said, "Let there be light;" and his condition would have been thick darkness, where not a ray of light would have beamed on his benighted way. Some idea of what this was, and would have continued to be, we have now in the heathen world, where thick darkness reigns over nations, though it has been somewhat broken in upon by the dim light which tradition has diffused there.

15. God has power to impart light to the most dark and benighted mind. There is no one to whom he cannot reveal himself and make his truth known, ver. 6. With as much ease as he commanded light to shine out of darkness at first can he command the pure light of truth to shine on the minds of men; and on minds most beclouded by sin he can cause the sun of righteousness to shine with healing in his beams.

16. We should implore the enlightening influence of the Spirit of truth, ver. 6. If God is the source of light, we should seek it at his hands. Nothing to man is so valuable as the light of truth; nothing of so much worth as the knowledge of the true God; and with the deepest solicitude, and the most fervent prayer, should we seek the enlightening influences of his Spirit, and the guidance of his grace.

17. There is no true knowledge of God except that which shines in the face of Jesus Christ, ver. 6. He came to make known the true God. He is the exact image of God. He resembles him in all things. And he who does not love the character of Jesus Christ, therefore, does not love the character of God; he who does not seek to be like Jesus Christ, does not desire to be like God. He who does not bear the image of the Redeemer, does not bear the image of God. To be a moral man merely, therefore, is not to be like God. To be amiable, and honest, merely, is not to be like God. Jesus Christ, the image of God, was more than this. He was *religious*. He was holy. He was, as a man, a man of prayer, and

filled with the love of God, and was always submissive to his holy will. He sought his honour and glory: and he made it the great purpose of his life and death to make known his existence, perfections, and name. To imitate him in this is to have the knowledge of the glory of God; and no man is *like* God who does not bear the image of the Redeemer. No man is like God, therefore, who is not a Christian. Of course, no man can be prepared for heaven who is not a friend and follower of Jesus Christ.

18. God designs to secure the promotion of his own glory in the manner in which religion is spread in the world, ver. 7. For this purpose, and with this view, he did not commit it to angels, nor has he employed men of rank, or wealth, or profound scientific attainments to be the chief instruments in its propagation. He has committed it to frail, mortal men; and often to men of humble rank, and even humble attainments—except attainments in piety. In fitting them for their work his grace is manifest; and in all the success which attends their labours it is apparent that it is by the mere grace and mercy of God that it is done.

19. We see what our religion has cost, ver. 8, 9. Its extension in the world has been everywhere connected with sufferings, and toil, and tears. It began in the labours, sorrows, self-denials, persecutions, and dying agonies of the Son of God; and to *introduce* it to the world cost his life. It was spread by the toils, and sacrafices, and sufferings of the apostles. It was kept up by the dying groans of martyrs. It has been preserved and extended on earth by the labours and prayers of the Reformers, and amidst scenes of persecution everywhere, and it is now extending through the earth by the sacrifices of those who are willing to leave country and home; to cross oceans and deserts; and to encounter the perils of barbarous climes, that they may make it known to distant lands. If estimated by what it has *cost*, assuredly no religion, no blessing is so valuable as Christianity. It is above all human valuation; and it should be a matter of unfeigned thankfulness to us that God has been pleased to raise up men who have been *willing* to suffer so much that it might be perpetuated and extended on the earth; and *we* should be willing also to imitate their example, and deny ourselves, that *we* may make its inestimable blessings known to those who are now destitute. To us, it is worth all it has cost—all the blood of apostles and martyrs; to others, also, it would be worth all that it *would* cost to send it to them. How can we better express our sense of its worth, and our gratitude to the dying Redeemer, and our veneration for the memory of self-denying apostles and martyrs, than by endeavouring to diffuse the religion for which they died all over the world?

20. We have in this chapter an illustration of the sustaining power of religion in trials, ver. 8, 9. The friends of Christianity have been called to endure every form of suffering. Poverty, want, tears, stripes, imprisonments, and deaths have been their portion. They have suffered under every form of torture which men could inflict on them. And yet the power of religion has never failed them. It has been amply tried; and has shown itself able to sustain them always, and to enable them always to triumph. Though troubled, they have not been so close pressed that they had no room to turn; though perplexed, they have not been without some resource; though persecuted by men, they have not been forsaken by God; though thrown down in the conflict, yet they have recovered strength, and been prepared to renew the strife, and to engage in new contentions with the foes of God. Who can estimate the value of a religion like this? Who does not see that it is adapted to man in a state of trial, and that it furnishes him with just what he needs in this world?

21. Christianity will live, ver. 8, 9. Nothing can destroy it. All the power that *could* be brought to bear on it to blot it from the earth *has* been tried, and yet it survives. No new attempt to destroy it can pre-

vail; and it is now settled that this religion is to live to the end of time. It has *cost* much to obtain this demonstration; but it is worth all it has cost, and the sufferings of apostles and martyrs, therefore, have not been for naught.

22. Christians should be willing to endure anything in order that they may become like Christ on earth, and be like him in heaven, ver. 10. It is worth all their efforts, and all their self-denials. It is the grand object before us; and we should deem no sufferings too severe, no self-denial or sacrifice too great, if we may become like him here below, and may live with him above, ver. 10, 11.

23. In order to animate us in the work to which God has called us; to encourage us in our trials; and to prompt us to a faithful discharge of our duties, especially those who like Paul are called to preach the gospel, we should have, like him, the following views and feelings—views and feelings adapted to sustain us in all our trials, and to uphold us in all the conflicts of life. (1.) A firm and unwavering belief of the truth of the religion which we profess, and of the truth which we make known to others, ver. 12. No man can preach successfully, and no man can do much good, whose mind is vacillating and hesitating; who is filled with doubts, and who goes timidly to work, or who declares that of which he has no practical acquaintance, and no deep-felt conviction, and who knows not whereof he affirms. A man to do good must have a faith which never wavers; a conviction of truth which is constant; a belief settled like the everlasting hills, which nothing can shake or overturn. With such a conviction of the truth of Christianity, and of the great doctrines which it inculcates, he *cannot but speak* of it, and make known his convictions. He that believes that men ARE in fact in danger of hell, WILL tell them of it; he that believes there is an awful bar of judgment, will tell them of it; he that believes that the Son of God became incarnate and died for men, will tell them of it; he that believes that there is a heaven, will invite them to it. And one reason why professing Christians are so reluctant to speak of these things, is, that they have no very settled and definite conviction of their truth, and no correct view of their relative importance. (2.) We should have a firm assurance that God has raised up the Lord Jesus, and that we also shall be raised from the dead, ver. 14. The hope and expectation of the resurrection of the dead was one of the sustaining principles which upheld Paul in his labours, and to attain to this was one of the grand objects of his life, Acts xxiii. 6; Phil. iii. 11. Under the influence of this hope and expectation, he was willing to encounter any danger, and to endure any trial. The prospect of being raised up to eternal life and glory was all that was needful to make trials welcome, and to uphold him in the midst of privations and toils. And so we, if we are assured of this great truth, shall welcome trial also, and shall be able to endure afflictions and persecutions. They will soon be ended, and the eternal glory in the morning of the resurrection shall be more than a compensation for all that we shall endure in this life. (3.) We should have a sincere desire to promote the glory of God, and to bring as many as possible to join in his praise, and to celebrate his saving mercy, ver. 15. It was this which sustained and animated Paul; and a man who has this as the leading object of his life, and his great purpose and aim, will be willing to endure much trial, to suffer much persecution, and to encounter many dangers. No object is so noble as that of endeavouring to promote the divine glory; and he who is influenced by that will care little how many sufferings he is called to endure in this life.

24. Christians should have such a belief of the truth of their religion as to be willing to speak of it at all times, and in all places, ver. 13. If we *have* such a belief we shall be willing to speak of it. We cannot help it. We shall so see its value, and so love it, and our hearts will be so full of it,

and we shall see so much the danger of our fellow-men, that we shall be instinctively prompted to go to them and warn them of their danger, and tell them of the glories of the Redeemer.

25. Christians may expect to be supported and comforted in the trials and toils of life, ver. 16. The "outward man" will indeed perish and decay. The body will become feeble, weary, jaded, decayed, decrepit. It will be filled with pain, and will languish under disease, and will endure the mortal agony, and will be corrupted in the tomb. But the "inward man" will be renewed. The faith will be invigorated, the hope become stronger, the intellect brighter, the heart better, the whole soul be more like God. While the body, therefore, the less important part, decays and dies, the immortal part shall live and ripen for glory. Of what consequence is it, therefore, how soon or how much the body decays; or when, and where, and how it dies? Let the immortal part be preserved, let that live, and all is well. And while this is done, we should not, we shall not "faint." We shall be sustained; and shall find the consolations of religion to be fitted to all our wants, and adapted to all the necessities of our condition as weak, and frail, and dying creatures.

26. We learn from this chapter how to bear affliction in a proper manner, ver. 17, 18. It is by looking at eternity and comparing our trials with the eternal weight of glory that awaits us. In themselves afflictions often seem heavy and long. Human nature is often ready to sink under them. The powers of the body fail, and the mortal frame is crushed. The day seems long while we suffer; and the night seems often to be almost endless, Deut. xxviii. 67. But compared with eternity how short are all these trials! Compared with the weight of glory which awaits the believer, what a trifle are the severest sufferings of this life. Soon the ransomed spirit will be released, and will be admitted to the full fruition of the joys of the world above. In that world all these sorrows will seem like the sufferings of childhood, that we have now almost forgotten, and that now seem to us like trifles.

27. We should not look to the things which are seen as our portion, ver. 17, 18. They are light in their character, and are soon to fade away. Our great interests are beyond the grave. There all is weighty, and momentous, and eternal. Whatever great interests we have are there. Eternity is stamped upon all the joys and all the sorrows which are beyond this life. Here all is temporary, changing, decaying, dying. There all is fixed, settled, unchanging, immortal. It becomes us then as rational creatures *to look* to that world, to act with reference to it, to feel and act *as if* we felt that all our interests were there. Were this life all, every thing in relation to us would be trifling. But when we remember that there is an eternity; that we are near it; and that our conduct here is to determine our character and destiny there, life becomes invested with infinite importance. Who can estimate the magnitude of the interests at stake? Who can appreciate aright the importance of every step we take, and every plan we form?

28. All here below is temporary, decaying, dying; ver. 17, 18. Afflictions are temporary. They are but for a moment, and will soon be passed away. Our sorrows here will soon be ended. The last sigh on earth will soon be heaved; the last tear will have fallen on the cheek; the last pain will have shot across the seat of life! The last pangs of parting with a beloved friend will soon have been endured; and the last step which we are to take in "the valley of the shadow of death," will soon have been trod. And in like manner we shall soon have tasted the last cup of earthly joy. All our comforts here below will soon pass from us. Our friends will die. Our sources of happiness will be dried up. Our health will fail, and darkness will come over our eyes, and we shall go down to the dead. All our property

CHAPTER V.

FOR we know, that if our earthly house of *this* tabernacle [a] were dissolved, we have a building of God, an house [b] not made with hands, eternal in the heavens.

a Job 4.19; 2 Pet.1.13,14. b 1 Pet.1.4.

must be left, and all our honours be parted with for ever. In a little time —O, how brief! we shall have gone from all these, and shall be engaged in the deep and awful solemnities of the unchanging world. How vain and foolish, therefore, the attachment to earthly objects! How important to secure an interest in that future inheritance which shall never fade away!

29. Let it not be inferred, however, that *all* affliction shall be light, and for a moment, or that all earthly trial shall of course work out a far more exceeding and eternal weight of glory. There are sorrows beyond the grave compared with which the most heavy and most protracted woes this side the tomb, are "light," and are "but for a moment." And there are sorrows *in* this life, deep and prolonged afflictions—which by no means tend to prepare the soul for the "far more exceeding and eternal weight of glory." Such are those afflictions where there is no submission to the will of God; where there is murmuring, repining, impatience, and increased rebellion; where there is no looking to God for comfort, and no contemplation of eternal glory. Such are those afflictions where men look to philosophy, or to earthly friends to comfort them; or where they plunge deeper into the business, the gayety, or the vices of the world, to drown their sorrows and to obliterate the sense of their calamities. This is "the sorrow of the world, which worketh death," 2 Cor. vii. 10. In afflictions, therefore, it should be to us a matter of deep and anxious solicitude to know whether we have the right feelings, and whether we are seeking the right sources of consolation. And in such seasons it shall be the subject of our deep and earnest prayer to God that our trials *may*, by his grace, be made to work out for us "a far more exceeding and eternal weight of glory." All are afflicted; all suffer in various ways; and all *may* find these trials terminate in eternal blessedness beyond the grave

CHAPTER V.

THIS chapter is closely connected with the former, and indeed has been improperly separated from it, as is manifest from the word "For" (γὰρ) with which it commences. It contains a further statement of *reasons* for what has been said in the previous chapter. The main subject there was the MINISTRY; the honesty and fidelity with which Paul and his fellow-labourers toiled (ver. 1—3); the trials and dangers which they encountered in the work of the ministry (ver. 7—12); and the consolations and supports which they had in its various trials, ver. 13—18. This chapter contains a continuation of the same subject, and a further statement of the motives which prompted them to their work, and of the supports which upheld them in the arduous duties to which they were called. It is a chapter full of exquisite beauties of sentiment and of language, and as well adapted to give consolation and support to all Christians now as it is to ministers; and the sentiments are as well adapted to sustain the humblest believer in his trials as they were to sustain the apostles themselves. The following are the points of consolation and support, and reasons for their zeal and self-denial, to which the apostle refers.

1. They had the assured prospect of the resurrection, and of eternal life, ver. 1—4. The body might decay, and be worn out; it might sigh and groan, but they had a better home, a mansion of eternal rest in the heavens. It was their earnest desire to reach heaven; though not such a desire as to make them unwilling to endure the toils and trials which God should appoint to them here below, but still an earnest, anxious wish to reach safely their eternal home in the skies. In the prospect of their heavenly home, and their eternal rest, they were willing

2 For in this we groan, [a] earnestly desiring to be clothed upon with our house which is from heaven:

a Rom.8.23.

to endure all the trials which were appointed to them.

2. God had appointed them to this; he had fitted them for these trials; he had endowed them with the graces of his Spirit; and they were, therefore, willing to be absent from the body, and to be present with the Lord; ver. 5—8. They had such a view of heaven as their home that they were willing at any time to depart and enter the world of rest, and they did not, therefore, shrink from the trials and dangers which would be likely soon to bring them there.

3. They had a deep and constant conviction that they must soon appear before the judgment-seat of Christ; ver. 9—11. They laboured that they might be accepted by him (ver. 9); they knew that they must give a solemn account to him (ver. 10); they had a clear view, and a deep impression of the awful terrors of that day, and they laboured, therefore, to save as many as possible from the condemnation of the great Judge of all, and endeavoured to "persuade" them to be prepared for that scene; ver. 11.

4. Though to some they might appear to be under the influence of improper excitement, and even to be deranged (ver. 14), yet they were acting only under the proper influence of the love of Christ; ver. 14, 15. They were constrained and urged on by his love; they knew that he had died for all, and that all men were dead in sin; and they felt themselves the constraining influence of that love prompting them to deny themselves, and to devote their all to his service and cause.

5. Their views of all things had been changed; ver. 16, 17. They had ceased to act under the influences which govern other men; but their own hearts had been changed, and they had become new creatures in Christ, and in their lives they evinced the spirit which should govern those who were thus renewed.

6. They had been solemnly commissioned by God as his ambassadors in this cause. They had been sent to make known the terms and the way of reconciliation, and they felt it to be their duty to proclaim those terms on as wide a scale as possible, and with the utmost zeal and self-denial. It was God's glorious plan of reconciliation; and on the ground of the atonement made by the Redeemer, they could now offer salvation to all mankind, and as all *might* be saved, they felt themselves bound to offer the terms of salvation to as many as possible; ver. 18—21. The grand argument for urging sinners to be reconciled to God, is the fact that Christ has died for their sins, and, therefore, the apostles apprized of this fact, sought to urge as many as possible to become his friends; ver. 21.

1. *For we know.* We who are engaged in the work of the gospel ministry. Paul is giving a reason why he and his fellow-labourers did not become weary and faint in their work. The reason was, that they knew that even if their body should die, they hac an inheritance reserved for them in heaven. The expression "we know" is the language of strong and unwavering assurance. They had no doubt on the subject. And it proves that there may be the assurance of eternal life; or such evidence of acceptance with God as to leave no doubt of a final admission into heaven. This language was often used by the Saviour in reference to the truths which he taught (John iii. 11; iv. 22); and it is used by the sacred writers in regard to the truths which they recorded, and in regard to their own personal piety; John xxi. 24; 1 John ii. 3, 5, 18; iii. 2, 14, 19, 24; iv. 6, 13; v. 2, 15, 19, 20. ¶ *That if our earthly house* The word "earthly" here (ἐπίγειος) stands opposed to "heavenly," or to the house eternal (ἐν τοῖς οὐρανοῖς) in the heavens." The word properly means "upon earth, terrestrial, belonging to the earth, or on the earth," and is applied to *bodies* (1

Cor. xv. 40); to earthly things (John iii. 12); to earthly, or worldly wisdom, James iii. 15. The word *house* here refers doubtless to the body, as the habitation, or the dwelling-place of the mind or soul. The soul dwells in it as we dwell in a house, or tent. ¶ *Of* this *tabernacle.* This word means a booth, or tent—a movable dwelling. The use of the word here is not a mere redundancy, but the idea which Paul designs to convey is, doubtless, that the body—the house of the soul—was not a *permanent* dwelling-place, but was of the same nature as a booth or tent, that was set up for a temporary purpose, or that was easily taken down in migrating from one place to another. It refers here to the body as the frail and temporary abode of the soul. It is not a permanent dwelling; a fixed habitation, but is liable to be taken down at any moment, and was fitted up with that view. Tindal renders it, "if our earthly mansion wherein we now dwell." The Syriac renders it, "for we know that if our house on earth, which is our body, were dissolved." The idea is a beautiful one, that the body is a mere unfixed, movable dwelling-place; liable to be taken down at any moment, and not designed, any more than a tent is, to be a permanent habitation. ¶ *Were dissolved* (καταλυθῇ). This word means properly to disunite the parts of any thing; and is applied to the act of throwing down, or destroying a building. It is applied here to the body, regarded as a temporary dwelling that might be taken down, and it refers, doubtless, to the dissolution of the body in the grave. The idea is, that if this body should moulder back to dust, and be resolved into its original elements; or if by great zeal and labour it should be exhausted and worn out. Language like this is used by Eliphaz, the Temanite, in describing the body of man. "How much less in those that dwell in houses of clay," &c; Job iv. 19; comp. 2 Pet. i. 13, 14. ¶ *We have a building of God.* Robinson (*Lexicon*) supposes that it refers to "the future spiritual body as the abode of the soul." Some have supposed that it refers to some "celestial vehicle" with which God invests the soul during the intermediate state. But the Scripture is silent about any such celestial vehicle. It is not easy to tell what was the precise idea which Paul here designed to convey. Perhaps a few remarks may enable us to arrive at the meaning. (1.) It was not to be temporary; not a tent or tabernacle that could be taken down. (2.) It was to be eternal in the heavens. (3.) It was to be such as to constitute a dwelling; *a clothing,* or such a protection as should keep the soul from being "naked." (4.) It was to be such as should constitute "life" in contradistinction from "mortality." These things will better agree with the supposition of its referring to the future *body* of the saints than any thing else; and probably the idea of Paul is, that the body there will be incorruptible and immortal. When he says it is a "building of God" (ἐκ Θεοῦ), he evidently means that it is made *by* God; that he is the architect of that future and eternal dwelling. Macknight and some others, however, understood this of the mansions which God has fitted up for his people in heaven, and which the Lord Jesus has gone to prepare for them; comp. John xiv. 2. But see Note on ver. 3. ¶ *An house.* A dwelling; an abode; that is, according to the interpretation above, a celestial, pure, immortal body; a body that shall have God for its immediate author, and that shall be fitted to dwell in heaven for ever. ¶ *Not made with hands.* Not constructed by man; a habitation not like those which are made by human skill, and which are therefore easily taken down or removed, but one that is made by God himself. This does not imply that the "earthly house" which is to be superseded by that in heaven is made with hands, but the idea is, that the earthly dwelling has things about it which *resemble* that which is made by man, or *as if* it were made with hands; *i. e.* it is temporary, frail, easily taken down or removed. But that which is in heaven is permanent, fixed, eternal, *as if* made by God.

3 If so be that being clothed we shall not be found naked.[a]

4 For we that are in *this* tabernacle do groan, being burdened;

a Re.3.18; 16.15.

¶ *Eternal in the heavens.* Immortal; to live for ever. The future body shall never be taken down or dissolved by death. It is eternal, of course, only in respect to the future, and not in respect to the past. And it is not only eternal, but it is to abide for ever *in* the heavens—in the world of glory. It is never to be subjected to a dwelling on the earth; never to be in a world of sin, suffering, and death.

2. *For in this.* In this tent, tabernacle, or dwelling. In our body here. ¶ *We groan;* comp. Note, Rom. viii. 22. The sense is, that we are subjected to so many trials and afflictions in the present body; that the body is subjected to so many pains and to so much suffering, as to make us earnestly desire to be invested with that body which shall be free from all susceptibility to suffering. ¶ *Earnestly desiring to be clothed upon with our house,* &c. There is evidently here a change of the metaphor which gives an apparent harshness to the construction. One idea of the apostle is, that the body here, and the spiritual body hereafter, is a house or a dwelling. Here he speaks of it as *a garment* which may be put on or laid off; and of himself as earnestly desiring to put on the immortal clothing or vestment which was in heaven. Both these figures are common in ancient writings, and a change in this manner in the popular style is not unusual. The Pythagoreans compared the body to a tent, or hut, for the soul; the Platonists liken it to a vestment.—*Bloomfield.* The Jews speak of a vestment to the soul in this world and the next. They affirm that the soul had a covering when it was under the throne of God, and before it was clothed with the body. This *vestment* they say was "the image of God" which was lost by Adam. After the fall, they say Adam and all his posterity were regarded as naked. In the future world they say the good will be clothed with a vestment for the soul which they speak of as lucid and radiant, and such as no one on earth can attain.—*Schoettgen.* But there is no reason to think that Paul referred to any such trifles as the Jews have believed on this subject. He evidently regarded man as composed of body and soul. The soul was the more important part, and the body constituted its mere habitation or dwelling. Yet a body was essential to the idea of the complete man; and since this was frail and dying, he looked forward to a union with the body that should be eternal in the heavens, as a more desirable and perfect habitation of the soul. Mr. Locke has given an interpretation of this in which he is probably alone, but which has so much appearance of plausibility that it is not improper to refer to it. He supposes that this whole passage has reference to the fact that at the coming of the Redeemer the body will be changed without experiencing death; (comp. 1 Cor. xv. 51, 52); that Paul expected that this might soon occur; and that he earnestly desired to undergo this transformation without experiencing the pains of dying. He therefore paraphrases it, "For in this tabernacle I groan, earnestly desiring, without putting off this mortal, earthly body by death, to have that celestial body superinduced, if so be the coming of Christ shall overtake me in this life, before I put off this body." ¶ *With our house.* The phrase "to be clothed upon with our house" seems to be harsh and unusual. The sense is plain, however, that Paul desired to be invested with that pure, spiritual, and undecaying body which was to be the eternal abode of his soul in heaven. That he speaks of as a house (οἰκητήριον), a more permanent and substantial dwelling than a *tent,* or tabernacle.

3. *If so be that being clothed.* This passage has been interpreted in a great many different ways. The view of Locke is given above. Rosenmüller renders it, "For in the other life we shall not be wholly destitute of a

not for that we would be unclothed, but clothed upon, that mortality [a] might be swallowed up of life.

a 1 Cor.15.33.

body, but we shall have a body." Tindal renders it, "If it happen that we be found clothed, and not naked." Doddridge supposes it to mean, "since being so clothed upon, we shall not be found naked, and exposed to any evil and inconvenience, how entirely soever we may be stripped of every thing we can call our own here below." Hammond explains it to mean, "If, indeed, we shall, happily, be among the number of those faithful Christians, who will be found clothed upon, not naked." Various other expositions may be seen in the larger commentaries. The meaning is probably this: (1.) The word "clothed" refers to the future spiritual body of believers; the eternal habitation in which they shall reside. (2.) The expression implies an earnest desire of Paul to be thus invested with that body. (3.) It is the language of humility and of deep solicitude, as if it were possible that they might fail, and as if it demanded their utmost care and anxiety that they *might* thus be clothed with the spiritual body in heaven. (4.) It means that in that future state, the soul will not be naked; *i. e.* destitute of any body, or covering. The present body will be laid aside. It will return to corruption, and the disembodied Spirit will ascend to God and to heaven. It will be disencumbered of the body with which it has been so long clothed. But we are not thence to infer that it will be destitute of a body; that it will remain a naked soul. It will be clothed there in its appropriate glorified body; and will have an appropriate habitation there. This does not imply, as Bloomfield supposes, that the souls of the wicked will be destitute of any such habitation as the glorified body of the saints; which may be true—but it means simply that the soul shall not be destitute of an appropriate body in heaven, but that the union of body and soul there shall be known as well as on earth.

4. *For we.* We who are Christians. All Christians. ¶ *That are in this tabernacle.* This frail and dying body; Note, ver. 1. ¶ *Do groan;* see ver. 2. This is a further explanation of what is said in ver. 2. It implies an ardent and earnest desire to leave a world of toil and pain, and to enter into a world of rest and glory. ¶ *Being burdened.* Being borne down by the toils, and trials, and calamities of this life; see Note, chap. iii. 7—10. ¶ *Not for that we would be unclothed.* Not that we are impatient, and unwilling to bear these burdens as long as God shall appoint. Not that we merely wish to lay aside this mortal body. We do not desire to die and depart merely because we suffer much, and because the body here is subjected to great trials. This is not the ground of our wish to depart. We are willing to bear trials. We are not impatient under afflictions. —The sentiment here is, that the mere fact that we may be afflicted much and long, should not be the principal reason why we should desire to depart. We should be willing to bear all this as long as God shall choose to appoint. The anxiety of Paul to enter the eternal world was from a higher motive than a mere desire to get away from trouble. ¶ *But clothed upon.* To be invested with our spiritual body. We desire to be clothed with that body. We desire to be in heaven, and to be clothed with immortality. We wish to have a body that shall be pure, undecaying, ever glorious. It was not, therefore, a mere desire to be released from sufferings; it was an earnest wish to be admitted to the glories of the future world, and partake of the happiness which we would enjoy there. This is *one* of the reasons why Paul wished to be in heaven. *Other* reasons he has stated elsewhere. Thus in Phil. i. 23, he says he had "a desire to depart and to *be with Christ.*" So in ver. 8 of this chapter, he says he was "willing rather to be absent from the body and to be pre-

5 Now he that hath wrought[a] us for the self-same thing, *is* God, who also hath given unto us the earnest[b] of the Spirit.

6 Therefore *we are* always confident, knowing that, whilst we are at home in the body, we are absent from the Lord:

a Is.29.23; Ep.2.10. b Ep.1.14.

sent with the Lord." In 2 Tim. iv. 6—8, he speaks of the "crown of righteousness" laid up for him as a reason why he was willing to die. ¶ *That mortality might be swallowed up of life.* On the meaning of the word rendered "swallowed up" (καταποθῇ); see Note on 1 Cor. xv. 54. The meaning here is, that it might be completely absorbed; that it might cease to be; that there might be no more mortality, but that he might pass to the immortal state—to the condition of eternal life in the heavens. The body here is mortal; the body there will be immortal; and Paul desired to pass away from the mortal state to one that shall be immortal, a world where there shall be no more death; comp. 1 Cor. xv. 53.

5. *Now he that hath wrought us for the self-same thing.* The phrase "self-same thing" here means *this very thing, i. e.* the thing to which he had referred—the preparation for heaven, or the heavenly dwelling. The word "wrought" here (κατεργασάμενος) means that God had *formed* or made them for this; that is, he had by the influences of the Spirit, and by his agency on the heart, created them, as it were, for this, and adapted them to it. God has destined us to this change from corruption to incorruption; he has adapted us to it; he has formed us for it. It does not refer to the original creation of the body and the soul for this end, but it means that God, by his own renewing, and sanctifying, and sustaining agency, had formed them for this, and adapted them to it. The *object* of Paul in stating that it was done by God, is to keep this truth prominently before the mind. It was not by any native inclination, or strength, or power which they had, but it was all to be traced to God; comp. Eph. ii. 10. ¶ *Who also hath given.* In addition to the fitting for eternal glory he has given us the earnest of the Spirit to sustain us here. We are not only prepared to enter into heaven, but we have here also the support produced by the earnest of the Spirit. ¶ *The earnest of the Spirit.* On the meaning of this, see Note on chap. i. 22. He has given to us the Holy Spirit as the pledge or assurance of the eternal inheritance.

6. *Therefore we are always confident.* The word here used (θαῤῥοῦντες) means to be of good cheer. To have good courage, to be full of hope The idea is, that Paul was not dejected, cast down, disheartened, discouraged. He was cheerful and happy. He was patient in his trials, and diligent in his calling. He was full of hope, and of the confident expectation of heaven; and this filled him with cheerfulness and with joy. Tindal renders it, "we are always of goud cheere." And this was not occasional and transitory, it was constant, it was uniform, it always (πάντοτε) existed.—This is an instance of the uniform *cheerfulness* which will be produced by the assured prospect of heaven. It is an instance too when the hope of heaven will enable a man to face danger with courage; to endure toil with patience; and to submit to trials in any form with cheerfulness. ¶ *Knowing;* see ver. 1. This is another instance in which the apostle expresses undoubted assurance. ¶ *Whilst we are at home in the body.* The word here used (ἐνδημοῦντες) means literally to be among one's own people, to be at home; to be present at any place. It is here equivalent to saying, "while we dwell in the body;" see ver. 1. Doddridge renders it, "sojourning in the body;" and remarks that it is improper to render it "at home in the body," since it is the apostle's design to intimate that this is *not* our home. But Bloomfield says that the word is never used in the sense of *sojourning.* The idea is not that of

7 (For [a] we walk by faith, not by sight:)

8 We are confident, *I say*, and [b] willing rather to be absent

a Rom. 8.24,25.

b Ph. 1.23.

being "at home"—for this is an idea which is the very opposite of that which the apostle wishes to convey. His purpose is not at all to represent the body here as our *home*, and the original word does not imply that. It means here simply to be *in* the body; to be present in the body; that is, while we are in the body. ¶ *We are absent from the Lord.* The Lord Jesus; see Notes, Acts i. 24; comp. Phil. i. 23. Here he was in a strange world, and among strangers. His great desire and purpose was to be *with* the Lord; and hence he cared little how soon the frail tabernacle of the body was taken down, and was cheerful amidst all the labours and sufferings that tended to bring it to the grave, and to release him to go to his eternal home where he would be present for ever with the Lord.

7. *For we walk.* To walk, in the Scriptures often denotes to live, to act, to conduct in a certain way; see Notes on Rom. iv. 12; vi. 4. It has reference to the fact that life is a journey, or a pilgrimage, and that the Christian is travelling to another country. The sense here is, that we conduct ourselves in our course of life with reference to the things which are unseen, and not with reference to the things which are seen. ¶ *By faith.* In the belief of those things which we do not see. We believe in the existence of objects which are invisible, and we are influenced by them. To walk by faith, is to live in the confident expectation of things that are to come; in the belief of the existence of unseen realities; and suffering them to influence us *as if* they were seen. The people of this world are influenced by the things that are *seen*. They live for wealth, honour, splendour, praise, for the objects which this world can furnish, and as if there were nothing which is unseen, or as if they ought not to be influenced by the things which are unseen. The Christian, on the contrary, has a firm conviction of the reality of the glories of heaven; of the fact that the Redeemer is there; of the fact that there is a crown of glory; and he lives, and acts *as if* that were all real, and *as if* he saw it all. The simple account of faith, and of living by faith is, that we live and act *as if* these things were true, and suffer them to make an impression on our mind according to their real nature; see Note on Mark xvi. 16. It is contradistinguished from living simply under the influence of things that are seen. God is unseen—but the Christian lives, and thinks, and acts *as if* there were a God, and *as if* he saw him. Christ is unseen now by the bodily eye; but the Christian lives and acts as if he were seen, *i. e.* as if his eye were known to be upon us, and *as if* he was now exalted to heaven and was the only Saviour. The Holy Spirit is unseen; but he lives, and acts *as if* there were such a Spirit, and as if his influences were needful to renew, and purify the soul. Heaven is unseen; but the Christian lives, and thinks, and acts *as if* there were a heaven, and as if he now saw its glories. He has confidence in these, and in kindred truths, and he acts as if they were real.—Could man *see* all these; were they visible to the naked eye as they are to the eye of faith, no one would doubt the propriety of living and acting with reference to them. But *if* they exist, there is no more impropriety in acting with reference to them than if they were seen. Our seeing or not seeing them does not alter their nature or importance, and the fact that they are not seen does not make it improper to act with reference to them.—There are many ways of being convinced of the existence and reality of objects besides *seeing* them; and it may be as rational to be influenced by the reason, the judgment, or by strong confidence, as it is to be influenced by sight. Besides, all men are influenced by things which they have not seen. They hope for objects that are future.

from the body, and to be present with the Lord.

9 Wherefore we [1] labour, that, whether present or absent, we may be accepted of him.

10 For [a] we must all appear

1 *endeavour.*

a Rom. 14.10.

They aspire to happiness which they have not yet beheld. They strive for honour and wealth which are unseen, and which is in the distant future. They live, and act—influenced by strong faith and hope—*as if* these things were attainable; and they deny themselves, and labour, and cross oceans and deserts, and breathe in pestilential air to obtain those things which they have not seen, and which to them are in the distant future. And why should not the Christian endure *like* labour, and be willing to suffer in like manner, to gain the *unseen* crown which is incorruptible, and to acquire the *unseen* wealth which the moth does not corrupt?—And further still, the men of this world strive for those objects which they have not beheld, without any promise or any assurance that they shall obtain them. No being able to grant them has promised them; no one has assured them that their lives shall be lengthened out to obtain them. In a moment they may be cut off and all their plans frustrated; or they may be utterly disappointed and all their plans fail; or *if* they gain the object, it may be unsatisfactory, and may furnish no pleasure such as they had anticipated. But not so the Christian. He has, (1.) The promise of life. (2.) He has the assurance that sudden death cannot deprive him of it. It at once removes him *to* the object of pursuit, not *from* it. (3.) He has the assurance that *when* obtained, it shall not disgust, or satiate, or decay, but that it shall meet all the expectations of the soul, and shall be eternal. ¶ *Not by sight.* This may mean either that we are not influenced by a sight of these future glories, or that we are not influenced by the things which we see. The main idea is, that we are not influenced and governed by the sight. We are not governed and controlled by the things which we see, and we do not see those things which actually influence and control us. In both it is *faith* that controls us, and not sight.

8. *We are confident,* ver. 6. We are cheerful, and courageous, and ready to bear our trial. Tindal renders it, "we are of good comfort." ¶ *And willing rather to be absent from the body.* We would prefer to die. The same idea occurs in Phil. i. 23. "Having a desire to depart and to be with Christ; which is far better." The sense is, that Paul would have *preferred* to die, and to go to heaven, rather than to remain in a world of sin and trial. ¶ *To be present with the Lord.* The Lord Jesus; see Note on Acts i. 24; comp. Phil. i. 23. The idea of Paul is, that the Lord Jesus would constitute the main glory of heaven, and that to be with him was equivalent to being in a place of perfect bliss. He had no idea of any heaven where the Lord Jesus was not; and to be with him was to be in heaven. That world where the Redeemer is, is heaven. This also proves that the spirits of the saints, when they depart, are with the Redeemer; *i. e.* are at once taken to heaven. It demonstrates, (1.) That they are not annihilated. (2.) That they do not *sleep*, and remain in an unconscious state, as Dr. Priestley supposes. (3.) That they are not in some intermediate state, either in a state of purgatory, as the Papists suppose, or a state where all the souls of the just and the unjust are assembled in a common abode, as many Protestants have supposed; but, (4.) That they *dwell* WITH Christ; they are WITH the Lord (πρὸς τὸν Κύριον). They abide in his presence; they partake of his joy and his glory; they are permitted to sit with him in his throne; Rev. iii. 21. The same idea the Saviour expressed to the dying thief, when he said, "to-day shalt thou be with me in paradise;" Luke xxiii. 43.

9. *Wherefore* (Διὸ). In view of the facts stated above. Since we have the prospect of a resurrection and of

before the judgment-seat of Christ; that every one may receive [a] the things *done* in *his* body, according to that he hath done, whether *it be* good or bad.

a chap. 7.3.

future glory; since we have the assurance that there is a house not made with hands, eternal in the heavens; and since God has given to us this hope, and has granted to us the earnest of the Spirit, we make it our great object so to live as to be accepted by him. ¶ *We labour.* The word here used (φιλοτιμούμεθα, from φίλος and τιμή, loving honour) means properly to love honour; to be ambitious. This is its usual classical signification. In the New Testament, it means to be ambitious to do any thing; to exert one's self; to strive, as if from a love or sense of honour. As in English, *to make it a point of honour* to do so and so.—*Robinson* (Lex.); see Rom. xv 20; 1 Thess. iv. 11. It means here, that Paul made it a point of constant effort; it was his leading and constant aim to live so as to be acceptable to God, and to meet his approbation wherever he was. ¶ *Whether present or absent.* Whether present with the Lord (ver. 8), or absent from him (ver. 6); that is, whether in this world or the next; whether we are here, or removed to heaven. Wherever we are, or may be, it is, and will be our main purpose and object so to live as to secure his favour. Paul did not wish to live on earth regardless of his favour or without evidence that he would be accepted by him. He did not make the fact that he was absent from him, and that he did not see him with the bodily eye, an excuse for walking in the ways of ambition, or seeking his own purposes and ends. The idea is, that *so far as this point was concerned,* it made no difference with him whether he lived or died; whether he was on earth or in heaven; whether in the body or out of the body; it was the great fixed principle of his nature so to live as to secure the approbation of the Lord. And this is the true principle on which the Christian should act, and will act. The fact that he is now absent from the Lord will be to him no reason why he should lead a life of sin and self-indulgence, any more than he would if he were in heaven; and the fact that he is soon to be with him is not the main reason why he seeks to live so as to please him. It is because this has become the fixed principle of the soul; the very purpose of the life; and this principle and this purpose will adhere to him, and control him wherever he may be placed, or in whatever world he may dwell. ¶ *We may be accepted of him.* The phrase here used (εὐάρεστοι εἶναι) means to be well-pleasing; and then to be acceptable, or approved; Rom. xii. 1; xiv. 18; Eph. v. 10; Phil. iv. 18; Tit. ii. 9 The sense here is, that Paul was earnestly desirous of so living as to please God, and to receive from him the tokens and marks of his favour. And the truth taught in this verse is, that this will be the great purpose of the Christian's life, and that it makes no difference as to the existence and operation of this principle whether a man is on earth or in heaven. He will equally desire it, and strive for it; and this is one of the ways in which religion makes a man conscientious and holy, and is a better guard and security for virtue than all human laws, and all the restraints which can be imposed by man.

10. *For we must* (δεῖ). It is proper, fit, necessary that we should all appear there. This fact, to which Paul now refers, is *another* reason why it was necessary to lead a holy life, and why Paul gave himself with so much diligence and self-denial to the arduous duties of his office. There is a necessity, or a fitness that we should appear there to give up our account, for we are here on trial; we are responsible moral agents; we are placed here to form characters for eternity. Before we receive our eternal allotment it is *proper* that we should render our account of the man-

ner in which we have lived, and of the manner in which we have improved our talents and privileges. In the nature of things, it is proper that we should undergo a trial before we receive our reward, or before we are punished; and God has made it necessary and certain, by his direct and positive appointment, that we should stand at the bar of the final judge; see Rom. xiv. 10. ¶ *All.* Both Jews and Gentiles; old and young; bond and free; rich and poor; all of every class, and every age, and every nation. None shall escape by being unknown; none by virtue of their rank, or wealth; none because they have a character too pure to be judged. All shall be arranged in one vast assemblage, and with reference to their eternal doom; see Rev. xx. 12. Rosenmüller supposes that the apostle here alludes to an opinion that was common among the Jews that the Gentiles only would be exposed to severe judgments in the future world, and that the Jews would be saved as a matter of course. But the idea seems rather to be, that as the trial of the great day was the most important that man could undergo, and as *all must* give account there, Paul and his fellow-labourers devoted themselves to untiring diligence and fidelity that they might be accepted in that great day. ¶ *Appear* (φανερωθῆναι). This word properly means, to make apparent, manifest, known; to show openly, &c. Here it means that we must be manifest, or openly shown; *i. e.* we must be seen there, and be *publicly* tried. We must not only *stand* there, but our character will be seen, our desert will be known, our trial will be public. All will be brought from their graves, and from their places of concealment, and will *be seen* at the judgment-seat. The secret things of the heart and the life will all be made manifest and known. ¶ *The judgment-seat of Christ.* The tribunal of Christ, who is appointed to be the judge of quick and dead; see Note on John v. 25; Acts x. 42; xvii. 31. Christ is appointed to judge the world; and for this purpose he will assemble it before him, and assign to all their eternal allotments; see Mat. xxv. ¶ *That every one may receive.* The word rendered *may receive* (κομίσηται) means properly to take care of, to provide for; and in the New Testament, to bear, to bring (Luke vii. 37); to acquire, to obtain, to receive. This is the sense here. Every individual shall take, receive, or *bear away* the appropriate reward for the transactions of this life of probation; see Eph. vi. 8; Col. iii. 25. ¶ *The things.* The appropriate *reward* of the actions of this life. ¶ Done *in* his *body.* Literally, "the things by or through (διὰ) the body." Tindal renders it, "the works of his body." The idea is, that every man shall receive an appropriate reward for the actions of this life. Observe here, (1.) That it is the works done *in* or *through* the body; not which the body itself has done. It is the *mind,* the man that has lived *in* the body, and acted by it, that is to be judged. (2.) It is to be for the deeds of this life; not for what is done *after* death. Men are not to be brought into judgment for what they do *after* they die. All beyond the grave is either reward or punishment; it is not probation. The destiny is to be settled for ever by what is done in this world of probation. (3.) It is to be for *all* the deeds done in the body; for all the thoughts, plans, purposes, words, as well as for all the *outward* actions of the man. All that has been thought or done must come into review, and man must give an account for all. ¶ *According to that he hath done.* As an exact retribution for all that has been done. It is to be a *suitable* and *proper* recompence. The retribution is to be measured by what has been done in this life. Rewards shall be granted to the friends, and punishments to the foes of God, just in proportion to, or suitably to their deeds in this life. Every man shall receive just what, under all the circumstances, he OUGHT to receive, and what will be impartial justice in the case. The judgment will be such that it will be capable of being *seen* to be right; and such as the universe at large, and as the individuals them-

11 Knowing therefore the terror [a] of the Lord, we persuade men; but [b] we are made manifest unto God, and I trust also are made manifest in your consciences.

a Heb. 10.31; Jude 23. b chap. 4.2.

selves will *see* OUGHT to be rendered. ¶ *Whether* it be *good or bad.* Whether the life has been good or evil. The good will have no wish to escape the trial; the evil will not be able. No power of wickedness, however great, will be able to escape from the trial of that day; no crime that has been concealed in this life will be concealed there; no transgressor of law who may have long escaped the punishment due to his sins, and who may have evaded all human tribunals, will be able to escape there.

11. *Knowing therefore.* We who are apostles, and who are appointed to preach the gospel, having the fullest assurance of the terrors of the day of judgment, and of the wrath of God, endeavour to persuade men to be prepared to meet Him, and to give up their account. ¶ *The terror of the Lord.* This is, of the Lord Jesus, who will be seated on the throne of judgment, and who will decide the destiny of all men, ver. 10; comp. Mat. xxv. The sense is, knowing how much the Lord is to be feared; what an object of terror and alarm it will be to stand at the judgment-seat; how fearful and awful will be the consequences of the trial of that day. The Lord Jesus will be an object of terror and alarm, or it will be a subject inspiring terror and alarm to stand there on that day, because, (1.) He has all power, and is appointed to execute judgment; (2.) Because all must there give a strict and impartial account of all that they have done; (3.) Because the wrath of God will be shown in the condemnation of the guilty. It will be a day of awful wailing and alarm when all the living and the dead shall be arraigned on trial with reference to their eternal destiny; and when countless hosts of the guilty and impenitent shall be thrust down to an eternal hell. Who can describe the amazing terror of the scene? Who can fancy the horrors of the hosts of the guilty and the wretched who shall then hear that their doom is to be fixed for ever in a world of unspeakable woe? The *influence* of the knowledge of the terror of the Lord on the mind of the apostle seems to have been two-fold; first, an apprehension of it as a personal concern, and a desire to escape it, which led him to constant self-denial and toil; and secondly, a desire to save others from being overwhelmed in the wrath of that dreadful day. ¶ *We persuade men.* We endeavour to persuade them to flee from the wrath to come; to be prepared to stand before the judgment-seat, and to be fitted to enter into heaven. Observe here the peculiarity of the statement. It is not, we drive men; or we endeavour to alarm men; or we frighten men; or we appeal merely to their fears, but it is, we PERSUADE men, we endeavour to induce them by all the arts of persuasion and argument to flee from the wrath to come. The future judgment, and the scenes of future woe, are not proper topics for mere declamation. To declaim constantly on hell-fire and perdition; to appeal merely to the fears of men, is not the way in which Paul and the Saviour preached the gospel. The knowledge that there would be a judgment, and that the wicked would be sent to hell, was a powerful motive for Paul to endeavour to "persuade" men to escape from wrath, and was a motive for the Saviour to weep over Jerusalem, and to lament its folly, and its doom; Luke xix. 41 But they who fill their sermons with the denunciations of wrath; who dwell on the words hell and damnation, for the purpose of rhetoric or declamation, to round a period, or merely to excite alarm; and who "deal damnation around the land" as if they rejoiced that men were to be condemned, and in a tone and manner as if they would be pleased to execute it, have yet to learn the true nature of the way to win men to God, and the proper effect

12 For [a] we commend not ourselves again unto you, but give you occasion to glory on our behalf, that ye may have somewhat to *answer* them which glory in [1] appearance, and not in heart.

a chap. 3.1.

1 *in the face.*

of those awful truths on the mind. The true effect is, to produce tenderness, deep feeling, and love; to prompt to the language of persuasion and of tender entreaty; to lead men to weep over dying sinners rather than to denounce them; to pray to God to have mercy on them rather than to use the language of severity, or to assume tones as if they would be pleased to execute the awful wrath of God. ¶ *But we are made manifest unto God.* The meaning of this is, probably, that God sees that we are sincere and upright in our aims and purposes. He is acquainted with our hearts. All our motives are known to him, and he sees that it is our aim to promote his glory, and to save the souls of men. This is probably said to counteract the charge which might have been brought against him by some of the disaffected in Corinth, that he was influenced by improper motives and aims. To meet this, Paul says, that God knew that he was endeavouring to save souls, and that he was actuated by a sincere desire to rescue them from the impending terrors of the day of judgment. ¶ *And I trust also,* &c. And I trust also you are convinced of our integrity and uprightness of aim. The same sentiment is expressed in other words in chap. iv. 2. It is an appeal which he makes to them, and the expression of an earnest and confident assurance that they knew and felt that his aim was upright, and his purpose sincere.

12. *For we commend not ourselves again unto you.* This refers to what he had said in the previous verse. He had there said that he had such a consciousness of integrity that he could appeal to God, and that he was persuaded that the Corinthians also approved his course, or admitted that he was influenced by right motives. He here states the reason why he had said this. It was not to commend himself to them. It was not to boast of his own character, nor was it in order to secure their praise or favour Some might be disposed to misrepresent all that Paul said of himself, and to suppose that it was said for mere vain-glory, or the love of praise. He tells them, therefore, that his sole aim was necessary self-defence, and in order that they might have the fullest evidence that he, by whom they had been converted, was a true apostle; and that he whom they regarded as their friend and father in the gospel was a man of whom they need not be ashamed. ¶ *But give you occasion.* This is a very happy turn of expression. The sense is, "You have been converted under my labours. You profess to regard me as your spiritual father and friend. I have no reason to doubt of your attachment to me. Yet you often hear my name slandered, and hear me accused of wanting the evidence of being an apostle, and of being vain-glorious, and self-seeking. I know your desire to vindicate my character, and to show that you are my friends. I, therefore, say these things in regard to myself in order that you may be thus able to show your respect for me, and to vindicate me from the false and slanderous accusations of my enemies. Thus doing, you will be able to answer them; to show that the man whom you thus respect is worthy of your confidence and esteem." ¶ *On your behalf.* For your own benefit, or as it were in self-vindication for adhering to me, and evincing attachment to me. ¶ *That ye may have somewhat to* answer *them.* That you may be furnished with a ready reply when you are charged with adhering to a man who has no claims to the apostleship, or who is slandered in any other way. ¶ *Which glory in appearance.* The false teachers in Corinth. Probably they boasted of their rank, their eloquence, their talents, their external advantages; but

13 For whether we be beside [a] ourselves, *it is* to God: or whether we be sober, *it is* for your cause.

[a] ch. 11. 1, 16, 17.

not in the qualities of the heart—in sincerity, honesty, real love for souls. Their consciences would not allow them to do this ; and they knew themselves that their boasting was mere vain pretence, and that there was no real and solid ground for it. The margin is, "in the face." The meaning is, probably, that their ground of boasting was external, and was such as can be seen of men, and was not rather the secret consciousness of right, which could exist only in the conscience and the heart. Paul, on the other hand, gloried mainly in his sincerity, his honesty, his desire for their salvation ; in his conscious integrity before God ; and not in any mere external advantages or professions, in his rank, eloquence, or talent. Accordingly all his argument here turns on his sincerity, his conscious uprightness, and his real regard for their welfare. And the truth taught here is, that sincerity and conscious integrity are more valuable than any or all external advantages and endowments.

13. *For whether we be beside ourselves.* This is probably designed to meet some of the charges which the false teachers in Corinth brought against him, and to furnish his friends there with a ready answer, as well as to show them the true principles on which he acted, and his real love for them. It is altogether probable that he was charged with being deranged ; that many who boasted themselves of prudence, and soberness, and wisdom, regarded him as acting like a madman. It has not been uncommon, by any means, for the cold and the prudent ; for formal professors and for hypocrites to regard the warm-hearted and zealous friends of religion as maniacs. Festus thought Paul was deranged, when he said, " Paul, thou art beside thyself; much learning doth make thee mad," (Acts xxvi. 24); and the Saviour himself was regarded by his immediate relatives and friends as beside himself, Mark iii. 21. And at all times there have been many, both in the church and out of it, who have regarded the friends of revivals, and of missions, and all those who have evinced any extraordinary zeal in religion, as deranged. The object of Paul here is to show, whatever might be the appearance or the estimate which they affixed to his conduct, what were the real principles which actuated him. These were zeal for God, love to the church, and the constraining influences of the love of Christ, ver. 14, 15. The word here rendered " be beside ourselves " (ἐξέστημεν, from ἐξίστημι) means properly, to put out of place ; to be put out of place ; and then to be put out of one's self, to astonish, to fill with wonder; Luke xxiv. 22; Acts viii. 9, 11; and then to be out of one's mind, to be deranged. Here it means that they were charged with being deranged, or that others esteemed, or professed to esteem Paul and his fellow-labourers deranged. ¶ It is *to God.* It is in the cause of God, and from love to him. It is such a zeal for him ; such an absorbing interest in his cause ; such love prompting to so great self-denial, and teaching us to act so much unlike other men as to lead them to think that we are deranged. The doctrine here is, that there may be such a zeal for the glory of God, such an active and ardent desire to promote his honour, as to lead others to charge us with derangement. It does not *prove* however that a man is deranged on the subject of religion because he is unlike others, or because he pursues a course of life that differs materially from that of other professors of religion, and from the man of the world. *He* may be the truly sane man after all ; and all the madness that may exist may be where there is a profession of religion without zeal ; a professed belief in the existence of God and in the realities of eternity, that produces no difference

14 For the love of [a] Christ constraineth us; because we thus judge, that if one died for all then [b] were all dead.

a Ca. 8. 6.

b Ro. 5. 15; 14. 7, 9.

in the conduct between the professor and other men; or an utter unconcern about eternal realities when a man is walking on the brink of death and of hell. There are few men that become deranged *by* religion; there are millions who act as madmen who have no religion. And the highest instances of madness in the world are those who walk over an eternal hell without apprehension or alarm. ¶ *Or whether we be sober.* Whether we are sane, or of sound mind; comp. Mark v. 15. Tindal renders this whole passage, "For if we be too fervent, to God we are too fervent; if we keep measure, for our cause keep we measure." The sense seems to be, "if we are esteemed to be sane, and sober-minded, as we trust you will admit us to be, it is for your sake. Whatever may be the estimate in which we are held, we are influenced by love to God, and love to man. In such a cause, we cannot but evince zeal and self-denial which may expose us to the charge of mental derangement; but still we trust that by you we shall be regarded as influenced by a sound mind. We seek your welfare. We labour for you. And we trust that you will appreciate our motives, and regard us as truly sober-minded."

14. *For the love of Christ.* In this verse, Paul brings into view *the principle* which actuated him; the reason of his extraordinary and disinterested zeal. That was, that he was influenced by the love which Christ had shown in dying for all men, and by the argument which was furnished by that death respecting the actual character and condition of man (in this verse); and of the obligation of those who professed to be his true friends, ver. 15. The phrase "the love of Christ" (ἀγάπη τοῦ Χριστοῦ) may denote either the love which Christ bears *toward us,* and which he has manifested, or our love *towards him.* In the former sense the phrase "the love of God" is used in Rom. v. 8; 2 Cor. xiii. 13, and the phrase "love of Christ" in Eph. iii. 14. The phrase is used in the latter sense in John xv. 9, 10, and Rom. viii. 35. It is impossible to determine the sense with certainty, and it is only by the view which shall be taken of the connection and of the argument which will in any way determine the meaning. Expositors differ in regard to it. It seems to me that the phrase here means the love which Christ had toward us. Paul speaks of his dying for all as the reason why he was urged on to the course of self-denial which he evinced. Christ died for all. All were dead. Christ evinced his great love for us, and for all, by giving himself to die; and it was this love which Christ had shown that impelled Paul to his own acts of love and self-denial. He gave himself to his great work impelled by that love which Christ had shown; by the view of the ruined condition of man which that work furnished; and by a desire to emulate the Redeemer, and to possess the same spirit which he evinced. ¶ *Constraineth us* (συνέχει). This word (συνέχω) properly means, to hold together, to press together, to shut up; then to press on, urge, impel, or excite. Here it means, that the impelling, or exciting motive in the labours and self-denials of Paul, was the love of Christ—the love which he had showed to the children of men. Christ so loved the world as to give himself for it. His love for the world was a demonstration that men were dead in sins. And we, being urged by the same love, are prompted to like acts of zeal and self-denial to save the world from ruin. ¶ *Because we thus judge.* Gr. "We judging this;" that is, we thus determine in our own minds, or we thus decide; or this is our firm conviction and belief—we come to this conclusion. ¶ *That if one died for all.* On the supposition that one died for all; or taking it for granted that one died for all, then it

follows that all were dead. The "one" who died for all here is undoubtedly the Lord Jesus. The word "for" (ὑπὲρ) means in the place of, instead of; see Phil. 13 ; ver. 20. of this chapter. It means that Christ took the place of sinners, and died in their stead ; that he endured what was an ample equivalent for all the punishment which would be inflicted if they were to suffer the just penalty of the law ; that he endured so much suffering, and that God by his great substituted sorrows made such an expression of his hatred of sin, as to answer *the same end* in expressing his sense of the evil of sin, and in restraining others from transgression, *as if* the guilty were personally to suffer the full penalty of the law. If this was done, of course, the guilty might be pardoned and saved, since all the ends which could be accomplished by their destruction have been accomplished by the substituted sufferings of the Lord Jesus ; see Notes on Rom. iii. 25, 26, where this subject is considered at length.—The phrase "for all," (ὑπὲρ πάντων) obviously means for all mankind; for every man. This is an exceedingly important expression in regard to the extent of the atonement which the Lord Jesus made, and while it proves that his death was vicarious, *i. e.*, in the place of others, and for their sakes, it *demonstrates* also that the atonement was *general,* and had, in itself considered, no limitation, and no particular reference to any class or condition of men ; and no particular applicability to one class more than to another. There was nothing in the *nature* of the atonement that limited it to any one class or condition ; there was nothing in the design that made it, in itself, any more applicable to one portion of mankind than to another. And whatever may be true in regard to *the fact* as to its actual applicability, or in regard to *the purpose of God* to apply it, it is demonstrated by this passage that his death had an original applicability to all, and that the merits of that death were sufficient to save all. The argument in favour of the general atonement, from this passage, consists in the following points. (1.) That Paul *assumes* this as a matter that was well known, indisputable, and universally admitted, that Christ died for all. He did not deem it necessary to enter into the argument to prove it, nor even to *state* it formally. It was so well known, and so universally admitted, that he made it a *first principle* — an elementary position — a maxim on which to base another important doctrine—to wit, that all were dead. It was a point which he assumed that no one would call in question ; a doctrine which might be laid down as the *basis* of an argument, like one of the first principles or maxims in science. (2.) It is the plain and obvious meaning of the expression—the sense which strikes *all* men, unless they have some theory to support to the contrary ; and it requires all the ingenuity which men can ever command to make it appear even *plausible,* that this is consistent with the doctrine of a limited atonement ; much more to make it out that it does not mean all. If a man is told that *all* the human family must die, the obvious interpretation is, that it applies to every individual. If told that all the passengers on board a steamboat were drowned, the obvious interpretation is, that every individual was meant. If told that a ship was wrecked, and that all the crew perished, the obvious interpretation would be that none escaped. If told that *all* the inmates of an hospital were sick, it would be understood that there was not an individual that was not sick. Such is the view which would be taken by nine hundred and ninety-nine persons out of a thousand, if told that Christ died for all ; nor could they conceive how this could be consistent with the statement that he died only for the elect, and that the elect was only a small part of the human family. (3.) This interpretation is in accordance with all the *explicit* declarations on the design of the death of the Redeemer. Heb. ii. 9, "That he, by the grace of God, should taste death for every man ;" comp. John iii. 16, "God so loved the world that he gave his only begotten Son, that *whosoever* believeth on him should not perish, but have everlasting life." 1 Tim. ii. 16, "Who gave himself a ransom for all." See Matt. xx. 28, "The Son of man came to give his life a ransom for many." 1 John ii. 2, "And he is the propitiation for our sins, and not for ours only, but also for the sins of the whole world." (4.) The fact also that on the ground of the atonement made by the Redeemer, salvation is offered to all men *by God*, is a proof that he died for all. The apostles were directed to go "into all the world and to preach the gospel *to every creature*," with the assurance that "he that believeth and is baptized shall be saved;" Mark xvi. 15, 16; and everywhere in the Bible the most full and free offers of salvation are made to all mankind; comp. Isa. lv. 1; John vii. 37; Rev. xxii. 17. These offers are made on the ground that the Lord Jesus died for men; John iii. 16. They are offers of salvation through the gospel, of the pardon of sin, and of eternal life to be made "to every creature." But if Christ died only for a part, if there is a large portion of the human family for whom he died in no sense whatever; if there is no provision of any kind made for them, then God must know this, and then the offers cannot be made with sincerity, and God is tantalising them with the offers of that which does not exist, and which he knows does not exist. It is of no use here to say that the preacher does not know who the elect are, and that he is obliged to make the offer to all in order that the elect may be reached. For it is not the preacher only who offers the gospel. It is God who does it, and he knows who the elect are, and yet *he* offers salvation to all. And if there is no salvation provided for all, and no possibility that all to whom the offer comes should be saved, then God is insincere; and there is no way possible of vindicating his character. (5.) If this interpretation is not correct, and if Christ did not die for all, then the argument of Paul here is a *non sequitur*, and is worthless. The demonstration that all are dead, according to him is, that Christ died for all. But suppose that he meant, or that he knew, that Christ died only for a part, for the elect, then how would the argument stand, and what would be its force? "Christ died only for a portion of the human race, *therefore* ALL are sinners. Medicine is provided only for a part of mankind, therefore all are sick. Pardon is offered to part only, therefore all are guilty." But Paul never reasoned in this way. He believed that Christ died for all mankind, and on the ground of that he inferred at once that all needed such an atonement; that all were sinners, and that all were exposed to the wrath of God. And the argument is in this way, and in this way only, sound. But still it may be asked, What *is* the force of this argument? How does the fact that Christ died for all, prove that all were sinners, or dead in sin?—I answer, (*a*) In the same way that to provide medicine for all, proves that all are sick, or liable to be sick; and to offer pardon to all who are in a prison, proves that all there are guilty. What insult is it to offer medicine to a man in health; or pardon to a man who has violated no law! And there would be the same insult in offering salvation to a man who was not a sinner, and who did not need forgiveness. (*b*) The dignity of the sufferer, and the extent of his sufferings, prove that all were under a deep and dreadful load of guilt. Such a being would not have come to die unless *the race* had been apostate; nor would he have endured so great sorrows unless a deep and dreadful malady had spread over the world. The deep anxiety; the tears; the toils; the sufferings, and the groans of the Redeemer, show what was *his* sense of the condition of man, and prove that *he* regarded them as degraded, fallen, and lost. And if the Son of God, who knows all hearts, regarded them as lost, they *are* lost. He was not mistaken in regard to the character of man, and he did not lay down his life under the influence of delusion and error. If to the view which has been taken of this important passage it be objected that the work of the atonement must have been to a large extent in vain; that it has actually been applied to but comparatively a small portion of the human family, and that it is unreasonable to suppose that God would suffer so great sorrows to be endured for naught, we may reply, (1.) That it may not have been in vain, though it may have been rejected by a large portion of mankind. There may have been other purposes accomplished by it besides the direct salvation of men. It was doing much when it rendered it consistent for God to offer salvation to all; it is much that God could be seen to be just and yet pardoning the sinner; it was much when his determined hatred of sin, and his purpose to honour his law, was evinced; and in regard to the benevolence and justice of God to other beings and to other worlds, much, very much was gained, though all the human race had rejected the plan and been lost, and in regard to *all* these objects, the plan was not in vain, and the sufferings of the Redeemer were not for naught. But, (2.) It is in accordance with what we see everywhere, when much that God does seems to our eyes, though not to his, to be in vain. How much rain falls on ever sterile sands or on barren rocks, to our eyes in vain! What floods of light are poured each day on barren wastes, or untraversed oceans, to our eyes in vain! How many flowers shed forth their fragrance in the wilderness, and 'waste their sweetness on the desert air," to us apparently for naught! How many pearls lie useless in the ocean; how much gold and silver in the earth; how many diamonds amidst rocks to us unknown, and apparently in vain! How many lofty trees rear their heads in the untraversed wilderness, and after standing for centuries fall on the earth and decay, to our eyes in vain! And how much *medicinal virtue* is created by God each year in the vegetable world that is unknown to man, and that decays and is lost without removing any disease, and that seems to be created in vain! And how long has it been before the most valuable medicines have been found out, and applied to alleviating pain, or removing disease! Year after year, and age after age, they existed in a suffering world, and men died perhaps within a few yards of the medicine which would have relieved or saved them, but it was unknown, or if known disregarded. But times were coming when their value would be appreciated, and when they would be applied to benefit the sufferer. So with the plan of salvation. It may be rejected, and the sufferings of the Redeemer may seem to have been for naught. But they will yet be of value to mankind; and when the time shall come for the whole world to embrace the Saviour, there will be found no want of sufficiency in the plan of redemption, and in the merits of the Redeemer to save all the race.

[A measure of truth is, doubtless, involved in this controversy concerning the universality of atonement; and the discussion of the subject in America, and more recently in this country, cannot fail ultimately to produce the most beneficial results. Yet we must express our conviction, that the seeming difference of opinion among evangelical men, has arisen from mutual misunderstanding, and that misunderstanding from the use of ambiguous phraseology. One says, Christ died for all men. No, says another, for the elect only. The dispute goes on and on, till at last the discovery is made, that while the same words were used by the disputants, each attached his own meaning to them. This ambiguity is painfully felt in the treatise of a distinguished writer, who has recently appeared on the limited side of the question. He does not explain, till he has advanced very far in the discussion, what sense he attaches to the common phraseology of "Christ dying for all men." He tells us afterwards, however, that he understands it in the highest sense of securing salvation for them; when we are convinced, that much of the argument might have been spared, or at all events better directed, than against a position which few or none maintain. The author is himself sensible of this. "The question," says he, "might, perhaps, have been settled at the outset by a careful definition of terms; but I have purposely deferred doing so, judging, that it might be done with better effect as the discussion proceeded. In speaking of the Saviour's dying for men, or dying for sinners, I have u ed the expression in what I conceive to be the strict and proper meaning, viz. as signifying his dying with an *intention* to save them. This, however, is not the only meaning the expression will bear.

For all men, for sinners in general, the Saviour died. He died in their *nature*, he died in their *stead*, he died doing honour to the law which they had violated; in other words, he died removing every legal obstruction that lay in the way of their obtaining life."—*The Death of Christ the Redemption of his People*, p. 70. Now, it is only in this last sense, that any rational advocate of general aspect in the atonement will maintain that Christ died for all men. Nor could he desire better language in which to express his views, than that which is furnished in the above quotation. That the atonement has certain general aspects is now nearly admitted on all hands. "General it must be in some sense," says the author already quoted, "if in some sense it be applicable to all, and that this is the case the foregoing statement undeniably proves," p. 68. The general aspect of the atonement is argued, from those well-known passages in which it is declared to have a reference to men, all men, the world, and the whole world. The reader will find some of these passages quoted above in the commentary. Of this universal phraseology various explanations have been given. Some have supplied the qualifying adjective "elect" in these places, where the design of atonement is said to embrace the "world." Modern writers of the highest name, however, and on both sides of the question, have vied with each other in their indignant repudiation of any such expletive. "I have felt myself," says Dr. Wardlaw, "far from satisfied with a common way of interpreting some of those texts which express the extent of the atonement in universal terms by means of a convenient supplement. According to this method of explanation, the world is, in such occurrences of it, made to signify the 'elect world,' the word 'elect' being inserted as a supplement, conceived to be necessary for the consistency of scripture. An 'elect world' indeed, has become a phrase in common use with a particular class of commentators and divines; being employed with as much matter of course freedom, as if it had actually had the sanction of ordinary usage in the sacred volume; but it is not to be found there." And subjoins Dr. Marshall, writing on the limited side of the question, "It certainly is not to be found there, and with every word of this well-deserved censure I cordially agree." Here then is one principle of interpretation fairly exploded, and few nowadays will have the hardihood to espouse it. Again, the phraseology has been explained of the world of Jews and Gentiles indiscriminately, Gentiles as well as Jews; and those who adopt this view tell us, that the Jewish system was narrow and exclusive, embracing only one people, the progeny of Abraham; that it was the design of God, in the fulness of time, to enlarge his church and to receive within her ample arms men of all nations, Jew and Gentile, Barbarian and Scythian, bond and free; that the death of Christ was at once the fulfilment and abrogation of the typical system with all its peculiar and exclusive rites; that by it the middle wall of partition between the Jew and the rest of the world was thrown down; that, therefore, it was natural to represent it as having a reference to all men and to the world, even when absolute universality was not and could not be intended. Such a vast enlargement of the scale on which spiritual blessings were now to be conferred, in consequence of the death of Christ, could not well have been expressed, it is alleged, in any other or in less universal terms. *See this view of the subject well exhibited in Hill's System*, vol. ii. chap. v. 3d. edit.

To this principle of interpretation we have no great objection. There is doubtless much truth in it. It lends valuable assistance in the investigation of many passages. But is there not some sense in which that atonement has an aspect absolutely to all, and every man? As much we have seen admitted above. Now, if the Saviour "died in the nature and stead of all, removing every legal obstruction that lay in the way of their obtaining life," how comes it to pass, that this universal aspect cannot be found in any of those confessedly the most universal passages in the Bible? If it be true, it must be found somewhere in the scriptures, and nowhere so likely, as in this class of texts; and the language, moreover, is just such as is naturally fitted to express this sense. While then we allow, that the phraseology in question may be in part explained by the admission of Gentiles as well as Jews into the kingdom of God; we maintain at the same time, that there is nothing in it which prevents us from including *all* in each of those divisions of mankind. Nay, if the apostles had wished to express this idea, how otherwise could they have done it? "Say if you will," says Dr. Wardlaw, commenting on John iii. 16, 17, "that the 'world' means Jews and Gentiles, still if it is not any definite number of Jews and Gentiles, it is Jews and Gentiles as together composing the world of mankind."

That the atonement, indeed, has a certain benign aspect towards all men, appears from its very nature. The exact equivalent view, as it has been not inappropriately termed, is now nearly abandoned. Rarely do we find any one affirming, that Christ endured exactly what the elect would have suffered and deserved, and that, therefore, there can be sufficiency in his death for that favoured number and for none besides. What then is the light in which the atonement of Christ ought to be viewed? We think the only rational and scriptural account of it, is that which regards it as a great remedial scheme, which rendered it consistent with the divine honour and all the interests of the divine administration, to extend mercy to *guilty men at large*, and which would have been equally requisite, had there been an intention to save one only, or millions; numbers indeed not forming any part of the question. Here then is something done, which removes legal obstructions and thereby opens the way to heaven for all. And if any do not enter in, their inability is moral, and lies not in any insufficiency of the divine provision. This view, however, seems to furnish a just foundation for the universality of gospel invitations, while it fastens the guilt of rejecting gospel provision on the sinner himself.

Thus far we feel disposed to agree with our author in his commentary, or rather dissertation on the verse and the subject it involves. We maintain, however, that the atonement has a *special* as well as a *general* aspect; that while it is gloriously true that it looks to all men, it has at the same time a special regard to some. We object, therefore, to the statement, "that the atonement in itself considered had no limitation and no particular reference to any class or condition of men, and no particular applicability to one class more than to another." This is similar to certain rash assertions that have recently been current in our own country; as that "while the atonement opens the door of mercy to all, it secures salvation to none;" that "Christ died as much for those who perish, as for those who are saved." We cannot envy that reputation for acuteness which may be gained by the free use of such language. Is it not God's design to save his people? Is not the atonement the means by which he does so, the means by which the purpose of electing love is fulfilled? And yet has that atonement no special reference to the elect? Further, if it be the means of saving *them*, does it not *secure* their salvation? Certainly, amongst men, if any effectual means were devised to accomplish a particular end, that end would be said to be secured by such means. The writer is aware of the ingenious evasion, that it is God's gracious purpose to apply the atonement, and not the atonement itself, that connects it with the elect, and secures their salvation. We are told, moreover, that we should look on the atonement by itself, and consider it in a philosophical way. The purpose to apply is an after arrangement. But *first*, a purpose to apply the atonement to a special class, differs in nothing from an original design to save such class by it, for that purpose must have been present to the mind of God in determining on atonement. To say that God saves a certain number by the atonement, and that yet in making it he had no special design in their favour, however it may recommend itself to philosophical refinement, will always be rejected by the common sense of mankind. *Second*. If we must consider the atonement apart from any special purpose connected with it, why not divest it also of any general purpose, that we may look on it steadily *per se*, and in this way reduce it to a mere abstraction, about which nothing could be either affirmed or denied?

The advocates of universal atonement, or some of the more forward among them, have recently carried out their views so far, as to deny that God in providing the atonement, or Christ in making it, had any special *love* to the elect. An eminent writer on that side, however, to whom reference has already been made, while he goes the length of denying special *design*, maintains the existence of special *love*, and administers a reproof to those of his own party, who go to this extreme. This is indeed an important concession, for *special love* is not very different from *special design*, nor is it easy to see how, in the mind of God, the one could subsist without the other. "The love of the Father is the same thing as election. Election is nothing but the love of the Father formed into a purpose."—*Marshall.* Or the point may be put in this way. Had God in providing the atonement special love to the elect? Where is the proof of it? Doubtless in that very provision. But if God in making it had no *design* to save them by it, the proof is not only weakened but destroyed. Special love, therefore, necessarily involves special design.

To do away with any thing like speciality of design, much has been said on the order of the divine decrees, especially as to whether the decree of atonement, or that of election, be first in order of nature. If that of atonement be first, it is asserted speciality is out of the question, as that is secured only by election, which is a posterior arrangement. On this subject it is more easy to darken counsel by words without knowledge, than to speak intelligibly. It may be fairly questioned, if those who have written most on it, fully understand themselves. Nor can we help lamenting, that so great a part of the controversy should have been made to turn on this point, which has hitherto eluded the grasp of the most profound, and drawn the controvertists into regions of thought, too high for the boldest flights of human intellect. After all that can be said on the subject, it must be allowed that the whole arrangement connected with the salvation of man, existed *simultaneously* in the mind of God, nor will any one rise much wiser from inquiries into which was first and which last.

The truth on the whole subject, then, seems to be, that while the atonement has a general reference towards all, it has at the same time a special reference to the elect of God, or as it is well expressed in a recent synodical decision, "The Saviour in making the atonement, bore special covenant relation to the elect; had a special love to them, and infallibly secured their everlasting salvation, whilst his obedience unto death, afforded such a satisfaction to the justice of God, as that on the ground of it, in consistency with his character and law, the door of mercy is open to all men, and a full and free salvation is presented for their acceptance." The special aspect, indeed, ought no more to be denied than the general. It rests on a large number of what may be called *special* texts; as, "Christ also loved *the Church* and gave himself for it, that he might sanctify and cleanse it," &c. "For the transgression of *my people* was he stricken." "I lay down my life for *the sheep*," Eph. v. 25; Isa. liii. 8; John x. 15. Nor will it do to say of this numerous class of passages, that they find a sufficient explanation in the purpose of application, which is connected with the remedy for sin, since most of them are of a kind that connect the salvation of the elect *directly with the atonement itself*, and not with any after design of applying it. This idea seems but an ingenious shift to sustain a favourite theory. How direct, for example, is this connection in the following passage: "who loved me and gave himself for me." No one who had not a theory to support, would ever think of introducing an after design of application to explain this. Indeed, as an able reviewer in one of our periodicals observes of the scheme that excludes a special design, "it separates too much the atonement from the salvation of man. It does not connect those that are saved, those that are regenerated by divine grace, at all specially with the sacrifice of Christ." Another important branch of evidence on this point, lies in the special relation which Christ in dying sustained towards his people, as that of shepherd, husband, surety, &c., and which cannot be explained on any other principle than that of special design.

If the question were put, how we preserve our consistency, in thus maintaining both the general and special view, we reply, first, that if *both* views are found in scripture, it matters not whether we can explain the consistency between them or no. But second, it is not so difficult as some would imagine, to conceive of God appointing a remedy with a general aspect towards the race, but specially intended to secure the salvation of his chosen people.]

¶ *Then were all dead.* All dead in sin; that is, all were sinners. The fact that he died for all proves that all were transgressors. The word "dead" is not unfrequently used in the scriptures to denote the condition of sinners; see Eph. ii. 1. It means not that sinners are in *all* senses, and in all respects like a lifeless corpse, for they are not. They are still moral agents, and have a conscience, and are capable of thinking, and speaking, and acting. It does not mean that they have no more power than one in the grave, for they *have* more power. But it means that there is a striking similarity, in some respects, between one who is dead and a sinner. That similarity does not extend to every thing, but in many respects it is very striking. (1.) The sinner is as insensible to the glories of the heavenly world, and the appeals of the gospel, as a corpse is to what is going on around or above it. The body that lies in the grave is insensible to the voice of friendship, and the charms of music, and the hum of business, and the plans of gain and ambition; and so the sinner is insensible to all the glories of the heavenly world, and to all the appeals that are made to him, and to all the warnings of God. He lives as though there were no heaven and no hell; no God and no Saviour. (2.) There is need of the same divine power to convert a sinner which is needful to raise up the dead. The same cause does not exist, making the existence of that power necessary, but it *is a fact* that a sinner *will* no more be converted by his own power than a dead man will rise from the grave by his own power. No man ever yet was converted without direct divine agency, any more than Lazarus was raised without divine agency. And there is no more just or melancholy description which can be given of man, than to say that he is *dead in sins.* He is insensible to all the appeals that God makes to him; he is insensible to all the sufferings of the Saviour, and to all the glories of heaven; he lives as though these did not exist, or as though he had no concern in them; his eyes see no more beauty in them than the sightless eyeballs of the dead do in the material world; his ear is as inattentive to the calls of God and the gospel as the ear of the dead is to the voice of friendship or the charms of melody; and in a world that is full of God, and that might be full of hope, he is living without God and without hope.

15 And *that* he died for all, that [a] they which live should not henceforth live unto themselves, but unto him which died for them, and rose again.

16 Wherefore henceforth know

a 1 Cor. 6. 19, 20.

15. *And* that *he died for all*, &c. This verse is designed still further to explain the reasons of the conduct of the apostle. He had not lived for himself. He had not lived to amass wealth, or to enjoy pleasure, or to obtain a reputation. He had lived a life of self-denial, and of toil; and he here states the reason why he had done it. It was because he felt that the great purpose of the death of the Redeemer was to secure this result. To that Saviour, therefore, who died for all, he consecrated his talents and his time, and sought in every way possible to promote *his* glory. ¶ *That they which live.* They who are true Christians, who are made alive unto God as the result of the dying love of the Redeemer. Sinners are dead in sins. Christians are alive to the worth of the soul, the presence of God, the importance of religion, the solemnities of eternity; *i. e.* they act and feel as if these things had a real existence, and as if they should exert a constant influence upon the heart and life.

["*They which live.*" This spiritual life, doubtless, implies that a man is alive to the worth of the soul, the presence of God, &c.; but it intimates something deeper too, which is the *foundation* of those things, and without which they could not exist. Scott paraphrases thus, "were *quickened* and pardoned, and so passed from death to life;" and Guyse still more explicitly, "were made supernaturally alive by his quickening spirit and by faith in him." *This* is the root; the things mentioned in the comment, the fruit; this the cause, these only the effects.]

It is observable that Paul makes a distinction here between those for whom Christ died and those who actually "live," thus demonstrating that there may be many for whom he died who do not live to God, or who are not savingly benefited by his death. The atonement was for all, but only a part are actually made alive to God. Multitudes reject it; but the fact that he died for all; that he tasted death for every man, that he not only died for the elect but for all others, that his benevolence was so great as to embrace the whole human family in the design of his death, is a reason why they who are actually made alive to God should consecrate themselves entirely to his service. The fact that he died for all evinced such unbounded and infinite benevolence that it should induce us who are actually benefited by his death, and who have any just views of it, to devote all that we have to his service. ¶ *Should not henceforth live unto ourselves.* Should not seek our own ease and pleasure; should not make it our great object to promote our own interest, but should make it the grand purpose of our lives to promote *his* honour, and to advance *his* cause. This is a vital principle in religion, and it is exceedingly important to know what is meant by living to ourselves, and whether we do it. It is done in the following, and perhaps in some other ways. (1.) When men seek pleasure, gain, or reputation as the controlling principle of their lives. (2.) When they are regardless of the *rights* of others, and sacrifice all the claims which others have on them in order to secure the advancement of their own purposes and ends. (3.) When they are regardless of the *wants* of others, and turn a deaf ear to all the appeals which charity makes to them, and have no time to give to serve them, and no money to spare to alleviate their wants; and especially when they turn a deaf ear to the appeals which are made for the diffusion of the gospel to the benighted and perishing. (4.) When their main purpose is the aggrandizement of their own families, for their families are but a diffusion of self. And, (5.) When they seek their own salvation only from selfish motives, and not from a desire to honour God. Multitudes are selfish even in their religion; and the main purpose which they have in view, is to promote their own objects, and not the honour of the Master whom they profess to serve. They seek and profess religion only because they desire to escape from wrath, and to obtain the happiness of heaven, and not from any love to the Redeemer or any desire to honour him. Or they seek to build up the interests of their own church and party, and all their zeal is expended on that and that alone, without any real desire to honour the Saviour. Or though *in* the church, they are still selfish, and live wholly to themselves. They live for fashion, for gain, for reputation. They practice no self-denial; they make no effort to advance the cause of God the Saviour. ¶ *But unto him,* &c. Unto the Lord Jesus Christ. To live to him is the opposite to living unto ourselves. It is to seek his honour; to feel that we belong to him; that all our time and talents; all our strength of intellect and body; all the avails of our skill and toil, all belong to him, and should be employed in his service. If we have talents by which we can influence other minds, they should be employed to honour the Saviour. If we have skill, or strength to labour by which we can make money, we should feel that it all belongs to him, and should be employed in his service. If we have property, we should feel that it is his, and that he has a claim upon it all, and that it should be honestly consecrated to his cause. And if we are endowed with a spirit of enterprise, and are fitted by nature to encounter perils in distant and barbarious climes, as Paul was, we should feel like him that we are bound to devote all entirely to his service, and to the promotion of his cause. A servant, a slave, does not live to himself but to his master. His person, his time, his limbs, his talents, and the avails of his industry are not regarded as his own. He is judged incapable of holding any property which is not at the disposal of his master. If he has strength, it is his master's. If he has skill, the avails of it are his master's. If he is an ingenious mechanic, or labours in any department; if he is amiable, kind, gentle, and faithful, and adapted to be useful in an eminent degree, it is regarded as all the property of his master. He is bound to go where his master chooses; to execute the task which he assigns; to deny himself at his master's will; and to come and lay the avails of all his toil and skill at his master's feet. He is regarded as having been purchased with money; and the purchase money is supposed to give a right to his time, his talents, his services, and his soul. Such as the slave is supposed to become by purchase, and by the operation of human laws, the Christian becomes by the purchase of the Son of God, and by the voluntary recognition of him as the master, and as having a right to all that we have and are. To him all belongs; and all should be employed in endeavouring to promote his glory, and in advancing his cause. ¶ *Which died for them, and rose again.* Paul here states the grounds of the obligation under which he felt himself placed, to live not unto himself but unto Christ. (1.) The first is, the fact that Christ had *died* for him, and for all his people. The effect of that death was the same as a purchase. It *was* a purchase; see Note, 1 Cor. vi. 20; vii. 23; comp. 1 Pet. i. 18, 19. (2.) The second is, that he had risen again from the dead. To this fact Paul traced all his hopes of eternal life, and of the resurrection from the dead; see Rom. iv. 25. As we have the hope of the resurrection from the dead only from the fact that he rose; as he has "brought life and immortality to light," and hath in this way "abolished death" (2 Tim. i. 10); as all the prospect of entering a world where there is no death and no grave is to be traced to the resurrection of the Saviour, so we are bound by every obligation of gratitude to devote ourselves without any reserve to him. To him, and him alone should we live; and in his cause our lives should be, as Paul's was, a living sacrifice, holy and acceptable in his sight.

16. *Wherefore henceforth.* In view of the fact that the Lord Jesus died for all men, and rose again. The effect of that has been to change all our feelings, and to give us entirely new views of men, of ourselves, and of

we no man after the flesh: yea, though we have known Christ after the flesh, yet now henceforth know we *him* no more.

---

the Messiah, so that we have become new creatures. The word "henceforth" (ἀπὸ τοῦ νῦν) means properly from the present time; but there is no impropriety in supposing that Paul refers to the time when he first obtained correct views of the Messiah, and that he means from that time. His mind seems to have been thrown back to the period when these new views burst upon his soul; and the sentiment is, that from the time when he obtained those new views, he had resolved to know no one after the flesh. ¶ *Know we no man.* The word *know* here (οἴδαμεν) is used in the sense of, we form our estimate of; we judge; we are influenced by. Our estimate of man is formed by other views than according to the flesh. ¶ *According to the flesh.* A great many different interpretations have been proposed of this expression, which it is not needful here to repeat. The meaning is, probably, that in his estimate of men he was not influenced by the views which are taken by those who are unrenewed, and who are unacquainted with the truths of redemption. It may include a great many things, and perhaps the following. (1.) He was not influenced in his estimate of men by a regard to their birth, or country. He did not form an attachment to a Jew because he was a Jew, or to a Gentile because he was a Gentile. He had learned that Christ died for all, and he felt disposed to regard all alike. (2.) He was not influenced in his estimate of men by their rank, and wealth, and office. Before his conversion he had been, but now he learned to look on their moral character, and to regard that as making the only permanent, and really important distinction among men. He did not esteem one man highly because he was of elevated rank, or of great wealth, and another less because he was of a different rank in life. (3.) It may also include the idea, that he had left his own kindred and friends on account of superior attachment to Christ. He had parted from them to preach the gospel. He was not restrained by their opinions; he was not kept from going from land to land by love to them. It is probable that they remained Jews. It may be, that they were opposed to him, and to his efforts in the cause of the Redeemer. It may be that they would have dismissed him from a work so self-denying, and so arduous, and where he would be exposed to so much persecution and contempt. It may be that they would have set before him the advantages of his birth and education; would have reminded him of his early brilliant prospects; and would have used all the means possible to dissuade him from embarking in a cause like that in which he was engaged. The passage here means that Paul was influenced by none of these considerations. In early life he had been. He had prided himself on rank, and on talent. He was proud of his own advantages as a Jew; and he estimated worth by rank, and by national distinction, Phil. iii. 4—6. He had despised Christians on account of their being the followers of the man of Nazareth; and there can be no reason to doubt that he partook of the common feelings of his countrymen and held in contempt the whole Gentile world. But his views were changed—so much changed as to make it proper to say that he was a new creature, ver. 17. When converted, he did not confer with flesh and blood (Gal. i. 16); and in the school of Christ, he had learned that if a man was his disciple, he must be willing to forsake father and mother, and sister and brother, and to hate his own life that he might honour him, Luke xiv. 26. He had formed his principle of action now from a higher standard than any regard to rank, or wealth, or national distinction; and had risen above them all, and now estimated men not by these external and factitious advantages, but by a reference to their personal character and moral worth. ¶ *Yea, though we have known Christ after the flesh.*

Though in common with the Jewish nation we expected a Messiah who would be a temporal prince, and who would be distinguished for the distinctions which are valued among men, yet we have changed our estimate of him, and judge of him in this way no longer. There can be no doubt that Paul, in common with his countrymen, had expected a Messiah who would be a magnificent temporal prince and conqueror, one who they supposed would be a worthy successor of David and Solomon. The coming of such a prince, Paul had confidently expected. He expected no other Messiah. He had fixed his hopes on that. This is what is meant by the expression 'to know Christ after the flesh.' It does not mean that he had seen him *in* the flesh, but that he had formed, so to speak, carnal views of him, and such as men of this world regard as grand and magnificent in a monarch and conqueror. He had had no correct views of his spiritual character, and of the pure and holy purposes for which he would come into the world. ¶ *Yet now henceforth know we him no more.* We know him no more in this manner. Our conceptions and views of him are changed. We no more regard him according to the flesh; we no longer esteem the Messiah who was to come as a temporal prince and warrior; but we look on him as a spiritual Saviour, a Redeemer from sin. The idea is, that his views of him had been entirely changed. It does not mean, as our translation would seem to imply, that Paul would have no further acquaintance with Christ, but it means that from the moment of his conversion he had laid aside all his views of his being a temporal sovereign, and all his feelings that he was to be honoured only because he supposed that he would have an elevated rank among the monarchs of the earth Locke and Macknight, it seems to me, have strangely mistaken this passage. The former renders it, "For if I myself have gloried in this, that Christ was himself circumcised as I am, and was of my blood and nation, I do so now no more any longer." The same substantially is the view of Macknight. Clarke as strangely mistakes it, when he says that it means that Paul could not prize now a man who was a sinner because he was allied to the royal family of David, nor prize a man because he had seen Christ in the flesh. The correct view, as it seems to me, is given above. And the *doctrine* which is taught here is, that at conversion, the views are essentially changed, and that the converted man has a view of the Saviour entirely different from what he had before. He may not, like Paul, have regarded him as a temporal prince; he may not have looked to him as a mighty monarch, but his views in regard to his person, character, work, and loveliness will be entirely changed. He will see a beauty in his character which he never saw before. Before, he regarded him as a root out of dry ground; as the despised man of Nazareth; as having nothing in his character to be desired, or to render him lovely (Isa. liii); but at conversion the views are changed. He is seen to be the chief among ten thousand and altogether lovely; as pure, and holy, and benevolent; as mighty, and great, and glorious; as infinitely benevolent; as lovely in his precepts, lovely in his life, lovely in his death, lovely in his resurrection, and as most glorious as he is seated on the right hand of God. He is seen to be a Saviour exactly adapted to the condition and wants of the soul; and the soul yields itself to him to be redeemed by him alone. There is no change of view so marked and decided as that of the sinner in regard to the Lord Jesus Christ at his conversion; and it is a clear proof that we have never been born again if our views in reference to him have never undergone any change. "What think ye of Christ?" is a question the answer to which will determine any man's character, and demonstrate whether he is or is not a child of God. Tindal has more correctly expressed the sense of this than our translation. "Though we have known Christ after the flesh, now henceforth know we him so no more."

17 Therefore if any man *be* in Christ, *he is* [1] a new [a] creature: old things are passed away; behold, [b] all things are become new.

1 *let him be.* a John. 3. 3; Gal. 6. 15. b Is. 65. 17; Re. 21. 5.

17. *Therefore if any man* be *in Christ.* The phrase to "be *in* Christ," evidently means to be united to Christ by faith; or to be in him as the branch is in the vine—that is, so united to the vine, or so in it, as to derive all its nourishment and support from it, and to be sustained entirely by it. John xv. 2, "Every branch *in* me." ver. 4, "Abide *in* me, and I in you." "The branch cannot bear fruit of itself except it abide *in* the vine; no more can ye except ye abide *in* me." See also ver. 5—7, see Note on John xv. 2. To be "in Christ" denotes a more tender and close union; and implies that all our support is from him. All our strength is derived from him; and denotes further that we shall partake of his fulness, and share in his felicity and glory, as the branch partakes of the strength and vigour of the parent vine. The word "therefore" (Ὥστε) here implies that the reason why Paul infers that any one is a new creature who is in Christ is that which is stated in the previous verse; to wit, the change of views in regard to the Redeemer to which he there refers, and which was so great as to constitute a change like a new creation. The affirmation here is universal, "if any man be in Christ;" that is, all who become true Christians—undergo such a change in their views and feelings as to make it proper to say of them that they are new creatures. No matter what they have been before, whether moral or immoral; whether infidels or speculative believers; whether amiable, or debased, sensual and polluted, yet if they become Christians they all experience such a change as to make it proper to say they are a new creation. ¶ *A new creature.* Marg. "Let him be." This is one of the instances in which the margin has given a less correct translation than is in the text. The idea evidently is, not that he *ought* to be a new creature, but that he is in fact; not that he *ought* to live as becomes a new creature—which is true enough—but that he will in fact live in that way, and manifest the characteristics of the new creation. The phrase "a new creature" (καινὴ κτίσις) occurs also in Gal. vi. 15. The word rendered "creature" (κτίσις) means properly in the New Testament, *creation.* It denotes, (1.) The act of creating (Rom. i. 20); (2.) A created thing, a creature (Rom. i. 25); and refers (*a*) To the universe, or creation in general; Mark x. 6; xiii 9—11; 1 Pet. iii. 4. (*b*) To man, mankind; Mark xvi. 15; Col. i. 23. Here it means a new creation in a moral sense, and the phrase new creature is equivalent to the expression in Eph. iv. 24, "The new man, which after God is created in righteousness and true holiness." It means, evidently, that there is a change produced in the renewed heart of man that is equivalent to the act of creation, and that bears a strong resemblance to it—a change, so to speak, as if the man was made over again, and had become new. The mode or manner in which it is done is not described, nor should the words be pressed to the quick, as if the process were the same in both cases—for the words are here evidently figurative. But the phrase implies evidently the following things. (1.) That there is an exertion of divine power in the conversion of the sinner as really as in the act of creating the world out of nothing, and that this is as indispensable in the one case as in the other. (2.) That a change is produced so great as to make it proper to say that he is a new man. He has new views, new motives, new principles, new objects and plans of life. He seeks new purposes, and he lives for new ends. If a drunkard becomes reformed, there is no impropriety in saying that he is a new man. If a man who was licentious becomes pure, there is no impropriety in saying that he is not the same man that he was

18 And all things *are* of God, who hath reconciled [a] us to himself by Jesus Christ, and hath given to us the ministry of reconciliation;

[a] Col. 1. 20.

before. Such expressions are common in all languages, and they are as proper as they are common. There *is* such a change as to make the language proper. And so in the conversion of a sinner. There *is* a change so deep, so clear, so entire, and so abiding, that it is proper to say, here is a new creation of God—a work of the divine power as decided and as glorious as when God created all things out of nothing. There is no other moral change that takes place on earth so deep, and radical, and thorough as the change at conversion. And there is no other where there is so much propriety in ascribing it to the mighty power of God. ¶ *Old things are passed away.* The old views in regard to the Messiah, and in regard to men in general, ver. 16. But Paul also gives this a general form of expression, and says that old things in general have passed away—referring to every thing. It was true of all who were converted that old things had passed away. And it may include the following things. (1.) In regard to the Jews—that their former prejudices against Christianity, their natural pride, and spirit of seducing others; their attachment to their rites and ceremonies, and dependence on them for salvation had all passed away. They now renounced that independence, relied on the merits of the Saviour, and embraced all as brethren who were of the family of Christ. (2.) In regard to the Gentiles—their attachment to idols, their love of sin and degradation, their dependence on their own works, had passed away, and they had renounced all these things, and had come to mingle their hopes with those of the converted Jews, and with all who were the friends of the Redeemer. (3.) In regard to all, it is also true that old things pass away. Their former prejudices, opinions, habits, attachments pass away. Their supreme love of self passes away. Their love of sins passes away. Their love of the world passes away. Their supreme attachment to their earthly friends rather than God passes away. Their love of sin, their sensuality, pride, vanity, levity, ambition, passes away. There is a deep and radical change on all these subjects,—a change which *commences* at the new birth; which is *carried on* by progressive sanctification; and which is *consummated* at death and in heaven. ¶ *Behold, all things are become new.* That is, all things in view of the mind. The purposes of life, the feelings of the heart, the principles of action, all become new. The understanding is consecrated to new objects, the body is employed in new service, the heart forms new attachments. Nothing can be more strikingly descriptive of the facts in conversion than this; nothing more entirely accords with the feelings of the new-born soul. All is new. There are new views of God, and of Jesus Christ; new views of this world and of the world to come; new views of truth and of duty; and every thing is seen in a new aspect and with new feelings. Nothing is more common in young converts than such feelings, and nothing is more common than for them to say that all things are new. The Bible seems to be a new book, and though they may have often read it before, yet there is a beauty about it which they never saw before, and which they wonder they have not before perceived. The whole face of nature seems to them to be changed, and they seem to be in a new world. The hills, and vales, and streams; the sun, the stars, the groves, the forests, seem to be new. A new beauty is spread over them all; and they now see them to be the work of God, and his glory is spread over them all, and they can *now* say,

"My Father made them all."

The heavens and the earth are filled with new wonders, and all things seem now to speak forth the praise of God. Even the very countenances of friends seem to be new; and there are new feelings towards all men; a new kind of love to kindred and friends; and a love before unfelt for enemies; and a new love for all mankind.

18. *And all things* are *of God.* This refers particularly to the things in question, the renewing of the heart, and the influences by which Paul had been brought to a state of willingness to forsake all, and to devote his life to the self-denying labours involved in the purpose of making the Saviour known. He makes the statement *general,* however, showing his belief that not only these things were produced by God, but that *all* things were under his direction, and subject to his control. Nothing that he had done was to be traced to his own agency or power, but God was to be acknowledged everywhere. This great truth Paul never forgot; and he never suffered himself to lose sight of it. It was in his view a cardinal and glorious truth; and he kept its influence always before his mind and his heart. In the important statement which follows, therefore, about the ministry of reconciliation, he deeply feels that the whole plan, and all the success which has attended the plan, was to be traced not to his zeal, or fidelity, or skill, but to the agency of God; see Note on 1 Cor. iii. 6, 7. ¶ *Who hath reconciled us to himself.* The word *us* here includes, doubtless, all who were Christians—whether Jews or Gentiles, or whatever was their rank. They had all been brought into a state of reconciliation, or agreement with God through the Lord Jesus Christ. Before they were opposed to God. They had violated his laws. They were his enemies. But by the means of the plan of salvation they had been brought into a state of agreement, or harmony, and were united in feeling and in aim with him. Two men who have been alienated by prejudice, by passion, or by interest, are reconciled when the cause of the alienation is removed, on whichever side it may have existed, or if on both sides, and when they lay aside their enmity and become friends. Thenceforward they are agreed, and live together without alienation, heart-burnings, jealousies, and strife. So between God and man. There was a variance; there was an alienation. Man was alienated from God. He had no love for him. He disliked his government and laws. He was unwilling to be restrained. He sought his own pleasure. He was proud, vain, self-confident. He was not pleased with the character of God, or with his claims, or his plans. And in like manner, God was *displeased* with the pride, the sensuality, the rebellion, the haughtiness of man. He was displeased that his law had been violated, and that man had cast off his government. Now reconciliation could take place only when these causes of alienation should be laid aside, and when God and man should be brought to harmony; when man should lay aside his love of sin, and should be pardoned, and when, therefore, God could consistently treat him as a friend. The Greek word which is here used (καταλλάσσω) means properly to change against any thing; to exchange for any thing, for money, or for any article.—*Robinson.* In the New Testament it means to change one person towards another; that is, to reconcile *to* any one; see Note on Rom. v. 10. It conveys the idea of producing a *change,* so that one who is alienated should be brought to friendship. Of course, all the *change* which takes place must be on the part of man, for God will not change, and the purpose of the plan of reconciliation is to effect such a *change* in man as to make him *in fact* reconciled to God, and at agreement with him. There were indeed obstacles to reconciliation on the part of God, but they did not arise from any unwillingness to be reconciled; from any reluctance to treat his creature as his friend; but they arose from the fact that man had sinned, and that God was just; that such is the perfection of God that he *cannot* treat the good and evil alike; and that, therefore, if he should treat man as his friend, it was

necessary that in some proper way he should maintain the honour of his law, and show his hatred of sin, and should secure the conversion and future obedience of the offender. All this God proposed to secure by the atonement made by the Redeemer, rendering it consistent for him to exercise the benevolence of his nature, and to pardon the offender. But God is not changed. The plan of reconciliation has made no change in his character. It has not made him a different being from what he was before. There is often a mistake on this subject; and men seem to suppose that God was *originally* stern, and unmerciful, and inexorable, and that he has been *made* mild and forgiving by the atonement. But it is not so. No change has been made in God; none needed to be made; none could be made. He was *always* mild, and merciful, and good; and the gift of a Saviour and the plan of reconciliation *is just an expression of his original willingness to pardon.* When a father sees a child struggling in the stream, and in danger of drowning, the peril and the cries of the child make no *change* in the character of the father, but such was his former love for the child that he would plunge into the stream at the hazard of his own life to save him. So it is with God. Such was his original love for man, and his disposition to show mercy, that he would submit to *any* sacrifice, except that of truth and justice, in order that he might save him. Hence he sent his only Son to die—not to change his own character; not to make himself a different being from what he was, but *in order* to show his love and his readiness to forgive when it could be consistently done. "*God so loved the world* THAT he sent his only begotten Son," John iii. 16. ¶ *By Jesus Christ.* By the agency, or medium of Jesus Christ. He was the mediator to interpose in the work of reconciliation. And he was abundantly qualified for this work, and was the *only* being that has lived in this world who was qualified for it. For, (1.) He was endowed with a divine and human nature—the nature of both the parties at issue—God and man, and thus, in the language of Job, could "lay his hand upon both," Job ix. 33. (2.) He was intimately acquainted with both the parties, and knew what was needful to be done. He knew God the Father so well that he could say, "No man knoweth the Father but the Son," Mat. xi. 27. And he knew man so well that it could be said of him, he "needed not that any should testify of man, for he knew what was in man," John ii. 25. No one can be a mediator who is not acquainted with the feelings, views, desires, claims, or prejudices of both the parties at issue. (3.) He was the *friend* of both the parties. *He loved God.* No man ever doubted this, or had any reason to call it in question, and he was always desirous of *securing* all that God claimed, and of vindicating him, and he never abandoned any thing that God had a right to claim. And *he loved man.* He showed this in all his life. He sought *his* welfare in every way possible, and gave himself for him. Yet no one is qualified to act the mediator's part who is not the common friend of both the parties at issue, and who will not seek the welfare, the right, or the honour of both. (4.) He was willing to suffer any thing from either party in order to produce reconciliation. From the hand of God he was willing to endure all that he deemed to be necessary, in order to show his hatred of sin by his vicarious sufferings, and to make an atonement; and from the hand of man he was willing to endure all the reproach, and contumely, and scorn which could be possibly involved in the work of inducing man to be reconciled to God.—And, (5.) He has removed all the obstacles which existed to a reconciliation. On the part of God, he has made it consistent for him to pardon. He has made an atonement, so that God can be just while he justifies the sinner. He has maintained his truth, and justice, and secured the stability of his moral government while he admits offenders to his favour. And on the part of man, he, by the agency of his Spirit, overcomes the unwillingness of the

19 To wit, that God was in Christ, reconciling the world unto himself, not imputing their trespasses [a] unto them; and hath

a Ro. 3. 24, 25.

sinner to be reconciled, humbles his pride, shows him his sin, changes his heart, subdues his enmity against God, and secures *in fact* a harmony of feeling and purpose between God and man, so that they shall be *reconciled* for ever. ¶ *And hath given to us.* To us the apostles and our fellow-labourers. ¶ *The ministry of reconciliation.* That is, of announcing to men the nature and the conditions of this plan of being reconciled. We have been appointed to make this known, and to press its acceptation on men; see ver. 20.

19. *To wit* (Greek, Ὡς ὅτι), *namely.* This verse is designed further to state the nature of the plan of reconciliation, and of the message with which they were intrusted. It contains an abstract, or an epitome of the whole plan; and is one of those emphatic passages in which Paul compresses into a single sentence the substance of the whole plan of redemption. ¶ *That God was in Christ.* That God was *by* Christ (ἐν Χριστῷ), by means of Christ; *by* the agency, or mediatorship of Christ. Or it may mean that God was united to Christ, and manifested himself by him. So Doddridge interprets it. Christ was the mediator by means of whom God designed to accomplish the great work of reconciliation. ¶ *Reconciling the world unto himself.* The *world* here evidently means the human race generally, without distinction of nation, age, or rank. The whole world was alienated from him, and he sought to have it reconciled. This is one *incidental* proof that God designed that the plan of salvation should be adapted to all men; see Note on ver. 14. It may be observed further, that *God* sought that the world should be reconciled. Man did not seek it He had no plan for it. He did not desire it. He had no way to effect it. It was the *offended* party, not the *offending*, that sought to be reconciled; and this shows the strength of his love. It was love for enemies and alienated beings, and love evinced to them by a most earnest desire to become their friend, and to be at agreement with them; comp. Note on Rom. v. 8. Tindal renders this very accurately, "For God was in Christ, and made agreement between the world and himself, and imputed not their sins unto them." ¶ *Not imputing their trespasses.* Not reckoning their transgressions to them; that is, forgiving them, pardoning them. On the meaning of the word *impute*, see Note, Rom. iv. 3. The idea here is, that God did not charge on them with inexorable severity and stern justice their offences, but graciously provided a plan of pardon, and offered to remit their sins on the conditions of the gospel. The plan of reconciliation demonstrated that he was not *disposed* to impute their sins to them, as he might have done, and to punish them with unmitigated severity for their crimes, but was more disposed to pardon and forgive. And it may be here asked, if God was not disposed to charge with unrelenting severity *their own sins* to their account, but was rather disposed to pardon them, can we believe that he is disposed to charge on them *the sin of another?* If he does not charge on them with inexorable and unmitigated severity *their own* transgressions, will he charge on them with unrelenting severity—*or at all*—the sin of Adam? see Note on Rom. v. 19. The sentiment here is, that God is not disposed or inclined to charge the transgressions of men upon them; he has no pleasure in doing it; and *therefore* he has provided a plan by which they may be pardoned. At the same time it is true that unless their sins *are* pardoned, justice will charge or impute their sins to them, and will exact punishment to the uttermost.

[See also the supplementary Notes on Romans v. 12, 19, where the subject of imputed sin is considered at length. The argument by which the author attempts here to set aside

[1] committed unto us the word of reconciliation.

1 *put in us.*

20 Now then we are [a] ambassadors for Christ; as though God

a Job 33.23; Mal. 2.7; Eph. 6.20.

that doctrine, is not of great force. Because God "graciously provided a plan of pardon," in consequence of which he can consistently remit or not reckon transgression, he cannot be supposed to hold us guilty of Adam's sin! This is substantially the argument. We might just reverse the matter, and would then certainly argue more conclusively thus: God does impute the first sin to us, and we are guilty, moreover, of actual sin, therefore in love he has provided a plan by which he can consistently deliver us from this accumulated load of sin. The deeper our guilt, the greater the necessity for the provision. But how the providing of atonement disproves the doctrine of imputed sin, it is impossible to see. Besides the non-imputation of trespasses here spoken of, can only be applied to such as accept the provision in the gospel, and can therefore be no reason for the denial of imputed sin. Neither this nor actual sin will be charged against the believer, and the glory of Christ's work is that it delivers him from both. Mr. Scott thus interprets, "When, therefore, sinners were brought to God, as 'in Christ reconciling the world unto himself in humble faith, he no more imputed their trespasses unto them, but blotted them out by a free forgiveness." Nor can the language mean any thing else; for while by the atonement all legal obstructions are removed, sinners are still charged with guilt, till they receive it. It ought also to be noticed, that the author changes the idea in the text into a mere *disposition* on the part of God not to charge trespasses, whereas the apostle speaks of their actual non-imputation. This last certainly cannot be strictly *universal* If that be intended, there should have accompanied it some explanation of the difficulties with which such an opinion is surrounded, and of the manner in which the passage can be reconciled with other passages which speak of non-imputation of guilt, as a privilege exclusively confined to believers. If the universality of the non-imputation could be made out, there might be something like foundation for the argument against imputed sin; though *even in that case*, it would not follow, that, because God had remitted the sins of all, or determined not to reckon them, imputed sin had not existed and been remitted too, as well as actual transgressions]

¶ *And hath committed unto us the word of reconciliation.* Margin, "put in us." Tindal renders this, "and hath committed unto us the preaching of the atonement." The meaning is, that the office of making known the nature of this plan, and the conditions on which God was willing to be reconciled to man, had been committed to the ministers of the gospel.

20. *Now then we are ambassadors for Christ.* We are the ambassadors whom Christ has sent forth to negotiate with men in regard to their reconciliation to God. Tindal renders this, "Now then are we messengers in the room of Christ." The word here used (πρεσβεύομεν, from πρέσβυς, an aged man, an elder, and then an ambassador) means to act as an ambassador, or sometimes merely to deliver a message for another, without being empowered to do any thing more than to explain or enforce it.—*Bloomfield.* See Thucyd. 7. 9. An ambassador is a minister of the highest rank, employed by one prince or state at the court of another, to manage the concerns of his own prince or state, and representing the dignity and power of his sovereign.—*Webster.* He is sent to do what the sovereign would himself do were he present. They are sent to make known the will of the sovereign, and to negotiate matters of commerce, of war, or of peace, and in general every thing affecting the interests of the sovereign among the people to whom they are sent. At all times, and in all countries, an ambassador is a sacred character, and his person is regarded as inviolable. He is bound implicitly to obey the instructions of his sovereign, and as far as possible to do only what the sovereign would do were he himself present. Ministers are ambassadors for Christ, as they are sent to do what he would do were he personally present. They are to make known, and to explain, and enforce the terms on which God is willing to be reconciled to men. They are not to negotiate on any new terms, nor to change those which God has proposed, nor to follow their own plans or devices, but they are simply to urge, explain, state, and enforce the terms on which God is willing to be reconciled. Of course

did beseech *you* by us, we pray *you* in Christ's stead, be ye reconciled to God.

21 For [a] he hath made him *to* be sin for us, who knew no sin; that we might be made [b] the righteousness of God in him.

[a] Is. 53.6,9,12; Ga. 3.13; 1 Pe. 2.22,24; 1 John 3.5.

[b] Ro. 5.19.

they are to seek the honour of the sovereign who has sent them forth, and to seek to do only his will. They go not to promote their own welfare; not to seek honour, dignity, or emolument; but they go to transact the business which the Son of God would engage in were he again personally on the earth. It follows that their office is one of great dignity, and great responsibility, and that respect should be showed them as the ambassadors of the King of kings. ¶ *As though God did beseech* you *by us.* Our message is to be regarded as the message of God. It is God who speaks. What we say to you is said in his name and on his authority, and should be received with the respect which is due to a message directly from God. The gospel message is God speaking to men through the ministry, and entreating them to be reconciled. This invests the message which the ministers of religion bear with infinite dignity and solemnity; and it makes it a fearful and awful thing to reject it. ¶ *We pray* you *in Christ's stead* (ὑπὲρ Χριστοῦ). In the place of Christ; or doing what he did when on earth, and what he would do were he where we are. ¶ *Be ye reconciled to God.* This is the sum and burden of the message which the ministers of the gospel bear to their fellow-men; see Note on ver. 19. It implies that *man* has something to do in this work. *He* is to be reconciled to God. He is to give up his opposition. He is to submit to the terms of mercy. All the change in the case is to be in him, for God cannot change. God has removed all the obstacles to reconciliation which existed on *his* part. He has done all that he will do, all that needed to be done, in order to render reconciliation easy as possible. And now it remains that man should lay aside his hostility, abandon his sins, embrace the terms of mercy, and become in fact reconciled to God. And the great object of the ministers of reconciliation is to urge this duty on their fellow-men. They are to do it in the name of Christ. They are to do it as if Christ were himself present, and were himself urging the message. They are to use the arguments which he would use; evince the zeal which he would show; and present the motives which he would present to induce a dying world to become in fact reconciled to God.

21. *For he hath made him* to be *sin for us.* The Greek here is, 'for him who knew no sin, he hath made sin, or a sin-offering for us.' The *design* of this very important verse is, to urge the strongest possible reason for being reconciled to God. This is implied in the word (γὰρ) *for.* Paul might have urged other arguments, and presented other strong considerations. But he chooses to present this fact, that Christ has been made sin for us, as embodying and concentrating all. It is the most affecting of all arguments; it is the one that is likely to prove most effectual. It is not indeed improper to urge on men every other consideration to induce them to be reconciled to God. It is not improper to appeal to them by the conviction of duty; to appeal to their reason and conscience; to remind them of the claims, the power, the goodness, and the fear of the Creator; to remind them of the awful consequences of a continued hostility to God; to persuade them by the hope of heaven, and by the fear of hell (ver. 11.) to become his friends: but, after all, the strongest argument, and that which is most adapted to melt the soul, is the fact that the Son of God has become incarnate for our sins, and has suffered and died in our stead. When all other appeals fail this is effectual; and this is in fact the strong argument by which the mass of those who

become Christians are induced to abandon their opposition and to become reconciled to God. ¶ To be *sin.* The words 'to be' are not in the original. Literally it is, 'he has made him sin, or a sin-offering' (ἁμαρτίαν ἐποίησεν). But what is meant by this? What is the exact idea which the apostle intended to convey? I answer, it cannot be, (1.) That he was literally *sin* in the abstract, or sin as such. No one can pretend this. The expression must be, therefore, in some sense, figurative. Nor, (2.) Can it mean that he was *a sinner*, for it is said in immediate connection that he "knew no sin," and it is everywhere said that he was holy, harmless, undefiled. Nor, (3.) Can it mean that he was, in any proper sense of the word, *guilty*, for no one is truly guilty who is not personally a transgressor of the law; and if he was, in any proper sense, *guilty*, then he deserved to die, and his death could have no more merit than that of any other guilty being; and if he was properly *guilty* it would make no difference in this respect whether it was by his own fault or by imputation: a *guilty* being *deserves* to be punished; and where there is desert of punishment there can be no merit in sufferings. But all such views as go to make the holy Redeemer a sinner, or guilty, or deserving of the sufferings which he endured, border on blasphemy, and are abhorrent to the whole strain of the Scriptures. In no form, in no sense possible, is it to be maintained that the Lord Jesus was sinful or guilty. It is a corner stone of the whole system of religion, that in all conceivable senses of the expression he was holy, and pure, and the object of the divine approbation. And every view which *fairly leads* to the statement that he was in any sense guilty, or which implies that he deserved to die, is *prima facie* a false view, and should be at once abandoned. But, (4.) If the declaration that he was made "sin" (ἁμαρτίαν) does not mean that he was sin itself, or a sinner, or guilty, then it must mean that he was a *sin-offering*,—an offering or a sacrifice for sin; and this is the interpretation which is now generally adopted by expositors; or it must be taken as an abstract for the concrete, and mean that God *treated him as if he were a sinner.* The former interpretation, that it means that God made him a sin-offering, is adopted by Whitby, Doddridge, Macknight, Rosenmüller, and others; the latter, that it means that God treated him as a sinner, is adopted by Vorstius, Schoettgen, Robinson (*Lex.*), Bishop Bull, and others. There are many passages in the Old Testament where the word "sin" (ἁμαρτία) is used in the sense of sin-offering, or a sacrifice for sin. Thus, Hos. iv. 8, "They eat up the sin of my people;" *i. e.* the sin-offerings; see Ezek. xliii. 22, 25; xliv. 29; xlv. 22, 23, 25. See Whitby's Note on this verse. But whichever meaning is adopted, whether it means that he was a sacrifice for sin, or that God treated him *as if* he were a sinner, *i. e.* subjected him to sufferings which, if he had been personally a sinner, would have been a proper expression of his hatred of transgression, and a proper punishment for sin, in either case it means that he made an atonement; that he died for sin; that his death was not merely that of a martyr; but that it was designed by substituted sufferings to make reconciliation between man and God. Locke renders this, probably expressing the true sense, "For God hath made him subject to suffering and death, the punishment and consequence of sin, as if he had been a sinner, though he were guilty of no sin." To me, it seems probable that the sense is, that God treated him *as if* he had been a sinner; that he subjected him to such pains and woes as would have been a proper punishment *if* he had been guilty; that while he was, in fact, in all senses perfectly innocent, and while God knew this, yet that in consequence of the voluntary assumption of the place of man which the Lord Jesus took, it pleased the Father to lay on him the deep sorrows which would be the proper expression of his sense of the evil of sin; that he endured so much suffering, as would answer the same great ends in maintaining the truth, and honour, and justice of God, as if the guilty had themselves endured the penalty of the law. This, I suppose, is what is usually meant when it is said "our sins were imputed to him;" and though this language is not used in the Bible, and though it is liable to great misapprehension and perversion, yet if this is its meaning, there can be no objection to it.

[Certainly Christ's being made sin, is not to be explained of his being made sin in the abstract, nor of his having actually become a sinner; yet it does imply, that sin was charged on Christ, or that it was imputed to him, and that he became answerable for it. Nor can this idea be excluded, even if we admit that "sin-offering" is the proper rendering of ἁμαρτία in the passage. "That Christ," says an old divine commenting on this place, "was made sin for us, because he was a sacrifice for sin, we confess; but therefore was he a sacrifice for sin because our sins were imputed to him, and punished in him." The doctrine of imputation of sin to Christ is here, by plain enough inference at least. The rendering in our Bibles, however, asserts it in a more direct form. Nor, after all the criticism that has been expended on the text, does there seem any necessity for the abandonment of that rendering, on the part of the advocate of imputation. For first ἁμαρτία in the Septuagint, and the corresponding אָשָׁם in the Hebrew, denote both the sin and the sin-offering, the piacular sacrifice and the crime itself. Second, the antithesis in the passage, so obvious and beautiful, is destroyed by the adoption of "sin-offering." Christ was made sin, we righteousness.

There seems in our author's comment on this place, and also on the fifth of the Romans, an attempt to revive the oft refuted objection against imputation, viz., that it involves something like a transference of moral character, an infusion, rather than an imputation of sin or righteousness. Nothing of this kind is at all implied in the doctrine. Its advocates with one voice disclaim it; and the reader will see the objection answered at length in the supplementary Notes on the fourth and fifth chapters of Romans. What then is the value of such arguments or insinuations as these: "All such views as go to make the holy Redeemer a sinner, or guilty, or deserving of the sufferings he endured, border on blasphemy," &c. Nor is it wiser to affirm that "if Christ was properly guilty, it would make no difference in this respect, whether it was by his own fault or by imputation." What may be meant in this connection by "properly guilty," we know not. But this is certain, that there is an immense difference between Christ's having the *guilt* of *our* iniquities charged on him, and having the guilt of his own so charged.

It is admitted in the commentary, that God "treated Christ as if he had been a sinner," and this is alleged as the probable sense of the passage. But this treatment of Christ on the part of God, must have some *ground*, and where shall we find it, unless in the imputation of sin to him? If the guilt of our iniquities, or which is the same thing, the law obligation to punishment, be not charged on Christ, how in justice can he be subjected to the punishment? If he had not voluntarily come under such obligation, what claim had law on him? That the very words "sin imputed to Christ" are not found in scripture, is not a very formidable objection. The words in this text are stronger and better "He was *made sin*," and says Isaiah, according to the rendering of Bishop Lowth, "The Lord made to meet upon him the iniquities of us all. It was required of him, and he was made answerable." Isa. liii. 6.]

¶ *Who knew no sin.* He was not guilty. He was perfectly holy and pure. This idea is thus expressed by Peter (1 Pet. ii. 22): "who did no sin, neither was guile found in his mouth;" and in Heb. vii. 26, it is said he was "holy, harmless, undefiled, separate from sinners." In all respects, and in all conceivable senses, the Lord Jesus was pure and holy. If he had not been, he would not have been qualified to make an atonement. Hence the sacred writers are everywhere at great pains to keep this idea prominent, for on this depends the whole superstructure of the plan of salvation. The phrase "*knew* no sin," is an expression of great beauty and dignity. It indicates his entire and perfect purity. He was altogether unacquainted with sin; he was a stranger to transgression; he was conscious of no sin; he committed none. He had a mind and heart perfectly free from pollution, and his whole life was perfectly pure and holy in the sight of God. ¶ *That we might be made the righteousness of God.* This is a Hebraism, meaning the same as *divinely righteous*. It means that we are made righteous in the sight of God; that is, that we are accepted as righteous, and treated as righteous by God on account of what the Lord Jesus has done. There is here an evident and beautiful contrast between what is said of Christ, and what is said of us. He was made *sin;* we are made *righteousness;* that is, he was treated *as if* he were a sinner, though he was perfectly holy and pure; we are treated *as if* we were righteous, though we are defiled and depraved. The idea is, that on account of what the Lord Jesus has endured in our behalf we are treated as if we had ourselves entirely fulfilled the law of God, and had never become exposed to its penalty. In the phrase "righteousness *of God,*" there is a reference to the fact that this is *his* plan of making men righteous, or of justifying them. They who thus become righteous, or are justified, are justified on his plan, and by a scheme which he has devised. Locke renders this, "that we, in and by him, might be made righteous, by a righteousness imputed to us by God." The idea is, that all our righteousness in the sight of God we receive in and through a Redeemer. All is to be traced to him. This verse contains a beautiful epitome of the whole plan of salvation, and the peculiarity of the Christian scheme. On the one hand, one who was perfectly innocent, by a voluntary substitution, is treated AS IF he were guilty; that is, is subjected to pains and sorrows which *if he were* guilty would be a proper punishment for sin: and on the other, they who *are* guilty and who deserve to be punished, are treated, through his vicarious sufferings, *as if* they were perfectly innocent; that is, in a manner which would be a proper expression of God's approbation if he had not sinned. The whole plan, therefore, is one of substitution; and without substitution, there can be no salvation. Innocence voluntarily suffers for guilt, and the guilty are thus made pure and holy, and are saved. The greatness of the divine compassion and love is thus shown for the guilty; and on the ground of this it is right and proper for God to call on men *to be* reconciled to him. It is the strongest argument that can be used. When God has given his only Son to the bitter suffering of death on the cross *in order* that we may be reconciled, it is the highest possible argument which can be used why we *should* cease our opposition to him, and become his friends.

[See the supplementary Notes on Rom. i. 17; iii. 21. See also the additional Note above, on the first clause of the verse. The "righteousness of God," is doubtless that righteousness which the divine Saviour wrought out, in his active and passive obedience, and if ever any of the guilty race of Adam are "treated as righteous" by God, it must be solely on the ground of its imputation.]

REMARKS.

1. It is possible for Christians to have the assurance that they shall enter into heaven, ver. 1. Paul said that *he* knew this; John knew this (see Note on ver. 1), and there is no reason why others should not know it. If a man hates sin he may know that as well as any thing else; if he loves God, why should he not know that as well as to know that he loves an earthly friend? If he desires to be holy, to enter heaven, to be eternally pure, why should we have any doubt about that? If he loves to pray, to read the Bible, to converse of heaven—if his heart is truly in these things, he may *know* it, as well as know any thing else about his own character or feelings.

2. If a Christian *may* know it, he *should* know it. No other knowledge is so desirable as this. Nothing will produce so much comfort as this. Nothing will contribute so much to make him firm, decided, and consistent in his Christian walk as this. No other knowledge will give him so much support in temptation; so much comfort in trial; so much peace in death. And *if* a man is a Christian, he should give himself no rest till he obtains assurance on this subject; if he is *not* a Christian he cannot know *that* too soon, or take too early measures to flee from the wrath to come.

3. The body will soon be dissolved in death, ver. 1. It is a frail crumbling, decaying dwelling, that must soon be taken down. It has none of the properties of a permanent abode. It *can* be held together but a little

time. It is like a nut or cottage, that is shaken by every gust of wind: like a tent when the pins are loose, and the cords unstranded, or rotten, and when the wind will soon sweep it away. And since this is the fact, we may as well know it, and not attempt to conceal it from the mind. All truth may be looked at calmly, and should be, and a man who is residing in a frail and shattered dwelling, should be looking out for one that is more permanent and substantial. Death should be looked at. The fact that this tabernacle shall be taken down should be looked at; and every man should be asking with deep interest the question whether there is not a more permanent dwelling for him in a better world.

4. This life is burdened, and is full of cares, ver. 2, 4. It is such as is fitted to make us desire a better state. We groan here under sin, amidst temptation, encompassed by the cares and toils of life. We are burdened with duties, and we are oppressed by trials; and under all we are sinking to the grave. Soon, under the accumulated burdens, the body will be crushed, and sink back to the dust. Man cannot endure the burden long, and he must soon die. These accumulated trials and cares are such as are adapted to make him desire a better inheritance, and to look forward to a better world God designs that this shall be a world of care and anxiety, in order that we may be led to seek a better portion beyond the grave.

5. The Christian has a permanent home in heaven, ver. 1, 2, 4. There is a house not made with hands; an eternal home; a world where mortality is unknown. There is his home; that is his eternal dwelling. Here he is a stranger, among strangers, in a strange world. In heaven is his home. The body here may be sick, feeble, dying; there it shall be vigorous, strong, immortal. He may have no comfortable dwelling here; he may be poor, and afflicted; there he shall have an undecaying dwelling, an unchanging home. Who in a world like this should not desire to be a Christian? What other condition of life is so desirable as that of the man who is *sure* that after a few more days he shall be admitted to an eternal home in heaven, where the body never dies, and where sin and sorrow are known no more?

6. The Christian should be willing to bear all the pain and sorrow which God shall appoint, ver. 1—4. Why should he not? He knows not only that God is good in all this; but he knows that it is but for a moment; that he is advancing toward heaven, and that he will soon be at home. Compared with that eternal rest what trifles are all the sufferings of this mortal life!

7. We should not desire to die merely to get rid of pain, or to be absent from the body, ver. 4. It is not merely in order that we may be "unclothed," or that we may get away from a suffering body, that we should be willing to die. Many a sinner suffers so much here that he is willing to plunge into an awful eternity, as he supposes, to get rid of pain, when, alas! he plunges only into deeper and eternal woe. We should be willing to bear as much pain, and to bear it as long as God shall be pleased to appoint. We should submit to all without a murmur. We should be anxious to be relieved only when God shall judge it best for us to be away from the body, and to be present with the Lord.

8. In a mere readiness to die there is no evidence that we are prepared for heaven; comp. ver. 4. Many a man supposes that because he is ready to die, that, therefore, he is prepared. Many a one takes comfort because a dying friend was ready and willing to die. But in a mere willingness to die there is no evidence of a preparation for death, because a hundred causes may conspire to produce this besides piety. And let us not be deceived by supposing that because we have no alarm about death, and are willing to go to another world, that therefore we are prepared. It may be either stupidity, or insensibility; it may be a mere desire to get rid of suffering; it may be because we are cherishing a

hope of heaven which is altogether vain and illusive.

9. The Christian should, and may desire to depart and to be in heaven, ver. 2. Heaven is his home; and it is his privilege to desire to be there. Here he is in a world of trial and of sin. There he shall be in a world of joy and of holiness. Here he dwells in a frail, suffering, decaying body. There he shall be clothed with immortality. It is his privilege, therefore, to desire, as soon as it shall be the will of God, to depart, and to enter on his eternal inheritance in heaven. He should have a strong, fixed, firm desire for that world; and should be ready at the shortest notice to go and to be for ever with the Lord.

10. The hopes and joys of Christians, and all their peace and calmness in the prospect of death, are to be traced to God, ver. 5. It is not that they are not naturally as timid and fearful of dying as others; it is not that they have any native courage or strength, but it is to be traced entirely to the mercy of God, and the influence of his Spirit, that they are enabled to look calmly at death, at the grave, at eternity. With the assured prospect of heaven, they have nothing to fear in dying; and if we have the "earnest of the Spirit"—the pledge that heaven is ours—we have nothing to fear in the departure from this world.

11. The Christian should be, and may be, always cheerful, ver. 6. Paul said that he was always confident, or cheerful. Afflictions did not depress him; trials did not cast him down. He was not disheartened by opposition; he did not lose his courage by being reviled and persecuted. In all this he was cheerful and bold. There is nothing in religion to make us melancholy and sad. The assurance of the favour of God, and the hope of heaven, should have, and will have, just the opposite effect. A sense of the presence of God, a conviction that we are sinners, a deep impression of the truth that we are to die, and of the infinite interest of the soul at stake, will indeed make us serious and solemn, and should do so. But this is not inconsistent with *cheerfulness*, but is rather fitted to produce it. It is favourable to a state of mind where all irritability is suppressed, and where the mind is made calm and settled; and this is favourable to cheerfulness. Besides, there is much, very much in religion to *prevent* sadness, and to remove gloom from the soul. The hope of heaven, and the prospect of dwelling with God and with holy beings for ever, is the best means of expelling the gloom which is caused by the disappointments and cares of the world. And much as many persons suppose that religion *creates* gloom, it is certain that nothing in this world has done so much to lighten care, to break the force of misfortune and disappointment, to support in times of trial, and to save from despair, as the religion of the Redeemer. And it is moreover certain that there are no persons so habitually calm in their feelings, and cheerful in their tempers, as consistent and devout Christians. If there are some Christians, like David Brainerd, who are melancholy and sad, as there are undoubtedly, it should be said, (1.) That they are few in number; (2.) That their gloom is to be traced to constitutional propensity, and not to religion; (3.) That they have, even with all their gloom, joys which the world never experiences, and which can never be found in sin; and, (4.) That their gloom is not produced *by* religion, but *by the want of more of it.*

12. It is noble to act with reference to things unseen and eternal, ver. 7. It elevates the soul; lifts it above the earth; purifies the heart; and gives to man a new dignity. It prevents all the grovelling effect of acting from a view of present objects, and with reference to the things which are just around us. "Whatever withdraws us," says Dr. Johnson, "from the power of our senses; whatever makes the past, the distant, or the future, predominate over the present, advances us in the dignity of thinking beings."—*Tour to the Hebrides*, p. 322, ed. Phil. 1810. Whatever directs the eye and the heart to heaven; whatever may make man feel and believe

that there is a God, a Saviour, a heaven, a world of glory, elevates him with the consciousness of his immortality, and raises him above the groveling objects that wither and debase the soul. Man should act with reference to eternity. He should be conscious of immortality. He should be deeply impressed with that high honour that awaits him of standing before God. He should feel that he *may* partake in the glories of the resurrection; that he may inherit an eternal heaven. Feeling thus, what trifles are the things of the earth! How little should he be moved by its trials! How little should he be influenced by its wealth, its pleasures, and its honours!

13. The Christian, when he leaves the body, is at once with the Lord Jesus, ver. 8. He rushes, as it were instinctively, to his presence, and casts himself at his feet. He has no other home than where the Saviour is; he thinks of no future joy or glory but that which is to be enjoyed with him. Why then should we fear death? Lay out of view, as we may, the momentary pang, the chilliness, and the darkness of the grave, and think of that which will be the moment *after* death—the view of the Redeemer, the sight of the splendours of the heavenly world, the angels, the spirits of the just made perfect, the river of the paradise of God, and the harps of praise, and what has man to fear in the prospect of dying?

> Why should I shrink at pain or woe,
> Or feel at death dismay?
> I've Canaan's goodly land in view,
> And realms of endless day.
>
> Apostles, martyrs, prophets there,
> Around my Saviour stand;
> And soon my friends in Christ below
> Will join the glorious band.
>
> Jerusalem! my happy home!
> My soul still pants for thee;
> When shall my labours have an end
> In joy, and peace, and thee!
>
> *C. Wesley.*

14. We should act feeling that we are in the immediate presence of God, and so as to meet his acceptance and approbation, whether we remain on earth, or whether we are removed to eternity, ver. 9. The prospect of being with him, and the consciousness that his eye is fixed upon us, should make us diligent, humble, and laborious. It should be the great purpose of our lives to secure his favour, and meet with his acceptance; and it should make no difference with us in this respect, where we are — whether on earth or in heaven; with the prospect of long life, or of an early death; in society or in solitude; at home or abroad; on the land or on the deep; in sickness or in health; in prosperity or in adversity, it should be our great aim so to live as to be "accepted of him." And the Christian *will* so act. To act in this manner is the very nature of true piety; and where this desire does not exist, there can be no true religion.

15. We must appear before the judgment-seat, ver. 10. We must *all* appear there. This is inevitable. There is not one of the human family that can escape. Old and young; rich and poor; bond and free; all classes, all conditions, all nations must stand there, and give an account for all the deeds done in the body, and receive their eternal doom. How solemn is the thought of being *arraigned!* How deeply affecting the idea that on the issue of *that one trial* will depend our eternal weal or woe! How overwhelming the reflection that from that sentence there can be no appeal; no power of reversing it; no possibility of afterwards changing our destiny!

16. We shall soon be there, ver. 10. No one knows when he is to die; and death when it comes will remove us at once to the judgment-seat. A disease that may carry us off in a few hours may take us there; or death that may come in an instant shall bear us to that awful bar. How many are stricken down in a moment; how many are hurried without *any* warning to the solemnities of the eternal world! So we may die. No one can *insure* our lives; no one can guard us from the approach of the invisible king of terrors.

17. We should be ready to depart

If we *must* stand at the awful bar; and if we may be summoned there any moment, assuredly we should lose no time in being ready to go. It is our great business in life; and it should claim our first attention, and all other things should be postponed that we may be ready to die. It should be the first inquiry every morning, and the last subject of thought every evening—for who knows when he rises in the morning but that before night he may stand at the judgment-seat! Who, when he lies down on his bed at night, knows but that in the silence of the night-watches he may be summoned to go alone—to leave his family and friends, his home and his bed, to answer for all the deeds done in the body?

18. We should endeavour to save others from eternal death, ver. 11. If we have ourselves any just views of the awful terrors of the day of judgment, and if we have any just views of the wrath of God, we should endeavour "to persuade" others to flee from the wrath to come. We should plead with them; we should entreat them; we should weep over them; we should pray for them, that they may be saved from going up to meet the awful wrath of God. If our friends are unprepared to meet God; if they are living in impenitence and sin, and if we have *any* influence over others in any way, we should exert it all to induce them to come to Christ, and to save themselves from the awful terrors of that day. Paul deemed no self-denial and no sacrifice too great, if he might persuade them to come to God, and to save their souls. And who that has any just views of the awful terrors of the day of judgment; of the woes of an eternal hell, and of the glories of an eternal heaven; can deem that labour too great which shall be the means of saving immortal souls? Not to frighten them should we labour, not to alarm them merely should we plead with them, but we should endeavour by all means to *persuade* them to come to the Redeemer. We should not use tones of harshness and denunciation; we should not speak of hell as if we would rejoice to execute the sentence, but we should speak with tenderness, earnestness, and with tears (comp. Acts xx. 31), that we may induce our friends and fellow-sinners to be reconciled to God.

19. We should not deem it strange or remarkable if we are charged with being deranged for being active and zealous in the subject of religion, ver. 13. There will always be enough, both *in* the church and *out* of it, to charge us with over-heated zeal; with want of prudence; or with decided mental alienation. But we are not to forget that Paul was accused of being "mad;" and even the Redeemer was thought to be "beside himself." "It is sufficient for the disciple that he be as his master, and the servant as his Lord;" and if the Redeemer was charged with derangement on account of his peculiar views and his zeal, we should not suppose that any strange thing had happened to us if we are accused in like manner.

20. The gospel should be offered to all men, ver. 14. If Christ died for all, then salvation is provided for all; and then it should be offered to all freely and fully. It should be done without any mental reservation, for God has no such mental reservation; without any hesitation or misgiving; without any statements that would break the force, or weaken the power of such an offer on the consciences of men. If they reject it, they should be left to see that they reject that which is *in good faith* offered to them, and that for this they must give an account to God. Every man who preaches the gospel should feel that he is not only *permitted* but REQUIRED to preach the gospel "to every creature;" nor should he embrace any opinion whatever which will in form or in fact cramp him or restrain him in thus offering salvation to all mankind. The fact that Christ died for all, and that all may be saved, should be a fixed and standing point in all systems of theology, and should be allowed to shape every other opinion, and to shed its influence over every other view of truth.

21 All men by nature are dead in sins, ver. 14. They are insensible to

their own good; to the appeals of God; to the glories of heaven, and to the terrors of hell. They do not act for eternity; they are without concern in regard to their everlasting destiny. They are as insensible to all these things, until aroused by the Spirit of God, as a dead man in his grave is to surrounding objects. And there is nothing that ever did arouse such a man, or ever could, but the same power that made the world, and the same voice that raised Lazarus from his grave. This melancholy fact strikes us everywhere; and we should be deeply humbled that it is *our* condition by nature, and should mourn that it is the condition of our fellow-men everywhere.

22. We should form our estimate of objects and of their respective value and importance by other considerations than those which are derived from their temporal nature, ver. 16. It should not be simply according to the flesh. It should not be as they estimate them who are living for this world. It should not be by their rank, their splendour, or their fashion. It should be by their reference to eternity, and their bearing on the state of things there.

23. It should be with us a very serious inquiry whether our views of Christ are such as they have who are living after the flesh, or such only as the unrenewed mind takes, ver. 16. The carnal mind has no just views of the Redeemer. To every impenitent sinner he is "a root out of a dry ground." There is no beauty in him. And to every hypocrite, and every deceived professor of religion, there is really no beauty seen in him. There is no spontaneous, elevated, glowing attachment to him. It is all forced and unnatural. But to the true Christian there is a beauty seen in his character that is not seen in any other; and the whole soul loves him, and embraces him. His character is seen to be most pure and lovely; his benevolence boundless; his ability and willingness to save, infinite. The renewed soul desires no other Saviour; and rejoices that he is just what he is—rejoices in his humiliation as well as his exaltation; in his poverty as well as his glory; rejoices in the privilege of being saved by him who was spit upon, and mocked, and crucified, as well as by him who is at the right hand of God. One thing is certain, unless we have just views of Christ we can never be saved.

24. The new birth is a great and most important change, ver. 17. It is not in name or in profession merely, but it is a deep and radical change of the heart. It is so great that it may be said of each one that he is *a new creation* of God; and in relation to each one, that old things are passed away, and all things are become new. How important it is that we examine our hearts and see whether this change has taken place, or whether we are still living without God and without hope. It is indispensable that we be born again; John iii. If we are not born again, and if we are not new creatures in Christ, we must perish for ever. No matter what our wealth talent, learning, accomplishment, reputation, or morality; unless we have been so changed that it may be said, and that we can say, "old things are passed away, and all things are become new," we must perish for ever. *There is no power in the universe that can save a man who is not born again.*

25. The gospel ministry is a most responsible and important work, ver. 18, 19. There is no other office of the same importance; there is no situation in which man can be placed more solemn than that of making known the terms on which God is willing to bestow favour on apostate man.

26. How amazing is the divine condescension, that God should have ever proposed such a plan of reconciliation, ver. 20, 21. That he should not only have been *willing* to be reconciled, but that he should have *sought*, and have been so *anxious* for it as to be willing to send his own Son to die to secure it! It was pure, rich, infinite benevolence. God was not to be *benefited* by it. He was infinitely blessed and happy even though man should have been lost. He was pure, and just, and holy, and it was not *necessary* to resort to this in order to

CHAPTER VI.

WE then, *as* workers[a] together *with him*, beseech *you*
also that ye receive not the grace of
God in vain.[b]
2 (For he saith,[c] I have heard

a chap.5.20. b He.12.15. c Is.49.8.

vindicate his own character. He had done man no wrong; and if man had perished in his sins, the throne of God would have been pure and spotless. It was love; mere love. It was pure, holy, disinterested, infinite benevolence. It was worthy of a God; and it has a claim to the deepest gratitude of man.

Let us then, in view of this whole chapter, seek to be reconciled to God. Let us lay aside all our opposition to him. Let us embrace his plans. Let us be willing to submit to him, and to become his ETERNAL FRIENDS. Let us seek to heaven to which he would raise us; and though our earthly house of this tabernacle *must* be dissolved, let us be prepared, as we may be, for that eternal habitation which he has fitted up for all who love him in the heavens.

CHAPTER VI.

THIS chapter, closely connected in sense with the preceding, is designed as an address to the Corinthian Christians, exhorting them to act worthily of their calling, and of their situation under such a ministry as they had enjoyed. In the previous chapters, Paul had discoursed at length of the design and of the labours of the ministry. The main drift of all this was to show them the nature of reconciliation, and the obligation to turn to God, and to live to him. This idea is pursued in this chapter; and in view of the labours and self-denials of the ministry, Paul urges on the Corinthian Christians the duty of coming out from the world, and of separating themselves entirely from all evil. The chapter may be conveniently contemplated in the following parts:

I. Paul states that he and his associates were fellow-labourers with God, and he exhorts the Corinthians not to receive the grace of God in vain. To induce them to make a wise improvement of the privileges which they enjoyed, he quotes a passage from Isaiah, and applies it as meaning that it was then an acceptable time, and that they might avail themselves of mercy, ver. 1, 2.

II. He enumerates the labours and self-denials of the ministry. He refers to their sincerity, zeal, and honesty of life. He shows how much they had been willing to endure in order to convey the gospel to others, and how much they had in fact endured, and how much they had benefited others. He speaks of their afflictions in a most tender and beautiful manner, and of the happy results which had followed from their self-denying labours, ver. 3—10. The design of this is, evidently, to remind them of what their religion had cost, and to appeal to them in view of all this to lead holy and pure lives.

III. Paul expresses his ardent attachment for them, and says that *if* they were straitened—if they did not live as they should do, it was not because he and his fellow-labourers had not loved them, and sought their welfare, but from a defect in themselves, ver. 11, 12.

IV. As a *reward* for all that he had done and suffered for them, he now asked only that they should live as became Christians, ver. 13—18. He sought not silver, or gold, or apparel. He had not laboured as he had done with any view to a temporal reward. And he now asked simply that they should come out from the world, and be dissociated from every thing that was evil. He demanded that they should be separated from all idolatry, and idolatrous practices; assures them that there can be no union between light and darkness; righteousness and unrighteousness; Christ and Belial; that there can be no agreement between the temple of God and idols; reminds them of the fact that they are the temple of God; and encourages them to do this by the assurance that God would be their God, and that they should be his adopted sons and daughters. The chapter is one of great

thee in a time accepted, and in the day of salvation have I succoured thee: behold, now *is* the accepted time; behold, now *is* the day of salvation.)
3 Giving no [a] offence in any

a 1Co.10.32.

beauty; and the argument for a holy life among Christians is one that is exceedingly forcible and tender.

1. *We then, as workers together* with him. On the meaning of this expression, see Note, 1 Cor. iii. 9. The Greek here is (συνεργοῦντες) "working together," and may mean either that the apostles and ministers to whom Paul refers were joint-labourers in entreating them not to receive the grace of God in vain; or it may mean that they *co-operated* with God, or were engaged *with* him in endeavouring to secure the reconciliation of the world to himself. Tindal renders it, "we as helpers." Doddridge, "we then as the joint-labourers of God." Most expositors have concurred in this interpretation. The word properly means, to work together; to cooperate in producing any result. Macknight supposes that the word here is in the vocative, and is an address to the fellow-labourers of Paul, entreating *them* not to receive the grace of God in vain. In this opinion he is probably alone, and has manifestly departed from the scope and design of the passage. Probably the most *obvious* meaning is that of our translators, who regard it as teaching that Paul was a joint-worker with God in securing the salvation of men. ¶ *That ye receive not the grace of God in vain.* The "grace of God" here means evidently the gracious offer of reconciliation and pardon. And the sense is, "We entreat you not to neglect or slight this offer of pardon, so as to lose the benefit of it, and be lost. It is offered freely and fully. It may be partaken of by all, and all may be saved. But it may also be slighted, and all the benefits of it will then be lost." The sense is, that it was possible that this offer might be made to them, they might hear of a Saviour, be told of the plan of reconciliation, and have the offers of mercy pressed on their attention and acceptance, and yet all be in vain. They might notwithstanding all this be lost, for simply *to hear* of the plan of salvation or the offers of mercy, will no more save a sinner than *to hear* of medicine will save the sick. It must be embraced and applied, or it will be in vain. It is true that Paul probably addressed this to those who were professors of religion; and the sense is, that they should use all possible care and anxiety lest these offers should have been made in vain. They should examine their own hearts; they should inquire into their own condition; they should guard against self-deception. The same persons (chap. v. 20) Paul had exhorted also to be reconciled to God; and the idea is, that he would earnestly entreat even professors of religion to give all diligence to secure an interest in the saving mercy of the gospel, and to guard against the possibility of being self-deceived and ruined.

2. *For he saith;* see Isaiah xlix. 8. In that passage the declaration refers to the Messiah, and the design is there to show that God would be favourable to him; that he would hear him when he prayed, and would make him the medium of establishing a covenant with his own people, and of spreading the true religion around the earth; see my Note on that place. Paul quotes the passage here not as affirming that he used it in exactly the sense, or with reference to the same design for which it was originally spoken, but as expressing the idea which he wished to convey, or in accordance with the general *principle* implied in its use in Isaiah. The general idea there, or the principle involved, was, that under the Messiah God would be willing to hear; that is, that he would be disposed to show mercy to the Jew and to the Gentile. This is the main idea of the passage as used by Paul. Under the Messiah, it is said by Isaiah, God would be willing to show mercy. That would be an acceptable time. That time,

says Paul, has arrived. The Messiah has come, and now God is willing to pardon and save. And the doctrine in this verse is, *that under the Messiah, or in the time of Christ, God is willing to show mercy to men.* In him alone is the throne of grace accessible, and now that he has come, God is willing to pardon, and men should avail themselves of the offers of mercy. ¶ *I have heard thee.* The Messiah. I have listened to thy prayer for the salvation of the heathen world. The *promise* to the Messiah was, that the heathen world should be given to him; but it was a promise that it should be in answer to *his* prayers and intercessions. "Ask of me, and I shall give thee the heathen for thine inheritance, and the uttermost parts of the earth for thy possession;" Ps. ii. 8. The salvation of the heathen world, and of all who are saved, is to be in answer to the prevalent intercession of the Lord Jesus. ¶ *In a time accepted.* In Isaiah, "in an acceptable time." The idea is, that he had prayed in a time when God was *disposed* to show mercy; the time when in his wise arrangements he had designed that his salvation should be extended to the world. It is a time which he had *fixed* as the appropriate period for extending the knowledge of his truth and his salvation; and it proves that there *was* to be a period which was the *favourable* period of salvation, that is, which God esteemed to be the proper period for making his salvation known to men. At such a period the Messiah would pray, and the prayer would be answered. ¶ *In the day of salvation.* In the time when I am disposed to show salvation. ¶ *Have I succoured thee.* The Messiah. I have sustained thee, that is, in the effort to make salvation known. God here speaks of there being an accepted time, a limited period, in which petitions in favour of the world would be acceptable to him. That time Paul says had come; and the idea which he urges is, that men should avail themselves of that, and embrace now the offers of mercy. ¶ *Behold, now is the accepted time,* &c. The meaning of this passage is, the "Messiah is come. The time referred to by Isaiah has arrived. It is now a time when God is ready to show compassion, to hear prayer, and to have mercy on mankind. Only through the Messiah, the Lord Jesus, does he show mercy, and men should therefore now embrace the offers of pardon." The doctrine taught here, therefore, is, that through the Lord Jesus, and where he is preached, God is willing to pardon and save men; and this is true *wherever* he is preached, and as long as men live under the sound of the gospel. The world is under a dispensation of mercy, and God is willing to show compassion, and while this exists, that is, while men live, the offers of salvation are to be freely made to them. The time *will* come when it will not be an acceptable time with God. The day of mercy will be closed; the period of trial will be ended; and men will be removed to a world where no mercy is shown, and where compassion is unknown. This verse, which should be read as a parenthesis, is designed to be connected with the argument which the apostle is urging, and which he presented in the previous chapter. The general doctrine is, that men should seek reconciliation with God. To enforce that, he here says, that it was *now* the acceptable time, the time when God was willing to be reconciled to men. The general sentiment of this passage may be thus expressed. (1.) Under the gospel it is an acceptable time, a day of mercy, a time when God is willing to show mercy to men. (2.) There may be special seasons which may be peculiarly called the acceptable, or accepted time. (*a*) When the gospel is pressed on the attention by the faithful preaching of his servants, or by the urgent entreaties of friends; (*b*) When it is brought to our attention by any striking dispensation of Providence; (*c*) When the Spirit of God strives with us, and brings us to deep reflection, or to conviction for sin; (*d*) In a revival of religion, when many are pressing into the kingdom—it is at all such seasons an accepted time, a day of salvation, a day which we should improve. It

thing, that the ministry be not blamed:

4 But in all *things* approving [1] ourselves as the ministers [a] of

[1] commending.

[a] 1 Co. 4. 1.

is "NOW" such a season, because, (1.) The time of mercy will pass by, and God will not be willing to pardon the sinner who goes unprepared to eternity. (2.) Because we cannot calculate on the future. We have no assurance, no evidence that we shall live another day, or hour. (3.) It is taught here, that the time *will* come when it will *not* be an accepted time. *Now* is the accepted time; at some future period it will NOT be. If men grieve away the Holy Spirit; if they continue to reject the gospel; if they go unprepared to eternity, no mercy can be found. God does not design to pardon beyond the grave. He has made no provision for forgiveness there; and they who are not pardoned in this life, must be unpardoned for ever.

3. *Giving no offence in any thing.* We the ministers of God, ver. 1. The word rendered *offence* means, properly, *stumbling;* then offence, or cause of offence, a falling into sin. The meaning here is, "giving no occasion for contemning or rejecting the gospel;" and the idea of Paul is, that he and his fellow-apostles so laboured as that no one who saw or knew them, should have occasion to reproach the ministry, or the religion which they preached; but so that in their pure and self-denying lives, the strongest argument should be seen for embracing it; comp. Matt. x. 16; 1 Cor. viii. 13; x. 32, 33. Notes, Phil. ii. 15; 1 Thes. ii. 10; v. 22. *How* they conducted so as to give no offence he states in the following verses. ¶ *That the ministry be not blamed.* The phrase, "the ministry," refers here not merely to the ministry of Paul, that is, it does not mean merely that *he* would be subject to blame and reproach, but that the *ministry itself* which the Lord Jesus had established would be blamed, or would be reproached by the improper conduct of any one who was engaged in that work. The idea is, that the misconduct of one minister of the gospel would bring a reproach upon the profession itself, and would prevent the usefulness and success of others, just as the misconduct of a physician exposes the profession to reproach, or the bad conduct of a lawyer reflects itself in some degree on the entire profession. And it is so everywhere. The errors, follies, misconduct, or bad example of one minister of the gospel brings a reproach upon the sacred calling itself, and prevents the usefulness of many others. Ministers do not stand alone. And though no one can be responsible for the errors and failings of others, yet no one can avoid suffering in regard to his usefulness by the sins of others. Not only, therefore, from a regard to his personal usefulness should every minister be circumspect in his walk, but from respect to the usefulness of all others who sustain the office of the ministry, and from respect to the success of religion all over the world. Paul made it one of the principles of his conduct so to act that no man should have cause to speak reproachfully of the ministry on his account. In order to this, he felt it to be necessary not only to *claim* and *assert* honour for the ministry, but to lead such a life as should deserve the respect of men. If a man wishes to secure respect for his calling, it must be by living in the manner which that calling demands, and then respect and honour will follow as a matter of course; see *Calvin.*

4. *But in all* things. In every respect. In all that we do. In every way, both by words and deeds. *How* this was done, Paul proceeds to state in the following verses. ¶ *Approving ourselves as the ministers of God.* Marg. "Commending." Tindal renders it, "In all things let us behave ourselves as the ministers of God." The idea is, that Paul and his fellow-labourers endeavoured to live as *became* the ministers of God, and so as to commend the ministry to the confidence and affection of men. They endeavoured to live as was appropri-

God, in much patience, in afflictions, in necessities, in distresses,

5 In stripes, [a] in imprisonments,
[1] in tumults, in labours, in watchings, in fastings.

a ch. 11. 23, &c.

1 or *in tossings to and fro.*

ate to those who were the ministers of God, and so that the world would be disposed to do honour to the ministry. ¶ *In much patience.* In the patient endurance of afflictions of all kinds. Some of his trials he proceeds to enumerate. The idea is, that a minister of God, in order to do good and to commend his ministry, should set an example of patience. He preaches this as a duty to others; and if, when he is poor, persecuted, oppressed, calumniated, or imprisoned, he should murmur, or be insubmissive, the consequence would be that he would do little good by all his preaching. And no one can doubt, that God often places his ministers in circumstances of peculiar trial, among other reasons, in order that they may illustrate their own precepts by their example, and show to their people with what temper and spirit they may and ought to suffer. Ministers often do a great deal more good by their example in suffering than they do in their preaching. It is easy to preach to others; it is not so easy to manifest just the right spirit in time of persecution and trial. Men too can resist preaching, but they cannot resist the effect and power of a good example in times of suffering. In regard to the *manner* in which Paul says that the ministry may commend itself, it may be observed, that he *groups* several things together; or mentions several *classes* of influences or means. In this and the next verse he refers to various kinds of afflictions. In the following verses he groups several things together, pertaining to a holy life, and a pure conversation. ¶ *In afflictions.* In all our afflictions; referring to *all* the afflictions and trials which they were called to bear. The following words, in the manner of a climax, specify more particularly the kinds of trials which they were called to endure. ¶ *In necessities.* This is a stronger term than afflictions, and denotes the distress which arose from *want.* He everywhere endured adversity. It denotes *unavoidable* distress and calamity. ¶ *In distresses.* The word here used (στενοχωρία) denotes properly *straitness of place,* want of room; then straits, distress, anguish. It is a stronger word than either of those which he had before used. See it explained in the Notes on Rom. ii. 9. Paul means that in all these circumstances he had evinced patience, and had endeavoured to act as became a minister of God.

5. *In stripes.* In this verse, Paul proceeds to *specifications* of what he had been called to endure. In the previous verse, he had spoken of his afflictions in general terms. In this expression, he refers to the fact that he and his fellow-labourers were scourged in the synagogues and cities as if they had been the worst of men. In 2 Cor. xi. 23—25, Paul says that he had been scourged five times by the Jews, and had been thrice beaten with rods. See Notes on that place. ¶ *In imprisonments.* As at Philippi; Acts xvi. 24. seq. It was no uncommon thing for the early preachers of Christianity to be imprisoned. ¶ *In tumults.* Marg. *Tossing to and fro.* The Greek word (ἀκαταστασία) denotes properly *instability,* thence disorder, tumult, commotion. Here it means that in the various tumults and commotions which were produced by the preaching of the gospel, Paul endeavoured to act as became a minister of God. Such tumults were excited at Corinth (Acts xviii. 6); at Philippi (Acts xvi. 19, 20); at Lystra and Derbe (Acts xiv. 19); at Ephesus (Acts xix.), and in various other places. The idea is, that if the ministers of religion are assailed by a lawless mob, they are to endeavour to show the spirit of Christ there, and to evince all patience, and to *do good* even in such a scene. Patience and the Christian spirit may often do more good in such scenes than much

6 By pureness, by knowledge, by long-suffering, by kindness, by the Holy Ghost, by love unfeigned,

preaching would do elsewhere. ¶ *In labours.* Referring probably to the labours of the ministry, and its incessant duties, and perhaps also to the labours which they performed for their own support, as it is well known that Paul and probably also the other apostles, laboured often to support themselves. ¶ *In watchings.* In wakefulness, or want of sleep. He probably refers to the fact that in these arduous duties, and in his travels, and in anxious cares for the churches, and for the advancement of religion, he was often deprived of his ordinary rest. He refers to this again in chap. xi. 27. ¶ *In fastings.* Referring probably not only to the somewhat frequent fasts to which he voluntarily submitted as acts of devotion, but also to the fact that in his travels, when abroad and among strangers, he was often destitute of food. To such trials, those who travelled as Paul did, among strangers, and without property, would be often compelled to submit; and *such* trials, almost without number, the religion which we now enjoy has cost. It at first cost the painful life, the toils, the anxieties, and the sufferings of the Redeemer; and it has been propagated and perpetuated amidst the deep sorrows, the sacrifices, and the tears and blood of those who have contributed to perpetuate it on earth. For such a religion, originated, extended, and preserved in such a manner, we can never express suitable gratitude to God. Such a religion we cannot overestimate in value; and for the extension and perpetuity of such a religion, *we* also should be willing to practise unwearied self-denial.

6. *By pureness.* Paul, having in the previous verses, grouped together some of the sufferings which he endured, and by which he had endeavoured to commend and extend the true religion, proceeds here to group together certain other influences by which he had sought the same object. The substance of what he here says is, that it had not only been done by sufferings and trials, but by a holy life, and by entire consecration to the great cause to which he had devoted himself. He begins by stating that it was by *pureness,* that is, by integrity, sanctity, a holy and pure life. All preaching, and all labours would have been in vain without this; and Paul well knew that if he succeeded in the ministry, he must be a good man. The same is true in all other professions. One of the essential requisites of an orator, according to Quintilian, is, that he must be a good man; and no man may expect ultimately to succeed in any calling of life unless he is *pure.* But however this may be in other callings, no one will doubt it in regard to the ministry of the gospel. ¶ *By knowledge.* Interpreters have differed much in the interpretation of this. Rosenmüller and Schleusner understand by it *prudence.* Grotius interprets it as meaning a knowledge of the law. Doddridge supposes that it refers to a solicitude to improve in the knowledge of those truths which they were called to communicate to others. Probably the idea is a very simple one. Paul is showing how he endeavoured to commend the gospel to others, ver. 4. He says, therefore, that one way was by communicating knowledge, true knowledge. He proclaimed that which was true, and which was real knowledge, in opposition to the false science of the Greeks, and in opposition to those who would substitute declamation for argument, and the mere ornaments of rhetoric for truth. The idea is, that the ministry should not be *ignorant,* but that if they wished to commend their office, they should be well informed, and should be men of good sense. Paul had no belief that an ignorant ministry was preferable to one that was characterized by true knowledge; and *he* felt that if he was to be useful it was to be by his imparting to others truth that would be useful. "The priest's lips should keep knowledge;" Mal. ii. 7. ¶ *By*

7 By the word [a] of truth, by the [b] power of God, by the armour [c] of righteousness on the right hand and on the left,

a ch. 4. 2. b 1 Co. 2. 4. c Eph 6. 11, &c.

long-suffering. By patience in our trials, and in the provocations which we meet with. We endeavour to obtain and keep a control over our passions, and to keep them in subjection. See this word explained in the Notes on 1 Cor. xiii. 4. ¶ *By kindness;* see Note, 1 Cor. xiii. 4. By gentleness of manner, of temper, and of spirit. By endeavouring to evince this spirit to all, whatever may be their treatment of us, and whatever may be our provocations. Paul felt that if a minister would do good he must be *kind*, and gentle to all. ¶ *By the Holy Ghost.* By the sanctifying influences of the Holy Spirit. By those graces and virtues which it is his office peculiarly to produce in the heart; comp. Gal. v. 22, 23. Paul here evidently refers not to the miraculous agency of the Holy Spirit, but he is referring to the Spirit which he and his fellow-ministers manifested, and means here, doubtless, that they evinced such feelings as the Holy Spirit produced in the hearts of the children of God. ¶ *By love unfeigned.* Sincere, true, ardent love to all. By undissembled, pure, and genuine affection for the souls of men. What good can a minister do if he does not love his people, and the souls of men? The prominent characteristic in the life of the Redeemer was *love*—love to all. So if we are like him, and if we do any good, we shall have love to men. No man is useful without it; and ministers, in general, are useful just in proportion as they have it. It will prompt to labour, self-denial, and toil; it will make them patient, ardent, kind; it will give them zeal, and will give them access to the heart; it will accomplish what no eloquence, labour, or learning will do without it. He who shows that he loves me has access at once to my heart; he who does not, cannot *make* a way there by any argument, eloquence, denunciation, or learning. No minister is useful without it; no one with it can be otherwise than useful.

7. *By the word of truth.* That is, by making known the truths of the gospel. It was his object to make known the simple truth. He did not corrupt it by false mixtures of philosophy and human wisdom, but communicated it as it had been revealed to him. The object of the appointment of the Christian ministry is to make known the truth, and when that is done it cannot but be that they will commend their office and work to the favourable regards of men. ¶ *By the power of God.* By the divine power which attended the preaching of the gospel. Most of the ancient commentators explain this of the power of working miracles.—*Bloomfield.* But it probably includes *all* the displays of divine power which attended the propagation of the gospel, whether in the working of miracles, or in the conversion of men. If it be asked how Paul used this power so as to give no offence in the work of the ministry, it may be replied, that the miraculous endowments bestowed upon the apostles, the power of speaking foreign languages, &c., seem to have been bestowed upon them to be employed in the same way as were their natural faculties; see Notes on 1 Cor. xiv. 32. The idea here is, that they used the great powers intrusted to them by God, not as impostors would have done, for the purposes of gain and ambition, or for vain display, but solely for the furtherance of the true religion, and the salvation of men. They thus showed that they were sent from God, as well by the nature of the powers with which they were intrusted, as by the manner in which they used them. ¶ *By the armour of righteousness on the right hand and on the left.* Interpreters have varied much in the exposition of this passage; and many have run into utter wildness. Grotius says, that it refers to the manner in which the ancient soldiers were armed. They bore a spear in their right hand, and a shield in the left. With the former they

8 By honour and dishonour, by evil report and good report: as deceivers, [a] and *yet* true;

a John. 7. 12, 17.

attacked their foes, with the latter they made defence. Some have supposed that it refers to the fact that they were taught to use the sword with the left hand as well as with the right. The simple idea is, that they were completely armed. To be armed on the right hand and on the left is to be well armed, or entirely equipped. They went forth to conflict. They met persecution, opposition, and slander. As the soldier went well armed to battle, so did they. But the armour with which *they* met their foes, and which constituted their entire panoply, was a holy life. With that they met all the assaults of their enemies; with that all slander and persecution. That was their defence, and by that they hoped and expected to achieve their conquests. They had no swords, and spears, and helmets, and shields; no carnal weapons of offence and defence; but they expected to meet all their assaults, and to gain all their victories, by an upright and holy life.

8. *By honour and dishonour.* The apostle is still illustrating the proposition that he and his fellow-labourers endeavoured to give no offence (ver. 3), and to commend themselves as the ministers of God, ver. 4. He here (ver. 8—10) introduces another *group* of particulars in which it was done. The main idea is, that they endeavoured to act in a manner so as to commend the ministry and the gospel, whether they were in circumstances of honour or dishonour, whether lauded or despised by the world. The word rendered "by" (διὰ) does not here denote the *means* by which they commended the gospel, but the *medium.* In the midst of honour and dishonour; whatever might be the esteem in which they were held by the world, they gave no offence. The first is, "by honour." They were not everywhere honoured, or treated with respect. Yet they *were* sometimes honoured by men. The churches which they founded would honour them, and as the ministers of religion they would be by them treated with respect. Perhaps occasionally also they might be treated with great attention and regard by the men of the world on account of their miraculous powers; comp. Acts xxviii. 7. So now, ministers of the gospel are often treated with great respect and honour. They are beloved and venerated; caressed and flattered, by the people of their charge. As ministers of God, as exercising a holy function, their office is often treated with great respect by the world. If they are eloquent or learned, or if they are eminently successful, they are often highly esteemed and loved. It is difficult in such circumstances to "commend themselves as the ministers of God." Few are the men who are not injured by honour; few who are not corrupted by flattery. Few are the ministers who are proof against this influence, and who in such circumstances can honour the ministry. If done, it is by showing that they regard such things as of little moment; by showing that they are influenced by higher considerations than the love of praise; by not allowing this to interfere with their duties, or to make them less faithful and laborious; but rather by making this the occasion of increased fidelity and increased zeal in their master's cause. Most ministers do more to "give offence" in times when they are greatly honoured by the world than when they are despised. Yet it is possible for a minister who is greatly honoured to make it the occasion of commending himself more and more as a minister of God. And he should do it; as Paul said he did.—The other situation was "in dishonour." It is needless to say, that the apostles were often in situations where they had opportunity thus to commend themselves as the ministers of God. If *sometimes* honoured, they were *often* dishonoured. If the world sometimes flattered and caressed them, it often despised them,

and cast out their names as evil; see Note, 1 Cor. iv. 13. And perhaps it is so substantially now with those who are faithful. In such circumstances, also, Paul sought to commend himself as a minister of God. It was by receiving all expressions of contempt with meekness; by not suffering them to interfere with the faithful discharge of his duties; by rising above them, and showing the power of religion to sustain him; and by returning good for evil, prayers for maledictions, blessings for curses, and by seeking to save, not injure and destroy those who thus sought to overwhelm him with disgrace. It may be difficult to do this, but it can be done; and *when* done, a man always does good. ¶ *By evil report.* The word here used (δυσφημία), means, properly, ill-omened language, malediction, reproach, contumely. It refers to the fact that they were often slandered and calumniated. Their motives were called in question, and their names aspersed. They were represented as deceivers and impostors, &c. The statement here is, that in such circumstances, and when thus assailed and reproached, they endeavoured to commend themselves as the ministers of God. Evidently they endeavoured to do this by not slandering or reviling in return; by manifesting a Christian spirit; by *living down* the slanderous accusation, and by doing good if possible even to their calumniators. It is more difficult, says Chrysostom, to bear such reports than it is pain of body; and it is consequently more difficult to evince a Christian spirit then. To human nature it is trying to have the name slandered and cast out as evil when we are conscious only of a desire to do good. But it is sufficient for the disciple that he be as his master, and if they called the master of the house Beelzebub, we must expect they will also those of his household. It is a fine field for a Christian minister, or any other Christian, to do good when his name is unjustly slandered. It gives him an opportunity of showing the true excellency of the Christian spirit; *and it gives him the inexpressible privilege of being like Christ*—like him in his suffering and in the moral excellence of character. A man should be willing to be any thing if it will make him like the Redeemer—whether it be in suffering or in glory; see Phil. iii. 10; 1 Pet. iv. 13. ¶ *And good report.* When men speak well of us; when we are commended, praised, or honoured. To honour the gospel then, and to commend the ministry, is, (1.) To show that the heart is not set on this, and does not seek it; (2.) To keep the heart from being puffed up with pride and self-estimation; (3.) *Not* to suffer it to interfere with our fidelity to others, and with our faithfully presenting to them the truth. Satan often attempts to *bribe* men by praise, and to neutralize the influence of ministers by flattery. It seems hard to go and proclaim to men painful truths who are causing the incense of praise to ascend around us. And it is commonly much easier for a minister of the gospel to commend himself as a minister of God when he is slandered than when he is praised, when his name is cast out as evil than when the breezes of popular favour are wafted upon him. Few men can withstand the influence of flattery, but many men can meet persecution with a proper spirit; few men comparatively can always evince Christian fidelity to others when they live always amidst the influence of "good report," but there are many who can be faithful when they are poor, and despised, and reviled. Hence it has happened, that God has so ordered it that his faithful servants have had but little of the "good report" which this world can furnish, but that they have been generally subjected to persecution and slander. ¶ *As deceivers.* That is, we are regarded and treated as if we were deceivers, and as if we were practising an imposition on mankind, and as if we would advance our cause by any trick or fraud that would be possible. We are regarded and treated as deceivers. Perhaps this refers to some charges which had been brought against them by the opposing faction at Corinth (*Locke*), or perhaps to the opinion

9 As [a] unknown and *yet* well known; as dying, and, behold, we live; [b] as chastened, and not killed;

a 1 Cor. 4 9. b Ps. 118. 18.

which the Jewish priests and heathen philosophers entertained of them. The idea is, that though they were extensively regarded and treated as impostors, yet they endeavoured to live as became the ministers of God. They bore the imputation with patience, and they applied themselves diligently to the work of saving souls. Paul seldom turned aside to vindicate himself from such charges, but pursued his master's work, and evidently felt that if he *had* a reputation that was worth any thing, or deserved any reputation, God would take care of it; comp. Ps. xxxvii. 1—4. A man, especially a minister, who is constantly endeavouring to vindicate his own reputation, usually has a reputation which is not worth vindicating. A man who deserves a reputation will ultimately obtain just as much as is good for him, and as will advance the cause in which he is embarked. ¶ *And* yet *true.* We are *not* deceivers and impostors. Though we are regarded as such, yet we show ourselves to be true and faithful ministers of Christ.

9. *As unknown.* As those who are deemed to be of an obscure and ignoble rank in life, unknown to the great, unknown to fame. The idea, I think, is, that they went as *strangers,* as persons unknown, in preaching the gospel. Yet, though thus unknown, they endeavour to commend themselves as the ministers of God. Though among strangers; though having no introduction from the great and the noble, yet they endeavoured so to act as to convince the world that they were the ministers of God. This could be done only by a holy life, and by the evidence of the divine approbation which would attend them in their work. And by this, the ministers of religion, if they are faithful, may make themselves known even among those who were strangers, and may live so as to "give no offence." Every minister and every Christian, even when they are "unknown" and when among strangers, should remember their high character as the servants of God, and should so live as to commend the religion which they profess to love, or which they are called on to preach. And yet how often is it that ministers when among strangers seem to feel themselves at liberty to lay aside their ministerial character, and to engage in conversation, and even partake of amusements which they themselves would regard as wholly improper if it were known that they were the ambassadors of God! And how often is it the case that professing Christians when travelling, when among strangers, when in foreign lands, forget their high calling, and conduct in a manner wholly different from what they did when surrounded by Christians; and when restrained by the sentiments and by the eyes of a Christian community! ¶ *And* yet *well known.* Our sentiments and our principles are well known. We have no concealments to make. We practise no disguise. We attempt to impose on no one. Though obscure in our origin; though without rank, or wealth, or power, or patronage, to commend ourselves to favour, yet we have succeeded in making ourselves known to the world. Though obscure in our origin, we are not obscure now. Though suspected of dark designs, yet our principles are all well known to the world. No men of the same obscurity of birth ever succeeded in making themselves more extensively known than did the apostles. The world at large became acquainted with them; and by their self-denial, zeal, and success, they extended their reputation around the globe. ¶ *As dying.* That is, regarded by others as dying. As condemned often to death; exposed to death; in the midst of trials that expose us to death, and that are ordinarily followed by death; see Note on 1 Cor. xv. 31, on the phrase, "I die daily." They passed through so many trials that it might be said that they were constantly dying. ¶ *And, behold, we live.* Strange

10 As sorrowful, yet alway rejoicing; as poor, yet mak-

as it may seem, we still survive. Through all our trials we are preserved, and though often exposed to death, yet we still live. The idea here is, that in all these trials, and in these exposures to death, they endeavoured to commend themselves as the ministers of God. They bore their trials with patience; submitted to these exposures without a murmur; and ascribed their preservation to the interposition of God. ¶ *As chastened.* The word *chastened* (παιδευόμενοι) means *corrected, chastised.* It is applied to the chastening which God causes by afflictions and calamities; 1 Cor. xi. 32; Rev. iii. 19; Heb. xii. 6. It refers here, not to the scourgings to which they were subjected in the synagogues and elsewhere, but to the chastisements which *God* inflicted; the trials to which *he* subjected them. And the idea is, that in the midst of these trials, they endeavoured to act as became the ministers of God. They bore them with patience. They submitted to them as coming from his hand. They felt that they were right; and they submitted without a murmur. ¶ *And not killed.* Though severely chastened, yet we are not put to death. We survive them—preserved by the interposition of God.

10. *As sorrowful* (λυπούμενοι). Grieving, afflicted, troubled, sad. Under these sufferings we seem always to be cast down and sad. We endure afflictions that usually lead to the deepest expressions of grief. If the world looks only upon our trials, we must be regarded as always suffering, and always sad. The world will suppose that we have cause for continued lamentation (*Doddridge*), and they will regard us as among the most unhappy of mortals. Such, perhaps, is the estimate which the world usually affixes to the Christian life. They regard it as a life of sadness and of gloom; of trial and of melancholy. They see little in it that is cheerful, and they suppose that a heavy burden presses constantly on the heart of the Christian. Joy they think pertains to the gayeties and pleasures of this life; sadness to religion. And perhaps a more comprehensive statement of the feelings with which the gay people of the world regard Christians cannot be found than in this expression, "*as sorrowful.*" True, they are not free from sorrow. They are tried like others. They have peculiar trials arising from persecution, opposition, contempt, and from the conscious and deep-felt depravity of their hearts. They ARE serious; and their seriousness is often interpreted as gloom. But there is another side to this picture, and there is much in the Christian character and feelings unseen or unappreciated by the world. For they are ¶ *Alway rejoicing.* So Paul was, notwithstanding the fact that he always appeared to have occasion for grief. Religion had a power not only to sustain the soul in trial, but to fill it with positive joy. The sources of his joy were doubtless the assurances of the divine favour and the hopes of eternal glory. And the same is true of religion always. There is an *internal* peace and joy which the world may not see or appreciate, but which is far more than a compensation for all the trials which the Christian endures. ¶ *As poor.* The idea is, we are poor, yet in our poverty we endeavour "to give no offence, and to commend ourselves as the ministers of God." This would be done by their patience and resignation; by their entire freedom from every thing dishonest and dishonourable, and by their readiness, when necessary, to labour for their own support. There is no doubt that the apostles were poor; comp. Acts iii. 6. The little property which some of them had, had all been forsaken in order that they might follow the Saviour, and go and preach his gospel. And there is as little doubt that the mass of ministers are still poor, and that God designs and desires that they should be. It is in such circumstances that he designs they should illustrate the beauty and the sustaining power of

ing many rich; as having nothing, and *yet* possessing all [a] things.

11 O *ye* Corinthians, our mouth is open unto you, our [b] heart is enlarged.

a Ps. 84. 11.

b Ep. 6. 8; Re. 22. 12.

religion, and be examples to the world. ¶ *Yet making many rich.* On the meaning of the word rich see Note, Rom. ii. 4. Here the apostle means that he and his fellow-labourers, though poor themselves, were the instruments of conferring durable and most valuable possessions on many persons. They had bestowed on them the true riches. They had been the means of investing them with treasures infinitely more valuable than any which kings and princes could bestow. They to whom they ministered were made partakers of the treasure where the moth doth not corrupt, and where thieves do not break through nor steal. ¶ *As having nothing.* Being utterly destitute. Having no property. This was true, doubtless, in a literal sense, of most of the apostles. ¶ *And* yet *possessing all things.* That is, (1.) Possessing a portion of all things that may be necessary for our welfare, as far as our heavenly Father shall deem to be necessary for us. (2.) Possessing an interest in all things, so that we can enjoy them. We can derive pleasure from the works of God—the heavens, the earth, the hills, the streams, the cattle on the mountains or in the vales, as the works of God. We have a *possession* in them so that we can enjoy them as his works, and can say, "Our Father made them all." They are given to man to enjoy. They are a part of the inheritance of man. And though we cannot call them our own in the legal sense, yet we can call them ours in the sense that we can derive pleasure from their contemplation, and see in them the proofs of the wisdom and the goodness of God. The child of God that *looks* upon the hills and vales; upon an extensive and beautiful farm or landscape, *may* derive more *pleasure* from the contemplation of them as the work of God and his gift to men, than the real owner does, if irreligious, from contemplating all this as his own. And so far as mere happiness is concerned, the friend of God who sees in all this the proofs of God's beneficence and wisdom, may have a more valuable *possession* in those things than he who holds the title-deeds. (3.) Heirs of all things. We have a title to immortal life—a promised part in all that the universe can furnish that can make us happy. (4.) In the possession of pardon and peace; of the friendship of God and the knowledge of the Redeemer, we have the possession of all things. This comprises all. He that has this, what need has he of more? This meets all the desires; satisfies the soul; makes the man happy and blessed. He that has God for his portion, may be said to have all things, for he is "all in all." He that has the Redeemer for his friend has all things that he needs, for "he that spared not his own Son, but gave him up for us all, how shall he not with him also freely give us all things?" Rom. viii. 32.

11. *O* ye *Corinthians, our mouth is open unto you.* We speak freely, and fully. This is an affectionate address to them, and has reference to what he had just said. It means that, when the heart was full on the subject, words would flow freely; and that he had given vent to the fervid language which he had just used because his heart was full. He loved them; he felt deeply; and he spoke to them with the utmost freedom of what he had thought, and purposed, and done. ¶ *Our heart is enlarged.* We have deep feelings, which naturally vent themselves in fervent and glowing language. The main idea here is, that he had a strong affection for them; a heart which embraced and loved them all, and which expressed itself in the language of deep emotion He had loved them so that he was willing to be reproached, and to be persecuted, and to be poor, and to have his name cast out

12 Ye are not straitened in us, but ye are straitened in your own bowels.

13 Now for a recompence in the same, (I speak as unto *my* children,) be ye also enlarged.

14 Be [a] ye not unequally yoked together with unbelievers; for

a De. 7. 2, 3; 1 Cor. 7. 39.

as evil. "I cannot be silent. I conceal or dissemble nothing. I am full of ardent attachment, and that naturally vents itself in the strong language which I have used." True attachment will find means of expressing itself. A heart full of love will give vent to its feelings. There will be no dissembling and hypocrisy there. And if a minister loves the souls of his people he will pour out the affections of his heart in strong and glowing language.

12. *Ye are not straitened in us.* That is, you do not possess a narrow or contracted place in our affections. We love you fully, ardently, and are ready to do all that can be done for your welfare. There is no want of room in our affections towards you. It is not narrow, confined, pent up. It is ample and free. ¶ *But ye are straitened in your own bowels.* That is, in the affections of your hearts. The word here used (σπλάγχνα) commonly means in the Bible the tender affections. The Greek word properly denotes the *upper* viscera; the heart, the lungs, the liver. It is applied by Greek writers to denote those parts of victims which were eaten during or after the sacrifice.—*Robinson* (*Lex.*). Hence it is applied to the *heart*, as the seat of the emotions and passions; and especially the gentler emotions, the tender affections, compassion, pity, love, &c. *Our* word "bowels" is applied usually to the lower viscera, and by no means expresses the idea of the word which is used in Greek. The idea here is, that they were straitened, or were *confined* in their affections for him. It is the language of reproof, meaning that he had not received from them the demonstrations of attachment which he had a right to expect, and which was a fair and proportionate return for the love bestowed on them. Probably he refers to the fact that they had formed parties; had admitted false teachers; and had not received his instructions as implicitly and as kindly as they ought to have done.

13. *Now for a recompence in the same.* "By way of recompence, open your hearts in the same manner towards me as I have done toward you. It is all the reward or compensation which I ask of you; all the return which I desire. I do not ask silver or gold, or any earthly possessions. I ask only a return of love, and a devotedness to the cause which I love, and which I endeavour to promote." ¶ *I speak as unto* my *children.* I speak as a parent addressing his children. I sustain toward you the relation of a spiritual father, and I have a right to require and expect a return of affection. ¶ *Be ye also enlarged.* Be not straitened in your affections. Love me as I love you. Give to me the same proofs of attachment which I have given you. The idea in this verse is, that the only compensation or remuneration which he expected for all the love which he had shown them, and for all his toils and self-denials in their behalf (ver. 4, 5), was, that they would love him, and yield obedience to the laws of the gospel requiring them to be separate from the world, ver. 14—18. One ground of the claim which he had to their affection was, that he sustained toward them the relation of a father, and that he had a right to require and to expect such a return of love. The Syriac renders it well, "Enlarge your love towards me." Tindal renders it, "I speak unto you as unto children, which have like reward with us; stretch yourselves therefore out; bear not the yoke with unbelievers."

14. *Be ye not unequally yoked together with unbelievers.* This is closely connected in sense with the previous verse. The apostle is there stating the nature of the remuneration or recompence which he asks for all the love which he had shown to

what fellowship hath righteousness with unrighteousness? and what communion hath light with darkness?

them. He here says, that one mode of remuneration would be to yield obedience to his commands, and to separate themselves from all improper alliance with unbelievers. "Make me this return for my love. Love me also, and as a proof of your affection, be not improperly united with unbelievers. Listen to me as a father addressing his children, and secure your own happiness and piety by not being unequally yoked with those who are not Christians." The word which is here used (ἑτεροζυγέω) means properly, to bear a different yoke, to be yoked heterogeneously. — *Robinson* (*Lex.*). It is applied to the custom of yoking animals of different kinds together (*Passow*); and as used here means not to mingle together, or be united with unbelievers. It is implied in the use of the word that there is a dissimilarity between believers and unbelievers so great that it is as improper for them to mingle together as it is to yoke animals of different kinds and species. The ground of the injunction is, that there is a difference between Christians and those who are not, so great as to render such unions improper and injurious. The direction here refers doubtless to all kinds of improper connections with those who were unbelievers. It has been usually supposed by commentators to refer particularly to marriage. But there is no reason for confining it to marriage. It doubtless includes that, but it may as well refer to any other intimate connection, or to intimate friendships, or to participation in their amusements and employments, as to marriage. The radical idea is, that they were to abstain from *all* connections with unbelievers — with infidels, and heathens, and those who were not Christians, which would *identify* them with them; or they were to have no connection with them *in any thing as* unbelievers, heathens, or infidels; they were to partake with them in nothing that was *peculiar* to them as such. They were to have no part with them in their heathenism, unbelief, and idolatry, and infidelity; they were not to be united with them in any way or sense where it would necessarily be understood that they were partakers with them in those things. This is evidently the principle here laid down, and this principle is as applicable now as it was then. In the remainder of this verse and the following verses (15, 16), he states *reasons* why they should have no such intercourse. There is no principle of Christianity that is more important than that which is here stated by the apostle; and none in which Christians are more in danger of erring, or in which they have more difficulty in determining the exact rule which they are to follow. The questions which arise are very important. Are we to have no intercourse with the people of the world? Are we cut loose from all our friends who are not Christians? Are we to become monks, and live a recluse and unsocial life? Are we never to mingle with the people of the world in business, in innocent recreation, or in the duties of citizens, and as neighbours and friends? It is important, therefore, in the highest degree, to endeavour to ascertain what are the principles on which the New Testament requires us to act in this matter. And in order to a correct understanding of this, the following principles may be suggested. I. There is a large field of action, pursuit, principle, and thought, over which infidelity, sin, heathenism, and the world as such, have the entire control. It is wholly without the range of Christian law, and stands opposed to Christian law. It pertains to a different kingdom; is conducted by different principles, and tends to destroy and annihilate the kingdom of Christ. It cannot be reconciled with Christian principle, and cannot be conformed to but in entire violation of the influence of religion. Here the prohibition of the New Testament is absolute and entire. Christians are not to mingle with the people of the world *in* these things;

and are not to partake of them. This prohibition, it is supposed, extends to the following, among other things. (1.) To idolatry. This was plain. On no account or pretence were the early Christians to partake of that, or to countenance it. In primitive times, during the Roman persecutions, all that was asked was that they should cast a little incense on the altar of a heathen god. They refused to do it, and because they refused to do it, thousands perished as martyrs. They judged rightly; and the world has approved their cause. (2.) Sin, vice, licentiousness. This is also plain. Christians are in no way to patronise them, or to lend their influence to them, or to promote them by their name, their presence, or their property. "Neither be partakers of other men's sins;" 1 Tim. v. 22; 2 John 11. (3.) Arts and acts of dishonesty, deception, and fraud in traffic and trade. Here the prohibition also must be absolute. No Christian can have a right to enter into partnership with another where the business is to be conducted on dishonest and unchristian principles, or where it shall lead to the violation of any of the laws of God. If it involves deception and fraud in the principles on which it is conducted; if it spreads ruin and poverty—as the distilling and vending of ardent spirits does; if it leads to the necessary violation of the Christian Sabbath, then the case is plain. A Christian is to have no "fellowship with such unfruitful works of darkness, but is rather to reprove them;" Eph. v. 11. (4.) The amusements and pleasures that are entirely worldly, and sinful in their nature; that are wholly under worldly influence, and which cannot be brought under Christian principles. Nearly all amusements are of this description. The true principle here seems to be, that if a Christian in such a place is expected to lay aside his Christian principles, and if it would be deemed indecorous and improper for him to introduce the subject of religion, or if religion would be regarded as entirely inconsistent with the nature of the amusement, then he is not to be found there. The world reigns there, and if the principles of his Lord and Master would be excluded, *he* should not be there. This applies of course to the theatre, the circus, the ball-room, and to large and splendid parties of pleasure. We are not to associate with idolaters *in* their idolatry; nor with the licentious *in* their licentiousness; nor with the infidel *in* his infidelity; nor with the proud *in* their pride; nor with the gay *in* their gayety; nor with the friends of the theatre, or the ball-room, or the circus *in* their attachment to these places and pursuits. And whatever *other* connection we are to have with them as neighbours, citizens, or members of our families, we are not to participate with them IN *these things*. Thus far all seems to be clear; and the rule is a plain one, whether it applies to marriage, or to business, or to religion, or to pleasure; comp. Note, 1 Cor. v. 10. II. There is a large field of action, thought, and plan which may be said to be *common* with the Christian and the world; that is, where the Christian is not expected to abandon his own principles, and where there will be, or need be, no compromise of the sternest views of truth, or the most upright, serious, and holy conduct. He may carry his principles with him; may always manifest them if necessary; and may even commend them to others. A few of these may be referred to. (1.) Commercial transactions and professional engagements that are conducted on honest and upright principles, even when those with whom we act are not Christians. (2.) Literary and scientific pursuits, which never, when pursued with a right spirit, interfere with the principles of Christianity, and never are contrary to it. (3.) The love and affection which are due to relatives and friends. Nothing in the Bible assuredly will prohibit a pious son from uniting with one who is not pious in supporting an aged and infirm parent, or a much loved and affectionate sister. The same remark is true also respecting the duty which a wife owes to a husband, a husband to a wife, or a parent to a child, though

15 And what concord hath Christ with Belial? or what

one of them should not be a Christian. And the same observation is true also of neighbours, who are not to be prohibited from uniting *as* neighbours in social intercourse, and in acts of common kindness and charity, though all not Christians. (4.) As citizens. We owe duties to our country, and a Christian need not refuse to act with others in the elective franchise, or in making or administering the laws. Here, however, it is clear that he is not at liberty to violate the laws and the principles of the Bible. He *cannot* be at liberty to unite with them in political schemes that are contrary to the law of God, or in elevating to office men whom he cannot vote for with a good conscience as qualified for the station. (5.) In plans of public improvement, in schemes that go to the advancement of the public welfare, when the schemes do not violate the laws of God. But *if* they involve the necessity of violating the Sabbath, or any of the laws of God, assuredly he cannot consistently participate in them. (6.) In doing good to others. So the Saviour was with sinners; so he ate, and drank, and conversed with them. So we may mingle with them, without partaking of their wicked feelings and plans, so far as we can do them good, and exert over them a holy and saving influence. In all the situations here referred to, and in all the duties growing out of them, the Christian may maintain his principles, and may preserve a good conscience. Indeed the Saviour evidently contemplated that his people would have *such* intercourse with the world, and that in it they would do good. But in none of these is there to be any compromise of principle; in none to be any yielding to the opinions and practices that are contrary to the laws of God. III. There is a large field of action, conduct, and plan, where Christians only will act together. These relate to the peculiar duties of religion—to prayer, Christian fellowship, the ordinances of the gospel, and most of the plans of Christian beneficence. Here the world will not intrude; and here assuredly there will be no necessity of any compromise of Christian principle. ¶ *For what fellowship.* Paul proceeds here to state *reasons* why there should be no such improper connection with the world. The main reason, though under various forms, is that there can be no fellowship, no communion, nothing *in common* between them; and that therefore they should be separate. The word fellowship (μετοχὴ) means partnership, participation. What is there in common; or how can the one partake with the other? The interrogative form here is designed to be emphatic, and to declare in the strongest terms that there can be no such partnership. ¶ *Righteousness.* Such as you Christians are required to practise; implying that all were to be governed by the stern and uncompromising principles of honesty and justice. ¶ *With unrighteousness.* Dishonesty, injustice, sin; implying that the world is governed by such principles. ¶ *And what communion* (κοινωνία). Participation; communion; that which is *in common.* What is there in common between light and darkness? What common principle is there of which they both partake? There is none. There is a total and eternal separation. ¶ *Light.* The emblem of truth, virtue, holiness; see Note, Mat. iv. 16; v. 16; John i. 4; Rom. ii. 19; 2 Cor. iv. 4, 6. It is implied here that Christians are enlightened, and walk in the light. Their principles are pure and holy—principles of which light is the proper emblem. ¶ *Darkness.* The emblem of sin, corruption, ignorance; implying that the world to which Paul refers was governed and influenced by these. The idea is, that as there is an entire separation between light and darkness in their nature; as they have nothing in common, so it is and should be, between Christians and sinners. There should be a separation. There can be nothing in common between holiness and sin; and Christians should have nothing to do "with the unfruitful works of darkness;" Eph. v. 11.

part hath he that believeth with an infidel?

16 And what agreement hath the temple of God with idols? for ye[a] are the temple of the living God; as God hath said,[b] I will

a 1 Cor. 3.16,17; 6.19; Ep. 2.21,22.

b Ex. 29.45: Le. 26.12; Je. 31.1,33; 32.38 Ez. 11.20; 36.28; 37. 26, 27.

---

15. *And what concord* (συμφώνησις). Sympathy, unison. This word refers properly to the unison or harmony produced by musical instruments, where there is *a chord.* What accordance, what unison is there; what strings are there which being struck will produce a chord or harmony? The idea is, then, there is *as much* that is discordant between Christ and Belial as there is between instruments of music that produce only discordant and jarring sounds. ¶ *Hath Christ.* What is there in common between Christ and Belial, implying that Christians are governed by the principles, and that they follow the example of Christ. ¶ *Belial.* Βελίαλ or Βελίαρ, as it is found in some of the late editions. The form Beliar is Syriac. The Hebrew word (בליעל) means literally *without profit; worthlessness; wickedness.* It is here evidently applied to Satan. The Syriac translates it "Satan." The idea is, that the persons to whom Paul referred, the heathen, wicked, unbelieving world, were governed by the principles of Satan, and were "taken captive by him at his will" (2 Tim. ii. 26; comp. John viii. 44), and that Christians should be separate from the wicked world, as Christ was separate from all the feelings, purposes, and plans of Satan. He had no participation in them; he formed no union with them; and so it should be with the followers of the one in relation to the followers of the other. ¶ *Or what part* (μερὶς). Portion, share, participation, fellowship. This word refers usually to a division of an estate; Luke x. 42; Note, Acts viii. 21; Col. i. 12. There is no participation; nothing in common. ¶ *He that believeth.* A Christian; a man the characteristic of whom it is that he believes on the Lord Jesus. ¶ *With an infidel.* A man who does not believe—whether a heathen idolater, a profane man, a scoffer, a philosopher, a man of science, a moral man, or a son or daughter of gayety. The idea is, that on the subject of religion there is no union; nothing in common; no participation. They are governed by different principles; have different feelings; are looking to different rewards; and are tending to a different destiny. The believer, therefore, should not select his partner in life and his chosen companions and friends from this class, but from those with whom he has sympathy, and with whom he has common feelings and hopes.

16. *And what agreement* (συγκατάθεσις). Assent, accord, agreement; what *putting or laying down together* is there? What is there in one that resembles the other? ¶ *The temple of God.* What has a temple of God to do with idol worship? It is erected for a different purpose, and the worship of idols in it would not be tolerated. It is implied here that Christians are themselves the temple of God, a fact which Paul proceeds immediately to illustrate; and that it is as absurd for them to mingle with the infidel world as it would be to erect the image of a heathen god in the temple of JEHOVAH. This is strong language, and we cannot but admire the energy and copiousness of the expressions used by Paul, "which cannot," says Bloomfield, "be easily paralleled in the best classical writers." ¶ *With idols.* Those objects which God hates, and on which he cannot look but with abhorrence. The sense is, that for Christians to mingle with the sinful world; to partake of their pleasures, pursuits, and follies, is as detestable and hateful in the sight of God as if his temple were profaned by erecting a deformed, and shapeless, and senseless block in it as an object of worship. And, assuredly, if Christians had such a sense of the abomination of mingling with the world, they would feel the obligation to be separate and pure. ¶ *For ye are the*

dwell in them, and walk in *them;* and I will be their God, and they shall be my people.

17 Wherefore[a] come out from among them, and be ye separate, saith the Lord, and touch not the

a Is. 52.11; chap. 7.1: Re. 18.4.

temple of the living God; see this explained in the Notes on 1 Cor. iii. 16, 17. The idea is, that as God dwells with his people, they ought to be separated from a sinful and polluted world. ¶ *As God hath said.* The words here quoted are taken substantially from Ex. xxxix. 45; Lev. xxvi. 12; Ezek. xxxvii. 27. They are not literally quoted, but Paul has thrown together the substance of what occurs in several places. The sense, however, is the same as occurs in the places referred to. ¶ *I will dwell in them* (ἐν οἰκήσω). I will take up my indwelling in them. There is an allusion doubtless to the fact that he would be present among his people by the *Sechinah,* or the visible symbol of his presence; see Note on 1 Cor. iii. 16, 17. It implies, when used with reference to Christians, that the Holy Spirit would abide with them, and that the blessing of God would attend them; see Rom. viii; Col. iii. 16; 2 Tim. i. 14. ¶ *And walk in* them. That is, I will walk among them. I will be one of their number. He was present among the Jews by the public manifestation of his presence by a symbol; he is present with Christians by the presence and guidance of his Holy Spirit. ¶ *And I will be their God.* Not only the God whom they worship, but the God who will protect and bless them. I will take them under my peculiar protection, and they shall enjoy my favour. This is certainly *as* true of Christians as it was of the Jews, and Paul has not departed from the spirit of the promise in applying it to the Christian character. His object in quoting these passages is, to impress on Christians the solemnity and importance of the truth that God dwelt among them and with them; that they were under his care and protection; that they belonged to him, and that they therefore should be separate from the world.

17. *Wherefore.* Since you are a peculiar people. Since God, the holy and blessed God, dwells with you and among you. ¶ *Come out from among them.* That is, from among idolaters and unbelievers; from a gay and vicious world. These words are taken, by a slight change, from Isaiah lii. 11. They are there applied to the Jews in Babylon, and are a solemn call which God makes on them to leave the place of their exile, to come out from among the idolaters of that city and return to their own land; see my Note on that place. Babylon, in the Scriptures, is the emblem of whatever is proud, arrogant, wicked, and opposed to God; and Paul, therefore, applies the words here with great beauty and force to illustrate the duty of Christians in separating themselves from a vain, idolatrous, and wicked world. ¶ *And be ye separate.* Separate from the world, and all its corrupting influences. ¶ *Saith the Lord;* see Isaiah lii. 11. Paul does not use this language as if it had original reference to Christians, but he applies it as containing an important principle that was applicable to the case which he was considering, or as language that would appropriately express the idea which he wished to convey. The language of the Old Testament is often used in this manner by the writers of the New. ¶ *And touch not the unclean* thing. In Isaiah, "touch no unclean thing;" that is, they were to be pure, and to have no connection with idolatry in any of its forms. So Christians were to avoid all unholy contact with a vain and polluted world. The sense is, "Have no close connection with an idolater, or an unholy person. Be pure; and feel that you belong to a community that is under its own laws, and that is to be distinguished in moral purity from all the rest of the world." ¶ *And I will receive you.* That is, I will receive and recognise you as my friends and my adopted children. This could not be done until they were separated from an

unclean *thing:* and I will receive you,

18 And [a] will be a Father unto you, and ye shall be my sons and daughters, saith the Lord Almighty.

a Je. 31.9; Re. 21.7.

idolatrous and wicked world. The fact of their being received by God, and recognised as his children, depended on their coming out from the world. These words with the verses following, though used evidently somewhat in the form of a quotation, yet are not to be found in any single place in the Old Testament. In 2 Sam. vii. 14, God says of Solomon, "I will be his Father, and he shall be my son." In Jer. xxxi. 9, God says, "For I am a Father to Israel, and Ephraim is my first-born." It is probable that Paul had such passages in his eye, yet he doubtless designed rather to express the general sense of the promises of the Old Testament than to quote any single passage. Or why may it not be that we should regard Paul here himself as speaking as an inspired man directly, and making a promise then first communicated immediately from the Lord? Paul was inspired as well as the prophets; and it may be that he meant to communicate a promise directly from God. Grotius supposes that it was not taken from any particular place in the Old Testament, but was a part of a hymn that was in use among the Hebrews.

18. *And I will be a Father unto you.* A father is the protector, counsellor, and guide of his children. He instructs them, provides for them, and counsels them in time of perplexity. No relation is more tender than this. In accordance with this, God says, that he will be to his people their protector, counsellor, guide, and friend. He will cherish towards them the feeling of a father; he will provide for them, he will acknowledge them as his children. No higher honour can be conferred on mortals than to be adopted into the family of God, and to be permitted to call the Most High *our Father.* No rank is so elevated as that of being the sons and the daughters of the Lord Almighty. Yet this is the common appellation by which God addresses his people; and the most humble in rank, the most poor and ignorant of his friends on earth, the most despised among men, may reflect that they are the children of the ever-living God, and have the Maker of the heavens and the earth as their Father and their eternal Friend. How poor are all the honours of the world compared with this! ¶ *The Lord Almighty.* The word here used (παντοκράτωρ) occurs nowhere except in this place and in the book of Revelation; Rev. i. 8; iv. 8; xi. 17; xv. 3; xvi. 7, 14; xix. 6. 16; xxi. 22. It means one who has all power; and is applied to God in contradistinction from idols that are weak and powerless. God is able to protect his people, and they who put their trust in him shall never be confounded. What has he to fear who has a friend of almighty power?

REMARKS.

1. It is right and proper to exhort Christians not to receive the grace of God in vain, ver. 1. Even they sometimes abuse their privileges; become neglectful of the mercy of God; undervalue the truths of religion, and do not make as much as they should do of the glorious truths that are fitted to sanctify and to save. *Every Christian should endeavour to make just as much as possible of his privileges, and to become just as eminent as he can possibly be in his Christian profession.*

2. The benefits of salvation to this world come through the intercession of Jesus Christ, ver. 2. It is because God is pleased to hear him; because *he* calls on God in an accepted time that *we* have any hope of pardon. The sinner enjoys no offer of mercy, and no possibility of pardon except what he owes to Jesus Christ. Should he cease to plead for men, the offers of salvation would be withdrawn, and the race would perish for ever.

3. The world is under a dispensation of mercy, ver. 2. Men may be

saved: God is willing to show compassion, and to rescue them from ruin.

4. How important is the present moment! ver. 2. How important is *each* moment! It may be the *last* period of mercy. No sinner can calculate with any certainty on another instant of time. God holds his breath, and with infinite ease he can remove him to eternity. Eternal results hang on the present—the fleeting moment, and yet how unconcerned are the mass of men about their present condition; how unanxious about what may possibly or probably occur the next moment! Now, the sinner may be pardoned. The next moment he may be beyond the reach of forgiveness. This instant, the bliss of heaven is offered him; the next, he may be solemnly excluded from hope and heaven!

5. The ministers of the gospel should give no occasion of offence to any one, ver. 3. On each one of them depends a portion of the honour of the ministry in this world, and of the honour of Jesus Christ among men. How solemn is this reponsibility! How pure, and holy, and unblameable should they be!

6. Ministers and all Christians should be willing to suffer in the cause of the Redeemer, ver. 4, 5. If the early ministers and other Christians were called to endure the pains of imprisonment and persecution for the honour of the gospel, assuredly we should be willing also to suffer. Why should there be any more reason for their suffering than for ours?

7. We see what our religion has cost, ver. 4, 5. It has come down to us through suffering. *All* the privileges that we enjoy have been the fruit of toil, and blood, and tears, and sighs. The best blood in human veins has flowed to procure these blessings; the holiest men on earth have wept, and been scourged, and tortured, that we might possess these privileges. What thanks should we give to God for all this! How highly should we prize the religion that has cost so much!

8. In trial we should evince such a spirit as not to dishonour, but to honour our religion, ver. 3—5. This is as incumbent on all Christians as it is on ministers of the gospel. It is in such scenes that the reality of religion is tested. It is then that its power is seen. It is then that its value may be known. Christians and Christian ministers often do good in circumstances of poverty, persecution, and sickness, which they never do in health, and in popular favour, and in prosperity. And God often places his people in trial that they may do good then, expecting that they will accomplish more then than they could in prosperous circumstances. They whose aim it is to do good have often occasion to bless God that they were subjected to trial. Bunyan wrote the "Pilgrim's Progress" in a dungeon, and almost all the works of Baxter were written when he was suffering under persecution, and forbidden to preach the gospel. The devil is often foiled in this way. He persecutes and opposes Christians; and on the rack and at the stake they do most to destroy his kingdom; he throws them into dungeons, and they make books which go down even to the millennium, making successful war on the empire of darkness. Christians, therefore, should esteem it a privilege to be permitted *to suffer* on account of Christ; Phil. i. 29.

9. If ministers and other Christians do any good they must be pure, ver. 6, 7. The gospel is to be commended by pureness, and knowledge, and the word of truth, and the armour of righteousness. It is in this way that they are to meet opposition; in this way that they are to propagate their sentiments. No man need expect to do good in the ministry or as a private Christian, who is not a holy man. No man who *is* a holy man can help doing good. It will be a matter of course that he will shed a healthful moral influence around him. And he will no more live without effect than the sun sheds its steady beams on the earth without effect. His influence may be very noiseless and still, like the sunbeams or the dew, but it will be felt in the world. Wicked men can resist any thing else better than they can a holy example. They can make a

mock of preaching; they can deride exhortation; they can throw away a tract; they can burn the Bible; but what can they do against a holy example? No more than they can against the vivifying and enlightening beams of the sun; and a man who leads a holy life cannot help doing good, and cannot be prevented from doing good.

10. They who are Christians must expect to meet with much dishonour, and to be subjected often to the influence of evil report, ver. 8. The world is unfriendly to religion, and its friends must never be surprised if their motives are impeached, and their names calumniated.

11. Especially is this the case with ministers, ver. 8. They should make up their minds to it, and they should not suppose that any strange thing had happened to them if they are called thus to suffer.

12. They who are about to make a profession of religion, and they who are about entering on the work of the ministry, or who are agitating the question whether they should be ministers, should ask themselves whether they are prepared for this. They should count the cost; nor should they either make a profession of religion or think of the ministry as a profession, unless they are willing to meet with dishonour, and to go through evil report; to be poor (ver. 10), and to be despised and persecuted, or to die in the cause which they embrace.

13. Religion has power to sustain the soul in trials, ver. 10. Why should he be sad who has occasion to rejoice always? Why should he deem himself poor, though he has slender earthly possessions, who is able to make many rich? Why should he be melancholy as if he had nothing, who has Christ as his portion, and who is an heir of all things? Let not the poor, who are rich in faith, despond as though they had nothing. They have a treasure which gold cannot purchase, and which will be of infinite value when all other treasure fails. He that has an everlasting inheritance in heaven cannot be called a poor man. And he that can look to such an inheritance should not be unwilling to part with his earthly possessions. Those who seem to be most wealthy are often the poorest of mortals; and those who seem to be poor, or who are in humble circumstances, often have an enjoyment of even this world which is unknown in the palaces and at the tables of the great. They look on all things as the work of their Father; and in their humble dwellings, and with their humble fare, they have an enjoyment of the bounties of their heavenly Benefactor, which is not experienced often in the dwellings of the great and the rich.

14. A people should render to a minister and a pastor a return of love and confidence that shall be proportionate to the love which is shown to them, ver. 12. This is but a reasonable and fair requital, and this is necessary not only to the comfort, but to the success of a minister. What good can he do unless he has the affections and confidence of his people?

15. The compensation or recompence which a minister has a right to expect and require for arduous toil is, that his people should be "enlarged" in love towards him, and that they should yield themselves to the laws of the Redeemer, and be separate from the world, ver. 13. And this is an ample reward. It is what he seeks, what he prays for, what he most ardently desires. If he is worthy of his office, he will seek not theirs but them (2 Cor. xii. 14), and he will be satisfied for all his toils if he sees them walking in the truth (3 John 4), and showing in their lives the pure and elevated principles of the gospel which they profess to love.

16. The welfare of religion depends on the fact that Christians should be separate from a vain, and gay, and wicked world, ver. 14—16. Why should they partake of those things in which they can, if Christians, have nothing in common? Why attempt to mingle light with darkness? to form a compact between Christ and Belial? or to set up a polluted idol in the temple of the living God? The truth is, there are great and eternal principles in the gospel which should not be sur-

CHAPTER VII.

HAVING therefore these[a] promises, dearly beloved, let us cleanse[b] ourselves from all filthiness of the flesh and spirit, perfecting holiness in the fear of God.

a chap.6.17,18; 1 John 3.3.

b Ps.51.10; Eze.36.25,26; 1 John 1.7, 9.

rendered, and which cannot be broken down. Christ intended to set up a kingdom that should be unlike the kingdoms of this world. And he designed that his people should be governed by different principles from the people of this world.

17. They who are about to make a profession of religion should resolve to separate themselves from the world, ver. 14, 15. Religion cannot exist where there is no such separation, and they who are unwilling to forsake infidel companions and the gay amusements and vanities of life, and to find their chosen friends and pleasures among the people of God, can have no evidence that they are Christians. The world with all its wickedness and its gay pleasures must be forsaken, and there must be an effectual line drawn between the friends of God and the friends of sin.

Let us, then, who profess to be the friends of the Redeemer remember how pure and holy we should be. It should not be indeed with the spirit of the Pharisee; it should not be with a spirit that will lead us to say, "stand by, for I am holier than thou;" but it should be, while we discharge all our duties to our impenitent friends, and while in all our intercourse with the world we should be honest and true, and while we do not refuse to mingle with them as neighbours and citizens as far as we can without compromitting Christian principles, still our chosen friends and our dearest friendships should be with the people of God. For, his friends should be our friends; our happiness should be with them, and the world should see that we *prefer* the friends of the Redeemer to the friends of gayety, ambition, and sin.

18. Christians are the holy temple of God, ver. 16. How pure should they be! How free should they be from sin! How careful to maintain consciences void of offence!

19. What an inestimable privilege it is to be a Christian! (ver. 18); to be a child of God! to feel that he is a Father and a Friend! to feel that though we may be forsaken by all others; though poor and despised, yet there is one who never forsakes; one who never forgets that he has sons and daughters dependent on him, and who need his constant care. Compared with this, how small the honour of being permitted to call the rich our friends, or to be regarded as the sons or daughters of nobles and of princes! Let the Christian then most highly prize his privileges, and feel that he is raised above all the elevations of rank and honour which this world can bestow. All these shall fade away, and the highest and the lowest shall meet on the same level in the grave, and alike return to dust. But the elevation of the child of God shall only begin to be visible and appreciated when all other honours fade away.

20. Let all seek to become the sons and daughters of the Lord Almighty. Let us aspire to this rather than to earthly honours; let us seek this rather than to be numbered with the rich and the great. All cannot be honoured in this world, and few are they who can be regarded as belonging to elevated ranks here. But *all* may be the children of the living God, and be permitted to call the Lord Almighty their Father and their Friend. O! if men could as easily be permitted to call themselves the sons of monarchs and princes; if they could as easily be admitted to the palaces of the great and sit down at their tables *as they can enter heaven,* how greedily would they embrace it! And yet how poor and paltry would be such honour and pleasure compared with that of feeling that we are the adopted children of the great and the eternal God!

CHAPTER VII.

THE first verse of this chapter properly belongs to the previous chapter, and should have been attached to that.

It is an exhortation made in view of the promises there referred to, to make every effort to obtain perfect purity, and to become entirely holy.

In ver. 2, 3, he entreats the Corinthians, in accordance with the wish which he had expressed in chap. vi. 13, to receive him as a teacher and a spiritual father; as a faithful apostle of the Lord Jesus. To induce them to do this, he assures them that he had given them, at no time, any occasion of offence. He had injured no man; he had wronged no man. Possibly some might suppose that he had injured them by the sternness of his requirements in forbidding them to contract friendships and alliances with infidels; or in the case of discipline in regard to the incestuous person. But he assures them that all his commands had been the fruit of most tender love for them, and that he was ready to live and die with them.

The remainder of the chapter (ver. 4—15) is occupied mainly in stating the *joy* which he had at the evidence which they had given that they were ready to obey his commands. He says, therefore (ver. 4), that he was full of comfort and joy; and that in all his tribulation, the evidence of their obedience had given him great and unfeigned satisfaction. In order to show them the extent of his joy, he gives a pathetic description of the anxiety of mind which he had on the subject; his troubles in Macedonia, and particularly his distress on not meeting with Titus as he had expected, ver. 5. But this distress had been relieved by his coming, and by the evidence which was furnished through him that they were ready to yield obedience to his commands, ver. 6, 7. This joy was greatly increased by his hearing from Titus the effect which his former epistle to them had produced, ver. 8—13. He had felt deep anxiety in regard to that. He had even regretted, it would seem (ver. 8), that he had sent it. He had been deeply pained at the necessity of giving them pain, ver. 8. But the effect had been all that he had desired; and when he learned from Titus the effect which it had produced—the deep repentance which they had evinced, and the thorough reformation which had occurred (ver. 9—11), he had great occasion to rejoice that he had sent the epistle to them. This new and distinguished instance of their obedience had given him great joy, and confirmed him in the proof that they were truly attached to him. The apostle adds, in the conclusion of the chapter, that his jo , was greatly increased by the joy which Titus manifested, and his entire satisfaction in the conduct of the Corinthians and the treatment which he had received from them (ver. 13), so that though he, Paul, had often had occasion to speak in the kindest terms of the Corinthians, all that he had ever said in their favour Titus had realized in his own case (ver. 14), and the affection of Titus for them had been greatly increased by his visit to them, ver. 15. The whole chapter, therefore, is eminently adapted to produce good feeling in the minds of the Corinthians toward the apostle, and to strengthen the bonds of their mutual attachment.

1. *Having therefore these promises.* The promises referred to in chap. vi 17, 18; the promise that God would be a Father, a protector, and a friend The idea is, that as we have a promise that God would dwell in us, that he would be our God, that he would be to us a Father, we should remove from us whatever is offensive in his sight, and become perfectly holy. ¶ *Let us cleanse ourselves.* Let us purify ourselves. Paul was not afraid to bring into view the agency of Christians themselves in the work of salvation. He, therefore, says, 'let us purify ourselves,' as if Christians had much to do; as if their own agency was to be employed; and as if their purifying was dependent on their own efforts. While it is true that all purifying influence and all holiness proceeds from God, it is also true that the effect of all the influences of the Holy Spirit is to excite us to diligence to purify our own hearts, and to urge us to make strenuous efforts to overcome our own sins. He who expects to be made pure without any effort of his own, will never become pure; and

he who ever becomes holy will become so in consequence of strenuous efforts to resist the evil of his own heart, and to become like God. The *argument* here is, that we have the promises of God to aid us. We do not go about the work in our own strength. It is not a work in which we are to have no aid. But it is a work which God desires, and where he will give us all the aid which we need. ¶ *From all filthiness of the flesh.* The noun here used (μολυσμὸς) occurs nowhere else in the New Testament. The *verb* occurs in 1 Cor. viii. 7; Rev. iii. 4; xiv. 4, and means to stain, defile, pollute, as a garment; and the word here used means *a soiling*, hence defilement, pollution, and refers to the defiling and corrupting influence of fleshly desires and carnal appetites. The filthiness of the flesh here denotes evidently the gross and corrupt appetites and passions of the body, including all such actions of all kinds as are inconsistent with the virtue and purity with which the body, regarded as the temple of the Holy Ghost, should be kept holy—all such passions and appetites as the Holy Spirit of God would not produce. ¶ *And spirit.* By "filthiness of the spirit," the apostle means, probably, all the thoughts or mental associations that defile the man. Thus the Saviour (Mat. xv. 19) speaks of evil thoughts, &c. that proceed out of the heart, and that pollute the man. And probably Paul here includes all the sins and passions which appertain particularly to mind or to the soul rather than to carnal appetites, such as the desire of revenge, pride, avarice, ambition, &c. These are in themselves as polluting and defiling as the gross sensual pleasures. They stand as much in the way of sanctification, they are as offensive to God, and they prove as certainly that the heart is depraved as the grossest sensual passions. The main difference is, that they are more *decent* in the external appearance; they can be better concealed; they are usually indulged by a more elevated class in society; but they are not the less offensive to God. It may be added, also, that they are often conjoined in the same person; and that the man who is defiled in his "spirit" is often a man most corrupt and sensual in his "flesh." Sin sweeps with a desolating influence through the whole frame, and it usually leaves no part unaffected, though some part may be more deeply corrupted than others. ¶ *Perfecting.* This word (ἐπιτελοῦντες) means properly to bring to an end, to finish, complete. The idea here is, that of carrying it out to the completion. Holiness had been commenced in the heart, and the exhortation of the apostle is, that they should make every effort that it might be complete in all its parts. He does not say that this work of perfection had ever been accomplished—nor does he say that it had not been. He only urges the obligation to make an effort to be entirely holy; and this obligation is not affected by the inquiry whether any one has been or has not been perfect. It is an obligation which results from the nature of the law of God and his unchangeable claims on the soul. The fact that no one has been perfect does not relax the claim; the fact that no one will be in this life does not weaken the obligation. It proves only the deep and dreadful depravity of the human heart, and should humble us under the stubbornness of guilt. The obligation to be perfect is one that is unchangeable and eternal; see Mat. v. 48; 1 Pet. i. 15. Tindal renders this, "and grow up to full holiness in the fear of God." The unceasing and steady aim of every Christian should be perfection—perfection in all things—in the love of God, of Christ, of man; perfection of heart, and feeling, and emotion; perfection in his words, and plans, and dealings with men; perfection in his prayers, and in his submission to the will of God. No man can be a Christian who does not sincerely desire it, and who does not constantly aim at it. No man is a friend of God who can acquiesce in a state of sin, and who is satisfied and contented that he is not as holy as God is holy. And any man who has no desire to be perfect as God is, and who does not make it his daily and constant aim to be as

2 Receive us; we have wronged no man, we have corrupted no man, [a] we have defrauded no man.

3 I speak not *this* to condemn *you;* for I have said [b] before, that ye are in our hearts to die and live with *you.*

a 1 Sa.12.3,4; Ac.20.33, chap.12.17.

b chap.6.11,12.

perfect as God, may set it down as demonstrably certain that he has no true religion. How can a man be a Christian who is willing to acquiesce in a state of sin, and who does not desire to be just like his Master and Lord? ¶ *In the fear of God.* Out of fear and reverence of God. From a regard to his commands, and a reverence for his name. The idea seems to be, that we are always in the presence of God; we are professedly under his law; and we should be awed and restrained by a sense of his presence from the commission of sin, and from indulgence in the pollutions of the flesh and spirit. There are many sins that the presence of a child will restrain a man from committing; and how should the conscious presence of a holy God keep us from sin! If the fear of man or of a child will restrain us, and make us attempt to be holy and pure, how should the fear of the all-present and the all-seeing God keep us not only from outward sins, but from polluted thoughts and unholy desires!

2. *Receive us.* Tindal renders this, "understand us." The word here used (χωρήσατε) means properly, give space, place, or room; and it means here evidently, make place or room for us in your affections; that is, admit or receive us as your friends. It is an earnest entreaty that they would do what he had exhorted them to do in chap. vi. 13; see Note on that verse. From that he had digressed in the close of the last chapter. He here returns to the subject, and asks an interest in their affections and their love. ¶ *We have wronged no man* We have done injustice to no man. This is given as a reason why they should admit him to their full confidence and affection. It is not improbable that he had been charged with injuring the incestuous person by the severe discipline which he had found it necessary to inflict on him; Note 1 Cor. v. 5. This charge would not improbably be brought against him by the false teachers in Corinth. But Paul here says, that whatever was the severity of the discipline, he was conscious of having done injury to no member of that church. It is possible, however, that he does not here refer to any such charge, but that he says in general that he had done no injury, and that there was no reason why they should not receive him to their entire confidence. It argues great consciousness of integrity when a man who has spent a considerable time, as Paul had, with others, is able to say that he had wronged no man in any way. Paul could not have made this solemn declaration unless he was certain he had lived a very blameless life; comp. Acts xx. 33. ¶ *We have corrupted no man.* This means that he had corrupted no man in his morals, either by his precept or his example. The word (φθείρω) means in general to bring into a worse state or condition, and is very often applied to morals. The idea is, here, that Paul had not by his precept or example made any man the worse. He had not corrupted his principles or his habits, or led him into sin. ¶ *We have defrauded no man.* We have taken no man's property by cunning, by trick, or by deception. The word πλεονεκτέω means literally to have more than another, and then to take advantage, to seek unlawful gain, to circumvent, defraud, deceive. The idea is, that Paul had taken advantage of no circumstances to extort money from them, to overreach them, or to cheat them. It is the conviction of a man who was conscious that he had lived honestly, and who could appeal to them all as full proof that his life among them had been blameless.

3. *I speak not* this *to condemn* you. I do not speak this with any desire to reproach you. I do not complain of you for the purpose of condemning, or because I have a desire to find fault,

4 Great *is* my boldness of speech
toward you, great[a] *is* my glorying of you: I am filled with comfort, I am exceeding joyful[b] in all
our tribulation.
5 For, when we were come into

a 1 Co.1.4; chap.1.14.

b Ph.2.17; Col.1.24.

though I am compelled to speak in some respect of your want of affection and liberality towards me. It is not because I have no love for you, and wish to have occasion to use words implying complaint and condemnation. ¶ *For I have said before;* chap. vii. 11, 12. ¶ *That ye are in our hearts.* That is, we are so much attached to you; or you have such a place in our affections. ¶ *To die and live with you.* If it were the will of God, we would be glad to spend our lives among you, and to die with you; an expression denoting most tender attachment. A similar well-known expression occurs in Horace:

Tecum vivere amem, tecum obeam libens.
Odes, B. III. IX. 24.
With the world I live, with the world I die.

This was an expression of the tenderest attachment. It was true that the Corinthians had not shown themselves remarkably worthy of the affections of Paul, but from the beginning he had felt towards them the tenderest attachment. And if it had been the will of God that he should cease to travel, and to expose himself to perils by sea and land to spread the knowledge of the Saviour, he would gladly have confined his labours to them, and there have ended his days.

4. *Great* is *my boldness of speech toward you.* This verse seems designed to soften the apparent harshness of what he had said (chap. vi. 12), when he intimated that there was a want of love in them towards him (*Bloomfield*), as well as to refer to the plainness which he had used all along in his letters to them. He says, therefore, that he speaks freely; he speaks as a friend; he speaks with the utmost openness and frankness; he conceals nothing from them. He speaks freely of their faults, and he speaks freely of his love to them; and he as frankly commends them and praises them. It is the open, undisguised language of a friend, when he throws open his whole soul and conceals nothing. ¶ *Great* is *my glorying of you.* I have great occasion to commend and praise you, and I do it freely. He refers here to the fact that he had boasted of their liberality in regard to the proposed collection for the poor saints of Judea (chap. ix. 4); that he had formerly boasted much of them to Titus, and of their readiness to obey his commands (ver. 14); and that now he had had abundant evidence, by what he had heard from Titus (ver. 5. seq.), that they were disposed to yield to his commands, and obey his injunctions. He had probably often had occasion to boast of their favourable regard for him. ¶ *I am filled with comfort.* That is, by the evidence which I have received of your readiness to obey me. ¶ *I am exceeding joyful.* I am overjoyed. The word here used occurs nowhere else in the New Testament except in Rom. v. 20. It is not found in the classic writers; and is a word which Paul evidently compounded (from ὑπὲρ and περισσεύω), and means to *superabound over*, to superabound greatly, or exceedingly. It is a word which would be used only when the heart was full, and when it would be difficult to find words to express its conceptions. Paul's heart was full of joy; and he pours forth his feelings in the most fervid and glowing language. I have joy which cannot be expressed. ¶ *In all our tribulation;* see Note, chap. i. 4.

5. *For when we were come into Macedonia.* For the reasons which induced Paul to go into Macedonia; see Notes on chap. i. 16; comp. Notes, chap. ii. 12, 13. ¶ *Our flesh had no rest.* We were exceedingly distressed and agitated. We had no rest. The causes of his distress he immediately states. ¶ *But we were troubled on every side.* In every way. We had no rest in any quarter. We were obliged to enter into harassing labours and strifes there, and we were full of

Macedonia, our flesh had no rest, but we were troubled on every side; without[a] *were* fightings, within *were* fears.

6 Nevertheless God, that comforteth those that are cast down, comforted us by the coming of Titus;[b]

7 And not by his coming only, but by the consolation wherewith he was comforted in you, when he told us your earnest desire, your

a De.32.25.

b chap.2.13.

anxiety in regard to you. ¶ *Without were fightings.* Probably he here refers to fierce opposition, which he met with in prosecuting his work of preaching the gospel. He met there, as he did everywhere, with opposition from Pagans, Jews, and false brethren. Tumults were usually excited wherever he went; and he preached the gospel commonly amidst violent opposition. ¶ *Within were fears.* Referring probably to the anxiety which he had in regard to the success of the epistle which he had sent to the church at Corinth. He felt great solicitude on the subject. He had sent Titus there to see what was the state of the church and to witness the effect of his instructions. Titus had not come to him as he had expected, at Troas (chap. ii. 13), and he felt the deepest anxiety in regard to him and to the success of his epistle. His fears were probably that they would be indisposed to exercise the discipline on the offender; or lest the severity of the discipline required should alienate them from him; or lest the party under the influence of the false teachers should prevail. All was uncertainty, and his mind was filled with the deepest apprehension.

6. *God that comforteth those that are cast down.* Whose characteristic is, that he gives consolation to those who are anxious and depressed. All his consolation was in God; and by whatever instrumentality comfort was administered, he regarded and acknowledged God as the author; see Note, chap. i. 4. ¶ *By the coming of Titus.* To Macedonia. He rejoiced not only in again seeing him, but especially in the intelligence which he brought respecting the success of his epistle, and the conduct of the church at Corinth.

7. *And not by his coming only.* Not merely by the fact that he was restored to me, and that my anxieties in regard to him were now dissipated. It is evident that Paul, not having met with Titus as he had expected, at Troas, had felt much anxiety on his account, perhaps apprehending that he was sick, or that he had died. ¶ *But by the consolation wherewith he was comforted in you.* Titus was satisfied and delighted with his interview with you. He had been kindly treated, and he had seen all the effect produced by the letter which he had desired. He had, therefore, been much comforted by his visit to Corinth, and this was a source of additional joy to Paul. He rejoiced at what he had witnessed among you, and he imparted the same joy to me also. The joy of one friend will diffuse itself through the heart of another. Joy is diffusive, and one Christian cannot well be happy without making others happy also. ¶ *When he told us of your earnest desire.* Either to rectify what was amiss (*Doddridge, Clarke*); or to see me.—*Macknight, Rosenmuller, Bloomfield.* It seems to me that the connection requires us to understand it of their desire, their anxiety to comply with his commands, and to reform the abuses which existed in the church, and which had given him so much pain. ¶ *Your mourning.* Produced by the epistle. Your deep repentance over the sins which had prevailed in the church. ¶ *Your fervent mind toward me.* Greek, 'Your *zeal* for me.' It denotes that they evinced great *ardour* of attachment to him, and an earnest desire to comply with his wishes. ¶ *So that I rejoiced the more.* I not only rejoiced at his coming, but I rejoiced the more at what he told me of you. Under any circumstances the coming of Titus would have been an occasion

mourning, your fervent mind toward me; so that I rejoiced the more.

8 For though I made you sorry with a letter, I do not repent, though I [a] did repent: for I perceive that the same epistle hath made you sorry, though *it were* but for a season.

9 Now I rejoice, not that ye

a chap.2.4.

---

of joy; but it was especially so from the account which he gave me of you.

8. *For though I made you sorry*, &c. That is, in the first epistle which he had sent to them. In that epistle he had felt it necessary to reprove them for their dissensions and other disorders which had occurred and which were tolerated in the church. That epistle was fitted to produce pain in them—as severe and just reproof always does; and Paul felt very anxious about its effect on them. It was painful to him to write it, and he was well aware that it must cause deep distress among them to be thus reproved. ¶ *I do not repent.* I have seen such happy effects produced by it; it has so completely answered the end which I had in view; it was so kindly received, that I do not regret now that I wrote it. It gives me no pain in the recollection, but I have occasion to rejoice that it was done. ¶ *Though I did repent.* Doddridge renders this, "however anxious I may have been." The word here used does not denote repentance in the sense in which that word is commonly understood, as if any wrong had been done. It is not the language of remorse. It can denote here nothing more than "that uneasiness which a good man feels, not from the consciousness of having done wrong, but from a tenderness for others, and a fear lest that which, prompted by duty, he had said, should have too strong an effect upon them."—*Campbell*, diss. vi. part iii. § 9. See the meaning of the word further illustrated in the same dissertation. The word (μεταμέλομαι) denotes properly to change one's purpose or mind after having done any thing (*Robinson*); or an uneasy feeling of regret for what has been done without regard either to duration or effects.—*Campbell.* Here it is not to be understood that Paul meant to say he had done any thing wrong. He was an inspired man, and what he had said was proper and right. But he was a man of deep feeling, and of tender affections. He was pained at the necessity of giving reproof. And there is no improbability in supposing that after the letter had been sent off, and he reflected on its nature and on the pain which it would cause to those whom he tenderly loved, there might be some misgiving of heart about it, and the deepest anxiety, and regret at the necessity of doing it. What parent is there who has not had the same feeling as this? He has felt it necessary to correct a beloved child, and has formed the purpose, and has executed it. But is there no misgiving of heart? No question asked whether it might not have been dispensed with? No internal struggle; no sorrow; no emotion which may be called *regret* at the resolution which has been taken? Yet there is no *repentance* as if the parent had done wrong. He feels that he has done what was right and necessary. He approves his own course, and has occasion of rejoicing at the good effects which follow. Such appears to have been the situation of the apostle Paul in this case; and it shows that he had a tender heart, that he did not delight in giving pain, and that he had no desire to overwhelm them with grief. When the effect was seen, he was not unwilling that they should be apprized of the pain which it had cost him. When a parent has corrected a child, no injury is done if the child becomes acquainted with the strugglings which it has cost him, and the deep pain and anxiety caused by the necessity of resorting to chastisement. ¶ *For I perceive*, &c. I perceive the good effect of the epistle. I perceive that it produced the kind of sorrow in you which I desired. I see that it has produced permanent good results. The sorrow which it caused in you is

were made sorry, but that ye sorrowed to repentance: for ye were made sorry, [1] after a godly manner, that ye might receive damage by us in nothing.

10 For godly sorrow [a] worketh

1 or, *according to God.*

a Je.31.9; Ez.7.16.

only for a season; the good effects will be abiding. I have, therefore, great occasion to rejoice that I sent the epistle. It produced permanent repentance and reformation (ver. 9), and thus accomplished all that I wished or desired.

9. *Now I rejoice, not that ye were made sorry,* &c. I have no pleasure in giving pain to any one, or in witnessing the distress of any. When men are brought to repentance under the preaching of the gospel, the ministers of the gospel do not find pleasure *in* their grief as such. They are not desirous of making men unhappy by calling them to repentance, and they have no pleasure in the deep distress of mind which is often produced by their preaching, in itself considered. It is only because such sorrow is an indication of their return to God, and will be followed by happiness and by the fruits of good living, that they find any pleasure in it, or that they seek to produce it. ¶ *But that ye sorrowed to repentance.* It was not mere grief; it was not sorrow producing melancholy, gloom, or despair; it was not sorrow which led you to be angry at him who had reproved you for your errors—as is sometimes the case with the sorrow that is produced by reproof; but it was sorrow that led to a change and reformation. It was sorrow that was followed by a putting away of the evil for the existence of which there had been occasion to reprove you. The word here rendered "repentance" (μετάνοιαν) is a different word from that which, in ver. 8, is rendered "I did repent," and indicates a different state of mind. It properly means a change of mind or purpose; comp. Heb. xii. 7. It denotes a change for the better; a change of mind that is durable and productive in its consequences; a change which amounts to a permanent reformation; see Campbell's Diss. ut supra. The sense here is, that it produced a change, a reformation. It was such sorrow for their sin as to lead them to reform and to put away the evils which had existed among them. It was this fact, and not that they had been made sorry, that led Paul to rejoice. ¶ *After a godly manner.* Marg. "according to God;" see Note on the next verse. ¶ *That ye might receive damage by us in nothing.* The Greek word rendered "receive damage" (ζημιωθῆτε) means properly to bring loss upon any one; to receive loss or detriment; see Note on 1 Cor. iii. 15; comp. Phil. iii. 8. The sense here seems to be, "So that on the whole no real injury was done you in any respect by me. You were indeed put to pain and grief by my reproof. You sorrowed. But it has done you no injury on the whole. It has been a benefit to you. If you had not reformed, if you had been pained without putting away the sins for which the reproof was administered, if it had been *mere* grief without any proper fruit, you might have said that you would have suffered a loss of happiness, or you might have given me occasion to inflict severer discipline. But now you are gainers in happiness by all the sorrow which I have caused." Sinners are gainers in happiness in the end by all the pain of repentance produced by the preaching of the gospel. No man suffers loss by being told of his faults if he repents; and men are under the highest obligations to those faithful ministers and other friends who tell them of their errors, and who are the means of bringing them to true repentance.

10. *For godly sorrow.* "Sorrow according to God" (Ἡ γὰρ κατὰ Θεὸν λύπη). That is, such sorrow as has respect to God, or is according to his will, or as leads the soul to him. This is a very important expression in regard to true repentance, and shows the exact nature of that sorrow which is connected with a return to God. The phrase may be regarded as implying the following things. (1.) Such sorrow as God *approves*, or such as is

suitable to, or conformable to his will and desires. It cannot mean that it is such sorrow or grief as God has, for he has none; but such as shall be in accordance with what God *demands* in a return to him. It is a sorrow which his truth is fitted to produce on the heart; such a sorrow as shall *appropriately* arise from viewing sin as God views it; such sorrow as exists in the mind when our views accord with his in regard to the existence, the extent, the nature, and the ill-desert of sin. Such views will lead to sorrow that it has ever been committed; and such views will be "according to God." (2.) Such sorrow as shall be exercised *towards* God in view of sin; which shall arise from a view of the evil of sin as committed against a holy God. It is not mainly that it will lead to pain; that it will overwhelm the soul in disgrace; that it will forfeit the favour or lead to the contempt of man; or that it will lead to an eternal hell; but it is such as arises from a view of the evil of sin as committed against a holy and just God, deriving its *main* evil from the fact that it is an offence against his infinite Majesty. Such sorrow David had (Ps. li. 4), when he said, "against thee, thee only have I sinned;" when the offence regarded as committed against man, enormous as it was, was lost and absorbed in its greater evil when regarded as committed against God. So all true and genuine repentance is that which regards sin as deriving its main evil from the fact that it is committed *against God*. (3.) That which leads *to God*. It leads *to* God to obtain forgiveness; to seek for consolation. A heart truly contrite and penitent seeks God, and implores pardon from him. Other sorrow in view of sin than that which is genuine repentance, leads the person *away* from God. He seeks consolation in the world; he endeavours to drive away his serious impressions or to drown them in the pleasures and the cares of life. But genuine sorrow for sin leads the soul *to* God, and conducts the sinner, through the Redeemer, to him to obtain the pardon and peace which he only can give to a wounded spirit. In God alone can pardon and true peace be found; and godly sorrow for sin will seek them there. ¶ *Worketh repentance.* Produces a change that shall be permanent; a reformation. It is not mere regret; it does not soon pass away in its effects, but it produces permanent and abiding changes. A man who mourns over sin as committed against God, and who seek *to* God for pardon, will reform his life and truly repent. He who has grief for sin only because it will lead to disgrace or shame, or because it will lead to poverty or pain, will not necessarily break off from it and reform. It is only when it is seen that sin is committed against God and is evil in his sight, that it leads to a change of life. ¶ *Not to be repented of* (ἀμεταμέλητον); see Note on ver. 8. Not to be regretted. It is permanent and abiding. There is no occasion to mourn over such repentance and change of life. It is that which the mind approves, and which it will always approve. There will be no reason for regretting it, and it will never be regretted. And it is so. Who ever yet repented of having truly repented of sin? Who is there, who has there ever been, who became a true penitent, and a true Christian, who ever regretted it? Not an individual has ever been known who regretted his having become a Christian. Not one who regretted that he had become one too soon in life, or that he had served the Lord Jesus too faithfully or too long. ¶ *But the sorrow of the world.* All sorrow which is not toward God, and which does not arise from just views of sin as committed against God, or lead to God. Probably Paul refers here to the sorrow which arises from worldly causes and which does not lead to God for consolation. Such may be the sorrow which arises from the loss of friends or property; from disappointment, or from shame and disgrace. Perhaps it may include the following things. (1.) Sorrow arising from losses of property and friends, and from disappointment. (2.) Sorrow for sin or vice when it overwhelms the mind with the consciousness of guilt, and when it does not lead to God, and when there is no repentance to salvation not to be repented of: but the sorrow of the world[a] worketh death.

11 For behold this self-same thing, that ye sorrowed after a godly[b] sort, what carefulness[c] it

a Pr.17.22. b Is.66.2. c Tit.3.8.

contrition of soul from viewing it as an offence against God. Thus a female who has wandered from the paths of virtue, and involved her family and herself in disgrace; or a man who has been guilty of forgery, or perjury, or any other disgraceful crime, and who is detected; a man who has violated the laws of the land, and who has involved himself and family in disgrace, will often feel regret, and sorrow, and also remorse, but it arises wholly from worldly considerations, and does not lead to God. (3.) When the sorrow arises from a view of worldly consequences merely, and when there is no looking to God for pardon and consolation. Thus men, when they lose their property or friends, often pine in grief without looking to God. Thus when they have wandered from the path of virtue and have fallen into sin, they often look merely to the *disgrace* among men, and see their names blasted, and their comforts gone, and pine away in grief. There is no looking to God for pardon or for consolation. The sorrow arises from this world, and it terminates there. It is the loss of what they valued pertaining to this world, and it is all which they had, and it produces death. It is sorrow such as the men of this world have, begins with this world, and terminates with this world. ¶ *Worketh death.* Tends to death, spiritual, temporal, and eternal. It does not tend to life. (1.) It produces distress only. It is attended with no consolation. (2.) It tends to break the spirit, to destroy the peace, and to mar the happiness. (3.) It often leads to death itself. The spirit is broken, and the heart pines away under the influence of the unalleviated sorrow; or under its influence men often lay violent hands on themselves and take their lives. Life is *often* closed under the influence of such sorrow. (4.) It tends to eternal death. There is no looking to God; no looking for pardon. It produces murmuring, repining, complaining, fretfulness against God, and thus leads to his displeasure and to the condemnation and ruin of the soul.

11. *For behold this self-same thing.* For see in your own case the happy effects of godly sorrow. See the effects which it produced; see an illustration of what it is fitted to produce. The construction is, "For lo! this very thing, to wit, your sorrowing after a godly manner, wrought carefulness, clearing of yourselves," &c. The object of Paul is to illustrate the effects of godly sorrow, to which he had referred in ver. 10. He appeals, therefore, to their own case, and says that it was beautifully illustrated among themselves. ¶ *What carefulness* (σπουδὴν). This word properly denotes *speed, haste;* then diligence, earnest effort, forwardness. Here it is evidently used to denote the diligence and the great anxiety which they manifested to remove the evils which existed among them. They went to work to remove them. They did not sit down to mourn over them merely, nor did they *wait* for God to remove them, nor did they plead that they could do nothing, but they set about the work as though they believed it might be done. When men are thoroughly convinced of sin, they will set about removing it with the utmost diligence. They will feel that this can be done, and must be done, or that the soul will be lost. ¶ What *clearing of yourselves* (ἀπολογίαν). Apology. This word properly means a plea or defence before a tribunal or elsewhere; Acts xxii. 1; 2 Tim. iv. 16. Tindal renders it, "Yea, it caused you to clear yourselves." The word here properly means *apology* for what had been done; and it probably refers here to the effort which would be made by the sounder part of the church to clear themselves from blame in what had occurred. It does not mean that the guilty, when convicted of sin, will attempt to

wrought in you, yea, *what* clearing [a] of yourselves, yea, *what* indignation, [b] yea, *what* fear, [c] yea, *what* vehement desire, [d] yea, *what* zeal, yea, *what* revenge! [e] In all *things* ye have approved yourselves [f] to be clear in this matter.

12 Wherefore, though I wrote unto you, *I did it* not for his

a Ep.5.11. b Ep.4 26. c He.4.1. d Ps.42.1; 130.6. e Re.3.19; Mat.5.29,30. f Ro.14.18.

vindicate themselves and to apologize to God for what they had done; but it means that the church at Corinth were anxious to state to Titus all the mitigating circumstances of the case: they showed great solicitude to free themselves, as far as could be done, from blame; they were anxious, as far as could be, to show that they had not approved of what had occurred, and perhaps that it had occurred only because it could not have been prevented. We are not to suppose that all the things here referred to occurred in the same individuals, and that the same persons precisely evinced diligence, and made the apology, &c. It was done by the church; all evinced deep feeling; but some manifested it in one way, and some in another. The whole church was roused, and all felt, and all endeavoured in the proper way to free themselves from the blame, and to remove the evil from among them. ¶ *Yea,* what *indignation.* Indignation against the sin, and perhaps against the persons who had drawn down the censure of the apostle. One effect of true repentance is to produce decided *hatred* of sin. It is not mere regret, or sorrow, it is positive *hatred.* There is a deep indignation against it as an evil and a bitter thing. ¶ *Yea,* what *fear.* Fear lest the thing should be repeated. Fear lest it should not be entirely removed. Or it may possibly mean fear of the displeasure of Paul, and of the punishment which would be inflicted if the evil were not removed. But it more probably refers to the anxious state of mind that the whole evil might be corrected, and to the dread of having any vestige of the evil remaining among them. ¶ *Yea,* what *vehement desire.* This may either mean their fervent wish to remove the cause of complaint, or their anxious desire to see the apostle. It is used in the latter sense in ver. 7, and according to Doddridge and Bloomfield this is the meaning here. Locke renders it, "desire of satisfying me." It seems to me more probable that Paul refers to their anxious wish to remove the sin, since this is the topic under consideration. The point of his remarks in this verse is not so much their affection for him as their indignation against their sin, and their deep grief that sin had existed and had been tolerated among them. ¶ *Yea,* what *zeal.* Zeal to remove the sin, and to show your attachment to me. They set about the work of reformation in great earnest. ¶ *Yea,* what *revenge!* Tindal renders this, "it caused punishment." The idea is, that they immediately set about the work of inflicting punishment on the offender. The word here used (ἐκδίκησις) probably denotes *maintenance of right, protection;* then it is used in the sense of *avengement,* or *vengeance;* and then of penal retribution or punishment; see Luke xxi. 22; 2 Thess. i. 8; 1 Pet. ii. 14. ¶ *In all* things, &c. The sense of this is, "You have entirely acquitted yourselves of blame in this business." The apostle does not mean that none of them had been to blame, or that the church had been free from fault, for a large part of his former epistle is occupied in reproving them for their faults in this business, but he means that by their zeal and their readiness to take away the cause of complaint, they had removed all necessity of further blame, and had pursued such a course as entirely to meet his approbation. They had cleared themselves of any further blame in this business, and had become, so far as this was concerned, "clear" (ἁγνοὺς) or pure.

12. *Wherefore, though I wrote unto you,* &c. In this verse Paul states the main reason why he had written to them on the subject. It was not

cause that had done the wrong, nor for his cause that suffered wrong, but that our care [a] for you in the sight of God might appear unto you.

13 Therefore we were comforted in your comfort: yea, and exceedingly the more joyed we for the joy of Titus, because his spirit was refreshed [b] by you all.

14 For if I have boasted any thing to him of you, I am not ashamed; but as we spake all things to you in truth, even so

a chap.2.4. b Ro.15.32.

principally on account of the man who had done the wrong, or of him who had been injured; but it was from tender anxiety for the whole church, and in order to show the deep interest which he had in their welfare. ¶ *Not for his cause that had done the wrong.* Not mainly, or principally on account of the incestuous person; 1 Cor. v. 1. It was not primarily with reference to him as an individual that I wrote, but from a regard to the whole church. ¶ *Nor for his cause that had suffered wrong.* Not merely that the wrong which he had suffered might be rectified, and that his rights might be restored, valuable and desirable as was that object. The offence was that a man had taken his father's wife as his own (1 Cor. v. 1), and the person injured, therefore, was his father. It is evident from this passage, I think, that the father was living at the time when Paul wrote this epistle. ¶ *But that our care,* &c. I wrote mainly that I might show the deep interest which I had in the church at large, and my anxiety that it might not suffer by the misconduct of any of its members. It is from a regard to the welfare of the whole earth that discipline should be administered, and not simply with reference to an individual who has done wrong, or an individual who is injured. In church discipline such *private* interests are absorbed in the general interest of the church at large.

13. *Therefore we were comforted in your comfort.* The phrase "your comfort," here seems to mean the happiness which they had, or might reasonably be expected to have in obeying the directions of Paul, and in the repentance which they had manifested. Paul had spoken of no other consolation or comfort than this; and the idea seems to be that they were a happy people, and would be happy by obeying the commands of God. This fact gave Paul additional joy, and he could not but rejoice that they had removed the cause of the offence, and that they would not thus be exposed to the displeasure of God. Had they not repented and put away the evil, the consequences to them must have been deep distress. As it was, they would be blessed and happy. ¶ *And exceedingly the more,* &c. Titus had been kindly received, and hospitably entertained, and had become much attached to them. This was to Paul an additional occasion of joy; see ver. 7.

14. *For if I have boasted any thing to him,* &c. This seems to imply that Paul had spoken most favourably to Titus of the Corinthians before he went among them. He had probably expressed his belief that he would be kindly received; that they would be disposed to listen to him, and to comply with the directions of the apostle; perhaps he had spoken to him of what he anticipated would be their liberality in regard to the collection which he was about to make for the poor saints at Jerusalem. ¶ *I am not ashamed.* It has all turned out to be true. He has found it as I said it would be. All my expectations are realized; and you have been as kind, and hospitable, and benevolent as I assured him you would be. ¶ *As we spake all things to you in truth.* Every thing which I said to you was said in truth. All my promises to you, and all my commands, and all my reasonable expectations expressed to you, were sincere. I practised no disguise, and all that I have said thus far turned out to be true. ¶ *Even so our boasting,* &c. My boasting of your character, and

our boasting, which *I made* before
Titus, is found a truth.
15 And his [1] inward affection is
more abundant toward you, whilst
he remembereth the obedience of
you all, how with fear [a] and trembling ye received him.
16 I rejoice, therefore, that I
have confidence [b] in you in all
things.

1 *bowels.* a Ph.2.12.

b 2 Th.3.4; Phile.8.21.

of your disposition to do right, which I made before Titus has turned out to be true. It was as I said it would be. I did not commend you too highly to him, as I did not overstate the matter to you in my epistle.

15. *And his inward affection,* &c. He has become deeply and tenderly attached to you. His affectionate regard for you has been greatly increased by his visit. On the meaning of the word here rendered "inward affection" (σπλαγχνα, Marg. *bowels*) see Note on chap. vi. 12. It denotes here deep, tender attachment, or love. ¶ *How with fear and trembling ye received him.* With fear of offending, and with deep apprehension of the consequences of remaining in sin. He saw what a fear there was of doing wrong, and what evidence there was, therefore, that you were solicitous to do right.

16. *I rejoice, therefore, that I have confidence,* &c. I have had the most ample proof that you are disposed to obey God, and to put away every thing that is offensive to him. The address of this part of the epistle, says Doddridge, is wonderful. It is designed, evidently, not merely to commend them for what they had done, and to show them the deep attachment which he had for them, but in a special manner to prepare them for what he he was about to say in the following chapter, respecting the collection which he had so much at heart for the poor saints at Jerusalem. What he here says was admirably adapted to introduce that subject. They had thus far showed the deepest regard for him. They had complied with all his directions. All that he had said of them had proved to be true. And as he had boasted of them to Titus (ver. 14), and expressed his entire confidence that they would comply with his requisitions, so he had also boasted of them to the churches of Macedonia, and expressed the utmost confidence that they would be liberal in their benefactions, chap. ix. 2. All that Paul here says in their favour, therefore, was eminently adapted to excite them to liberality, and prepare them to comply with his wishes in regard to that contribution.

REMARKS.

1. Christians are bound by every solemn and sacred consideration to endeavour to purify themselves, ver. 1. They who have the promises of eternal life, and the assurance that God will be to them a father, and evidence that they are his sons and daughters, should not indulge in the filthiness of the flesh and spirit.

2. Every true Christian will aim at perfection, ver. 1. He will desire to be perfect; he will strive for it; he will make it a subject of unceasing and constant prayer. No man can be a Christian to whom it would not be a pleasure to be at once as perfect as God. And if any man is conscious that the idea of being made *at once* perfectly holy would be unpleasant or painful, he may set it down as certain evidence that he is a stranger to religion.

3. No man can be a Christian who voluntarily indulges in sin, or in what he knows to be wrong, ver. 1. A man who does that cannot be aiming at perfection. A man who does that shows that he has no real desire to be perfect.

4. How blessed will be heaven, ver. 1. There we shall be perfect. And the crowning glory of heaven is not that we shall be *happy*, but that we shall be *holy*. Whatever there is in the heart that is good shall there be perfectly developed; whatever there is that is evil shall be removed, and the whole soul will be like God. The Christian desires heaven because he will be there perfect. He desires no other

heaven. He could be induced to accept no other if it were offered to him. He blesses God day by day that there *is* such a heaven, and that there is no other: that there is *one* world which sin does not enter, and where evil shall be unknown.

5. What a change will take place at death, ver. 1. The Christian will be there made perfect. *How* this change will be there produced we do not know. Whether it will be by some extraordinary influence of the Spirit of God on the heart, or by the mere removal from the body, and from a sinful world to a world of glory, we know not. The fact seems to be clear, that at death the Christian will be made at once as holy as God is holy, and that he will ever continue to be in the future world.

6. What a desirable thing it is to die, ver. 1. Here, should we attain to the age of the patriarchs, like them we should continue to be imperfect. Death only will secure our perfection; and death, therefore, is a desirable event. The perfection of our being could not be attained but for death; *and every Christian should rejoice that he is to die.* It is better to be in heaven than on earth; better to be with God than to be away from him; better to be made perfect than to be contending here with internal corruption, and to struggle with our sins. "I would not live always," was the language of holy Job; "I desire to depart and to be with Christ," was the language of holy Paul.

7. It is often painful to be compelled to use the language of reproof, ver. 8. Paul deeply regretted the necessity of doing it in the case of the Corinthians, and expressed the deepest anxiety in regard to it. No man, no minister, parent, or friend can use it but with deep regret that it is necessary But the painfulness of it should not prevent our doing it. It should be done tenderly but faithfully. If done with the deep feeling, with the tender affection of Paul, it will be done right; and when so done, it will produce the desired effect, and do good. No man should use the language of reproof with a hard heart, or with severity of feeling. If he is, like Paul, ready to weep when he does it, it will do good. If he does it because he *delights* in it, it will do evil.

8. It is a subject of rejoicing where a people exercise repentance, ver. 8. A minister has pleasure not *in* the pain which his reproofs cause; not in the deep anxiety and distress of the sinner, and not in the pain which Christians feel under his reproofs, but he has joy in the happy results or the fruits which follow from it. It is only from the belief that those tears will produce abundant joy that he has pleasure in causing them, or in witnessing them.

9. The way to bring men to repentance is to present to them the simple and unvarnished truth, ver. 8, 9. Paul stated simple and plain truths to the Corinthians. He did not abuse them; he did not censure them in general terms; he stated things just as they were, and *specified* the things on account of which there was occasion for repentance. So if ministers wish to excite repentance in others, they must *specify* the sins over which others should weep; if we wish, as individuals, to feel regret for our sins, and to have true repentance toward God, we must dwell on those *particular* sins which we have committed, and should endeavour so to reflect on them that they may make an appropriate impression on the heart. No man will truly repent by *general* reflections on his sin; no one who does not endeavour so to dwell on his sins as that they shall make the proper impression which each one is fitted to produce on the soul. Repentance is that state of mind which a view of the truth in regard to our own depravity is fitted to produce.

10. There is a great difference between godly sorrow and the sorrow of the world, ver. 10. All men feel sorrow. All men, at some period of their lives, grieve over their past conduct. Some in their sorrow are pained because they have offended God, and go to God, and find pardon and peace in him. That sorrow is unto salvation. But the mass do not look to God. They turn away from him even in their

CHAPTER VIII.

MOREOVER, brethren, we do you to wit of the grace of God bestowed on the churches of Macedonia;[a]

2 How that, in a great trial

a chap.9.2,4.

disappointments, and in their sorrows, and in the bitter consciousness of sin. They seek to alleviate their sorrows in worldly company, in pleasure, in the intoxicating bowl; and such sorrow works death. It produces additional distress, and deeper gloom here, and eternal woe hereafter.

11. We may learn what constitutes true repentance, ver. 11. There should be, and there will be, deep feeling. There will be "carefulness," deep anxiety to be freed from the sin; there will be a desire to remove it; "indignation" against it; "fear" of offending God; "earnest desire" that all that has been wrong should be corrected; "zeal" that the reformation should be entire; and a wish that the appropriate "revenge," or expression of displeasure, should be excited against it. The true penitent hates nothing so cordially as he does his sin. He hates nothing but sin. And his warfare with that is decided, uncompromising, inexorable, and eternal.

12. It is an evidence of mercy and goodness in God that the sorrow which is felt about sin *may* be made to terminate in our good, and to promote our salvation, ver. 10, 11. If sorrow for sin had been suffered to take its own course, and had proceeded unchecked, it would in all cases have produced death. If it had not been for the merciful interposition of Christianity, by which even sorrow might be turned to joy, this world would have been everywhere a world of sadness and of death. Man would have suffered. Sin always produces, sooner or later, woe. Christianity has done nothing to make men wretched, but it has done every thing to bind up broken hearts. It has revealed a way by which sorrow may be turned into joy, and the bitterness of grief may be followed by the sweet calm and sunshine of peace.

13. The great purpose of Christian discipline is to benefit the whole church, ver. 12. It is not merely on account of the offender, nor is it merely that the injured may receive a just recompense. It is primarily that the church may be pure, and that the cause of religion may not be dishonoured. When the work of discipline is entered on from any private and personal motives, it is usually attended with bad feeling, and usually results in evil. When it is entered on with a desire to honour God, and to promote the purity of the church, when the whole aim is to deliver the church from opprobrium and scandal, and to have just such a church as Jesus Christ desires, then it will be prosecuted with good temper, and with right feeling, and then it will lead to happy results. Let no man institute a process of discipline on an offending brother from private, personal, and revengeful feelings. Let him first examine his own heart, and let him be sure that his aim is solely the glory of Christ, before he attempts to draw down the censure of the church on an offending brother. How many cases of church discipline would be arrested if this simple rule were observed! And while the case before us shows that it is important in the highest degree that discipline should be exercised on an offending member of the church; while no consideration should prevent us from exercising that discipline; and while every man should feel desirous that the offending brother should be reproved or punished, yet this case also shows that it should be done with the utmost tenderness, the most strict regard to justice, and the deepest anxiety that the general interests of religion should not suffer by the manifestation of an improper spirit, or by improper motives in inflicting punishment on an offending brother.

CHAPTER VIII.

In the previous chapter the apostle had expressed his entire confidence in the ready obedience of the Corinth-

of affliction, the abundance of their joy and their deep [a] poverty abounded unto the riches of their [1] liberality.

a Mar.12.44.

1 *simplicity.*

ians in all things. To this confidence he had been led by the promptitude with which they had complied with his commands in regard to the case of discipline there, and by the respect which they had shown to Titus, whom he had sent to them. All that he had ever said in their favour had been realized; all that had ever been asked of them had been accomplished The object of his statement in the close of chap. vii. seems to have been to excite them to diligence in completing the collection which they had begun for the poor and afflicted saints of Judea. On the consideration of that subject, which lay so near his heart, he now enters; and this chapter and the following are occupied with suggesting arguments, and giving directions for a liberal contribution.

Paul had given directions for taking up this collection in the first epistle; see chap. xvi. 1. seq.; comp. Rom. xv. 26. This collection he had given Titus direction to take up when he went to Corinth; see ver. 6—17 of this chapter. But from some cause it had not been completed, ver. 10, 11. What that cause was, is not stated, but it may have been possibly the disturbances which had existed there, or the opposition of the enemies of Paul, or the attention which was necessarily bestowed in regulating the affairs of the church. But in order that the contribution might be made, and might be a liberal one, Paul presses on their attention several considerations designed to excite them to give freely. The chapter is, therefore, of importance to us, as it is a statement of the duty of giving liberally to the cause of benevolence, and of the motives by which it should be done. In the presentation of this subject, Paul urges upon them the following considerations.

He appeals to the very liberal example of the churches of Macedonia, where, though they were exceedingly poor, they had contributed with great cheerfulness and liberality to the object, ver. 1—5.

From their example he had been induced to desire Titus to lay the subject before the church at Corinth, and to finish the collection which he had begun, ver. 6.

He directs them to abound in this, not as a matter of commandment, but excited by the example of others, ver. 7, 8.

He appeals to them by the love of the Saviour; reminds them that though he was rich yet he became poor, and that they were bound to imitate his example, ver. 9.

He reminds them of their intention to make such a contribution, and of the effort which they had made a year before; and though they had been embarrassed in it, and might find it difficult still to give as much as they had intended, or as much as they would wish, still it would be acceptable to God. For if there was a willing mind, God accepted the offering, ver. 10—12.

He assures them that it was not his wish to burden or oppress them. All that he desired was that there should be an equality in all the churches, ver. 13—15.

To show them how much he was interested in this, he thanks God that he had put it into the heart of Titus to engage in it. And in order more effectually to secure it, he says that he had sent with Titus a brother who was well known, and whose praise was in all the churches. He had done this in order that the churches might have entire confidence that the contribution would be properly distributed. Paul did not wish it to be intrusted to himself. He would leave no room for suspicion in regard to his own character; he would furnish the utmost security to the churches that their wishes were complied with. He desired to act honestly not only in the sight of the Lord, but to furnish evidence of his entire honesty to men, ver. 16—21.

To secure the same object he had also sent *another* brother, and these three brethren he felt willing to recommend as faithful and tried; as men in whom the church at Corinth might repose the utmost confidence, ver. 22—24.

1. *Moreover, brethren, we do you to wit.* We make known to you; we inform you. The phrase "we do you to wit," is used in Tindal's translation, and means "we cause you to know." The *purpose* for which Paul informed them of the liberality of the churches of Macedonia was to excite them to similar liberality. ¶ *Of the grace of God, &c.* The favour which God had shown them in exciting a spirit of liberality, and in enabling them to contribute to the fund for supplying the wants of the poor saints at Jerusalem. The word "grace" (χάρις) is sometimes used in the sense of *gift*, and the phrase "gift of God" some have supposed *may* mean *very great gift*, where the words "of God" may be designed to mark any thing very eminent or excellent, as in the phrase "cedars of God," "mountains of God," denoting very great cedars, very great mountains. Some critics (as Macknight, Bloomfield, Locke, and others) have supposed that this means that the churches of Macedonia had been able to contribute largely to the aid of the saints of Judea. But the more obvious and correct interpretation, as I apprehend, is that which is implied in the common version, that the phrase "grace of God," means that God had bestowed on them grace to give according to their ability in this cause. According to this it is implied, (1.) That a disposition to contribute to the cause of benevolence is to be traced to God. He is its author. He excites it. It is not a plant of native growth in the human heart, but a large and liberal spirit of benevolence is one of the effects of his grace, and is to be traced to him. (2.) It is a *favour* bestowed on a church when God excites in it a spirit of benevolence. It is one of the evidences of his love. And indeed there cannot be a higher proof of the favour of God than when by his grace he inclines and enables us to contribute largely to meliorate the condition, and to alleviate the wants of our fellow-men. Perhaps the apostle here meant delicately to hint this. He did not therefore say coldly that the churches of Macedonia had contributed to this object, but he speaks of it as *a favour* shown to them by God that they were able to do it. And he meant, probably, gently to intimate to the Corinthians that it would be an evidence that they were enjoying the favour of God if they should contribute in like manner. ¶ *The churches of Macedonia.* Philippi, Thessalonica, Berea. For an account of Macedonia, see Notes, Acts xvi. 9; Rom. xv. 26. Of these churches, that at Philippi seems to have been most distinguished for liberality (Phil. iv. 10, 15, 16, 18), though it is probable that other churches contributed according to their ability, as they are commended (comp. chap. ix. 2) without distinction.

2. *How that, in a great trial of affliction.* When it might be supposed they were unable to give; when many would suppose they needed the aid of others; or when it might be supposed their minds would be wholly engrossed with their own concerns. The trial to which the apostle here refers was doubtless some persecution which was excited against them, probably by the Jews; see Acts xvi. 20; xvii. 5. ¶ *The abundance of their joy.* Their joy arising from the hopes and promises of the gospel. Notwithstanding their persecutions, their joy has abounded, and the effect of their joy has been seen in the liberal contribution which they have made. Their joy could not be repressed by their persecution, and they cheerfully contributed largely to the aid of others. ¶ *And their deep poverty.* Their very low estate of poverty was made to contribute liberally to the wants of others. It is implied here, (1.) That they were very poor—a fact arising probably from the consideration that the poor generally embraced the gospel first, and also because it is probable that they were molested and stripped of their property in persecutions (comp. Heb. x. 34); (2.) That notwithstanding this they were enabled to make a

3 For to *their* power, (I bear record,) yea, and beyond *their* power, *they were* willing of themselves;

4 Praying us with much entreaty that we would receive the gift, and *take upon us* the fellowship [a] of the ministering to the saints.

5 And *this they did*, not as we hoped, but first gave their ownselves to the Lord, and unto us by the will of God.

a Acts 11,29; Ro. 15.25, 26.

liberal contribution—a fact demonstrating that a people *can* do much even when poor if all feel disposed to do it, and that afflictions are favourable to the effort; and, (3.) That one cause of this was the *joy* which they had even in their trials. If a people have the joys of the gospel; if they have the consolations of religion themselves, they will somehow or other find means to contribute to the welfare of others. They will be willing to labour with reference to it, or they will find something which they can sacrifice or spare. Even their deep poverty will abound in the fruits of benevolence. ¶ *Abounded.* They contributed liberally. Their joy was manifested in a large donation, notwithstanding their poverty. ¶ *Unto the riches of their liberality.* Marg. "Simplicity." The word (ἁπλότης) here used means properly sincerity, candour, probity; then Christian simplicity, integrity; then liberality; see Rom. xii. 8 (Marg.); 2 Cor. ix. 11, 13. The phrase "riches of liberality," is a Hebraism, meaning rich, or abundant liberality. The sense is, their liberality was much greater than could be expected from persons so poor; and the object of the apostle is, to excite the Corinthians to give liberally by their example.

3. *For to* their *power.* To the utmost of their ability ¶ *I bear record.* Paul had founded those churches and had spent much time with them. He was therefore well qualified to bear testimony in regard to their condition. ¶ *Yea, and beyond* their *power.* Beyond what could have been expected; or beyond what it would have been thought possible in their condition. Doddridge remarks that this is a noble hyperbole, similar to that used by Demosthenes when he says, "I have performed all, even with an industry beyond my power." The sense is, they were willing to give more than they were well able. It shows the strong interest which they had in the subject, and the anxious desire which they had to relieve the wants of others. ¶ *Of themselves* (αὐθαίρετοι). Acting from choice, self-moved, voluntarily, of their own accord. They did not wait to be urged and pressed to do it. They rejoiced in the opportunity of doing it. They came forward of their own accord and made the contribution. "God loveth a cheerful giver" (chap. ix. 7); and from all the accounts which we have of these churches in Macedonia it is evident that they were greatly distinguished for their cheerful liberality.

4. *Praying us with much entreaty.* Earnestly entreating me to receive the contribution and convey it to the poor and afflicted saints in Judea. ¶ *And* take upon us *the fellowship of the ministering to the saints.* Greek, "that we would take the gift and the fellowship of the ministering to the saints." They asked of us to take part in the labour of conveying it to Jerusalem. The occasion of this distress which made the collection for the saints of Judea necessary, was probably the famine which was predicted by Agabus, and which occurred in the time of Claudius Cæsar; see Note on Acts xi. 28. Barnabas was associated with Paul in conveying the contribution to Jerusalem; Acts vi. 30. Paul was unwilling to do it unless they particularly desired it, and he seems to have insisted that some person should be associated with him; ver. 20; 1 Cor. xvi. 3, 4.

5. *And this they did*, &c. They did not give what we expected only. We knew their poverty, and we expected only a small sum from them. ¶ *Not as we hoped.* Not according to the utmost of our hopes. We were

6 Insomuch that we desired Titus, that as he had begun, so he would also finish in you the same [1] grace also.

7 Therefore, as ye abound [a] in every *thing*, *in* faith, and utterance, and knowledge, and *in* all diligence, and *in* your love to us, *see* that ye abound in this grace also.

8 I speak not [b] by commandment, but by occasion of the for-

1 or *gift*. a 1 Cor.1.5. b 1 Cor.7.6.

greatly disappointed in the amount which they gave, and in the manner in which it was done. ¶ *But first gave their ownselves to the Lord.* They first made an entire consecration of themselves and all that they had to the Lord. They kept nothing back. They felt that all they had was his. And where a people honestly and truly devote *themselves* to God, they will find no difficulty in having the means to contribute to the cause of charity. ¶ *And unto us by the will of God.* That is, they gave themselves to us to be directed in regard to the contribution to be made. They complied with our wishes and followed our directions. The phrase "by the will of God," means evidently that God moved them to this, or that it was to be traced to his direction and providence. It is one of the instances in which Paul traces every thing that is right and good to the agency and direction of God.

6. *Insomuch.* The sense of this passage seems to be this, "We were encouraged by this unexpected success among the Macedonians. We were surprised at the extent of their liberality. And encouraged by this, we requested Titus to go among you and finish the collection which you had proposed and which you had begun. Lest you should be outstripped in liberality by the comparatively poor Macedonian Christians, we were anxious that you should perform what you had promised and contemplated, and we employed Titus, therefore, that he might go at once and finish the collection among you." ¶ *The same grace also.* Marg. "*Gift;*" see Note on ver. 1. The word refers to the contribution which he wished to be made.

7. *Therefore as ye abound in every* thing; see Note, 1 Cor. i. 5. Paul never hesitated to commend Christians where it could be done with truth; and the fact that they were eminent in some of the Christian duties and graces, he makes the ground of the exhortation that they would abound in all. From those who had so many eminent characteristics of true religion he had a right to expect much; and he therefore exhorts them to manifest a symmetry of Christian character. ¶ In *faith.* In the full belief of the truth and obligation of the gospel. ¶ *And utterance.* In the ability to instruct others; perhaps referring to their power of speaking foreign languages; 1 Cor. xiv. ¶ *And knowledge.* The knowledge of God, and of his truth. ¶ *And in all diligence.* Diligence or readiness in the discharge of every duty. Of this, Paul had full evidence in their readiness to comply with his commands in the case of discipline to which so frequent reference is made in this epistle. ¶ *And* in *your love to us.* Manifested by the readiness with which you received our commands; see chap. vii. 4, 6, 7, 11, 16. ¶ See *that ye abound in this grace also.* The idea here is, that eminence in spiritual endowments of any kind, or in any of the traits of the Christian character should lead to great benevolence, and that the character is not complete unless benevolence be manifested toward every good object that may be presented.

8. *I speak not by commandment.* This does not mean that he had no express command of God in the case, but that he did not mean *to command* them; he did not speak authoritatively; he did not intend to prescribe what they should give. He used only moral motives, and urged the considerations which he had done to *persuade* rather than to *command* them to give; see ver. 10. He was endeavouring to

wardness of others, and to prove the sincerity of your love.

9 For ye know the grace of our Lord Jesus Christ, that, though he was [a] rich, yet for your sakes he became poor, [b] that ye through his poverty might be rich. [c]

a John 1.1. b Luke 9.58; Phil.2.6, 7. c Rev.3.18.

induce them to give liberally, not by abstract command and law, but by showing them what others had given who had much less ability and much fewer advantages than they had. Men cannot be induced to give to objects of charity by command, or by a spirit of dictation and authority. The only successful, as well as the only lawful appeal, is to their hearts and consciences, and sober judgments. And if an apostle did not take upon himself the language of authority and command in matters of Christian benevolence, assuredly ministers and ecclesiastical bodies now have no right to use any such language. ¶ *But by occasion of the forwardness of others.* I make use of the example of the churches of Macedonia as an argument to induce you to give liberally to the cause. ¶ *And to prove the sincerity of your love.* The apostle does not specify here what "love" he refers to, whether love to God, to Christ, to himself, or to the church at large. It may be that he designedly used the word in a general sense, to denote love to any good object; and that he meant to say that liberality in assisting the poor and afflicted people of God would be the best evidence of the sincerity of their love to God, to the Redeemer, to him, and to the church. Religion is love; and that love is to be manifested by doing good to all men as we have opportunity. The most *substantial* evidence of that love is when we are willing to part with our property, or with whatever is valuable to us, to confer happiness and salvation on others.

9. *For ye know,* &c. The apostle Paul was accustomed to illustrate every subject, and to enforce every duty where it could be done, by a reference to the life and sufferings of the Lord Jesus Christ. The design of this verse is apparent. It is, to show the duty of giving liberally to the objects of benevolence, from the fact that the Lord Jesus was willing to become poor in order that he might benefit others. The idea is, that he who was Lord and proprietor of the universe, and who possessed all things, was willing to leave his exalted station in the bosom of the Father and to become poor, in order that we might become rich in the blessings of the gospel, in the means of grace, and as heirs of all things; and that we who are thus benefited, and who have such an example, should be willing to part with our earthly possessions in order that we may benefit others. ¶ *The grace.* The benignity, kindness, mercy, goodness. His coming in this manner was a proof of the highest benevolence. ¶ *Though he was rich.* The riches of the Redeemer here referred to, stand opposed to that poverty which he assumed and manifested when he dwelt among men. It implies, (1.) His pre-existence, for he *became* poor. He had been rich. Yet not in this world. He did not lay aside wealth here on earth after he had possessed it, for he had none. He was not first rich and then poor on earth, for he had no earthly wealth. The Socinian interpretation is, that he was "rich in power and in the Holy Ghost;" but it was not true that he laid these aside, and that he became poor in either of them. He *had* power, even in his poverty, to still the waves, and to raise the dead, and he was always full of the Holy Ghost. His family was poor; and his parents were poor; and he was himself poor all his life. This then *must* refer to a state of antecedent riches before his assumption of human nature; and the expression is strikingly parallel to that in Phil. ii. 6, seq. "Who being in the form of God, thought it not robbery to be equal with God, but made himself of no reputation," &c.. (2.) He was rich as the Lord and proprietor of all things.

He was the Creator of all (John i. 3; Col. i. 16), and as Creator he had a right to all things, and the disposal of all things. The most absolute right which can exist is that acquired by the act of creation; and this right the Son of God possessed over all gold, and silver, and diamonds, and pearls; over all earth and lands; over all the treasures of the ocean, and over all worlds. The extent and amount of his riches, therefore, is to be measured by the extent of his dominion over the universe; and to estimate his riches, therefore, we are to conceive of the sceptre which he sways over the distant worlds. What wealth has man that can compare with the riches of the Creator and Proprietor of all? How poor and worthless appears all the gold that man can accumulate compared with the wealth of him whose are the silver, and the gold, and the cattle upon a thousand hills? ¶ *Yet for your sakes.* That is, for your sakes as a part of the great family that was to be redeemed. In what respect it was for their sake, the apostle immediately adds when he says, it was that they might be made rich. It was not for his own sake, but it was for ours. ¶ *He became poor.* In the following respects. (1.) He chose a condition of poverty, a rank of life that was usually that of poverty. He "took upon himself the form of a servant;" Phil. ii. 7. (2.) He was connected with a poor family. Though of the family and lineage of David (Luke ii. 4), yet the family had fallen into decay, and was poor. In the Old Testament he is beautifully represented as a shoot or sucker that starts up from the root of a decayed tree; see my Note on Isa. xi. 1. (3.) His whole life was a life of poverty. He had no home; Luke ix. 58. He chose to be dependent on the charity of the few friends that he drew around him, rather than to *create* food for the abundant supply of his own wants. He had no farms or plantations; he had no splendid palaces; he had no money hoarded in useless coffers or in banks; he had no property to distribute to his friends. His mother he commended when he died to the charitable attention of one of his disciples (John xix. 27), and all his personal property seems to have been the raiment which he wore, and which was divided among the soldiers that crucified him. Nothing is more remarkable than the difference between the plans of the Lord Jesus and those of many of his followers and professed friends. He formed no plan for becoming rich, and he always spoke with the deepest earnestness of the dangers which attend an effort to accumulate property. He was among the most poor of the sons of men in his life; and few have been the men on earth who have not had *as much* as he had to leave to surviving friends, or to excite the cupidity of those who should fall heirs to their property when dead. (4.) He died poor. He made no will in regard to his property, for he had none to dispose of. He knew well enough the effect which would follow if he had amassed wealth, and had left it to be divided among his followers. They were *very* imperfect; and even around the cross there might have been anxious discussion, and perhaps strife about it, as there is often now over the coffin and the unclosed grave of a rich and foolish father who has died. Jesus intended that his disciples should never be turned away from the great work to which he called them by any wealth which he would leave them; and he left them not even a *keepsake* as a memorial of his name. All this is the more remarkable from two considerations. (*a*) That he had it in his power to choose the manner in which he would come. He might have come in the condition of a splendid prince. He might have rode in a chariot of ease, or have dwelt in a magnificent palace. He might have lived with more than the magnificence of an oriental prince, and might have bequeathed treasures greater than those of Crœsus or Solomon to his followers. But he *chose* not to do it. (*b*) It would have been as right and proper for *him* to have amassed wealth, and to have sought princely possessions, as for any of his followers. What is right for them would have been right for him. Men often mistake on this

10 And herein I give *my* advice: for this is expedient for you, who have begun before, not only to do, but also to be [1] forward a year ago.

[1] *willing.*

subject; and though it cannot be demonstrated that all his followers should aim to be as poor as he was, yet it is undoubtedly true that he meant that his example should operate constantly to check their desire of amassing wealth. In him it was *voluntary;* in us there should be always a *readiness to be poor* if such be the will of God; nay, there should be rather a *preference* to be in moderate circumstances that we may thus be like the Redeemer. ¶ *That ye through his poverty might be rich.* That is, might have durable and eternal riches, the riches of God's everlasting favour. This includes, (1.) The present possession of an interest in the Redeemer himself. "Do you see these extended fields?" said the owner of a vast plantation to a friend. "They are mine. All this is mine." "Do you see yonder poor cottage?" was the reply of the friend as he directed his attention to the abode of a poor widow. "She has more than all this. She has CHRIST as her portion; and that is more than all." He who has an interest in the Redeemer has a possession that is of more value than all that princes can bestow. (2.) The heirship of an eternal inheritance, the prospect of immortal glory; Rom. viii. 17. (3.) Everlasting treasures in heaven. Thus the Saviour compares the heavenly blessings to *treasures;* Mat. vi. 20. Eternal and illimitable wealth is theirs in heaven; and to raise us to that blessed inheritance was the design of the Redeemer in consenting to become poor. This, the apostle says, was to be secured by his poverty. This includes probably the two following things, viz. (1.) That it was to be by the *moral influence* of the fact that he was poor that men were to be blessed He designed by his example to counteract the effect of wealth; to teach men that this was not the thing to be aimed at; that there were more important purposes of life than to obtain money; and to furnish a perpetual reproof of those who are aiming to amass riches. The example of the Redeemer thus stands before the whole church and the world as a living and constant memorial of the truth that men need other things than wealth; and that there are objects that demand their time and influence other than the accumulation of property. It is well to have such an example; well to have before us the example of one who *never* formed any plan for gain, and who constantly lived above the world. In a world where gain is the great object, where all men are forming plans for it, it is well to have one great model that shall continually demonstrate the folly of it, and that shall point to better things. (2.) The word "poverty" here may include more than a mere want of property. It may mean all the circumstances of his low estate and humble condition; his sufferings and his woes. The whole train of his privations was included in this; and the idea is, that he gave himself to this lowly condition in order that by his sufferings he might procure for us a part in the kingdom of heaven. His *poverty* was a part of the sufferings included in the work of the atonement. For it was not the sufferings of the garden merely, or the pangs of the cross, that constituted the atonement; it was the series of sorrows and painful acts of humiliation which so thickly crowded his life. By all these he designed that we should be made rich; and in view of all these the argument of the apostle is, we should be willing to deny ourselves to do good to others.

10. *And herein I give my advice.* Not undertaking to *command* them, or to prescribe how much they should give. Advice will go much farther than commands on the subject of charities. ¶ *For this is expedient for you* (συμφέρει). That is, this will be of advantage to you; it will be profitable; it will be becoming. The idea is, that they were bound by a regard to consistency and to their own

11 Now therefore perform [a] the doing *of it;* that as *there was* a readiness to will, so *there may be* a performance also out of that which ye have.

12 For if [b] there be first a

a 1 Ti.6.19; Heb.13.16; James 2.15,16. b Luke 21.3.

welfare, to perform what they had purposed. It became them; it was proper, and was demanded; and there would have been manifest disadvantages if it had not been done. ¶ *Who have begun before.* Who commenced the collection a year before; see ver. 6. It had been commenced with fair prospects of success, but had been interrupted probably by the dissensions which arose in the church there. ¶ *Not only to do.* Not merely to accomplish it as if by constraint, or as a matter of compulsion and drudgery. ¶ *But also to be forward.* Marg. "*Willing.*" So the Greek (τὸ θέλειν). They were voluntary in this, and they set about it with vigorous and determined zeal and courage. There was a resolute determination in the thing, and a willingness and heartiness in it which showed that they were actuated by Christian principle. Consistency, and their own reputation and advantage, now demanded that they should complete what they had begun.

11. *As* there was *a readiness to will.* Now accomplish the thing, and be not satisfied with having begun it. Do not suppose that the intention was sufficient, or that you are now released from the obligation. A year indeed has elapsed; but the necessity of the aid for the poor has not ceased. The sentiment here is, that if we have felt it our duty to aid in a cause of benevolence, and have commenced it, and have then been interrupted in executing our purpose, we should seize the first favourable opportunity to accomplish what we had designed. We should not regard ourselves as released from our obligation, but should, from a regard to consistency and our obligation to God, accomplish what we had intended. ¶ *Out of that which ye have.* According to your ability; see ver. 12. It should be in proportion to your means.

12. *For if there be first a willing mind.* If there is a *readiness* (προθυμία), a disposition to give; if the heart is in it, then the offering will be acceptable to God, whether you be able to give much or little. A willing mind is the first consideration. No donation, however large, can be acceptable where that does not exist; none, however small, can be otherwise than acceptable where that is found. This had relation as used by Paul to the duty of almsgiving; but the *principle* is as applicable to every thing in the way of duty. A willing mind is the first and main thing. It is that which God chiefly desires, and that without which every thing else will be offensive, hypocritical, and vain; see Note, chap. ix. 7. ¶ It is *accepted.* Doddridge, Rosenmüller, Macknight, and some others apply this to the person, and render it, "*he* is accepted;" but the more usual, and the more natural interpretation is to apply it to the gift—*it* is accepted. God will approve of it, and will receive it favourably. ¶ *According to that a man hath,* &c. He is not required to give what he has not. His obligation is proportioned to his ability. His offering is acceptable to God according to the largeness and willingness of his heart, and not according to the narrowness of his fortune.—*Locke.* If the means are small, if the individual is poor, and if the gift shall be, therefore, small in amount, yet it may be proof of a larger heart and of more true love to God and his cause than when a much more ample benefaction is made by one in better circumstances. This sentiment the Saviour expressly stated and defended in the case of the poor widow; Mark xii. 42—44; Luke xxi. 1—4. She who had cast in her two mites into the treasury had put in more than all which the rich men had contributed, for they had given of their abundance, but she had cast in all that she had, even all her living. The great and obviously just and equal principle here stated, was originally applied by Paul to the duty of giving alms. But it is

willing mind, *it is* accepted according to that a man hath, *and* not according to that he hath not.

13 For *I mean* not that other men be eased, and ye burdened:

14 But by an equality, *that* now at this time your abundance

---

equally true and just as applied to all the duties which we owe to God. He demands, (1.) A willing mind, a heart disposed to yield obedience. He claims that our service should be voluntary and sincere, and that we should make an unreserved consecration of what we have. Secondly, he demands only what we have power to render. He requires a service strictly according to our ability, and to be measured by that. He demands no more than our powers are fitted to produce; no more than we are able to render. *Our obligations in all cases are limited by our ability.* This is obviously the rule of equity, and this is all that is anywhere demanded in the Bible, and this *is* everywhere demanded. Thus our love to him is to be in proportion to *our* ability, and not to be graduated by the ability of angels or other beings. "And thou shalt love the Lord thy God with ALL THY heart, and with *all* THY soul, and with *all* THY mind, and with *all* THY strength;" Mark xii. 30. Here the obligation is limited by the ability, and the love is to be commensurate with the ability. So of repentance, faith, and of obedience in any form. None but a tyrant ever demands more than can be rendered; and to demand more is the appropriate description of a tyrant, and cannot appertain to the ever-blessed God. Thirdly, if there is any service rendered to God, according to the ability, it is accepted of him. It may not be as much or as valuable as may be rendered by beings of higher powers; it may not be as much as we would desire to render, but it is all that God demands, and is acceptable to him. The poor widow was not able to give as much as the rich man; but her offering was equally acceptable, and *might* be more valuable, for it would be accompanied with her prayers. The service which *we* can render to God may not be equal to that which the angels render; but it may be equally appropriate to our condition and our powers, and may be equally acceptable to God. God may be *as well pleased* with the sighings of penitence as the praises of angels; with the offerings of a broken and a contrite heart as with the loud hallelujahs of unfallen beings in heaven.

13. *For* I mean *not that other men be eased,* &c. I do not intend that others should be eased in order to relieve you. Literally, "Not that there should be *rest* (*ἄνεσις, a letting loose, remission, relaxation*) to others, but *affliction* (θλίψις) to you." Probably the Corinthians were able to contribute more than many other churches, certainly more than the churches of Macedonia (ver. 2), and Paul therefore presses upon them the duty of giving according to their means, yet he by no means intended that the entire burden should come on them.

14. *But by an equality.* On just and equal principles. ¶ That *now at this time,* &c. That at the present time your abundance may be a supply for their wants, so that at some future time, if there should be occasion for it, their abundance may be a supply for your wants. The idea is this. Corinth was then able to give liberally, but many of the other churches were not. They were poor, and perhaps persecuted and in affliction. But there might be great reverses in their condition. Corinth might be reduced from its affluence, and might itself become dependent on the aid of others, or might be unable to contribute any considerable amount for the purposes of charity. The members of the church in Corinth, therefore, should so act in their circumstances of prosperity, that others would be disposed to aid them should their condition ever be such as to demand it. And the doctrine here taught is, (1.) That the support of the objects of benevolence should be on *equal* principles. The rich should bear an equal

may be a supply for their want, that their abundance also may be *a supply* for your want, that there may be equality:

15 As it is written, [a] He that *had gathered* much had nothing over; and he that *had gathered* little had no lack.

a Ex.16.18.

and fair proportion, and if more frequent demands are made on their benefaction than on others they should not complain. (2.) Christians should contribute liberally while they have the means. In the vicissitudes of life no one can tell how soon he may be unable to contribute, or may even be dependent on the charity of others himself. A change in the commercial world; losses by fire or at sea; want of success in business; loss of health, and the failure of his plans, may soon render him unable to aid the cause of benevolence. While he is prospered he should embrace every opportunity to do good to all. Some of the most painful regrets which men ever have, arise from the reflection that when prospered they were indisposed to give to benefit others, and when their property is swept away they become unable. God often sweeps away the property which they were *indisposed* to contribute to aid others, and leaves them to penury and want. Too late they regret that they were not the liberal patrons of the objects of benevolence when they were able to be. ¶ *That there may be equality.* That all may be just and equal. That no unjust burden should be borne by any one portion of the great family of the redeemed. Every Christian brother should bear his due proportion.

15. *As it is written;* see Ex. xvi. 18. ¶ *He that* had gathered *much,* &c. This passage was originally applied to the gathering of manna by the children of Israel. The manna which fell around the camp of Israel was gathered every morning. All that were able were employed in gathering it; and when it was collected it was distributed in the proportion of an omer, or about five pints to each man. Some would be more active and more successful than others. Some by age or infirmity would collect little; probably many by being confined to the camp would collect none. They who had gathered more than an omer, therefore, would in this way contribute to the wants of others, and would be constantly manifesting a spirit of benevolence. And such was their willingness to do good in this way, such their readiness to collect more than they knew would be demanded for their own use, and such the arrangement of Providence in furnishing it, that there was no want; and there was no more gathered than was needful to supply the demands of the whole. Paul applies this passage, therefore, in the very spirit in which it was originally penned. He means to say that the rich Christians at Corinth should impart freely to their poorer brethren. They had gathered more wealth than was immediately necessary for their families or themselves. They should, therefore, impart freely to those who had been less successful. Wealth, like manna, is the gift of God. It is like that spread by his hand around us every day. Some are able to gather much more than others. By their skill, their health, their diligence, or by providential arrangements, they are eminently successful. Others are feeble, or sick, or aged, or destitute of skill, and are less successful. All that is obtained is by the arrangement of God. The health, the strength, the skill, the wisdom by which we are enabled to obtain it, are all his gift. That which is thus honestly obtained, therefore, should be regarded as *his* bounty, and we should esteem it a privilege daily to impart to others less favoured and less successful. Thus society will be bound more closely together. There will be, as there was among the Israelites, the feelings of universal brotherhood. There will be on the one hand the happiness flowing from the constant exercise of the benevolent feelings; on the other the strong ties of gratitude. On the one hand the evils of poverty will be prevented,

16 But thanks *be* to God, which put the same earnest care into the heart of Titus for you.

17 For indeed he accepted the exhortation; [a] but being more forward, of his own accord he went unto you.

18 And we have sent with him the brother, [b] whose praise *is* in the gospel throughout all the churches:

a ver.6. b chap.12 18.

and on the other the not less, though different evils resulting from superabundant wealth. Is it a forced and unnatural analogy also to observe, that wealth, like manna, corrupts by being kept in store? Manna if kept more than a single day became foul and loathsome. Does not wealth hoarded up when it might be properly employed; wealth that *should* have been distributed to relieve the wants of others, become corrupting in its nature, and offensive in the sight of holy and benevolent minds? comp. James v. 2—4. Wealth, like manna, should be employed in the service which God designs—employed to diffuse everywhere the blessings of religion, comfort, and peace.

16. *But thanks* be *to God.* Paul regarded every right feeling, and every pure desire; every inclination to serve God or to benefit a fellow mortal, as the gift of God. He, therefore, ascribes the praise to him that Titus was disposed to show an interest in the welfare of the Corinthians. ¶ *The same earnest care.* The earnest care here referred to was that the Corinthians might complete the collection, and finish what they had proposed. Titus was willing to undertake this, and see that it was done. ¶ *For you.* For your completing the collection. Paul represents it as being done *for* them, or for their welfare. The poor saints in Judea indeed were to have the immediate benefit of the contribution, but it was a privilege for them to give, and Paul rejoiced that they had that privilege. A man who presents to Christians a feasible object of benevolence, and who furnishes them an opportunity of doing good to others, is doing good to them, and they should esteem it an act of kindness done to them.

17. *For indeed he accepted the exhortation.* He cheerfully complied with the exhortation which I gave him, to wit, to visit you, and excite you to this good work. ¶ *But being more forward.* More disposed to do this than I had supposed. The idea here is, that he was very ready to engage in this; he was more ready to engage in it than Paul was to exhort him to it; he anticipated his request; he had already resolved to engage in it. ¶ *Of his own accord he went,* &c. He went voluntarily and without urging. The ground of Paul's thankfulness here seems to have been this. He apprehended probably some difficulty in obtaining the collection there He was acquainted with the distracted state of the church, and feared that Titus might have some reluctance to engage in the service. He was therefore very agreeably surprised when he learned that Titus was willing to make another journey to Corinth and to endeavour to complete the collection.

18. *And we have sent with him the brother.* It has been generally supposed that this anonymous brother was Luke. Some have supposed however that it was Mark, others that it was Silas or Barnabas. It is impossible to determine with certainty who it was; nor is it material to know. Whoever it was, it was some one well known, in whom the church at Corinth could have entire confidence. It is remarkable that though Paul mentions him again (chap. xii. 18), he does it also in the same manner, without specifying his name. The only circumstances that can throw any light on this are, (1.) That Luke was the companion and intimate friend of Paul, and attended him in his travels. From Acts xvi. 10, 11, where Luke uses the term "*we,*" it appears that he was with Paul when he first went into Macedonia, and from ver. 15 it is clear that he went with Paul to Philippi. From Acts xvii. 1, where Luke alters his style and uses the term "they," it is evident that he did

19 And not *that* only, but who was also chosen [a] of the churches to travel with us with this [1] grace, which is administered by us to [b] the glory of the same Lord, and *declaration of* your ready mind:

20 Avoiding this, that no man should blame us in this abun-

a 1 Cor.16.3,4. 1 or, *gift*. b chap.4.15.

not accompany Paul and Silas when they went to Thessalonica, but either remained at Philippi or departed to some other place. He did not join them again until they went to Troas on the way to Jerusalem; Acts xx. 5. In what manner Luke spent the interval is not known. Macknight supposes that it might have been in multiplying copies of his gospel for the use of the churches. Perhaps also he might have been engaged in preaching, and in services like that in the case before us. (2.) It seems probable that Luke is the person referred to by the phrase "whose praise is in the gospel throughout all the churches." This would be more likely to be applied to one who had written a gospel, or a life of the Redeemer that had been extensively circulated, than to any other person. Still it is by no means *certain* that he is the person here referred to, nor is it of material consequence. ¶ *Whose praise.* Who is well known and highly esteemed. ¶ Is *in the gospel.* Either for writing the gospel, or for preaching the gospel. The Greek will bear either construction. In some way he was celebrated for making known the truths of the gospel.

19. *And not* that *only.* Not only is he esteemed on account of other services which he has rendered by his preaching and writings; but he has had a new mark of the confidence of the churches in being appointed to convey the collection to Jerusalem. ¶ *Chosen of the churches.* Chosen by the churches. Many concurred in the choice, showing that they had entire confidence in him. Paul had been unwilling to have charge of this contribution alone (1 Cor. xvi. 3, 4; comp. ver. 20), and he had procured the appointment of some one to undertake it. Probably he expected that the church at Corinth would concur in this appointment. ¶ *With this grace.* Marg. "*Gift;*" see ver. 1. The word here refers to the alms, or the collection which had been made. ¶ *Which is administered by us.* That is, which is undertaken by us. Paul had been the instrument of procuring it. ¶ *To the glory of the same Lord.* The Lord of us all. The design was to promote the glory of the Lord by showing the influence of religion in producing true benevolence. ¶ *And* declaration of *your ready mind.* That is, to afford you an opportunity of evincing your readiness to do good to others, and to promote their welfare.

20. *Avoiding this.* That is, I intend to prevent any blame from being cast upon me in regard to the management of these funds. For this purpose Paul had refused to have the entire management of the funds (see 1 Cor. xii. 3, 4), and had secured the appointment of one who had the entire confidence of all the churches. ¶ *That no man should blame us.* That no one should have any occasion to say that I had appropriated it to my own use or contrary to the will of the donors. Paul felt how dangerous it was for ministers to have much to do with money matters. He had a very deep impression of the necessity of keeping his own character free from suspicion on this subject. He knew how easy it might be for his enemies to raise the charge that he had embezzled the funds and appropriated them to his own use. He therefore insisted on having associated with him some one who had the entire confidence of the churches, and who should be appointed by them, and thus he was certain of being for ever free from blame on the subject. A most important example for all ministers in regard to the pecuniary benefactions of the churches. ¶ *In this abundance,* &c. In this large amount which is contributed by the churches and committed to our disposal Large sums of money are in our time committed to the ministers of the gospel in the

dance which is administered by us:
21 Providing for honest[a] things, not only in the sight of the Lord, but also in the sight of men.
22 And we have sent with them

a Ro.12.17; Ph.4.8; 1 Pe.2.12.

execution of the objects of Christian benevolence. Nothing can be more wise than the example of Paul here, that they should have associated with them others who have the entire confidence of the churches, that there may not be occasion for slander to move her poisonous tongue against the ministers of religion.

21. *Providing for honest things.* The expression here used occurs in Rom. xii. 17; see the Note on that place. In that place, however, it refers to the manner in which we are to treat those who injure us; here it refers to the right way of using property; and it seems to have been a kind of maxim by which Paul regulated his life, a *vade mecum* that was applicable to every thing. The sentiment is, that we are to see to it beforehand that all our conduct shall be comely or honest. The word rendered "providing for" (προνοούμενοι) means foreseeing, or perceiving beforehand; and the idea is, that we are to make it a matter of previous calculation, a settled plan, a thing that is to be attended to of set design. In the middle voice, the form in which it occurs here, it means to provide for in one's own behalf; to apply oneself to any thing; to practise diligently.—*Robinson.* The word rendered "things honest" (καλὰ) means properly beautiful, or comely. The idea which is presented here is, that we are to see beforehand, or we are to make it a matter of set purpose that what we do shall be comely, *i. e.* just, honourable, correct, not only in the sight of the Lord, but in the sight of men. Paul applies this in his own case to the alms which were to be intrusted to him. His idea is, that he meant so to conduct in the whole transaction as that his conduct should be approved by God, but that it should also be regarded as *beautiful* or correct in the sight of men. He knew how much his own usefulness depended on an irreproachable character. He, therefore, procured the appointment of one who had the entire confidence of the churches to travel with him. But there is no reason for confining this to the particular case under consideration. It seems to have been the leading maxim of the life of Paul, and it should be of ours. The maxim may be applied to every thing which we have to do; and should constantly regulate us. It may be applied to the acquisition and use of property; to the discharge of our professional duties; to our intercourse with others; to our treatment of inferiors and dependents; to our charities, &c.—in all of which we should make it a matter of previous thought, of earnest diligence, that our conduct should be perfectly honest and comely before God and man. Let us learn from this verse also, that ministers of the gospel should be especially careful that their conduct in money matters, and especially in the appropriation of the charities of the church, should be above suspicion. Much is often intrusted to their care, and the churches and individual Christians often commit much to their discretion. Their conduct in this should be without reproach; and in order to this, it is well to follow the example of Paul, and to insist that others who have the entire confidence of the churches should be associated with them. Nothing is easier than to raise a slanderous report against a minister of the gospel; and nothing gratifies a wicked world more than to be able to do it—and perhaps especially if it pertains to some improper use of money. It is not easy to meet such reports when they are started; and a minister, therefore, should be guarded, as Paul was, at every possible point, that he may be freed from that "whose breath outvenoms all the worms of Nile"—SLANDER.

22. *And we have sent with them our brother.* Who this was is wholly unknown, and conjecture is useless.

our brother, whom we have oftentimes proved diligent in many things, but now much more diligent, upon the great confidence which [1] *I have* in you.
23 Whether *any do inquire* of Titus, *he is* my partner and fellow-helper concerning you; or our brethren *be inquired of, they are* the messengers [a] of the churches, *and* the glory of Christ.

1 or, *he hath.*

a Ph.2.25.

Some have supposed that it was Apollos, others Silas, others Timothy. But there are no means of ascertaining who it was; nor is it material. It was some one in whom Paul had entire confidence. ¶ *Whom we have oftentimes proved diligent.* Of whom we have evidence that he has been faithful. It is evident, therefore, that he had been the companion and fellow-labourer of Paul. ¶ *But now much more diligent,* &c. Who will now prove himself much more diligent than ever before. ¶ *Upon the confidence,* &c. Marg. "he hath." The margin is doubtless the more correct reading here. The idea is, that this brother had great confidence in the Corinthians that they would give liberally, and that he would, therefore, evince special diligence in the business.

23. *Whether* any do inquire *of Titus.* It is to be observed that the words "any do inquire" are not in the original; nor is it clear that these are the most proper words to be introduced here. The Greek may mean either, "if any do inquire about Titus," or it may mean "if any thing is to be said about Titus." The sense of the passage may either be, that some of the faction at Corinth might be disposed to inquire about the authority of Titus to engage in this work, or that Paul having said so much in commendation of the persons who went with Titus, it seemed proper also to say something in his favour also. The idea is, "If any inquiry is made from any quarter about him, or if it is necessary from any cause to say any thing about him, I would say he is my partner," &c. ¶ He is *my partner,* &c. He partakes with me in preaching the gospel, and in establishing and organizing churches; comp. Tit. i 5. To the Corinthians this fact would be a sufficient commendation of Titus. ¶ *Or our brethren* be inquired of. That is, the brethren who accompanied Titus. If any inquiry was made about their character, or if it was necessary to say any thing in regard to them. ¶ They are *the messengers of the churches.* They have the entire confidence of the churches, having been selected and appointed by them to a work of labour and responsibility; comp. Phil. ii. 25. The words here rendered "messengers of the churches," are in the original "apostles of the churches," (ἀπόστολοι ἐκκλησιῶν). The word *apostles* here is used evidently in its proper sense, to denote one who is sent out to transact any business for others, or as an agent or legate. These persons were not *apostles* in the technical sense, and this is an instance where the word is applied in the New Testament to those who had no claim to the apostolic office. It is also applied in a similar way to Apollos and Barnabas, though neither, strictly speaking, were apostles. ¶ And *the glory of Christ.* That is, they have a character so well known and established for piety; they are so eminent Christians and do such honour to the Christian name and calling, that they may be called the glory of Christ. It is an honour to Christ that he has called such persons into his church, and that he has so richly endowed them. Every Christian should so live as that it would appear to all the world that it was an honour and glory to the Redeemer that he had such followers; an honour to his gospel that it had converted such and brought them into his kingdom. It is sufficient honour, moreover, to any man to say that he is "the glory of Christ." Such a character should be, and will be, as it was here, a recommendation sufficient for any to secure them the confidence of others.

24 Wherefore shew ye to them, and before the churches, the proof of your love, and of our boasting[a] on your behalf.

a chap.7.14.

24. *Wherefore show ye to them*, &c. By a liberal contribution in the cause in which they are engaged and for which they have come among you now, furnish the evidence that you love me and the Christian cause, and show that I have not boasted of you in vain. ¶ *The proof of your love.* Your love to me, to God, to the cause of religion; see Note on ver. 8. ¶ *And of our boasting*, &c. My boasting that you would give liberally to the object; see Note, chap. vii. 14. Let it now be seen that my boasting was well founded, and that I properly understood your character, and your readiness to contribute to the objects of Christian benevolence.

REMARKS.

1. Let us bear in mind that a disposition to be liberal proceeds only from God, ver. 1. The human heart is by nature selfish, and indisposed to benevolence. It is only by the grace of God that men are excited to liberality; and we should therefore *pray* for this as well as for all other graces. We should beseech God to remove selfishness from our minds; to dispose us to feel as we should feel for the wants of others, and to incline us to give just what we *ought* to give to relieve them in trouble, and to promote their temporal and eternal welfare.

2. It is an inestimable blessing when God gives a spirit of liberality to the church, ver. 1. It should be regarded as a proof of his special favour; and as an evidence of the prevalence of the principles of true religion.

3. Men are often most liberal when in circumstances of distress, perplexity, and affliction, ver. 2. Prosperity often freezes the heart, but adversity opens it. Success in life often closes the hand of benevolence, but adversity opens it. We are taught to feel for the sufferings of others by suffering ourselves; and in the school of adversity we learn invaluable lessons of benevolence which we should never acquire in prosperity. If you want the tear of sympathy: if you want aid in a good cause, go to a man in affliction, and his heart is open. And hence it is that God often suffers his people to pass through trials in order that they may possess the spirit of large and active benevolence.

4. If Christians desire to be liberal they must *first* devote themselves to God, ver. 5. If this is not done they will have no heart to give, and they will not give. They will have a thousand excuses ready, and there will be no ground of appeal which we can make to them. True liberality is always based on the fact that we have given ourselves wholly to God.

5. When Christians have honestly devoted *themselves* to God, it will be easy to contribute liberally to the cause of benevolence, ver. 5. They will find *something* to give; or if they have nothing now they will labour and deny themselves in order that they may have something to give. If every professed Christian on earth had honestly given *himself* to God, and should act in accordance with this, the channels of benevolence would never be dry.

6. We should compare ourselves in the matter of benevolence with the churches here referred to, ver. 3. They were poor; they were in deep affliction, and yet they contributed all in their power, and beyond their power. Do we do this? Do we give according to our ability? Do we deny ourselves of one comfort? withhold one gratification? curtail one expense which fashion demands, in order that we may have the means of doing good? O! if every Christian would give according to his ability to the sacred cause of charity, how soon would the means be ample to place the Bible in every family on the globe, to preach the gospel in every country, and to maintain all the institutions which the cause of humanity needs in this and in other lands.

7. The Christian character is in-

complete unless there is a spirit of large and liberal beneficence, ver. 7. This is indispensable to the proper symmetry of the Christian graces, and this should be cultivated in order to give beauty and completeness to the whole. Yet it cannot be denied that there are true Christians where this is wanting. There are those who give every other evidence of piety; who are men of prayer, and who evince humility, and who are submissive in trials, and whose conversation is that of Christians, who are yet sadly deficient in this virtue. Either by an original closeness of disposition, or by a defect of education, or by want of information in regard to the objects of Christian benevolence, they are most stinted in their benefactions, and often excite the amazement of others that they give so little to the cause of benevolence. Such persons should be entreated to carry out their Christian character to completion. As they abound in other things, they should abound in this grace also. They are depriving themselves of much comfort, and are bringing much injury on the cause of the Redeemer while they refuse to sustain the great objects of Christian charity. No Christian character is symmetrical or complete unless it is crowned with the spirit of large and comprehensive benevolence towards every object that tends to promote the temporal and eternal welfare of man.

8. The sincerity of our love should be tested, and will be, by our readiness to deny ourselves to do good to others, ver. 8. The love of the Lord Jesus was tested in that way; and there can be no true love to God or man where there is not a readiness to contribute of our means for the welfare of others. If we love the Redeemer we shall devote all to his service; if we love our fellow-men we shall evince our "sincerity" by being willing to part with our earthly substance to alleviate their woes, enlighten their ignorance, and save their souls.

9. Let us imitate the example of the Lord Jesus, ver. 9. He was rich, yet he became poor; and, O! HOW POOR! Let the rich learn to copy his example, and be willing to part with their abundant and superfluous wealth in order that they may relieve and benefit others. That man is most happy as well as most useful, who most resembles the Redeemer; that man will be most happy who stoops from the highest earthly elevation to the lowest condition that he may minister to the welfare of others.

10. Charity should be voluntary, ver. 12. It should be the free and spontaneous offering of the heart; and the first promptings of the heart, before the pleadings of avarice come in, and the heart grows cold by the influence of returning covetousness, are likely to be the most correct.

11. Charity should be in an honest proportion to our means, ver. 12. It should be according to what a man hath. God hath left the determination of this proportion to every individual, responsible to him alone. He has not told us how much we shall give, or in what proportion we shall give; but he has left it for every individual to decide what he *may* give, and what he *ought* to give.

12. If men do not give according to their means they must answer for it to God. Every man may have opportunity to contribute to relieve others if he will open his heart and ears to the cries of a suffering and a dying world. No man can complain that he has no opportunity to give; or that he may not procure for his own soul all the blessings which can be produced by the most large and liberal benevolence.

13. Men have no excuse for being lost, ver. 12. If God required more of them than they could render they would have excuse. They would not be to blame. They might be sufferers and martyrs in hell, but no one would blame them. But the sinner can never have any such excuse. God never required any more of him than he had power to render; and if he dies it will be his own fault, and the throne of God will still be spotless and pure.

14. God's government is an equal, and just, and good government, ver. 12. What can be more equitable than

CHAPTER IX.

FOR as touching the ministering[a] to the saints, it is superfluous for me to write to you:

2 For I know the forwardness

a chap.8.4, &c.

the principle that a man is accepted according to what he has? What ground of complaint can the sinner have in regard to this administration?

15. The churches should bear their just proportion in the cause of Christian beneficence, ver. 13—15. There *are* great interests of charity which MUST be sustained. The world cannot do without them. Not only must the poor be provided for, but the cause of temperance, and of Sabbath-schools, and of missions must be sustained. Bibles *must* be distributed, and men must be educated for the ministry, and the widow and the fatherless must be the objects of Christian benevolence. These burdens, if they are burdens, should be equally distributed. The rich should furnish *their fair proportion* in sustaining them; and those in more moderate circumstances must do *their* fair proportion also in sustaining them. If this were done, all the objects of Christian benevolence could be sustained, and they would in fact not be burdensome to the churches. With infinite ease all might be contributed that is necessary to send the gospel around the world.

16. Ministers of the gospel should have as little as possible to do with money matters, ver. 19—21. While they should be willing, if it is necessary, to be the almoners of the churches, and should esteem it a privilege to be the means of conveying to the poor and needy, and to the great cause of benevolence, what the churches may choose to commit to them, yet they should not covet this office; they should not show any particular desire for it; nor should they do it unless, like Paul, they have the most ample security that the voice of slander can never be raised in regard to their management. Let them see to it that they have persons associated with them who have the entire confidence of the churches; men who will be responsible also, and who will be competent witnesses of the manner in which they discharge their duty. In all things ministers should be pure. On few points is there more danger that the enemy will endeavour to take advantage, and to injure their character, than in regard to their abuse of funds intrusted to their care.

17. Let all Christians so live that it may be honestly said of them they are "the glory of Christ," ver. 23. Let them aim so to live that it will be esteemed to be an honour to the Redeemer that he called them into his kingdom, and that he so richly endowed them by his grace. *This* would be a commendation to all men where they might go; to say this is enough to say of any man. None can have a higher character than to have it said with truth of him "he is the glory of Christ; he is an honour to his Redeemer and to his cause."

CHAPTER IX.

IN this chapter the apostle continues the subject which he had discussed in chap. viii.—the collection which he had purposed to make for the poor saints in Judea. The deep anxiety which he had that the collection should be liberal; that it should not only be such as to be really an aid to those who were suffering, but be such as would be an expression of tender attachment to them on the part of the Gentile converts, was the reason, doubtless, why Paul urged this so much on their attention. His primary wish undoubtedly was, to furnish aid to those who were suffering. But in connection with that, he also wished to excite a deep interest among the Gentile converts in behalf of those who had been converted to Christianity among the Jews. He wished that the collection should be so liberal as to show that they felt that they were united as brethren, and that they were grateful that they had received the true religion from the Jews. And he doubtless wished to cement as much as possible the great body of the Christian brotherhood, and to impress

of your mind, for which I boast of you to them of Macedonia, that Achaia was ready a year ago; and your zeal hath provoked very many.

3 Yet have I sent the brethren, lest our boasting of you should be in vain in this behalf; that, as I said, ye may be ready:

4 Lest haply if they of Macedonia come with me, and find you unprepared, we (that we say not, ye) should be ashamed in this same confident boasting. [a]

[a] chap.8.24.

on their minds the great truths that whatever was their national origin, and whatever were their national distinctions, yet in Christ they were one. For this purpose he presses on their attention a great variety of considerations why they should give liberally, and this chapter is chiefly occupied in stating reasons for that in addition to those which had been urged in the previous chapter. The following view will present the main points in the chapter.

(1.) He was aware of their readiness to give, and knowing this, he had boasted of it to others, and others had been excited to give liberally from what the apostle had said of them, ver. 1, 2. The *argument* here is, that Paul's veracity and their own character were at stake and depended on their now giving liberally.

(2.) He had sent the brethren to them in order that there might by no possibility be a *failure*, ver. 3—5. Though he had the utmost confidence in them, and fully believed that they were disposed to give liberally, yet he knew also that something might prevent it unless messengers went to secure the contributions, and that the consequence might be, that he and they would be "ashamed" that he had boasted so much of their readiness to give.

(3.) To excite them to give liberally, Paul advances the great principles that the reward in heaven will be in proportion to the liberality evinced on earth, and that God loves one who gives cheerfully, ver. 6, 7. By the prospect, therefore, of an ample reward, and by the desire to meet with the approbation of God, he calls upon them to contribute freely to aid their afflicted Christian brethren.

(4.) He further excites them to liberal giving by the consideration that if they contributed liberally, God was able to furnish them abundantly with the means of doing good on a large scale in time to come, ver. 8—11. In this way he would enable them to do good hereafter in proportion as they were disposed to do good now, and the result of all would be, that abundant thanks would be rendered to God—thanks from those who were aided, and thanks from those who had aided them that they had been enabled to contribute to supply their wants.

(5.) As a final consideration inducing them to give, the apostle states that not only would they thus do good, but would show the power of the gospel, and the affection which they had for the Jewish converts, and would thus contribute much in promoting the glory of God. The Jewish converts would see the power of the gospel on their Gentile brethren; they would feel that they now appertained to one great family; they would praise God for imparting his grace in this manner; and they would be led to pray much for those who had thus contributed to alleviate their wants, ver. 12—14.

(6.) Paul closes the whole chapter, and the whole discussion respecting the contribution about which he had felt so deep an interest, by rendering thanks to God for his "unspeakable gift," JESUS CHRIST, ver. 15. Paul was ever ready, whatever was the topic before him, to turn the attention to him. He here evidently regards him as the author of all liberal feeling, and of all true charity; and seems to imply that all that *they* could give would be small compared with the "unspeakable gift" of God, and that the fact that God had imparted *such* a gift to the world was a reason why *they* should be willing to devote all they had to his service.

1. *For as touching the ministering to the saints.* In regard to the collection that was to be taken up for the aid of the poor Christians in Judea; see Notes on Rom. xv. 26; 1 Cor. xvi. 1; 2 Cor. viii. ¶ *It is superfluous,* &c. It is needless to urge that matter on you, because I know that you acknowledge the obligation to do it, and have already purposed it. ¶ *For me to write to you.* That is, to write more, or to write largely on the subject. It is unnecessary for me to urge arguments why it should be done; and all that is proper is to offer some suggestions in regard to the *manner* in which it shall be accomplished.

2. *For I know the forwardness of your mind.* I know your promptitude, or your readiness to do it; see chap. viii. 10. Probably Paul here means that he had had opportunity before of witnessing their readiness to do good, and that he had learned in particular of Titus that they had formed the plan to aid in this contribution. ¶ *For which I boast of you to them of Macedonia.* To the church in Macedonia; see chap. viii. 1. So well assured was he that the church at Corinth would make the collection as it had proposed, that he boasted of it to the churches of Macedonia as if it were already done, and made use of this as an argument to stimulate them to make an effort. ¶ *That Achaia was ready a year ago.* Achaia was that part of Greece of which Corinth was the capital; see Note, Acts xviii. 12. It is probable that there were Christians in other parts of Achaia besides Corinth, and indeed it is known that there was a church in Cenchrea (see Rom. xvi. 1.) which was one of the ports of Corinth. Though the contribution would be chiefly derived from Corinth, yet it is probable that the others also would participate in it. The phrase "was ready" means that they had been preparing themselves for this collection, and doubtless Paul had stated that the collection was already made and was waiting. He had directed them (1 Cor. xvi. 1.) to make it on the first day of the week, and to lay it by in store, and he did not doubt that they had complied with his request. ¶ *And your zeal.* Your ardour and promptitude. The readiness with which you entered into this subject, and your desire to relieve the wants of others. ¶ *Hath provoked.* Has roused, excited, impelled to give. We use the word *provoke* commonly now in the sense of *to irritate*, but in the Scriptures it is confined to the signification of exciting, or rousing. The ardour of the Corinthians would excite others not only by their promptitude, but because Corinth was a splendid city, and their example would be looked up to by Christians at a distance. This is one instance of the effect which will be produced by the example of a church in a city.

3. *Yet have I sent the brethren.* The brethren referred to in chap. viii. 18, 22, 23. ¶ *Lest our boasting of you.* That you were disposed to contribute, and that you were already prepared, and that the contribution was ready. ¶ *Should be in vain.* Lest any thing should have occurred to prevent the collection. I have sent them that they may facilitate it, and that it may be secure and certain. ¶ *In this behalf.* In this respect. That is, lest our boasting of you, in regard to your readiness to contribute to relieve the wants of others, should be found to have been ill-grounded.

4. *Lest haply if they of Macedonia.* If any of the Macedonians should happen to come with me, and should find that you had done nothing. He does not say that they *would* come with him, but it was by no means improbable that they would. It was customary for some of the members of the churches to travel with Paul from place to place, and the intercourse was constant between Macedonia and Achaia. Paul had, therefore, every reason to suppose that some of the Macedonians would accompany him when he should go to Corinth. At all events it was probable that the Macedonians would learn from some quarter whether the

5 Therefore I thought it necessary to exhort the brethren, that
they would go before unto you, and
make up beforehand your [1] bounty,
[2] whereof ye had notice before, that
the same might be ready, as *a mat-*
ter of bounty, and not as *of* covetousness.
6 But this *I say*, He [a] which soweth sparingly shall reap also sparingly; and he which soweth bountifully shall reap also bountifully.

1 *blessing*. 2 or, *which hath been so much spoken of before*.

a Ps.41.1—3; Pr.11.24,25; 19.17; 22.9; Ga. 6.7,9.

Corinthians were or were not ready when Paul should go to them ¶ *We* (*that we say not ye*) *should be ashamed*, &c. "In this," says Bloomfield, "one cannot but recognise a most refined and delicate turn, inferior to none of the best classical writers." Paul had boasted confidently that the Corinthians would be ready with their collection. He had excited and stimulated the Macedonians by this consideration. He had induced them in this way to give liberally, chap. viii. 1—4. If now it should turn out after all that the Corinthians had given nothing, or had given stintedly, the character of Paul would suffer. His veracity and his judgment would be called in question, and he would be accused of trick, and artifice, and fraud in inducing them to give. Or if he should not be charged with dishonesty, yet he would be humbled and mortified himself that he had made representations which had proved to be so unfounded. But this was not all. The character of the Corinthians was also at stake. They had purposed to make the collection. They had left the impression in the mind of Paul that it would be done. They had hitherto evinced such a character as to make Paul confident that the collection would be made. If now by any means this should fail, their character would suffer, and they would have occasion to be ashamed that they had excited so confident expectations of what they would do.

5. *Therefore I thought it necessary*, &c. In order to *secure* the collection, and to avoid all unpleasant feeling on all hands. ¶ *That they would go before unto you.* Before I should come. ¶ *And make up beforehand your bounty.* Prepare it before I come. The word "bounty" is in the Marg. rendered "blessing." The Greek (εὐλογία) means properly commendation, *eulogy*. Then it means blessing, praise applied to God. Then *that which blesses*—a gift, donation, favour, bounty—whether of God to men, or of one man to another. Here it refers to their contribution as that which would be adapted to confer *a blessing* on others, or fitted to produce happiness. ¶ *That the same might be ready as* a matter of *bounty*. That it may truly appear as a liberal and voluntary offering; as an act of generosity and not as *wrung* or extorted from you. That it may be truly a *blessing*—a *thank-offering* to God and adapted to do good to men. ¶ *And not as* of *covetousness*. "And not like a sort of extortion, wrung from you by mere dint of importunity."—*Doddridge*. The word here used (πλεονεξία) means usually covetousness, greediness of gain, which leads a person to defraud others. The idea here is, that Paul would have them give this as an act of bounty, or liberality on their part, and not as an act of covetousness on his part, not as extorted by him from them.

6. *But this* I say. This I say in order to induce you to give liberally. This I say to prevent your supposing that because it is to be a voluntary offering you may give only from your superfluity, and may give sparingly. ¶ *He which soweth sparingly.* This expression has all the appearance of a proverb, and doubtless is such. It does not occur indeed elsewhere in the Scriptures, though substantially the same sentiment exciting to liberality often occurs; see Ps. xli. 1—3; Prov. xi. 24, 25; xix. 17; xxii. 9. Paul here says that it is in giving as it is in agriculture. A man that sows little must expect to reap little. If he sows a small piece of land he will reap a small harvest; or if he is niggardly in sowing and wishes to *save* his seed and

will not commit it to the earth, he must expect to reap little. So it is in giving. Money given in alms, money bestowed to aid the poor and needy, or to extend the influence of virtue and pure religion, is money bestowed in a way similar to the act of committing seed to the earth. It will be returned again in some way with an abundant increase. It shall not be lost. The seed may be buried long. It may lie in the ground with no indication of a return or of increase. One who knew not the arrangements of Providence might suppose it was lost and dead. But in due time it shall spring up and produce an ample increase. So with money given to objects of benevolence. To many it may seem to be a waste, or may appear to be thrown away. But in due time it will be repaid in some way with abundant increase. And the man who wishes to make the most out of his money for future use and personal comfort will give liberally to deserving objects of charity—just as the man who wishes to make the most out of his grain will not suffer it to lie in his granary, but will commit the seed to the fertile earth. "Cast thy bread upon the waters: for thou shalt find it again after many days" (Eccl. xi. 1); that is, when the waters as of the Nile have overflown the banks and flooded the whole adjacent country, then is the time to cast abroad thy seed. The waters will retire, and the seed will sink into the accumulated fertile mud that is deposited, and will spring up in an abundant harvest. So it is with that which is given for objects of benevolence. ¶ *Shall reap also sparingly.* Shall reap in proportion to what he sowed. This every one knows is true in regard to grain that is sowed. It is also no less true in regard to deeds of charity. The idea is, that God will bestow rewards in proportion to what is given. These rewards may refer to results in this life, or to the rewards in heaven, or both. All who have ever been in the habit of giving liberally to the objects of benevolence can testify that they have lost nothing, but have reaped in proportion to their liberality. This follows in various ways. (1.) In the *comfort* and peace which results from giving. If a man wishes to *purchase* happiness with his gold, he can secure the most by bestowing it liberally on objects of charity. It will produce him more immediate peace than it would to spend it in sensual gratifications, and far more than to hoard it up useless in his coffers. (2.) In reflection on it hereafter. It will produce more happiness in remembering that he has done good with it, and promoted the happiness of others, than it will to reflect that he has hoarded up useless wealth, or that he has squandered it in sensual gratification. The one will be unmingled pleasure when he comes to die; the other will be unmingled self-reproach and pain. (3.) In subsequent life, God will in some way repay to him far more than he has bestowed in deeds of charity. By augmented prosperity, by health and future comfort, and by raising up for us and our families, when in distress and want, friends to aid us, God can and often does abundantly repay the liberal for all their acts of kindness and deeds of beneficence. (4.) God can and will reward his people in heaven abundantly for all their kindness to the poor, and all their self-denials in endeavouring to diffuse the influence of truth and the knowledge of salvation. Indeed the rewards of heaven will be in no small degree apportioned in this manner, and determined by the amount of benevolence which we have shown on earth; see Mat. xxv. 34—40. On all accounts, therefore, we have every inducement to give liberally. As a farmer who desires an ample harvest scatters his seed with a liberal hand; as he does not grudge it though it falls into the earth; as he scatters it with the expectation that in due time it will spring up and reward his labours, so should we give with a liberal hand to aid the cause of benevolence, nor should we deem what we give to be lost or wasted though we wait long before *we* are recompensed, or though *we* should be in no other way rewarded than by the comfort which arises from the act of doing good.

7 Every man according as he purposeth in his heart, *so let him give;* not [a] grudgingly, or of necessity: for God loveth a cheerful [b] giver.

a De.15.7,8. b Ex.35 5; Ro.12 8.

7. *Every man according as he purposeth in his heart,* &c. The main idea in this verse is, that the act of giving should be voluntary and cheerful. It should not seem to be extorted by the importunity of others (ver. 6); nor should it be given from urgent necessity, but it should be given as an offering of the heart. On this part of the verse we may remark, (1.) That the heart is usually more concerned in the business of giving than the head. If liberality is evinced, it will be the heart which prompts to it; if it is not evinced, it will be because the heart has some bad passions to gratify, and is under the influence of avarice, or selfishness, or some other improper attachment. Very often a man is convinced he *ought* to give liberally, but a narrow heart and a parsimonious spirit prevents it. (2.) We should follow the dictates of the heart in giving. I mean that a man will usually give more correctly who follows the first promptings of his heart when an object of charity is presented, than he will if he takes much time to deliberate. The instinctive prompting of a benevolent heart is to give liberally. And the *amount* which should be given will usually be suggested to a man by the better feelings of his heart. But if he resolves to deliberate much, and if he suffers the heart to grow cold, and if he defers it, the pleadings of avarice will come in, or some object of attachment or plan of life will rise to view, or he will begin to compare himself with others, and he will give much *less* than he would have done if he had followed the first impulse of feeling. God implanted the benevolent feelings in the bosom that they should prompt us to do good; and he who acts most in accordance with them is most likely to do what he ought to do; and in general it is the safest and best rule for a man to give just what *his heart* prompts him to give when an object of charity is presented. Man at best is too selfish to be likely to give too much or to go beyond his means; and if in a few instances it should be done, more would be gained in value in the cultivation of benevolent feeling than would be lost in money. I know of no better rule on the subject, than to cultivate as much as possible the benevolent feelings, and then to throw open the soul to every proper appeal to our charity, and to give just according to the instinctive prompting of the heart. (3.) Giving should be voluntary and cheerful. It should be from the heart. Yet there is much, very much that is not so, and there is, therefore, much benevolence that is *spasmodic* and spurious; that cannot be depended on, and that will not endure. No dependence can be placed on a man in regard to giving who does not do it from the steady influences of a benevolent heart. But there is much obtained in the cause of benevolence that is produced by a kind of *extortion* It is given because others give, and the man would be ashamed to give less than they do. Or, it is given because he thinks his rank in life demands it, and he is prompted to do it by pride and vanity. Or, he gives from respect to a pastor or a friend, or because he is warmly importuned to give; or because he is shut up to a kind of necessity to give, and must give or he would lose his character and become an object of scorn and detestation. In all this there is nothing cheerful and voluntary; and there can be nothing in it acceptable to God. Nor can it be depended on permanently. The heart is not in it, and the man will evade the duty as soon as he can, and will soon find excuses for not giving at all. ¶ *Not grudgingly.* Greek, "Not of grief" (μὴ ἐκ λύπης). Not as if he were sorry to part with his money. Not as if he were constrained to do a thing that was extremely painful to him. ¶ *Or of necessity.* As if he were compelled to do it. Let him do it cheerfully. ¶ *For God loveth a cheerful giver.* And who does not? Valuable

8 And [a] God *is* able to make all grace abound toward you: that ye, always having all sufficiency in all *things*, may abound to every good work:

9 (As it is written, [b] He hath

a Ph 4.19. b Ps.112.9.

as any gift may be in itself, yet if it is forced and constrained; if it can be procured only after great importunity and persevering effort, who can esteem it as desirable? God desires the heart in every service. No service that is not cheerful and voluntary; none that does not arise from true love to him can be acceptable in his sight. God loves it because it shows a heart like his own—a heart disposed to give cheerfully and do good on the largest scale possible; and because it shows a heart attached from principle to his service and cause. The expression here has all the appearance of a proverb, and expressions similar to this occur often in the Scriptures. In an uninspired writer, also, this idea has been beautifully expanded. "In all thy gifts show a cheerful countenance, and dedicate thy tithes with gladness. Give unto the Most High according as he hath enriched thee: and as thou hast gotten give with a cheerful eye. For the Lord recompenseth, and will give thee seven times as much."—Wisdom of the Son of Sirach, chap. xxxv. 9—11. In nothing, therefore, is it more important than to examine the motives by which we give to the objects of benevolence. However liberal may be our benefactions, yet God may see that there is no sincerity, and may hate the spirit with which it is done.

8. *And God is able*, &c. Do not suppose that by giving liberally you will be impoverished and reduced to want. You should rather confide in God, who is able to furnish you abundantly with what is needful for the supply of your necessities. Few persons are ever reduced to poverty by liberality. Perhaps in the whole circle of his acquaintance it would be difficult for an individual to point out *one* who has been impoverished or made the poorer in this way. Our selfishness is generally a sufficient guard against this; but it is also to be added, that the divine blessing rests upon the liberal man, and that God keeps him from want. But in the mean time there are multitudes who are made poor by the want of liberality. They are parsimonious in giving, but they are extravagant in dress, and luxury, and in expenses for amusement or vice, and the consequence is poverty and want. "There is that withholdeth more than is meet, and it tendeth to poverty;" Prov. xi. 24. The divine blessing rests upon the liberal; and while every person should make a proper provision for his family, every one should give liberally, confiding in God that he will furnish the supplies for our future wants. Let this maxim be borne in mind, that no one is usually made the poorer by being liberal. ¶ *All grace.* All kinds of favour. He is able to impart to you those things which are needful for your welfare. ¶ *That ye always*, &c. The sense is, "If you give liberally you are to expect that God will furnish you with the means, so that you will be able to abound more and more in it." You are to expect that he will abundantly qualify you for doing good in every way, and that he will furnish you with all that is needful for this. The man who gives, therefore, should have faith in God. He should *expect* that God will bless him in it; and the experience of the Christian world may be appealed to in proof that men are *not* made poor by liberality.

9. *As it is written.* Ps. cxii. 9. The idea is, "in this way will the saying in the Scriptures be verified, or the promise confirmed." The psalmist is describing the character of the righteous man. One of his characteristics, he says, is, that he has scattered abroad, he has given liberally to the poor. On such a man a blessing is pronounced (ver. 1); and one of the blessings will be that he shall be prospered. Some difficulty has been felt by commentators to see how the quotation here made sustains the position of Paul that the liberal man

dispersed abroad; he hath given to the poor: his righteousness remaineth for ever.

10 Now he[a] that ministereth seed to the sower both minister bread for *your* food, and multiply your seed sown, and increase the fruits[b] of your righteousness;)

11 Being enriched in every thing to all bountifulness,[1] which

a Is.55.10. b Hos.10.12.

1 *simplicity, or liberality.*

would be blessed of God, and would receive an increase according to his liberality. In order to this, they have supposed (see Doddridge, Bloomfield, and Clarke) that the word "righteousness" means the same as almsgiving, or that "he would always have something to bestow." But I would suggest that perhaps Paul quoted this, as quotations are frequently made in the Scriptures, where a passage was familiar. He quotes only a part of the passage, meaning that the whole passage confirms the point under consideration. Thus the whole passage in the psalm is, "He hath dispersed; he hath given to the poor; his righteousness endureth for ever; *his horn shall be exalted with honour;*" that is, he shall be abundantly blessed with prosperity and with the favour of God. Thus the entire promise sustains the position of Paul, that the liberal man would be abundantly blessed. The phrase "he hath dispersed" (Ἐσκόρπισεν), may refer either to the act of sowing, as a man scatters seed on the earth; or there may be an allusion to the oriental custom of scattering money among an assembled company of paupers; comp. Prov. xi. 24. ¶ *His righteousness.* His deeds of beneficence. ¶ *Remaineth.* In its fruits and consequences; that is, either in its effects on others, or on himself. It *may* mean that the sums so distributed will remain with him for ever, inasmuch as he will be supplied with all that is needful to enable him to do good to others. This interpretation accords with the connection.

10. *Now he that ministereth seed to the sower.* This is an expression of an earnest wish. In the previous verses he had stated the promises, or had shown what we had a right to *expect* as a consequence of liberality. He here unites the expression of an earnest desire that they might experience this themselves. The allusion is to the act of sowing seed. The idea is, that when a man scatters seed in his field God provides him with the means of *sowing again.* He not only gives him a harvest to supply his wants, but he blesses him also *in giving him the ability to sow again.* Such was the benevolent wish of Paul. He desired not only that God would supply their returning wants, but he desired also that he *would give them the ability to do good again;* that he would furnish them the means of future benevolence. He acknowledges God as the source of all increase, and wishes that they may experience the results of such increase. Perhaps in this language there is an allusion to Isa. lv. 10; and the idea is, that it is God who furnishes by his providence the seed to the sower. In like manner he will furnish you the means of doing good. ¶ *Minister bread for* your *food.* Furnish you with an ample supply for your wants. ¶ *Multiply your seed sown.* Greatly increase your means of doing good; make the result of all your benefactions so to abound that you may have the means of doing good again, and on a larger scale, as the seed sown in the earth is so *increased* that the farmer may have the means of sowing more abundantly again. ¶ *And increase the fruits of your righteousness.* This evidently means, the results and effects of their benevolence. The word "righteousness" here refers to their liberality; and the wish of the apostle is, that the results of their beneficence might greatly abound, that they might have the means of doing extensive good, and that they might be the means of diffusing happiness from afar.

11. *Being enriched in every thing,* &c. In all respects your riches are conferred on you for this purpose. The design of the apostle is to state to them the true reason why wealth was

[a] causeth through us thanksgiving to God.

12 For the administration of this service not only supplieth [b] the want of the saints, but is abundant also by many thanksgivings unto God;

13 Whiles by the experiment of this ministration they glorify [c] God for your professed subjection

a chap.1.11; 4.15. b chap.8.14. c Mat.5.16.

bestowed. It was not for the purposes of luxury and self-gratification; not to be spent in sensual enjoyment, not for parade and display; it was that it might be distributed to others in such a way as to cause thanksgiving to God. At the same time, this implies the expression of an earnest wish on the part of Paul. He did not desire that they should be rich for their own gratification or pleasure; he desired it only as the means of their doing good to others. Right feeling will desire property only as the means of promoting happiness and producing thanksgiving to God. They who truly love their children and friends will wish them to be successful in acquiring wealth only that they may have the means and the disposition to alleviate misery, and promote the happiness of all around them. No one who has true benevolence will desire that any one in whom he feels an interest should be enriched for the purpose of living amidst luxury, and encompassing himself with the indulgences which wealth can furnish. If a man has not a disposition to do good with money, it is not true benevolence to desire that he may not possess it. ¶ *To all bountifulness.* Marg. Simplicity, or liberality. The word (ἁπλότης) means properly sincerity, candour, probity; then also simplicity, frankness, fidelity, and especially as manifesting itself in liberality; see Rom. xii. 8; 2 Cor. viii. 2. Here it evidently means *liberality,* and the idea is, that property is given for this purpose, in order that there may be liberality evinced in doing good to others. ¶ *Which causeth through us,* &c. That is, we shall so distribute your alms as to cause thanksgiving to God. The result will be that by our instrumentality, thanks will be given to the great Source and Giver of all wealth. Property should *always* be so employed as to produce thanksgiving. If it is made to contribute to our own support and the support of our families, it should excite thanksgiving. If it is given to others, it should be *so* given, if it is possible, that the recipient should be more grateful *to God* than *to us;* should feel that though we may be the honoured instrument in distributing it, yet the true benefactor is God.

12. *For the administration of this service.* The distribution of this proof of your liberality. The word *service* here, says Doddridge, intimates that this was to be regarded not merely as an act of *humanity,* but *religion.* ¶ *The want of the saints.* Of the poor Christians in Judea on whose behalf it was contributed. ¶ *But is abundant also by many thanksgivings unto God.* Will abound unto God in producing thanksgivings. The result will be that it will produce abundant thanksgiving in their hearts to God.

13. *Whiles by the experiment,* &c. Or rather, by the *experience* of this ministration; the proof (δοκιμῆς), the evidence here furnished of your liberality. They shall in this ministration have *experience* or *proof* of your Christian principle. ¶ *They glorify God.* They will praise God as the source of your liberality, as having given you the means of being liberal, and having inclined your hearts to it. ¶ *For your professed subjection,* &c. Literally, "For the obedience of your profession of the gospel." It does not imply merely that there was a profession of religion, but that there was a *real* subjection to the gospel which they professed. This is not clearly expressed in our translation. Tindal has expressed it better, "Which praise God for your obedience in acknowledging the gospel of Christ." There was a real and sincere submission to the gospel of Christ, and that was manifested by their giving liberally to supply the wants of

unto the gospel of Christ, and for
your liberal distribution unto them,
and unto all *men;*
14 And by their prayer for you,
which long after you for the exceeding grace[a] of God in you.
15 Thanks[b] *be* unto God for his
unspeakable gift.[c]

a chap.8.1. b James 1.17. c John 3.16.

others. The doctrine is, that one evidence of true subjection to the gospel; one proof that our profession is sincere and genuine, is a willingness to contribute to relieve the wants of the poor and afflicted friends of the Redeemer. *And unto all* men. That is, all others whom you may have the opportunity of relieving.

14. *And by their prayer for you.* On the grammatical construction of this difficult verse, Doddridge and Bloomfield may be consulted. It is probably to be taken in connection with ver. 12, and ver. 13 is a parenthesis. Thus interpreted, the sense will be, "The administration of this service (ver. 12) will produce abundant thanks to God. It will also (ver. 14) produce *another effect.* It will tend to excite the prayers of the saints for *you,* and thus produce important benefits to yourselves. They will earnestly desire your welfare, they will anxiously pray to be united in Christian friendship with those who have been so signally endowed with the grace of God." The sentiment is, that charity should be shown to poor and afflicted Christians because it will lead them to pray for us and to desire our welfare. The prayers of the poorest Christian for us are worth more than all we usually bestow on them in charity; and he who has secured the pleadings of a child of God, however humble, in his behalf, has made a good use of his money. ¶ *Which long after you.* Who earnestly desire to see and know you. Who will sincerely desire your welfare, and who will thus be led to pray for you. ¶ *For the exceeding grace of God in you.* On account of the favour which God has shown to you: the strength and power of the Christian principle, manifesting itself in doing good to those whom you have never seen. The apostle supposes that the exercise of a charitable disposition is to be traced entirely to God. God is the author of all grace; he alone excites in us a disposition to do good to others.

15. *Thanks* be *unto God.* Whitby supposes that this refers to the charitable disposition which they had manifested, and that the sense is, that God was to be adored for the liberal spirit which they were disposed to manifest, and the aid which they were disposed to render to others. But this, it is believed, falls far below the design of the apostle. The reference is rather to the inexpressible gift which God had granted to them in bestowing his Son to die for them; and this is one of the most striking instances which occur in the New Testament, showing that the mind of Paul was *full* of this subject; and that wherever he *began,* he was sure to *end* with a reference to the Redeemer. The invaluable gift of a Saviour was so familiar to his mind, and he was so accustomed to dwell on that in his private thoughts, that the mind naturally and easily glanced on that whenever any thing occurred that by the remotest allusion would suggest it. The idea is, "Your benefactions are indeed valuable; and for them, for the disposition which you have manifested, and for all the good which you will be enabled thus to accomplish, we are bound to give thanks to God. All this will excite the gratitude of those who shall be benefited. But how small is all this compared with the *great gift* which *God* has imparted in bestowing a Saviour! That is unspeakable. No words can express it, no language convey an adequate description of the value of the gift, and of the mercies which result from it." ¶ *His unspeakable gift.* The word here used (ἀνεκδιηγήτῳ) means, what cannot be related, unutterable. It occurs nowhere else in the New Testament. The idea is, that no words can properly express the greatness of the gift thus bestowed on man. It is higher than the mind

can conceive; higher than language can express. On this verse we may observe, (1.) That the Saviour is a *gift* to men. So he is uniformly represented; see John iii. 16; Gal. i. 4; ii. 20; Eph. i. 22; Tim. ii. 6; Tit. ii. 14. Man had no claim on God. He could not *compel* him to provide a plan of salvation; and the whole arrangement—the selection of the Saviour, the sending him into the world, and all the benefits resulting from his work, are all an undeserved gift to man. (2.) This is a gift unspeakably great, whose value no language can express, no heart fully conceive. It is so because, (*a*) Of his own greatness and glory; (*b*) Because of the inexpressible love which he evinced; (*c*) Because of the unutterable sufferings which he endured; (*d*) Because of the inexpressibly great benefits which result from his work. No language can do justice to this work in either of these respects; no heart in this world fully conceives the obligation which rests upon man in virtue of his work. (3.) Thanks should be rendered to God for this. We *owe* him our highest praises for this. This appears, (*a*) Because it was *mere benevolence* in God. We had no claim; we could not compel him to grant us a Saviour. The gift might have been withheld, and his throne would have been spotless. We owe no thanks where we have a claim; where we deserve nothing, then he who benefits us has a *claim on* our thanks. (*b*) Because of the benefits which we have received from him. Who can express this? All our peace and hope; all our comfort and joy in this life; all our prospect of pardon and salvation; all the offers of eternal glory are to be traced to him. Man has *no* prospect of being happy when he dies but in virtue of the "unspeakable gift" of God. And when he thinks of his sins, which may now be freely pardoned; when he thinks of an agitated and troubled conscience, which may now be at peace; when he thinks of his soul, which may now be unspeakably and eternally happy; when he thinks of the hell from which he is delivered, and of the heaven to whose eternal glories he may now be raised up by the gift of a Saviour, his heart should overflow with gratitude, and the language should be continually on his lips and in his heart, "THANKS BE UNTO GOD FOR HIS UNSPEAKABLE GIFT." Every other mercy should seem small compared with this; and every manifestation of right feeling in the heart should lead us to contemplate the source of it, and to feel, as Paul did, that *all* is to be traced to the unspeakable gift of God.

REMARKS.

1. This chapter, with the preceding, derives special importance from the fact that it contains the most extended discussion of the principles of Christian charity which occurs in the Bible. No one can doubt that it was intended by the Redeemer that his people should be distinguished for benevolence. It was important, therefore, that there should be some portion of the New Testament where the principles on which charity should be exercised, and the motives by which Christians should be induced to give, should be fully stated. Such a discussion we have in these chapters; and they therefore demand the profound and prayerful attention of all who love the Lord Jesus.

2. We have here a striking specimen of the manner in which the Bible is written. Instead of abstract statements and systematic arrangement, the principles of religion are brought out in connection *with a case* that actually occurred. But it follows that it is important to study attentively the Bible, and to be familiar with every part of it. In some part of the Scriptures, statements of the principles which should guide us in given circumstances will be found; and Christians should, therefore, be familiar with every part of the Bible.

3. These chapters are of special importance to the ministers of religion, and to all whose duty it is to press upon their fellow Christians the duty of giving liberally to the objects of benevolence. The principles on which it should be done are fully developed

CHAPTER X.

NOW I Paul myself beseech[a] you by the meekness and gentleness of Christ, who[1] in presence[b] *am* base among you, but being absent am bold toward you :

a Ro.12.1.

1 or, *in outward appearance.*
b ver.10.

here. The motives which it is lawful to urge are urged here by Paul. It may be added, also, that the chapters are worthy of our profound study on account of the admirable tact and address which Paul evinces in inducing others to give. Well he knew human nature. Well he knew the motives which would influence others to give. And well he knew exactly how to shape his arguments and adapt his reasoning to the circumstances of those whom he addressed.

4. The *summary* of the motives presented in this chapter contains still the most important argument which can be urged to produce liberality. We cannot but admire the felicity of Paul in this address—a felicity not the result of craft and cunning, but resulting from his amiable feelings, and the love which he bore to the Corinthians and to the cause of benevolence. He reminds them of the high opinion which he had of them, and of the honourable mention which he had been induced to make of them (ver. 1, 2); he reminds them of the painful result to his own feelings and theirs if the collection should in any way fail, and it should appear that his confidence in them had been misplaced (ver. 3—5); he refers them to the abundant reward which they might anticipate as the result of liberal benefactions, and of the fact that God loved those who gave cheerfully (ver. 6, 7); he reminds them of the abundant grace of God, who was able to supply all their wants and to give them the means to contribute liberally to meet the wants of the poor (ver. 8); he reminds them of the joy which their liberality would occasion, and of the abundant thanksgiving to God which would result from it (ver. 12, 13); and he refers them to the unspeakable gift of God, Jesus Christ, as an example, and an argument, and as urging the highest claims in them, ver. 15. "Who," says Doddridge, "could withstand the force of such oratory?" No doubt it was effectual in that case, and it should be in all others.

5. May the motives here urged by the apostle be effectual to persuade us all to liberal efforts to do good! Assuredly there is no *less* occasion for Christian liberality now than there was in the time of Paul. There are still multitudes of the poor who need the kind and efficient aid of Christians. And the whole world now is a field in which Christian beneficence may be abundantly displayed, and every land may, and should experience the benefits of the charity to which the gospel prompts, and which it enjoins. Happy are they who are influenced by the principles of the gospel to do good to all men! Happy they who have any opportunity to illustrate the power of Christian principle in this; any ability to alleviate the wants of one sufferer, or to do any thing in sending that gospel to benighted nations which alone can save the soul from eternal death!

6. Let us especially thank God for his unspeakable gift, Jesus Christ. Let us remember that to him we owe every opportunity to do good: that it was because he came that there is any possibility of benefiting a dying world; and that all who profess to love him are bound to imitate his example and to show their sense of their obligation to God for giving a Saviour. How poor and worthless are all our gifts compared with the great gift of God; how slight our expressions of compassion, even at the best, for our fellow-men, compared with the compassion which he has shown for us! When God has given his Son to die for us, what should we not be willing to give that we may show our gratitude, and that we may benefit a dying world!

CHAPTER X.

PAUL, having finished the subject of

the duty of alms-giving in the previous chapter, enters into this on a vindication of himself from the charges of his enemies. His general design is to vindicate his apostolic authority, and to show that he had a right, as well as others, to regard himself as sent from God. This vindication is continued through chap. xi. and xii. In this chapter the stress of the argument is, that he did not depend on any thing *external* to recommend him —on any "carnal weapons;" on any thing which commended itself by the outward appearance; or on any thing that was so much valued by the admirers of human eloquence and learning. He seems willing to admit all that his enemies could say of him on that head, and to rely on other proofs that he was sent from God. In chap. xi. he pursues the subject, and shows by a comparison of himself with others, that he had as good a right certainly as they to regard himself as sent by God. In chap. xii. he appeals to another argument, to which none of his accusers were able to appeal, that he had been permitted to see the glories of the heavenly world, and had been favoured in a manner unknown to other men.

It is evident that there was one or more false teachers among the Corinthians who called in question the divine authority of Paul. These teachers were native Jews (chap. xi. 13, 22), and they boasted much of their own endowments. It is impossible, except from the epistle itself, to ascertain the nature of their charges and objections against him. From the chapter before us it would seem that one principal ground of their objection was, that though he was bold enough in his letters and had threatened to exercise discipline, yet that he would not dare to do it. They accused him of being, when present with them, timid, weak, mild, pusillanimous, of lacking moral courage to inflict the punishment which he had threatened in his letters. To this he replies in this chapter.

(1.) He appeals to the meekness and gentleness of Christ; thus indirectly and delicately vindicating his own mildness from their objections, and entreats them not to give him occasion to show the boldness and severity which he had purposed to do He had no *wish* to be bold and severe in the exercise of discipline, ver. 1, 2.

(2.) He assures them that the weapons of his warfare were not carnal, but spiritual. He relied on the truth of the gospel and on the power of motives; and these weapons were mighty by the aid of God to cast down all that offend him. Yet he was ready to revenge and punish all disobedience by severe measures if it were necessary, ver. 3—6.

(3.) They looked on the outward appearance. He cautioned them to remember that he had as good claims to be regarded as belonging to Christ at they had, ver. 7. He had given proofs that he was an apostle, and the false teachers should look at those proofs lest they should be found to be opposing God. He assured them that *if* he had occasion to exercise his power he would have no reason to be ashamed of it, ver. 8. It would be found to be ample to execute punishment on his foes.

(4.) The false teachers had said that Paul was terrible only in his letters. He boasted of his power, but it was, they supposed, only *epistolary bravery*. He would not dare to execute his threatening. In reply to this, Paul, in a strain of severe irony, says that he would not seem to terrify them by mere letters. It would be by something far more severe. He advised such objectors, therefore, to believe that he would prove himself to be such as he had shown himself to be in his letters; to look at the *evidence*, since they boasted of their talent for reasoning, that he would show himself in fact to be what he had threatened to be, ver. 9—12.

(5.) He pursues the strain of severe irony by secretly comparing himself with them, ver. 12—16. They boasted much, but it was only by comparing themselves with one another, and not with any elevated standard of excellence. Paul admitted that he had not the *courage* to do that, ver. 12. Nor did he *dare* to boast of things wholly

2 But I beseech *you*, that I may not be bold when I am present

beyond his ability as they had done. He was contented to act only within the proper limits prescribed to him by his talents and by the appointment of God. Not so they. They had boldness and courage to go far *beyond* that, and to boast of things wholly *beyond* their ability, and beyond the proper measure, ver. 13, 14. Nor had he courage to boast of entering into other men's labours. It required more courage than he had, to make a boast of what he had done if he had availed himself of things made ready to his hand as if they were the fruit of his own labours, implying that *they* had done this; that they had come to Corinth, a church founded by his labours, and had quietly set themselves down there, and then, instead of going into other fields of labour, had called in question the authority of him who had founded the church, and who was labouring indefatigably elsewhere, ver. 15, 16. Paul adds, that such was not *his* intention. He aimed to preach the gospel beyond, to carry it to regions where it had not been spread. Such was the nature of *his* courage; such the kind of boldness which *he* had, and he was not ambitious to join them in *their* boasting.

(6.) He concludes this chapter with a very serious admonition. Leaving the strain of irony, he seriously says that if any man were disposed to boast, it should be only in the Lord. He should glory not in self-commendation, but in the fact that he had evidence that the Lord approved him; not in his own talents or powers, but in the excellence and glory of the Lord, ver. 17, 18.

1. *Now I Paul myself beseech you.* I entreat you who are members of the church not to give me occasion for the exercise of severity in discipline. I have just expressed my confidence in the church in general, and my belief that you will act in accordance with the rules of the gospel. But I cannot thus speak of all. There are some among you who have spoken with contempt of my authority and my claims as an apostle. Of them I cannot speak in this manner; but instead of *commanding* them I *entreat* them not to give me occasion for the exercise of discipline. ¶ *By the meekness and gentleness of Christ.* In view of the meekness and mildness of the Redeemer; or desiring to imitate his gentleness and kindness. Paul wished to imitate that. He did not wish to have occasion for severity. He desired at all times to imitate, and to exhibit the gentle feelings of the Saviour. He had no pleasure in severity; and he did not desire to exhibit it. ¶ *Who in presence.* Marg. *In outward appearance.* It may either mean that when present among them he appeared, according to their representation, to be humble, mild, gentle (ver. 10); or that in his external appearance he had this aspect; see on ver. 10. Most probably it means that they had represented him as *timid* when among them, and afraid to exercise discipline, however much he had threatened it. ¶ Am *base among you.* The word here used (ταπεινὸς) usually means low, humble, poor. Here it means *timid, modest,* the opposite of boldness. Such was formerly the meaning of the English word *base.* It was applied to those of low degree or rank; of humble birth; and stood opposed to those of elevated rank or dignity. Now it is commonly used to denote that which is degraded or worthless; of mean spirit; vile; and stands opposed to that which is manly and noble. But Paul did not mean to use it here in that sense. He meant to say that they regarded him as *timid* and afraid to execute the punishment which he had threatened, and as manifesting a spirit which was the opposite of boldness. This was doubtless a *charge* which they brought against him; but we are not necessarily to infer that it was true. All that it proves is, that he was modest and unobtrusive, and that they interpreted this as timidity and want of spirit. ¶ *But being absent am bold toward you.* That is, in my letters; see on ver. 10. This they charged him with, that he was bold enough when away from

with that confidence, wherewith [a] I think to be bold against some, which [1] think of us as if we walked according to the flesh.

3 For though we walk in the flesh, we do not war after [a] the flesh:

4 (For the weapons [b] of our

a 1 Cor.4.21; chap.13.2,10. 1 or, reckon.

a Ro.8.13. b Ep.6.13; 1 Th.5.8.

them, but that he would be tame enough when he should meet them face to face, and that they had nothing to fear from him.

2. *That I may not be bold.* I entreat you so to act that I may not have occasion to exercise the severity which I fear I shall be compelled to use against those who accuse me of being governed wholly by worldly motives and policy. ¶ *That I may not be bold.* That I may not be compelled to be bold and decisive in my measures by your improper conduct. ¶ *Which think of us.* Marg. *Reckon.* They suppose this; or, they accuse me of it. By the word "us" here Paul means himself, though it is possible also that he speaks in the name of his fellow-apostles and labourers who were associated with him, and the objections *may* have referred to all who acted with him. ¶ *As if we walked.* As if we lived or acted. The word "walk" in the Scriptures is often used to denote the course or manner of life; Notes, Rom. iv. 12; 2 Cor. v. 7. ¶ *According to the flesh;* see Note on chap. i. 17. As if we were governed by the weak and corrupt principles of human nature. As if we had no higher motive than carnal and worldly policy. As if we were seeking our own advantage and not the welfare of the world. The charge was, probably, that he was not governed by high and holy principles, but by the principles of mere worldly policy; that he was guided by personal interests, and by worldly views—by ambition, or the love of dominion, wealth, or popularity, and that he was destitute of every supernatural endowment and every evidence of a divine commission.

3. *For though we walk in the flesh.* Though we are mortal like other men; though we dwell like them in mortal bodies, and necessarily must devote some care to our temporal wants; and though, being in the flesh, we are conscious of imperfections and frailties like others. The sense is, that he did not claim exemption from the common wants and frailties of nature. The best of men are subject to these wants and frailties; the best of men are liable to err. ¶ *We do not war after the flesh.* The warfare in which he was engaged was with sin, idolatry, and all forms of evil. He means that in conducting this he was not actuated by worldly views or policy, or by such ambitious and interested aims as controlled the men of this world. This refers primarily to the warfare in which Paul was himself engaged as an apostle; and the idea is, that he went forth as a soldier under the great Captain of his salvation to fight his battles and to make conquests for him. A similar allusion occurs in 2 Tim. ii. 3, 4. It is true, however, that not only all ministers, but all Christians are engaged in a warfare; and it is equally true that they do not maintain their conflict "after the flesh," or on the principles which govern the men of this world. The warfare of Christians relates to the following points. (1.) It is a warfare with the corrupt desires and sensual propensities of the heart; with eternal corruption and depravity, with the remaining unsubdued propensities of a fallen nature. (2.) With the powers of darkness; the mighty spirits of evil that seek to destroy us; see Eph. vi. 11—17. (3.) With sin in all forms; with idolatry, sensuality, corruption, intemperance, profaneness, wherever they may exist. The Christian is opposed to all these, and it is the aim and purpose of his life as far as he may be able to resist and subdue them. He is a soldier enlisted under the banner of the Redeemer to oppose and resist all forms of evil. But his warfare is not conducted on worldly principles. Mahomet propagated his religion with the sword; and the men of this world seek for victory by arms and violence;

warfare [a] *are* not carnal, but mighty [1] through [b] God to the pulling down [c] of strong holds;)

5 Casting down [2] imaginations, [d] and every high [e] thing that exalteth itself against the knowledge

a 1 Ti.1.18. 1 or, *to*. b chap.13.3,4. c Jer.1.10.

2 or, *reasonings*. d 1 Co.1.19. e Ps.18.27; Ez.17.24.

The Christian looks for his conquests only by the force and the power of truth, and by the agency of the Spirit of God.

4. *For the weapons of our warfare* The means by which we hope to achieve our victory. ¶ Are *not carnal*. Not those of the flesh. Not such as the men of the world use. They are not such as are employed by conquerors; nor are they such as men in general rely on to advance their cause. We do not depend on eloquence, or talent, or learning, or wealth, or beauty, or any of the external aids on which the men of this world rely. They are not such as derive advantage from any power inherent in themselves. Their strength is derived from God alone. ¶ *But mighty through God*. Marg. "*to*." They are rendered mighty or powerful by the agency of God. They depend on him for their efficacy. Paul has not here specified the weapons on which he relied; but he had before specified them (chap. vi. 6, 7), so that there was no danger of mistake. The weapons were such as were furnished by truth and righteousness, and these were rendered mighty by the attending agency of God. The sense is, that God is the author of the doctrines which we preach, and that he attends them with the agency of his Spirit, and accompanies them to the hearts of men. It is important for all ministers to feel that *their* weapons are mighty ONLY through God. Conquerors and earthly warriors go into battle depending on the might of their own arm, and on the wisdom and skill which plans the battle. The Christian goes on his warfare, feeling that however well adapted the truths which he holds are to accomplish great purposes, and however wisely his plans are formed, yet that the efficacy of all depends on the agency of God. He has no hope of victory but in God. And if God does not attend him, he is sure of inevitable defeat. ¶ *To the pulling down of strongholds*. The word here rendered "strongholds" (ὀχύρωμα) means properly a fastness, fortress, or strong fortification. It is here beautifully used to denote the various obstacles *resembling* a fortress which exist, and which are designed and adapted to oppose the truth and the triumph of the Christian's cause. All those obstacles are strongly *fortified*. The sins of his heart are fortified by long indulgence and by the hold which they have on his soul. The wickedness of the world which he opposes is strongly fortified by the fact that it has seized on strong human passions; that one point strengthens another; that great numbers are united. The idolatry of the world was strongly fortified by prejudice, and long establishment, and the protection of laws, and the power of the priesthood; and the opinions of the world are entrenched behind false philosophy and the power of subtle argumentation. The whole world is fortified against Christianity; and the nations of the earth have been engaged in little else than in raising and strengthening such strongholds for the space of six thousand years. The Christian religion goes forth against all the combined and concentrated powers of resistance of the whole world; and the warfare is to be waged against every strongly fortified place of error and of sin. These strong fortifications of error and of sin are to be battered down and laid in ruins by our spiritual weapons.

5. *Casting down imaginations*. Marg. *reasonings*. The word is probably used here in the sense of *device*, and refers to all the plans of a wicked world; the various systems of false philosophy; and the reasonings of the enemies of the gospel. The various systems of false philosophy were so intrenched that they might be called the stronghold of the enemies of God. The foes of Christianity pretend to a

of God, and bringing into captivity [a] every thought to [b] the obedience of Christ;

6 And having in a readiness to revenge all disobedience, when your obedience [c] is fulfilled.

7 Do ye look on things after the outward [d] appearance? If any man

a Mat.11.29.30. b Ge.8.21: Mat.15.19: He.4.12.

c chap.7.15. d John 7.24.

great deal of *reason*, and rely on that in resisting the gospel. ¶ *And every high thing*, &c. Every exalted opinion respecting the dignity and purity of human nature; all the pride of the human heart and of the understanding. All this is opposed to the knowledge of God, and all exalts itself into a vain self-confidence. Men entertain vain and unfounded opinions respecting their own excellency, and they feel that they do not need the provisions of the gospel and are unwilling to submit to God. ¶ *And bringing into captivity*, &c. The figure here is evidently taken from military conquests. The idea is, that all the strongholds of heathenism, and pride, and sin would be demolished; and that when this was done, like throwing down the walls of a city or making a breach, all the plans and purposes of the soul, the reason, the imagination, and all the powers of the mind would be subdued or led in triumph by the gospel, like the inhabitants of a captured city. Christ was the great Captain in this warfare. In his name the battle was waged, and by his power the victory was won. The captives were made for him and under his authority; and all were to be subject to his control. Every power of thought in the heathen world; all the systems of philosophy and all forms of opinion among men; all the purposes of the soul; all the powers of reason, memory, judgment, fancy in an individual, were all to come under the laws of Christ. All *doctrines* were to be in accordance with his will; philosophy should no longer control them, but they should be subject to the will of Christ. All the *plans of life* should be controlled by the will of Christ, and formed and executed under his control—as captives are led by a conqueror. All *the emotions and feelings of the heart* should be controlled by him, and led by him as a captive is led by a victor. The sense is, that it was the aim and purpose of Paul to accomplish this, and that it would certainly be done. The strongholds of philosophy, heathenism, and sin should be demolished, and all the opinions, plans, and purposes of the world should become subject to the all-conquering Redeemer.

6. *And having in a readiness*, &c. I am ready to punish all disobedience, notwithstanding all that is said to the contrary; see Notes on ver. 1, 2. Clothed as I am with this power; aiming to subdue all things to Christ, though the weapons of my warfare are not carnal, and though I am modest or timid (ver. 1) when I am with you, I am prepared to take any measures of severity required by my apostolic office, in order that I may inflict deserved punishment on those who have violated the laws of Christ. The design of this is, to meet the objection of his enemies, that he would not *dare* to execute his threatenings. ¶ *When your obedience is fulfilled.* Doddridge renders this, "now your obedience is fulfilled, and the sounder part of your church restored to due order and submission." The idea seems to be, that Paul was ready to inflict discipline when the church had showed a readiness to obey his laws, and to do its own duty—delicately intimating that the reason why it was not done was the want of entire promptness in the church itself, and that it could not be done on any offender as long as the church itself was not prepared to sustain him. The church was to discountenance the enemies of the Redeemer; to show an entire readiness to sustain the apostle, and to unite with him in the effort to maintain the discipline of Christ's house.

7. *Do ye look on things after the outward appearance?* This is addressed evidently to the members of the church, and with reference to the

trust to himself that he is Christ's, let him of himself think this again, that, as he *is* Christ's, even so *are* we Christ's.

8 For though I should boast somewhat more of our authority, [a] which the Lord hath given us for edification, [b] and not for your destruction, I should not be ashamed:

9 That I may not seem as if I would terrify you by letters.

a chap. 13.2,3. b chap. 13.8.

claims which had been set up by the false teachers. There can be no doubt that they valued themselves on their external advantages, and laid claim to peculiar honour in the work of the ministry, because they were superior in personal appearance, in rank, manners, or eloquence to Paul. Paul reproves them for thus judging, and assures them that this was not a proper criterion by which to determine on qualifications for the apostolic office. Such things were highly valued among the Greeks, and a considerable part of the effort of Paul in these letters is to show that these things constitute no evidence that those who possessed them were sent from God. ¶ *If any man trust to himself*, &c. This refers to the false teachers who laid claims to be the followers of Christ by way of eminence. Whoever these teachers were, it is evident that they claimed to be on the side of Christ, and to be appointed by him. They were probably Jews, and they boasted of their talents and eloquence, and possibly that they had seen the Saviour. The phrase "trust to himself," seems to imply that they relied on some special merit of their own, or some special advantage which they had.—*Bloomfield.* It may have been that they were of the same tribe that he was, or that they had seen him, or that they confided in their own talents or endowments as a proof that they had been sent by him. It is not an uncommon thing for men to have such confidence in their own gifts, and particularly in a power of fluent speaking, as to suppose that this is a sufficient evidence that they are sent to preach the gospel. ¶ *Let him of himself think this again.* Since he relies so much on himself; since he has such confidence in his own powers, let him look at the evidence that I also am of Christ. ¶ *That as he is Christ's, even so are we Christ's.* That I have given as much evidence that I am commissioned by Christ as they can produce. It may be of a different kind. It is not in eloquence. and rank, and the gift of a rapid and ready elocution, but it may be superior to what they are able to produce. Probably Paul refers here to the fact that he had seen the Lord Jesus, and that he had been directly commissioned by him. The sense is, that no one could produce more proofs of being called to the ministry than he could.

8. *For though I should boast*, &c. If I should make even higher claims than I have done to a divine commission. I could urge higher evidence than I have done that I am sent by the Lord Jesus. ¶ *Of our authority.* Of my authority as an apostle, my power to administer discipline, and to direct the affairs of the church. ¶ *Which the Lord hath given us for edification.* A power primarily conferred to build up his people and save them and not to destroy. ¶ *I should not be ashamed.* It would be founded on good evidence and sustained by the nature of my commission. I should also have no occasion to be ashamed of the manner in which it has been exercised—a power that has in fact been employed in extending religion and edifying the church, and not in originating and sustaining measures fitted to destroy the soul.

9. *That I may not seem*, &c. The meaning of this verse seems to be this. "I say that I might boast more of my power in order that I may not appear disposed to terrify you with my letters merely. I do not threaten more than I can perform. I have it in my power to execute all that I have threatened, and to strike an awe not only by my letters, but by the infliction of extraordinary miraculous punishments. And if I should boast that I had done

10 For *his* letters, [1] say they, *are* weighty and powerful; but *his* bodily presence *is* weak, and *his* speech contemptible

[1] said he.

this, and could do it again, I should have no reason to be ashamed. It would not be vain and empty boasting; not boasting which is not well-founded."

10. *For his letters.* The letters which he has sent to the church when absent. Reference is had here probably to the first epistle to the Corinthians. They might also have seen some of Paul's other epistles, and been so well acquainted with them as to be able to make the general remark that he had the power of writing in an authoritative and impressive manner. ¶ *Say they.* Marg. *Said he.* Greek (φησί) in the singular. This seems to have referred to some one person who had uttered the words—perhaps some one who was the principal leader of the faction opposed to Paul. ¶ *Are weighty and powerful.* Tindal renders this, "Sore and strong." The Greek is, "heavy and strong" (βαρεῖαι καὶ ἰσχυραί). The sense is, that his letters were energetic and powerful. They abounded with strong argument, manly appeals, and impressive reproof. This even his enemies were compelled to admit, and this no one can deny who ever read them. Paul's letters comprise a considerable portion of the New Testament; and some of the most important doctrines of the New Testament are those which are advocated and enforced by him; and his letters have done more to give shape to the theological doctrines of the Christian world than any other cause whatever. He wrote fourteen epistles to churches and individuals on various occasions and on a great variety of topics; and his letters soon rose into very high repute among even the inspired ministers of the New Testament (see 2 Pet. iii. 15, 16), and were regarded as inculcating the most important doctrines of religion. The general characteristics of Paul's letters are, (1.) They are strongly argumentative. See especially the epistles to the Romans and the Hebrews. (2.) They are distinguished for boldness and vigour of style. (3.) They are written under great energy of feeling and of thought—a rapid and impetuous torrent that bears him forcibly along. (4.) They abound more than most other writings in parentheses, and the sentences are often involved and obscure. (5.) They often evince rapid transitions and departures from the regular current of thought. A thought strikes him suddenly, and he pauses to illustrate it, and dwells upon it long, before he returns to the main subject. The consequence is, that it is often difficult to follow him. (6.) They are powerful in reproof—abounding with strokes of great boldness of denunciation, and also with specimens of most withering sarcasm and most delicate irony. (7.) They abound in expressions of great tenderness and pathos. Nowhere can be found expressions of a heart more tender and affectionate than in the writings of Paul. (8.) They dwell much on great and profound doctrines, and on the application of the principles of Christianity to the various duties of life. (9.) They abound with references to the Saviour. He illustrates every thing by his life, his example, his death, his resurrection. It is not wonderful that letters composed on such subjects and in such a manner by an inspired man produced a deep impression on the Christian world; nor that they should be regarded now as among the most important and valuable portions of the Bible. Take away Paul's letters, and what a chasm would be made in the New Testament! What a chasm in the religious opinions and in the consolations of the Christian world! ¶ *But his bodily presence.* His personal appearance. ¶ *Is weak.* Imbecile, feeble (ἀσθενής)—a word often used to denote infirmity of body, sickness, disease; Mat. xxv. 39, 43, 44; Luke x. 9; Acts iv. 9; v. 15, 16; 1 Cor. xi. 30. Here it is to be observed that this is a mere charge which was brought against him, and it is not of necessity to be supposed that it was

11 Let such an one think this, that, such as we are in word by letters when we are absent, such *will we be* also in deed when we are present.

12 For [a] we dare not make our-

a chap.3.1.

true, though the presumption is, that there was some foundation for it. It is supposed to refer to some bodily imperfections, and possibly to his diminutive stature. Chrysostom says that his stature was low, his body crooked, and his head bald. Lucian, in his Philopatris, says of him, Corpore erat parvo, contracto, incurvo, tricubitali—probably an exaggerated description, perhaps a caricature—to denote one very diminutive and having no advantages of personal appearance. According to Nicephorus, Paul "was a little man, crooked, and almost bent like a bow; with a pale countenance, long and wrinkled; a bald head; his eyes full of fire and benevolence; his beard long, thick, and interspersed with gray hairs, as was his head," &c. But there is no certain evidence of the truth of these representations. Nothing in the Bible would lead us to suppose that Paul was remarkably diminutive or deformed; and though there may be some foundation for the charge here alleged that his bodily presence was weak, yet we are to remember that this was the accusation of his enemies, and that it was doubtless greatly exaggerated. Nicephorus was a writer of the sixteenth century, and his statements are worthy of no regard. That Paul was eminently an eloquent man may be inferred from a great many considerations; some of which are, (1.) His recorded discourses in the Acts of the Apostles, and the effect produced by them. No one can read his defence before Agrippa or Felix and not be convinced that as an orator he deserves to be ranked among the most distinguished of ancient times. No one who reads the account in the Acts can believe that he had any remarkable impediment in his speech or that he was remarkably deformed. (2.) Such was somehow his grace and power as an orator that he was taken by the inhabitants of Lycaonia as *Mercury*, the god of eloquence; Acts xvi. 12. Assuredly the evidence here is, that Paul was not deformed. (3.) It may be added, that Paul is mentioned by Longinus among the principal orators of antiquity. From these circumstances, there is no reason to believe that Paul was remarkably deficient in the qualifications requisite for an orator, or that he was in any way remarkably deformed. ¶ *And his speech contemptible.* To be despised. Some suppose that he had an impediment in his speech. But conjecture here is vain and useless. We are to remember that this is a charge made by his adversaries, and that it was made by the fastidious Greeks, who professed to be great admirers of eloquence, but who in his time confided much more in the mere art of the rhetorician than in the power of thought, and in energetic appeals to the reason and conscience of men. Judged by their standard it may be that Paul had not the graces in voice or manner, or in the knowledge of the Greek language which they esteemed necessary in a finished orator; but judged by his power of thought, and his bold and manly defence of truth, and his energy of character and manner, and his power of impressing truth on mankind, he deserves, doubtless, to be ranked among the first orators of antiquity. No man has left the impress of his own mind on more other minds than Paul.

11. *Let such an one think this*, &c. Let them not flatter themselves that there will be any discrepancy between my words and my deeds. Let them feel that all which has been threatened will be certainly executed unless there is repentance. Paul here designedly contradicts the charge which was made against him; and means to say that all that he had threatened in his letters would be certainly executed unless there was a reform. I think that the evidence here is clear that Paul does not intend to admit what they said about his bodily presence to

selves of the number, or compare ourselves with some that commend themselves: but they measuring themselves by themselves, and comparing themselves among themselves, [1] are not wise.[a]

1 understand it not.

a Pr.26.12.

be true; and most probably all that has been recorded bout his deformity is mere fable.

12. *For we dare not make ourselves of the number.* We admit that we are not bold enough for that. They had accused him of a want of boldness and energy when present with them, ver. 1, 10. Here in a strain of severe but delicate irony, he says he was *not* bold enough to do things which they had done. He did not *dare* to do the things which had been done among them. To such boldness of character, present or absent, he could lay no claim. ¶ *Or compare ourselves,* &c. I am not bold enough for that. That requires a stretch of boldness and energy to which I can lay no claim. ¶ *That commend themselves.* That put themselves forward, and that boast of their endowments and attainments. It is probable that this was commonly done by those to whom the apostle here refers; and it is certain that it is everywhere the characteristic of pride. To do this, Paul says, required greater boldness than he possessed, and on this point he yielded to them the palm. The satire here is very delicate, and yet very severe, and was such as would doubtless be felt by them. ¶ *But they measuring themselves by themselves.* Whitby and Clarke suppose that **this** means that they compare themselves with each other; and that they made the false apostles particularly their standard. Doddridge, Grotius, Bloomfield, and some others suppose the sense to be, that they made themselves the standard of excellence. They looked continually on their own accomplishments, and did not look at the excellences of others. They thus formed a disproportionate opinion of themselves, and undervalued all others. Paul says that he had not boldness enough for that. It required a moral courage to which he could lay no claim. Horace (Epis. i. 7. 98) has an expression similar to this:—

Metiri se quemque suo modulo ac pede verum est.

The sense of Paul is, that they made themselves the standard of excellence; that they were satisfied with their own attainments; and that they overlooked the superior excellence and attainments of others. This is a graphic description of pride and self-complacency; and, alas! it is what is often exhibited. How many there are, and it is to be feared even among professing Christians, who have no other standard of excellence than themselves. Their views are the standard of orthodoxy; their modes of worship are the standard of the proper manner of devotion; their habits and customs are in their own estimation perfect; and their own characters are the models of excellence, and they see little or no excellence in those who differ from them. They look on themselves as the true measure of orthodoxy, humility, zeal, and piety; and they condemn all others, however excellent they may be, who differ from them. ¶ *And comparing themselves,* &c. Or rather comparing themselves *with* themselves. Themselves they make to be the standard, and they judge of everything by that. ¶ *Are not wise.* Are stupid and foolish. Because, (1.) They had no such excellence as to make themselves the standard. (2.) Because this was an indication of pride. (3.) Because it made them blind to the excellences of others. It was to be presumed that others *had* endowments not inferior to theirs. (4.) Because the requirements of God, and the character of the Redeemer, were the proper standard of conduct. Nothing is a more certain indication of folly than for a man to make himself the standard of excellence. Such an individual must be blind to his own real character; and the only thing certain about his attainments is, that he is inflated with pride. And yet how common! How self-satisfied are most persons! How

13 But we will not boast of things without *our* measure, but according to the measure of the [1] rule which God hath distributed to us, a measure to reach even unto you.

1 or, *line*.

pleased with their own character and attainments! How grieved at any comparison which is made with others implying their inferiority! How prone to undervalue all others simply because they differ from them!—The margin renders this, "understand it not," that is, they do not understand their own character or their inferiority.

13. *But we will not boast of things without* our *measure.* Tindal renders this, "But we will not rejoice above measure." There is great obscurity in the language here, arising from its brevity. But the general idea seems to be plain. Paul says that he had not boldness as they had to boast of things wholly *beyond* his proper rule and his actual attainments and influence: and, especially, that he was not disposed to enter into other men's labours; or to boast of things that had been done by the mere influence of his name, and beyond the proper limits of his personal exertions. He made no boast of having done any thing where he had not been himself on the ground and laboured assiduously to secure the object. *They*, it is not improbable, had boasted of what had been done in Corinth as though it were really their work though it had been done by the apostle himself. Nay more, it is probable that they boasted of what had been done by the mere influence of their name. Occupying a central position, they supposed that their reputation had gone abroad, and that the mere influence of their *reputation* had had an important effect. Not so with Paul. He made no boast of any thing but what God had enabled him to do by his evangelical labours, and by personal exertions. He entered into no other men's labours, and claimed nothing that others had done as his own. He was not bold enough for that. ¶ *But according to the measure of the rule,* &c. Marg. Or, *line*. The word rendered "rule" (Greek, κανών, whence our English word *canon*) means properly a *reed, rod*, or *staff* employed to keep any thing stiff, erect, asunder (Hom. Il. 8. 103); then a measuring rod or line; then any standard or rule—its usual meaning in the New Testament, as, *e. g.*, of life and doctrine, Gal. vi. 16; Phil. iii. 16.—*Robinson's Lex.* Here it means the limit, boundary line, or sphere of action assigned to any one. Paul means to say that God had appropriated a certain line or boundary as the proper limit of his sphere of action; that his appropriate sphere extended to them; that in going to them, though they were far distant from the field of his early labours, he had confined himself within the proper limits assigned him by God; and that in boasting of his labours among them he was not boasting of any thing which did not properly fall within the sphere of labour assigned to him. The meaning is, that Paul was especially careful not to boast of any thing beyond his proper bounds. ¶ *Which God hath distributed to us.* Which in assigning our respective fields of labour God has assigned unto me and my fellow-labourers. The Greek word here rendered "distributed" (ἐμέρισεν) means properly to measure; and the sense is, that God had measured out or apportioned their respective fields of labour; that by his providence he had assigned to each one his proper sphere, and that in the distribution Corinth had fallen to the lot of Paul. In going there he had kept within the proper limits; in boasting of his labours and success there he did not boast of what did not belong to him. ¶ *A measure to reach even unto you.* The sense is, "the limits assigned me include you, and I may therefore justly boast of what I have done among you as within my proper field of labour." Paul was the apostle to the Gentiles (Acts xxvi. 17, 18); and the whole country of Greece therefore he regarded as falling within the limits assigned to him. No one therefore

14 For we stretch not ourselves beyond *our measure*, as though we reached unto you, for we are come as far as to you also in *preaching* the gospel of Christ:

15 Not boasting of things without *our* measure, *that is*, of [a] other men's labours; but having hope when your faith is increased, that we shall be [1] enlarged by

a Ro.15.20.

1 or, *magnified in you.*

could blame him for going there as if he was an intruder; no one assert that he had gone beyond the proper bounds.

14. *For we stretch not ourselves beyond* our measure. In coming to preach to you we have not gone beyond the proper limits assigned us. We have not endeavoured to enlarge the proper boundaries, to *stretch the line* which limited us, but have kept honestly within the proper limits. ¶ *As though we reached not unto you.* That is, as if our boundaries did not extend so far as to comprehend you. We have not overstepped the proper limits, as if Greece was not within the proper sphere of action. ¶ *For we are come as far as to you,* &c. In the regular work of preaching the gospel we have come to you. We have gone from place to place preaching the gospel where we had opportunity; we have omitted no important places, until in the regular discharge of our duties in preaching we have reached you and have preached the gospel to you. We have not omitted other places in order to come to you and enter into the proper field of labour of others, but in the regular work of making the gospel known as far as possible to all men we have come to Corinth. Far as it is, therefore, from the place where we started, we have approached it in a regular manner, and have not gone out of our proper province in doing it.

15. *Not boasting of things without* our *measure.* There is here probably an allusion to the false teachers at Corinth. They had come *after* Paul had been there, and had entered into his labours. When he had founded the church; when he had endured trials and persecutions in order to reach Corinth; when he had laboured there for a year and a half (Acts xviii. 11), *they* came and entered the quiet and easy field, formed parties, and claimed the field as their own. Paul says that he had not courage to do that; see Note, ver. 12. That requirea a species of boldness to which he could lay no claim; and he did not assume honour to himself like that ¶ That is, *of other men's labours.* Not intruding into churches which we did not establish, and claiming the right to direct their affairs, and to exclude the founders from all proper honours and all influence, and endeavouring to alienate the affections of Christians from their spiritual father and guide. ¶ *But having hope,* &c. So far from this; so far from a desire to enter into the labours of others and quietly enjoying the avails of their industry; and so far even from a desire to sit down ourselves and enjoy the fruit of our own labours, I desire to penetrate other untrodden regions; to encounter new dangers; to go where the gospel has not been planted, and to rear other churches there. I do not, therefore, make these remarks as if I wished even to dispossess the teachers that have entered into my labours. I make them because I wish to be aided by you in extending the gospel further; and I look to your assistance in order that I may have the means of going into the regions where I have not made known the name of the Redeemer. ¶ *When your faith is increased.* When you become so strong as not to need my presence and my constant care; and when you shall be able to speed me on my way and to aid me on my journey. He expected to be assisted by them in his efforts to carry the gospel to other countries. ¶ *That we shall be enlarged.* Marg. *Magnified by you.* Bloomfield supposes that this means, "to gain fame and glory by you;" that is, as the teacher may justly by his pupils. So Robinson renders it, "to make great, to praise." But to me the idea seems to be that he wished them to enlarge

you according to our rule abundantly.

16 To preach the gospel in the *regions* beyond you, *and* not to boast in another man's line [1] of things made ready to our hand.

17 But [a] he that glorieth, let him glory in the Lord.

1 or, *rule*. *a* Je.9.24.

or magnify him by introducing him to larger fields of action; by giving him a wider sphere of labour. It was not that he wished to be magnified by obtaining a wider reputation, not as a matter of praise or ambition, but he wished to have his work and success greatly enlarged. This he hoped to be enabled to do partly by the aid of the church at Corinth. When they became able to manage their own affairs; when his time was not demanded to superintend them; when their faith became so strong that his presence was not needed; and when they should assist him in his preparations for travel, then he would enter on his wider field of labour. He had no intention of sitting down in ease as the false teachers in Corinth seem disposed to have done. ¶ *According to our rule.* Greek, "According to our canon;" see on ver. 13. The sense is, according to the rule by which the sphere of his labours had been marked out. His rule was to carry the gospel as far as possible to the heathen world. He regarded the regions lying far beyond Corinth as coming properly within his limits; and he desired to occupy that field. ¶ *Abundantly.* Greek, Unto abundance. So as to abound; that is, to occupy the field assigned as far as possible.

16. *To preach the gospel in the regions beyond you.* What regions are referred to here can be only a matter of conjecture. It may be that he wished to preach in other parts of Greece, and that he designed to go to Arcadia or Lacedæmon. Rosenmüller supposes that as the Corinthians were engaged in commerce, the apostle hoped that by them some tidings of the gospel would reach the countries with which they were engaged in traffic. But I think it most probable that he alludes to Italy and Spain. It is certain that he had formed the design of visiting Spain (Rom. xv. 24, 28); and he doubtless wished the Corinthians to aid him in that purpose, and was anxious to do this as soon as the condition of the eastern churches would allow it. ¶ And *not to boast in another man's line of things*, &c. Marg. *Rule*, the same word (κανὼν) which occurs in ver. 13. The meaning is, that Paul did not mean to boast of what properly belonged to others. He did not claim what they had done as his own. He did not intend to labour within what was properly their bounds, and then to claim the field and the result of the labour as his. He probably means here to intimate that this had been done by the false teachers of Corinth; but so far was he from designing to do this, that he meant soon to leave Corinth, which was properly within his limits, and the church which he had founded there, to go and preach the gospel to other regions. Whether Paul ever went to Spain has been a question (see Note on Rom. xv. 24); but it is certain that he went to Rome, and that he preached the gospel in many other places after this besides Corinth.

17. *But he that glorieth.* He that boasts. Whatever may be the occasion of his boasting, whether in planting churches or in watering them; whether in his purposes, plans, toils, or success. Paul himself did not deem it improper on some occasions to boast (chap. xi. 16; xii. 5), but it was not of his own power, attainments, or righteousness. He was disposed to trace all to the Lord, and to regard him as the source of all blessing and all success. ¶ *Let him glory in the Lord.* In this serious and weighty admonition, Paul designs, doubtless, to express the manner in which *he* was accustomed to glory, and to furnish an admonition to the Corinthians. In the previous part of the chapter there had been some severe irony. He closes the chapter with the utmost

18 For not he that commendeth himself is approved, but [a] whom the Lord commendeth.

a Ro.2.29.

seriousness and solemnity of manner, in order to show on his part that he was not disposed to glory in his own attainments and to admonish them not to boast of theirs. If they had any thing valuable they should regard the Lord as the author of it. In this admonition it is probable that Paul had in his eye the passage in Jer. ix. 23, 24; though he has not expressly quoted it. "Let not the wise man glory in his wisdom, neither let the mighty man glory in his might, let not the rich man glory in his riches; but let him that glorieth glory in this, that he understandeth and knoweth me, that I am the LORD which exercise loving-kindness, judgment, and righteousness in the earth." The sentiment is a favourite one with Paul, as it should be with all Christians; see Note on 1 Cor. i. 31. On this verse we may *here* remark, I. That nothing is more common than for men to boast or glory. Little as they really have in which to glory, yet there is no one probably who has not *something* of which he is proud, and of which he is disposed to boast. It would be difficult or impossible to find a person who had not something on which he prided himself; something in which he esteemed himself superior to others. II. The things of which they boast are very various. (1.) Many are proud of their personal beauty; many, too, who would be unwilling to be thought proud of it. (2.) Many glory in their accomplishments; or, what is more likely, in the accomplishments of their children. (3.) Many glory in their talents; talents for any thing, valuable or not, in which they suppose they surpass others. They glory in their talent for eloquence, or science, or gaining knowledge; or in their talent for gaining property or keeping it; for their skill in their professions or callings; for their ability to run, to leap, or to practise even any trick or sleight of hand. There is nothing so worthless that it does not constitute a subject of glorying, *provided it be ours*. If it belong to others it may be valueless. (4.) Many glory in their property; in fine houses, extended plantations, or in the reputation of being rich; or in gorgeous dress, equipage, and furniture. In short, there is nothing which men possess in which they are not prone to glory. Forgetful of God the giver; forgetful that all may be soon taken from them, or that they soon must leave all; forgetful that none of these things can constitute a distinction in the grave or beyond, they boast as if these things were to remain for ever, and as if they had been acquired independently of God. How prone is the man of talents to forget that God has given him his intellect, and that for its proper use he must give account! How prone is the rich man to forget that he must die! How prone the gay and the beautiful to forget that they will lie undistinguished in the grave; and that death will consume them as soon as the most vile and worthless of the species! III. If we glory it should be in the Lord. We should ascribe our talents, wealth, health, strength, and salvation to him. We should rejoice, (1.) That we *have* such a Lord, so glorious, so full of mercy, so powerful, so worthy of confidence and love. (2.) We should rejoice in our endowments and possessions as his gift. We should rejoice that we may come and lay every thing at his feet, and whatever may be our rank, or talents, or learning, we should rejoice that we may come with the humblest child of poverty, and sorrow, and want, and say, "Not unto us, not unto us, but unto thy name give glory, for thy mercy and for thy truth's sake;" Ps. cxv. 1; see Note on 1 Cor. i. 31.

18. *For not he who commendeth himself*, &c. Not he who boasts of his talents and endowments. He is not to be judged by the estimate which he shall place on himself, but by the estimate which God shall form and express. ¶ *Is approved*. By God.

It is no evidence that we shall be saved that we are prone to commend ourselves; see Rom. xvi. 10. ¶ *But whom the Lord commendeth:* see Note on Rom. ii. 29. The idea here is, that men are to be approved or rejected by God. He is to pass judgment on them, and that judgment is to be in accordance with his estimate of their character, and not according to their own If he approves them they will be saved; if he does not, vain will be all their empty boasting; vain all their reliance on their wealth, eloquence, learning, or earthly honours. None will save them from condemnation; not all these things can purchase for them eternal life. Paul thus seriously shows that we should be mainly anxious to obtain the divine favour. It should be the grand aim and purpose of our life; and we should repress all disposition for vain-glory or self-confidence; all reliance on our talents, attainments, or accomplishments for salvation. OUR BOAST IS THAT WE HAVE SUCH A REDEEMER; AND IN THAT WE ALL MAY GLORY.

REMARKS.

1. We should have no *desire* to show off any peculiar boldness or energy of character which we may have; ver. 1, 2. We should greatly prefer to evince the gentleness and meekness of Christ. Such a character is in itself of far more value than one that is merely energetic and bold; that is rash, authoritative, and fond of display.

2. They who are officers in the church should have no *desire* to administer discipline; ver. 2. Some men are so fond of power that they always love to exercise it. They are willing to show it even by inflicting punishment on others; and "dressed in a little brief authority" they are constantly seeking occasion to show their consequence; they magnify trifles; they are unwilling to pass by the slightest offences. The reason is not that they love the truth, but that they love their own consequence, and they seek every opportunity to show it.

3. All Christians and all Christian ministers are engaged in a warfare; ver. 3. They are at war with sin in their own hearts, and with sin wherever it exists on earth, and with the powers of darkness. With foes so numerous and so vigilant, they should not expect to live a life of ease or quietness. Peace, perfect peace, they may expect in heaven, not on earth. Here they are to fight the good fight of faith and thus to lay hold on eternal life. It has been the common lot of all the children of God to maintain such a war, and shall *we* expect to be exempt?

"Shall *I* be carried to the skies
On flowery beds of ease,
While others fought to win the prize,
And sailed through bloody seas?

"Are there no foes for me to face,
Must I not stem the flood?
Is this vile world a friend to grace,
To help me on to God?"

4. The weapons of the Christian are not to be carnal, but are to be spiritual; ver. 4. He is not to make his way by the exhibition of human passion; in bloody strife; and by acting under the influence of ambitious feelings. Truth is his weapon; and armed with truth, and aided by the Spirit of God, he is to expect the victory. How different is the Christian warfare from others! How different is Christianity from other systems! Mahomet made his way by arms, and propagated his religion amidst the din of battle. But not so Christianity. That is to make its way by the silent, but mighty operation of truth; and there is not a rampart of idolatry and sin that is not yet to fall before it.

5. The Christian should be a man of a pure spirit; ver. 4. He is to make his way by the truth. He should therefore love the truth, and he should seek to diffuse it as far as possible. In propagating or defending it, he should be *always* mild, gentle, and kind. Truth is never advanced, and an adversary is never convinced, where passion is evinced; where there is a haughty manner or a belligerent spirit. The apostolic precepts are *full of wisdom,* "speaking the truth in love" Eph. iv. 15), "in MEEKNESS INSTRUCTING those that oppose themselves; if

God peradventure will give them repentance to the acknowledging of the truth;" 2 Tim. ii. 25.

6. In his warfare the Christian shall conquer; ver. 4, 5. Against the truth of Christianity nothing has been able to stand. It made its way against the arrayed opposition of priests and emperors; against customs and laws; against inveterate habits and opinions; against all forms of sin, until it triumphed, and "the banners of the faith floated from the palaces of the Cesars." So it will be in all the conflicts with evil. Nothing is more certain than that the powers of darkness in this world are destined to fall before the power of Christian truth, and that every stronghold of sin shall yet be demolished. So it is in the conflicts of the individual Christian. He may struggle long and hard. He may have many foes to contend with. But he shall gain the victory. His triumph shall be secure; and he shall yet be enabled to say, "I have fought a good fight—*henceforth there is laid up for me* A CROWN."

"The saints in all this glorious war
Shall conquer though they die;
They see the triumph from afar,
And seize it with their eye."

7. Yet all should feel their dependence on God; ver. 4. It is only through him and by his aid that we have any power. Truth itself has no power except as it is attended and directed by God; and we should engage in our conflict feeling that none but God can give us the victory. If forsaken by him, we shall fall; if supported by him, we may face without fear a "frowning world," and all the powers of the "dark world of hell."

8. We should not judge by the outward appearance; ver. 7. It is the heart that determines the character; and by that God shall judge us, and by that we should judge ourselves.

9. We should aim to extend the gospel as far as possible; ver. 14—16. Paul aimed to go beyond the regions where the gospel had been preached, and to extend it to far distant lands. So the "field" still "is the world." A large portion of the earth is yet unevangelized. Instead, therefore, of sitting down quietly in enjoyment and ease, let us, like him, earnestly desire to extend the influence of pure religion, and to bring distant nations to the saving knowledge of the truth.

10. Let us not boast in ourselves; ver. 17. Not of our talents, wealth, learning, or accomplishments let us glory. But let us glory that we have such a God as JEHOVAH. Let us glory that we have such a Redeemer as Jesus Christ. Let us glory that we have such a sanctifier as the Holy Spirit. Let us acknowledge God as the source of all our blessings, and to him let us honestly consecrate our hearts and our lives.

11. What a reverse of judgment there will yet be on human character! ver. 17. 18. How many now *commend* themselves who will be *condemned* in the last day. How many men boast of their talents and morals, and even their religion, who will then be involved in indiscriminate condemnation with the most vile and worthless of the race. How anxious should we be, therefore, to secure the approbation of God; and whatever our fellow-men may say of us, how infinitely desirable is it to be commended then by our heavenly Father.

CHAPTER XI.

THIS chapter is connected in its general design with the preceding. The object of Paul is to vindicate himself from the charges which had been brought against him, and especially to vindicate his claims to the apostolic office. It is *ironical* in its character, and is of course severe upon the false teachers who had accused him in Corinth. The main purpose is to state his claims to the office of an apostle, and especially to show that when he mentioned those claims, or even boasted of his labours, he had ground for doing so. It would seem that they had charged him with "*folly*" in boasting as he had done. Probably the false teachers were loud in proclaiming their own praise, but represented Paul as guilty of folly in praising himself. He therefore (ver. 1) asks them if they could bear with him a little further in his folly, and entreats them to do it. This verse contains the scope of the chapter; and the remainder of the chapter is an enumeration of the causes which he had for his boasting, though probably each reason is adapted to some form of accusation brought against him.

Having entreated them to bear with him a little further, he states the *reasons* why he was disposed to go into this subject at all; ver. 2—4. It was not because he was disposed to sound his own praise, but it was from love to them. He had espoused them as a chaste virgin to Christ. He was afraid that their affections would be alienated from the Redeemer. He reminded them of the manner in which Eve was tempted; and he reminded them that by the same smooth and plausible arts their affections might also be stolen away, and that they might be led into sin. He reminds them that there was danger of their receiving another gospel, and expresses the apprehension that they had done it, and that they had embraced a deceiver; ver. 4.

Having made this general statement of his design, Paul now goes more into detail in answering the objections against him, and in showing the reasons which he had for boasting as he had done. The statement in answer to their objections relates to the following points.

(1.) He had supposed that he was not behind the chiefest of the apostles. He had supposed that he had claims to the apostolic office of as high an order as any of them. Called to the work as he had been, and labouring as he had done, he had regarded himself as having an indisputable claim to the office of an apostle. True, they had charged him with being rude in speech, a charge which he was not disposed to deny, but in a far more important point than that he had showed that he was not disqualified for the apostolic office. In *knowledge*, the main qualification, he had not been deficient, as probably even his opponents were disposed to admit; ver. 5, 6.

(2.) He had not deprived himself of the claims to the office and honours of an apostle by declining to receive from them a compensation, and by preaching the gospel without charge; ver. 7—9. Probably they had alleged that this was a proof that he *knew* that he had no claim to the honours of an apostle. He, therefore, states exactly how this was. He had *received* a support, but he had robbed other churches to do it. And even when he was with them, he had received supplies from a distant church in order that he might not be burdensome to them. The charge was therefore groundless, that he *knew* that he had no right to the support due to an apostle.

(3.) He declares it to be his fixed purpose that no one should prevent his boasting in that manner. And this he did because he loved them, and because he would save them from the snares of those who would destroy them. He therefore stated the true character of those who attempted to deceive them. They were the ministers of Satan, appearing as the ministers of righteousness, as Satan himself was transformed into an angel of light; ver 10—15.

(4.) Paul claims the privilege of boasting as a fool a little further; ver. 16. And he claims that as others boasted, and as they were allowed to do so by the Corinthians, he had also a right to do the same thing. They suffered them to boast; they allowed them to do it even if they devoured them, and smote them, and took their property. It was but fair, therefore, that he should be allowed to boast a little of what he was and of what he had done; ver. 17—20.

(5.) He goes, therefore, into an extended and most tender description of what he had suffered, and of his claims to their favourable regard. He had all the personal advantages arising from birth which they could pretend to. He was a Hebrew, of the seed of Abraham, and a minister of Christ; ver. 21—23. He had endured far more labours and dangers than they had done; and in order to set this before them he enumerates the trials through which he had pas-

CHAPTER XI.

WOULD to God ye could bear with me a little in *my* folly: and indeed bear[1] with me.

2 For I am jealous over you

[1] or, *ye do bear.*

sed, and states the labours which constantly came upon him; ver. 23—30. Of these things, of his sufferings, and trials, and infirmities, he felt that he had a right to speak, and these constituted a far higher claim to the confidence of the Christian church than the endowments of which his adversaries boasted.

(6.) As another instance of peril and suffering, he refers to the fact that his life was endangered when he was in Damascus, and that he barely escaped by being lowered down from the wall of the city, ver. 31—33. The conclusion which Paul doubtless intends should be derived from all this is, that he had far higher grounds of claim to the office of an apostle than his adversaries would admit, or than they could furnish themselves. He admitted that he was weak and subject to infirmities; he did not lay claim to the graces of a polished elocution, as they did; but if a life of self-denial and toil, of an honest devotion to the cause of truth at imminent and frequent hazard of life, constituted an evidence that he was an apostle, he had that evidence. They appealed to their birth, their rank, their endowments as public speakers. In the quiet and comfort of a congregation and church established to their hands; in reaping the avails of the labours of others; and in the midst of enjoyments, they coolly laid claims to the honours of the ministerial office, and denied his claims. In trial, and peril, and labour, and poverty; in scourges, and imprisonments, and shipwrecks; in hunger and thirst; in unwearied travelling from place to place; and in the care of all the churches, were *his* claims to their respect and confidence, and he was willing that any one that chose should make the comparison between them. Such was *his* "foolish" boasting; such his claims to their confidence and regard.

1. *Would to God.* Greek, "I would" (Ὄφελον). This expresses earnest desire, but in the Greek there is no appeal to God. The sense would be well expressed by "O that," or "I earnestly wish." ¶ *Ye could bear with me,* That you would bear patiently with me; that you would hear me patiently, and suffer me to speak of myself. ¶ *In my folly.* Folly in boasting. The idea seems to be, "I know that boasting is generally foolish, and that it is not to be indulged in. But though it is to be generally regarded as folly, yet circumstances compel me to it, and I ask your indulgence in it." It is possible also that his opponents accused him of folly in boasting so much of himself. *And indeed bear with me.* Marg. *Ye do bear.* But the text has probably the correct rendering. It is the expression of an earnest wish that they would tolerate him a little in this. He entreats them to bear with him because he was constrained to it.

2. *For I am jealous over you.* This verse expresses the reason why he was disposed to speak of his attainments, and of what he had done. It was because he loved them, and because he feared that they were in danger of being seduced from the simplicity of the gospel. The phrase "I am jealous" (ζηλῶ) means properly, I ardently love you; I am full of tender attachment to you. The word was usual among the Greeks to denote an ardent affection of any kind (from ζέω, to boil, to be fervid or fervent). The precise meaning is to be determined by the connection; see Note on 1 Cor. xii. 31. The *word* may denote the jealousy which is felt by an apprehension of departure from fidelity on the part of those whom we love; or it may denote a fervid and glowing attachment. The meaning here probably is, that Paul had a strong attachment to them. ¶ *With godly jealousy.* Greek, "with the zeal of God" (Θεοῦ ζήλῳ). That is, with very great or vehement zeal—in accordance with the Hebrew custom when

with godly jealousy: for I have espoused you [a] to one husband, that I may present *you as* a chaste virgin [b] to Christ.

3 But I fear, lest by any means, as the serpent beguiled Eve through his subtilty, so your minds should be corrupted from the simplicity that is in Christ.

a Hos.2.19,20.

b Le.21.13.

the name God is used to denote any thing signally great, as the phrase "mountains of God," meaning very elevated or lofty mountains. The mention of this ardent attachment suggested what follows. His mind reverted to the tenderness of the marriage relation, and to the possibility that in that relation the affections might be estranged. He makes use of this figure, therefore, to apprize them of the change which he apprehended. ¶ *For I have espoused you,* &c. The word here used (ἁρμόζω) means properly to adapt, to fit, to join together. Hence to join in wedlock, to marry. Here it means to marry to another; and the idea is, that Paul had been the agent employed in forming a connection, similar to the marriage connection, between them and the Saviour. The *allusion* here is not certain. It may refer to the custom which prevailed when friends made and procured the marriage for the bridegroom; or it may refer to some custom like that which prevailed among the Lacedemonians where persons were employed to form the lives and manners of virgins and prepare them for the duties of the married life. The sense is clear. Paul claims that it was by *his* instrumentality that they had been united to the Redeemer. Under him they had been brought into a relation to the Saviour similar to that sustained by the bride to her husband; and he felt all the interest in them which naturally grew out of that fact and from a desire to present them blameless to the pure Redeemer. The relation of the Church to Christ is often represented by marriage; see Eph. v. 23—33; Rev. xix. 7; xxi. 9. ¶ *To one husband.* To the Redeemer. ¶ *That I may present* you as *a chaste virgin to Christ.* The allusion here, according to Doddridge, is, to the custom among the Greeks "of having an officer whose business it was to educate and form young women, especially those of rank and figure, designed for marriage, and then to *present* them to those who were to be their husbands, and if this officer through negligence permitted them to be corrupted between the espousals and the consummation of the marriage, great blame would fall upon him." Such a responsibility Paul felt. So anxious was he for the entire purity of that church which was to constitute "the bride, the Lamb's wife;" so anxious that all who were connected with that church should be presented pure in heaven.

3. *But I fear.* Paul had just compared the church to a virgin, soon to be presented as a bride to the Redeemer. The mention of this seems to have suggested to him the fact that the first woman was deceived and led astray by the tempter, and that the same thing might occur in regard to the church which he was so desirous should be preserved pure. The grounds of his fear were, (1.) That Satan had seduced the first woman, thus demonstrating that the most holy were in danger of being led astray by temptation; and, (2.) That special efforts were made to seduce them from the faith. The persuasive arts of the false teachers; the power of philosophy; and the attractive and corrupting influences of the world, he had reason to suppose might be employed to seduce them from simple attachment to Christ. ¶ *Lest by any means.* Lest somehow (μήπως). It is implied that many means would be used; that all arts would be tried; and that in some way, which perhaps they little suspected, these arts would be successful, unless they were constantly put upon their guard. ¶ *As the serpent beguiled Eve;* see Gen. iii. 1—11. The word serpent here refers doubtless to Satan, who was the agent by whom Eve was

beguiled; see John viii. 44; 1 John iii. 8; Rev. xii. 9; xx. 2. Paul did not mean that they were in danger of being corrupted in the same way, but that similar efforts would be made to seduce them. Satan adapts his temptations to the character and circumstances of the tempted. He varies them from age to age, and applies them in such a way as best to secure his object. Hence all should be on their guard. No one knows the mode in which he will approach him, but all may know that he will approach them in *some* way. ¶ *Through his subtilty;* see Gen. iii. 1. By his craft, art, wiles (ἐν τῇ πανουργίᾳ). The word implies that shrewdness, cunning, craft was employed. A tempter always employs cunning and art to accomplish his object. The precise *mode* in which Satan accomplished his object is not certainly known. *Perhaps* the cunning consisted in assuming an attractive form—a fascinating manner—a manner fitted to charm; perhaps in the idea that the eating of the forbidden fruit had endowed a serpent with the power of reason and speech above all other animals, and that it might be expected to produce a similar transformation in Eve. At all events there were false pretences and appearances, and such Paul apprehended would be employed by the false teachers to seduce and allure them; see on ver. 13, 14. ¶ *So your minds should be corrupted.* So your thoughts should be perverted. So your hearts should be alienated. The mind is corrupted when the affections are alienated from the proper object, and when the soul is filled with unholy plans, and purposes, and desires. ¶ *From the simplicity that is in Christ.* (1.) From simple and single-hearted *devotedness* to him—from pure and unmixed attachment to him. The fear was that their affections would be fixed on other objects, and that the *singleness* and *unity* of their devotedness to him would be destroyed. (2.) From his *pure doctrines.* By the admixture of philosophy; by the opinions of the world there was danger that their minds should be turned away from their hold on the simple truths which Christ had taught. (3.) From that simplicity of mind and heart; that childlike candour and docility; that freedom from all guile, dishonesty, and deception which so eminently characterized the Redeemer. Christ had a single aim; was free from all guile; was purely honest; never made use of any improper arts; never resorted to false appearances, and never deceived. His followers should in like manner be artless and guileless. There should be no mere cunning, no trick, no craft in advancing their purposes. There should be nothing but honesty and truth in all that they say. Paul was afraid that they would lose this beautiful simplicity and artlessness of character and manner; and that they would insensibly be led to adopt the maxims of mere cunning, of policy, of expediency, of seductive arts which prevailed so much in the world—a danger which was imminent among the shrewd and cunning people of Greece; but which is confined to no time and no place. Christians should be more guileless than even children are; *as* pure and free from trick, and from art and cunning as was the Redeemer himself. (4.) From the simplicity *in worship* which the Lord Jesus commended and required. The worship which the Redeemer designed to establish was simple, unostentatious, and pure—strongly in contrast with the gorgeousness and corruption of the pagan worship, and even with the imposing splendour of the Jewish temple service. He intended that it should be adapted to all lands, and such as could be offered by all classes of men—a pure worship, claiming first the homage of the heart, and then such simple external expressions as should best exhibit the homage of the heart. How easily might this be corrupted! What temptations were there to attempt to corrupt it by those who had been accustomed to the magnificence of the temple service, and who would suppose that the religion of the Messiah *could* not be less gorgeous than that which was designed to shadow forth his coming; and by those who had been accustomed to

4 For if he that cometh preacheth another Jesus, whom we have not preached, or *if* ye receive another spirit, which ye

---

the splendid rites of the pagan worship, and who would suppose that the true religion *ought* not to be less costly and splendid than the false religion had been. If so much expense had been lavished on false religions, how natural to suppose that equal costliness at least should be bestowed on the true religion. Accordingly the history of the church for a considerable part of its existence has been little more than a record of the various forms in which the simple worship instituted by the Redeemer has been corrupted, until all that was gorgeous in pagan ceremonies and splendid in the Jewish ritual has been introduced as a part of Christian worship. (5.) From simplicity in dress and manner of living. The Redeemer's dress was simple. His manner of living was simple. His requirements demand great simplicity and plainness of apparel and manner of life ; 1 Pet. iii. 3—6 ; 1 Tim. ii. 9, 10. Yet how much proneness is there at all times to depart from this! What a besetting sin has it been in all ages to the church of Christ! And how much pains should there be that the very simplicity that is in Christ should be observed by all who bear the Christian name!

4. *For if he that cometh,* &c. There is much difficulty in this verse in ascertaining the true sense, and expositors have been greatly perplexed and divided in opinion, especially with regard to the true sense of the last clause, "ye might well bear with *him*." It is difficult to ascertain whether Paul meant to speak ironically or seriously ; and different views will prevail as different views are taken of the design. If it be supposed that he meant to speak seriously, the sense will be, "If the false teacher could recommend a better Saviour than I have done, or a Spirit better able to sanctify and save, then there would be a propriety in your receiving him and tolerating his doctrines." If the former, then the sense will be, "You cannot well bear with *me;* but if a man comes among you preaching a false Saviour, and a false Spirit, and a false doctrine, then you bear with him without any difficulty." Another interpretation still has been proposed, by supposing that the word "me" is to be supplied at the close of the verse instead of "him," and then the sense would be, "If you receive so readily one who preaches another gospel, one who comes with far less evidence that he is sent from God than I have, and if you show yourselves thus ready to fall in with any kind of teaching that may be brought to you, you might at least bear with *me* also." Amidst this variety it is not easy to ascertain the true sense. To me it seems probable, however, that Paul spoke *seriously,* and that our translation has expressed the true sense. The main idea doubtless is, that Paul felt that there was danger that they would be corrupted. If they could bring a better gospel, a more perfect system, and proclaim a more perfect Saviour, there would be no such change. But that could not be expected. It could not be done. If therefore they preached *any other* Saviour or any other gospel; if they departed from the truths which *he* had taught them, *it would be for the worse.* It could not be otherwise. The Saviour whom he preached was perfect, and was able to save. The Spirit which he preached was perfect, and able to sanctify. The gospel which he preached was perfect, and there was no hope that it could be improved. Any change must be for the worse ; and as the false teachers varied from his instructions, there was every reason to apprehend that their minds would be corrupted from the simplicity that was in Christ. The principal idea, therefore, is, that the gospel which *he* preached was as perfect as it could be, and that any change would be for the worse. No doctrine which others brought could be recommended *because* it was better. By the phrase "he that cometh" is meant doubtless the false teacher in Corinth. ¶ *Preacheth another Jesus.*

have not received, or another [a] gospel, which ye have not accepted, ye might well bear [1] with *him*.

5 For I suppose I [b] was not a whit behind the very chiefest apostles.

6 But though [c] *I be* rude in

a Ga.1.7,8.
1 or, *with me*.

b 1 Co.15.10; chap.12.11.
c 1 Co.1.17;2.1,13.

Proclaims one who is more worthy of your love and more able to save. If he that comes among you and claims your affections can point out another Christ who is more worthy of your confidence, then I admit that you do well to receive him. It is *implied* here that this could not be done. The Lord Jesus in his character and work is perfect. No Saviour superior to him has been provided; none but he is necessary. ¶ *Whom we have not preached.* Let them show, if they can, that they have any Saviour to tell of whom we have not preached. We have given all the evidence that we are sent by God, and have laid all the claim to your confidence, which they can do for having made known the Saviour. They with all their pretensions have no Saviour to tell you of with whom we have not already made you acquainted. They have no claims, therefore, from this quarter which we have not also. ¶ *Or if ye receive another spirit,* &c. If they can preach to you another Sanctifier and Comforter; or if under their ministry you have received higher proofs of the power of the Spirit in performing miracles; in the gift of tongues; in renewing sinners and in comforting your hearts. The idea is, that Paul had proclaimed the existence and agency of the same Holy Spirit which they did; that his preaching had been attended with as striking proofs of the presence and power of that Spirit; that he had all the evidence of a divine commission from such an influence attending his labours which they could possibly have. They could reveal no spirit better able to sanctify and save; none who had more power than the Holy Spirit which they had received under the preaching of Paul, and there was therefore no reason why they should be "corrupted" or seduced from the simple doctrines which they had received, and follow others. ¶ *Or another gospel,* &c. A gospel more worthy of your acceptance—one more free, more full, more rich in promises; one that revealed a better plan of salvation, or that was more full of comfort and peace. ¶ *Ye might well bear with him.* Marg. "*with me.*" The word *him* is not in the Greek; but is probably to be supplied. The sense is, there would then be some excuse for your conduct. There would be some reason why you should welcome such teachers. But if this cannot be done; if they can preach no other and no better gospel and Saviour than I have done, then there is no excuse. There is no reason why you should follow such teachers and forsake those who were your earliest guides in religion. —Let us never forsake the gospel which we have till we are sure we can get a better. Let us adhere to the simple doctrines of the New Testament until some one can furnish better and clearer doctrines. Let us follow the rules of Christ in our opinions and our conduct; our plans, our mode of worship, our dress, and our amusements, engagements, and company, until we can *certainly* ascertain that there are better rules. A man is foolish for making any change until he has evidence that he is likely to better himself; and it remains yet to be proved that any one has ever bettered himself or his family by forsaking the simple doctrines of the Bible, and embracing a philosophical speculation; by forsaking the scriptural views of the Saviour as the incarnate God, and embracing the views which represent him as a mere man; by forsaking the simple and plain rules of Christ about our manner of life, our dress, and our words and actions, and embracing those which are recommended by mere fashion and by the customs of a gay world.

5. *For I suppose,* &c. I think that

speech, yet not[a] in knowledge; but we have been thoroughly made manifest[b] among you in all things.

7 Have I committed an offence in abasing myself that ye might be exalted, because I have preached to you the gospel of God freely?

a Ep.3.4. b chap.12.12.

I gave as good evidence that I was commissioned by God as the most eminent of the apostles. In the miracles which I performed; in the abundance of my labours, and in my success, I suppose that I did not fall behind any of them. If so, I ought to be regarded and treated as an apostle; and if so, then the false teachers should not be allowed to supplant me in your affections, or to seduce you from the doctrines which I have taught. On the evidence that Paul was equal to others in the proper proof of a commission from God; see Notes on ver. 21—30.

6. *But though* I be *rude in speech;* see Note, chap. x. 10. The word rendered *rude* here (ἰδιώτης) means properly a private citizen, in opposition to one in a public station; then a plebeian, or one unlettered or unlearned, in opposition to one of more elevated rank, or one who is learned; see Notes on Acts iv. 13; 1 Cor. xiv. 16. The idea is, my language is that of a plain unlettered person. This was doubtless charged upon him by his enemies, and it may be that he designed in part to admit the truth of the charge. ¶ *Yet not in knowledge.* I do not admit that I am ignorant of the religion which I profess to teach. I claim to be acquainted with the doctrines of Christianity. It does not appear that they charged him with ignorance. If it be asked how the admission that he was rude in speech consists with the fact that he was endowed by the Holy Spirit with the power of speaking languages, we may observe that Paul had undoubtedly learned to speak Greek in his native place (Tarsus in Cilicia), and that the Greek which he had learned there was probably a corrupt kind, such as was spoken in that place. It was this Greek which he probably continued to speak; for there is no more reason to suppose that the Holy Spirit would aid him in speaking a language which he had thus early learned than he would in speaking Hebrew. The endowments of the Holy Spirit were conferred to enable the apostles to speak languages which they had never learned, not in perfecting them in languages with which they were before acquainted. It may have been true, therefore, that Paul may have spoken some languages which he never learned with more fluency and perfection than he did those which he had learned to speak when he was young. See the remarks of the Archbishop of Cambray, as quoted by Doddridge *in loc.* It may be remarked, also, that some estimate of the manner of Paul on this point may be formed from his writings. Critics profoundly acquainted with the Greek language remark, that while there is great energy of thought and of diction in the writings of Paul; while he chooses or *coins* most expressive words, yet that there is everywhere a want of Attic elegance of manner, and of the smoothness and beauty which were so grateful to a Grecian ear. ¶ *But we have been thoroughly made manifest,* &c. You have known all about me. I have concealed nothing from you, and you have had ample opportunity to become thoroughly acquainted with me. The meaning is, "I need not dwell on this. I need speak no more of my manner of speech or knowledge. With all that you are well acquainted."

7. *Have I committed an offence.* Have I done wrong. Greek, "Have I committed a sin." There is here a somewhat abrupt transition from the previous verse; and the connection is not very apparent. *Perhaps* the connection is this. "I admit my inferiority in regard to my manner of speaking. But this does not interfere with my full understanding of the doctrines which I preach, nor does it interfere with the numerous evidences

8 I robbed other churches, taking wages *of them*, to do you service.

9 And when I was present with you, and wanted, I [a] was chargeable to no man: for that

a Ac.18.3; 1Th.2.9.

which I have furnished that I am called to the office of an apostle. What then *is* the ground of offence? In what *have* I erred? Wherein have I shown that I was not qualified to be an apostle? Is it in the fact that I have not chosen to press my claim to a support, but have preached the gospel without charge?" There can be no doubt that they urged this as an objection to him, and as a proof that he was *conscious* that he had no claim to the office of an apostle; see Notes on 1 Cor. ix. 3—18. Paul here answers this charge; and the sum of his reply is, that he *had* received a support, but that it had come from others, a support which they had furnished because the Corinthians had neglected to do it. ¶ *In abasing myself.* By labouring with my own hands; by submitting to voluntary poverty, and by neglecting to urge my reasonable claims for a support. ¶ *That ye might be exalted.* In spiritual blessings and comforts. I did it because I could thus better promote religion among you. I could thus avoid the charge of aiming at the acquisition of wealth; could shut the mouths of gainsayers, and could more easily secure access to you. Is it now to be seriously urged as a fault that I have sought your welfare, and that in doing it I have submitted to great self-denial and to many hardships? See Notes on 1 Cor. ix. 18, seq.

8. *I robbed other churches.* The churches of Macedonia and elsewhere, which had ministered to his wants. Probably he refers especially to the church at Philippi (see Phil. iv. 15, 16), which seems to have done more than almost any other church for his support. By the use of the word "robbed" here Paul does not mean that he had obtained any thing from them in a violent or unlawful manner, or any thing which they did not give voluntarily. The word (ἐσύλησα) means properly, "I spoiled, plundered, robbed," but the idea of Paul here is, that he, *as it were,* robbed them, because he did not render an equivalent for what they gave him. They supported him when he was labouring for another people. A conqueror who plunders a country gives *no equivalent* for what he takes. In this sense only could Paul say that he had plundered the church at Philippi. His general principle was, that "the labourer was worthy of his hire," and that a man was to receive his support from the people for whom he laboured (see 1 Cor. ix. 7—14), but this rule he had not observed in this case. ¶ *Taking wages* of them. Receiving a support from them. They bore my expenses. ¶ *To do you service.* That I might labour among you without being supposed to be striving to obtain your property, and that I might not be compelled to labour with my own hands, and thus to prevent my preaching the gospel as I could otherwise do. The supply from other churches rendered it unnecessary in a great measure that his time should be taken off from the ministry in order to obtain a support.

9. *And when I was present with you.* When I was labouring in order to build up the church in Corinth. ¶ *I was chargeable to no man.* I was burdensome to no one; or more literally, "I did not lie as a dead weight upon you." The word here used, which occurs nowhere else in the New Testament (κατενάρκησα), means, literally, *to become torpid against, i. e.* to the detriment of any one; and hence to be burdensome. According to Jerome, its use here is a Cilicism of Paul. The idea is that he did not lead a torpid, inactive life at the expense of others. He did not expect a support from them when he was doing nothing; nor did he demand support which would in any sense be a burden to them. By his own hands (Acts xviii. 3), and by the aid which he received from abroad, he was supported without deriving aid from the people

which was lacking to me, the [a] brethren which came from Macedonia supplied: and in all *things* I have kept myself from being burdensome unto you, and *so* will I keep *myself*.

10 As the truth of Christ is in me, [1] no man shall stop me of this boasting in the regions of Achaia.

11 Wherefore? because I love you not? God knoweth.

12 But what I do, that I will do,

a Ph.4.10,15.

1 *this boasting shall not be stopped in me.*

of Corinth. ¶ *And in all* things, &c. In all respects I have carefully kept myself from being a burden on the church. Paul had no idea of living at other men's expense when he was doing nothing. He did not, as a general thing, mean to receive any thing for which he had not rendered a fair equivalent; a just principle for ministers and for all other men; see chap. xii. 13.

10. *As the truth of Christ is in me.* That is, I solemnly declare this as in the presence of Christ. As I am a Christian man; as I feel bound to declare **the** truth, and as I must answer to Christ. It is a solemn form of asseveration, equal to an oath; see Note on Rom. ix. 1; comp. 1 Tim. ii. 7. ¶ *No man shall stop me,* &c. Marg. *This boasting shall not be stopped in me;* see Note on 1 Cor. ix. 15. The idea here is, that Paul was solemnly determined that the same thing should continue. He had not been burdensome to any, and he was resolved that he would not be. Rather than be burdensome he had laboured with his own hands, and he meant to do it still. No man in all Achaia should ever have reason to say that he had been an idler, and had been supported by the churches when he was doing nothing. It was the fixed and settled purpose of his life never to be burdensome to any man. What a noble resolution! How fixed were the principles of his life! And what an instance of magnanimous self-denial and of elevated purpose! Every man, minister or otherwise, should adopt a similar resolution. He should resolve to receive nothing for which he has not rendered a fair equivalent, and resolve if he has health *never* to be a burden to his friends or to the church of God. And even if sick he may yet feel that he is not burdensome to others. If he is gentle and grateful; if he makes no unnecessary care; and especially if he furnishes an example of patience and piety, and seeks the blessing of God on his benefactors, he furnishes them what they will usually esteem an ample equivalent. No man *need* be burdensome to his friends; and all should resolve that by the grace of God they never will be. There is considerable variety in the MSS. here (see Mill on the place), but in regard to the general sense there can be no doubt. Nothing should ever hinder this boasting; nothing should deprive him of the privilege of saying that he had not been a burden. ¶ *In the regions of Achaia.* Achaia was that part of Greece of which Corinth was the capital; see Note on Acts xviii. 12.

11. *Wherefore,* &c. It is not because I do not love you. It is not from pride, or because I would not as willingly receive aid from you as from any other. It is not because I am more unwilling to be under obligation to you than to others. I have a deep and tender attachment to you; but it is because I can thus best promote the gospel and advance the kingdom of the Redeemer. Possibly it might have been thought that his unwillingness to receive aid from *them* was some proof of reserve towards them or want of affection, and this may have been urged against him. This he solemnly denies.

12. *But what I do.* The course of life which I have been pursuing I will continue to pursue. That is, I will continue to preach as I have done without demanding a support. I will labour with my own hands if necessary; I will preach without *demanding* rigidly what I might be entitled to. ¶ *That I may cut off occasion.* That I might give them no opportun-

that I may cut off occasion from them *a* which desire occasion; that wherein they glory, they may be found even as we.

13 For such *are* false *b* apostles, deceitful *c* workers, transforming themselves into the apostles of Christ.

a Ga.1.7; Ph.1.15,&c. *b* Ga.2.4; 2 Pet.2.1; 1 John 4.1; Re.2.2. *c* Ph.3.2; Tit.1.10,11.

ity of accusing me of desiring to grow rich, and of calumniating me. Paul meant that they should have no plausible pretext even for accusing him; that no man should be able to say that he was preaching merely for the hire. ¶ *Which desire occasion.* No doubt his enemies eagerly sought opportunities of accusing him, and greatly wished for some plausible reason for charging him with that which would be disgraceful and ruinous to his character. Or it may mean that they desired opportunity from the example of Paul to justify themselves in their course; that they took wages from the church at Corinth largely, and desired to be able to say that they had his example. ¶ *That wherein they glory.* Probably meaning that they boasted that they preached the gospel gratis; that they received nothing for their labours. Yet while they did this, it is not improbable that they received presents of the Corinthians, and under various pretences contrived to get from them an ample support, perhaps much more than would have been a reasonable compensation. Men who *profess* to preach the gospel *gratis,* usually contrive in various ways to get more from the people than those who receive a regular and stipulated compensation. By taxing pretty liberally their hospitality; by accepting liberal presents; by frequent proclamation of their self-denial and their poverty, they usually filch large amounts from the people. No people were ever louder in praise of poverty, or in proclamation of their own self-denials than some orders of monks, and that when it might be said almost that the richest possessions of Europe were passing into their hands. At all events, Paul meant that these men should have no opportunity from *his* course to take any such advantage. He knew what he had a right to (1 Cor. ix.), but he had not urged the right. He had received nothing from the church at Corinth, and he meant to receive nothing. He had honestly preached the gospel to them without charge, and he meant still to do it, 1 Cor. ix. 18. They should, therefore, have no opportunity from his conduct either to accuse him of preaching for money, or of sheltering themselves under his example in pretending to preach for nothing when they were in fact obtaining large sums from the people. ¶ *They may be found even as we.* That they may be compelled honestly to pursue such a course as I do, and be found to be in fact what they pretend to be. The sense is, "I mean so to act that if they follow my example, or plead my authority, they may be found to lead an honest life; and that if they boast on this subject, they shall boast strictly according to truth. There shall be no trick; nothing underhanded or deceptive in what they do so far as my example can prevent it."

13. *For such are false apostles.* They have no claim to the apostolic office. They are deceivers. They *pretend* to be apostles; but they have no divine commission from the Redeemer. Paul had thus far argued the case without giving them an explicit designation as deceivers. But here he says that men who had conducted thus; who attempted to impose on the people; who had brought another gospel, whatever pretences they might have—and he was not disposed to deny that there was much that was plausible,—were really impostors and the enemies of Christ. It is morally certain, from ver. 22, that these men were Jews; but why they had engaged in the work of preaching, or why they had gone to Corinth, cannot with certainty be determined. ¶ *Deceitful workers.* Impostors. Men who practise various

14 And no marvel; for Satan [a] himself is transformed into an angel of light.

[a] Ge.3.1,5; Re.12.9.

arts to impose on others. They were crafty, and fraudulent, and hypocritical. It is probable that they were men who saw that great advantage might be taken of the new religion; men who saw the power which it had over the people, and who saw the confidence which the new converts were inclined to repose in their teachers; perhaps men who had seen the disciples to the Christian faith commit all their property to the hands of the apostles, or who had heard of their doing it (comp. Acts iv. 34, 35), and who supposed that by pretending to be apostles also they might come in for a share of this confidence, and avail themselves of this disposition to commit their property to their spiritual guides. To succeed, it was needful as far as possible to undermine the influence of the true apostles, and take their place in the confidence of the people. Thence they were "*deceitful* (δόλιοι) workers," full of trick, and cunning, and of plausible arts to impose on others. ¶ *Transforming themselves,* &c. Pretending to be apostles. Hypocritical and deceitful, they yet pretended to have been sent by Christ. This is a direct charge of hypocrisy. They knew they were deceivers; and yet they assumed the high claims of apostles of the Son of God.

14. *And no marvel.* And it is not wonderful, ver. 15. Since Satan himself is capable of appearing to be an angel of light, it is not to be deemed strange that those who are in his service also should resemble him. ¶ *For Satan himself is transformed,* &c. That is, he who is an apostate angel; who is malignant and wicked; who is the prince of evil, assumes the appearance of a holy angel. Paul assumes this as an indisputable and admitted truth, without attempting to prove it, and without referring to any particular instances. Probably he had in his eye cases where Satan put on false and delusive appearances for the purpose of deceiving, or where he assumed the appearance of great sanctity and reverence for the authority of God. Such instances occurred in the temptation of our first parents (Gen. iii. 1—6), and in the temptation of the Saviour, Mat. iv. The phrase "an angel of light," means a pure and holy angel, light being the emblem of purity and holiness. Such are all the angels that dwell in heaven; and the idea is, that Satan assumes such a form as to appear to be such an angel. Learn here, (1.) His power. He can *assume* such an aspect as he pleases. He can dissemble and appear to be eminently pious. He is the prince of duplicity as well as of wickedness; and it is the consummation of bad power for an individual to be able to assume any character which he pleases. (2.) His art. He is long practised in deceitful arts. For six thousand years he has been practising the art of delusion. And with him it is perfect. (3.) We are not to suppose that all that *appears* to be piety is piety. Some of the most plausible appearances of piety are assumed by Satan and his ministers. None ever professed a profounder regard for the authority of God than Satan did when he tempted the Saviour. And if the prince of wickedness can *appear* to be an angel of light, we are not to be surprised if those who have the blackest hearts appear to be men of most eminent piety. (4.) We should be on our guard. We should not listen to suggestions merely because they *appear* to come from a pious man, nor because they *seem* to be prompted by a regard to the will of God. We may be *always* sure that, if we are to be tempted, it will be by some one having a great appearance of virtue and religion. (5.) We are not to expect that Satan will *appear* to man to be as bad as he is. He never shows himself openly to be a spirit of pure wickedness; or black and abominable in his character; or full of evil and hateful. He would thus defeat himself. It is for this reason that wicked men do not believe that there is such a being as Satan. Though continually under

15 Therefore *it is* no great thing if his ministers also be transformed as the ministers of righteousness; whose end[a] shall be according to their works.

16 I say again, Let no man think me a fool;[b] if otherwise, yet as a fool [1] receive me, that I may boast myself a little.

17 That which I speak, I

a Ph.3.19. b chap. 12.6,11. 1 or, *suffer*.

his influence and "led captive by him at his will," yet they neither see him nor the chains which lead them, nor are they willing to believe in the existence of the one or the other.

15. *Therefore* it is *no great thing*, &c. It is not to be deemed surprising. You are not to wonder if men of the basest, blackest character put on the appearance of the greatest sanctity, and even become eminent as professed preachers of righteousness. ¶ *Whose end shall be*, &c. Whose final destiny. Their doom in eternity shall not be according to their fair professions and plausible pretences, for they cannot deceive God; but shall be according to their real character, and their works. Their work is a work of deception, and they shall be judged according to that. What revelations there will be in the day of judgment, when all impostors shall be unmasked, and when all hypocrites and deceivers shall be seen in their true colours! And how desirable is it that there should be such a day to disclose all beings in their true character, and FOR EVER to remove imposture and delusion from the universe!

16. *I say again.* I repeat it. He refers to what he had said in ver. 1. The sense is, "I have said much respecting myself which may seem to be foolish. I admit that to boast in this manner of one's own self in general is folly. But circumstances compel me to it. And I entreat you to look at those circumstances and not regard me as a fool for doing it." ¶ *If otherwise.* If you think otherwise. If I cannot obtain this of you that you will not regard me as acting prudently and wisely. If you *will* think me foolish, still I am constrained to make these remarks in vindication of myself. ¶ *Yet as a fool receive me.* Marg. "Suffer;" see ver. 1. Bear with me as you do with others. Consider how much I have been provoked to this; how necessary it is to my character; and do not reject and despise me because I am constrained to say that of myself which is usually regarded as foolish boasting. ¶ *That I may boast myself a little.* Since others do it and are not rebuked, may I be permitted to do it also; see ver. 18, 19. There is something sarcastic in the words "*a little.*" The sense is, "Others are allowed to boast a great deal. Assuredly I may be allowed to boast *a little* of what I have done."

17. *That which I speak.* In praise of myself. ¶ *I speak* it *not after the Lord;* see Note on 1 Cor. vii. 12. The phrase here may mean either, I do not speak this by inspiration or claiming to be inspired by the Lord; or more probably it may mean, I do not speak this imitating the example of the Lord Jesus or strictly as becomes his follower. He was eminently modest, and never vaunted or boasted. And Paul probably means to say, "I do not in this profess to follow him entirely. I admit that it is a departure from his pure example in this respect. But circumstances have compelled me; and much as I would prefer another strain of remark, and sensible as I am in general of the folly of boasting, yet a regard to my apostolic office and authority urges me to this course." Bloomfield supposes that the apostle is not speaking seriously, but that he has an allusion to their view of what he was saying. "Be it so, if you think that what I speak, I speak not as I profess to do according to the Lord, or with a view to subserve the purposes of his religion, but *as it were* in folly, in the confidence of boasting, yet permit me to do it notwithstanding, since you allow others to do it." It is not easy to settle which is the true sense of the passage. I see no

speak *it*[a] not after the Lord, but
as it were foolishly, in this confidence[b] of boasting.
18 Seeing[c] that many glory
after the flesh, I will glory also.

a 1 Co.7.12. b chap.9.4.

19 For ye suffer fools gladly,
seeing ye *yourselves* are wise.
20 For ye suffer, if a man bring
you into bondage, if a man devour
you, if a man take *of you*, if a man

c Ph.3.3,4; 1 Co.4.10.

conclusive evidence against either. But the former seems to me to be most in accordance with the scope of the whole. Paul admitted that what he said was not in exact accordance with the spirit of the Lord Jesus; and in admitting this he designed probably to administer a delicate hint that all *their* boasting was a wide departure from that spirit. ¶ *As it were foolishly.* As in folly. It is to be admitted that to boast is in general foolish; and I admit that my language is open to this general charge ¶ *In this confidence of boasting.* In confident boasting. I speak confidently and I admit in the spirit of boasting.

18. *Seeing that many glory*, &c. The false teachers in Corinth. They boasted of their birth, rank, natural endowments, eloquence, &c.; see ver. 22. Comp. Phil. iii. 3, 4. ¶ *I will glory also.* I also will boast of my endowments, which though somewhat different yet pertain in the main to the *flesh* also; see ver. 23, seq. *His* endowments *in the flesh*, or what *he* had to boast of pertaining to the flesh, related not so much to birth and rank, though not inferior to them in these, but to what *the flesh* had endured—to stripes and imprisonments, and hunger and peril. This is an exceedingly delicate and happy turn given to the whole subject.

19. *For ye suffer fools gladly.* You tolerate or endure those who are really fools. This is perhaps, says Dr. Bloomfield, the most sarcastic sentence ever penned by the apostle Paul. Its sense is, "You profess to be wondrous wise. And yet you who are so wise a people, freely tolerate those who are foolish in their boasting; who proclaim their own merits and attainments. You may allow me, therefore, to come in for my share, and boast also, and thus obtain your favour." Or it may mean, "You are so profoundly wise as easily to see who are fools. You have great power of discernment in this, and have found out that I am a fool, and also that other boasters are fools. Yet knowing this, you bear patiently with such fools; have admitted them to your favour and friendship, and I may come in among the rest of the fools, and partake also of your favours." They *had* borne with the false apostles who had boasted of their endowments, and yet they claimed to be eminent for wisdom and discernment.

20. *For ye suffer*, &c. You bear patiently with men who impose on you in every way, and who are constantly defrauding you, though you profess to be so wise, and you may bear with me a little, though I have no such intention. Seriously, if you bear with boasters who intend to delude and deceive you in various ways, you may bear with one who comes to you with no such intention, but with an honest purpose to do good. ¶ *If a man bring you into bondage* (καταδουλοῖ). If a man, or if any one (εἴ τις) *make a slave of you*, or reduce you to servitude. The idea is, doubtless, that the false teachers set up a lordship over their consciences; destroyed their freedom of opinion; and made them subservient to their will. They really took away their Christian freedom as much as if they had been slaves. In what way this was done is unknown. It may be that they imposed on them rites and forms, commanded expensive and inconvenient ceremonies, and required arduous services merely at their own will. A false religion always makes slaves. It is only true Christianity that leaves perfect freedom. All heathens are slaves to their priests; all fanatics are slaves to some fanatical leader; all those who embrace error are slaves to those who claim to be their guides. The papist every-

exalt himself, if a man smite you on the face.

21 I speak as concerning reproach, as though we had been

where is the slave of the priest, and the despotism there is as great as in any region of servitude whatever. ¶ *If a man devour* you. This is exceedingly sarcastic. The idea is, "Though you are so wise, yet you in fact tolerate men who impose on you—no matter though they eat you up, or consume all that you have. By their exorbitant demands they would consume all you have—or, as we would say, eat you out of house and home." All this they took patiently; and freely gave all that they demanded. False teachers are always rapacious. They seek the *property*, not the *souls* of those to whom they minister. Not satisfied with a maintenance, they aim to obtain *all*, and their plans are formed to secure as much as possible of those to whom they minister. ¶ *If a man take* of you. If he take and seize upon your possessions. If he comes and takes what he pleases and bears it away as his own. ¶ *If a man exalt himself.* If he set himself up as a ruler and claim submission. No matter how arrogant his claims, yet you are ready to bear with him. You *might* then bear with me in the very moderate demands which I make on your obedience and confidence. ¶ *If a man smite you on the face.* The word here rendered "smite" (δέρω) means properly to skin, to flay; but in the New Testament it means to beat, to scourge—especially so as to take off the skin; Mat. xxi. 35; Mark xii. 3, 5. The idea here is, if any one treats you with contumely and scorn—since there can be no higher expression of it than to smite a man on the face; Mat. xxvi. 67. It is not to be supposed that this occurred literally among the Corinthians; but the idea is, that the false teachers really treated them with as little respect as if they smote them on the face. In what way this was done is unknown; but probably it was by their domineering manners, and the little respect which they showed for the opinions and feelings of the Corinthian Christians. Paul says that as they bore this very patiently, they might allow *him* to make some remarks about himself in self-commendation.

21. *I speak as concerning reproach.* I speak of disgrace. That is, says Rosenmüller, "I speak of your disgrace, or, as others prefer it, of the disgrace of the false apostles." Doddridge regards it as a question. "Do I speak this by way of dishonour, from an envious desire to derogate from my superiors so as to bring them down to my own level?" But to me it seems that Paul refers to what he had been admitting respecting himself—to what he had evinced in rudeness of speech (ver. 6), and to his not having urged his claims to the support which an apostle had a right to receive—to things, in short, which *they* esteemed to be disgraceful or reproachful. And his idea, it seems to me, is this: "I have been speaking of reproach or disgrace *as if* I was weak, *i. e.* as if I was disposed to admit as true all that has been said of me as reproachful or disgraceful; all that has been said of my want of qualifications for the office, of my want of talent, or elevated rank, or honourable birth, &c. I have not pressed my claims, but have been reasoning as if all this were true—*as if* all that was honourable in birth and elevated in rank belonged to them—all that is mean and unworthy pertained to me. But it is not so. Whatever *they* have *I* have. Whatever they can boast of, I can boast of in a more eminent degree. Whatever advantage there is in birth is mine; and I can tell of toils, and trials, and sufferings in the apostolic office which far surpass theirs." Paul proceeds, therefore, to a full statement of his advantages of birth and of his labours in the cause of the Redeemer. ¶ *As though we had been weak.* As if I had no claims to urge; as if I had no just cause of boldness, but must submit to this reproach. ¶ *Howbeit* (δέ). *But.* The sense is, if any one is disposed to boast, I am ready for him. I can

weak. Howbeit whereinsoever any is bold, (I speak foolishly,) I am bold also.
22 Are they Hebrews? so *am* I. Are they Israelites? so *am* I. Are they the seed of Abraham? so *am* I.
23 Are they ministers of Christ?

---

tell also of things that have as high claims to confidence as they can. If they are disposed to go into a comparison on the points which qualify a man for the office of an apostle, I am ready to compare myself with them. ¶ *Whereinsoever* (ἐν ᾧ). In what. Whatever they have to boast of I am prepared also to show that I am equal to them. Be it pertaining to birth, rank, education, labours, they will find that I do not shrink from the comparison. ¶ *Any is bold* (τις τολμᾷ). Any one *dares* to boast; any one is bold. ¶ *I speak foolishly.* Remember now that I speak as a fool. I have been charged with this folly. Just now keep that in mind; and do not forget that it is only a fool who is speaking. Just recollect that I have no claims to public confidence: that I am destitute of all pretensions to the apostolic office; that I am given to a vain parade and ostentation, and to boasting of what does not belong to me, and when you recollect this let me tell my story. The whole passage is ironical in the highest degree. The sense is, "It is doubtless all nonsense and folly for a man to boast who has only the qualifications which I have. But there is a great deal of wisdom in *their* boasting who have so much more elevated endowments for the apostolic office." ¶ *I am bold also.* I can meet them on their own ground, and speak of qualifications not inferior to theirs.

22. *Are they Hebrews?* This proves that the persons who had made the difficulty in Corinth were those who were of Hebrew extraction, though it may be that they had been born in Greece and had been educated in the Grecian philosophy and art of rhetoric. It is also clear that they prided themselves on being Jews—on having a connection with the people and land from whence the religion which the Corinthian church now professed had emanated. Indications are apparent everywhere in the New Testament of the superiority which the Jewish converts to Christianity claimed over those converted from among the heathen. Their boast would probably be that they were the descendants of the patriarchs; that the land of the prophets was theirs; that they spake the language in which the oracles of God were given; that the true religion had proceeded from them, &c. ¶ *So am I.* I have as high claims as any of them to distinction on this head. Paul had all their advantages of birth. He was an Israelite; of the honoured tribe of Benjamin; a Pharisee, circumcised at the usual time (Phil. iii. 5), and educated in the best manner at the feet of one of their most eminent teachers; Acts xxii. 3. ¶ *Are they Israelites?* Another name, signifying substantially the same thing. The only difference is, that the word "Hebrew" signified properly one who was from beyond (עִבְרִי from עָבַר, to pass, to pass over—hence applied to Abraham, because he had come from a foreign land; and the word denoted properly *a foreigner*—a man from the land or country *beyond*, עֵבֶר) the Euphrates. The name *Israelite* denoted properly one descended from Israel or Jacob, and the difference between them was, that the name *Israelite*, being a patronymic derived from one of the founders of their nation, was in use among themselves; the name *Hebrew* was applied by the Canaanite to them as having come from *beyond* the river, and was the current name among foreign tribes and nations. See Gesenius's Lexicon on the word (עִבְרִי) *Hebrew*. Paul in the passage before us means to say that he had as good a claim to the honour of being a native born descendant of Israel as could be urged by any of them. ¶ *Are they the seed of Abraham?* Do they boast that they are descended from Abraham? This with all the Jews was regarded as a distinguished honour (see Mat. iii. 9;

(I speak as a fool) I *am* more; in labours [a] more abundant, in stripes [b] above measure, in prisons more frequent, in deaths [c] oft.

24 Of the Jews five times received I forty *stripes* [d] save one.
25 Thrice was I beaten [e] with rods, once was I [f] stoned, thrice

a 1 Co.15.10. b Ac.9.16, 20.23; 21.11. c 1 Co.15.30,32.

d De. 25.3. e Ac.16.22. f Ac.14.19.

John viii. 39), and no doubt the false teachers in Corinth boasted of it as eminently qualifying them to engage in the work of the ministry. ¶ *So am I.* Paul had the same qualification. He was a Jew also by birth. He was of the tribe of Benjamin; Phil. iii. 5.

23. *Are they ministers of Christ?* Though Jews by birth yet they claimed to be the ministers of the Messiah. ¶ *I speak as a fool.* As if he had said, "Bear in mind, in what I am now about to say, that he who speaks is accused of being a fool in boasting. Let it not be deemed improper that I should act in this character, and since you regard me as such, let me speak like a fool." His frequent reminding them of this charge was eminently fitted to humble them that they had ever made it, especially when they were reminded by an enumeration of his trials, of the character of the man against whom the charge was brought. ¶ *I* am *more.* Paul was not disposed to deny that they were true ministers of Christ. But he had higher claims to the office than they had. He had been called to it in a more remarkable manner, and he had shown by his labours and trials that he had more of the true spirit of a minister of the Lord Jesus than they had. He therefore goes into detail to show what he had endured in endeavouring to diffuse the knowledge of the Saviour; trials which he had borne probably while they had been dwelling in comparative ease, and in a comfortable manner, free from suffering and persecution. ¶ *In labours more abundant.* In the kind of labour necessary in propagating the gospel. Probably he had now been engaged in the work a much longer time than they had, and had been far more indefatigable in it. ¶ *In stripes.* In receiving stripes; *i. e.*, I have been more frequently scourged; ver. 24. This was a proof of his being a minister of Christ, because eminent devotedness to him at that time, of necessity subjected a man to frequent scourging. The ministry is one of the very few places, perhaps it stands alone in this, where it is proof of peculiar qualification for office that a man has been treated with all manner of contumely, and has even been often publicly whipped. What other office admits such a qualification as this? ¶ *Above measure.* Exceedingly; far exceeding them. He had received far more than they had, and he judged, therefore, that this was one evidence that he had been called to the ministry. ¶ *In prisons more frequent.* Luke, in the Acts of the Apostles, mentions only one imprisonment of Paul before the time when this epistle was written. That was at Philippi with Silas, Acts xvi. 23, seq. But we are to remember that many things were omitted by Luke. He does not profess to give an account of *all* that happened to Paul; and an omission is not a contradiction. For any thing that Luke says, Paul may have been imprisoned often. He *mentions* his having been in prison once; he does not *deny* that he had been in prison many times besides; see on ver. 24. ¶ *In deaths oft.* This is, exposed to death; or suffering pain equal to death; see on chap. i. 9. No one familiar with the history of Paul can doubt that he was often in danger of death.

24. *Of the Jews,* &c. On this verse and the following verse it is of importance to make a few remarks preliminary to the explanation of the phrases. (1.) It is admitted that the particulars here referred to cannot be extracted out of the Acts of the Apostles. A few can be identified, but there are many more trials referred to here than are specified there. (2.) This *proves* that this epistle was

not framed from the history, but that they are written independently of one another.—*Paley.* (3.) Yet they are not inconsistent one with the other. For there is no article in the enumeration here which is contradicted by the history, and the history, though silent with respect to many of these transactions, has left *space* enough to suppose that they may have occurred. (*a*) There is no *contradiction* between the accounts. Where it is said by Paul that he was *thrice* beaten with rods, though in the Acts but *one* beating is mentioned, yet there is no contradiction. It is only the *omission* to record *all* that occurred to Paul. But had the history, says Paley, contained an account of *four* beatings with rods, while Paul mentions here but *three,* there would have been a contradiction. And so of the other particulars. (*b*) Though the Acts of the Apostles be silent concerning many of the instances referred to, yet that silence may be accounted for on the plan and design of the history. The date of the epistle synchronizes with the beginning of the twentieth chapter of the Acts. The part, therefore, which precedes the twentieth chapter is the only place in which can be found any notice of the transactions to which Paul here refers. And it is evident from the Acts that the author of that history was not with Paul until his departure from Troas, as related in chap. xvi. 10 ; see Note on that place. From that time Luke attended Paul in his travels. From that period to the time when this epistle was written occupies but four chapters of the history, and it is here if anywhere that we are to look for the minute account of the life of Paul. But here much may have occurred to Paul before Luke joined him. And as it was the design of Luke to give an account of Paul mainly *after* he had joined him, it is not to be wondered at that many things may have been omitted of his previous life. (*c*) The period of time after the conversion of Paul to the time when Luke joined him at Troas is very succinctly given. That period embraced sixteen years, and is comprised in a few chapters. Yet in that time Paul was constantly travelling. He went to Arabia, returned to Damascus, went to Jerusalem, and then to Tarsus, and from Tarsus to Antioch, and thence to Cyprus, and then through Asia Minor, &c. In this time he must have made many voyages, and been exposed to many perils. Yet all this is comprised in a few chapters, and a considerable portion of them is occupied with an account of public discourses. In that period of sixteen years, therefore, there was ample opportunity for all the occurrences which are here referred to by Paul ; see Paley's Horæ Paulinæ on 2 Cor. No. ix. (*d*) I may add, that from the account which *follows* the time when Luke joined him at Troas (from Acts xvi. 10), it is altogether probable that he *had* endured much before. After that time there is mention of *just such* transactions of scourging, stoning,&c., as are here specified, and it is altogether probable that he had been called to suffer them before. When Paul says "of the Jews," &c., he refers to this because this was a Jewish mode of punishment. It was usual with them to inflict but thirty-nine blows. The Gentiles were not limited by law in the number which they inflicted. ¶ *Five times.* This was doubtless in their synagogues and before their courts of justice. They had not the power of capital punishment, but they had the power of inflicting minor punishments. And though the *instances* are not specified by Luke in the Acts, yet the statement here by Paul has every degree of probability. We know that he often preached in their synagogues (Acts ix. 20 ; xiii. 5, 14, 15 ; xiv. 1 ; xvii. 17 ; xviii. 4); and nothing is more probable than that they would be enraged against him, and would vent their malice in every way possible. They regarded him as an apostate, and a ringleader of the Nazarenes, and they would not fail to inflict on him the severest punishment which they were permitted to inflict. ¶ *Forty* stripes *save one.* The word *stripes* does not occur in the original, but is necessarily understood. The law of Moses (Deut. xxv

I suffered shipwreck, a night [a] and a day I have been in the deep;

26 *In* journeyings often, *in* perils of waters, *in* perils of rob-

a Ac.xxvii.

3) expressly limited the number of stripes that might be inflicted to forty. In no case might this number be exceeded. This was a humane provision, and one that was not found among the heathen, who inflicted any number of blows at discretion. Unhappily it is not observed among professedly Christian nations where the practice of whipping prevails, and particularly in slave countries, where the master inflicts any number of blows at his pleasure. In practice among the Hebrews, the number of blows inflicted was in fact limited to thirty-nine, lest by any accident in counting, the criminal should receive more than the number prescribed in the law. There was another reason still for limiting it to thirty-nine. They usually made use of a scourge with three thongs, and this was struck thirteen times. That it was usual to inflict but thirty-nine lashes is apparent from Josephus, Ant. book iv. chap. viii. § 21.

25. *Thrice was I beaten with rods.* In the Acts of the Apostles there is mention made of his being beaten in this manner but once before the time when this epistle was written. That occurred at Philippi; Acts xvi. 22, 23. But there is no reason to doubt that it was more frequently done. This was a frequent mode of punishment among the ancient nations, and as Paul was often persecuted, he would be naturally subjected to this shameful punishment. ¶ *Once I was stoned.* This was the usual mode of punishment among the Jews for blasphemy. The instance referred to here occurred at Lystra; Acts xiv. 19. Paley (Horæ Paulinæ) has remarked that this, when confronted with the history, furnished the nearest approach to a contradiction without a contradiction being actually incurred, that he ever had met with. The history (Acts xiv. 19) contains but one account of his being actually stoned. But prior to this (Acts xiv. 5), it mentions that "an assault was made both of the Gentiles, and also of the Jews with their rulers, to use them despitefully and to stone them, but they were aware of it, and fled to Lystra and Derbe." "Now," Paley remarks, "had the assault been completed; had the history related that a stone was thrown, as it relates that preparations were made both by Jews and Gentiles to stone Paul and his companions; or even had the account of this transaction stopped without going on to inform us that Paul and his companions were aware of their danger and fled, a contradiction between the history and the epistle would have ensued. Truth is necessarily consistent; but it is scarcely possible that independent accounts, not having truth to guide them, should thus advance to the very brink of contradiction without falling into it." ¶ *Thrice I suffered shipwreck.* On what occasions, or where, is now unknown, as these instances are not referred to in the Acts of the Apostles. The instance of shipwreck recorded there (chap. xxvii.), which occurred when on his way to Rome, happened *after* this epistle was written, and should not be supposed to be one of the instances referred to here. Paul made many voyages in going from Jerusalem to Tarsus, and to Antioch, and to various parts of Asia Minor, and to Cyprus; and shipwrecks in those seas were by no means such unusual occurrences as to render this account improbable. ¶ *A night and a day,* &c. The word here used (νυχθήμερον) denotes a complete natural day, or twenty-four hours. ¶ *In the deep.* To what this refers we do not now certainly know. It is probable, however, that Paul refers to some period when, having been shipwrecked, he was saved by supporting himself on a plank or fragment of the vessel until he obtained relief. Such a situation is one of great peril, and he mentions it, therefore, among the trials which he had endured. The supposition of some commentators

ners, *in* perils [a] by *mine own* countymen, *in* perils by the heathen, *in* perils in the city, *in* perils in the wilderness, *in* perils in the sea, *in* perils among false brethren;

a Ac.14.5.

27 In weariness and painfulness, in watchings [b] often, in hunger [c] and thirst, in fastings often, in cold and nakedness.
28 Besides those things that

b Ac.20.31. c 1 Cor.4.11.

---

that he spent his time on some rock in the deep; or of others that this means some deep dungeon; or of others that he was swallowed by a whale, like Jonah, shows the extent to which the fancy is often indulged in interpreting the Bible.

26. *In journeyings often.* Of course subject to the fatigue, toil, and danger which such a mode of life involves. ¶ In *perils of waters.* In danger of losing my life at sea, or by floods, or by crossing streams. ¶ *Of robbers.* Many of the countries, especially Arabia, through which he travelled, were then infested, as they are now, with robbers. It is not impossible or improbable that he was often attacked and his life endangered. It is still unsafe to travel in many of the places through which he travelled. ¶ *By* mine own *countrymen.* The Jews. They often scourged him; laid wait for him and were ready to put him to death. They had deep enmity against him as an apostate, and he was in constant danger of being put to death by them. ¶ *By the heathen.* By those who had not the true religion. Several instances of his danger from this quarter are mentioned in the Acts. ¶ *In the city.* In cities, as in Derbe, Lystra, Philippi, Jerusalem, Ephesus, &c. ¶ *In the wilderness.* In the desert, where he would be exposed to ambushes, or to wild beasts, or to hunger and want. Instances of this are not recorded in the Acts, but no one can doubt that they occurred. The idea here is, that he had met with constant danger wherever he was, whether in the busy haunts of men or in the solitude and loneliness of the desert. ¶ *In the sea;* see ver. 25. ¶ *Among false brethren.* This was the crowning danger and trial to Paul, as it is to all others. A man can better bear danger by land and water, among robbers and in deserts, than he can bear to have his confidence abused, and to be subjected to the action and the arts of spies upon his conduct. *Who* these were he has not informed us. He mentions it as the chief trial to which he had been exposed, that he had met those who pretended to be his friends, and who yet had sought every possible opportunity to expose and destroy him. Perhaps he has here a delicate reference to the danger which he apprehended from the false brethren in the church at Corinth.

27. *In weariness.* Resulting from travelling, exposure, labour, and want. The word κόπος (from κόπτω, to beat, to cut) means, properly, wailing and grief, accompanied with beating the breast. Hence the word means toil, labour, wearisome effort. ¶ *And painfulness.* This word (μόχθος) is a stronger term than the former. It implies painful effort; labour producing sorrow, and in the New Testament is uniformly connected with the word rendered "weariness" (1 Thess. ii. 9; 2 Thess. iii. 8), rendered in both those places "travail." ¶ *In watchings often.* In loss of sleep, arising from abundant toils and from danger; see Note on chap. vi. 5. ¶ *In hunger and thirst.* From travelling among strangers, and being dependent on them and on his own personal labours; see Note, 1 Cor. iv. 11. ¶ *In fastings often.* Either voluntary or involuntary; see Note on chap. vi. 5. ¶ *In cold and nakedness;* see Note, 1 Cor. iv. 11.

28. *Besides those things that are without.* In addition to these external trials, these trials pertaining to the body, I have mental trials and anxieties resulting from the necessary care of all the churches. But on the meaning of these words commentators are not agreed. Rosenmüller supposes that the phrase means "besides

are without, that which cometh upon me daily, the care [a] of all the churches.

29 Who [b] is weak, and I am not weak? who is offended, and I burn not?

a Ac.15.36.40.

b 1 Co.9.22.

those things that come from other sources," "that I may omit other things." Beza, Erasmus, Bloomfield, and some others suppose that the passage means those things out of the regular routine of his office. Doddridge, "besides foreign affairs." Probably the sense is, "Apart from the things beside" (Χωρὶς τῶν παρεκτὸς); "not to mention other matters; or if other matters should be laid aside, there is this continually rushing anxiety arising from the care of all the churches." That is, this would be enough in itself. Laying aside all that arises from hunger, thirst, cold, &c., this continual care occupies my mind and weighs upon my heart. ¶ *That which cometh upon me daily.* There is great force in the original here. The phrase rendered "that which cometh upon me" means properly, "that which *rushes* upon me." The word (ἐπισύστασις) means properly a concourse, a crowd, hence a tumult; and the idea here is, that these cares rushed upon him, or pressed upon him like a crowd of men or a mob that bore all before it. This is one of Paul's most energetic expressions, and denotes the incessant anxiety of mind to which he was subject. ¶ *The care of all the churches.* The care of the numerous churches which he had established, and which needed his constant supervision. They were young; many of them were feeble; many were made up of heterogeneous materials; many composed of Jews and Gentiles mingled together, with conflicting prejudices, habits, preferences; many of them were composed of those who had been gathered from the lowest ranks of life; and questions would be constantly occurring relating to their order and discipline in which Paul would feel a deep interest, and which would naturally be referred to him for decision. Besides this, they had many trials. They were persecuted, and would suffer much. In their sufferings Paul would feel deep sympathy, and would desire, as far as possible, to afford them relief. In addition to the churches which *he* had planted, he would feel an interest in all others, and doubtless many cases would be referred to him as an eminent apostle for counsel and advice. No wonder that all this came rushing on him like a tumultuous assembly ready to overpower him.

29. *Who is weak,* &c. I sympathize with all. I feel where others feel, and their sorrows excite deep sympathetic emotions in my bosom. Like a tender and compassionate friend I am affected when I see others in circumstances of distress. The word *weak* here may refer to any want of strength, any infirmity or feebleness arising either from body or mind. It may include all who were feeble by persecution or by disease; or it may refer to the weak in faith and doubtful about their duty (see 1 Cor. ix. 22), and to those who were burdened with mental sorrows. The idea is, that Paul had a deep sympathy in all who *needed* such sympathy from any cause. And the statement here shows the depth of feeling of this great apostle; and shows what should be the feeling of every pastor; see Note on Rom. xii. 15. ¶ *And I am not weak?* I share his feelings and sympathize with him. If he suffers, I suffer. Bloomfield supposes that Paul means that in the case of those who were weak in the faith he *accommodated* himself to their weakness and thus became all things to all men; see my Note on 1 Cor. ix. 22. But it seems to me probable that he uses the phrase here in a more *general* sense, as denoting that he sympathized with those who were weak and feeble in all their circumstances. ¶ *Who is offended* (σκανδαλίζεται). Who is *scandalized.* The word means properly to cause to stumble and fall; hence to be a stumbling-block to any one; to give or cause offence to any one. The idea here seems to be, "who is liable to be led astray; who

30 If I must needs glory, I will [a] glory of the things which concern mine infirmities.
31 The God [b] and Father of our Lord Jesus Christ, which [c] is blessed for evermore, knoweth [d] that I lie not.
32 In Damascus [e] the governor

a chap.12.5,9,10. b Ga.1.3. c Ro.9.5. d 1 Th.2.5. e Ac.9.24,25.

has temptations and trials that are likely to lead him to sin or to cause him to fall, and I do not burn with impatience to restore him, or with indignation against the tempter?" In all such cases Paul deeply sympathized with them, and was prompt to aid them. ¶ *And I burn not?* That is, with anger or with great agitation of mind at learning that any one had fallen into sin. This may either mean that he would burn with indignation against those who had led them into sin, or be deeply excited in view of the disgrace which would be thus brought on the Christian cause. In either case it means that his mind would be in a glow of emotion; he would feel deeply; he could not look upon such things with indifference or without being deeply agitated. With all he sympathized; and the condition of all, whether in a state of feeble faith, or feeble body, or falling into sin, excited the deepest emotions in his mind. The truth here taught is, that Paul felt a deep sympathy for all others who bore the Christian name, and this sympathy for others greatly increased the cares and toils of the apostolic office which he sustained. But having given this exposition, candour compels me to acknowledge that the whole verse *may* mean, "Who is feeble in the faith in regard to certain observances and rites and customs (1 Cor. ix. 22), and I do not also evince the same? I do not rouse their prejudices, or wound their feelings, or alarm them. On the other hand, who is scandalized, or led into sin by the example of others in regard to such custom; who is led by the example of others into transgression, and I do not burn with indignation?" In either case, however, the general sense is, that he sympathized with all others.

30. *If I must needs glory.* It is unpleasant for me to boast, but circumstances have compelled me. But since I am compelled, I will not boast of my rank, or talents, but of that which is regarded by some as an infirmity. ¶ *Mine infirmities.* Greek, "The things of my weakness." The word here used is derived from the same word which is rendered weak," in ver. 29. He intends doubtless to refer here to what had preceded in his enumeration of the trials which he had endured. He had spoken of *sufferings.* He had endured much. He had also spoken of that tenderness of feeling which prompted him to sympathize so deeply when others suffered. He admitted that he often wept, and trembled, and glowed with strong feelings on occasions which perhaps to many would not seem to call for such strong emotions, and which they might be disposed to set down as a weakness or infirmity. This might especially be the case among the Greeks, where many philosophers, as the Stoics, were disposed to regard *all* sympathetic feeling, and all sensitiveness to suffering as an infirmity. But Paul admitted that he was disposed to glory in this alone. He gloried that he *had suffered* so much; that he had endured so many trials on account of Christianity, and that he *had* a mind that was capable of feeling for others and of entering into their sorrows and trials. Well might he do this, for there is no more lovely feature in the mind of a virtuous man, and there is no more lovely influence of Christianity than this, that it teaches us to "bear a brother's woes," and to sympathize in all the sorrows and joys of others. Philosophy and infidelity may be dissocial, cheerless, cold; but it is not so with Christianity. Philosophy may snap asunder all the cords which bind us to the living world, but Christianity strengthens these cords; cold and cheerless atheism and scepticism may teach us to look with unconcern on a suffering world, but it is the glory of Christianity that it teaches us to feel an interest in the weal or woe of

under Aretas the king kept the city of the Damascenes with a garrison, desirous to apprehend me:

---

the obscurest man that lives, to rejoice in his joy, and to weep in his sorrows.

31. *The God and Father*, &c. Paul was accustomed to make solemn appeals to God for the truth of what he said, especially when it was likely to be called in question; see ver. 10; comp. Rom. ix. 1. The solemn appeal which he here makes to God is made in view of what he had just said of his sufferings, not of what follows—for there was nothing in the occurrence at Damascus that demanded so solemn an appeal to God. The *reason* of this asseveration is probably that the transactions to which he had referred were known to but few, and perhaps not all of them to even his best friends; that his trials and calamities had been so numerous and extraordinary that his enemies would say that they were improbable, and that all this had been the mere fruit of exaggeration; and as he had no *witnesses* to appeal to for the truth of what he said, he makes a solemn appeal to the ever-blessed God. This appeal is made with great *reverence.* It is not rash, or bold, and is by no means irreverent or profane. He appeals to God as the Father of the Redeemer whom he so much venerated and loved, and as himself blessed for evermore. If all appeals to God were made on as important occasions as this, and with the same profound veneration and reverence, such appeals would never be improper, and we should never be shocked as we are often now when men appeal to God. This passage *proves* that an appeal to God on great occasions is not improper; it proves also that it should be done with profound veneration.

32. *At Damascus.* This circumstance is mentioned as an additional trial. It is evidently mentioned as an instance of peril which had escaped his recollection in the rapid account of his dangers enumerated in the previous verses. It is designed to show what imminent danger he was in, and how narrowly he escaped with his life. On the situation of Damascus, see Note, Acts ix. 2. The transaction here referred to is also related by Luke (Acts ix. 24, 25), though without mentioning the name of the king, or referring to the fact that the governor kept the city with a garrison. ¶ *The governor.* Greek, ὁ ἐθνάρχης, *The ethnarch;* properly a ruler of the people, a prefect, a ruler, a chief. Who he was is unknown, though he was evidently some officer under the king. It is not improbable that he was a Jew, or at any rate he was one who could be influenced by the Jews, and he was doubtless excited by the Jews to guard the city, and if possible to take Paul as a malefactor. Luke informs us (Acts ix. 23, 24) that the Jews took counsel against Paul to kill him, and that they watched the gates night and day to effect their object. They doubtless represented Paul as an apostate, and as aiming to overthrow their religion. He had come with an important commission to Damascus and had failed to execute it; he had become the open friend of those whom he came to destroy; and they doubtless claimed of the civil authorities of Damascus that he should be given up and taken to Jerusalem for trial. It was not difficult, therefore, to secure the co-operation of the governor of the city in the case, and there is no improbability in the statement. ¶ *Under Aretas the king.* There were three kings of this name who are particularly mentioned by ancient writers. The first is mentioned in 2 Mac. v. 8, as the "king of the Arabians." He lived about 170 years before Christ, and of course could not be the one referred to here. The second is mentioned in Josephus, Ant. b. xiii. chap. xv. § 2. He is first mentioned as having reigned in Cœlo-Syria, but as being called to the government of Damascus by those who dwelt there, on account of the hatred which they bore to Ptolemy Meneus. Whiston remarks in a note on Josephus, that this was the first king of the Arabians who took Damascus and reigned there, and that this name

33 And through a window in a basket was I let down by the wall, and escaped his hands.

---

afterwards became common to such Arabian kings as reigned at Damascus and at Petra; see Josephus, Ant. b. xvi. chap. ix. § 4. Of course this king reigned some time before the transaction here referred to by Paul. A third king of this name, says Rosenmüller, is the one mentioned here. He was the father-in-law of Herod Antipas. He made war with his son-in-law Herod because he had repudiated his daughter, the wife of Herod. This he had done in order to marry his brother Philip's wife; see Note, Mat. xiv. 3. On this account Aretas made war with Herod, and in order to resist him, Herod applied to Tiberius the Roman emperor for aid. Vitellius was sent by Tiberius to subdue Aretas, and to bring him dead or alive to Rome. But before Vitellius had embarked in the enterprise, Tiberius died, and thus Aretas was saved from ruin. It is supposed that in this state of things, when thus waging war with Herod, he made an incursion to Syria and seized upon Damascus, where he was reigning when Paul went there; or if not reigning there personally, he had appointed an *ethnarch* or governor who administered the affairs of the city in his place. ¶ *Kept the city*, &c. Luke (Acts ix. 24) says that they watched the gates day and night to kill him. This was probably the Jews. Meantime the ethnarch guarded the city, to prevent his escape. The Jews would have killed him at once; the ethnarch wished to apprehend him and bring him to trial. In either case Paul had much to fear, and he, therefore, embraced the only way of escape. ¶ *With a garrison*. The word which is used here in the original (φρουρέω) means simply to watch; to guard; to keep. Our translation would seem to imply that there was a body of men *stationed* in order to guard the city. The true idea is, that there were men who were appointed to guard the gates of the city and to keep watch lest he should escape them. Damascus was surrounded, as all ancient cities were, with high walls, and it did not occur to them that he could escape in any other way than by the gates.

33. *And through a window.* That is, through a little door or aperture in the wall; perhaps something like an embrasure, that might have been large enough to allow a man to pass through it. Luke says (Acts ix. 25) that they let him down "by the wall." But there is no inconsistency. They doubtless first passed him *through* the embrasure or loop-hole in the wall, and then let him down gently by the side of it. Luke does not say it was *over* the top of the wall, but merely that he descended *by* the wall. It is not probable that an embrasure or opening would be near the bottom, and consequently there would be a considerable distance for him to descend by the side of the wall after he had passed through the window. Bloomfield, however, supposes that the phrase employed by Luke and rendered "*by* the wall," means properly "*through* the wall." But I prefer the former interpretation. ¶ *In a basket.* The word here used (σαργάνη) means any thing braided or twisted; hence a rope-basket, a net-work of cords, or a wicker hamper. It might have been such an one as was used for catching fish, or it might have been made for the occasion. The word used by Luke (Acts ix. 25) is σπυρὶς—a word usually meaning a basket for storing grain, provisions, &c. Where Paul went immediately after he had escaped them, he does not here say. From Gal. i. 17, it appears that he went into Arabia, where he spent some time, and then returned to Damascus, and after three years he went up to Jerusalem. It would not have been safe to have gone to Jerusalem at once, and he therefore waited for the passions of the Jews to have time to cool, before he ventured himself again in their hands.

REMARKS.

1. There may be circumstances, but they are rare, in which it may be proper to speak of our own attainments,

and of our own doings; ver. 1. Boasting is in general nothing but folly—the fruit of pride—but there may be situations when to state what we have done may be necessary to the vindication of our own character, and may tend to honour God. Then we should do it; not to trumpet forth our own fame, but to glorify God and to advance his cause. Occasions occur however but rarely in which it is proper to speak in this manner of ourselves.

2. The church should be pure. It is the bride of the Redeemer; the "Lamb's wife;" ver. 2. It is soon to be presented to Christ, soon to be admitted to his presence. How holy should be that church which sustains such a relation! How anxious to be worthy to appear before the Son of God!

3. All the individual members of that church should be holy; ver. 2. They as individuals are soon to be presented in heaven as the fruit of the labours of the Son of God, and as entitled to his eternal love. How pure should be the lips that are soon to speak his praise in heaven; how pure the eyes that are soon to behold his glory; how holy the feet that are soon to tread his courts in the heavenly world!

4. There is great danger of being corrupted from the simplicity that is in Christ; ver. 3. Satan desires to destroy us; and his great object is readily accomplished if he can seduce Christians from simple devotedness to the Redeemer; if he can secure corruption in doctrine or in the manner of worship, and can produce conformity in dress and in the style of living to this world. Formerly he excited persecution. But in that he was foiled. The more the church was persecuted the more it grew. Then he changed his ground. What he could not do by persecution he sought to do by corrupting the church; and in this he has been by far more successful. This can be done slowly but certainly; effectually but without exciting suspicion. And it matters not to Satan whether the church is crippled by persecution or its zeal destroyed by false doctrine and by conformity to the world. *His* aim is secured; and the power of the church destroyed. The form in which he *now* assails the church is by attempting to seduce it from simple and hearty attachment to the Saviour. And, O! in how many instances is he successful.

5. Our religion has cost much suffering. We have in this chapter a detail of extraordinary trials and sorrows in establishing it; and we have reason to be thankful, in some degree, that the enemies of Paul made it necessary for him to boast in this manner. We have thus some most interesting details of facts of which otherwise we should have been ignorant; and we see that the life of Paul was a life of continual self-denial and toil. By sea and land; at home and abroad; among his own countrymen and strangers, he was subjected to continued privations and persecution. So it has been always in regard to the establishment of the gospel. It began its career in the sufferings of its great Author, and the foundation of the church was laid in his blood. It progressed amidst sufferings, for all the apostles, except John, it is supposed were martyrs. It continued to advance amidst sufferings—for ten fiery persecutions raged throughout the Roman empire, and thousands died in consequence of their professed attachment to the Saviour. It has been always propagated in heathen lands by self-denials and sacrifices, for the life of a missionary is that of sacrifice and toil. How many such men as David Brainerd and Henry Martyn have sacrificed their lives in order to extend the true religion around the world!

6. All that *we* enjoy is the fruit of the sufferings, toils, and sacrifices of others. We have not one Christian privilege or hope which has not cost the life of many a martyr. How thankful should we be to God that he was pleased to raise up men who would be *willing* thus to suffer, and that he sustained and kept them until their work was accomplished!

7. We may infer the *sincerity* of the men engaged in propagating the Christian religion. What had Paul to

gain in the sorrows which he endured? Why did he not remain in his own land and reap the honours which were then fully within his grasp? The answer is an easy one. It was because he believed that Christianity was true; and believing that, he believed that it was of importance to make it known to the world. Paul did not endure these sorrows, and encounter these perils for the sake of pleasure, honour, or gain. No man who reads this chapter can doubt that he was sincere, and that he was an honest man.

8. The Christian religion is, therefore, true. Not because the first preachers were sincere—for the advocates of error are often sincere, and are willing to suffer much or even to die as martyrs; but because this was a case when their sincerity proved *the facts* in regard to the truth of Christianity. It was not sincerity in regard *to opinions* merely, it was in regard *to facts*. They not only *believed* that the Messiah had come and died and risen again, but they *saw him—saw* him when he lived; *saw* him die; *saw* him after he was risen; and it was in relation to these *facts* that they were sincere. But how could they be deceived here? Men may be deceived in their opinions; but how could *John, e. g.*, be deceived in affirming that he was intimately acquainted—the bosom friend—with Jesus of Nazareth; that he saw him die; and that he conversed with him *after* he had died? In this he could not be mistaken; and sooner than deny this, John would have spent his whole life in a cave in Patmos, or have died on the cross or at the stake. But if John *saw* all this, then the Christian religion is true.

9. We should be willing to suffer now. If Paul and the other apostles were willing to endure so much, why should not we be? If they were willing to deny themselves so much in order that the gospel should be spread among the nations, why should not we be? It is now just as important that it should be spread as it was then; and the church should be just as willing to sacrifice its comforts to make the gospel known as it was in the days of Paul. We may add, also, that if there was the same devotedness to Christ evinced by all Christians now which is described in this chapter; if there was the same zeal and self-denial, the time would not be far distant when the gospel would be spread all around the world. May the time soon come when all Christians shall have the same self-denial as Paul; and especially when all who enter the ministry shall be WILLING to forsake country and home, and to encounter peril in the city and the wilderness; on the sea and the land; to meet cold, and nakedness, hunger, thirst, persecution, and death in any way in order that they may make known the name of the Saviour to a lost world.

CHAPTER XII.

THIS chapter is a continuation of the same general subject which was discussed in the two previous chapters. The general design of the apostle is, to defend himself from the charges brought against him in Corinth, and especially, as it would appear, from the charge that he had no claims to the character of an apostle. In the previous chapters he had met these charges, and had shown that he had just cause to be bold towards them; that he had in his life given evidence that he was called to this work, and especially that by his successes and by his sufferings he had showed that he had evidence that he had been truly engaged in the work of the Lord Jesus.

This chapter contains the following subjects.

1. Paul appeals to another evidence that he was engaged in the apostolic office—an evidence to which none of his accusers could appeal—that he had been permitted to behold the glories of the heavenly world; ver. 1—10. In the previous chapter he had mentioned his trials. Here he says (ver. 1), that as they had compelled him to boast, he would mention the revelation which he had had of the Lord. He details, therefore, the remarkable vision which he had had several years before (ver. 2—4), when he was caught up to heaven, and permitted to behold the wonders there.

CHAPTER XII.

IT is not expedient for me doubtless to glory. [1] I will come to visions and revelations of the Lord.

2 I knew a man in [a] Christ

1 *For I will.*

a Rom.16.7.

Yet he says, that lest such an extraordinary manifestation should exalt him above measure, he was visited with a sore and peculiar trial—a trial from which he prayed earnestly to be delivered, but that he received answer that the grace of God would be sufficient to support him; ver. 5—9. It was in view of this, he says (ver. 10) that he had pleasure in infirmities and sufferings in the cause of the Redeemer.

2. He then (ver. 11, 12) sums up what he had said; draws the conclusion that he had given every sign or evidence that he was an apostle; that in all that pertained to toil, and patience, and miracles, he had shown that he was commissioned by the Saviour; though with characteristic modesty he said *he was nothing*.

3. He then expresses his purpose to come again and see them, and his intention then not to be burdensome to them; ver. 13—15. He was willing to labour for them, and to exhaust his strength in endeavouring to promote their welfare without receiving support from them, for he regarded himself in the light of a father to them, and it was not usual for children to support their parents.

4. In connection with this, he answers another charge against himself. Some accused him of being crafty; that though he did not burden them, yet he knew well how to manage so as to secure what he wanted without burdening them, or seeming to receive any thing from them; ver. 16. To this he answers by an appeal to fact. Particularly he appeals to the conduct of Titus when with them, in full proof that he had no such design; ver. 17—19.

5. In the conclusion of the chapter, he expresses his fear that when he should come among them he would find much that would humble them, and give him occasion for severity of discipline; ver. 20, 21. This apprehension is evidently expressed in order that they might be led to examine themselves, and to put away whatever was wrong.

1. *It is not expedient.* It is not well; it does not become me. This may either mean that he felt and admitted that it did not become him to boast in this manner; that there was an impropriety in his doing it though circumstances had compelled him, and in this sense it is understood by nearly, or quite, all expositors; or it may be taken ironically. "Such a man as I am ought not to boast. So you say, and so it would seem. A man who has done no more than I have; who has suffered nothing; who has been idle and at ease as I have been, ought surely not to boast. And since there is such an evident impropriety in *my* boasting and speaking about myself, I will turn to another matter, and inquire whether the same thing may not be said about visions and revelations. I will speak, therefore, of a man who had some remarkable revelations, and inquire whether *he* has any right to boast of the favours imparted to him." This seems to me to be the probable interpretation of this passage. ¶ *To glory.* To boast; chap. x. 8, 13; xi. 10. One of the charges which they alleged against him was, that he was given to boasting without any good reason. After the enumeration in the previous chapter of what he had done and suffered, he says that this was doubtless very true. Such a man has nothing to boast of. ¶ *I will come.* Marg. "For I will." Our translators have omitted the word (γὰρ) *for* in the text, evidently supposing that it is a mere expletive. Doddridge renders it, "nevertheless." But it seems to me that it contains an important sense, and that it should be rendered by THEN. "Since it is not fit that I should glory, *then* I will refer to visions, &c. I will turn away then from that subject, and come to another." Thus the word (γὰρ) is used in John vii. 41. "Shall THEN

about fourteen [1] years ago, (whether in the body, I cannot tell; or whether out of the body, I cannot tell: God knoweth;) such an one caught up to the third heaven.

1 *A.D.*46; Acts 22.17.

(μὴ γὰρ) Christ come out of Galilee?" Acts viii. 31. "How can I THEN (πῶς γὰρ) except some man should guide me?" see also Acts xix. 35; Rom. iii. 3; Phil. i. 18. ¶ *To visions.* The word *vision* is used in the Scriptures often to denote the mode in which divine communications were usually made to men. This was done by causing some scene to appear to pass before the mind as in a landscape, so that the individual seemed to *see* a representation of what was to occur in some future period. It was usually applied to *prophecy*, and is often used in the Old Testament; see my Note on Isa. i. 1, and also on Acts ix. 10. The vision which Paul here refers to was that which he was permitted to have of the heavenly world; ver. 4. He was permitted to *see* what perhaps no other mortal had seen, the glory of heaven. ¶ *And revelations of the Lord.* Which the Lord had made. Or it may mean manifestations which the Lord had made of himself to him. The word rendered *revelations* means properly an *uncovering* (ἀποκάλυψις, from ἀποκαλύπτω, to uncover), and denotes a removal of the veil of ignorance and darkness, so that an object may be clearly seen; and is thus applied to truth revealed, because the obscurity is removed and the truth becomes manifest.

2. *I knew a man in Christ.* I was acquainted with a Christian; the phrase "in Christ" meaning nothing more than that he was united to Christ or was a Christian; see Rom. xvi. 7. The reason why Paul did not speak of this directly as a vision which he had himself seen was probably that he was accused of boasting, and he had admitted that it did not become *him* to glory. But though it did not become *him* to boast directly, yet he could tell them of a man concerning whom there would be no impropriety evidently in boasting. It is not uncommon, moreover, for a man to speak of himself in the third person. Thus Cesar in his Commentaries uniformly speaks of himself. And so John in his Gospel speaks of himself, chap. xiii. 23, 24; xix. 26; xxi. 20. John did it on account of his modesty, because he would not appear to put himself forward, and because the mention of his own name as connected with the friendship of the Saviour in the remarkable manner in which he enjoyed it, might have savoured of pride. For a similar reason Paul may have been unwilling to mention his own name here; and he may have abstained from referring to this occurrence elsewhere, because it might savour of pride, and might also excite the envy or ill-will of others. Those who have been most favoured with spiritual enjoyments will not be the most ready to proclaim it. They will cherish the remembrance in order to excite gratitude in their own hearts and support them in trial; they will not blazon it abroad as if they were more the favourites of heaven than others are. That this refers to Paul himself is evident for the following reasons. (1.) His argument required that he should mention something that had occurred to himself. Any thing that had occurred to another would not have been pertinent. (2.) He applies it directly to himself (ver. 7), when he says that God took effectual measures that he should not be unduly exalted in view of the abundant revelations bestowed on him. ¶ *About fourteen years ago.* On what occasion or where this occurred, or why he concealed the remarkable fact so long, and why there is no other allusion to it, is unknown; and conjecture is useless. If this epistle was written, as is commonly supposed, about the year 58, then this occurrence must have happened about the year 44. This was several years after his conversion, and of course this does not refer to the *trance* mentioned in Acts ix. 9, at the time when

he was converted. Dr. Benson supposes that this vision was made to him when he was praying in the temple after his return to Jerusalem, when he was directed to go from Jerusalem to the Gentiles (Acts xxii. 17), and that it was intended to support him in the trials which he was about to endure. There can be little danger of error in supposing that its object was to support him in those remarkable trials, and that God designed to impart to him such views of heaven and its glory, and of the certainty that he would soon be admitted there, as to support him in his sufferings, and make him willing to bear all that should be laid upon him. God often gives to his people some clear and elevated spiritual comforts *before* they enter into trials as well as while *in* them; he *prepares* them for them before they come. This vision Paul had kept secret for fourteen years. He had doubtless *often* thought of it; and the remembrance of that glorious hour was doubtless one of the reasons why he bore trials so patiently and was willing to endure so much. But before this he had had no occasion to mention it. He had other proofs in abundance that he was called to the work of an apostle; and to mention this would savour of pride and ostentation. It was only when he was *compelled* to refer to the evidences of his apostolic mission that he refers to it here. ¶ *Whether in the body, I cannot tell.* That is, I do not pretend to explain it. I do not know how it occurred. With the *fact* he was acquainted; but *how* it was brought about he did not know. Whether the body was caught up to heaven; whether the soul was for a time separated from the body; or whether the scene passed before the mind in a vision, so that he *seemed* to have been caught up to heaven, he does not pretend to know. The evident idea is, that at the time he was in a state of insensibility in regard to surrounding objects, and was unconscious of what was occurring, as if he had been dead. Where Paul confesses his own ignorance of what occurred to himself it would be vain for us to inquire; and the question *how* this was done is immaterial. No one can doubt that God had power if he chose to transport the body to heaven; or that he had power for a time to separate the soul from the body; or that he had power to represent to the mind so clearly the view of the heavenly world that he would appear to see it; see Acts vii. 56. It is clear only that he lost all consciousness of any thing about him at that time, and that he saw only the things in heaven. It may be added here, however, that Paul evidently supposed that his soul *might* be taken to heaven without the body, and that it might have separate consciousness and a separate existence. He was not, therefore, a materialist, and he did not believe that the existence and consciousness of the soul was dependent on the body. ¶ *God knoweth.* With the mode in which it was done God only could be acquainted. Paul did not attempt to explain that. That was to him of comparatively little consequence, and he did not lose his time in a vain attempt to explain it. How happy would it be if all theologians were as ready to be satisfied with the knowledge of *a fact*, and to leave the mode of explaining it with God, as this prince of theologians was. Many a man would have busied himself with a vain *speculation* about the way in which it was done; Paul was contented with the *fact* that it had occurred. ¶ *Such an one caught up.* The word which is here used (ἁρπάζω) means, to seize upon, to snatch away, as wolves do their prey (John xii. 10); or to seize with avidity or eagerness (Mat. xi. 12); or to carry away, to hurry off by force or involuntarily; see John vi. 15; Acts vii. 39; xxiii. 10. In the case before us there is implied the idea that Paul was conveyed by a foreign force; or that he was suddenly seized and snatched up to heaven. The word expresses the suddenness and the rapidity with which it was done. Probably it was instantaneous, so that he appeared at once to be in heaven. Of the mode in which it was done Paul has given no explanations; and conjecture would

3 And I knew such a man, (whether in the body, or out of the body, I cannot tell: God knoweth;)

4 How that he was caught up into paradise,[a] and heard unspeakable words, which it is not [1] lawful for a man to utter.

a Lu.23.43; Re.2.7. 1 or, *possible*.

be useless. ¶ *To the third heaven.* The Jews sometimes speak of seven heavens, and Mahomet has borrowed this idea from the Jews. But the Bible speaks of but three heavens, and among the Jews in the apostolic ages also the heavens were divided into three. (1.) The aerial, including the clouds and the atmosphere, the heavens above us, *until* we come to the stars. (2.) The starry heavens, the heavens in which the sun, moon, and stars appear to be situated. (3.) The heavens *beyond* the stars. That heaven was supposed to be the residence of God, of angels, and of holy spirits. It was this upper heaven, the dwelling-place of God, to which Paul was taken, and whose wonders he was permitted to behold—this region where God dwelt; where Christ was seated at the right hand of the Father, and where the spirits of the just were assembled. The fanciful opinions of the Jews about seven heavens may be seen detailed in Schoettgen or in Wetstein, by whom the principal passages from the Jewish writings relating to the subject have been collected. As their opinions throw no light on this passage, it is unnecessary to detail them here.

3. *And I knew such a man.* It is not uncommon to repeat a solemn affirmation in order that it may be made more emphatic. This is done here. Paul repeats the idea, that he was intimately acquainted with such a man, and that he did not know whether he was in the body or out of the body. All that was known to God.

4. *Into paradise.* The word paradise (παράδεισος) occurs but three times in the New Testament; Luke xxiii. 43; 2 Cor. xii. 4; Rev. ii. 7. It occurs often in the Septuagint, as the translation of the word *garden;* Gen. ii. 8—10, 15, 16; iii. 1—3, 8, 16, 23, 24; xiii. 10; Num. xxiv. 6; Isa. li. 3; Ezek. xxviii. 13; xxxi. 8, 9; Joel ii. 3. And also Isa. i. 30; Jer. xxix. 5; and of the word (פרדס) *Pardes* in Neh. ii. 8; Eccl. ii. 5; Cant. ii. 13. It is a word which had its origin in the language of eastern Asia, and which has been adopted in the Greek, the Roman, and other western languages. In Sanscrit the word *paradêsha* means a land elevated and cultivated; in Armenian, *pardes* denotes a garden around the house planted with trees, shrubs, grass for use and ornament. In Persia, the word denotes the *pleasure gardens* and *parks* with wild animals around the country residences of the monarchs and princes. Hence it denotes in general a garden of pleasure; and in the New Testament is applied to the abodes of the blessed after death, the dwelling-place of God and of happy spirits; or to heaven as a place of blessedness. Some have supposed that Paul here by the word "paradise" means to describe a different place from that denoted by the phrase "the third heaven;" but there is no good reason for this supposition. The only difference is that this word implies the idea of a place of blessedness; but the same place is undoubtedly referred to. ¶ *And heard unspeakable words.* The word which is here rendered "unspeakable" (ἄῤῥητα) may either mean what *cannot* be spoken, or what *ought* not to be spoken. The word means unutterable, ineffable; and whichever idea we attach to it, Paul meant to say that he could not attempt by words to do justice to what he saw and heard. The use of the word "*words*" here would seem to imply that he heard the *language* of exalted praise; or that there were truths imparted to his mind which he could not hope to convey in any language spoken by men. ¶ *Which it is not lawful for a man to utter.* Marg. "*Possible.*" Witsius supposes that the word ἐξὸν may include both, and Doddridge accords with the interpretation. See also Robinson's Lex. The word is most commonly

used in the signification of *lawful*. Thus, Mat. xiv. 4, "It is not *lawful* for thee to have her." Acts xvi. 21, "Which it is not *lawful* for us to observe;" xxii. 25, "Is it *lawful* for you to scourge a man that is a Roman," &c. In the same sense of *lawful* it is used in Mat. xii. 2, 10, 12; xx. 15; Mark ii. 26; x. 2. When it refers to *possibility* it probably means *moral* possibility; that is, propriety, or it means that it is right. It seems to me, therefore, that the word here rather means that it was not *proper* to give utterance to those things; it would not be *right* to attempt it. It might be also true that it would not have been possible for language to convey clearly the ideas connected with the things which Paul was then permitted to see; but the main thought is, that there was some reason why it would not be *proper* for him to have attempted to communicate those ideas to men at large. The Jews held that it was unlawful to pronounce the *Tetragrammaton*, *i. e.* the name of four letters (יהוה), JEHOVAH; and whenever that name occurred in their scriptures, they substituted the name *Adonai* in its place. They maintain indeed that the true pronunciation is utterly lost, and none of them to this day attempt to pronounce it. But this was mere superstition; and it is impossible that Paul should have been influenced by any such reason as this.

The transaction here referred to is very remarkable. It is the only instance in the scriptures of any one who was taken to heaven, either in reality or in vision, and who returned again to the earth and was then qualified to communicate important truths about the heavenly world from personal observation. Enoch and Elijah were taken to heaven; but they returned not to converse with men. Elijah appeared with Moses in conversation with Jesus on the mount of transfiguration; but they conversed with him only about his decease, which he was about to accomplish at Jerusalem; Luke ix. 31. There would have been no propriety for them to have spoken to Jesus of heaven, for he came down from heaven and was *in* heaven (John iii. 13), and they were not permitted to speak to the disciples of heaven. Lazarus was raised from the dead (John xi.), and many of the saints which had slept in their graves arose at the death of Jesus (Mat. xxvii. 52), but there is no intimation that they communicated any thing to the living about the heavenly world. Of all the millions who have been taken to heaven, not one has been permitted to return to bear his testimony to its glories; to witness for God that he is faithful to his promises; to encourage his pious friends to persevere; or to invite his impenitent friends to follow him to that glorious world. And so fixed is the law; so settled is the principle, that even Lazarus was not permitted to go, though at the earnest request of the rich man in hell, and warn his friends not to follow him to that world of woe; Luke xvi. 27—31. Mahomet indeed feigned that he had made a journey to heaven, and he attempts to describe what he saw; and the difference between *true inspiration* and *false* or *pretended inspiration* is strikingly evinced by the difference between Paul's dignified silence—*verba sacro digna silentio* (*Horace*) and the puerilities of the prophet of Mecca. See the Koran, chap. xvii. As the difference between the true religion and imposture is strikingly illustrated by this, we may recur to the principal events which happened to the impostor on his celebrated journey. The whole account may be seen in Prideaux's Life of Mahomet, p. 43. seq. He solemnly affirmed that he had been translated to the heaven of heavens; that on a white beast, less than a mule, but larger than an ass, he had been conveyed from the temple of Mecca to that of Jerusalem; had successively ascended the seven heavens with his companion Gabriel, receiving and returning the salutations of its blessed inhabitants; had then proceeded alone within two bow-shots of the throne of the Almighty, when he felt a cold which pierced him to the heart, and was touched on the shoulder by the hand of God, who commanded him to pray fifty times a day, but with the advice of Moses he was prevailed on to have the number reduced to five; and that he then returned to Jerusalem and to Mecca, having performed a journey of thousands of years in the tenth part of a night.

The fact that Paul was not permitted to communicate what he had seen is very remarkable. It is natural to ask why it is so? Why has not God sent down departed saints to *tell* men of the glories of heaven? Why does he not permit them to come and bear testimony to what they have seen and enjoyed? Why not come and clear up the doubts of the pious; why not come and convince a thoughtless world; why not come and bear honourable testimony for God that he is faithful to reward his people? And especially why did he not suffer Paul, whom he had permitted to behold the glories of paradise, to testify simply to what he had seen, and tell us what was there?

To these questions, so obvious, it is impossible to give an answer that we can demonstrate to be the true one. But we may suggest *some* reasons which may furnish a *plausible* answer, and which may serve to remove some of the perplexity in the case. I would, therefore, suggest that the following may have been some of the reasons why Paul was not permitted to communicate what he saw to men. (1.) It was designed for the support of Paul himself in view of the very remarkable trials which he was about to endure. God had called him to great toils and self-denials. He was to labour much alone; to go to foreign lands; to be persecuted, and ultimately put to death; and it was his purpose to qualify him for this work by some peculiar manifestation of his favour. He accordingly gave him such views of heaven that he would be supported in his trials by a conviction of the undoubted truth of what he taught, and by the prospect of certain glory when his labours should end. It was one instance when God gave peculiar views to prepare for trials, as he often does to his people now, preparing them in a peculiar manner for peculiar trials. Christians, from some cause, often have more elevated views and deeper feeling *before* they are called to endure trials than they have at other times—peculiar grace to prepare them for suffering. But as this was designed in a peculiar manner for Paul alone, it was not proper for him to communicate what he saw to others. (2.) It is probable that if there were a full revelation of the glories of heaven we should not be able to comprehend it; or even if we did, we should be incredulous in regard to it. So unlike what we see; so elevated above our highest comprehension; probably so unlike what we now anticipate is heaven, that we should be slow to receive the revelation. It is always difficult to describe what we have not seen, even on earth, so that we shall have *any* very clear idea of it: how much more difficult must it be to describe heaven. We are often incredulous about what is reported to exist in foreign lands on earth which we have not seen, and a long time is often necessary before we will believe it. The king of Siam, when told by the Dutch ambassador that water became so hard in his country that men might walk on it, said, "I have often suspected you of falsehood, but now I *know* that you lie." So incredulous might we be, with our weak faith, if we were told what actually exists in heaven. We should not improbably turn away from it as wholly incredible. (3.) There are great truths which it is not the design of God to reveal to men. The object is to communicate *enough* to win us, to comfort us, to support our faith, not to reveal *all*. In eternity there must be boundless truths and glories which are not *needful* for us to know now, and which, on many accounts, it would not be proper to be revealed to men. The question is not, do we know *all*, but have we *enough* safely to guide us to heaven, and to comfort us in the trials of life. (4.) There *is* enough revealed of heaven for our guidance and comfort in this world. God has told us what it will be in general. It will be a world without sin; without tears;

5 Of such an one will I glory: yet[a] of myself I will not glory, but in mine infirmities.

6 For though I would desire to glory, I shall not be a fool; for I will say the truth: but *now*

a chap.11.30; ver.9,10.

without wrong, injustice, fraud, or wars; without disease, pestilence, plague, death; and it is easy to fill up the picture sufficiently for all our purposes. Let us think of a world where all shall be pure and holy; of a world free from all that we now behold that is evil; free from pain, disease, death; a world where "friends never depart, foes never come;" a world where all shall be harmony and love —and where all this shall be ETERNAL, and we shall see that God has revealed *enough* for our welfare here. The highest *hopes* of man are met when we anticipate AN ETERNAL HEAVEN; the heaviest trials may be cheerfully borne when we have the prospect of EVERLASTING REST. (5.) One other reason may be assigned why it was not proper for Paul to disclose what he saw, and why God has withheld more full revelations from men about heaven. It is, that his purpose is that we shall here walk by faith and not by sight. We are not to see the reward, nor to be told fully what it is. We are to have such confidence in God that we shall assuredly believe that he will fully reward and bless us, and under this confidence we are to live and act here below. God designs, therefore, to try our faith, and to furnish an abundant evidence that his people are *disposed* to obey his commands and to put their trust in his faithfulness. Besides, if *all* the glories of heaven were revealed; if all were told that might be; and if heaven were made as attractive to mortal view as possible, then it might appear that his professed people were influenced *solely* by the hope of the reward. As it is, there is enough to support and comfort; not enough to make it the main and only reason why we serve God. It may be added, (*a*) That we have *all* the truth which we shall ever have about heaven here below. No other messenger will come; none of the pious dead will return. If men, therefore, are not willing to be saved in view of the truth which they have, they must be lost. God will communicate no more. (*b*) The Christian will soon know all about heaven. He will *soon* be there. He begins no day with any certainty that he may not close it in heaven; he lies down to rest at no time with any assurance that he will not wake in heaven amidst its full and eternal splendours. (*c*) The sinner will soon know fully what it is *to lose heaven*. A moment may make him fully sensible of his loss—for he may die; and a moment may put him for ever beyond the possibility of reaching a world of glory.

5. *Of such an one will I glory.* Of such a man it would be right to boast. It would be admitted that it is right to exult in such a man, and to esteem him to be peculiarly favoured by God. I will boast of him as having received peculiar honour from the Lord. Bloomfield, however, supposes that the words rendered "of such an one" should be translated "of such a thing," or of such a transaction; meaning "I can indeed justly boast of my being caught up to heaven as of a thing the whole glory of which pertains to him who has thus exalted me; but of myself, or of any thing in me, I will not boast." So Rosenmüller explains it. But it seems to me that the connection requires that we should understand it of a person, and that the passage is partly ironical. Paul speaks in the third person. He chooses to keep himself *directly* out of view. And though he refers really to himself, yet he would not say this directly, but says that of such a man they would admit it would be proper to boast. ¶ *Yet of myself.* Directly. It is not expedient for me to boast of myself. "You would allow me to boast of such a man as I have referred to; I admit that it is not proper for me to boast directly of myself." ¶ *But in mine infirmities.* My weaknesses, trials, pains, sufferings; such as many

I forbear, lest any man should think of me above that which he seeth me *to be*, or *that* he heareth of me.

---

regard as infirmities; see Note on chap. xi. 30.

6. *For though I would desire to glory.* I take this to be a solemn and serious declaration of the *irony* which precedes; and that Paul means to say seriously, that if he had a wish to boast as other men boasted, if he chose to make much of his attainments and privileges, he would have enough of which to make mention. It would not be mere empty boasting without any foundation or any just cause, for he had as much of which to speak in a confident manner pertaining to his labours as an apostle, and his evidence of the divine favour, as could be urged by any one. "I might go on to speak much more than I have done, and to urge claims which all would admit to be well-founded." ¶ *I shall not be a fool.* "It would not be foolish boasting; for it would be according to truth. I could urge much more than I have done; I could speak of things which no one would be disposed to call in question as laying the foundation of just claims to my being regarded as eminently favoured of God; I could seriously state what all would admit to be such." ¶ *For I will say the truth.* That is, "Whatever I should say on this subject would be the simple truth. I should mention nothing which has not actually occurred. But I forbear, lest some one should form an improper estimate of me." The apostle seems to have intended to have added something more, but he was checked by the apprehension to which he here refers. Or perhaps he means to say that if he should boast of the vision to which he had just referred; if he should go on to say how highly he had been honoured and exalted by it, there would be no impropriety in it. It was so remarkable that if he confined himself strictly to the truth, as he would do, still it would be regarded by all as a very extraordinary honour, and one to which no one of the false teachers could refer as laying a foundation for *their* boasting. ¶ *Lest any man should think of me*, &c. The idea in this part of the verse I take to be this. "I desire and expect to be estimated by my public life. I expect to be judged of men by my deeds, by what they see in me, and by my general reputation in respect to what I have done in establishing the Christian religion. I am willing that my character and reputation, that the estimate in which I shall be held by mankind, shall rest on that. I do not wish that my character among men shall be determined by my *secret* feelings; or by any secret extraordinary communication from heaven which I may have, and which cannot be subjected to the observation of my fellow-men. I am willing to be estimated by my public life; and however valuable such extraordinary manifestations may be to me as an individual; or however much they may comfort me, I do not wish to make the basis of my public reputation. I expect to stand and be estimated by my public deeds; by what all men see and hear of me; and I would not have them form even a favourable opinion of me beyond that." This is the noble language of a man who was willing to enjoy such a reputation as his public life entitled him to. He wished to have the basis of his reputation such that all men could see and examine it. Unlike enthusiasts and fanatics, he appealed to no secret impulses; did not rest his claims for public confidence on any peculiar communications from heaven; but wished to be estimated by his public deeds. And the important truth taught is, that however much the communion we may have with God; however much comfort and support in prayer and in our favoured moments of fellowship with God; or however much we may fancy in this way that we are the favourites of heaven; and however much this may support us in trial: still this should not be made the foundation of claim to the favourable opinions of our fellow-men. By our public character; by our well-known actions; by

7 And lest I should be exalted above measure through the abundance of the revelations, there was given to me a thorn [a] in the flesh,

[a] Eze.28. 24; Ga.4.14.

our lives as seen by men, we should desire to be estimated, and we should be *satisfied* with such a measure of public esteem as our deportment shall fairly entitle us to. We should seldom, perhaps, refer to our moments of secret, happy, and most favoured communion with God Paul kept his most elevated joys in this respect, secret *for fourteen years :*—what an example to those who are constantly blazoning their Christian experience abroad, and boasting of what they have enjoyed! We should *never* refer to such moments as a foundation for the estimate in which our character shall be held by our fellow-men. We should never make this the foundation of a claim to the public confidence in us. For all such claims; for all the estimate in which we shall be held by men, we should be willing to be tried by our lives. Paul would not even make *a vision of heaven;* not even *the privilege of having beheld the glories of the upper world, though a favour conferred on no other living man*, a ground of the estimate in which his character should be held! What an example to those who wish to be estimated by secret raptures, and by special communications to their souls from heaven! No. Let us be willing to be estimated *by men* by what they see in us; to enjoy such a reputation as our conduct shall fairly entitle us to. Let our communion with God cheer our own hearts; but let us not obtrude this on men as furnishing a claim for an exalted standard in their estimation.

7. *And lest I should be exalted.* Lest I should be spiritually proud; lest I should become self-confident and vain, and suppose that I was a special favourite of Heaven. If Paul was in danger of spiritual pride, who is not? If it was necessary for God to adopt some special measures to keep him humble, we are not to be surprised that the same thing should occur in other cases. There is abundant reason to believe that Paul was naturally a proud man. He was by nature self-confident; trusting in his own talents and attainments, and eminently ambitious. When he became a Christian, therefore, one of his besetting sins would be pride; and as he had been peculiarly favoured in his call to the apostleship; in his success as a preacher; in the standing which he had among the other apostles, and in the revelations imparted to him, there was also peculiar danger that he would become self-confident and proud of his attainments. There is no danger that more constantly besets Christians, and even eminent Christians, than pride. There is no sin that is more subtile, insinuating, deceptive; none that lurks more constantly around the heart and that finds a more ready entrance, than pride. He who has been characterized by pride before his conversion will be in special danger of it afterwards; he who has eminent gifts in prayer, or in conversation, or in preaching, will be in special danger of it; he who is eminently successful will be in danger of it; and he who has any extraordinary spiritual comforts will be in danger of it. Of this sin he who lives nearest to God may be in most special danger; and he who is most eminent in piety should feel that he also occupies a position where the enemy will approach him in a sly and subtile manner, and where he is in peculiar danger of a fall. Possibly the fear that he might be in danger of being made proud by the flattery of his friends may have been one reason why Paul kept this thing concealed for fourteen years; and if men wish to keep themselves from the danger of this sin, they should not be forward to speak even of the most favoured moments of their communion with God. ¶ *Through the abundance of the revelations.* By my being raised thus to heaven, and by being permitted to behold the wonders of the heavenly world, as well as by the

the [a] messenger of Satan, to buffet me, lest I should be exalted above measure.

a Job 2.7; Lu.13.16.

8 For this [a] thing I besought the Lord thrice, that it might depart from me.

a De.3.23,27; Ps 77.2,11; La.3.8; Mat.26.44.

numerous communications which God had made to me at other times. ¶ *There was given to me.* That is, God was pleased to appoint me. The word which Paul uses is worthy of special notice. It is that this "thorn in the flesh" was *given* to him, implying that it was a favour. He does not complain of it; he does not say it was sent in cruelty; he does not even speak of it as an affliction; he speaks of it as a *gift*, as any man would of a favour that had been bestowed. Paul had so clear a view of the *benefits* which resulted from it that he regarded it as a favour, as Christians should every trial. ¶ *A thorn in the flesh.* The word here used (σκόλοψ) occurs nowhere else in the New Testament. It means properly any thing pointed or sharp, *e. g.* a stake or palisade (Xen. Anab. v. 2, 5); or the point of a hook. The word is used in the Septuagint to denote a *thorn* or prickle, as a translation of סִיר (*sir*), in Hos. ii. 6, "I will hedge up thy way with *thorns*;" to denote a pricking briar in Ezek. xxviii. 24, as a translation of סִלּוֹן (*sillon*), meaning a thorn or prickle, such as is found in the shoots and twigs of the palm-tree; and to denote "pricks in the eyes" (Num. xxxiii. 55), as a translation of שִׂכִּים (*sikkim*), thorns or prickles. So far as the *word* here used is concerned, it means a sharp thorn or prickle; and the idea is, that the trial to which he refers was as troublesome and painful as such a thorn would be in the flesh But whether he refers to some infirmity or pain in the flesh or the body is another question, and a question in which interpreters have been greatly divided in opinion. Every one who has become familiar with commentaries knows that almost every expositor has had his own opinion about this, and also that no one has been able to give any good reason for his own. Most of them have been fanciful; and many of them eminently ridiculous. Even Baxter, who was subject himself to some such disorder, supposes that it might be the stone or gravel; and the usually very judicious Doddridge supposes that the view which he had of the glories of heavenly objects so affected his nerves as to produce a *paralytic* disorder, and particularly a stammering in his speech, and perhaps also a ridiculous distortion of the countenance. This opinion was suggested by Whitby, and has been adopted also by Benson, Macknight, Slade, and Bloomfield. But though sustained by most respectable names, it would be easy to show that it is mere conjecture, and perhaps quite as improbable as any of the numerous opinions which have been maintained on the subject. If Paul's speech had been affected, and his face distorted, and his nerves shattered by such a sight, how could he doubt whether he was in the body or out of it when this occurred? Many of the Latin fathers supposed that some unruly and ungovernable lust was intended. Chrysostom and Jerome suppose that he meant the headache; Tertullian an earache; and Rosenmüller supposes that it was the gout in the head, *kopfgicht*, and that it was a periodical disorder such as affected him when he was with the Galatians; Gal. iv. 13. But all conjecture here is vain; and the numerous strange and ridiculous opinions of commentators is a melancholy attestation of their inclination to fanciful conjecture where it is *impossible* in the nature of the case to ascertain the truth. All that can be known of this is, that it was some infirmity of the flesh, some bodily affliction or calamity, that was *like* the continual piercing of the flesh with a thorn (Gal. iv. 13); and that it was something that was *designed* to prevent spiritual pride. It is not indeed an improbable supposition that it was something that could be seen by others, and that thus tended to humble him when with them. ¶ *The messenger of Satan.* Among the Hebrews it was customary to attribute severe and painful diseases to Satan; comp. Job ii. 6, 7; comp. Note on Luke xiii. 16. In the time of the Saviour malignant spirits are known to have taken possession of the body in numerous cases, and to have produced painful bodily diseases, and Paul here says that Satan was permitted to bring this calamity on him. ¶ *To buffet me.* To buffet, means to smite with the hand; then to maltreat in any way. The meaning is, that the effect and design of this was deeply to afflict him. Doddridge and Clarke suppose that the reference is here to the false teacher whom Satan had sent to Corinth, and who was to him the source of perpetual trouble. But it seems more probable to me that he refers to some bodily infirmity. The general truth taught in this verse is, that God will take care that his people shall not be unduly exalted by the manifestations of his favour, and by the spiritual privileges which he bestows on them. He will take measures to humble them; and a large part of his dealings with his people is designed to accomplish this. Sometimes it will be done, as in the case of Paul, by bodily infirmity or trial, by sickness, or by long and lingering disease; sometimes by great poverty and by an humble condition of life; sometimes by *reducing* us from a state of affluence where we were in danger of being exalted above measure; sometimes by suffering us to be slandered and calumniated, by suffering foes to rise up against us who shall blacken our character and in such a manner that we cannot meet it; sometimes by persecution; sometimes by want of success in our enterprises, and if in the ministry, by withholding his Spirit; sometimes by suffering us to fall into sin, and thus greatly humbling us before the world. Such was the case with David and with Peter; and God often permits us to see in this manner our own weakness, and to bring us to a sense of our dependence and to proper humility by suffering us to perform some act that should be ever afterward *a standing source* of our humiliation; some act so base, so humiliating, so evincing the deep depravity of our hearts as *for ever* to make and keep us humble. How could David be lifted up with pride after the murder of Uriah? How could Peter after having denied his Lord with a horrid oath? Thus many a Christian is *suffered* to fall by the temptation of Satan to show him his weakness and to keep him from pride; many a fall is made the occasion of the permanent benefit of the offender. And perhaps every Christian who has been much favoured with elevated spiritual views and comforts can recall something which shall be to him a standing topic of regret and humiliation in his past life. We should be thankful for *any* calamity that will humble us; and we should remember that clear and elevated views of God and heaven are, after all, *more* than a compensation for all the sufferings which it may be necessary to endure in order to make us humble.

8. *For this thing.* On account of this; in order that this calamity might be removed. ¶ *I besought the Lord.* The word "Lord" in the New Testament, when it stands without any other word in connection to limit its signification, commonly denotes the Lord Jesus Christ; see Note on Acts i. 24. The following verse here shows conclusively that it was the Lord Jesus to whom Paul addressed this prayer. The answer was that his grace was sufficient for him; and Paul consoled himself by saying that it was a sufficient support if the power of Christ implied in that answer, should rest on him. He would glory in trials if *such* was their result. Even Rosenmüller maintains that it was the Lord Jesus to whom this prayer was addressed, and says that the Socinians themselves admit it. So Grotius (on ver. 9) says that the answer was given by Christ. But if this refers to the Lord Jesus, then it proves that it is right to go to him in times of trouble, and that it is right to worship him. Prayer is the most solemn act of adoration which we can perform; and no better authority can be required

9 And he said unto me, My grace is sufficient for thee: for my strength is made perfect in weakness. Most gladly therefore

for paying divine honours to Christ than the fact that Paul worshipped him and called upon him to remove a severe and grievous calamity. ¶ *Thrice.* This may either mean that he prayed for this *often*, or that he sought it on three set and solemn occasions. Many commentators have supposed that the former is meant. But to me it seems probable that Paul on three special occasions earnestly prayed for the removal of this calamity. It will be recollected that the Lord Jesus prayed three times in the garden of Gethsemane that the cup might be removed from him, Mat. xxvi. 44. At the third time he ceased, and submitted to what was the will of God. There is some reason to suppose that the Jews were in the habit of praying three times for any important blessing or for the removal of any calamity; and Paul in this would not only conform to the usual custom, but especially he would be disposed to imitate the example of the Lord Jesus. Among the Jews *three* was a sacred number, and repeated instances occur where an important transaction is mentioned as having been done thrice; see Num. xxii. 28; xxiv. 10; 1 Sam. iii. 8; xx. 41; 1 Kings xviii. 44; Prov. xxii. 20; Jer. vii. 4; xxii. 29; John xxi. 17. The probability, therefore, is, that Paul on three different occasions earnestly besought the Lord Jesus that this calamity might be removed from him. It might have been exceedingly painful, or it might, as he supposed, interfere with his success as a preacher; or it might have been of such a nature as to expose him to ridicule; and he prayed, therefore, if it were possible that it might be taken away. The passage proves that it is *right* to pray earnestly and repeatedly for the removal of any calamity. The Saviour so prayed in the garden; and Paul so prayed here. Yet it also proves that there should be a *limit* to such prayers. The Saviour prayed three times; and Paul limited himself to the same number of petitions and then submitted to the will of God. This does not prove that we should be limited to exactly this number in our petitions; but it proves that there should be a limit; that we should not be over-anxious, and that when it is plain from any cause that the calamity will not be removed, we should submit to it. The Saviour in the garden knew that the cup would not be removed, and he acquiesced. Paul was *told* indirectly that *his* calamity would not be removed, and he submitted. *We* may expect no such revelation from heaven, but we may know in other ways that the calamity will not be removed; and *we* should submit. The child or other friend for whom we prayed may die; or the calamity, as, *e. g.* blindness, or deafness, or loss of health, or poverty, may become permanent, so that there is no hope of removing it; and we should then cease to pray that it may be removed, and we should cheerfully acquiesce in the will of God. So David prayed most fervently for his child when it was alive; when it was deceased, and it was of no further use to pray for it, he bowed in submission to the will of God, 2 Sam. xii. 20.

9. *And he said unto me.* The Saviour replied. In what way this was done, or whether it was done at the time when the prayer was offered, Paul does not inform us. It is possible, as Macknight supposes, that Christ appeared to him again and spake to him in an audible manner. Grotius supposes that this was done by the בת קול (*Bath-qol*)—"daughter of the voice," so frequently referred to by the Jewish writers, and which they suppose to be referred to in 1 Kings xix. 12, by the phrase, "a still small voice." But it is impossible to determine in what way it was done, and it is not material. Paul was in habits of communion with the Saviour, and was accustomed to receive revelations from him. The material fact here is, that the request was *not* granted in the exact form in which he presented it, but that he received as-

surance of grace to support him in his trial. It is one of the instances in which the fervent prayer of a good man, offered undoubtedly in faith, was not answered in the form in which he desired, though substantially answered in the assurance of grace sufficient to support him. It furnishes, therefore, a very instructive lesson in regard to prayer, and shows us that we are not to expect as a matter of course that all our prayers will be literally answered, and that we should not be disappointed or disheartened if they are not. It is *a matter of fact* that not all the prayers even of the pious, and of those who pray having faith in God as a hearer of prayer, are literally answered. Thus the prayer of David (2 Sam. xii. 16—20) was not literally answered; the child for whose life he so earnestly prayed died. So the Saviour's request was not literally answered, Mark xiv. 36. The cup of suffering which he so earnestly desired should be taken away was not removed. So in the case before us; comp. also Deut. iii. 23—27; Job xxx. 20; Lam. iii. 8. So in numerous cases now, Christians pray with fervour and with faith for the removal of some calamity which is not removed; or for something which they regard as desirable for their welfare which is withheld. Some of the *reasons* why this is done are obvious. (1.) The grace that will be imparted if the calamity is not removed will be of greater value to the individual than would be the direct answer to his prayer. Such was the case with Paul; so it was doubtless with David; and so it is often with Christians now The removal of the calamity might be apparently a blessing, but it might also be attended with danger to our spiritual welfare; the grace imparted may be of permanent value and may be connected with the development of some of the loveliest traits of Christian character. (2.) It might not be for the good of the individual who prays that the exact thing should be granted. When a parent prays with great earnestness and with *insubmission* for the life of a child, he knows not what he is doing. If the child lives, he may be the occasion of much more grief to him than if he had died. David had far more trouble from Absalom than he had from the death of the child for which he so earnestly prayed. At the same time it may be better for the child that he should be removed. If he dies in infancy he will be saved. But who can tell what will be his character and destiny should he live to be a man? So of other things. (3.) God has often some better thing in store for us than would be the immediate answer to our prayer Who can doubt that this was true of Paul? The promised grace of Christ as sufficient to support us is of more value than would be the mere removal of any bodily affliction. (4.) It would not be well for us, probably, should our petition be literally answered. Who can tell what is best for himself? If the thing were obtained, who can tell how soon we might forget the benefactor and become proud and self-confident? It was the design of God to *humble* Paul; and this could be much better accomplished by continuing his affliction and by imparting the promised grace, than by withdrawing the affliction and withholding the grace. The very thing to be done was to keep him humble; and this affliction could not be withdrawn without also foregoing the benefit. It is true, also, that where things are in themselves proper to be asked, Christians sometimes ask them in an improper manner, and this is one of the reasons why *many* of their prayers are not answered. But this does not pertain to the case before us. ¶ *My grace is sufficient for thee.* A much better answer than it would have been to have removed the calamity; and one that seems to have been entirely satisfactory to Paul. The meaning of the Saviour is, that he would support him; that he would not suffer him to sink exhausted under his trials; that he had nothing to fear. The infliction was not indeed removed; but there was a promise that the favour of Christ would be shown to him constantly, and that he would find his support to be ample. If Paul

will I rather glory [a] in my infirmities, that the power [b] of Christ may rest upon me.

10 Therefore I take pleasure in infirmities, in reproaches, in necessities, in persecutions, in

a ver.5. b 1Pe.4 14

had this support, he might well bear the trial; and if we have this assurance, as we may have, we may welcome affliction, and rejoice that calamities are brought upon us. It is a sufficient answer to our prayers if we have the solemn promise of the Redeemer that we shall be upheld and never sink under the burden of our heavy woes. ¶ *My strength is made perfect in weakness.* That is, the strength which I impart to my people is more commonly and more completely manifested when my people feel that they are weak. It is not imparted to those who feel that they are strong and who do not realize their need of divine aid. It is not so completely manifested to those who *are* vigorous and strong as to the feeble. It is when we are conscious that we are feeble, and when we feel our need of aid, that the Redeemer manifests his power to uphold, and imparts his purest consolations. Grotius has collected several similar passages from the classic writers which may serve to illustrate this expression. Thus Pliny, vii. Epis. 26, says, "We are best where we are weak." Seneca says, "Calamity is the occasion of virtue." Quintilian, "All temerity of mind is broken by bodily calamity." Minutius Felix, "Calamity is often the discipline of virtue." There are few Christians who cannot bear witness to the truth of what the Redeemer here says, and who have not experienced the most pure consolations which they have known, and been most sensible of his comforting presence and power in times of affliction. ¶ *Most gladly, therefore,* &c. I count it a privilege to be afflicted, if my trials may be the means of my more abundantly enjoying the favour of the Redeemer. His presence and imparted strength are more than a compensation for all the trials that I endure. ¶ *That the power of Christ.* The strength which Christ imparts; his power manifested in supporting me in trials. ¶ *May rest upon me* (ἐπισκηνώσῃ). The word properly means *to pitch a tent upon;* and then to dwell in or upon. Here it is used in the sense of abiding upon, or remaining with. The sense is, that the power which Christ manifested to his people rested with them, or abode with them in their trials, and *therefore* he would rejoice in afflictions, in order that he might partake of the aid and consolation thus imparted. Learn hence, (1.) That a Christian never *loses* any thing by suffering and affliction. If he may obtain the favour of Christ by his trials he is a gainer. The favour of the Redeemer is more than a compensation for all that we endure in his cause. (2.) The Christian is a *gainer* by trial. I never knew a Christian that was not ultimately benefited by trials. I never knew one who did not find that he had *gained* much that was valuable to him in scenes of affliction. I do not know that I have found one who would be willing to exchange the advantages he has gained in affliction for all that the most uninterrupted prosperity and the highest honours that the world could give would impart. (3.) Learn to bear trials with joy. They are good for us. They develope some of the most lovely traits of character. They injure no one if they are properly received. And a Christian should *rejoice* that he *may* obtain what he *does* obtain in affliction, cost what it may. It is worth more than it costs; and when we come to die, the things that we shall have most occasion to thank God for will be our afflictions. And, O! if they are the means of raising us to a higher seat in heaven, and placing us nearer the Redeemer there who will not rejoice in his trials?

10. *Therefore I take pleasure.* Since so many benefits result from trials; since my afflictions are the occasion of obtaining the favour of Christ in

distresses for Christ's sake: for when I am weak, then am I strong.

11 I am become a fool in glorying: ye have compelled me: for I ought to have been commended of you: for [a] in nothing am I behind the very

a chap.11.5.

so eminent a degree, I rejoice in the privilege of suffering. There is often real *pleasure* in affliction, paradoxical as it may appear. Some of the happiest persons I have known are those who have been deeply afflicted; some of the purest joys which I have witnessed have been manifested on a sick-bed, and in the prospect of death. And I have no doubt that Paul, in the midst of all his infirmities and reproaches, had a joy above that which all the wealth and honour of the world could give. See here the power of religion. It not only supports, it comforts. It not only enables one to bear suffering with resignation, but it enables him to *rejoice.* Philosophy blunts the feelings; infidelity leaves men to murmur and repine in trial; the pleasures of this world have no power even to support or comfort in times of affliction; but Christianity furnishes positive pleasure in trial, and enables the sufferer to smile through his tears. ¶ *In infirmities.* In my weaknesses; see Note on chap. xi. 30. ¶ *In reproaches.* In the contempt and scorn with which I meet as a follower of Christ, Note, chap. xi. 21. ¶ *In necessities.* In want; see Notes on chap. vi. 4, 5. ¶ *In distresses for Christ's sake;* Note, chap. vi. 4. In the various wants and difficulties to which I am exposed on account of the Saviour, or which I suffer in his cause. ¶ *For when I am weak, then am I strong.* When I feel weak; when I am subjected to trial, and nature faints and fails, then strength is imparted to me, and I am enabled to bear all. The more I am borne down with trials, the more do I feel my need of divine assistance, and the more do I feel the efficacy of divine grace. Such was the promise in Deut. xxxiii. 25: "As thy days, so shall thy strength be." So in Heb. xi. 24: "Who out of weakness were made strong." What Christian has not experienced this, and been able to say that when he felt himself weak and felt like sinking under the accumulation of many trials, he has found his strength according to his day, and felt an arm of power supporting him? It is then that the Redeemer manifests himself in a peculiar manner; and then that the excellency of the religion of Christ is truly seen and its power appreciated and felt.

11. *I am become a fool in glorying.* The meaning of this expression I take to be this. "I have been led along in speaking of myself until I admit I appear foolish in this kind of boasting. It is folly to do it, and I would not have entered on it unless I had been driven to it by my circumstances and the necessity which was imposed on me of speaking of myself." Paul doubtless desired that what he had said of himself should not be regarded as an example for others to follow. Religion repressed all vain boasting and self-exultation; and to prevent others from falling into a habit of boasting, and then pleading his example as an apology, he is careful to say that he regarded it as folly; and that he would by no means have done it if the circumstances of the case had not constrained him. If any one, therefore, is disposed to imitate Paul in speaking of himself and what he has done, let him do it only when he is in circumstances like Paul, and when the honour of religion and his usefulness imperiously demand it; and let him not forget that it was the deliberate conviction of Paul that boasting was the characteristic of a fool! ¶ *Ye have compelled me.* You have made it necessary for me to vindicate my character and to state the evidence of my divine commission as an apostle. ¶ *For I ought to have been commended of you.* By you. Then this boasting, so foolish, would have been unnecessary. What a delicate reproof! All the fault of this

chiefest apostles, though [a] I be nothing.

12 Truly the signs [b] of an apostle were wrought among you in all

a Lu.17.10; 1Co.3.7; Ep.3.7.

b 1 Co.9.2.

foolish boasting was theirs. They knew him intimately. They had derived great benefits from his ministry, and they were bound in gratitude and from a regard to right and truth to vindicate him. But they had not done it; and hence, through their fault, he had been compelled to go into this unpleasant vindication of his own character. ¶ *For in nothing am I behind the very chiefest apostles.* Neither in the evidences of my call to the apostolic office (see 1 Cor. ix. 1, seq.); nor in the endowments of the Spirit; nor in my success; nor in the proofs of a divine commission in the power of working miracles; see Note on chap. xi. 5. ¶ *Though I be nothing.* This expression was either used in sarcasm or seriously. According to the former supposition it means, that he was regarded as nothing; that the false apostles spoke of him as a mere nothing, or as having no claims to the office of an apostle. This is the opinion of Clarke, and many of the recent commentators. Bloomfield inclines to this. According to the latter view, it is an expression of humility on the part of Paul, and is designed to express his deep sense of his unworthiness in view of his past life—a conviction deepened by the exalted privileges conferred on him, and the exalted rank to which he had been raised as an apostle. This was the view of most of the early commentators. Doddridge unites the two. It is not possible to determine with certainty which is the true interpretation; but it seems to me that the latter view best accords with the scope of the passage, and with what we have reason to suppose the apostle *would* say at this time. It is true that in this discussion (chap. x. seq.) there is much that is sarcastic. But in the whole strain of the passage before us he is serious. He is speaking of his sufferings, and of the evidences that he was raised to elevated rank as an apostle, and it is not quite natural to suppose that he would throw in a sarcastic remark just in the midst of this discussion. Besides, this interpretation accords exactly with what he says, 1 Cor. xv. 9: "For I am the least of all the apostles, that am not meet to be called an apostle." If this be the correct interpretation, then it teaches, (1.) That the highest attainments in piety are not inconsistent with the deepest sense of our nothingness and unworthiness. (2.) That the most distinguished favours bestowed on us by God are consistent with the lowest humility. (3.) That those who are most favoured in the Christian life, and most honoured by God, should not be unwilling to take a low place, and to regard and speak of themselves as nothing. Compared with God, what are they?—Nothing. Compared with the angels, what are they?—Nothing. As creatures compared with the vast universe, what are we?—Nothing. An atom, a speck. Compared with other Christians, the eminent saints who have lived before us, what are we? Compared with what we ought to be, and might be, what are we?—Nothing. Let a man look over his past life, and see how vile and unworthy it has been; let him look at God, and see how great and glorious he is; let him look at the vast universe, and see how immense it is; let him think of the angels, and reflect how pure they are; let him think of what he might have been, of how much more he might have done for his Saviour; let him look at his body, and think how frail it is, and how soon it must return to the dust; and no matter how elevated his rank among his fellow-worms, and no matter how much God has favoured him as a Christian or a minister, he will feel, if he feels right, that he is nothing. The most elevated saints are distinguished for the deepest humility; those who are nearest to God feel most their distance; they who are to occupy the highest place in

patience, in signs, and wonders, and
mighty deeds.
13 For what is it wherein you
were inferior to other churches,
except *it be* that I [a] myself was
not burdensome to you? forgive
me this wrong.
14 Behold, the third time I

a chap.11.9.

heaven feel most deeply that they are unworthy of the lowest.

12. *Truly the signs of an apostle.* Such miracles as the acknowledged apostles worked. Such "signs" or evidences that they were divinely commissioned; see Note on Mark xvi. 17; Acts ii. 22; Rom. xv. 19. ¶ *Were wrought among you.* That is, by me; see Note, 1 Cor. ix. 2. ¶ *In all patience.* I performed those works notwithstanding the opposition which I met with. I patiently persevered in furnishing the evidence of my divine commission. There was a succession of miracles demonstrating that I was from God, notwithstanding the unreasonable opposition which I met with, until I *convinced* you that I was called to the office of an apostle. ¶ *In signs and wonders.* In working miracles; comp. Note, Acts ii. 22. What these miracles at Corinth were, we are not distinctly informed. They probably, however, were similar to those wrought in other places, in healing the sick, &c.; the most *benevolent* as it was one of the most *decisive* proofs of the divine power.

13. *For what is it, &c.* This verse contains a striking mixture of sarcasm and irony, not exceeded, says Bloomfield, by any example in Demosthenes. The sense is, "I have given among you the most ample proof of my apostolic commission. I have conferred on you the highest favours of the apostolic office. In these respects you are superior to all other churches. In one respect only are you *inferior* —it is in this, that you have not been *burdened* with the privilege of supporting me. If you had had this, you would have been inferior to no others. But this was owing to me; and I pray that you will forgive me this I might have urged it; I might have claimed it; I might have given you the privilege of becoming equal to the most favoured in all respects. But I have not pressed it, and you have not done it, and I ask your pardon." There is a delicate insinuation that they had not contributed to his wants (see Note, chap. xi. 8); an intimation that it was a privilege to contribute to the support of the gospel, and that Paul *might* have been "burdensome to them" (see Notes on 1 Cor. ix. 1—12); and an admission that he was in part to blame for this, and had not in this respect given them an opportunity to equal other churches in all respects. ¶ *Was not burdensome to you;* see this explained in the Notes on chap. x. 8. ¶ *Forgive me this wrong.* "If it be a fault, pardon it. Forgive me that I did not give you this opportunity to be equal to other churches. It is a privilege to contribute to the support of the gospel, and they who are permitted to do it should esteem themselves highly favoured. I pray you to pardon me for depriving you of any of your Christian privileges." What the feelings of the Corinthians were about forgiving Paul for this we know not; but most churches would be as ready to forgive a minister for this as for any other offence.

14. *Behold, the third time I am ready to come to you.* That is, this is the third time that I have *purposed* to come and see you, and have made preparation for it. He does not mean that he had been twice with them and was now coming the third time, but that he had twice before intended to go and had been disappointed; see 1 Cor. xvi. 5; 2 Cor. i. 15, 16. His purpose had been to visit them on his way to Macedonia, and again on his return from Macedonia. He had now formed a third resolution, which he had a prospect of carrying into execution. ¶ *And I will not be burdensome to you.* I resolve still, as I have done before, not to receive a compensation that shall be oppressive to you,

am ready to come to you; and I will not be burdensome to you: for [a] I seek not yours, but you: for the children ought not to lay up for the parents, but the parents for the children.

15 And I will very gladly spend and be spent for [1] you; though

a 1 Co.10 33; 1 Th.2.8.

1 *your souls.*

see Notes on chap. xi. 9, 10. ¶ *For I seek not yours, but you.* I desire not to obtain your property, but to save your souls. This was a noble resolution; and it is the resolution which should be formed by every minister of the gospel. While a minister of Christ has a claim to a competent support, his main purpose should not be to obtain such a support. It should be the higher and nobler object of winning souls to the Redeemer. See Paul's conduct in this respect explained in the Notes on Acts xx. 33. ¶ *For the children,* &c. There is great delicacy and address in this sentiment. The meaning is, "It is not natural and usual for children to make provisions for their parents. The common course of events and of duty is, for parents to make provision for their offspring. I, therefore, your spiritual father, choose to act in the same way. I make provision for your spiritual wants; I labour and toil for you as a father does for his children. I seek your welfare, as he does, by constant self-denial. In return, I do not ask you to provide for me, any more than a father ordinarily expects his children to provide for him. I am willing to labour as he does, content with doing my duty, and promoting the welfare of those under me." The words rendered "ought out" (οὐ ὀφείλει) are to be understood in a *comparative* sense. Paul does not mean that a child ought *never* to provide for his parents, or to lay any thing up for a sick, a poor, and an infirm father, but that the duty of doing that was slight and unusual compared with the duty of a parent to provide for his children. The one was of comparatively rare occurrence; the other was constant and was the ordinary course of duty It *is* a matter of obligation for a child to provide for an aged and helpless parent; but commonly the duty is that of a parent to provide for his children. Paul felt like a father toward the church in Corinth; and he was willing, therefore, to labour for them without compensation.

15. *And I will very gladly spend.* I am willing to spend my strength, and time, and life, and all that I have, for your welfare, as a father cheerfully does for his children. Any expense which may be necessary to promote your salvation I am willing to submit to. The labour of a father for his children is cheerful and pleasant. Such is his love for them that he delights in toil for their sake, and that he may make them happy. The toil of a pastor for his flock should be cheerful. He should be willing to engage in unremitted efforts for their welfare; and if he has any right feeling he will find *a pleasure* in that toil He will not grudge the time demanded; he will not be grieved that it exhausts his strength, or his life, any more than a father will who toils for his family. And as the pleasures of a father who is labouring for his children are among the purest and most pleasant which men ever enjoy, so it is with a pastor. Perhaps, on the whole, the pleasantest employment in life is that connected with the pastoral office; the happiest moments known on earth are the duties, arduous as they are, of the pastoral relation. God thus, as in the relation of a father, tempers toil and pleasure together; and accompanies most arduous labours with present and abundant reward. ¶ *Be spent.* Be exhausted and worn out in my labours. So the Greek word means. Paul was willing that his powers should be entirely exhausted and his life consumed in this service. ¶ *For you.* Marg. as in the Greek, for *your souls.* So it should have been rendered. So Tindal renders it. The sense is, that he was willing to become wholly exhausted if by it he might secure the salvation of their

the more abundantly I love you, the less I be loved.
16 But be it so, I did not burden you: nevertheless, being crafty, I caught you with guile.
17 Did I make a gain of you by

souls. ¶ *Though the more abundantly I love you,* &c. This is designed doubtless as a gentle reproof. It refers to the fact that notwithstanding the tender attachment which he had evinced for them, they had not manifested the love in return which he had a right to expect. It is *possible* that there may be an allusion to the case of a fond, doting parent. It sometimes happens that a parent fixes his affections with undue degree on some one of his children; and in such cases it is not uncommon that the child evinces *special* ingratitude and want of love. Such *may* be the allusion here—that Paul had fixed his affections on them like a fond, doting father, and that he had met with a return by no means corresponding with the fervour of his attachment; yet still he was willing, like such a father, to exhaust his time and strength for their welfare. The doctrine is, that we should be willing to labour and toil for the good of others, even when they evince great ingratitude. The proper end of labouring for their welfare is not to excite their gratitude, but to obey the will of God; and no matter whether others are grateful or not; whether they love us or not; whether we can promote our popularity with them or not, let us do them good always. It better shows the firmness of our Christian principle to endeavour to benefit others when they love us the less for all our attempts, than it does to attempt to do good on the swelling tide of popular favour.

16. *But be it so.* This is evidently a charge of his enemies; or at least a charge which it might be supposed they would make. Whether they ever in fact made it, or whether the apostle merely anticipates an objection, it is impossible to determine. It is clearly to be regarded as *the language* of objectors; for, (1.) It can never be supposed that Paul would state as a serious matter that he had caught them with deceit or fraud. (2.) He *answers* it as an objection in the following verse. The meaning is, "We admit that you did not burden us. You did not exact a support from us. But all this was mere trick. You accomplished the same thing in another way. You professed when with us not to seek our property but our souls. But in various ways you contrived to get our money, and to secure your object. You made others the agents for doing this, and sent them among us under various pretexts to gain money from us." It will be remembered that Paul had sent Titus among them to take up the collection for the poor saints in Judea (chap. viii. 6), and it is not at all improbable that some there had charged Paul with making use of this pretence only to obtain money for his own private use. To guard against this charge, was one of the reasons why Paul was so anxious to have some persons appointed by the church to take charge of the contribution; see 1 Cor. xvi. 3; comp. Notes on 2 Cor. viii. 19—21. ¶ *Being crafty.* Being cunning That is, by sending persons to obtain money on different pretences. ¶ *I caught you with guile.* I took you by deceit or fraud. That is, making use of fraud in pretending that the money was for poor and afflicted saints, when in reality it was for my own use. It is impossible that Paul should have ever admitted this of himself; and they greatly pervert the passage who suppose that it applies to him, and then plead that it is right to make use of guile in accomplishing their purposes. Paul never carried his measures by dishonesty, nor did he ever justify fraud; comp. Notes on Acts xxiii. 6.

17. *Did I make a gain,* &c. In refuting this slander, Paul appeals boldly to the facts, and to what they knew. "Name the man," says he, "who has thus defrauded you under my instructions. If the charge is

any of them whom I sent unto you?

18 I desired Titus, [a] and with *him* I sent a brother: [b] Did Titus make a gain of you? walked we not in the same spirit? *walked we* not in the same steps?

19 Again, think ye that we excuse ourselves [c] unto you? we speak before God in Christ: but *we do* all things, dearly beloved, for your edifying.

20 For I fear, lest, when[d] I come, I shall not find you such as I would, and *that* I shall be found unto you

a chap.7.2. b chap.8.6. c chap.5.12. d 1 Co.4 21; chap.13.2.10.

well-founded, let him be specified, and let the mode in which it was done be distinctly stated." The phrase "make a gain" (from πλεονεκτέω), means properly to have an advantage; then to take advantage, to seek unlawful gain. Here Paul asks whether he had defrauded them by means of any one whom he had sent to them.

18. *I desired Titus.* To go and complete the collection which you had commenced; see chap. viii. 6. ¶ *And with him I sent a brother;* see Note on chap. viii. 18. ¶ *Did Titus make a gain of you?* They knew that he did not. They had received him kindly, treated him with affection, and sent him away with every proof of confidence and respect; see chap. vii. 7. How then could they now pretend that he had defrauded them? ¶ *Walked we not in the same spirit?* Did not all his actions resemble mine? Was there not the same proof of honesty, sincerity, and love which I have ever manifested? This is a very delicate turn. Paul's course of life when *with* them they admitted was free from guile and from any attempt to get money by improper means. They charged him only with attempting it by means of others. He now boldly appeals to them and asks whether Titus and he had not *in fact* acted in the same manner; and whether they had not alike evinced a spirit free from covetousness and deceit?

19. *Again, think ye that we excuse ourselves unto you?* see Note on chap. v. 12. The sense is, Do not suppose that this is said from mere anxiety to obtain your favour, or to ingratiate ourselves into your esteem. This is said doubtless to keep himself from the suspicion of being actuated by improper motives. He had manifested great solicitude certainly in the previous chapter to vindicate his character; but he here says that it was not from a mere desire to show them that his conduct was right; it was from a desire to honour Christ. ¶ *We speak before God in Christ.* We declare the simple and undisguised truth as in the presence of God. I have no mere desire to palliate my conduct; I disguise nothing; I conceal nothing; I say nothing for the mere purpose of self-vindication, but I can appeal to the Searcher of hearts for the exact truth of all that I say. The phrase "before God in Christ," means probably, "I speak as in the presence of God, and as a follower of Christ, as a Christian man." It is the solemn appeal of a Christian to his God for the truth of what he said, and a solemn asseveration that what he said was not for the mere purpose of excusing or *apologizing for* (Greek) his conduct. ¶ *But we do all things, dearly beloved, for your edifying.* All that I have done has been for your welfare. My vindication of my character, and my effort to disabuse you of your prejudices, has been that you might have unwavering confidence in the gospel and might be built up in holy faith. On the word *edify,* see Notes on Rom. xiv. 19; 1 Cor. viii. 1; x. 23.

20. *For I fear lest, when I come;* see ver. 14. ¶ *I shall not find you such as I would.* That is, walking in the truth and order of the gospel. He had feared that the disorders would not be removed, and that they would not have corrected the errors which prevailed, and for which he had rebuked them. It was on this ac-

such as ye would not; lest *there*
be debates, envyings, wraths, strifes,
backbitings, whisperings, swellings,
tumults:
21 *And* lest, when I come
again, my God will humble [a] me
among you, and *that* I shall bewail many which have sinned
already, and have not repented [b]
of the uncleanness, and fornication, [c] and lasciviousness which
they have committed.

[a] chap.2.1. [b] Re.2.21. [c] 1 Co.5.1.

count that he had said so much to them. His desire was that all these disorders might be removed, and that he might be saved from the necessity of exercising severe discipline when he should come among them. ¶ *And* that *I shall be found unto you such as ye would not.* That is, that I shall be compelled to administer discipline, and that my visit may not be as pleasant to you as you would desire. For this reason he wished all disorder corrected, and all offences removed; that every thing might be pleasant when he should come; see 1 Cor. iv. 21; comp. Note on chap. x. 2. ¶ *Lest* there be *debates.* I fear that there may be existing there debates, &c., which will require the interposition of the authority of an apostle. On the meaning of the word *debate,* see Note on Rom. i. 29. ¶ *Envyings;* see Note on 1 Cor. iii. 3. ¶ *Wraths.* Anger or animosities between contending factions, the usual effect of forming parties. ¶ *Strifes.* Between contending factions; see Note on 1 Cor. iii. 3. ¶ *Backbitings;* see Note on Rom. i. 30. ¶ *Whisperings;* see Note on Rom. i. 29. ¶ *Swellings.* Undue elation; being puffed up (see Note on chap viii. 1; 1 Cor. iv. 6, 18, 19; v. 2)—such as would be produced by vain self-confidence. ¶ *Tumults.* Disorder and confusion arising from this existence of parties. Paul, deeply sensible of the evil of all this, had endeavoured in this correspondence to suppress it, that all things might be pleasant when he should come among them.

21. And *lest, when I come again, my God will humble me,* &c. Lest I should be compelled to inflict punishment on those whom I suppose to have been converted under my ministry. I had rejoiced in them as true converts: I had counted them as among the fruit of my ministry. Now to be compelled to inflict punishment on them as having no religion would mortify me and humble me. The infliction of punishment on members of the church is a sort of punishment to him who inflicts it as well as to him who is punished. Members of the church should walk uprightly, lest they overwhelm the ministry in shame. ¶ *And that I shall bewail many,* &c. If they repented of their sin he could still rejoice in them. If they continued in their sin till he came, it would be to him a source of deep lamentation. It is evident from the word "many" here that the disorders had prevailed very extensively in the church at Corinth. The word rendered "have sinned already" means "who have sinned *before,*" and the idea is, that they were old offenders, and that they had not yet repented. ¶ *The uncleanness;* see Note, Rom. i. 24. ¶ *And fornication and lasciviousness,* &c.; see Notes on 1 Cor. v. 1; vi. 18. This was *the* sin to which they were particularly exposed in Corinth, as it was *the* sin for which that corrupt city was particularly distinguished. See the Introduction to the first epistle. Hence the frequent cautions in these epistles against it; and hence it is not to be wondered at that some of those who had become professing Christians had fallen into it. It may be added that it is still the sin to which converts from the corruptions and licentiousness of paganism are particularly exposed.

CHAPTER XIII.

This closing chapter of the epistle relates to the following subjects.

I. The assurance of Paul that he was about to come among them (ver. 1—4), and that he would certainly inflict punishment on all who deserved it, His enemies had reproached him

CHAPTER XIII.

THIS *is* the third *time* I am coming to you. In [a] the mouth of two or three witnesses shall every word be established.

a De.19.15; He.10.28,29

as being timid and pusillanimous; see Notes on chap. x. 1, 2, 10, 11. They had said that he was powerful to threaten, but afraid to execute. It is probable that they had become more bold in this from the fact that he had twice proposed to go there and had failed. In reply to all this, he now in conclusion solemnly assures them that he was coming, and that in *all* cases where an offence was proved by two or three witnesses, punishment would be inflicted; ver. 1. He assures them (ver. 2) that he would not spare; and that since they sought a proof that Christ had sent him, they should *witness* that proof in the punishment which he would inflict (ver. 3); for that Christ was now clothed with power and was able to execute punishment, though he had been crucified; ver. 4.

II. Paul calls on them solemnly to examine themselves and to see whether they had any true religion; ver. 5, 6. In the state of things which existed there; in the corruption which had abounded in the church, he solemnly commands them to institute a faithful inquiry, to know whether they had not been deceived; at the same time expressing the hope that it would appear as the result of their examination that they were not reprobates.

III. He earnestly prays to God that they might do no evil · that they might be found to be honest and pure, whatever might be thought of Paul himself or whatever might become of him; ver. 7. Their repentance would save Paul from exerting his miraculous power in their punishment, and might thus prevent the proof of his apostolic authority which they desired, and the consequence might be that they *might* esteem him to be a reprobate, for he could not exert his miraculous power except in the cause of truth; ver. 8. Still he was willing to be esteemed an impostor if *they* would do no evil

IV. He assures them that he earnestly wished their perfection, and that the design of his writing to them severe as he had appeared, was their edification; ver. 9, 10.

V. Then he bids them an affectionate and tender farewell, and closes with the usual salutations and benedictions; ver. 11—14.

1. *This* is *the third* time, &c.; see Note on chap. xii. 14. For an interesting view of this passage, see Paley's Horæ Paulinæ on this epistle, No. xi. It is evident that Paul had been to Corinth but once before this, but he had resolved to go before a second time, but had been disappointed. ¶ *In the mouth of two or three witnesses*, &c. This was what the law of Moses required; Deut. xx. 16; see Note on John viii. 17; comp. Mat. xviii. 16. But in regard to its application here, commentators are not agreed. Some suppose that Paul refers to his own epistles which he had sent to them as the two or three witnesses by which his promise to them would be made certain; that he had purposed it and promised it two or three times, and that as this was all that was required by the law, it would certainly be established. This is the opinion of Bloomfield, Rosenmüller, Grotius, Hammond, Locke, and some others. But, with all the respect due to such great names, it seems to me that this would be trifling and childish in the extreme. Lightfoot supposes that he refers to Stephanas, Fortunatus, and Achaicus, who would be witnesses to them of his purpose; see 1 Cor. xvi. 17. But the more probable opinion, it seems to me, is that of Doddridge, Macknight, and others, that he anticipated that there would be necessity for the administration of discipline there, but that he would feel himself under obligation in administering it to adhere to the reasonable maxim of the Jewish law. No one should be condemned or punished where there was not at least two

2 I told you before, and foretell you, as if I were present, the second time; and being absent now I write to them [a] which heretofore have sinned, and to all other, that, if I come again, I will not spare:

3 Since ye seek a proof of Christ speaking in me, which to you-ward is not weak, but is mighty [b] in you.

4 For though [c] he was crucified through weakness, yet he liveth

a chap.12.21. b 1 Co.9.2. c Ph.2.7,8; 1 Pe.3.18.

or three witnesses to prove the offence. But where there were, discipline would be administered according to the nature of the crime.

2. *I told you before.* That I would not spare offenders; that I would certainly punish them. He had intimated this before in the first Epis. chap. iv. 21; chap. v. ¶ *And foretell you.* Now apprise you of my fixed determination to punish every offender as he deserves. ¶ *As if I were present the second time.* The mention of the *second time* here proves that Paul had been with them but *once* before. He had formed the resolution to go to them, but had been disappointed. The time when he had been with them is recorded in Acts xviii. 1, seq. He now uses the same language to them which he says he would use if he were with them, as he had expected to be, the second time. See the remarks of Paley on this passage, referred to above. ¶ *And being absent;* see Note on 1 Cor. v. 3. ¶ *To them which have heretofore sinned.* To all the offenders in the church. They had supposed that he would not come to them (1 Cor. iv. 18), or that if he came he would not dare to inflict punishment, 2 Cor. 9—11. They had, therefore, given themselves greater liberty, and had pursued their own course, regardless of his authority and commands. ¶ *I will not spare.* I will punish them. They shall not escape.

3. *Since ye seek a proof of Christ speaking in me;* see the Notes on the previous chapters. They had called in question his apostolic authority; they had demanded the evidence of his divine commission. He says that he would now furnish such evidence by inflicting just punishment on all offenders, and they should have abundant proof that Christ spoke by him, or that he was inspired. ¶ *Which to you-ward is not weak.* Or *who,* that is, Christ, is not weak, &c. Christ has manifested his power abundantly towards you, that is, either by the miracles that had been wrought in his name; or by the diseases and calamities which they had suffered on account of their disorders and offences (see Note on 1 Cor. xi. 30; v.); or by the force and efficacy of his doctrine. The connection, it seems to me, requires that we should understand it of the calamities which had been inflicted by Christ on them for their sins, and which Paul says would be inflicted again if they did not repent. The idea is, that they had had ample demonstration of the power of Christ to inflict punishment, and they had reason to apprehend it again.

4. *For though he was crucified through weakness.* Various modes have been adopted of explaining the phrase "through weakness." The most probable explanation is that which refers it to the human nature which he had assumed (Phil. ii. 7, 8; 1 Pet. iii. 18), and to the *appearance* of weakness which he manifested. He did not choose to exert his power. He *appeared* to his enemies to be weak and feeble. This idea would be an *exact* illustration of the point before the apostle. He is illustrating his own conduct, and especially in the fact that he had not exerted his miraculous powers among them in the punishment of offenders; and he does it by the example of Christ, who though abundantly *able* to have exerted his power and to have rescued himself from his enemies, yet was willing to *appear* weak, and to be crucified. It is very clear, (1.) That the Lord Jesus *seemed* to his enemies to be weak and incapable of resistance. (2.) That he did not put forth his power to protect his life. He in

by the power of God. For we also are weak [1] in him, but we shall live with him by the power of God towards you.

5 Examine [a] yourselves, whether ye be in the faith; prove your own selves. Know ye not your own selves, how that Jesus Christ [b] is in you, except ye be reprobates? [c]

1 or, *with*.
a 1 Cor.11.28; 1 John 3.20,21.
b Ro.8.10; Ga.4.19.
c 1 Co.9.27; 2 Ti.3.8.

fact offered no resistance, *as if* he had no power. (3.) He had a human nature that was peculiarly sensitive, and sensible to suffering; and that was borne down and crushed under the weight of mighty woes; see my Notes on Isa. liii. 2, 3. From all these causes he *seemed* to be weak and feeble; and these appear to me to be the principal ideas in this expression. ¶ *Yet he liveth.* He is not now dead. Though he was crucified, yet he now lives again, and is now capable of exerting his great power He furnishes proof of his being alive, in the success which attends the gospel, and in the miracles which are wrought in his name and by his power. There is a *living* Redeemer in heaven; a Redeemer who is able to exert all the power which he ever exerted when on earth; a Redeemer, therefore, who is able to save the soul; to raise the dead; to punish all his foes. ¶ *By the power of God.* In raising him from the dead and placing him at his own right hand; see Eph. i. 19—21. Through the power of God he was brought from the tomb, and has a place assigned him at the head of the universe. ¶ *For we also are weak in him.* Marg. "*with* him." We his apostles, also, are weak in virtue of our connection with him. We are subject to infirmities and trials; we seem to have no power; we are exposed to contempt; and we appear to our enemies to be destitute of strength. Our enemies regard us as feeble; and they despise us. ¶ *But we shall live with him, &c.* That is, we shall show to you that we are *alive.* By the aid of the power of God we shall show that we are *not* as weak as our foes pretend; that we *are* invested with power; and that we are able to inflict the punishment which we threaten. This is one of the numerous instances in which Paul illustrated the case before him by a reference to the example and character of Christ. The idea is, that Christ did not exert *his* power, and appeared to be weak, and was put to death. So Paul says that he had not exerted *his* power, and seemed to be weak. But, says he, Christ lives, and is clothed with strength; and so we, though we appear to be weak, shall exert among you, or toward you, the power with which he has invested us, in inflicting punishment on our foes.

5. *Examine yourselves;* see Note on 1 Cor. xi. 28. The particular reason why Paul calls on them to examine themselves was, that there was occasion to fear that many of them had been deceived. Such had been the irregularities and disorders in the church at Corinth; so ignorant had many of them shown themselves of the nature of the Christian religion, that it was important, in the highest degree, for them to institute a strict and impartial examination to ascertain whether they had not been altogether deceived. This examination, however, is never unimportant or useless for Christians; and an exhortation to do it is *always* in place. So important are the interests at stake, and so liable are the best to deceive themselves, that all Christians should be often induced to examine the foundation of their hope of eternal salvation. ¶ *Whether ye be in the faith.* Whether you are true Christians. Whether you have any true faith in the gospel. Faith in Jesus Christ, and in the promises of God through him, is one of the distinguishing characteristics of a true Christian; and to ascertain whether we have any true faith, therefore, is to ascertain whether we are sincere Christians. For some reasons for such an examination, and some remarks on the mode of doing it; see Note

or. 1 Cor. xi. 28. ¶ *Prove your own selves.* The word here used (δοκιμάζετε) is stronger than that before used, and rendered "examine" (πειράζετε). This word, *prove*, refers to assaying or trying metals by the powerful action of heat; and the idea here is, that they should make the *most thorough* trial of their religion, to see whether it would stand the test; see Note on 1 Cor. iii. 13. The *proof* of their piety was to be arrived at by a faithful examination of their own hearts and lives; by a diligent comparison of their views and feelings with the word of God; and especially by making *trial* of it in life. The best way to *prove* our piety is to subject it to *actual trial* in the various duties and responsibilities of life. A man who wishes to *prove* an axe to see whether it is good or not, does not sit down and look at it, or read all the treatises which he can find on axe-making, and on the properties of iron and steel, valuable as such information would be; but he shoulders his axe and goes into the woods, and puts it to the trial there. If it cuts well; if it does not break; if it is not soon made dull, he understands the quality of his axe better than he could in any other way. So if a man wishes to know what his religion is worth, let him *try* it in the places where religion is of any value. Let him go into the world with it. Let him go and *try* to do good; to endure affliction in a proper manner; to combat the errors and follies of life; to admonish sinners of the error of their ways; and to urge forward the great work of the conversion of the world, and he will soon see there what his religion is worth—as easily as a man can test the qualities of an axe. Let him not merely sit down and think, and compare himself with the Bible and look at his own heart—valuable as this may be in many respects—but let him treat his religion as he would any thing else—let him subject it to actual experiment. That religion which will enable a man to imitate the example of Paul or Howard, or the great Master himself, *in doing good*, is genuine. That religion which will enable a man to endure persecution for the name of Jesus; to bear calamity without murmuring; to submit to a long series of disappointments and distresses for Christ's sake, is genuine. That religion which will prompt a man unceasingly to a life of prayer and self-denial; which will make him ever conscientious, industrious, and honest; which will enable him to warn sinners of the errors of their ways, and which will dispose him to seek the friendship of Christians, and the salvation of the world, is pure and genuine. *That will answer the purpose.* It is like the good axe with which a man can chop all day long, in which there is no flaw, and which does not get dull, *and which answers all the purposes of an axe.* Any other religion than this is worthless. ¶ *Know ye not your own selves.* That is, "Do you not know yourselves?" This does not mean, as some may suppose, that they might know *of* themselves, without the aid of others, what their character was; or that they might themselves ascertain it; but it means that they might know *themselves*, *i. e.* their character, principles, conduct. This *proves* that Christians *may know* their true character. If they are Christians, they may know it with as undoubted certainty as they may know their character on any other subject. Why should not a man be as able to determine whether he loves God as whether he loves a child, a parent, or a friend? What greater difficulty need there be in understanding the character on the subject of religion than on any other subject; and why should there be any more reason for doubt on this than on any other point of character? And yet it is remarkable, that while a child has no doubt that he loves a parent, or a husband a wife, or a friend a friend, almost all Christians are in very great doubt about their attachment to the Redeemer and to the great principles of religion. Such was not the case with the apostles and early Christians. "I KNOW," says Paul, "whom I have believed, and am persuaded that he is able to keep that which I have committed to him," &c.; 2 Tim. i. 12. "We KNOW,' says

6 But I trust that ye shall know that we are not reprobates.

7 Now I pray to God that ye do no evil; not that we should appear approved, but that ye

John, speaking in the name of the body of Christians, "that we have passed from death unto life;" 1 John iii. 14. "We KNOW that we are of the truth;" 19. "We KNOW that he abideth in us;" 24. "We KNOW that we dwell in him;" 1 John iv. 13; see also v. 2, 19, 20. So Job said, "I KNOW that my Redeemer liveth, and that he shall stand in the latter day upon the earth," &c.; Job xix. 25. Such is the current language of scripture. Where, in the Bible, do the sacred speakers and writers express doubts about their attachment to God and the Redeemer? Where is such language to be found as we hear from almost all professing Christians, expressing entire *uncertainty* about their condition; absolute doubt whether they love God or hate him; whether they are going to heaven or hell; whether they are influenced by good motives or bad; and even *making it a matter of merit* to be in such doubt, and thinking it wrong *not* to doubt? What would be thought of a husband that should make it a matter of merit to doubt whether he loved his wife; or of a child that should think it wrong *not* to doubt whether he loved his father or mother? Such attachments *ought* to be doubted—but they do not occur in the common relations of life. On the subject of religion men often act as they do on no other subject; and if it is right for one to be satisfied of the sincerity of his attachments to his best earthly friends, and to *speak* of such attachment without wavering or misgiving, it cannot be wrong to be satisfied with regard to our attachment to God, and to *speak* of that attachment, as the apostles did, in language of undoubted confidence. ¶ *How that Jesus Christ is in you.* To be in Christ, or for Christ to be in us, is a common mode in the scriptures of expressing the idea that we are Christians. It is language derived from the close union which subsists between the Redeemer and his people; see the phrase explained in the Note on Rom. viii. 10. ¶ *Except ye be reprobates;* see Note on Rom. i. 28. The word rendered "reprobates" (ἀδόκιμοι) means properly *not approved, rejected:* that which will not stand the trial. It is properly applicable to metals, as denoting that they will not bear the tests to which they are subjected, but are found to be base or adulterated. The sense here is, that they might know that they were Christians, unless their religion was base, false, adulterated; or such as would not bear the test. There is no allusion here to the sense which is sometimes given to the word *reprobate,* of being cast off or abandoned by God, or doomed by him to eternal ruin in accordance with an eternal purpose. Whatever may be the truth on that subject, nothing is taught in regard to it here. The simple idea is, that they might know that they were Christians, unless their religion was such as would not stand the test, or was worthless.

6. *But I trust,* &c. The sense of this verse is, "Whatever may be the result of your examination of yourselves, I trust (Gr. *I hope*) you will not find us false and to be rejected; that is, I trust you will find in me evidence that I am commissioned by the Lord Jesus to be his apostle." The idea is, that they would find when he was among them, that he was endowed with all the qualifications needful to confer a claim to the apostolic office.

7. *Now I pray to God that ye do no evil.* I earnestly desire that you may do right, and only right; and I beseech God that it may be so, whatever may be the result in regard to me, and whatever may be thought of my claims to the apostolic office. This is designed to mitigate the apparent severity of the sentiment in ver. 6. There he had said that they would find him fully endowed with the power of an apostle. They would see that he was able abundantly to punish

should do that which is honest, though we be as reprobates.

8 For [a] we can do nothing against the truth, but for the truth.

9 For we are glad, when we

a Pr.21.30.

the disobedient. They would have ample demonstration that he was endowed by Christ with all the powers appropriate to an apostle, and that all that he had claimed had been well-founded, all that he threatened would be executed. But this *seemed* to imply that he *desired* that there should be occasion for the exercise of that power of administering discipline; and he, therefore, in this verse, removes all suspicion that such was his wish, by saying solemnly, that he prayed to God that they might never do wrong; that they might never give him occasion for the exercise of his power in that way, though as a consequence he would be regarded as a reprobate, or as having no claims to the apostolic office. He would rather be regarded as an impostor; rather lie under the reproach of his enemies that he had no claims to the apostolic character, than that they, by doing wrong, should give him occasion to show that he was not a deceiver. ¶ *Not that we should appear approved.* My great object, and my main desire, is not to urge my claims to the apostolic office and clear up my own character; it is that you should lead honest lives, whatever may become of me and my reputation. ¶ *Though we be as reprobates.* I am willing to be regarded as rejected, disapproved, worthless, like base metal, provided you lead honest and holy lives. I prefer to be so esteemed, and to have you live as becomes Christians, than that you should dishonour your Christian profession, and thus afford me the opportunity of demonstrating, by inflicting punishment, that I am commissioned by the Lord Jesus to be an apostle. The sentiment is, that a minister of the gospel should desire that his people should walk worthy of their high calling, whatever may be the estimate in which he is held. He should never desire that they should do wrong—how *can* he do it?—in order that he may take occasion from their wrong-doing to vindicate, in any way, his own character, or to establish a reputation for skill in administering discipline or in governing a church. What a miserable condition it is—and as wicked as it is miserable—for a man to wish to take advantage of a state of disorder, or of the faults of others, in order to establish his own character, or to obtain reputation. Paul spurned and detested such a thought; yet it is to be feared it is sometimes done.

8. *For we.* That is, we the apostles. ¶ *Can do nothing against the truth,* &c. That is, we who are under the influence of the Spirit of God; who have been commissioned by him as apostles, can do nothing that shall be against the great system of truth which we are appointed to promulgate and defend. You need, therefore, apprehend no partial or severe discipline from us; no unjust construction of your conduct. Our aim is to promote the truth, and to do what is right; and we cannot, therefore, by any regard to our own reputation, or to any personal advantage, do what is wrong, or countenance, or desire what is wrong in others. We *must* wish that which is right to be done by others, whatever may be the effect on us—whether we are regarded as apostles or deceivers. I suppose, therefore, that this verse is designed to qualify and confirm the sentiment in the previous verse, that Paul meant to do only right; that he wished all others to do right; and that whatever might be the effect on his own reputation, or however he might be regarded, he *could not* go against the great system of gospel truth which he preached, or even *desire* that others should ever do wrong, though it might in any way be for his advantage. It was a *fixed principle* with him to act only in accordance with truth; to do what was right.

9. *For we are glad when we are weak,* &c. We rejoice in your wel-

are weak, and ye are strong: and
this also we wish, *even* your perfection.[a]
10 Therefore I write these things
being absent, lest being present I
should use sharpness, [b] according [c]
to the power which the Lord hath
given me to edification, and not to
destruction.
11 Finally, brethren, farewell.
Be perfect, [d] be of good comfort,
be [e] of one mind, live in peace;

a 1 Th.3.10; He.6.1. b Tit.1.13. c chap.10.8. d ver.9. e Ro.12.16; 15.5; Ep.4.3; Ph.2.2; 1 Pe.3.8.

fare, and are willing to submit to self-denial and to infirmity if it may promote your spiritual strength. In the connection in which this stands it seems to mean, "I am content to appear *weak,* provided you do no wrong; I am willing *not* to have occasion to exercise my power in punishing offenders, and had rather lie under the reproach of being actually weak, than to have occasion to exercise my power by punishing you for wrong-doing; and provided you are strong in the faith and in the hope of the gospel, I am very willing, nay, I rejoice that I am under this necessity of appearing weak." ¶ *And this also we wish.* I desire this in addition to your doing no evil. ¶ Even *your perfection.* The word here used (κατάρτισις) occurs nowhere else in the New Testament, though the verb from which it is derived (καταρτίζω) occurs often; Mat. iv. 21; xxi. 16; Mark i. 19; Luke vi. 40; Rom. ix. 22; 1 Cor. i. 10; 2 Cor. xiii. 11; Gal. vi. 1; 1 Thess. iii. 10, *et al.*; see Note on ver. 11. On the meaning of the word see Rom. ix. 22. The idea of *restoring,* putting in order, fitting, repairing, is involved in the word always, and hence the idea of making perfect; *i. e.* of *completely restoring* any thing to its proper place. Here it evidently means that Paul wished their *entire* reformation—so that there should be no occasion for exercising discipline. Doddridge renders it, "perfect good order." Macknight, "restoration." For this restoration of good order Paul had diligently laboured in these epistles; and this was an object near to his heart.

10. *Therefore I write these things,* &c. This is a kind of apology for what he had said, and especially for the apparently harsh language which he had felt himself constrained to use. He had reproved them; he had admonished them of their faults; he had threatened punishment, all of which was designed to prevent the necessity of severe measures when he should be with them. ¶ *Lest being present I should use sharpness.* In order that when I come I may not have occasion to employ severity; see the sentiment explained in the Note on chap. x. 2. ¶ *According to the power,* &c. That I may not use the power with which Christ has invested me for maintaining discipline in his church. The same form of expression is found in chap. x. 8; see Note on that place.

11. *Finally, brethren* (λοιπόν). The remainder; all that remains is for me to bid you an affectionate farewell. The word here rendered "farewell" (χαίρετε), means usually to joy and rejoice, or to be glad; Luke i. 14; John xvi. 20, 22; and it is often used in the sense of "joy to you," "hail!" as a salutation; Mat. xxvi. 49; xxvii. 29. It is also used as a salutation at the beginning of an epistle, in the sense of *greeting;* Acts xv. 23; xxiii. 26; James i. 1. It is generally agreed, however, that it is here to be understood in the sense of *farewell,* as a parting salutation, though it may be admitted that there is included in the word an expression of a wish for their happiness. This was among the last words which Cyrus, when dying, addressed to his friends. ¶ *Be perfect.* See this word explained in the Notes on ver. 9, and Rom. ix. 22 It was a wish that every disorder might be removed; that all that was *out of joint* might be restored; that every thing might be in its proper place; and that they might be just what they ought to be. A command to be perfect, however, does not prove that it has ever in fact been obeyed: and an earnest wish on the part of an apostle that

and the God of love and peace
shall be with you.
12 Greet [a] one another with an
holy kiss.
13 All the saints salute you.
14 The [b] grace of the Lord
Jesus Christ, and the love of
God, and the [c] communion of the

a Ro.16.16. b Ro.16.24. c Ph.2.1.

---

others *might* be perfect, does not demonstrate that they were; and this passage should not be adduced to prove that any *have* been free from sin. It may be adduced, however, to prove that an obligation rests on Christians to be perfect, and that there is no natural obstacle to their becoming such, since God never can command us to do an impossibility. Whether any one, but the Lord Jesus, *has been* perfect, however, is a question on which different denominations of Christians have been greatly divided. It is incumbent on the advocates of the doctrine of sinless perfection to produce *some one instance* of a perfectly sinless character. This has not *yet* been done. ¶ *Be of good comfort.* Be consoled by the promises and supports of the gospel. Take comfort from the hopes which the gospel imparts. Or the word may possibly have a reciprocal sense, and mean, *comfort one another;* see Schleusner. Rosenmüller renders it, "receive admonition from all with a grateful mind, that you may come to greater perfection." It is, at any rate, the expression of an earnest wish on the part of the apostle, that they might be happy. ¶ *Be of one mind.* They had been greatly distracted, and divided into different parties and factions. At the close of the epistle he exhorts them as he had repeatedly done before, to lay aside these strifes, and to be united, and manifest the same spirit; see Note on Rom. xii. 16; xv. 5; see Note also on 1 Cor. i. 10. The sense is, that Paul desired that dissensions should cease, and that they should be united in opinion and feeling as Christian brethren. ¶ *Live in peace.* With each other. Let contentions and strifes cease. To promote the restoration of peace had been the main design of these epistles. ¶ *And the God of love and peace.* The God who is all love, and who is the author of all peace. What a glorious appellation is this! There can be no more beautiful expression, and it is as true as it is beautiful, that God is a God of *love* and of *peace.* He is infinitely benevolent; he delights in exhibiting his love; and he delights in the love which his people evince for each other. At the same time he is the author of peace, and he delights in peace among men. When Christians love each other they have reason to expect that the God of love will be with them; when they live in peace, they may expect the God of peace will take up his abode with them. In contention and strife we have no reason to expect his presence; and it is only when we are willing to lay aside all animosity that we may expect the God of peace will fix his abode with us.

12. *Greet.* Salute; see Note, Rom. xvi. 3. ¶ *With an holy kiss.* Note, Rom. xvi. 16.

13. *All the saints salute you.* That is, all who were with Paul, or in the place where he was. The epistle was written from Macedonia, probably from Philippi. See Intro. § 3.

14. *The grace of our Lord Jesus Christ;* see Note, Rom xvi. 20. This verse contains what is usually called *the apostolic benediction;* the form which has been so long, and which is almost so universally used, in dismissing religious assemblies. It is properly *a prayer,* and it is evident that the Optative εἴη, "*May* the grace," &c., is to be supplied. It is the expression of a desire that the favours here referred to may descend on all for whom they are thus invoked. ¶ *And the love of God.* May the love of God *towards* you be manifest. This must refer peculiarly to the *Father,* as the Son and the Holy Spirit are mentioned in the other members of the sentence. The "love of God" here referred to is the manifestation of his goodness and favour in the pardon of sin, in the communi-

Holy Ghost, *be* with you all. Amen.

The second *epistle* to the Corinthians was written from Philippi, *a city* of Macedonia, by Titus and Lucas.

---

cation of his grace, in the comforts and consolations which he imparts to his people, in all that constitutes an expression of love. The love of God brings salvation; imparts comfort; pardons sin; sanctifies the soul; fills the heart with joy and peace; and Paul here prays that all the blessings which are the fruit of that love may be with them. ¶ *And the communion of the Holy Ghost;* comp. Note, 1 Cor. x. 16. The word *communion* (κοινωνία) means properly participation, fellowship, or having any thing *in common;* Acts ii. 42; Rom. xv. 26; 1 Cor. i. 9; x. 16; 2 Cor. vi. 14; viii. 4; ix. 13; Gal. ii. 9; Eph. iii. 9; 1 John i. 3. This is also a wish or prayer of the apostle Paul; and the desire is either that they might partake of the views and feelings of the Holy Ghost; that is, that they might have fellowship *with him;* or that they might all in common partake of the gifts and graces which the Spirit of God imparts. He gives love, joy, peace, long-suffering, gentleness, goodness, faith (Gal. v. 22), as well as miraculous endowments; and Paul prays that these things might be imparted freely to *all* the church *in common,* that all might participate in them; all might share them. ¶ *Amen.* This word is wanting, says Clarke, in almost every MS. of any authority. It was however early affixed to the epistle.

In regard to this closing verse of the epistle, we may make the following remarks. (1.) It is *a prayer;* and if it is a prayer addressed to God, it is no less so to the Lord Jesus and to the Holy Spirit. If so, it is right to offer worship to the Lord Jesus and to the Holy Spirit. (2.) There is a distinction in the divine nature; or there is the existence of what is usually termed three persons in the Godhead. If not, why are they mentioned in this manner? If the Lord Jesus is not divine and equal with the Father, why is he mentioned in this connection? How strange it would be for Paul, an inspired man, to pray in the same breath, "the grace of a man or an angel" and "the love of God" be with you! And if the "Holy Spirit" be merely an *influence* of God or an *attribute* of God, how strange to pray that the "love of God" and the participation or fellowship of an "influence of God," or an "attribute of God" might be with them! (3.) The Holy Spirit is *a person,* or has a distinct personality. He is not an attribute of God, nor a mere divine influence. How could prayer be addressed to *an attribute,* or *an influence?* But here, nothing can be plainer than that there were favours which the Holy Ghost, as an intelligent and conscious agent, was expected to bestow. And nothing can be plainer than that they were favours in some sense *distinct* from those which were conferred by the Lord Jesus, and by the Father. Here is a *distinction* of some kind *as real* as that between the Lord Jesus and the Father; here are favours expected from him distinct from those conferred by the Father and the Son; and there is, therefore, here all the proof that there can be, that there is in some respects a distinction between the persons here referred to, and that the Holy Spirit is an intelligent, conscious agent. (4.) The Lord Jesus is not *inferior* to the Father, that is, he has an equality with God. If he were *not* equal, how could he be mentioned, as he here is, as bestowing favours like God, and especially why is he mentioned *first?* Would Paul, in invoking blessings, mention the name of a mere man or an angel before that of the eternal God? (5.) The passage, therefore, furnishes a proof of the doctrine of the Trinity that has not yet been answered, and, it is believed, cannot be. On the supposition that there are three persons in the adorable Trinity, united in essence and yet distinct in some respects, all is plain and clear. But on the supposition that the Lord

Jesus is a mere man, an angel, or an archangel, and that the Holy Spirit is an attribute, or an influence from God, how unintelligible, confused, strange does all become! That Paul, in the solemn close of the epistle, should at the same time invoke blessings from a mere creature, and from God, and from an *attribute*, surpasses belief. But that he should invoke blessings from him who was the equal with the Father, and from the Father himself, and from the Sacred Spirit sustaining the same rank, and in like manner imparting important blessings, is in accordance with all that we should expect, and makes all harmonious and appropriate. (6.) Nothing could be a more proper close of the epistle; nothing is a more appropriate close of public worship, than such an invocation. It is a prayer to the ever-blessed God, that all the rich influences which he gives as Father, Son, and Holy Ghost, may be imparted; that all the benefits which God confers in the interesting relations in which he makes himself known to us may descend and bless us. What more appropriate prayer can be offered at the close of public worship? How seriously should it be pronounced, as a congregration is about to separate, perhaps to come together no more! With what solemnity should all join in it, and how devoutly should all pray, as they thus separate, that these rich and inestimable blessings may rest upon them! With hearts uplifted to God it should be pronounced and heard; and every worshipper should leave the sanctuary deeply feeling that what he most needs as he leaves the place of public worship; as he travels on the journey of life; as he engages in its duties or meets its trials; as he looks at the grave and eternity, is the grace of the Lord Jesus Christ, the love of God, and the blessings which the Holy Spirit imparts in renewing, and sanctifying, and comforting his people. What more appropriate prayer than this for the writer and reader of these Notes! May that blessing rest alike upon us, though we may be strangers in the flesh, and may those divine and heavenly influences guide us alike to the same everlasting kingdom of glory

In regard to the subscription at the end of this epistle, it may be observed, that it is wanting in a great part of the most ancient MSS., and is of no authority whatever; see Notes at the end of the epistle to the Romans, and 1 Corinthians. In this case, however, this subscription is in the main correct, as there is evidence that it was written from Macedonia, and not improbably from Philippi. See the Introduction to the epistle.

THE EPISTLE OF PAUL THE APOSTLE

TO THE

GALATIANS.

INTRODUCTION.

§ 1. *The Situation of Galatia, and the Character of the People.*

GALATIA was a province of Asia Minor, having Pontus on the east, Bithynia and Paphlagonia north, Cappadocia and Phrygia south, and Phrygia west. See the map prefixed to the Acts of the Apostles. In Tanner's Classical Atlas, however, it extends on the north to the Euxine or Black sea. It was probably about two hundred miles in its greatest extent from east to west, and varied in breadth from twelve to an hundred and fifty miles. It was one of the largest provinces of Asia Minor, and covered an extent of country almost as large as the State of New Jersey. It is probable, however, that the boundaries of Galatia varied at different times as circumstances dictated. It had no *natural* boundary, except on the north; and of course the limits may have been varied by conquests, or by the will of the Roman emperor, when it was erected into a province.

The name *Galatia* is derived from the word *Gaul*, and was given to it because it had been conquered by the Gauls, who, having subdued the country, settled in it.—*Pausanias*, Attic. cap. iv. These were mixed with various Grecian families, and the country was also called *Gallogræcia*.—*Justin*, lib. xxiv. 4; xxv. 2; xxvii. 3. This invasion of Asia Minor was made, according to Justin (lib. xxv. cap. 2), about the four hundred and seventy-ninth year after the founding of Rome, and, of course, about 272 years before Christ. They invaded Macedonia and Greece; and subsequently invaded Asia Minor, and became an object of terror to all that region. This expedition issued from Gaul, passed over the Rhine, along the Danube, through Noricum, Pannonia, and Mœsia, and at its entrance into Germany, carried along with it many of the Tectosages. On their arrival in Thrace, Lutarius took them with him, crossed the Bosphorus, and effected the conquest of Asia Minor.—Liv. lib xxxviii. c. 16. Such was their number, that Justin says, "they filled all Asia (*i. e.* all Asia Minor) like swarms of bees. Finally, they became so numerous that no kings of the east could engage in war without an army of Gauls; neither when driven from their kingdom could they flee to any other than to the Gauls. Such was the terror of the name of Gauls, and such the invincible felicity of their arms—*et armorum invicta felicitas erat*—that they supposed that in no other way could their own majesty be protected, or being lost, could be recovered, without the aid of Gallic courage. Their being called in by the king of Bithynia for aid, when they had gained the victory, they divided the kingdom with him, and called that region *Gallogræcia.*"—Justin, xxv. 2. Under the reign of Augustus Cesar, about 26 years before the birth of Christ, this region was reduced into the form of a Roman colony, and was governed by a *proprætor*, appointed by the emperor.

Their original Gaulish language they retained so late as the fifth century, as appears from the testimony of Jerome, who says that their dialect was nearly the same as that of the Treviri.—Tom. iv. p. 256. ed. Benedict. At the same time, they also spoke the Greek language in common with all the inhabitants of Lesser Asia, and therefore the epistle to them was written in Greek, and was intelligible to them as well as to others.

The Galatians, like the inhabitants of the surrounding country, were heathens, and their religion was of a gross and debasing kind. They are said to have worshipped "the mother of the gods," under the name of *Agdistis.* Callimachus, in his hymns, calls them "a foolish people." And Hillary, himself a Gaul, calls them *Gallos indociles*—expressions which, says Calmet, may well excuse Paul's addressing them as "foolish," chap. iii. 1. There were few cities to be found among them, with the exception of Ancyra, Tavium, and Pessinus, which carried on some trade.

The possessors of Galatia were of three different nations or tribes of Gauls; the Tolistobogi, the Trocmi, and the Tectosagi. There are imperial medals extant, on which these names are found. It is of some importance to bear in mind these distinctions. It is possible that while Peter was making converts in one part of Galatia, the apostle Paul was in another; and that some, claiming authority as from Peter, propagated opinions not conformable to the views of Paul, to correct and expose which was one design of this epistle.—*Calmet.*

The Gauls are mentioned by ancient historians as a tall and valiant people. They went nearly naked. Their arms were only a sword and buckler. The impetuosity of their attack, it is said, was irresistible, and hence they became so formidable, and were usually so victorious.

It is not possible to ascertain the number of the inhabitants of Galatia, at the time when the gospel was preached there, or when this epistle was written. In 2 Macc. viii. 20, it is said that Judas Maccabeus, exhorting his followers to fight manfully against the Syrians, referred to several instances of divine interposition to encourage them; and among others, "he told them of the battle which they had in Babylon with the *Galatians;* how they came but eight thousand in all to the business, with four thousand Macedonians; and that the Macedonians being perplexed, the eight thousand destroyed an hundred and twenty thousand, because of the help which they had from heaven, and so received a great booty." But it is not certain that this refers to those who dwelt in Galatia. It may refer to *Gauls* who at that time had overrun Asia Minor; the Greek word here used, (Γαλάτας) being taken equally for either. It is evident, however, that there was a large population that went under this general name; and it is probable that Galatia was thickly settled at the time when the gospel was preached there. It was in the central part of Asia Minor, then one of the most densely populated parts of the world, and was a region singularly fertile.—Strabo, lib. xii. p. 567, 568, ed. Casaub. Many persons, also, were attracted there for the sake of commerce. That there were many Jews also, in all the provinces of Asia Minor, is apparent not only from the Acts of the Apostles, but is expressly declared by Josephus, Ant. xvi. 6.

§ 2. *The time when the Gospel was preached in Galatia.*

There is no certain information as to the time when the gospel was first preached in Galatia, or the persons by whom it was done. There is mention, however, of Paul's having preached there several times, and several circumstances lead us to suppose that those churches were established by him, or that he was the first to carry the gospel to them, or that he and Barnabas together preached the gospel there on the *mission* on which they were sent from Antioch, Acts xiii. 2. seq. In Acts xvi. 5, 6, it is expressly said that they went "throughout Phrygia and the region of Galatia." This journey was for the purpose of confirming the churches, and was undertaken at the suggestion of Paul (Acts xv. 36), with the design of visiting their brethren in every city where they had preached the word of the Lord. It is true, that in the account of the mission of Paul and Barnabas (Acts xiv.), it is not expressly said that they went into Galatia; but it is said (Acts xiv. 5, 6), that when they were in Iconium, an assault was made on them, or a purpose formed to stone them, and that, being apprized of it, they fled unto Lystra and Derbe, cities of Lycaonia, "and unto the region that lieth round about." Pliny, lib. v. c. 27, says, that a part of Lycaonia bordered on Galatia, and contained fourteen cities, of which Iconium was the most celebrated. Phrygia also was contiguous to Galatia, and to Lycaonia, and these circumstances render it probable that when Paul proposed to Barnabas to visit again the churches where they had preached, Galatia was included. and that they had been there before this visit referred to in Acts xvi. 6.

It may be, also, that Paul refers to himself in the epistle (chap. i. 6), where he says, "I marvel that ye are so soon removed from him that CALLED YOU into the grace of Christ unto another gospel;" and if so, then it is plain that he preached to them first, and founded the churches there. The same thing may be evinced also from the expression in chap. iv. 15, where he says, "I bear you record, that if it had been possible, ye would have plucked out your own eyes, and have given them to me;" an expression which leads us to suppose that they had formed for him a peculiar attachment, because he had first preached the gospel to them, and that there had existed all the ardour of attachment implied in their *first love.* It is quite evident, therefore, I think, that the gospel was preached among the Galatians first by Paul, either alone or in company with some other one of the apostles. It is possible, however, as has been intimated above, that Peter also may have preached in one part of Galatia at the time that Paul was preaching in other parts. It is a circumstance also of some importance on this point, that Paul speaks in this epistle in a tone of authority, and with a severity of reproof which he would hardly have used unless he had at first preached there, and had a right to be regarded as the founder of the church, and to address it as its father. In this respect the tone here is quite different, as Mr. Locke has remarked, from what is observable in the epistle to the Romans. Paul had not been at Rome when he addressed the church there by letter, and his language differs materially from that which occurs in the epistles to the Corinthians and Galatians. It was to them the very respectful and mild language of a stranger; here it is respectful, but it is the authoritative language of a father having a right to reprove.

§ 3. *The date of this Epistle.*

Many have supposed that this was the first epistle which Paul wrote. Tertullian maintained this (see Lardner, vol. vi. p. 7. ed. Lond. 1829), and Epiphanius also. Theodoret and others suppose it was written at Rome, and was consequently written near the close of the life of Paul, and was one of his last epistles. Lightfoot supposes also that it was written from Rome, and that it was among the first which Paul wrote there. Chrysostom says that this epistle was written before that to the Romans. Lewis Capellus, Witsius, and Wall suppose that it was written from Ephesus after the apostle had been a second time in Galatia. This also was the opinion of Pearson, who places it in the year 57, after the first epistle to the Corinthians, and before

Paul left Ephesus. Grotius thought it difficult to assign the date of the epistle, but conjectures that it was written about the same time as that to the Romans. Mill supposes that it was not written until after that to the Romans, probably at Troas, or some other place in Asia, as Paul was going to Jerusalem. He dates the epistle in the year 58. Dr. Benson supposes that it was written at Corinth, when the apostle was first there, and made a long stay of a year and six months. While there, he supposes that Paul received tidings of the instability of the converts in Galatia, and wrote this epistle and sent it by one of his assistants. See these opinions examined in Lardner as quoted above. Lardner himself supposes that it was written from Corinth about the year 52, or the beginning of the year 53. Macknight supposes it was written from Antioch, after the council at Jerusalem, and before Paul and Silas undertook the journey in which they delivered to the churches the decrees which were ordained at Jerusalem; Acts xvi. 4. Hug, in his Introduction, supposes that it was written at Ephesus in the year 57, and after the I. and II. Thess., and the epistle to Titus had been written. Mr. Locke supposes that Paul established churches in Galatia, in the year 51; and that this epistle was written between that time and the year 57. These opinions are mostly mere conjecture; and amidst such a variety of sentiment, it is evidently impossible to determine exactly at what time it was written. The only mark of time in the epistle itself occurs in chap. i. 6, where the apostle says, "I marvel that ye are *so soon* (οὕτω ταχέως) removed from him that called you," &c.; where the words "so soon" would lead us to suppose that it was at no distant period after he had been among them. Still it might have been several years. The date assigned to it in the Polyglott Bible (Bagster's) is the year 58.

The exact date of the epistle is of very little importance. In regard to the time when it was written the only arguments which seem to me to be of much weight, are those advanced by Paley in his Horæ Paulinæ. "It will hardly be doubted," says he, "but that it was written whilst the dispute concerning the circumcision of Gentile converts was fresh in men's minds; for even supposing it to have been a forgery, the only credible motive that can be assigned for the forgery, was to bring the name and authority of the apostle into this controversy. No design can be so insipid, or so unlikely to enter into the thoughts of any man, as to produce an epistle written earnestly and pointedly on one side of a controversy, when the controversy itself was dead, and the question no longer interesting to any class of readers whatever. Now the controversy concerning the circumcision of Gentiles was of such a nature, that, if it arose at all, it must have arisen in the beginning of Christianity." Paley then goes on to show that it was natural that the Jews, and converts from the Jews, should start this question, and agitate it; and that this was much more likely to be insisted on while the temple was standing, and they continued as a nation, and sacrifices were offered, than after their city and temple were destroyed. It is therefore clear that the controversy must have been started, and the epistle written *before* the invasion of Judea, by Titus, and the destruction of Jerusalem. The *internal* evidence leads to this conclusion. On the whole, it is probable that the epistle was written somewhere about the year 53, or between that and 57; and was evidently designed to settle an important controversy in the churches of Galatia. The *place* where it was written, must be, I think, wholly a matter of conjecture. The subscription at the end that it was written from Rome is of no authority whatever; and there are no internal circumstances, which, so far as I can see, throw any light on the subject.

§ 4. *The design of the Epistle.*

It is easy to discern from the epistle itself that the following circumstances existed in the churches of Galatia, and that it was written with reference to them.

(1.) That they had been at first devotedly attached to the apostle Paul, and had received his commands and instructions with implicit confidence when he was among them; chap. iv. 14, 15; comp. chap. i. 6.

(2.) That they had been perverted from the doctrine which he taught them soon after he had left them; chap. i. 6.

(3.) That this had been done by persons who were of Jewish origin, and who insisted on the observance of the rites of the Jewish religion.

(4.) That they claimed to have come directly from Jerusalem, and to have derived their views of religion and their authority from the apostles there.

(5.) That they taught that the apostle Paul was inferior to the apostles there; that he had been called more recently into the apostolic office; that the apostles at Jerusalem must be regarded as the source of authority in the Christian church; and that, therefore, the teaching of Paul should yield to that which was derived directly from Jerusalem.

(6.) That the laws of Moses were binding, and were necessary in order to justification. That the rite of circumcision especially was of binding obligation; and it is probable (chap. vi. 12), that they had prevailed on many of the Galatians to be circumcised, and certain that they had induced them to observe the Jewish festivals; chap. iv. 10.

(7.) It would seem, also, that they urged that Paul himself had changed his views since he had been among the Galatians, and now maintained the necessity of circumcision; chap. v. 11. Perhaps they alleged this, from the undoubted fact that Paul, when at Jerusalem (Acts xxi. 26), had complied with some of the customs of the Jewish ritual.

(8.) That they urged that all the promises of God were made to Abraham, and that whoever would partake of those promises, must be circumcised as Abraham was. This Paul answers, chap. iii. 7; iv. 7.

(9.) That in consequence of the promulgation of these views, great dissensions had arisen in the church, and strifes of an unhappy nature existed, greatly contrary to the spirit which should be manifested by those who bore the Christian name.

From this description of the state of things in the churches of Galatia, the design of the epistle is apparent, and the scope of the argument will be easily seen. Of this state of things the apostle had been undoubtedly apprised, but whether by letters, or by messengers from the churches there, is not declared. It is not improbable, that some of his friends in the churches there had informed him of it, and he immediately set about a remedy to the evils existing there.

I. The first object, therefore, was to show that he had received his commission as an apostle, *directly from God*. He had not received it at all from man; he had not even been instructed by the other apostles; he had not acknowledged their superiority; he had not even consulted them. He did not acknowledge, therefore, that the apostles at Jerusalem possessed any superior rank or authority. His commission, though he had not seen the Lord Jesus before he was crucified, he had, nevertheless, derived immediately from him. The doctrine, therefore, which he had taught them, that the Mosaic laws were not binding, and that there was no necessity of being circumcised, was a doctrine which had been derived directly from God. In proof of this, he goes into an extended statement (chap. i.), of the manner in which he had been called, and of the fact, that he had not consulted with the apostles at Jerusalem, or confessed his inferiority to them; of the fact that when they had become acquainted with the manner in which he preached, they approved his course (chap. i. 24; ii. 1—10); and of the fact that on one occasion, he had actually been constrained to differ from Peter, the oldest of the apostles, on a point in which he was manifestly wrong, and on one of the very points then under consideration.

II. The second great object, therefore, was to show the real nature and design of the law of Moses, and to prove that the peculiar rites of the Mosaic ritual, and especially the rite of circumcision, were not necessary to justification and salvation ; and that they who observed that rite, did in fact renounce the Scripture method of justification ; make the sacrifice of Christ of no value, and make slaves of themselves. This leads him into a consideration of the true nature of the doctrine of justification, and of the way of salvation by a Redeemer.

This point he shows in the following way,

(1.) By showing that those who lived before Christ, and especially Abraham, were in fact justified, not by obedience to the ritual law of Moses, but by faith in the promises of God ; chap. iii. 1—18.

(2.) By showing that the design of the Mosaic ritual was only temporary, and that it was intended to lead to Christ; chap. iii. 19—29 ; iv. 1—8.

(3.) In view of this, he reproves the Galatians for having so readily fallen into the observance of these customs ; chap. iv. 9—21.

(4.) This view of the design of the Mosaic law, and of its tendency, he illustrates by an allegory drawn from the case of Hagar ; chap. iv. 21—31.

This whole discourse is succeeded by an affectionate exhortation to the Galatians, to avoid the evils which had been engendered ; reproving them for the strifes existing in consequence of the attempt to introduce the Mosaic rites, and earnestly entreating them to stand firm in the liberty which Christ had vouchsafed to them from the servitude of the Mosaic institutions, chap. v. vi.

The design of the whole epistle, therefore, is to state and defend the true doctrine of justification, and to show that it did not depend on the observance of the laws of Moses. In the general purpose, therefore, it accords with the design of the epistle to the Romans. In one respect, however, it differs from the design of that epistle. That was written, to show that man could not be justified by *any works of the law*, or by conformity to *any* law, moral or ceremonial ; the object of this is, to show that justification cannot be obtained by *conformity to the ritual* or *ceremonial law;* or that the observance of the ceremonial law is not necessary to salvation. In this respect, therefore, this epistle is of less general interest than that to the Romans. It is also, in some respects, more difficult. The argument, if I may so express myself, is more *Jewish.* It is more in the Jewish manner; is designed to meet a Jew in his own way, and is, therefore, somewhat more difficult for all to follow. Still it contains great and vital statements on the doctrines of salvation, and, as such, demands the profound and careful attention of all who desire to be saved, and who would know the way of acceptance with God

EPISTLE TO THE GALATIANS.

CHAPTER I.

PAUL, an apostle, (not of men, neither by man, but *a* by Jesus Christ, and God the Father, who *b* raised him from the dead ;)

a Ac.9.6,15. *b* Ac.2.24.

CHAPTER I.

ANALYSIS.

THE main design of Paul in this chapter, is to show that he had received his call to the apostleship, not from man, but from God. It had been alleged (see the Introduction above) that the apostles at Jerusalem possessed the most elevated rank, and the highest authority in the Christian church ; that they were to be regarded as the fountains and the judges of the truth ; that Paul was inferior to them as an apostle ; and that they who inculcated the necessity of circumcision, and the observance of the rites of Moses, were sustained by the authority and the examples of the apostles at Jerusalem.

To meet this statement was the design of this first chapter. Paul's grand object was to show that he was not appointed by men ; that he had not been commissioned by men ; that he had not derived his instructions from men ; that he had not even consulted with them ; but that he had been commissioned and taught expressly by Jesus Christ, and that when the apostles at Jerusalem had become acquainted with him, and with his views and plans of labour, long after he had begun to preach, they had fully concurred with him. This argument comprises the following parts :

I. The solemn declaration that he was not commissioned by men, and that he was not, in any sense, an apostle of man, together with the general salutation to the churches in Galatia ; ver. 1—5..

II. The expression of his astonishment that the Galatians had so soon forsaken his instruction, and embraced another gospel ; and a solemn declaration that whoever preached another gospel was to be held accursed ; ver. 6—10. Twice he anathematizes those who attempt to declare any other way of justification than that which consisted in faith in Christ, and says that it was no gospel at all. It was to be held as a great and fixed principle, that there was but one way of salvation ; and no matter who attempted to preach any other, he was to be held accursed.

III. To show, therefore, that *he* was not appointed by men, and that he had not received his instructions from men, but that he had preached the truth directly revealed to him by God, and that which was, therefore, immutable and eternal, he goes into a statement of the manner in which he was called into the ministry, and made acquainted with the gospel ; ver. 11—24.

(*a*) He affirms, that he was not taught it by man, but by the express revelation of Jesus Christ ; ver. 11, 12.

(*b*) He refers to his former well-known life, and his zeal in the Jewish religion ; showing how much he had been formerly opposed to the gospel ; ver. 13, 14.

(*c*) He says that he had been separated, by the divine purpose, from his mother's womb, to be a preacher of the gospel, and that when he was called to the ministry, he had no conference with any human being, as to what he was to preach ; he did not go up to Jerusalem to consult with those who were older apostles, but he retired far from them into Arabia, **and** thence again returned to Damascus; ver. 15—17.

(*d*) After three years, he says, he did indeed go to Jerusalem; but he remained there but fifteen days, and saw none of the apostles but Peter and James; ver. 18, 19. His views of the gospel were formed before that; and that he did not submit implicitly to Peter, and learn of him, he shows in ch. ii., where he says, he "withstood him to the face."

(*e*) After that, he says, he departed into the regions of Cilicia, in Asia Minor, and had no opportunity of conference with the churches which were in Judea. Yet they heard that he who had been formerly a persecutor, had become a preacher, and they glorified God for it; ver. 20—24. Of course, he had had no opportunity of deriving his views of religion from them; he had been in no sense dependent on them; but so far as they were acquainted with his views, they concurred in them. The sum of the argument, therefore, in this chapter is, that when Paul went into Cilicia and the adjacent regions, he had never seen but two of the apostles, and that but for a short time; he had never seen the apostles together; and he had never received any instructions from them. His views of the gospel, which he had imparted to the Galatians, he had derived directly from God.

1. *Paul an apostle;* see Note, Rom. i. 1. This is the usual form in which he commences his epistles; and it was of special importance to commence this epistle in this manner, because it was one design to vindicate his apostleship, or to show that he had received his commission directly from the Lord Jesus. ¶ *Not of men.* "*Not from* (ἀπ') *men.*" That is, he was not *from* any body of men, or commissioned by men. The word apostle means *sent,* and Paul means to say, that he was not *sent* to execute any purpose of men, or commissioned by them. His was a higher calling; a calling of God, and he had been sent directly *by* him. Of course, he means to exclude here all classes of men as having had any thing to do in sending him forth; and, especially, he means to affirm, that he had not been sent out by the body of apostles at Jerusalem. This, it will be remembered (see the Introduction), was one of the charges of those who had perverted the Galatians from the faith which Paul had preached to them. ¶ *Neither by man.* "Neither *by* or *through* (δι') the instrumentality of any man." Here he designs to exclude all men from having had any agency in his appointment to the apostolic office. He was neither sent out *from* any body of men to execute their purposes; nor did he receive his commission, authority, or ordination through the medium of any man. A minister of the gospel now receives his call from God, but he is ordained or set apart to his office by man. Matthias, the apostle chosen in the place of Judas (Acts i. 26), received his call from God, but it was by the vote of the body of the apostles. Timothy was also called of God, but he was appointed to his office by the laying on the hands of the presbytery; 1 Tim. iv. 14. But Paul here says, that *he* received no such commission as that from the apostles. They were not the means or the medium of ordaining him to his work. He had, indeed, together with Barnabas, been set apart at Antioch, by the brethren there (Acts xiii. 1—3), for a *special mission* in Asia Minor; but this was not an appointment to the apostleship. He had been restored to sight after the miraculous blindness produced by seeing the Lord Jesus on the way to Damascus, by the laying on of the hands of Ananias, and had received important instruction from him (Acts ix. 17), but his commission as an apostle had been received directly from the Lord Jesus, without any intervening medium, or any form of human authority, Acts ix. 15; xxii. 17—21; 1 Cor. ix. 1. ¶ *But by Jesus Christ.* That is, directly by Christ. He had been called by him, and commissioned by him, and sent by him, to engage in the work of the gospel. ¶ *And God the Father.* These words were omitted by Marcion, because, says Jerome he

2 And all the brethren which are with me, unto the churches of Galatia: [a]

3 Grace [b] *be* to you, and peace, from God the Father, and *from* our Lord Jesus Christ,

4 Who gave [c] himself for our sins, that he might deliver us [d] from this present evil [e] world, according [f] to the will of God and our Father:

a Ac.16.6; 18.23. *b* Ro.1.7,&c. *c* John 10.17,18; Tit.2.14. *d* John 17.14. *e* 1 John 2.16. *f* Ro.8.27.

held that Christ raised himself from the dead. But there is no authority for omitting them. The sense is, that he had the highest possible authority for the office of an apostle; he had been called to it by God himself, who had raised up the Redeemer. It is remarkable here, that Paul associates Jesus Christ and God the Father, as having called and commissioned him. We may ask here, of one who should deny the divinity of Christ, how Paul could mention him as being equal with God in the work of commissioning him? We may further ask, how could he say that he had not received his call to this office from a man, if Jesus Christ was a mere man? That he *was* called by Christ, he expressly says, and strenuously maintains as a point of great importance. And yet, the very point and drift of his argument is, to show that he was not called by *man*. How could this be if Christ was a mere man? ¶ *Who raised him from the dead;* see Notes on Acts ii. 24, 32. It is not quite clear, why Paul introduces this circumstance here. It may have been, (1.) Because his mind was full of it. and he wished on all occasions to make that fact prominent; (2.) Because this was the distinguishing feature of the Christian religion, that the Lord Jesus had been raised up from the dead, and he wished, in the outset, to present the superiority of that religion which had brought life and immortality to light; and, (3.) Because he wished to show that he had received his commission from that same God who had raised up Jesus, and who was, therefore, the author of the true religion. His commission was from the source of life and light, the God of the living and the dead; the God who was the author of the glorious scheme which revealed life and immortality.

2. *And all the brethren which are with me.* It was usual for Paul to associate with him the ministers of the gospel, or other Christians who were with him, in expressing friendly salutations to the churches to which he wrote, or as uniting with him, and concurring in the sentiments which he expressed. Though Paul claimed to be inspired, yet it would do much to conciliate favour for what he advanced, if others also concurred with what he said, and especially if they were known to the churches to which the epistles were written. Sometimes the names of others were associated with his in the epistle; see Note, 1 Cor. i. 1; Phil. i. 1; Col. i. 1; 1 Thess. i. 1. As we do not know where this epistle was written, of course we are ignorant who the "brethren" were, who are here referred to. They may have been ministers with Paul, or they may have been the private members of the churches. Commentators have been much divided in opinion on the subject; but all is conjecture. It is obviously impossible to determine. ¶ *Unto the churches.* How many churches there were in Galatia, is unknown. There were several *cities* in Galatia, as Ancyria, Tavia, Pessinus, &c. It is not improbable that a church had been established in each of the cities, and as they were not far distant from each other, and the people had the same general character and habits, it is not improbable that they had fallen into the same errors. Hence the epistle is directed to them in common.

3. *Grace be unto you,* &c. This is the usual apostolic salutation, imploring for them the blessing of God. See it fully explained in the Notes on Rom. i. 7.

4. *Who gave himself for our sins.* The reason why Paul so soon introduces this important doctrine, and

makes it here so prominent, probably is, that this was the cardinal doctrine of the Christian religion, the great truth which was ever to be kept before the mind, and because this truth had been in fact lost sight of by them. They had embraced doctrines which tended to obscure it, or to make it void. They had been led into error by the Judaizing teachers, who held that it was necessary to be circumcised, and to conform to the whole Jewish ritual. Yet the tendency of all this was to obscure the doctrines of the gospel, and particularly the great truth that men can be justified only by faith in the blood of Jesus; chap. v. 4; comp. chap. i. 6, 7. Paul, therefore, wished to make this prominent—the very *starting point* in their religion; a truth never to be forgotten, that Christ gave himself for their sins, that he might deliver them from all the bad influences of this world, and from all the false systems of religion engendered in this world. The expression "*who gave*" (τοῦ δόντος) is one that often occurs in relation to the work of the Redeemer, where it is represented as a *gift*, either on the part of God, or on the part of Christ himself; see Note on John iii. 16; comp. John iv. 10; Rom. iv. 25; 2 Cor. ix. 15; Gal. ii. 20; Eph. v. 25; Tit. ii. 14. This passage proves, (1.) That it was wholly *voluntary* on the part of the Lord Jesus. No one compelled him to come; no one could compel him. It is not too much to say, that God *could* not, and *would* not COMPEL any innocent and holy being to undertake the great work of the atonement, and endure the bitter sorrows which were necessary to redeem man. God will *compel* the guilty to suffer, but he never will compel the innocent to endure sorrows, even in behalf of others. The whole work of redemption must be *voluntary*, or it could not be performed. (2.) It evinced great benevolence on the part of the Redeemer. He did not come to take upon himself unknown and unsurveyed woes. He did not go to work in the dark. He knew what was to be done. He knew just what sorrows were to be endured—how long, how keen, how awful. And yet, knowing this, he came resolved and prepared to endure all those woes, and to drink the bitter cup to the dregs. (3.) If there had not been this benevolence in his bosom, man must have perished for ever. He could not have saved himself; and he had no power or right to compel another to suffer in his behalf; and even God would not lay this mighty burden on any other, unless he was entirely willing to endure it. How much then do we owe to the Lord Jesus; and how entirely should we devote our lives to him who loved us, and gave himself for us. The word *himself*, is rendered by the Syriac, *his life* (*N phsh*); and this is in fact the sense of the Greek, that he gave his *life* for our sins, or that he died in our stead. He gave his *life* up to toil, tears, privation, sorrow, and death, that he might redeem us. The phrase, "*for our sins*" (ὑπὲρ τῶν ἁμαρτιῶν ἡμῶν), means the same as *on account of*; meaning, that the cause or reason why he gave himself to death, was our sins; that is, he died because we are sinners, and because we could be saved only by his giving himself up to death. Many MSS. instead of ὑπὲρ, here read περὶ, but the sense is not materially varied. The Syriac translates it, "who gave himself *instead of*," by a word denoting that there was a *substitution* of the Redeemer in our place. The sense is, that the Lord Jesus became a vicarious offering, and died in the stead of sinners. It is not possible to express this idea more distinctly and unambiguously than Paul has done, in this passage. Sin was the procuring cause of his death; to make expiation for sin was the design of his coming; and sin is pardoned and removed only by his substituted suffering. ¶ *That he might deliver us.* The word here used (ἐξέληται) properly means, to pluck out, to tear out; to take out from a number, to select; then to rescue or deliver. This is the sense here. He came and gave himself that he might *rescue* or *deliver* us from this present evil world. It does not mean to take away by death, or to remove to another world, but that he might

5 To whom *be* glory for ever and ever. Amen.

6 I marvel that ye are so soon removed [a] from him that called you into the grace of Christ unto another gospel;

[a] chap. 5. 4, 7, 8.

effect a separation between us and what the apostle calls here, "this present evil world." The grand purpose was, to rescue sinners from the dominion of this world, and separate them unto God. ¶ *This present evil world;* see John xvii. 15, 16. Locke supposes, that by this phrase is intended the Jewish institutions, or the Mosaical age, in contradistinction from the age of the Messiah. Bloomfield supposes, that it means "the present state of being, this life, filled as it is with calamity, sin, and sorrow; or, rather, the *sin itself,* and the misery consequent upon it." Rosenmüller understands by it, "the men of this age, Jews, who reject the Messiah; and Pagans, who are devoted to idolatry and crime." The word rendered *world* (αἰών), means properly *age,* an indefinitely long period of time; then eternity, for ever. It then comes to mean the world, either present or future; and then the present world, as it is, with its cares, temptations, and desires; the idea of evil, physical and moral, being everywhere implied. —*Robinson, Lex.;* Mat. xiii. 22; Luke xvi. 8; xx. 34; Rom. xii. 2. Here it means the world as it is, without religion, a world of bad passions, false opinions, corrupt desires; a world full of ambition, and of the love of pleasure, and of gold; a world where God is not loved or obeyed; a world where men are regardless of right, and truth, and duty; where they live for themselves, and not for God; in short, that great community, which in the Scriptures is called THE WORLD, in contradistinction from the kingdom of God. That world, that evil world, is full of sin; and the object of the Redeemer was to *deliver* us from that; that is, to effect a separation between his followers and that. It follows, therefore, that his followers constitute a peculiar community, not governed by the prevailing maxims, or influenced by the peculiar feelings of the people of this world. And it follows, also, that if there is not *in fact* such a separation, then the purpose of the Redeemer's death, in regard to us, has not been effected, and we are still a part of that great and ungodly community, *the world.* ¶ *According to the will of God,* &c. Not by the will of man, or by his wisdom, but in accordance with the will of God. It was his purpose that the Lord Jesus should thus give himself; and his doing it was in accordance with his will, and was pleasing in his sight. The whole plan originated in the divine purpose, and has been executed in accordance with the divine will. If in accordance with *his* will, it is good, and is worthy of universal acceptation.

5. *To whom* be *glory,* &c. Let him have all the praise and honour of the plan and its execution. It is not uncommon for Paul to introduce an ascription of praise in the midst of an argument: see Note on Rom. i. 25. It results from the strong desire which he had, that all the glory should be given to God, and showed that he believed that all blessings had their origin in him, and that he should be always acknowledged.

6. *I marvel.* I wonder. It is remarked by Luther (Comm. in loco), that Paul here uses as mild a word as possible. He does not employ the language of severe reproof, but he expresses his astonishment that the thing should have occurred. He was deeply affected and amazed, that such a thing could have happened. They had cordially embraced the gospel; they had manifested the tenderest attachment for him; they had given themselves to God, and yet in a very short time they had been led wholly astray, and had embraced opinions which tended wholly to pervert and destroy the gospel. They had shown an instability and inconstancy of character, which was to him perfectly surprising. ¶ *That ye are so soon.* This proves that the epistle was written not long

after the gospel was first preached to them. According to the general supposition, it could not have been more than from two to five years. Had it been a long and gradual decline; had they been destitute for years of the privileges of the gospel; or had they had time to forget him who had first preached to them, it would not have been a matter of surprise. But when it occurred in a few months; when their once ardent love for Paul, and their confidence in him had so soon vanished, or their affections become alienated, and when they had so soon embraced opinions tending to set the whole gospel aside, it could not but excite his wonder. Learn hence, that men, professedly pious, and apparently ardently attached to the gospel, *may* become soon perverted in their views, and alienated from those who had called them into the gospel, and whom they professed tenderly to love. The ardour of the affections becomes cool, and some artful, and zealous, and plausible teachers of error seduce the mind, corrupt the heart, and alienate the affections. Where there is the ardour of the first love to God, there is also an effort soon made by the adversary, to turn away the heart from him; and young converts are commonly *soon* attacked in some plausible manner, and by art and arguments adapted to turn away their minds from the truth, and to alienate the affections from God. ¶ *So soon removed.* This also, Luther remarks, is a mild and gentle term. It implies that *foreign* influence had been used, to turn away their minds from the truth. The word here used (μετατίθεσθε) means, to transpose, put in another place; and then, to go over from one party to another. Their affections had become transferred to other doctrines than those which they had at first embraced, and they had moved off from the only true foundation, to one which would give them no support. ¶ *From him that called you.* There has been great difference of opinion in regard to the sense of this passage. Some have supposed, that it refers to God; others to Christ; others to Paul himself. Either supposition makes good sense, and conveys an idea not contrary to the Scriptures in other places. Doddridge, Chandler, Clarke, Macknight, Locke, and some others refer it to Paul; Rosenmüller, Koppe, and others, suppose it refers to God; and others refer it to the Redeemer. The Syriac renders it thus: "I marvel that ye are so soon turned away from that Messiah (Christ) who has called you." &c. It is not possible, perhaps, to determine the true sense. It does not seem to me to refer to Paul, as the main object of the epistle is, not to show that they had removed from *him*, but from the *gospel*—a far more grievous offence; and it seems to me that it is to be referred to God. The reasons are, (1.) That he who had called them, is said to have called them "into the grace of Christ," which would be hardly said of Christ himself; and, (2.) That the work of calling men is usually in the Scriptures attributed to God; 1 Thess. ii. 12; v. 24; 2 Thess. ii. 14; 2 Tim. i. 9. ¶ *Into the grace of Christ.* Locke renders this, "into the covenant of grace which is by Christ." Doddridge understands it of the method of salvation which is *by* or *through* the grace of Christ. There is no doubt that it refers to the plan of salvation which is by Christ, or in Christ; and the main idea is, that the scheme of salvation which they had embraced under his instruction, was one which contemplated salvation only by the grace or favour of Christ; and that from that they had been removed to another scheme, essentially different, where the grace of Christ was made useless and void. It is Paul's object to show that the true plan makes Christ the great and prominent object; and that the plan which they had embraced was in this respect wholly different. ¶ *Unto another gospel.* A gospel which destroys the grace of Christ; which proclaims salvation on other terms than simple dependence on the merits of the Lord Jesus; and which has introduced the Jewish rites and ceremonies as essential, in order to obtain salvation. The apostle calls that scheme the *gospel*

7 Which [a] is not another; but
there be some that trouble you, and
would pervert [b] the gospel of Christ.
8 But though we, or an angel
from heaven, preach any other
gospel unto you than that which
we have preached unto you, let [c]
him be accursed.

a 2 Co.11.4. b Ac.15.1,24; 2 Co.2.17; chap.5.10,12. c 1 Co.16.22.

because it pretended to be; it was preached by those who claimed to be preachers of the gospel; who alleged that they had come direct from the apostles at Jerusalem, and who pretended to declare the method of salvation. It claimed to be the gospel, and yet it was essentially unlike the plan which he had preached as constituting the gospel. That which *he* preached, inculcated the entire dependence of the sinner on the merits and grace of Christ; that system had introduced dependence on the observance of the rites of the Mosaic system, as necessary to salvation.

7. *Which is not another.* There is also a great variety of views in regard to the meaning of this expression. Tindal translates it, "which is nothing else but there be some that trouble you." Locke, "which is not owing to any thing else but only this, that ye are troubled with a certain sort of men who would overturn the gospel of Christ." But Rosenmüller, Koppe, Bloomfield, and others, give a different view; and according to them the sense is, "which, however, is not another gospel, nor indeed the gospel at all, or true," &c. According to this, the design was to state, that what they taught had none of the elements or characteristics of the gospel. It was a different system, and one which taught an entirely different method of justification before God. It seems to me that this is the true sense of the passage, and that Paul means to teach them that the system, though it was called the gospel, was essentially different from that which he had taught, and which consisted in simple reliance on Christ for salvation. The system which *they* taught, was in fact the Mosaic system; the Jewish mode, depending on the rites and ceremonies of religion; and which, therefore, did not deserve to be called the *gospel.* It would load them again with burdensome rites, and with cumbrous institutions, from which it was the great purpose of the gospel to relieve them. ¶ *But there be some that trouble you.* Though this is most manifestly another system, and not the gospel at all, yet there are some persons who are capable of giving trouble and of unsettling your minds, by making it plausible. They pretend that they have come direct from the apostles at Jerusalem; that they have received their instructions from them, and that they preach the true gospel as they teach it. They pretend that Paul was called into the office of an apostle after them; that he had never seen the Lord Jesus; that he had derived his information only from others; and thus they are able to present a plausible argument, and to unsettle the minds of the Galatians. ¶ *And would prevent.* That is, the tendency of their doctrine is wholly to *turn away* (μεταστρέψαι), to destroy, or render useless the gospel of Christ. It would lead to the denial of the necessity of dependence on the merits of the Lord Jesus for salvation, and would substitute dependence on rites and ceremonies. This does not of necessity mean that such was the *design* of their teaching, for they might have been in the main honest; but that such was the *tendency* and *result* of their teaching. It would lead men to *rely* on the Mosaic rites for salvation.

8. *But though we.* That is, we the apostles. Probably, he refers particularly to himself, as the plural is often used by Paul when speaking of himself. He alludes here, possibly, to a charge which was brought against him by the false teachers in Galatia, that he had changed his views since he came among them, and now preached differently from what he did then; see the Introduction. They endeavoured probably to fortify their own opinions in regard to the obligations of the

Mosaic law, by affirming, that though Paul when he was among them had maintained that the observance of the law was not necessary to salvation, yet that he had changed his views, and now held the same doctrine on the subject which they did. What they relied on in support of this opinion is unknown. It is certain, however, that Paul *did*, on some occasions (see Note on Acts xxi. 21—26), comply with the Jewish rites, and it is not improbable that they were acquainted with that fact, and interpreted it as proving that he had changed his sentiments on the subject. At all events, it would make their allegation plausible that Paul was *now* in favour of the observance of the Jewish rites, and that if he had ever taught differently, he must now have changed his opinion. Paul therefore begins the discussion by denying this in the most solemn manner. He affirms that the gospel which he had at first preached to them was the true gospel. It contained the great doctrines of salvation. It was to be regarded by them as a fixed and settled point, that there was no other way of salvation but by the merits of the Saviour. No matter who taught any thing else; no matter though it be alleged that he had changed his mind; no matter even though he *should* preach another gospel; and no matter though an angel from heaven should declare any other mode of salvation, it was to be held as a fixed and settled position, that the true gospel had been preached to them at first. We are not to suppose that Paul admitted that he had changed his mind, or that the inferences of the false teachers there were well-founded, but we are to understand this as affirming in the most solemn manner that the true gospel, and the only method of salvation, had been preached among them at first. ¶ *Or an angel from heaven.* This is a very strong rhetorical mode of expression. It is not to be supposed that an angel from heaven would preach any other than the true gospel. But Paul wishes to put the strongest possible case, and to affirm in the strongest manner possible, that the true gospel had been preached to them. The great system of salvation had been taught; and no other was to be admitted, no matter who preached it; no matter what the character or rank of the preacher: and no matter with what imposing claims he came. It follows from this, that the mere rank, character, talent, eloquence, or piety of a preacher does not of necessity give his doctrine a claim to our belief, or prove that his gospel is true. Great talents may be prostituted; and great sanctity of manner, and even holiness of character, may be in error; and no matter what may be the rank, and talents, and eloquence, and piety of the preacher, if he does not accord with the gospel which was first preached, he is to be held accursed. ¶ *Preach any other gospel*, &c.; see Note on ver. 6. Any gospel that differs from that which was first preached to you, any system of doctrines which goes to deny the necessity of simple dependence on the Lord Jesus Christ for salvation. ¶ *Let him be accursed.* Gr. ἀνάθεμα (*anathema*). On the meaning of this word, see Notes on 1 Cor. xii. 3; xvi. 22. It is not improperly here rendered "accursed," or "devoted to destruction." The object of Paul is to express the greatest possible abhorrence of any other doctrine than that which he had himself preached. So great was his detestation of it, that, says Luther, "he casteth out very flames of fire, and his zeal is so fervent, that he beginneth almost to curse the angels." It follows from this, (1.) That any other doctrine than that which is proclaimed in the Bible on the subject of justification, is to be rejected and treated with abhorrence, no matter what the rank, talent, or eloquence of him who defends it. (2.) That we are not to patronise or countenance such preachers. No matter what their zeal or their apparent sincerity, or their apparent sanctity, or their apparent success, or their real boldness in rebuking vice, we are to withdraw from them. "Cease, my son," said Solomon, "to hear the instruction that causes to err from the words of know-

9 As we said before, so say I now again, If any *man* preach any other [a] gospel unto you than that ye have received, let him be accursed.

10 For do I now persuade

a De.4.2; Re.22.18.

ledge; Prov. xix. 27. Especially are we to withdraw wholly from that instruction which goes to deny the great doctrines of salvation; that pure gospel which the Lord Jesus and the apostle taught. If Paul would regard even an angel as doomed to destruction, and as held accursed, should he preach any other doctrine, assuredly *we* should not be found to lend our countenance to it, nor should we patronise it by attending on such a ministry. Who would desire to attend on the ministry of even an angel if he was to be held accursed? How much less the ministry of a man preaching the same doctrine!—It does not follow from this, however, that we are to treat others with severity of language or with the language of *cursing*. They must answer to God. *We* are to withdraw from their teaching; we are to regard the *doctrines* with abhorrence; and we are not to lend our countenance to them. To their own master they stand or fall; but what *must* be the doom of a teacher whom an inspired man has said should be regarded as "ACCURSED!"—It may be added, how responsible is the ministerial office! How fearful the account which the ministers of religion must render! How much prayer, and study, and effort are needed that they may be able to understand the true gospel, and that they may not be led into error, or lead others into error.

9. *As we said before.* That is, in the previous verse. It is equivalent to saying, "as I have just said;" see 2 Cor. vii. 3. It cannot be supposed that he had said this when he was with them, as it cannot be believed that he then anticipated that his doctrines would be perverted, and that another gospel would be preached to them. The sentiment of ver. 8 is here repeated on account of its importance. It is common in the scriptures, as indeed it is everywhere else, to *repeat* a declaration in order to deepen the impression of its importance and its truth. Paul would not be misunderstood on this point. He would leave no doubt as to his meaning. He would not have it supposed that he had uttered the sentiment in ver. 8 hastily; and he therefore repeats it with emphasis. ¶ *Than that ye have received.* In the previous verse, it is, "that which we have preached." By this change in the phraseology he designs, probably, to remind them that they had once solemnly professed to embrace that system. It had not only been *preached* to them, it had been *embraced* by them. The teachers of the new system, therefore, were really in opposition to the once avowed sentiments of the Galatians; to what they knew to be true. They were not only to be held accursed, therefore, because Paul so declared, but because they preached what the Galatians themselves knew to be false, or what was contrary to that which they had themselves professed to be true.

10. *For do I now persuade men, or God?* The word "now" (ἄρτι) is used here, evidently, to express a contrast between his present and his former purpose of life. Before his conversion to Christianity, he impliedly admits, that it *was* his object to conciliate the favour of men; that he derived his authority from them (Acts ix. 1, 2); that he endeavoured to act so as to please them and gain their good esteem. But *now* he says, this was not his object. He had a higher aim. It was to please God, and to conciliate his favour. The object of this verse is obscure; but it seems to me to be connected with what follows, and to be designed to introduce that by showing that he had not *now* received his commission from men, but had received it from God. *Perhaps* there may be an allusion to an implied allegation in regard to him. It *may* have been alleged (see Notes on the previous verses) that even *he* had changed his mind, and was now himself an observer of the laws of Moses

men, or God? or do I seek[a] to please men? for if I yet pleased men, I should not[b] be the servant of Christ.

a 2 Co.12.19; 1 Th.2.4. *b* Ja.4.4.

To this, perhaps, he replies; by this question, that such conduct would not have been inconsistent in his view, when it was his main purpose to please *men*, and when he derived his commission from them; but that *now* he had a higher aim. His purpose was to please God; and he was not aiming in any way to gratify men. The word which is rendered "persuade" here (πείθω), has been very variously interpreted. Tindal renders it, "seek now the favour of men or of God?" Doddridge: "Do I now solicit the favour of men or of God?" This also is the interpretation of Grotius, Hammond, Elsner, Koppe, Rosenmüller, Bloomfield, &c. and is undoubtedly the true explanation. The word properly means to *persuade*, or to *convince;* Acts xviii. 4; xxviii. 23; 2 Cor. v. 11. But it also means, to bring over to kind feelings, to conciliate, to pacify, to quiet. Sept. 1 Sam. xxiv. 8; 2 Macc. iv. 25; Acts xii. 20; 1 John iii. 19. By the *question* here, Paul means to say, that his great object was now to *please God.* He desired his favour rather than the favour of man. He acted with reference to his will. He derived his authority from him, and not from the Sanhedrim or any earthly council. And the purpose of all this is to say, that he had not received his commission to preach from man, but had received it directly from God. ¶ *Or do I seek to please men?* It is not my aim or purpose to please men, and to conciliate their favour; comp. 1 Thess. ii. 4. ¶ *For if I yet pleased men.* If I made it my aim to please men; if this was the regulating principle of my conduct. The word "*yet*" here (ἔτι) has reference to his former purpose. It implies that this had once been his aim. But he says if he had *pursued* that purpose to please men; if this had *continued* to be the aim of his life, he would not *now* have been a servant of Christ. He had been constrained to *abandon* that purpose in order that he might be a servant of Christ; and the sentiment is, that in order that a man may become a Christian, it is necessary for him to abandon the purpose of pleasing men as the rule of his life. It may be implied also that if *in fact* a man makes it his aim to please men, or if this is the purpose for which he lives and acts, and if he shapes his conduct with reference to that, he cannot be a Christian or a servant of Christ. A Christian *must* act from higher motives than those, and he who aims supremely at the favour of his fellow-men has full evidence that he is not a Christian. A friend of Christ must do his duty, and must regulate his conduct by the will of God, whether men are pleased with it or not. And it may be further implied that the life and deportment of a sincere Christian *will not* please men. It is not that which they love. A holy, humble, spiritual life they do not love. It is true, indeed, that their consciences tell them that such a life is right; that they are often constrained to speak well of the life of Christians, and to commend it; it is true that they are constrained to respect a man who is a sincere Christian, and that they often repose confidence in such a man; and it is true also that they often speak with respect of them when they are dead; but the life of an humble, devoted, and zealous Christian they do not *love.* It is contrary to their views of life. And especially if a Christian so lives and acts as to reprove them either by his words or by his life; or if a Christian makes his religion so prominent as to interfere with their pursuits or pleasures, they do not love it. It follows from this, (1.) That a Christian is not to *expect* to please men. He must not be disappointed, therefore, if he does not. His Master did not please the world; and it is enough for the disciple that he be as his master. (2.) A professing Christian, and especially a minister, should be alarmed when the world flatters and caresses him. He

11 But I certify you, brethren, that the gospel which was preached of me, is not after man.

a 1 Co.15.1—3

12 For[a] I neither received it of man, neither was I taught *it*, but by the revelation[b] of Jesus Christ.

b Ep.3.3.

should fear either, (*a*) That he is not living as he ought to do, and that sinners love him *because* he is so much like them, and keeps them in countenance; or, (*b*) That they *mean* to make him betray his religion and become conformed to them. It is a great point gained for the gay world, when it can, by its caresses and attentions, get a Christian to forsake a prayer-meeting for a party, or surrender his deep spirituality to engage in some political project. "Woe unto you," said the Redeemer, "when all men speak well of you," Luke vi. 26. (3.) One of the main differences between Christians and the world is, that others *aim* to please men; the Christian *aims* to please God. And this is a *great* difference. (4.) It follows that if men would become Christians, they must cease to make it their object to please men. They must be willing to be met with contempt and a frown; they must be willing to be persecuted and despised; they must be willing to lay aside all hope of the praise and the flattery of men, and be content with an honest effort to please God. (5.) True Christians must differ from the world. Their aims, feelings, purposes must be unlike the world. They are *to be* a peculiar people; and they should be willing to be esteemed such. It does not follow, however, that a true Christian should not desire the good esteem of the world, or that he should be indifferent to an honourable reputation (1 Tim. iii. 7); nor does it follow that a consistent Christian will not often command the respect of the world. In times of trial, the world will repose confidence in Christians; when any work of benevolence is to be done, the world will instinctively look to Christians; and notwithstanding sinners will not *love* religion, yet they will secretly feel assured that some of the brightest ornaments of society are Christians, and that they have a *claim* to the confidence and esteem of their fellow-men. ¶ The *servant of Christ*. A Christian.

11. *But I certify you.* I make known to you; or, I declare to you; see 1 Cor. xv. 1. Doubtless this had been known to them before, but he now assures them of it, and goes into an extended illustration to show them that he had not received his authority from *man* to preach the gospel To state and prove this is the main design of this chapter. ¶ *Is not after man.* Gr. Not according to man; see ver. 1. That is, he was not appointed by man, nor had he any human instructor to make known to him what the gospel was. He had neither received it from man, nor had it been debased or adulterated by any human admixtures. He had received it directly from the Lord Jesus.

12. *For I neither received it of man.* This is very probably said in reply to his opponents, who had maintained that Paul had derived his knowledge of the gospel from other men, as he had not been personally known to the Lord Jesus, or been of the number of those whom he called to be his apostles. In reply to this, he says, that he did not receive his gospel in any way from man. ¶ *Neither was I taught* it. That is, by man. He was not taught it by any written account of it, or by the instruction of man in any way. The only plausible objection to this statement which could be urged would be the fact that Paul had an interview with Ananias (Acts ix. 17) before his baptism, and that he would probably receive instructions from him. But to this it may be replied, (1.) That there is no evidence that Ananias went into an explanation of the nature of the Christian religion in his interview with Paul; (2.) Paul had *before* this been taught what Christianity was by his interview with the Lord Jesus on the way to Damascus (Acts ix. 5; xxvi. 14—18); (3.) The purpose for which Ananias

13 For ye have heard of my conversation in time past in the Jews' religion, how that beyond measure I persecuted the church[a] of God, and wasted it.

14 And profited in the Jews'

a Ac.8.1,3; 9.1,2; 26.9.

was sent to him in Damascus was that he might receive his sight, and be filled with the Holy Ghost, Acts ix. 17. Whatever instructions he may have received through Ananias, it is still true that his call was *directly* from the Lord Jesus, and his information of the nature of Christianity from *his* revelation. ¶ *But by the revelation of Jesus Christ.* On his way to Damascus, and subsequently in the temple, Acts xxii. 17—21. Doubtless he received communications at various times from the Lord Jesus with regard to the nature of the gospel and his duty. The sense here is, that he was not indebted to *men* for his knowledge of the gospel, but had derived it entirely from the Saviour.

13. *For ye have heard of my conversation.* My conduct, my mode of life, my deportment; see Note on 2 Cor. i. 12. Probably Paul had himself made them acquainted with the events of his early years. The *reason* why he refers to this is, to show them that he had not derived his knowledge of the Christian religion from any instruction which he had received in his early years, or any acquaintance which he had formed with the apostles. He had at first been decidedly opposed to the Lord Jesus, and had been converted only by his wonderful grace. ¶ *In the Jews' religion.* In the belief and practice of *Judaism;* that is, as it was understood in the time when he was educated. It was not merely in the religion of Moses, but it was in that religion as understood and practised by the Jews in his time, when opposition to Christianity constituted a very material part of it. In *that* religion Paul proceeds to show that he had been more distinguished than most persons of his time. ¶ *How that beyond measure.* In the highest possible degree; beyond all limits or bounds; exceedingly. The phrase which Paul here uses (καθ' ὑπερβολὴν), *by hyperbole,* is one which he frequently employs to denote any thing that is *excessive,* or that cannot be expressed by ordinary language; see the Greek in Rom. vii. 13; 1 Cor. xii. 31; 2 Cor. i. 8; iv. 7, 17. ¶ *I persecuted the church;* see Acts viii. 3; ix. 1, seq. ¶ *And wasted it.* Destroyed it. The word which is here used, means properly to waste or destroy, as when a city or country is ravaged by an army or by wild beasts. His *purpose* was utterly to root out and destroy the Christian religion.

14. *And profited.* Made advances and attainments. He made advances not only in the knowledge of the Jewish religion, but also he surpassed others in his zeal in defending its interests. He had had better advantages than most of his countrymen; and by his great zeal and characteristic ardour he had been able to make higher attainments than most others had done. ¶ *Above many my equals.* Marg. *Equal in years.* This is the true sense of the original. It means that he surpassed those of the same age with himself. Possibly there may be a reference here to those of the same age who attended with him on the instructions of Gamaliel. ¶ *Being more exceedingly zealous.* More studious of; more ardently attached to them; more anxious to distinguish himself in attainments in the religion in which he was brought up. All this is fully sustained by all that we know of the character of Paul, as at all times a man of singular and eminent zeal in all that he undertook. ¶ *Of the traditions of my fathers.* Or the traditions of the Jews; see Note, Mat. xv. 2. A large part of the doctrines of the Pharisees depended on mere tradition; and Paul doubtless made this a special matter of study, and was particularly tenacious in regard to it. It was to be learned, from the very nature of it, only by *oral* teaching, as there is no evidence that it was then recorded. Subsequently these traditions were recorded in the *Mishna,* and are found in the Jewish

religion above many my [1] equals in mine own nation, being [a] more exceedingly zealous of the traditions [b] of my fathers.

15 But when it pleased God, [c] who separated me from my mother's womb, and called *me* by his grace,

1 *equal in years.* a Ac.22,3, Ph.3.6. b Mar.7 5—13.

c Is.49.1; Je.1.5.

writings. But in the time of Paul they were to be learned as they were handed down from one to another; and hence the utmost diligence was requisite to obtain a knowledge of them. Paul does not here say that he was zealous then for the practice of the new religion, nor for the study of the Bible. His object in going to Jerusalem and studying at the feet of Gamaliel was doubtless to obtain a knowledge of the traditions of the sect of the Pharisees. Had he been studying the Bible all that time, he would have kept from the fiery zeal which he evinced in persecuting the church, and would, if he had studied it right, been saved from much trouble of conscience afterwards.

15. *But when it pleased God.* Paul traced all his hopes of eternal life, and all the good influences which had ever borne upon his mind, to God. ¶ *Who separated me,* &c. That is, who destined me; or who purposed from my very birth that I should be a preacher and an apostle. The meaning is, that God had in his secret purposes set him apart to be an apostle. It does not mean that he had actually called him in his infancy to the work, for this was not so, but that he designed him to be an important instrument in his hands in spreading the true religion. Jeremiah (i. 5) was thus set apart, and John the Bapist was thus early designated for the work which they afterwards performed. It follows from this, (1.) That God often, if not always, has *purposes* in regard to men from their very birth. He *designs* them for some important field of labour, and endows them at their creation with talents adapted to that. (2.) It does not follow that because a young man has gone far astray; and has become even a blasphemer and a persecutor, that God has not destined him to some important and holy work in his service. How many men have been called, like Paul, and Newton, and Bunyan, and Augustine, from a life of sin to the service of God. (3.) God is often training up men in a remarkable manner for future usefulness. His eye is upon them, and he watches over them, until the time comes for their conversion. His providence was concerned in the education and training of Paul. It was by the divine intention with reference to his future work that he had so many opportunities of education, and was so well acquainted with the "traditions" of that religion which he was yet to demonstrate to be unfounded and false. He gave him the opportunity to cultivate his mind, and prepare to grapple with the Jew in argument, and show him how unfounded were his hopes. So it is often now. He gives to a young man an opportunity of a finished education. Perhaps he suffers him to fall into the snares of infidelity, and to become familiar with the arguments of sceptics, that he may thus be better prepared to meet their sophisms, and to enter into their feelings. His eye is upon them in their wanderings, and they are suffered often to wander far; to range the fields of science; to become distinguished as scholars, as Paul was; until the time comes for their conversion, and then, in accordance with the purpose which set them apart from the world, God converts them, and consecrates all their talents and attainments to his service. (4.) We should never despair of a young man who has wandered far from God. If he has risen high in attainments; if his whole aim is ambition; or if he has become an infidel, still we are not to despair of him. It is *possible* still that God "separated" that talent to his service from the very birth, and that he means yet to call it all to his service. How easy it was to convert Saul of Tarsus when the proper period

16 To reveal [a] his Son in me, that [b] I might preach him among

a 2 Co.4.6. b Ac.9.15.

arrived. So it is of the now unconverted and unconsecrated, but cultivated talent among the young men of our land Far as they may have wandered from God and virtue, yet much of that talent has been devoted to him in baptism, and by parental purposes and prayers; and, it may be—*as is morally certain from the history of the past*—that much of it is consecrated also by the divine purpose and intention for the noble cause of virtue and pure religion. In that now apparently wasted talent; in that learning now apparently devoted to other aims and ends, there is much that *will* yet adorn the cause of virtue and religion; and how fervently should we pray that it may be "called" by the grace of God and actually devoted to his service. ¶ *And called me by his grace.* On the way to Damascus. It was special *grace*, because he was then engaged in bitterly opposing him and his cause.

16. *To reveal his Son in me.* This is to be regarded as connected with the first part of ver. 15, "When it pleased God to reveal his Son in me," *i. e.* on the way to Damascus. The phrase evidently means, to make me acquainted with the Lord Jesus, or to reveal his Son *to* me; comp. the Greek in Mat. x. 32, for a similar expression. The *revelation* here referred to was the miraculous manifestation which was made to Paul on his way to Damascus; comp. 2 Cor. iv. 6. That revelation was in order to convince him that he was the Messiah; to acquaint him with his nature, rank, and claims; and to qualify him to be a preacher to the heathen. ¶ *That I might preach him.* In order that I might so preach him; or with a view to my being appointed to this work. This was the leading purpose for which Paul was converted, Acts ix. 15; xxii. 21. ¶ *The heathen.* The Gentiles; the portion of the world that was not Jewish, or that was destitute of the true religion. ¶ *Immediately.* Koppe supposes that this is to be connected with "I went into Arabia" (ver. 17). Rosenmüller supposes it means, "Immediately *I consented.*" Dr. Wells and Locke suppose that it refers to the fact that he immediately went to Arabia. But this seems to me to be an unnatural construction. The words are too remote from each other to allow of it. The evident sense is, that he was at once *decided.* He did not take time to deliberate whether he should or should not become a Christian. He made up his mind at once and on the spot. He did not consult with any one; he did not ask advice of any one; he did not wait to be instructed by any one. He was convinced by the vision in an overpowering manner that Jesus was the Messiah, and he yielded at once. The main idea is, that there was no delay, no consultation, no deferring it, that he might see and consult with his friends, or with the friends of Christianity. The object for which he dwells on this is. to show he did not receive his views of the gospel from man. ¶ *I conferred not.* I did not *lay the case* (προσανεθέμην) before any man; I did not confer with any one. ¶ *Flesh and blood.* Any human being, for so the phrase properly signifies; see Note, Mat. xvi. 17. This does not mean here, that Paul did not consult his own ease and happiness; that he was regardless of the sufferings which he might be called to endure; that he was willing to suffer, and was not careful to make provision for his own comfort—which was true in itself—but that he did not lay the case before any man, or any body of men for instruction or advice. He acted promptly and decisively. He was not disobedient to the heavenly vision (Acts xxvi. 19), but resolved at once to obey. Many suppose that this passage means that Paul did not take counsel of the evil passions and suggestions of his own heart, or of the feelings which would have prompted him to lead a life of ambition, or a life under the influence of corrupt desires. But however true this was in fact, no such thing is intended here.

the heathen; immediately I conferred not with flesh and [a] blood:

17 Neither went I up to Jerusalem to them which were apostles

a 2 Co.5.16.

It means simply that he did not take counsel of any human being. He resolved at once to follow the command of the Saviour, and at once to obey him. The passage shows, (1.) That when the Lord Jesus calls us to follow him we should promptly and decidedly obey. (2.) We should not delay even to take counsel of earthly friends, or wait for human advice, or consult their wishes, but should *at once* resolve to follow the Lord Jesus. Most persons, when they are awakened to see their guilt, and their minds are impressed on the subject of religion, are prone to *defer*, it; to resolve to think of it at some future time; or to engage in some other business before they become Christians; or, at least, they wish to finish what they have on hand before they yield to God. Had Paul pursued this course, he would probably never have become a Christian. It follows, therefore, (3.) That when the Lord Jesus calls us, we should at once abandon any course of life, however pleasant, or any plan of ambition, however brilliant, or any scheme of gain, however promising, in order that we may follow him. What a brilliant career of ambition did Paul abandon! and how promptly and decidedly did he do it! He did not pause or hesitate a moment; but brilliant as were his prospects, he at once forsook all; paused in mid-career in his ambition; and without consulting a human being, at once gave his heart to God. Such a course should be pursued by all. Such a promptness and decision will prepare one to become an eminent Christian, and to be eminently useful.

17. *Neither went I up to Jerusalem.* That is, I did not go there at once. I did not go to consult with the apostles there, or to be instructed by them in regard to the nature of the Christian religion. The design of this statement is, to show that in no sense did he derive his commission from man. ¶ *To them which were apostles before me.* This implies that Paul *then* regarded himself to be an apostle. They were, he admits, apostles *before* he was; but he felt also that he had original authority with them, and he did not go to them to receive instruction, or to derive his commission from them. Several of the apostles remained in Jerusalem for a considerable time after the ascension of the Lord Jesus, and it was regarded as the principal place of authority; see Acts xv. ¶ *But I went into Arabia.* Arabia was south of Damascus, and at no great distance. The line indeed between Arabia Deserta and Syria is not very definitely marked, but it is generally agreed that Arabia extends to a considerable distance into the great Syrian desert. To what part of Arabia, and for what purpose Paul went, is wholly unknown. Nothing is known of the circumstances of this journey; nor is the time which he spent there known. It is known indeed (ver. 18) that he did not go to Jerusalem until three years after his conversion, but how large a part of this time was spent in Damascus, we have no means of ascertaining. It is probable that Paul was engaged during these three years in preaching the gospel in Damascus and the adjacent regions, and in Arabia; comp. Acts ix. 20, 22, 27. The account of this journey into Arabia is wholly omitted by Luke in the Acts of the Apostles, and this fact, as has been remarked by Paley (Horæ Paulinæ, chap. v. No. 2), demonstrates that the Acts and this epistle were not written by the same author, or that the one is independent of the other; because "if the Acts of the Apostles had been a forged history made up from the epistle, it is impossible that this journey should have been passed over in silence; if the epistle had been composed out of what the author had read of St. Paul's history in the Acts, it is unaccountable that it should have been inserted." As to the reason why Luke omitted to mention the journey into Arabia, nothing is known. Various conjec-

before me; but I went into Arabia, and returned again into Damascus.
18 Then [a] after three years I
went [1] up to Jerusalem to see
Peter, and abode with him fifteen
days.
19 But other of the apostles

a Ac.9.26.

1 or, *returned*.

tures have been entertained, but they are *mere* conjectures. It is sufficient to say, that Luke has by no means recorded *all* that Paul or the other apostles did, nor has he pretended to do it. He has given the leading events in the public labours of Paul; and it is not at all improbable that he has omitted not a few short excursions made by him for the purpose of preaching the gospel. The journey into Arabia, probably, did not furnish any incidents *in regard to the success of the gospel there* which required particular record by the sacred historian, nor has Paul himself referred to it for any such reason, or intimated that it furnished any incidents, or any facts, that required particularly the notice of the historian. He has mentioned it for a different purpose altogether, to show that he did not receive his commission from the apostles, and that he did not go at once to consult them. He went directly the other way. As Luke, in the Acts, had no occasion to illustrate this; as he had no occasion to refer to this *argument*, it did not fall in with the design to mention the fact. Nor is it known *why* Paul went into Arabia. Bloomfield supposes that it was in order to recover his health after the calamity which he suffered on the way to Damascus. But every thing in regard to this is mere conjecture. I should rather think it was more in accordance with the general character of Paul that he made this short excursion for the purpose of preaching the gospel. ¶ *And returned again unto Damascus.* He did not go to Jerusalem to consult with the apostles after his visit to Arabia, but returned again to the place where he was converted and preached there, showing that he had not derived his commission from the other apostles.

18. *Then after three years.* Probably three years after his departure from Jerusalem to Damascus, not after his return to Arabia. So most commentators have understood it. ¶ *Went up to Jerusalem.* More correctly, as in the margin, *returned.* ¶ *To see Peter.* Peter was the oldest and most distinguished of the apostles. In chap. ii. 9, he, with James and John, is called a *pillar*. But why Paul went particularly to see *him* is not known. It was probably, however, from the celebrity and distinction which he knew Peter had among the apostles that he wished to become particularly acquainted with him. The word which is here rendered *to see* (ἱστορῆσαι) is by no means that which is commonly employed to denote that idea. It occurs nowhere else in the New Testament; and properly means to ascertain by personal inquiry and examination, and then to *narrate*, as a historian was accustomed to do, whence our word *history*. The notion of personally seeing and examining, is one that belongs essentially to the word, and the idea here is that of seeing or visiting Peter in order to a personal acquaintance. ¶ *And abode with him fifteen days.* Probably, says Bloomfield, including three Lord's-days. Why he departed then is unknown. Beza supposes that it was on account of the plots of the Grecians against him, and their intention to destroy him (Acts ix. 29); but this is not assigned by Paul himself as a reason. It is probable that the purpose of his visit to Peter would be accomplished in that time, and he would not spend more time than was necessary with him. It is clear that in the short space of *two weeks* he could not have been very extensively taught by Peter the nature of the Christian religion, and probably the time is mentioned here to show that he had not been under the teaching of the apostles.

19. *Save James the Lord's brother.* That the James here referred to was an apostle, is clear. The whole con-

saw I none, save James[a] the Lord's brother.

a Mar.6.3.

20 Now the things which I write unto you, behold, before God, I lie not.

struction of the sentence demands this supposition. In the list of the apostles in Mat. x. 2,3, two of this name are mentioned, James the son of Zebedee and brother of John, and James the son of Alpheus. From the Acts of the Apostles, it is clear that there were two of this name in Jerusalem. Of these, James the brother of John was slain by Herod (Acts xii. 2), and the other continued to reside in Jerusalem, Acts xv. 13; xxi. 13. This latter James was called James the Less (Mark xv. 40), to distinguish him from the other James, probably because he was the younger. It is probable that this was the James referred to here, as it is evident from the Acts of the Apostles that he was a prominent man among the apostles in Jerusalem. Commentators have not been agreed as to what is meant by his being the brother of the Lord Jesus. Doddridge understands it as meaning that he was "the near kinsman" or cousin-german to Jesus, for he was, says he, the son of Alpheus and Mary, the sister of the virgin; and if there were but two of this name, this opinion is undoubtedly correct. In the Apostolical Constitutions (see Rosenmüller) three of this name are mentioned as apostles or eminent men in Jerusalem; and hence many have supposed that one of them was the son of Mary the mother of the Lord Jesus. It is said (Mat. xiii. 55) that the brothers of Jesus were James and Joses, and Simon, and Judas; and it is remarkable that three of the apostles bear the same names; James the son of Alpheus, Simon Zelotes, and Judas; John xiv. 22. It is indeed *possible*, as Bloomfield remarks, that three brothers of our Lord and three of his apostles might bear the same names, and yet be different persons; but such a coincidence would be very remarkable, and not easily explained. But if it were not so, then the James here was the son of Alpheus, and consequently a cousin of the Lord Jesus. The word *brother* may, according to scripture usage, be understood as denoting a *near kinsman*. See Schleusner (Lex. 2) on the word ἀδελφός. After all, however, it is not quite certain who is intended. Some have supposed that neither of the apostles of the name of James is intended, but another James who was the son of Mary the mother of Jesus. See Koppe *in loc.* But it is clear, I think, that one of the apostles is intended. Why James is particularly mentioned here is unknown. As, however, he was a prominent man in Jerusalem, Paul would naturally seek his acquaintance. It is possible that the other apostles were absent from Jerusalem during the fifteen days when he was there.

20. *Behold, before God I lie not.* This is an oath, or a solemn appeal to God; see Note, Rom. ix. 1. The design of this oath here is to prevent all suspicion of falsehood. It may seem to be remarkable that Paul should make this solemn appeal to God in this argument, and in the narrative of a plain fact, when his statement could hardly be called in question by any one. But we may remark, (1.) That the oath here refers not only to the fact that he was with Peter and James but fifteen days, but to the *entire group* of facts to which he had referred in this chapter. "The things which I wrote unto you." It included, therefore, the narrative about his conversion, and the direct revelation which he had from the Lord Jesus. (2.) There were no *witnesses* which he could appeal to in this case, and he could, therefore, only appeal to God. It was probably not practicable for him to appeal to Peter or James, as neither of them were in Galatia, and a considerable part of the transactions here referred to occurred where there were no witnesses. It pertained to the direct revelation of truth from the Lord Jesus. The only way, therefore, was for Paul to appeal directly to God for the truth of what he said. (3.) The importance of the truth here affirmed

21 Afterwards I [a] came into the regions of Syria and Cilicia;
22 And was unknown by face unto the churches [b] of Judea which were in Christ:
23 But they had heard [c] only, That he which persecuted us in times past, now preacheth the faith which once he destroyed.
24 And they glorified[d] God in me.

a Ac.9.30. b 1 Th.2.14. c Ac.9.13,26. d Ac.21.19,20.

was such as to justify this solemn appeal to God. It was an extraordinary and miraculous revelation of the truth by Jesus Christ himself. He received information of the truth of Christianity from no human being. He had consulted no one in regard to its nature. That fact was so extraordinary, and it was so remarkable that the system thus communicated to him should harmonize so entirely with that taught by the other apostles with whom he had had no intercourse, that it was not improper to appeal to God in this solemn manner. It was, therefore, no trifling matter in which Paul appealed to God; and a solemn appeal of the same nature and in the same circumstances can never be improper.

21. *Afterwards I came,* &c. In this account he has omitted a circumstance recorded by Luke (Acts ix. 29), of the controversy which he had with the Grecians or Hellenists. It was not material to the purpose which he has here in view, which is to state that he was not indebted to the apostles for his knowledge of the doctrines of Christianity. He therefore merely states that he left Jerusalem soon after he went there, and travelled to other places. ¶ *The regions of Syria.* Syria was between Jerusalem and Cilicia. Antioch was the capital of Syria, and in that city and the adjacent places he spent considerable time; comp. Acts xv. 23, 41. ¶ *Cilicia.* This was a province of Asia Minor, of which Tarsus, the native place of Paul, was the capital; see Note on Acts vi. 9.

22. *And was unknown by face,* &c. Paul had visited Jerusalem only, and he had formed no acquaintance with any of the churches in the other parts of Judea. He regarded himself at the first as called to preach particularly to the Gentiles, and he did not remain even to form an acquaintance with the Christians in Judea. ¶ *The churches of Judea.* Those which were out of Jerusalem. Even at the early period of the conversion of Paul there were doubtless many churches in various parts of the land. ¶ *Which were in Christ.* United to Christ; or which were Christian churches. The *design* of mentioning this is, to show that he had not derived his views of the gospel from any of them. He had neither been instructed by the apostles, nor was he indebted to the Christians in Judea for his knowledge of the Christian religion.

23. *But they had heard only,* &c They had not seen me; but the remarkable fact of my conversion had been reported to them. It was a fact that could hardly be concealed; see Note, Acts xxvi. 26.

24. *And they glorified God in me.* They praised God on my account. They regarded me as a true convert and a sincere Christian; and they praised God that he had converted such a persecutor, and had made him a preacher of the gospel. The *design* for which this is mentioned is, to show that though he was personally unknown to them, and had not derived his views of the gospel from them, yet that he had their entire confidence. They regarded him as a convert and an apostle, and they were disposed to praise God for his conversion. This fact would do much to conciliate the favour of the Galatians, by showing them that he had the confidence of the churches in the very land where the gospel was first planted, and which was regarded as the source of ecclesiastical authority. In view of this we may remark, (1.) That it is the duty of Christians kindly and affectionately to receive among their number those who have been converted from a career of persecution or of sin in any form. And it is always done by true Christians. It is easy to forgive a

man who has been actively engaged in persecuting the church, or a man who has been profane, intemperate, dishonest, or licentious, if he becomes a true penitent, and confesses and forsakes his sins. No matter what his life has been; no matter how abandoned, sensual, or devilish; if he manifests true sorrow and gives evidence of a change of heart, he is cordially received into any church, and welcomed as a fellow-labourer in the cause which he once destroyed. Here, at least, is one place where forgiveness is cordial and perfect. His former life is not remembered, except to praise God for his grace in recovering a sinner from such a course; the evils that he has done are forgotten; and he is henceforward regarded as entitled to all the privileges and immunities of a member of the household of faith. There is not on earth an infuriated persecutor or blasphemer who would not be cordially welcomed to any Christian church on the evidence of his repentance; not a man so debased and vile that the most pure, and elevated, and learned, and wealthy Christians would not rejoice to sit down with him at the same communion table on the evidence of his conversion to God. (2.) We should "glorify" or praise God for all such instances of conversion. We should do it because, (*a*) Of the abstraction of the talents of the persecutor from the cause of evil. Paul could have done, and would have done immense service to the enemies of Christianity if he had pursued the career which he had commenced. But when he was converted, all that bad influence ceased. So when an infidel or a profligate man is converted now, (*b*) Because now his talents will be consecrated to a better service. They will be employed in the cause of truth and salvation. All the power of the matured and educated talent will now be devoted to the interests of religion; and it is a fact for which we should thank God, that he often takes educated talent, and commanding influence, and an established reputation for ability, learning, and zeal, and devotes it to his own service. (*c*) Because there will be a change of destiny; because the enemy of the Redeemer will now be saved. The moment when Saul of Tarsus was converted, was the moment which determined a change in his eternal destiny. Before, he was in the broad way to hell; henceforward he walked in the path of life and salvation. Thus we should always rejoice over a sinner returning from the error of his ways; and should praise God that he who was in danger of eternal ruin is now an heir of glory. Christians are not jealous in regard to the *numbers* who shall enter heaven. They feel that there is "room" for all; that the feast is ample for all; and they rejoice when *any* can be induced to come with them and partake of the happiness of heaven. (3.) *We* may still glorify and praise God for the grace manifested in the conversion of Saul of Tarsus. What does not the world owe to him! What do we not owe to him! No man did as much in establishing the Christian religion as he did; no one among the apostles was the means of converting and saving so many souls; no one has left so many and so valuable writings for the edification of the church. To him we owe the invaluable epistles—so full of truth, and eloquence, and promises, and consolations—on which we are commenting; and to him the church owes, under God, some of its most elevated and ennobling views of the nature of Christian doctrine and duty. After the lapse, therefore, of eighteen hundred years, we should not cease to glorify God for the conversion of this wonderful man, and should feel that *we* have cause of thankfulness that he changed the infuriated persecutor to a holy and devoted apostle. (4.) Let us remember that God has the same power now. There is not a persecutor whom he could not convert with the same ease with which he changed Saul of Tarsus. There is not a vile and sensual man that he could not make pure; not a dishonest man that his grace could not make honest; not a blasphemer that he could not teach to venerate his name; not a lost and abandoned sinner that he cannot receive to himself. Let us

CHAPTER II.

THEN, fourteen years after, [a] I went up again to Jerusalem with Barnabas, and took Titus with *me* also.

a Ac.15.2,&c.

then without ceasing cry unto him that his grace may be continually manifested in reclaiming such sinners from the error of their ways, and bringing them to the knowledge of the truth, and to a consecration of their lives to his service.

CHAPTER II.

ANALYSIS.

THE second chapter is closely connected *in sense* with the first, and is indeed a part of the same argument. Injury has been done by the division which is made. The proper division would have been at the close of the 10th verse of this chapter. The general scope of the chapter, like the first, is to show that he did not receive the gospel from man; that he had not derived it from the apostles; that he did not acknowledge his indebtedness to them for his views of the Christian religion; that they had not even set up *authority* over him; but that they had welcomed him as a fellow-labourer, and acknowledged him as a coadjutor in the work of the apostleship. In confirmation of this he states (ver. 1) that he had indeed gone to Jerusalem, but that he had done it by express revelation (ver. 2); that he was cordially received by the apostles there—especially by those who were pillars in the church; and that so far from regarding himself as inferior to the other apostles, he had resisted Peter to his face at Antioch on a most important and vital doctrine.

The chapter, therefore, may be regarded as divided into two portions, viz.:—

I. *The account of his visit to Jerusalem and of what occurred there*, ver. 1—10.

(*a*) He had gone up fourteen years after his conversion, after having laboured long among the Gentiles in his own way, and without having felt his dependence on the apostles at Jerusalem, ver. 1, 2.

(*b*) When he was there, there was no attempt made to compel him to submit to the Jewish rites and customs; and what was conclusive in the case was, that they had not even required Titus to be circumcised, thus proving that they did not assert jurisdiction over Paul, and that they did not intend to impose the Mosaic rites on the converts from among the Gentiles, ver. 3—5.

(*c*) The most distinguished persons among the apostles at Jerusalem, he says, received him kindly, and admitted him to their confidence and favour without hesitation. They added no heavy burdens to him (ver. 6); they saw evidence that he had been appointed to bear the gospel to the Gentiles (ver. 7, 8); they gave to him and Barnabas the right hand of fellowship (ver. 9); and they asked only that they should remember and show kindness to the poor saints in Judea, and thus manifest an interest in those who had been converted from Judaism, or contribute their proper proportion to the maintenance of all, and show that they were not disposed to abandon their own countrymen, ver. 10. In this way they gave the fullest proof that they approved the course of Paul, and admitted him into entire fellowship with them as an apostle.

II. *The scene at Antioch, where Paul rebuked Peter for his dissimulation;* ver 11—21. The main object of mentioning this seems to be to show, first, that he did not regard himself as inferior to the other apostles, or that he had not derived his views of the gospel from them; and, secondly, to state that the observance of the Jewish rites was not necessary to salvation, and that he had maintained that from the beginning. He had strongly urged it in a controversy with Peter, and in a case where Peter was manifestly wrong; and it was no new doctrine on the subject of justification which he had preached to the Galatians. He states, therefore,

(*a*) That he had opposed Peter at Antioch, because he had dissembled there, and that even Barnabas had been carried away with the course which Peter had practised; ver. 11—14.

(*b*) That the Jews must be justified by faith, and not by dependence on their own law; ver. 15, 16.

(*c*) That they who are justified by faith should act consistently, and not attempt to build again the things which they had destroyed; ver. 17, 18.

(*d*) That the effect of justification by faith was to make one dead to the law that he might live unto God; that the effect of it was to make one truly alive and devoted to the cause of true religion; and to show this, he appeals to the effect of his own heart and life (ver. 19, 20).

(*e*) And that if justification could be obtained by the law, then Christ had died in vain; ver. 21. He thus shows that the effect of teaching the necessity of the observance of the Jewish rites was to destroy the gospel, and to render it vain and useless.

1. *Then fourteen years after.* That is, fourteen years after his first visit there subsequent to his conversion. Some commentators, however, suppose that the date of the fourteen years is to be reckoned from his conversion. But the more obvious construction is, to refer it to the time of his visit there, as recorded in the previous chapter; ver 18. This time was spent in Asia Minor chiefly in preaching the gospel. ¶ *I went up again to Jerusalem.* It is commonly supposed that Paul here refers to the visit which he made as recorded in Acts xv. The circumstances mentioned are substantially the same; and the object which he had at that time in going up was one whose mention was entirely pertinent to the argument here. He went up with Barnabas to submit a question to the assembled apostles and elders at Jerusalem, in regard to the necessity of the observance of the laws of Moses. Some persons who had come among the Gentile converts from Judea had insisted on the necessity of being circumcised in order to be saved. Paul and Barnabas had opposed them; and the dispute had become so warm that it was agreed to submit the subject to the apostles and elders at Jerusalem. For that purpose Paul and Barnabas had been sent, with certain others, to lay the case before all the apostles. As the question which Paul was discussing in this epistle was about the necessity of the observance of the laws of Moses in order to justification, it was *exactly in point* to refer to a journey when this very question had been submitted to the apostles. Paul indeed had made another journey to Jerusalem before this with the collection for the poor saints in Judea (Acts xi. 29, 30; xii. 25), but he does not mention that here, probably because he did not then see the other apostles, or more probably because that journey furnished no illustration of the point now under debate. On the occasion here referred to (Acts xv.), the very point under discussion here constituted the main subject of inquiry, and was definitely settled. ¶ *And took Titus with me also.* Luke, in the Acts of the Apostles (xv. 2), says, that there were others with Paul and Barnabas on that journey to Jerusalem. But who they were he does not mention. It is by no means certain that Titus was *appointed* by the church to go to Jerusalem; but the contrary is more probable. Paul seems to have taken him with him as a private affair; but the reason is not mentioned. It may have been to show his Christian liberty, and his sense of what he had a right to do; or it may have been *to furnish a case* on the subject of inquiry, and submit the matter to them whether Titus was *to be* circumcised. He was a Greek; but he had been converted to Christianity. Paul had not circumcised him; but had admitted him to the full privileges of the Christian church. Here then was *a case in point;* and it may have been important to have had such a case before them, that they might fully understand it. This, as Doddridge properly remarks, is the first mention which occurs of Titus. He is not mentioned by Luke in the Acts of the Apostles, and though his name occurs several times in the second epistle to the Corinthians (ii. 13; vii. 6; viii. 6, 16, 23, xii. 18), yet it is to be remembered that that epistle was written a consid-

2 And I went up by revelation, and communicated unto them that gospel which I preach among the Gentiles; but [1] pri-

[1] or, *severally.*

erable time after this to the Galatians. Titus was a Greek, and was doubtless converted by the labours of Paul, for he calls him his own son, Tit. i. 4. He attended Paul frequently in his travels; was employed by him in important services (see 2 Cor. in the places referred to above); was left by him in Crete to set in order the things that were wanting, and to ordain elders there (Tit. i. 5); subsequently he went into Dalmatia (2 Tim. iv. 10), and is supposed to have returned again to Crete, whence it is said he propagated the gospel in the neighbouring islands, and died at the age of 94.—*Calmet.*

2. *And I went up by revelation.* Not for the purpose of receiving instruction from the apostles there in regard to the nature of the Christian religion. It is to be remembered that the design for which Paul states this is, to show that he had not received the gospel from men. He is careful, therefore, to state that he went up by the express command of God. He did not go up to receive instructions from the apostles there in regard to his own work, or to be confirmed by them in his apostolic office, but he went to submit an important question pertaining to the church at large. In Acts xv. 2, it is said that Paul and Barnabas went up by the appointment of the church at Antioch. But there is no discrepancy between that account and this, for though he was designated by the church there, there is no improbability in supposing that he was directed by a special revelation to comply with their request. The reason why he says that he went up by direct revelation seems to be, to show that he did not *seek* instruction from the apostles; he did not go of his own accord to consult with them as if he were dependent on them; but even in a case when he went to advise with them he was under the influence of express and direct revelation, proving that he was as much commissioned by God as they were. ¶ *And communicated unto them that gospel, &c.* Made them acquainted with the doctrines which he preached among the heathen. He stated fully the principles on which he acted; the nature of the gospel which he taught; and his doctrine about the exemption of the Gentiles from the obligations of the law of Moses. He thus satisfied them in regard to his views of the gospel; and showed them that he understood the system of Christianity which had been revealed. The result was, that they had entire confidence in him, and admitted him to entire fellowship with them; ver. 9. ¶ *But privately.* Marg. *Severally.* Gr. κατ' ἰδίαν. The phrase means that he did it not in a public manner; not before a promiscuous assembly; not even before all the apostles collected together, but in a private manner to a few of the leaders and chief persons. He made a private explanation of his motives and views, that they might understand it before it became a matter of public discussion. The *point* on which Paul made this private explanation was not whether the gospel was to be preached to the Gentiles, for on that they had no doubt after the revelation to Peter (Acts x.); but whether the rites of the Jews were to be imposed on the Gentile converts. Paul explained his views and his practice on that point, which were that he did not *impose* those rites on the Gentiles; that he taught that men might be justified without their observance; and that they were not necessary in order to salvation. The *reasons* why he sought this private interview with the leading men in Jerusalem he has not stated. But we may suppose that they were something like the following. (1.) The Jews in general had very strong attachment to their own customs, and this attachment was found in a high degree among those who were converted from among them to the Christian faith. They would be strongly excited, therefore, by the doctrine that those customs were not necessary

vately to them which were of reputation, lest by any means I [a] should run, or had run, in vain.

a Ph.2.16.

to be observed. (2.) If the matter were submitted to a promiscuous assembly of converts from Judaism, it could not fail to produce great excitement. They could not be made readily to understand the reasons why Paul acted in this manner; there would be no possibility in an excited assemblage to offer the explanations which might be desirable; and after every explanation which could be given in this manner, they might have been unable to understand all the circumstances of the case. (3.) If a few of the principal men were made to understand it, Paul felt assured that their influence would be such as to prevent any great difficulty. He therefore sought an early opportunity to lay the case before them in private, and to secure their favour; and this course contributed to the happy issue of the whole affair; see Acts xv. There was indeed much disputation when the question came to be submitted to "the apostles and elders" (Acts xv. 7); many of the sect of the Pharisees in that assembly maintained that it was needful to teach the Gentiles that the law of Moses was to be kept (Acts xv. 5); and no one can tell what would have been the issue of that discussion among the excitable minds of the converts from Judaism, had not Paul taken the precaution, as he here says, to have submitted the case in private to those who were of "reputation," and if Peter and James had not in this manner been satisfied, and had not submitted the views which they did, as recorded in Acts xv. 7—21, and which terminated the whole controversy. We may just remark here that this fact furnishes an argument such as Paley has dwelt so much on in his Horæ Paulinæ—though he has not referred to this—of what he calls *undesigned coincidences*. The affair in Acts xv. and the course of the debate, *looks very much* as if Peter and James had had some conference with Paul in private, and had had an opportunity of understanding fully his views on the subject before the matter came before the "apostles and elders" in public, though no such private conference is there referred to by Luke. But on turning to the epistle to the Galatians, we find in fact that he had on one occasion before seen the same Peter and James (chap. i. 18, 19); and that he had had a private interview with those "of reputation" on these very points, and particularly that James, Peter, and John had approved his course, and given to him and Barnabas the right hand of fellowship; chap. ii. 9. Thus understood, the case here referred to was one of the most consummate instances of prudence that occurred in the life of Paul; and from this case we may learn, (1.) That when a difficulty is to be settled involving great principles, and embracing a great many points, it is better to seek an opportunity *of private explanation* than to submit it to a promiscuous multitude or to public debate. It is not well to attempt to settle important points when the passions of a promiscuous assembly may be excited, and where prejudices are strong. It is better to do it by private explanations, when there is an opportunity coolly to ask questions and to state the facts just as they are. (2.) The importance of securing the countenance of influential men in a popular assembly; of having men *in* the assembly who would understand the whole case. It was morally certain that if such men as Peter and James were made to understand the case, there would be little difficulty in arriving at an amicable adjustment of the difficulty. (3.) Though this passage does not refer to preaching the gospel in general, since the gospel here submitted to the men of reputation was the question referred to above, yet we may remark, that great prudence should be used in preaching; in stating truths that may excite prejudices, or when we have reason to apprehend prejudices; and that it is

3 But neither Titus, who was with me, being a Greek, was compelled to be circumcised:

4 And that because of false [a] brethren unawares brought in, who came in privily to spy out our

a Ac.15.1,24.

often best to preach the gospel to men of reputation (κατ' ἰδίαν) *separately*, or *privately*. In this way the truth can be made to bear on the conscience; it may be better adapted to the character of the individual; he may put himself less in a state of defence, and guard himself less against the proper influences of truth. And especially is this true in *conversing* with persons on the subject of religion. It should be if possible *alone*, or *privately*. Almost any man may be approached on the subject of religion if it be done when he is alone; when he is at leisure, and if it be done in a kind spirit. Almost any man will become irritated if you address him personally in a promiscuous assembly, or even with his family around him. I have never in more than in one or two instances been unkindly treated when I have addressed an individual on the subject of religion if he was alone; and though a minister should never shrink from stating the truth, and should never be afraid of man, however exalted his rank, or great his talents, or vast his wealth, yet he will probably meet with most success when he discourses *privately* to "them which are of reputation." ¶ *To them which were of reputation.* Meaning here the leading men among the apostles. Tindal renders this, "which are counted chefe." Doddridge, "those of greatest *note* in the church." The Greek is, literally, "those who seem," more fully in ver. 6; "who seem to be something," *i. e.* who are persons of note, or who are distinguished. ¶ *Lest by any means I should run, or had run in vain.* Lest the effects of my labours and journeys should be lost. Paul feared that if he did not take this method of laying the case before them privately, they would not understand it. Others might misrepresent him, or their prejudices might be excited, and when the case came before the assembled apostles and elders, a decision might be adopted which would go to prove that he had been entirely wrong in his views, or which would lead those whom he had taught, to believe that he was, and which would greatly hinder and embarrass him in his future movements. In order to prevent this, therefore, and to secure a just decision, and one which would not hinder his future usefulness, he had sought this private interview, and thus his object was gained.

3. *But neither Titus, who was with me.* Paul introduces this case of Titus undoubtedly to show that circumcision was not necessary to salvation. It was a case just in point. He had gone up to Jerusalem with express reference to this question. Here was a man whom he had admitted to the Christian church without circumcising him. He claimed that he had a right to do so; and that circumcision was not *necessary* in order to salvation. If it were necessary, it would have been proper that Titus should have been compelled to submit to it. But Paul says this was not demanded; or if demanded by any, the point was yielded, and he was not compelled to be circumcised. It is to be remembered that this was at Jerusalem; that it was a case submitted to the apostles there; and that consequently the determination of this case settled the whole controversy about the obligation of the Mosaic laws on the Gentile converts. It is quite evident from the whole statement here, that Paul did not intend that Titus should be circumcised; that he maintained that it was not necessary; and that he resisted it when it was demanded; ver. 4, 5. Yet on another occasion he himself performed the act of circumcision on Timothy; Acts xvi. 3. But there is no inconsistency in his conduct. In the case of Titus it was *demanded* as a matter of right and as obligatory on him, and he resisted the principle as dangerous. In the case of Timothy, it was a voluntary

liberty [a] which we have in Christ Jesus, that they might bring us into bondage: [b]

a chap.5.1.13. b 2 Co.11.20: chap.4.3,9.

compliance on his part with the usual customs of the Jews, where it was not pressed as a matter of obligation, *and where it would not be understood as indispensable to salvation.* No danger would follow from compliance with the custom, and it might do much to conciliate the favour of the Jews, and he therefore submitted to it. Paul would not have hesitated to have circumcised Titus in the same circumstances in which it was done to Timothy; but the circumstances were different; and when it was insisted on as a matter of principle and of obligation, it became a matter of principle and of obligation with him to oppose it. ¶ *Being a Greek.* Born of Gentile parents, of course he had not been circumcised. Probably both his parents were Greeks. The case with Timothy was somewhat different. His mother was a Jewess, but his father was a Greek; Acts xvi. 3. ¶ *Was compelled to be circumcised.* I think it is implied here that this was demanded and insisted on by some that he should be circumcised. It is also implied that Paul resisted it, and the point was yielded, thus settling the great and important principle that it was not necessary in order to salvation; see ver. 5.

4. *And that because of false brethren.* Who these false brethren were is not certainly known, nor is it known whether he refers to those who were at Jerusalem or to those who were at Antioch. It is probable that he refers to *Judaizing Christians,* or persons who claimed to be Christians and to have been converted from Judaism. Whether they were dissemblers and hypocrites, or whether they were so imperfectly acquainted with Christianity, and so obstinate, opinionated, and perverse, though really in some respects good men, that they were conscientious in this, it is not easy to determine. It is clear, however, that they opposed the apostle Paul; that they regarded him as teaching dangerous doctrines; that they perverted and misstated his views; and that they claimed to have clearer views of the nature of the true religion than he had. Such adversaries he met everywhere (2 Cor. xi. 26); and it required all his tact and skill to meet their plausible representations. It is evident here that Paul is assigning a *reason* for something which he had done, and that reason was to counteract the influence of the "false brethren" in the case. But what is the thing concerning which he assigns a reason? It is commonly supposed to have been on account of the fact that he did not submit to the circumcision of Titus, and that he means to say that he resisted that in order to counteract their influence, and defeat their designs. But I would submit whether ver. 3 is not to be regarded as a parenthesis, and whether the fact for which he assigns *a reason* is not that he sought a private interview with the leading men among the apostles? ver. 2. The *reason* of his doing that would be obvious. In this way he could more easily counteract the influence of the false brethren. He could make a full statement of his doctrines. He could meet their inquiries, and anticipate the objections of his enemies. He could thus secure the influence of the leading apostles in his favour, and effectually prevent all the efforts of the false brethren to impose the Jewish rites on Gentile converts. ¶ *Unawares brought in.* The word rendered "unawares" (παρεισάκτους) is derived from a verb meaning to lead in by the side of others, to introduce along with others; and then to lead or bring in by stealth, to smuggle in.—*Robinson, Lex.* The verb occurs nowhere in the New Testament but in 2 Pet. ii. 1, where it is applied to heresies, and is rendered "Who privily shall bring in." Here it refers probably to men who had been artfully introduced into the ministry, who made pretensions to piety, but who were either strangers to it, or who were greatly ignorant of the true nature of the Christian system; and who were disposed to take

5 To whom we gave place by subjection, no, not for an hour; that the truth of the gospel might continue with you.

---

every advantage, and to impose on others the observance of the peculiar rites of the Mosaic economy. *Into what* they were brought, the apostle does not say. It may have been that they had been introduced into the ministry in this manner (*Doddridge*); or it may be that they were introduced into the "assembly" where the apostles were collected to deliberate on the subject.—*Chandler.* I think it probable that Paul refers to the occurrences in Jerusalem, and that these false brethren had been introduced *from* Antioch or some other place where Paul had been preaching, or that they were persons whom his adversaries had introduced to *demand* that Titus should be circumcised, under the plausible pretence that the laws of Moses required it, but really in order that there might be such proof as they desired that this rite was to be imposed on the Gentile converts. If Paul was compelled to submit to this; if they could carry this point, it would be just such an instance as they needed, and would settle the whole inquiry, and prove that the Mosaic laws were to be imposed on the Gentile converts. This was the reason why Paul so strenuously opposed it. ¶ *To spy out our liberty which we have in Christ Jesus.* In the practice of the Christian religion. The liberty referred to was, doubtless, the liberty from the painful, expensive, and onerous rites of the Jewish religion; see chap. v. 1. Their object in spying out the liberty which Paul and others had, was, undoubtedly, to be witnesses of the fact that they did not observe the peculiar rites of the Mosaic system; to make report of it; to insist on their complying with those customs, and thus to secure the imposition of those rites on the Gentile converts. Their first object was to satisfy themselves of *the fact* that Paul did not insist on the observance of their customs; and then to secure, by the authority of the apostles, an injunction or order that Titus should be circumcised, and that Paul and the converts made under his ministry should be required to comply with those laws. ¶ *That they might bring us into bondage.* Into bondage to the laws of Moses; see Note, Acts xv. 10.

5. *To whom we gave place by subjection, no, not for an hour.* We did not submit to this at all. We did not yield even for the shortest time. We did not waver in our opposition to their demands, or in the slightest degree become subject to their wishes. We steadily opposed their claims, in order that the great principle might be forever settled, that the laws of Moses were not to be imposed as obligatory on the Gentile converts. This I take to be the clear and obvious sense of this passage, though there has been a great variety of opinions on it. A considerable number of MSS. omit the words οἷς οὐδὲ, "to whom neither" (see Mill, Koppe, and Griesbach), and then the sense would be reversed, that Paul *did* yield to them for or after a short time, in order that he might in this way better consult the permanent interests of the gospel. This opinion has been gaining ground for the last century, that the passage here has been corrupted; but it is by no means confirmed. The ancient versions, the Syriac, the Vulgate, and the Arabic, accord with the usual reading of the text. So also do by far the largest portion of MSS.; and such, it seems to me, is the sense demanded by the connection. Paul means, in the whole passage, to say, that a *great principle* was settled. That the question came up fairly whether the Mosaic rites were to be imposed on Gentile converts. That false brethren were introduced who demanded it; and that he steadily mantained his ground. He did not yield a moment. He felt that a great principle was involved; and though on all proper occasions he was willing to yield and to become all things to all men, yet here he did not court them, or temporize with them in the least. The phrase "by subjec-

6 But of those who seemed *a*
to be somewhat, whatsoever they
were, it maketh no matter to me:
God *b* accepteth no man's person: for they who seemed *to be*
somewhat, in conference added nothing to me;
7 But contrariwise, when they
saw that the gospel of the uncircumcision was committed unto me,

a chap.6.3. *b* Ac.10.34; Ro.2.11.

tion" here means, that he did not suffer himself to be *compelled* to yield. The phrase "for an hour" is equivalent to the shortest period of time. He did not waver, or yield at all. ¶ *That the truth of the gospel might continue with you.* That the great principle of the Christian religion which had been taught you might continue, and that you might enjoy the full benefit of the pure gospel, without its being intermingled with any false views. Paul had defended these same views among the Galatians, and he now sought that the same views might be confirmed by the clear decision of the college of apostles at Jerusalem.

6. *But of those who seemed to be somewhat*; see ver. 2. This undoubtedly refers to those who were the most eminent among the apostles at Jerusalem. There is an apparent harshness in our common translation which is unnecessary. The word here used (δοκούντων) denotes those who were thought to be, or who were of reputation; that is, men who were of note and influence among the apostles. The object of referring to them here is, to show that he had the concurrence and approbation of the most eminent of the apostles to the course which he had pursued. ¶ *Whatsoever they were, it maketh no matter to me.* Tindal renders this, "What they were in time passed, it maketh no matter to me." The idea seems to be this. Paul means to say that whatever was their real rank and standing, it did not in the least affect his authority as an apostle, or his argument. While he rejoiced in their concurrence, and while he sought their approbation, yet he did not admit for a moment that he was inferior to them as an apostle, or dependent on them for the justness of his views. What they were, or what they might be thought to be, was immaterial to his claims as an apostle, and immaterial to the authority of his own views as an apostle. He had derived his gospel from the Lord Jesus; and he had the fullest assurance that his views were just. Paul makes this remark evidently *in keeping* with all that he had said, that he did not regard himself as in any manner dependent on them for his authority. He did not treat them with disrespect; but he did not regard them as having a *right* to claim an authority over him. ¶ *God accepteth no man's person*; see Notes, Acts x. 34; Rom. ii. 11. This is a general truth, that God is not influenced in his judgment by a regard to the rank, or wealth, or external condition of any one. Its *particular* meaning here is, that the authority of the apostles was not to be measured by their external rank, or by the measure of reputation which they had among men. If, therefore, it were to be admitted that he himself was not in circumstances of so much external honour as the other apostles, or that they were esteemed to be of more elevated rank than he was, still he did not admit that this gave them a claim to any higher authority. God was not influenced in *his* judgment by any such consideration; and Paul therefore claimed that all the apostles were in fact on a level in regard to their authority. ¶ *In conference.* When I conferred with them, ver. 2. They did not then impose on me any new obligations; they did not communicate any thing to me of which I was before ignorant.

7. *The gospel of the uncircumcision.* The duty of preaching the gospel to the uncircumcised part of the world; that is, to the Gentiles. Paul had received this as his peculiar office when he was converted and called to the ministry (see Acts ix. 15; xxii. 21); and they now perceived that he had been specially intrusted with this office, from the remarkable success

[a] as *the gospel* of the circumcision *was* unto Peter;

8 (For he that wrought effectually in Peter to the apostleship of the circumcision, the same was mighty in me toward the Gentiles;)

9 And when James, Cephas,

a 1Th.2.4; 1Ti.2.7.

which had attended his labours. It is evidently not meant here that Paul was to preach *only* to the Gentiles and Peter *only* to the Jews, for Paul often preached in the synagogues of the Jews, and Peter was the first who preached to a Gentile (Acts x.); but it is meant that it was the *main* business of Paul to preach to the Gentiles, or that this was especially intrusted to him. ¶ *As* the gospel *of the circumcision.* As the office of preaching the gospel to the Jews. ¶ Was *unto Peter.* Peter was to preach principally to the circumcised Jews. It is evident that until this time Peter had been principally employed in preaching to the Jews. Paul selects Peter here particularly, doubtless because he was the oldest of the apostles, and in order to show that he was himself regarded as on a level in regard to the apostleship with the most aged and venerable of those who had been called to the apostolic office by the personal ministry of the Lord Jesus.

8. *For he that wrought effectually in Peter,* &c. Or by the means or agency of Peter. The argument here is, that the same effects had been produced under the ministry of Paul among the Gentiles which had been under the preaching of Peter among the Jews. It is inferred, therefore, that God had called both to the apostolic office; see this argument illustrated in the Notes on Acts xi. 17. ¶ *The same was mighty in me,* &c. In enabling me to work miracles, and in the success which attended the ministry.

9. *And when James, Cephas, and John, who seemed to be pillars* That is, pillars or supports in the church. The word rendered *pillars* (στύλοι) means properly firm support; then persons of influence and authority, as in a church, or that support a church as a pillar or column does an edifice. In regard to James, see Note on chap 19; comp. Acts xv. 13. Cephas or Peter was the most aged of the apostles, and regarded as at the head of the apostolical college. John was the beloved disciple, and his influence in the church must of necessity have been great. Paul felt that if he had the countenance of these men, it would be an important proof to the churches of Galatia that he had a right to regard himself as an apostle. Their countenance was expressed in the most full and decisive manner. ¶ *Perceived the grace that was given unto me.* That is, the favour that had been shown to me by the great Head of the church, in so abundantly blessing my labours among the Gentiles. ¶ *They gave unto me and Barnabas the right-hands of fellowship.* The right-hand in token of fellowship or favour. They thus publicly acknowledged us as fellow-labourers, and expressed the utmost confidence in us. To give the right-hand with us is a token of friendly salutation, and it seems that it was a mode of salutation not unknown in the times of the apostles. They were thus recognised as associated with the apostles in the great work of spreading the gospel around the world. Whether this was done in a public manner is not certainly known; but it was probably in the presence of the church, or possibly at the close of the council referred to in Acts xv. ¶ *That we* should *go unto the heathen.* To preach the gospel, and to establish churches. In this way the whole matter was settled, and settled as Paul desired it to be. A delightful harmony was produced between Paul and the apostles at Jerusalem; and the result showed the wisdom of the course which he had adopted. There had been no harsh contention or strife. No jealousies had been suffered to arise. Paul had sought an opportunity of a full statement of his views to them in private (ver. 2), and they had been entirely satisfied that God had called him and

and John, who seemed to be pillers, [a] perceived the grace [b] that was given unto me, they gave to me and Barnabas the right-hands of fellowship; that we *should go* unto the heathen, and they unto the circumcision.

10 Only *they would* that we

a Mat.16.18; Ep.2.20. b Ro.1.5; 12.3,6.

Barnabas to the work of making known the gospel among the heathen. Instead of being jealous at their success, they had rejoiced in it; and instead of throwing any obstacle in their way, they cordially gave them the right-hand. How easy would it be always to prevent jealousies and strifes in the same way! If there was, on the one hand, the same readiness for a full and frank explanation; and if, on the other, the same freedom from envy at remarkable success, how many strifes that have disgraced the church might have been avoided! The true way to avoid strife is just that which is here proposed. Let there be on both sides perfect frankness; let there be a willingness to explain and state things just as they are; and let there be a disposition to rejoice in the talents, and zeal, and success of others, even though it should far outstrip our own, and contention in the church would cease, and every devoted and successful minister of the gospel would receive the right-hand of fellowship from all—however venerable by age or authority—who love the cause of true religion.

10. *Only* they would *that we should remember the poor.* That is, as I suppose, the poor Christians in Judea. It can hardly be supposed that it would be necessary to make this an express stipulation in regard to the converts from among the Gentiles, and it would not have been very pertinent to the case before them to have done so. The object was, to bind together the Christians from among the heathen and from among the Jews, and to prevent alienation and unkind feeling. It might have been alleged that Paul was disposed to forget his own countrymen altogether; that he regarded himself as so entirely the apostle of the Gentiles that he would become wholly alienated from those who were his "kinsmen according to the flesh," and thus it might be apprehended that unpleasant feelings would be engendered among those who had been converted from among the Jews. Now nothing could be better adapted to allay this than for him to pledge himself to feel a deep interest in the poor saints among the Jewish converts; to remember them in his prayers; and to endeavour to secure contributions for their wants. Thus he would show that he was not alienated from his countrymen; and thus the whole church would be united in the closest bonds. It is probable that the Christians in Judea were at that time suffering the ills of poverty arising either from some public persecution, or from the fact that they were subject to the displeasure of their countrymen. All who know the peculiar feelings of the Jews at that time in regard to Christians, must see at once that many of the followers of Jesus of Nazareth would be subjected to great inconveniences on account of their attachment to him. Many a wife might be disowned by her husband; many a child disinherited by a parent; many a man might be thrown out of employment by the fact that others would not countenance him; and hence many of the Christians would be poor. It became, therefore, an object of special importance to provide for them; and hence this is so often referred to in the New Testament. In addition to this, the church in Judea was afflicted with famine; comp. Acts xi. 30; Rom. xv. 25—27; 1 Cor. xvi. 1, 2; 2 Cor. viii. 1—7. ¶ *The same which I also was forward to do.* See the passages just referred to. Paul interested himself much in the collection for the poor saints at Jerusalem, and in this way he furnished the fullest evidence that he was not alienated from them, but that he felt the deepest interest in those who were his kindred. One of the proper ways of securing *union*

should remember the poor; the same which I [a] also was forward to do.

11 But when Peter was come to [b] Antioch, I withstood him to the face, because he was to be blamed.

12 For before that certain

a Ac.11.30; Ro.15.25.

b Ac.15.35.

in the church is to have the poor with them and depending on them for support; and hence every church has some poor persons as one of the bonds of union. The best way to unite *all* Christians, and to prevent alienation, and jealousy, and strife, is to have *a great common object of charity*, in which all are interested and to which all may contribute. Such a common object for all Christians is a sinful world. All who bear the Christian name may unite in promoting its salvation, and nothing would promote union in the now divided and distracted church of Christ like a deep and common interest in the salvation of all mankind.

11. *But when Peter was come to Antioch.* On the situation of Antioch, see Note, Acts xi. 19. The *design* for which Paul introduces this statement here is evident. It is to show that he regarded himself as on a level with the chief apostles, and that he did not acknowledge his inferiority to any of them. Peter was the eldest, and probably the most honoured of the apostles. Yet Paul says that he did not hesitate to resist him in a case where Peter was manifestly wrong, and thus showed that he was an apostle of the same standing as the others. Besides, what he said to Peter on that occasion was exactly pertinent to the strain of the argument which he was pursuing with the Galatians, and he therefore introduces it (ver. 14—21) to show that he had held the same doctrine all along, and that he had defended it in the presence of Peter, and in a case where Peter did not reply to it. The *time* of this journey of Peter to Antioch cannot be ascertained; nor the occasion on which it occurred. I think it is evident that it was after this visit of Paul to Jerusalem, and the occasion *may* have been to inspect the state of the church at Antioch, and to compose any differences of opinion which may have existed there. But every thing in regard to this is mere conjecture; and it is of little importance to know when it occurred. ¶ *I withstood him to the face.* I openly opposed him, and reproved him. Paul thus showed that he was equal with Peter in his apostolical authority and dignity. The instance before us is one of faithful public reproof; and every circumstance in it is worthy of special attention, as it furnishes a most important illustration of the manner in which such reproof should be conducted. The *first* thing to be noted is, that it was done openly, and with candour. It was reproof addressed to the offender himself. Paul did not go to others and whisper his suspicions; he did not seek to undermine the influence and authority of another by slander; he did not calumniate him and then justify himself on the ground that what he had said was no more than true: he went to him at once, and he frankly stated his views and reproved him in a case where he was manifestly wrong. This too was a case so public and well known that Paul made his remarks before the church (ver. 14) because the church was interested in it, and because the conduct of Peter led the church into error. ¶ *Because he was to be blamed.* The word used here may either mean because he had *incurred* blame, or because he *deserved* blame. The essential idea is, that he had done wrong, and that he was by his conduct doing injury to the cause of religion.

12. *For before that certain came.* Some of the Jews who had been converted to Christianity. They evidently observed in the strictest manner the rites of the Jewish religion. ¶ *Came from James;* see Note on chap. i. 19. Whether they were sent by James, or whether they came of their own accord, is unknown. It is evident only that they had been intimate with James at Jerusalem, and

came from James, he did eat
[a] with the Gentiles: but when
they were come, he withdrew
and separated himself, fearing
them which were of the circumcision.
13 And the other Jews dissembled likewise with him; in-

a Ac.11.3.

they doubtless pleaded his authority. James had nothing to do with the course which they pursued; but the sense of the whole passage is, that James was a leading man at Jerusalem, and that the rites of Moses were observed there. When they came down to Antioch, they of course observed those rites, and insisted that others should do it also. It is very evident that at Jerusalem the peculiar rites of the Jews were observed for a long time by those who became Christian converts. They would not at once cease to observe them, and thus needlessly shock the prejudices of their countrymen; see Notes on Acts xxi. 21—25. ¶ *He did eat with the Gentiles.* Peter had been taught that in the remarkable vision which he saw as recorded in Acts x. He had learned that God designed to break down the wall of partition between the Jews and the Gentiles, and he familiarly associated with them, and partook with them of their food. He evidently disregarded the peculiar laws of the Jews about meats and drinks, and partook of the common food which was in use among the Gentiles. Thus he showed his belief that all the race was henceforward to be regarded as on a level, and that the peculiar institutions of the Jews were not to be considered as binding, or to be imposed on others. ¶ *But when they were come, he withdrew and separated himself.* He withdrew from the Gentiles, and probably from the Gentile converts to Christianity. The reason why he did this is stated. He feared those who were of the circumcision, or who had been Jews. Whether they demanded this of him; whether they encountered him in debate; or whether he silently separated himself from the Gentiles without their having said any thing to him, is unknown. But he feared the effect of their opposition; he feared their reproaches; he feared the report which would be made to those at Jerusalem; and perhaps he apprehended that a tumult would be excited and a persecution commenced at Antioch by the Jews who resided there. This is a melancholy illustration of Peter's characteristic trait of mind. We see in this act the same Peter who trembled when he began to sink in the waves; the same Peter who denied his Lord. Bold, ardent, zealous, and forward; he was at the same time timid and often irresolute; and he often had occasion for the deepest humility, and the most poignant regrets at the errors of his course. No one can read his history without loving his ardent and sincere attachment to his Master; and yet no one can read it without a tear of regret that he was left thus to do injury to his cause. No man loved the Saviour more sincerely than he did, yet his constitutional timidity and irresoluteness of character often led him to courses of life fitted deeply to wound his cause.

13. *And the other Jews.* That is, those who had been converted to Christianity. It is probable that they were induced to do it by the example of Peter, as they would naturally regard him as a leader. ¶ *Dissembled likewise with him.* Dissembled or concealed their true sentiments. That is, they attempted to conceal from those who had come down from James the fact that they had been in the habit of associating with the Gentiles, and of eating with them. From this it would appear that they intended to conceal this wholly from them, and that they withdrew from the Gentiles before any thing had been said to them by those who came down from James. ¶ *Insomuch that Barnabas also was carried away,* &c. Concerning Barnabas, see Note, Acts iv. 36. Barnabas was the intimate friend of Paul. He had been associated with him in very important labours; and the fact,

somuch that Barnabas also was carried away with their dissimulation.

14 But when I saw that they walked not uprightly, according to the truth [a] of the gospel, I said unto Peter [b] before *them* all, If thou, being a Jew, livest after the

a ver.5. b 1 Ti.5.20.

therefore, that the conduct of Peter was exciting so unhappy an influence as even to lead so worthy and good a man as he was into hypocrisy and error, made it the more proper that Paul should publicly notice and reprove the conduct of Peter. It could not but be a painful duty, but the welfare of the church and the cause of religion demanded it, and Paul did not shrink from what was so obvious a duty.

14. *But when I saw that they walked not uprightly.* To *walk*, in the Scriptures, is usually expressive of conduct or deportment; and the idea here is, that their conduct in this case was not honest. ¶ *According to the truth of the gospel.* According to the true spirit and design of the gospel. That requires perfect honesty and integrity; and as that was the rule by which Paul regulated his life, and by which he felt that all ought to regulate their conduct, he felt himself called on openly to reprove the principal person who had been in fault. The spirit of the world is crafty, cunning, and crooked. The gospel would correct all that wily policy, and would lead man in a path of entire honesty and truth. ¶ *I said unto Peter before* them *all.* That is, probably, before all the church, or certainly before all who had offended with him in the case. Had this been a *private affair,* Paul would doubtless have sought a private interview with Peter, and would have remonstrated with him in private on the subject. But it was public. It was a case where many were involved, and where the interests of the church were at stake. It was a case where it was very important to establish some fixed and just principles, and he therefore took occasion to remonstrate with him in public on the subject. This might have been at the close of public worship; or it may have been that the subject came up for debate in some of their public meetings, whether the rites of the Jews were to be imposed on the Gentile converts. This was a question which agitated all the churches where the Jewish and Gentile converts were intermingled; and it would not be strange that it should be the subject of public debate at Antioch. The fact that Paul reproved Peter before "them all," proves, (1.) That he regarded himself, and was so regarded by the church, as on an equality with Peter, and as having equal authority with him. (2.) That public reproof is right when an offence has been public, and when the church at large is interested, or is in danger of being led into error; comp. 1 Tim. v. 20, " Them that sin rebuke before all, that others also may fear." (3.) That it is a duty to reprove those who err. It is a painful duty, and one much neglected; still it is a duty often enjoined in the Scriptures, and one that is of the deepest importance to the church. He does a favour to another man who, in a kind spirit, admonishes him of his error, and reclaims him from a course of sin. He does another the deepest injury, who suffers sin unrebuked to lie upon him, and who sees him injuring himself and others, and who is at no pains to admonish him for his faults. (4.) If it is the duty of one Christian to admonish another who is an offender, and to do it in a kind spirit, it is the duty of him who has offended to *receive* the admonition in a kind spirit, and with thankfulness. Excitable as Peter was by nature, yet there is no evidence that he became angry here, or that he did not receive the admonition of his brother Paul with perfect good temper, and with an acknowledgment that Paul was right and that he was wrong. Indeed, the case was so plain,—as it usually is if men would be honest,—that he seems to have felt that it was right, and to have received the rebuke as became a Christian. Peter, unhappily, was accustomed to

manner of Gentiles, and not as do
the Jews, why compellest thou
the Gentiles to live as do the
Jews?

a Ep.2.3,12.

15 We *who are* Jews by nature, and not sinners [a] of the Gentiles,
16 Knowing that [b] a man is

b Ac.13.38,39; Ro.3.20.

rebukes; and he was at heart too good a man to be offended when he was admonished that he had done wrong. A good man is willing to be reproved when he has erred, and it is usually proof that there is much that is wrong when we become excited and irritable if another admonishes us of our faults. It may be added here, that nothing should be inferred from this in regard to the *inspiration* or apostolic authority of Peter. The fault was not that he taught error *of doctrine*, but that he sinned *in conduct.* Inspiration, though it kept the apostles from teaching *error*, did not keep them necessarily from sin. A man may always *teach* the truth, and yet be far from perfection in practice. The case here proves that Peter was not perfect, a fact proved by his whole life; it proves that he was sometimes timid, and even, for a period, time-serving, but it does not prove that what he wrote for our guidance was false and erroneous. ¶ *If thou, being a Jew.* A Jew by birth. ¶ *Livest after the manner of the Gentiles.* In eating, &c., as he had done before the Judaizing teachers came from Jerusalem, ver. 12. ¶ *And not as do the Jews.* Observing their peculiar customs, and their distinctions of meats and drinks. ¶ *Why compellest thou the Gentiles*, &c. As he would do, if he insisted that they should be circumcised, and observe the peculiar Jewish rites. The charge against him was gross inconsistency in doing this. "Is it not at least as lawful for them to neglect the Jewish observances, as it was for thee to do it but a few days ago?"—*Doddridge.* The word here rendered "compellest," means here *moral* compulsion or persuasion. The idea is, that the conduct of Peter was such as to lead the Gentiles to the belief that it was necessary for them to be circumcised in order to be saved. For a similar use of the word, see Mat. xiv. 22; Luke xiv. 23; Acts xxviii. 19.

15. *We* who are *Jews by nature.* It has long been a question whether this and the following verses are to be regarded as a part of the address of Paul to Peter, or the words of Paul as a part of the epistle to the Galatians. A great variety of opinion has prevailed in regard to this. Grotius says, "Here the narrative of Paul being closed, he pursues his argument to the Galatians." In this opinion Bloomfield and many others concur. Rosenmüller and many others suppose that the address to Peter is continued to ver. 21. Such *seems* to be the most obvious interpretation, as there is no break or change in the style, nor any vestige of a transfer of the argument to the Galatians. But, on the other hand, it may be urged, (1.) That Paul in his writings often changes his mode of address without indicating it. —*Bloomfield.* (2.) That it is rather improbable that he should have gone into so long a discourse with Peter on the subject of justification. His purpose was answered by the reproof of Peter for his dissimulation; and there is something incongruous, it is said, in his instructing Peter at such length on the subject of man's justification. Still it appears to me probable that this is to be rgarded as a part of the discourse of Paul to Peter, to the close of ver. 21. The following reasons seem to me to require this interpretation:—(1.) It is the most natural and obvious—usually a safe rule of interpretation. The discourse proceeds *as if* it were an address to Peter. (2.) There *is* a change at the beginning of the next chapter, where Paul expressly addresses himself to the Galatians. (3.) As to the impropriety of Paul's addressing Peter at length on the subject of justification, we are to bear in mind that he did not address him *alone.* The *reproof* was addressed to Peter particularly,

not justified by the works of the law, but by the faith [a] of Jesus Christ, even we have believed in Jesus Christ, that we might be justified by the faith of Christ, and not by the works of the law: for [b] by the works of the law shall no flesh be justified.

a Ro.5.1; chap.3.11,24.

b Ps.143.2; He.7.18,19.

but it was "before them all" (ver. 14); that is, before the assembled church, or before the persons who had been led astray by the conduct of Peter, and who were in danger of error on the subject of justification. Nothing, therefore, was more proper than for Paul to continue his discourse for *their* benefit, and to state to them fully the doctrine of justification. And nothing was more pertinent or proper for him now than to report this to the Galatians as a part of his argument to them, showing that he had *always*, since his conversion, held and defended the same doctrine on the subject of the way in which men are to be justified in the sight of God. It is, therefore, I apprehend, to be regarded as an address to Peter and the other Jews who were present. "*We* who were born Jews." ¶ *By nature.* By birth; or, we were born Jews. We were not born in the condition of the Gentiles. ¶ *And not sinners of the Gentiles.* This cannot mean that Paul did not regard the Jews as sinners, for his views on that subject he has fully expressed in Rom. ii. iii. But it must mean that the Jews were not born under the disadvantages of the Gentiles in regard to the true knowledge of the way of salvation. They were not left wholly in ignorance about the way of justification, as the Gentiles were. They knew, or they might know, that men could not be saved by their own works. It was also true that they were under more restraint than the Gentiles were, and though they were sinners, yet they were not abandoned to so gross and open sensuality as was the heathen world. They were not idolaters, and wholly ignorant of the law of God.

16. *Knowing.* We who are Jews by nature, or by birth. This cannot mean that *all* the Jews knew this, or that he who was a Jew knew it as a matter of course, for many Jews were ignorant of it, and many opposed it. But it means that the persons here referred to, those who had been born Jews, and who had been converted to Christianity, had had an opportunity to learn and understand this, which the Gentiles had not. This gospel had been preached to them, and they had professedly embraced it. They were not left to the gross darkness and ignorance on this subject which pervaded the heathen world, and they had had a better opportunity to learn it than the converts from the Gentiles. They ought, therefore, to act in a manner becoming their superior light, and to show in all their conduct that they fully believed that a man could not be justified by obedience to the law of Moses. This rendered the conduct of Peter and the other Jews who "dissembled" with him so entirely inexcusable. They could not plead ignorance on this vital subject, and yet they were pursuing a course, the tendency of which was to lead the Gentile converts to believe that it was indispensable to observe the laws of Moses, in order to be justified and saved. ¶ *That a man is not justified by the works of the law;* see Notes on Rom. i. 17; iii. 20, 26; iv. 5. ¶ *But by the faith of Jesus Christ.* By believing on Jesus Christ; see Notes, Mark xvi. 16; Rom. iii. 22. ¶ *Even we have believed in Jesus Christ.* We are therefore justified. The object of Paul here seems to be to show, that as they had believed in the Lord Jesus, and thus had been justified, there was no necessity of obeying the law of Moses with any view to justification. The thing had been fully done without the deeds of the law, and it was now unreasonable and unnecessary to insist on the observance of the Mosaic rites. ¶ *For by the works of the law,* &c; see Notes on Rom. iii. 20, 27. In this verse, the apostle has stated in few words the important doctrine of justification by faith—the doctrine which

Luther so justly called, *Articulus stantis, vel cadentis ecclesiæ.* In the notes referred to above, particularly in the Notes on the Epistle to the Romans, I have stated in various places what I conceive to be the true doctrine on this important subject. It may be useful, however, to throw together in one connected view, as briefly as possible, the leading ideas on the subject of justification, as it is revealed in the gospel. I. Justification is properly a word applicable to courts of justice, but is used in a similar sense in common conversation among men. An illustration will show its nature. A man is charged, *e. g.* with an act of trespass on his neighbour's property. Now there are two ways which he may take *to justify himself*, or to meet the charge, so as to be regarded and treated as innocent. He may, (*a*) Either *deny* that he performed the act charged on him, or he may, (*b*) Admit that the deed was done, and set up as a defence, that he *had a right* to do it. In either case, if the point be made out, he will be *just* or *innocent* in the sight of the law. The law will have nothing against him, and he will be regarded and treated in the premises as an innocent man; or he has justified himself in regard to the charge brought against him. II. Charges of a very serious nature are brought against man by his Maker. He is charged with violating the law of God; with a want of love to his Maker; with a corrupt, proud, sensual heart; with being entirely alienated from God by wicked works; in one word, with being entirely depraved. This charge extends to all men; and to the entire life of every unrenewed man. It is not a charge merely affecting the external conduct, nor merely affecting the heart; it is a charge of entire alienation from God; a charge, in short, of total depravity; see, especially, Rom. i., ii., iii. That this charge is a very serious one, no one can doubt. That it deeply affects the human character and standing, is as clear. It is a charge brought in the Bible; and God appeals in proof of it to the history of the world, to every man's conscience, and to the life of every one who has lived; and on these facts, and on his own power in searching the hearts, and in knowing what is in man, he rests the proofs of the charge. III. It is impossible for man to vindicate himself from this charge. *He can neither show that the things charged have not been committed, nor that, having been committed, he had a right to do them.* He cannot *prove* that God is not right in all the charges which he has made against him in his word; and he cannot prove that it was right for him to do as he has done. The charges against him are facts which are undeniable, and the facts are such as cannot be vindicated. But if he can do neither of these things, then he cannot be justified by the law. The law will not acquit him. It holds him guilty. It condemns him. No *argument* which he can use will show that he is right, and that God is wrong. No *works* that he can perform will be any compensation for what he has already done. No *denial* of the existence of the facts charged will alter the case; and he must stand condemned by the law of God. In the legal sense he cannot be justified; and justification, if it ever exist at all, must be in a mode that is a departure from the regular operation of law, and in a mode which the law did not contemplate, for no *law* makes any provision for the *pardon* of those who violate it. It must be by some system which is distinct from the law, and in which man may be justified on different principles than those which the law contemplates. IV. This other system of justification is that which is revealed in the gospel by the faith of the Lord Jesus. It does NOT consist in either of the following things. (1.) It is *not* a system or plan where the Lord Jesus takes the part of the sinner *against* the law or *against* God. He did not come to show that the sinner was right, and that God was wrong. He admitted most fully, and endeavoured constantly to show, that God was right, and that the sinner was wrong; nor can an instance be referred to where the Saviour took the part of the sinner against God in any such sense that he endeavoured to show that the sinner had not done the things charged on him, or that he had a right to do them. (2.) It is not that we *are* either innocent, or are declared to be innocent. God justifies the "ungodly," Rom. iv. 5. We are not innocent; we never have been; we never shall be; and it is not the design of the scheme to declare any such *untruth* as that we are not personally undeserving. It will be *always* true that the justified sinner has no claims to the mercy and favour of God. (3.) It is not that we cease to be undeserving personally. He that is justified by faith, and that goes to heaven, will go there admitting that he *deserves* eternal death, and that he is saved wholly by favour and not by desert. (4.) It is *not* a declaration on the part of God that *we* have wrought out salvation, or that *we* have any claim for what the Lord Jesus has done. Such a declaration would not be true, and would not be made. (5.) It is not that the righteousness of the Lord Jesus is *transferred* to his people. Moral character cannot be transferred. It adheres to the moral agent as much as colour does to the rays of light which cause it. It is not true that *we* died for sin, and it cannot be so reckoned or imputed. It is not true that *we* have any merit, or any claim, and it cannot be so reckoned or imputed. All the imputations of God are according to truth; and he will always reckon us to be personally undeserving and sinful. But if justification be none of these things, it may be asked, what is it? I answer—*It is the declared purpose of God to regard and treat those sinners who believe in the Lord Jesus Christ as if they had not sinned, on the ground of the merits of the Saviour.* It is not mere pardon. The main difference between pardon and justification respects the sinner contemplated in regard to his *past* conduct, and to God's *future dealings* with him. Pardon is a free forgiveness of past offences. It has reference to those sins *as* forgiven and blotted out. It is an act of remission on the part of God. Justification has respect to the law, and to God's *future dealings* with the sinner. It is an act by which God determines to treat him hereafter *as* a righteous man, or *as if* he had not sinned. The ground or reason of this is, the merit of the Lord Jesus Christ; merit such that we can plead it *as if* it were our own. The *rationale* of it is, that the Lord Jesus has accomplished by his death the same happy effects in regard to the law and the government of God, which would have been accomplished by the death of the sinner himself. In other words, nothing would be gained to the universe by the everlasing punishment of the offender himself, which will not be secured by his salvation on the ground of the death of the Lord Jesus. He has taken our place, and died in our stead; and he has met the descending stroke of justice, which would have fallen on our own head if he had not interposed (see my Notes on Isa. liii.); and now the great interests of justice will be as firmly secured if we are saved, as they would be if we were lost. The law has been fully obeyed by one who came to save us, and *as much* honour has been done to it by his obedience as could have been by our own; that is, it *as much* shows that the law is *worthy* of obedience to have it perfectly obeyed by the Lord Jesus, as it would if it were obeyed by us. It *as much* shows that the law of a sovereign is worthy of obedience to have it obeyed by an only son and an heir to the crown, as it does to have it obeyed by his subjects. And it has *as much* shown the evil of the violation of the law to have the Lord Jesus suffer death on the cross, as it would if the guilty had died themselves. If transgression whelm the innocent in calamity; if it extends to those who are perfectly *guiltless*, and inflicts pain and woe on them, it is as certainly an expression of the evil of transgression *as if* the guilty themselves suffer. And an impression as deep has been made of the evil of sin by the sufferings of the Lord Jesus in our stead, *as if* we had suffered ourselves. He endured on the cross as intense agony as we can conceive it possible for a sinner ever to endure; and the dignity of the person who suffered, THE INCARNATE GOD, is more than an equivalent for the more lengthened sorrows which the penalty of the law exacts in hell. Besides, from the very dignity of the sufferer in our place, an impression has gone abroad on the universe more deep and important than would have been by the sufferings of the individual himself in the world of woe. The sinner who is lost will be unknown to other worlds. His *name* may be unheard beyond the gates of the prison of despair. The *impression* which will be made on distant worlds by his individual sufferings will be as a part of *the aggregate of woe*, and his individual sorrows may make *no* impression on distant worlds. But not so with him who took our place. He stood in the centre of the universe. The sun grew dark, and the dead arose, and angels gazed upon the scene, and from his cross *an impression* went abroad to the farthest part of the universe, showing the tremendous effects of the violation of law, when not one soul could be saved from its penalty without such sorrows of the Son of God. In virtue of all this, the offender, by believing on him, may be treated *as if* he had not sinned; and this constitutes justification. God admits him to favour *as if* he had himself obeyed the law, or borne its penalty, since as many good results will now follow from his salvation as could be derived from his punishment; and since all the additional happy results will follow which can be derived from the exercise of pardoning mercy. The character of God is thus revealed. His mercy is shown. His determination to maintain his law is evinced. The truth is maintained; and yet he shows the fulness of his mercy and the richness of his benevolence.

[The reader will find the above objections to the doctrine of imputation fully considered in the supplementary Notes on Rom. iv. 5; see especially the Note on Rom. iv. 3, in which it is observed, that almost every objection against the imputation of righteousness may be traced to two sources. The first of these is the idea that Christ's righteousness becomes ours, in the same sense that it is his, viz., of personal achievement; an idea continually rejected by the friends, and as often proceeded on by the enemies, of imputation. The second source is the idea that imputation involves a transference of moral character, whereas the *imputing* and the *infusing* of righteousness are allowed to be two very different things. Now, in this place, the commentator manifestly proceeds on these mistaken views. What does he mean by "transference of the righteousness of Christ" when he says, "justification is not that the righteousness of the Lord Jesus is transferred to his people?" What follows, at once explains. "Moral character," he continues, "cannot be transferred. It adheres to the moral agent, as much as colour does to the rays of light which cause it." But this is quite aside from the subject, and proves what never had been denied. The same remarks apply with equal force to what is said about our being "always personally undeserving," and never regarded as having ourselves actually "wrought out salvation." These objections belong to the first source of misconception noticed above.

It has been asked a thousand times, and the question is most pertinent, How can God treat believers as innocent, if there be not some sense in which they are so? "The imputations of God are according to truth," so is his treatment. The author tells us, that the ground of justification is the "merits of the Saviour," which phrase he prefers throughout, to the more scriptural and more appropriate one of the righteousness of Christ; more appropriate, because the subject is forensic, belonging to judicature and dealing in matters of law; see Hervey's reply to Wesley, vol. iv. p. 33. Yet if these merits, or this righteousness, be not imputed to us—held as ours - *how can we be justified on any such ground?* "I would further observe," says Mr. Hervey, replying to Wesley in the publication just quoted, "that you have dropt the word imputed," which inclines me to suspect you would cashier the thing. But let me ask, Sir, how can we be justified by the merits of Christ, unless they are imputed to us? Would the payment made by a surety procure a discharge for the debtor, unless it were placed to his account? It is certain the sacrifices of old could not make an atonement, unless they were imputed to each offerer respectively. This was an ordinance settled by Jehovah himself, Lev. vii. 18. And were not the sacrifices, was not their imputation, typical of Christ and things pertaining to Christ, the former prefiguring his all-sufficient expiation; the latter shadowing forth the way whereby we are partakers of its efficacy?

The language of President Edwards, the prince of American divines, indeed of theolo-

17 But if, while we seek to be justified by Christ, we [a] ourselves

a 1 John 3.9,10.

gians universally, is decisive enough, and one would think that the opinion of this master in reasoning should have its weight on the other side of the Atlantic. "It is absolutely necessary," says he, "that in order to a sinner's being justified, the righteousness of some other should be reckoned to his account; for it is declared, that the person justified is looked on as, in himself, ungodly: but God neither will nor can justify a person without a righteousness; for justification is manifestly a forensic term, as the word is used in scripture, and a judicial thing or the act of a judge; so that if a person should be justified without a righteousness, the judgment would not be according to truth. The sentence of justification would be a false sentence, unless there be a righteousness performed, that is, by the judge properly looked upon as his."

Nor are we sure, if our author's distinction between pardon and justification be altogether accurate. By those who deny imputed righteousness, justification is frequently said to consist in the *mere remission of sin*. In a recent American publication, the views of the "new school party" are thus given: "Though they retain the word justification, they make it consist in mere pardon. In the eye of the law, the believer, according to their views, is not justified at all, and never will be throughout eternity. Though on the ground of what Christ has done, God is pleased to forgive the sinner upon his believing, Christ's righteousness is not reckoned in any sense as his, or set down to his account. He believes, and his *faith* or *act of believing* is accounted to him for righteousness; that is, faith is so reckoned to his account that God *treats* him as if he were righteous."—*Old and New Theology, by James Wood.* Now Mr. Barnes does not exactly say that justification and pardon are the same, for he makes a distinction. "The main difference between the two respects the sinner contemplated in regard to his *past* conduct, and to God's *future* dealings with him." "Pardon is a free forgiveness of *past* offences. Justification has respect to the law and to God's *future* dealings." But this difference is not respecting the *nature* of the things. It is simply a matter of time, of past and future; and justification, after all, is neither more nor less than pardon of sins past and to come. A criminal is often pardoned while yet his guilt is allowed. To exalt pardon to justification, there must be supposed a righteousness, on the ground of which not only is sin forgiven, but *the person accepted and declared legally righteous*. And in this lies the main difference between the two. In the case of the believer however these are never found apart. Whoever is pardoned is at the same time justified. Earthly princes sometimes remit the punishment of crime, but seldom or never dream of honouring the criminal; but wherever God pardons, he dignifies and ennobles.]

17. *But if, while we seek to be justified by Christ.* The connection here is not very clear, and the sense of the verse is somewhat obscure. Rosenmüller supposes that this is an objection of a Jew, supposing that where the law of Moses is not observed there is no rule of life, and that therefore there must be sin; and that since the doctrine of justification by faith taught that there was no necessity of obeying the ceremonial law of Moses, therefore Christ, who had introduced that system, must be regarded as the author and encourager of sin. To me it seems probable that Paul here has reference to an objection which has in all ages been brought against the doctrine of justification by faith, and which seems to have existed in his time, that the doctrine leads to licentiousness. The objections are, that it does not teach the necessity of the observance of the law in order to acceptance with God. That it pronounces a man justified and accepted who is a violator of the law. That his acceptance does not depend on moral character. That it releases him from the obligation of law, and that it teaches that a man may be saved though he does not conform to law. These objections existed early, and have been found everywhere where the doctrine of justification by faith has been preached. I regard this verse, therefore, as referring to these objections, and not as being peculiarly the objection of a Jew. The idea is, "You seek to be justified by faith without obeying the law. You professedly reject that, and do not hold that it is necessary to yield obedience to it. If now it shall turn out that you are sinners; that your lives are not holy; that you are free from the wholesome restraint of the law, and are given up to lives of sin, will it not follow that Christ is

also are found sinners, *is* therefore Christ the minister of sin? God forbid.

18 For if I build again the things which I destroyed, I make myself a transgressor.

19 For I [a] through the law am dead to the law, that I might live [b] unto God.

20 I am crucified [c] with Christ: nevertheless I live; yet not I, but Christ liveth in [d] me: and the

a Ro.7.4,10; 8.2. b Ro.6.11,14. c chap.5.24; 6.14. d 1 Th.5.10; 1 Pe.4.2.

---

the cause of it; that he taught it; and that the system which he introduced is responsible for it? And is not the gospel therefore responsible for introducing a system that frees from the restraint of the law, and introduces universal licentiousness?" To this Paul replies by stating distinctly that the gospel has no such tendency, and particularly by referring in the following verses to his own case, and to the effect of the doctrine of justification on his own heart and life. ¶ *We ourselves are found sinners.* If it turns out that we are sinners, or if others discover by undoubted demonstration that we lead lives of sin; if they see us given up to a lawless life, and find us practising all kinds of evil; if it shall be seen not only that we are not pardoned and made better by the gospel, but are actually made worse, and are freed from all moral restraint. ¶ Is *therefore Christ the minister of sin?* Is it to be traced to him? Is it a fair and legitimate conclusion that this is the tendency of the gospel? Is it to be charged on him, and on the plan of justification through him, that a lax morality prevails, and that men are freed from the wholesome restraints of law? ¶ *God forbid.* It is not so. This is not the proper effect of the gospel of Christ, and of the doctrine of justification by faith. The system is not fitted to produce such a freedom from restraint, and if such a freedom exists, it is to be traced to something else than the gospel.

18. *For if I build again the things which I destroyed.* Paul here uses the first person; but he evidently intends it as a general proposition, and means that if *any one* does it he becomes a transgressor. The sense is, that if a man, having removed or destroyed that which was evil, again introduces it or establishes it, he does wrong, and is a transgressor of the law of God. The particular application here, as it seems to me, is to the subject of circumcision and the other rites of the Mosaic law. They had been virtually abolished by the coming of the Redeemer, and by the doctrine of justification by faith. It had been seen that there was no necessity for their observance, and of that Peter and the others had been fully aware. Yet they were lending their influence again to establish them or to "build" them up again. They complied with them, and they insisted on the necessity of their observance. Their conduct, therefore, was that of building up again that which had once been destroyed, destroyed by the ministry, and toils, and death of the Lord Jesus, and by the fair influence of his gospel. To rebuild that again; to re-establish those customs, was wrong, and now involved the guilt of a transgression of the law of God. Doddridge supposes that this is an address to the Galatians, and that the address to Peter closed at the previous verse. But it is impossible to determine this; and it seems to me more probable that this is all a part of the address to Peter; or rather perhaps *to the assembly* when Peter was present; see Note on ver. 15.

19. *For I through the law.* On this passage the commentators are by no means agreed. It is agreed that in the phrase "am dead to the law," the law of Moses is referred to, and that the meaning is, that Paul had become dead to that as a ground or means of justification. He acted as though it were not; or it ceased to have influence over him. A dead man is insensible to all around him. He hears nothing; sees nothing; and nothing affects him. So when we are said to be dead to any thing, the meaning is, that it does not have an influence over us. In this sense Paul

life which I now live in the flesh, I live by the faith of the Son of God, who loved me, and gave himself [a] for me.

[a] John 10.11; Ep.5.2.

was dead to the law of Moses. He ceased to observe it as a ground of justification. It ceased to be the grand aim and purpose of his life, as it had been formerly, to obey it. He had higher purposes than that, and truly lived to God; see Note, Rom. vi. 2. But on the meaning of the phrase "through the law" (διὰ νόμου) there has been a great variety of opinion. Bloomfield, Rosenmüller, and some others suppose that he means the Christian religion, and that the meaning is, "by one law, or doctrine, I am dead to another;" that is, the Christian doctrine has caused me to cast aside the Mosaic religion. Doddridge, Clarke, Chandler, and most others, however, suppose that he here refers to the law of Moses, and that the meaning is, that by contemplating the true character of the law of Moses itself; by considering its nature and design; by understanding the extent of its requisitions, he had become dead to it; that is, he had laid aside all expectations of being justified by it. This seems to me to be the correct interpretation. Paul had formerly expected to be justified by the law. He had endeavoured to obey it. It had been the object of his life to comply with all its requisitions in order to be saved by it; Phil. iii. 4—6. But all this while he had not fully understood its nature; and when he was made fully to feel and comprehend its spiritual requirements, then all his hopes of justification by it died, and he became dead to it; see this sentiment more fully explained in the Note on Rom. vii. 9. ¶ *That I might live unto God.* That I might be truly alive, and might be found engaged in his service. He was dead to the law, but not to every thing. He had not become literally inactive and insensible to all things, like a dead man, but he had become truly sensible to the commands and appeals of God, and had consecrated himself to his service; see Note, Rom. vi. 11.

20. *I am crucified with Christ.* In the previous verse, Paul had said that he was *dead.* In this verse he states what he meant by it, and shows that he did not wish to be understood as saying that he was inactive, or that he was literally insensible to the appeals made to him by other beings and objects. In respect to one thing he was dead; to all that was truly great and noble he was alive. To understand the remarkable phrase, "I am crucified with Christ," we may remark, (1.) That this was the way in which Christ was put to death. He suffered on a cross, and thus became literally dead. (2.) In a sense *similar* to this, Paul became dead to the law, to the world, and to sin. The Redeemer by the death of the cross became insensible to all surrounding objects, as the dead always are. He ceased to see, and hear, and was as though they were not. He was laid in the cold grave, and they did not affect or influence him. So Paul says that *he* became insensible to the law as a means of justification; to the world; to ambition and the love of money; to the pride and pomp of life, and to the dominion of evil and hateful passions. They lost their power over him; they ceased to influence him. (3.) This was *with* Christ, or by Christ. It cannot mean *literally* that he was put to death with him, for that is not true. But it means that the effect of the death of Christ on the cross was to make him dead to these things, in like manner as he, when he died, became insensible to the things of this busy world. This may include the following things. (*a*) There was an *intimate union* between Christ and his people, so that what affected *him*, affected *them*; see John xv. 5, 6. (*b*) The death of the Redeemer on the cross involved as a consequence the death of his people to the world and to sin; see chap. v. 24; vi. 14. It was like a blow at the root of a vine or a tree, which would affect every branch and tendril or like a blow at

the head which affects every member of the body. (*c*) Paul felt *identified* with the Lord Jesus; and he was willing to share in all the ignominy and contempt which was connected with the idea of the crucifixion. He was willing to regard himself as one with the Redeemer. If there was disgrace attached to the manner in which he died, he was willing to share it with him. He regarded it as a matter to be greatly desired to be made *just like Christ* in all things, and even in the manner of his death. This idea he has more fully expressed in Phil. iii. 10, "That I may know him, [*i. e.* I desire earnestly to know him,] and the power of his resurrection, and the fellowship of his sufferings, *being made conformable unto his death*;" see also Col. i. 24; comp. 1 Pet. iv. 13. ¶ *Nevertheless I live.* This expression is added, as in ver. 19, to prevent the possibility of mistake. Paul, though he was crucified with Christ, did not wish to be understood that he felt himself to be *dead*. He was not inactive; not insensible, as the dead are, to the appeals which are made from God, or to the great objects which ought to interest an immortal mind. He was still actively employed, and the more so from the fact that he was crucified with Christ. The object of all such expressions as this is, to show that it was no design of the gospel to make men inactive, or to annihilate their energies. It was not to cause men to do nothing. It was not to paralyse their powers, or stifle their own efforts. Paul, therefore, says, "I am not dead. I am truly alive, and I live a better life than I did before." Paul was *as* active after conversion as he was before. Before, he was engaged in persecution; now, he devoted his great talents with as much energy, and with as untiring zeal, to the cause of the great Redeemer. Indeed the whole narrative would lead us to suppose that he was *more* active and zealous *after* his conversion than he was before. The effect of religion is not to make one dead in regard to the putting forth of the energies of the soul. True religion never made one lazy man; it has converted many a man of indolence, and effeminacy, and self-indulgence to a man actively engaged in doing good. If a professor of religion is *less* active in the service of God than he was in the service of the world; less laborious, and zealous, and ardent than he was before his supposed conversion, he ought to set it down as full proof that he is an utter stranger to true religion. ¶ *Yet not I.* This is also designed to prevent misapprehension. In the previous clause he had said that he lived, or was actively engaged. But lest this should be misunderstood, and it should be inferred that he meant to say it was by his own energy or powers, he guards it, and says it was not at all from himself. It was by no native tendency; no power of his own; nothing that could be traced to himself. He assumed no credit for any zeal which he had shown in the true life. He was disposed to trace it all to another. He had ample proof in his past experience that there was no tendency in himself to a life of true religion, and he therefore traced it all to another. ¶ *Christ liveth in me.* Christ was the *source* of all the life that he had. Of course this cannot be taken literally that Christ had a residence in the apostle, but it must mean that his grace resided in him; that his principles actuated him; and that he derived all his energy, and zeal, and life from his grace. The union between the Lord Jesus and the disciple was so close that it might be said the one lived in the other. So the juices of the vine are in each branch, and leaf, and tendril, and live in them and animate them; the vital energy of the brain is in each delicate nerve—no matter how small—that is found in any part of the human frame. Christ was in him as it were the vital principle. All his life and energy were derived from him. ¶ *And the life which I now live in the flesh.* As I now live on the earth surrounded by the cares and anxieties of this life. I carry the life-giving principles of my religion to all my duties and all my trials. ¶ *I live by the faith of the Son of God.* By confidence in the

21 I do not frustrate the grace of God: for if [a] righteousness *come* by the law, then Christ is dead in vain.

[a] He.7.11.

CHAPTER III.

O FOOLISH [b] Galatians, who [c] hath bewitched you, that

[b] Mat.7.26. [c] chap.5.7.

Son of God, looking to him for strength, and trusting in his promises, and in his grace. *Who loved me,* &c. He felt under the highest obligation to him from the fact that he had loved him, and given himself to the death of the cross in his behalf. The conviction of obligation on this account Paul often expresses; see Notes on Rom. vi. 8—11; Rom. viii. 35—39; 2 Cor. v. 15. There is no higher sense of obligation than that which is felt towards the Saviour; and Paul felt himself bound, as we should, to live entirely to him who had redeemed him by his blood.

21. *I do not frustrate the grace of God.* The word rendered "frustrate" (ἀθετῶ) means properly to displace, abrogate, abolish; then to make void, to render null; Mark vii. 9; Luke vii. 30; 1 Cor. i. 19. The phrase "the grace of God," here refers to the favour of God manifested in the plan of salvation by the gospel, and is another name for the gospel. The sense is, that Paul would not take any measures or pursue any course that would render that vain or inefficacious. Neither by his own life, by a course of conduct which would show that it had no influence over the heart and conduct, nor by the observance of Jewish rites and customs, would he do any thing to render that inefficacious. The design is to show that he regarded it as a great principle that the gospel was efficacious in renewing and saving man, and he would do nothing that would tend to prevent that impression on mankind. A life of sin, of open depravity and licentiousness, would do that. And in like manner a conformity to the rites of Moses as a ground of justification would tend to frustrate the grace of God, or to render the method of salvation solely by the Redeemer nugatory. This is to be regarded, therefore as at the same time a reproof of Peter for complying with customs which tended to frustrate the plan of the gospel, and a declaration that he intended that his own course of life should be such as to confirm the plan, and show its efficacy in pardoning the sinner and rendering him alive in the service of God. ¶ *For if righteousness* come *by the law.* If justification can be secured by the observance of *any* law—ceremonial or moral—then there was no need of the death of Christ as an atonement. This is plain. If man by conformity to *any* law could be justified before God, what need was there of an atonement? The work would then have been wholly in his own power, and the merit would have been his. It follows from this, that man cannot be justified by his own morality, or his alms-deeds, or his forms of religion, or his honesty and integrity. If he can, he needs no Saviour, he can save himself. It follows also that when men depend on their own amiableness, and morality, and good works, they would feel no need of a Saviour; and this is the true reason why the mass of men reject the Lord Jesus. They suppose they do not deserve to be sent to hell. They have no deep sense of guilt. They confide in their own integrity, and feel that God *ought* to save them. Hence they feel no need of a Saviour; for why should a man in health employ a physician? And confiding in their own righteousness, they reject the grace of God, and despise the plan of justification through the Redeemer. To feel the need of a Saviour it is necessary to feel that we are lost and ruined sinners; that we have no merit on which we can rely; and that we are entirely dependent on the mercy of God for salvation. Thus feeling, we shall receive the salvation of the gospel with thankfulness and joy, and show that in regard to us Christ is not "dead in vain."

CHAPTER III.

ANALYSIS.

THE address of Paul to Peter, as I suppose, was closed at the last verse

ye should not obey the truth, before whose eyes Jesus Christ hath been evidently set forth, crucified among you?

of chapter ii. The apostle in this chapter, in a direct address to the Galatians, pursues the argument on the subject of justification by faith. In the previous chapters he had shown them fully that he had received his views of the gospel directly from the Lord Jesus, and that he had the concurrence of the most eminent among the apostles themselves. He proceeds to state more fully what his views were; to confirm them by the authority of the Old Testament; and to show the necessary effect of an observance of the laws of Moses on the great doctrine of justification by faith. This subject is pursued through this chapter and the following. This chapter comprises the following subjects.

(1.) A severe reproof of the Galatians for having been so easily seduced by the arts of cunning men from the simplicity of the gospel, ver. 1. He says that Christ had been plainly set forth crucified among them, and it was strange that they had so soon been led astray from the glorious doctrine of salvation by faith.

(2.) He appeals to them to show that the great benefits which *they* had received had not been in consequence of the observance of the Mosaic rites, but had come solely by the hearing of the gospel, ver. 2—5. Particularly the Holy Spirit, with all his miraculous and converting and sanctifying influences, had been imparted only in connection with the gospel. This was the most rich and most valuable endowment which they had ever received; and this was solely by the preaching of Christ and him crucified.

(3.) In illustration of the doctrine of justification by faith, and in proof of the truth of it, he refers to the case of Abraham, and shows that he was justified in this manner, and that the scripture had promised that others would be justified in the same way, ver. 6—9.

(4.) He shows that the law pronounced a curse on all those who were under it, and that consequently it was impossible to be justified by it. But Christ had redeemed us from that curse, having taken the curse on himself, so that now we might be justified in the sight of God. In this way, says he, the blessing of Abraham might come on the Gentiles, and they all might be saved in the same manner that he was, ver. 10—14.

(5.) This view he confirms by showing that the promise made to Abraham was made *before* the giving of the law. It was a mode of justification in existence *before* the law of Moses was given. It was of the nature of a solemn compact or covenant on the part of God. It referred particularly to the Messiah, and to the mode of justification in him. And as it was of the nature of a covenant, it was impossible that the law given many years after could disannul it, or render it void, ver. 15—18.

(6.) It might then be asked, what was the use of the law? Why was it given? It was *added*, Paul says, on account of transgressions, and was designed to restrain men from sin, and to show them their guilt. It was, further, not *superior* to the promise of a Mediator, or to the Mediator, for it was appointed by the instrumentality of *angels*, and it was in the hand of the Mediator himself, *under him*, and subject to him. It could not therefore be *superior* to him, and to the plan of justification through him, ver. 19, 20.

(7.) Yet Paul answers an important objection here, and a very obvious and material inquiry. It is, whether he means to teach that the law of God is contradictory to his promises? Whether the law and the gospel are rival systems? Whether it is necessary, in order to hold to the excellency of the one to hold that the other is contradictory, evil, and worthless? To all this he answers; and says, by no means. He says the fault was not in the law. The view which he had taken, and which was revealed in the Bible, arose from the nature of the case. The law was as good a law as could be made, and it answered all the purposes of law. It was *so* excellent, that if it had been possible that men could be justified by law at all, that was the law by which it would have been done. But it was not possible. The effect of the law, therefore, was to show that all men were sinners, and to shut them up to the plan of justification by the work of a Redeemer. It was appointed, therefore, not to justify men, but to lead them to the Saviour, ver. 21—24.

(8.) The effect of the plan of justification by faith in the Lord Jesus was to make the mind free. It was no longer under a schoolmaster. They who are justified in this way become the children of God. They all become one in the Redeemer. There is neither Jew nor Greek, but they constitute one great family, and are the children of Abraham, and heirs according to the promise, ver. 25—29.

1. *O foolish Galatians.* That is, foolish for having yielded to the influence of the false teachers, and for having embraced doctrines that tended to subvert the gospel of the Redeemer. The original word here used (ἀνόητοι) denotes void of understanding; and they had shown it in a remarkable manner in rejecting the doctrine of the apostles, and in embracing the errors into which they had fallen. It will be remembered that this is an expression similar to what was applied to them by others; see the Introduction, § I. Thus Callimachus in his hymns calls them "a foolish people," and Hillary, himself a Gaul, calls them *Gallos indociles*, expressions remarkably in accordance with that used here by Paul. It is implied that they were without stability of character. The particular thing to which Paul refers here is, that they were so easily led astray by the arguments of the false teachers. ¶ *Who hath bewitched you.* The word here used (ἐβάσκανε) properly means, to prate about any one; and then to mislead by pretences, as if by magic arts; to fascinate; to influence by a charm. The idea here is, that they had not been led by *reason* and by *sober judgment*, but that there must have been some charm or fascination to have taken them away in this manner from what they had embraced as true, and what they had the fullest evidence was true. Paul had sufficient confidence in them to believe that they had not embraced their present views under the unbiassed influence of judgment and reason, but that there must have been some fascination or charm by which it was done. It was in fact accomplished by the arts and the plausible pretences of those who came from among the Jews. ¶ *That ye should not obey the truth.* The truth of the gospel. That you should yield your minds to falsehood and error. It should be observed, however, that this phrase is wanting in many MSS. It is omitted in the Syriac version; and many of the most important Greek and Latin Fathers omit it. Mill thinks it should be omitted; and Griesbach has omitted it. It is not essential to the passage in order to the sense; and it conveys no truth which is not elsewhere taught fully. It is apparently added to show what was the effect of their being bewitched or enchanted. ¶ *Before whose eyes.* In whose very presence. That is, it has been done so clearly that you may be said to have *seen* it. ¶ *Jesus Christ hath been evidently set forth.* By the preaching of the gospel. He has been so fully and plainly preached that you may be said to have seen him. The effect of his being preached in the manner in which it has been done, ought to have been as great as if you had seen him crucified before your eyes. The word rendered "hath been evidently set forth" (προεγράφη), means properly *to write before;* and then to announce beforehand in writing; or *to announce by posting up on a tablet.* The meaning here is, probably, that Christ has been announced among them crucified, as if the doctrine was set forth in a public written tablet—*Robinson's Lex.* There was the utmost clearness and distinctness of view, so that they need not make any mistake in regard to him. The Syriac renders it, "Christ has been crucified before your eyes as if he had been represented by paint-

2 This only would I learn of you, Received[a] ye the Spirit by the works of the law, or[b] by the hearing of faith?

a Ep.1.13. b Rom.10.17.

ing." According to this, the idea is, that it was as plain as if there had been a representation of him by a picture. This has been done chiefly by preaching. I see no reason, however, to doubt that Paul means also to include the celebration of the Lord's supper, in which the Lord Jesus is so clearly exhibited as a crucified Saviour. ¶ *Crucified among you.* That is, represented among you *as* crucified. The words "among you," however, are wanting in many MSS. and obscure the sense. If they are to be retained, the meaning is, that the representations of the Lord Jesus as crucified had been as clear and impressive among them as if they had seen him with their own eyes. The *argument* is, that they had so clear a representation of the Lord Jesus, and of the design of his death, that it was strange that they had so soon been perverted from the belief of it. Had they *seen* the Saviour crucified; had they stood by the cross and witnessed his agony in death on account of sin, how could they doubt what was the design of his dying, and how could they be seduced from faith in his death, or be led to embrace any other method of justification? How could they *now* do it, when, although they had not *seen* him die, they had the fullest knowledge of the object for which he gave his precious life? The *doctrine* taught in this verse is, that a faithful exhibition of the sufferings and death of the Saviour *ought* to exert an influence over our minds and hearts *as if* we had seen him die; and that they to whom such an exhibition has been made should avoid being led astray by the blandishments of false doctrines, and by the arts of man. Had we *seen* the Saviour expire, we could never have forgotten the scene. Let us endeavour to cherish a remembrance of his sufferings and death *as if* we had seen him die.

2. *This only would I learn of you.* I would ask this of you; retaining still the language of severe reproof. The design here, and in the following verses, is, to *prove* to them that the views which they had at first embraced were correct, and that the views which they *now* cherished were false. To show them this, he asks them the simple question, by what means they had obtained the exalted privileges which they enjoyed? Whether they had obtained them by the simple gospel, or whether by the observance of the law? The word "only" here (μόνον) implies that this was enough to settle the question. The argument to which he was about to appeal was *enough* for his purpose. He did not need to go any further. They had been converted. They had received the Holy Spirit. They had had abundant evidence of their acceptance with God, and the simple matter of inquiry now was, whether this had occurred as the regular effect of the gospel, or whether it had been by obeying the law of Moses? ¶ *Received ye the Spirit.* The Holy Spirit. He refers here, doubtless, to *all* the manifestations of the Spirit which had been made to them, in renewing the heart, in sanctifying the soul, in comforting them in affliction, and in his miraculous agency among them. The Holy Spirit had been conferred on them at their conversion (comp. Acts x. 44; xi. 17) and this was to them proof of the favour of God, and of their being accepted by him. ¶ *By the works of the law.* By obeying the law of Moses or of *any* law. It was in no way connected with their obeying the law. This must have been so clear to them that no one could have any doubt on the subject. The inestimably rich and precious gift of the Holy Spirit had *not* been conferred on them in consequence of their obeying the law. ¶ *Or by the hearing of faith.* In connection with hearing the gospel requiring faith as a condition of salvation. The Holy Spirit was sent down only in connection with the preaching of the gospel. It was a matter of truth, and which could not be denied,

3 Are ye so foolish? having [a] begun in the Spirit, are ye now made perfect [b] by the flesh?

a chap.4.9. *b* He.9.10.

that those influences had not been imparted under the law, but had been connected with the gospel of the Redeemer; comp. Acts ii. The doctrine taught in this verse is, that the benefits resulting to Christians from the gift of the Holy Spirit are enough to prove that the gospel is from God, and therefore true. This was the case with regard to the miraculous endowments communicated in the early ages of the church by the Holy Spirit; for the miracles which were wrought, the knowledge of languages imparted, and the conversion of thousands from the error of their ways, proved that the system was from heaven; and it is true now. Every Christian has had ample proof, from the influences of the Spirit on his heart and around him, that the system which is attended with such benefits is from heaven. His own renewed heart; his elevated and sanctified affections; his exalted hopes; his consolations in trial; his peace in the prospect of death, and the happy influences of the system around him in the conversion of others, and in the intelligence, order, and purity of the community, are ample proof that the religion is true. Such effects do not come from any attempt to keep the law; they result from no other system. No system of infidelity produces them; no mere system of infidelity can produce them. It is only by that pure system which proclaims salvation by the grace of God; which announces salvation by the merits of the Lord Jesus, that such effects are produced. The Saviour promised the Holy Spirit to descend after his ascension to heaven to apply his work; and everywhere, under the faithful preaching of the simple gospel, that Spirit keeps up the evidence of the truth of the system by his influences on the hearts and lives of men.

3. *Are ye so foolish?* Can it be that you are so unwise? The idea is, that Paul hardly thought it credible that they *could* have pursued such a course. They had so cordially embraced the gospel when he preached to them, they had given such evidences that they were under its influence, that he regarded it as hardly possible that they should have so far abandoned it as to embrace such a system as they had done. ¶ *Having begun in the Spirit.* That is, when the gospel was first preached to them. They had commenced their professedly Christian life under the influence of the Holy Spirit, and with the pure and spiritual worship of God. They had known the power and spirituality of the glorious gospel. They had been renewed by the Spirit; sanctified in some measure by him; and had submitted themselves to the spiritual influences of the gospel. ¶ *Are ye now made perfect.* Tindal renders this, "ye would now end." The word here used (ἐπιτελέω) means properly, to bring through to an end, to finish; and the sense here has probably been expressed by Tindal. The idea of *perfecting*, in the sense in which we now use that word, is not implied in the original. It is that of finishing, ending, completing; and the sense is: "You began your Christian career under the elevated and spiritual influences of Christianity, a system so pure and so exalted above the carnal ordinances of the Jews. Having begun thus, can it be that you are *finishing* your Christian course, or carrying it on to completion by the observance of those ordinances, as if they were more pure and elevating than Christianity? Can it be that you regard them as *an advance* on the system of the gospel?" ¶ *By the flesh.* By the observance of the carnal rites of the Jews, for so the word here evidently means. This has not ever been an uncommon thing. Many have been professedly converted by the Spirit, and have soon fallen into the observance of mere rites and ceremonies, and depended mainly on them for salvation. Many *churches* have commenced their career in an elevated and spiritual manner, and have *ended* in the observance of mere forms. So

4 Have ye suffered so [1] many things in vain? [a] if *it be* yet in vain.
5 He therefore that ministereth [b] to you the Spirit, and worketh miracles among you, *doeth he it* by the works of the law, or by the hearing of faith?

1 or, *great*. *a* 2 John 8. *b* 2 Cor.3.8.

many Christians begin their course in a spiritual manner, and end it "in the flesh" in another sense. They soon conform to the world. They are brought under the influence of worldly appetites and propensities. They forget the spiritual nature of their religion; and they live for the indulgence of ease, and for the gratification of the senses. They build them houses, and they "plant vineyards," and they collect around them the instruments of music, and the bowl and the wine is in their feasts, and they surrender themselves to the luxury of living: and it seems as if they intended to *perfect* their Christianity by drawing around them as much of the world as possible. The beautiful simplicity of their early piety is gone. The blessedness of those moments when they lived by simple faith has fled. The times when they sought all their consolation in God are no more; and they now seem to differ from the world only in form. I dread to see a Christian inherit much wealth, or even to be thrown into very prosperous business. I see in it a temptation to build himself a splendid mansion, and to collect around him all that constitutes luxury among the people of the world. How natural for him to feel that if he has wealth like others, he should show it in a similar manner! And how easy for the most humble and spiritually-minded Christian, in the beginning of his Christian life, to become conformed to the world (such is the weakness of human nature in its best forms); and having begun in the spirit, to end in the flesh!

4. *Have ye suffered so many things in vain?* Paul reminds them of what they had endured on account of their attachment to Christianity. He assures them, that if the opinions on account of which they had suffered were false, then their sufferings had been in vain. They were of no use to them—for what advantage was it to suffer for a false opinion? The opinions for which they had suffered had not been those which they now embraced. They were not those connected with the observance of the Jewish rites. They had suffered on account of their having embraced *the gospel*, the system of justification by a crucified Redeemer; and now, if those sentiments were wrong, why, their sufferings had been wholly in vain; see this argument pursued at much greater length in 1 Cor. xv. 18, 19, 29—32. *If* it be *yet in vain*. That is, I trust it is not in vain. I hope you have not so far abandoned the gospel, that all your sufferings in its behalf have been of no avail. I believe the system is true; and if true, and you are sincere Christians, it will not be in vain that you have suffered in its behalf, though you have gone astray. I trust, that although your principles have been shaken, yet they have not been wholly overthrown, and that you will not reap the reward of your having suffered so much on account of the gospel.

5. *He therefore that ministereth*, &c. This verse contains substantially a repetition of the argument in ver. 2. The argument is, that the gift of the Holy Spirit to them was not imparted in consequence of the observance of the law of Moses, but in connection with the preaching of the gospel. By the word "he" in this place, Clarke, Doddridge, Bloomfield, Chandler, Locke and many others, suppose that the apostle means himself. Bloomfield says, that it is the common opinion of "all the ancient commentators." But this seems to me a strange opinion. The obvious reference, it seems to me, is to God, who had furnished or imparted to them the remarkable influences of the Holy Spirit, and this had been done in connection with the preaching of the gospel, and not by the observance of the law. If, however, it refers to Paul, it means that

6 Even as Abraham [a] believed
God, and it was [1] accounted to him
for righteousness.
7 Know ye therefore, that they
which are of faith, the same are the
children [b] of Abraham.
8 And the Scripture, foreseeing that God would justify [c] the

a Ge.15.6. 1 or, *imputed*. *b* John 8.39; Ro.4.11—16. *c* ver.22.

he had been made the agent or instrument in imparting to them those remarkable endowments, and that this had been done by one who had not enforced the necessity of obeying the law of Moses, but who had preached to them the simple gospel.

6. *Even as Abraham believed God,* &c.; see this passage fully explained in the Notes on Rom. iv. 3. The passage is introduced here by the apostle to show that the most eminent of the patriarchs was not saved by the deeds of the law. He was saved by faith, and this fact showed that it was possible to be saved in that way, and that it was the design of God to save men in this manner. Abraham believed God, and was justified, *before* the law of Moses was given. It could not, therefore, be pretended that the law was *necessary* to justification; for if it had been, Abraham could not have been saved. But if not necessary in his case, it was in no other; and this instance demonstrated that the false teachers among the Galatians were wrong even according to the Old Testament.

7. *Know ye therefore,* &c. Learn from this case. It is an inference which follows, that all they who believe are the children of Abraham. ¶ *They which are of faith.* Who believe, and who are justified in this manner. ¶ *Are the children of Abraham.* Abraham was the "father of the faithful." The most remarkable trait in his character was his unwavering confidence in God. They who evinced the same trait, therefore, were worthy to be called his children. They would be justified in the same way, and in the same manner meet the approbation of God. It is *implied* here, that it was sufficient for salvation to have a character which would render it proper to say that we are the children of Abraham. If we are like him, if we evince the same spirit and character, we may be sure of salvation.

8. *And the Scripture.* The word Scripture refers to the Old Testament; see Note, John v. 39. It is here personified, or spoken of as *foreseeing.* The idea is, that he by whom the scriptures were inspired, foresaw that. It is agreeable, the meaning is, to the account on the subject in the Old Testament. The Syriac renders this, "Since God foreknew that the Gentiles would be justified by faith, he before announced to Abraham, as the scripture saith, In thee shall all nations be blessed." ¶ *Foreseeing.* That is, this doctrine is contained in the Old Testament. It was foreseen and predicted that the heathen would be justified by faith, and not by the works of the law. ¶ That *God would justify the heathen.* Gr. The nations—τὰ ἔθνη—the Gentiles. The fact that the heathen, or the Gentiles would be admitted to the privileges of the true religion, and be interested in the benefits of the coming of the Messiah, is a fact which is everywhere abundantly predicted in the Old Testament. As an instance, see Isa. xlix. 6, 22, 23; lx. I do not know that it is anywhere distinctly foretold that the heathen would be justified by *faith*, nor does the argument of the apostle require us to believe this. He says that the scriptures, *i. e.* he who inspired the scriptures, *foresaw* that fact, and that the scriptures were written *as if* with the knowledge of that fact; but it is not directly affirmed. The whole structure and frame of the Old Testament, however, proceeds on the supposition that it would be so; and this is all that the declaration of the apostle requires us to understand. ¶ *Preached before the gospel.* This translation does not convey quite the idea to us, which the language of Paul, in the original, would to the people to whom he addressed it. We have affixed a *technical sense* to the phrase "to preach the gospel." It is applied to the formal

heathen through faith, preached before the gospel unto Abraham, *saying,* [a] In thee shall all nations be blessed.

a Ge.12.3; 22.18; Ac.3.25.

9 So then [b] they which be of
faith are blessed with faithful
Abraham.
10 For as many as are of the

b chap.4.28.

and public annunciation of the truths of religion, especially the "good news" of a Saviour's birth, and of redemption by his blood. But we are not required by the language used here to suppose that this was done to Abraham, or that "the gospel" was preached to him in the sense in which we all now use that phrase. The expression, in Greek (προευηγγελίσατο), means merely, "the joyful news was announced beforehand to Abraham;" *scil.* that in him should all the nations of the earth be blessed. It was *implied,* indeed, that it would be by the Messiah; but the distinct point of the "good news" was not the "*gospel*" as we understand it, but it was that somehow through him all the nations of the earth would be made happy. Tindal has well translated it, "Showed beforehand glad tidings unto Abraham." This translation should have been adopted in our common version. ¶ *In thee shall all nations be blessed;* see Notes on Acts iii. 25; Rom. iv. 13. All nations should be made happy in him, or through him. The sense is, that the Messiah was to be descended from him, and the religion of the Messiah, producing peace and salvation, was to be extended to all the nations of the earth; see Gen. xii. 3; comp. Note on ver. 16 of this chapter.

[Εὐαγγελίζω doubtless here, as elsewhere, signifies to announce glad tidings. And in all the passages where this word occurs, even in those where the author might be disposed to allow that the "gospel technically" was meant, the translation which he proposes here would be very suitable and exact. It was certainly the same gospel that was preached to Abraham, that is now preached to us, *though not with the same fulness of revelation,* in his case. The apostle here affirms that the gospel, *i. e.,* the way of justification through Christ, in opposition to the legal system he had been condemning—was, *in few words,* preached to Abraham, being contained in that promise, "in thee shall all nations be blessed;" see Gen. xxii. 17. The full meaning of the promise, indeed, could not be gathered from the words themselves, but Abraham must have understood their application in a far more extensive sense than that "somehow through him all the nations of the earth would be made happy." Whether the true import were made known to him directly by the Spirit of God, or discerned by him in typical representation, it is certain that Abraham's faith terminated on the promised Seed, *i. e.,* Christ whose day he desired to see, and seeing it afar, was glad, John viii. 56. "Hereof it followeth," says Luther on the place, "that the blessing and faith of Abraham is the same that ours is, that Abraham's Christ is our Christ, that Christ died as well for the sins of Abraham as for us."]

9. *So then they which be of faith.* They whose leading characteristic it is that they *believe.* This was the leading trait in the character of Abraham, and this is the leading thing required of those who embrace the gospel, and in the character of a true Christian. ¶ *Are blessed with faithful Abraham.* In the same manner they are interested in the promises made to him, and they will be treated as he was. They are justified in the same manner, and admitted to the same privileges on earth and in heaven.

10. *For as many as are of the works of the law.* As many as are seeking to be justified by yielding obedience to the law—whether the moral law, or the ceremonial law. The proposition is general; and it is designed to show that, from the nature of the case, it is impossible to be justified by the works of the law, since, under all circumstances of obedience which we can render, we are still left with its heavy curse resting on us. ¶ *Are under the curse.* The curse which the law of God denounces. Having failed by all their efforts to yield perfect obedience, they must, of course, be exposed to the curse which the law denounces on the guilty. The word rendered curse (κατάρα) means, as with us, properly, *imprecation,* or *cursing.* It is used in the Scriptures particularly in the sense of the Hebrew

works of the law, are under the curse: for it is written, [a] Cursed *is* every one that continueth not in all things which are written in the book of the law to do them.

11 But that no man is justified

a De.27.26.

אלה, malediction, or execration (Job xxxi. 30; Jer. xxix. 18; Dan. ix. 11); of the word מארה (Mal. ii. 2; Rev. iii. 33); and especially of the common Hebrew word קללה, a curse; Gen. xxvii. 12, 13; Deut. xi. 26, 28, 29; xxiii. 5; xxvii. 13, *et sæpe al.* It is here used evidently in the sense of devoting to punishment or destruction; and the idea is, that all who attempt to secure salvation by the works of the law, must be exposed to its penalty. It denounces a curse on all who do not yield entire obedience; and no partial compliance with its demands can save from the penalty. ¶ *For it is written.* The substance of these words is found in Deut. xxviii. 26: "Cursed be he that confirmeth not all the words of this law to do them." It is the solemn close of a series of maledictions, which Moses denounces in that chapter on the violators of the law. In this quotation, Paul has given the sense of the passage, but he has quoted literally neither from the Hebrew nor from the Septuagint. The *sense*, however, is retained. The word "cursed" here means, that the violator of the law shall be devoted to punishment or destruction. The phrase "that continueth not," in the Hebrew is "that confirmeth not"—that does not establish or confirm by his life. He would *confirm* it by *continuing* to obey it; and thus the sense in Paul and in Moses is substantially the same. The word "all" is not expressed in the Hebrew in Deuteronomy, but it is evidently implied, and has been inserted by the English translators. It is found, however, in six MSS. of Kennicott and De Rossi; in the Samaritan text; in the Septuagint; and in several of the Targums.—*Clarke.* ¶ *The book of the law.* That is, in the law. This phrase is not found in the passage in Deuteronomy. The expression there is, "the words of this law." Paul gives it a somewhat larger sense, and applies it to the whole of the law of God. The meaning is, that the *whole* law must be obeyed, or man cannot be justified by it, or will be exposed to its penalty and its curse. This idea is expressed more fully by James (ii. 10); "Whosoever shall keep the whole law, and yet offend in one point, he is guilty of all;" that is, he is guilty of breaking the law *as a whole,* and must be held responsible for such violation. The sentiment here is one that is common to *all* law, and must be, from the nature of the case. The idea is, that a man who does not yield compliance to a whole law, is subject to its penalty, or to a curse. All law is sustained on this principle. A man who has been honest, and temperate, and industrious, and patriotic, if he commits a single act of murder, is subject to the curse of the law, and must meet the penalty. A man who has been honest and honourable in all his dealings, yet if he commit a single act of forgery, he must meet the curse denounced by the laws of his country, and bear the penalty. So, in all matters pertaining to law: no matter what the integrity of the man; no matter how upright he has been, yet, for *the one offence* the law denounces a penalty, and he must bear it. It is out of the question for him to be justified by it. He cannot plead as a reason why he should not be condemned for the act of murder or forgery, that he has in all other respects obeyed the law, or even that he has been guilty of no such offences before. Such is the idea of Paul in the passage before us. It was clear to his view that man had not in all respects yielded obedience to the law of God. If he had not done this, it was impossible that he should be justified by the law, and he must bear its penalty.

11. *But that no man is justified,* &c. The argument which Paul has been pursuing he proceeds to confirm by an express declaration of the Bible. The argument is this: "It is impos-

by the law in the sight of God, *it*
is evident: for, The [a] just shall
live by faith.
12 And the law [b] is not of faith:
but, The [c] man that doeth them
shall live in them.
13 Christ [d] hath redeemed us
from the curse of the law, being

a Hab.2.4. b Rom.10.5,6. c Le.18.5; Eze.20.11. d 2 Co.5.21; chap.4.5.

sible that a man should be justified by the law, because God has appointed another way of justification." But there cannot be two ways of obtaining life, and as he has appointed *faith* as the condition on which men shall *live*, he has precluded from them the possibility of obtaining salvation in any other mode. ¶ *For, The just shall live by faith.* This is quoted from Hab. ii. 4. This passage is also quoted by Paul in Rom. i. 17; see it explained in the Note on that verse. The sense here is, that life is promised to man only in connection with faith. It is not by the works of the law that it is done. The condition of life is faith: and he lives who believes. The meaning is not, I apprehend, that the man who is justified by faith shall live, but that life is promised and exists only in connection with faith, and that the just or righteous man obtains it only in this way. Of course it cannot be obtained by the observance of the law, but must be by some other scheme.

12. *And the law is not of faith.* The law is not a matter of faith; it does not relate to faith; it does not require faith; it deals in other matters, and it pertains to another system than to faith. ¶ *But, The man*, &c. This is the language of the law, and this is what the law teaches. It does not make provision for faith, but it requires unwavering and perpetual obedience, if man would obtain life by it; see this passage explained in the Notes on Rom. x. 5.

13. *Christ hath redeemed us.* The word used here (ἐξηγόρασεν) is not that which is usually employed in the New Testament to denote redemption. That word is λυτρόω. The difference between them mainly is, that the word used here more usually relates to *a purchase* of any kind; the other is used strictly with reference to *a ransom*. The word here used is more *general* in its meaning; the other is strictly appropriated to a ransom. This distinction is not observable here, however, and the word here used is employed in the proper sense of redeem. It occurs in the New Testament only in this place, and in chap. iv. 5; Eph. v. 16; Col. iv. 5. It properly means, to purchase, to buy up; and then to purchase any one, to redeem, to set free. Here it means, that Christ had purchased, or set us free from the curse of the law, by his being made a curse for us. On the meaning of the words redeem and ransom, see my Notes on Rom. iii. 25; Isa. xliii. 3; comp. 2 Cor. v. 21. ¶ *From the curse of the law.* The curse which the law threatens, and which the execution of the law would inflict; the punishment due to sin. This must mean, that he has rescued us from the consequences of transgression in the world of woe; he has saved us from the punishment which our sins have deserved. The word, "us" here, must refer to *all* who are redeemed; that is, to the Gentiles as well as the Jews. The curse of the law is a curse which is due to sin, and cannot be regarded as applied particularly to any one class of men. All who violate the law of God, however that law may be made known, are exposed to its penalty. The word "law" here, relates to the law of God in general, to all the laws of God made known to man. The law of God denounced death as the wages of sin. It threatened punishment in the future world for ever. That would certainly have been inflicted, but for the coming and death of Christ. The world is lying by nature under this curse, and it is sweeping the race on to ruin. ¶ *Being made a curse for us.* This is an exceedingly important expression. Tindal renders it, "And was made a curse for us." The Greek word is κατάρα, the same word which is used in ver. 10; see Note on that verse. There is scarcely any

made a curse for us: for it is written, *a* Cursed *is* every one that hangeth on a tree:

a De.21.23.

passage in the New Testament on which it is more important to have correct views than this; and scarcely any one on which more erroneous opinions have been entertained. In regard to it, we may observe that it does not mean, (1.) That by being made *a curse,* his character or work were in any sense displeasing to God. He approved always of what the Lord Jesus did, and he regarded his whole character with love and approbation. The passage should never be so interpreted as to leave the impression that he was in any conceivable sense the object of the divine displeasure. (2.) He was not *ill-deserving.* He was not blame-worthy. He had done no wrong. He was holy, harmless, undefiled. No crime charged upon him was proved; and there is no clearer doctrine in the Bible than that in all his character and work the Lord Jesus was perfectly holy and pure. (3.) He was not *guilty* in any proper sense of the word. The word guilty means, properly, to be bound to punishment for crime. It does not mean properly, to be exposed to suffering, but it always, when properly used, implies the notion of personal crime. I know that theologians have used the word in a somewhat different sense, but it is contrary to the common and just apprehensions of men. When we say that a man is *guilty,* we instinctively think of his having committed a crime, or having done something wrong. When a jury finds a man *guilty,* it implies that the man has committed a crime, and *ought* to be punished. But in this sense, and in no conceivable sense, where the word is properly used, was the Lord Jesus guilty. (4.) It cannot be meant that the Lord Jesus properly bore the penalty of the law. His sufferings were *in the place* of the penalty, not *the penalty itself.* They were a *substitution* for the penalty, and were, therefore, strictly and properly vicarious, and were not the identical sufferings which the sinner would himself have endured. There are some things in the penalty of the law, which the Lord Jesus did not endure, and which a substitute or a vicarious victim could not endure. Remorse of conscience is a part of the inflicted penalty of the law, and will be a vital part of the sufferings of the sinner in hell—but the Lord Jesus did not endure that. *Eternity of sufferings* is an essential part of the penalty of the law—but the Lord Jesus did not suffer for ever. Thus there are numerous sorrows connected with the consciousness of personal guilt, which the Lord Jesus did not and cannot endure. (5.) He was not sinful, or a sinner, in any sense. He did not *so* take human guilt upon him, that the words *sinful* and *sinner* could with any propriety be applied to him. They are *not* applied to him any way in the Bible; but the language there is undeviating. It is, that in all senses he was holy and undefiled. And yet language is often used on this subject which is horrible and but little short of blasphemy, as if he was guilty, and as if he was even the greatest sinner in the universe. I have heard language used which sent a thrill of horror to my heart; and language may be found in the writings of those who hold the doctrine of imputation in the strictest sense, which is but little short of blasphemy. I have hesitated whether I should copy expressions here on this subject from one of the greatest and best of men,—I mean Luther,—to show the nature of the views which men sometimes entertain on the subject of the imputation of sin to Christ. But as Luther deliberately published them to the world in his favourite book, which he used to call his "Catharine de Bora," after the name of his wife; and as similar views are sometimes entertained now; and as it is important that such views should be held up to universal abhorrence,—no matter how respectable the source from which they emanate,—I will copy a few of his expressions on this subject. "And this, no doubt, all the prophets did foresee in spirit, *that*

Christ should become the greatest transgressor, murderer, adulterer, thief, rebel, and blasphemer, THAT EVER WAS OR COULD BE IN THE WORLD. For he being made a sacrifice for the sins of the whole world, is not now an innocent person and without sins; is not now the Son of God, born of the Virgin Mary; but a sinner which hath and carrieth the sin of Paul, who was a blasphemer, an oppressor, and a persecutor; of Peter, which denied Christ; of David, which was an adulterer, a murderer, and caused the Gentiles to blaspheme the name of the Lord; and, briefly, which hath and beareth all the sins of all men in his body: not that he himself committed them, but for that he received them, being committed or done of us, and laid them upon his own body, that he might make satisfaction for them with his own blood. Therefore, this general sentence of Moses comprehendeth him also (albeit in his own person he was innocent), because it found him amongst sinners and transgressors; like as the magistrate taketh him for a thief, and punisheth him whom he findeth among other thieves and transgressors, though he never committed any thing worthy of death. When the law, therefore, found him among thieves it condemned and killed him as a thief." "If thou wilt deny him to be a sinner and accursed, deny, also, that he was crucified and dead." "But if it be not absurd to confess and believe that Christ was crucified between two thieves, then it is not absurd to say that he was accursed, and OF ALL SINNERS, THE GREATEST."* "God, our most merciful Father, sent his only Son into the world, and laid upon him all the sins of all men, saying, be thou Peter, that denier; Paul, that persecutor, blasphemer, and cruel oppressor; David, that adulterer; that sinner which did eat the apple in paradise; that thief which hanged upon the cross; and, briefly, be thou the person which hath committed the sins of all men; see, therefore, that thou pay and satisfy for them."—*Luther on the Galatians*, chap. iii. 13. [pp. 213—215. Ed. Lond. 1838.] Luther was a great and holy man. He held, as firmly as any one can, to the personal holiness of the Redeemer. But this language shows how imperfect and erroneous views may warp the language of holy men; and how those sentiments led him to use language which is little less than blasphemy. Indeed, we cannot doubt that if Luther had heard this very language used by one of the numerous enemies of the gospel in his time, as applicable to the Saviour, he would have poured out the full torrent of his burning wrath, and all the stern denunciations of his most impassioned eloquence, on the head of the scoffer and the blasphemer. It is singular, it is one of the remarkable facts in the history of mind, that a man with the New Testament before him, and accustomed to contemplate daily its language, could ever have allowed himself to use expressions like these of the holy and unspotted Saviour. But what *is* the meaning of the language of Paul, it will be asked, when he says that he was "made a curse for us?" In reply, I answer, that the meaning must be ascertained from the passage which Paul quotes in support of his assertion, that Christ was "made a curse for us." That passage is, "Cursed is every one that hangeth on a tree." This passage is found in Deut. xxi. 23. It occurs in a law respecting one who was hanged for a "sin worthy of death," ver. 22. The law was, that he should be buried the same day, and that the body should not remain suspended over the night, and it is added, as a reason for this, that "he that is hanged is accursed of God;" or, as it is in the margin, "the curse of God." The meaning is, that when one was executed for crime in this manner, he was the object of the Divine displeasure and malediction. Regarded thus as an object accursed of God, there was a propriety that the man who was executed for crime should be *buried* as soon as possible, that the offensive object should be hidden from the view In quoting this passage, Paul leaves out the words "of God," and simply says, that the one who was hanged on a tree was held accursed. The sense

* The underscoring is mine.

of the passage before us is, therefore, that Jesus was subjected to what was regarded as an accursed death. *He was treated in his death* AS IF *he had been a criminal.* He was put to death in the same manner as he would have been if he had himself been guilty of the violation of the law. Had he been a thief or a murderer; had he committed the grossest and the blackest crimes, this would have been the punishment to which he would have been subjected. This was the mode of punishment adapted to those crimes, and he was treated *as if* all these had been committed by him. Or, in other words, had he been guilty of all these, or any of these, he could not have been treated in a more shameful and ignominious manner than he was; nor could he have been subjected to a more cruel death. As has already been intimated, it does not mean that he was guilty, nor that he was not the object of the approbation and love of God, but that his death was the same that it would have been if he had been the vilest of malefactors, and that that death was regarded by the law as accursed. It was by such substituted sorrows that we are saved; and he consented to die the most shameful and painful death, *as if* he were the vilest malefactor, in order that the most guilty and vile of the human race might be saved. In regard to the way in which his death is connected with our justification, see Note on chap. ii. 16. It may be observed, also, that the punishment of the cross was unknown to the Hebrews in the time of Moses, and that the passage in Deut. xxi. 23, did not refer originally to that. Nor is it known that hanging criminals alive was practised among the Hebrews. Those who were guilty of great crimes were first stoned or otherwise put to death, and then their bodies were suspended for a few hours on a gibbet. In many cases, however, merely the *head* was suspended after it had been severed from the body, Gen. xl. 17—19; Num. xxv. 4, 5. Crucifixion was not known in the time of the giving of the law; but the Jews gave such an extent to the law in Deut. xxi. 23, as to include this mode of punishment; see John xix. 31, seq. The force of the argument here, as used by the apostle Paul, is, that if to be suspended on a gibbet after having been put to death, was regarded as a curse, it should not be regarded as a curse in a less degree to be suspended alive on a cross, and to be put to death in this manner. If this interpretation of the passage be correct, then it follows that this should never be used as implying, *in any sense,* that Christ was guilty, or that he was ill-deserving, or that he was an object of the divine displeasure, or that he poured out on him all his wrath. He was, throughout, an object of the divine love and approbation. God never loved him more, or approved what he did more, than when he gave himself to death on the cross. He had no hatred towards him; he had no displeasure to express towards him. And it is this which makes the atonement so wonderful and so glorious. Had he been displeased with him; had the Redeemer been properly an object of his wrath; had he in any sense *deserved* those sorrows, there would have been no merit in his sufferings; there would have been no atonement. What merit can there be when one suffers only what he deserves? But what made the atonement so wonderful, so glorious, so benevolent; what made it *an atonement at all,* was, that innocence was treated AS IF it were guilt; that the most pure, and holy, and benevolent, and lovely being on earth should *consent* to be treated, and should be treated by God and man, AS IF he were the most vile and ill-deserving. This is the mystery of the atonement; this shows the wonders of the divine benevolence; this is the nature of substituted sorrow; and this lays the foundation for the offer of pardon, and for the hope of eternal salvation.

[The curse of the law is doubtless the sentence of condemnation it has pronounced against sinners. Christ being made a curse for us signifies, therefore, his appointment of God to endure the penalty denounced by the law, in our room. *He* intercepted the curse that must have fallen on us, and ruined us for ever. This quotation, and the original passage in Deuteronomy, certainly do intimate something like *wrath* or *displeasure* in the divine mind. Our author's criticism, here, seems to have but a slender foundation. He affirms, that though Moses in Deut. xxi. 23, speaks of the criminal that hung on a tree being "accursed of God," Paul leaves out "of God," thereby intimating "that Jesus was subjected to what was regarded (by man) as an accursed death." This criticism is employed to get rid of the idea that the Holy Jesus was the object of the divine malediction, and gives opportunity for affirming, what is indeed true, that never was Jesus regarded with greater complacency by his Father, than when he hung on the cross and died in the room of sinners. Yet some meaning must be attached to those scriptures which allege, or seem to allege, that the wrath of God was the bitterest ingredient in the Saviour's cup; see his complaints in the xxii. xl. lxix. and lxxx. Psalms. Nor can the agony in the garden, and the exclamation on the cross, be otherwise accounted for. Speaking of this last, an author of whom America has some reason to boast, says, "In the language of the psalmist, God hid his face from him, that is, if I mistake not, withdrew from him wholly, those manifestations of supreme complacency in his character and conduct, which he had always before made. As this was in itself a most distressing testimony of the divine anger against sin, so it is naturally imagined, and I think, when we are informed that it pleased Jehovah to bruise him, directly declared in the scriptures, that this manifestation was accompanied by other disclosures of the anger of God against sin, and against him as the substitute of sinners."—*Dwight's sermon on the Priesthood of Christ.* It is not with very much reason or modesty, therefore, that the commentator objects to the passage being understood as *in any sense* implying that God "poured out on Christ all his wrath;" such certainly was the fact. And the simple omission by Paul here of the words "of God" is too slender ground for the assertion, that that awful truth is not only not affirmed by him, but tacitly denied.

But this extraordinary criticism is by no means new. Luther thus speaks of it as an objection in his day, "that Paul omitted this word (of God) which is in Moses"—therefore they ask this question, how this sentence may be applied to Christ, that he is accursed of God, and hanged on a tree, seeing that he is no malefactor or thief, but righteous and holy? "This," says the reformer—and the language may be held as his reply to much that is said of him above—"this may peradventure move the simple and the ignorant, thinking that the Sophisters do speak it not only wittily, *but also very godly*, and thereby do defend the honour and glory of Christ, and give warning to all Christians to beware that they think not so wickedly of Christ, that he should be made a curse."—*Luther's comment in loco.*

The passage certainly does intimate, if there be any meaning in language, that Christ, *as the substitute of sinners*, was accursed of God. "We cannot but consider his choosing to hang upon a tree, a situation declared by the ceremonial law to be accursed of God, as intended to demonstrate to the world, that although he himself continued in all things written in the law to do them, his death was not merely the infliction of human law upon an innocent man, but a suffering which in the sight of God was penal."—*Hill*, vol. ii. p. 117, 3d edit. Indeed all the objections and difficulties which Mr. Barnes has stated on this verse, would disappear, if the distinction in the above quotation, and carefully marked also by Luther, were duly attended to, viz., *that*, between Christ, viewed in his own person, and viewed as the substitute of sinners. By overlooking this distinction in such passages as that before us, we not only stumble at the doctrine of imputation, but play into the hands of the Socinians, and well nigh yield the fortress to them; it being just about as difficult to suppose that an innocent being can suffer for sin, as that sin should be imputed to him. "Many expositors," Mr. Scott has well observed, "who contend against the imputation of Christ's righteousness to believers, in disputing against Socinians argue for the vicarious sufferings of Christ in our stead. Now what is this but imputation? *He*, though perfectly holy, paid the debt which *we* sinners had contracted. It was exacted and he became answerable; *we* sinners, on believing, are made the righteousness of God in him, and receive the inheritance which *he* merited. This then is a reciprocal imputation."—*Comment in loco.* The objections which our author has again in this place urged against the doctrine of imputation, have already been considered, in previous supplementary Notes; see on 2 Cor. v. 21; Rom. iv. v. throughout. It is never supposed, for a moment, by the advocates of that doctrine, that Christ was personally guilty, or that he was guilty in any other sense than having sin charged on him, and being in consequence thereof under obligation to suffer the penalty.

A word now on Luther's language, which sends such a thrill of horror to the commentator's heart, although he knew all the while that the reformer was as zealous for the spotless purity of the Redeemer as himself. Luther was the great reviver of a forgotten, though vital, doctrine; a doctrine which he believed to be "articulus stantis vel cadentis ecclesiæ," viz. the doctrine of justification by faith, through the imputed righteousness of Christ. With this was inseparably connected the imputation of our sin to him. Considering the importance of this doctrine, and the almost

14 That [a] the blessing of Abraham might come on the Gentiles through Jesus Christ; that we might receive the promise [b] of the Spirit through faith.

15 Brethren, I speak after the

a Ro.4.9,16.

b Is.44.3; Eze.36.27; Joel 2.28,29.

universal neglect into which it had fallen, it is not to be wondered at, that Luther should express himself strongly on the subject, nor do those authors increase their claim on our confidence, who depart very far from the doctrine of the reformation on this subject. Luther's expressions may possibly be *too* strong, but might the same charge not be brought against the words of that apostle, who has ventured to affirm, not that Christ has been made a *sinner* but *sin* itself, in the very abstract, as if no force of language could be too much on such a subject; see 2 Cor. v. 21, supplementary Note, in which the common rendering of "sin-offering," by which this passage is weakened, is shown to be inadmissable. To the same effect, we are entitled to cite this very passage, notwithstanding every attempt to distort it, in which Paul not only says that Christ was accursed, but a curse, καταρα for καταρατος, as in the other place 'αμαρτια for 'αμαρτωλος. Moreover, the reader will find, if he choose to consult Luther's commentary, that he takes great care to affirm "that Christ is innocent as concerning his own person," so that mistake is impossible. It is worthy of notice, too, that the reason why he has introduced such names as thief, malefactor, &c., is that such were the parties who were hanged on a tree under the law, and the "Sophisters" had asked how this sentence could be applied to Christ, who was no thief or malefactor? He resolves it by a reference to the doctrine of imputation, and affirms that Christ "sustained the person" or stood in the room of such. Nor does our author do great justice to the reformer in his second and third quotation. Immediately before the sentence beginning "if thou wilt deny," &c., Luther has, "But some man will say it is very absurd and slanderous to call the Son of God accursed sinner;" and to this the sentence quoted is an answer—an answer to the very objection in the commentary, and therefore ought in justice to have been placed in that light, when it affirms no more than that the fact of Christ being crucified and dead, necessarily implied that sin was charged to his account, otherwise, under the administration of a just God, these things never could have happened to him. The same remarks apply to the third quotation, which is but part of one and the same sentence with the second, and the reader has only to consult the commentary of Luther to be satisfied on the point.]

14. *That the blessing of Abraham.* The blessing which Abraham enjoyed, to wit, that of being justified by faith. ¶ *Might come on the Gentiles.* As well as on the Jews. Abraham was blessed in this manner *before* he was circumcised (Rom. iv. 11), and the same blessing might be imparted to others also who were not circumcised; see this argument illustrated in the Notes on Rom. iv. 10—12. ¶ *Through Jesus Christ.* Since he has been made a curse for all, and since he had no exclusive reference to the Jews or to any other class of men, all may come and partake alike of the benefits of his salvation. ¶ *That we might receive the promise of the Spirit.* That all we who are Christian converts. The promise of the Spirit, or the promised Spirit, is here put for all the blessings connected with the Christian religion. It includes evidently the miraculous agency of the Holy Spirit; and all his influences in renewing the heart, in sanctifying the soul, and in comforting the people of God. These influences had been obtained in virtue of the sufferings and death of the Lord Jesus in the place of sinners, and these influences were the sum of all the blessings promised by the prophets.

15. *Brethren, I speak after the manner of men.* I draw an illustration from what actually occurs among men. The illustration is, that when a contract or agreement is made by men involving obligations and promises, no one can add to it or take from it. It will remain as it was originally made. So with God. He made a solemn promise to Abraham. That promise pertained to his posterity. The blessing was connected with that promise, and it was of the nature of a compact with Abraham. But if so, then this could not be effected by the law which was four hundred years after, and the law must have been given to secure some different object from that designed by the promise made to Abraham, ver. 19. But the promise made to Abraham was designed to secure the "in-

manner of men; Though *it be* but a man's[1] covenant, yet *if it be* confirmed, no man disannulleth, or addeth thereto.

[1] testament.

heritance," or the favour of God; and if so, then the same thing could not be secured by the observance of the law, since there could not be two ways so unlike each other of obtaining the same thing. God cannot have two ways of justifying and saving men; and if he revealed a mode to Abraham, and that mode was by faith, then it could not be by the observance of the law which was given so long after. The main design of the argument and the illustration here (ver. 15, seq.) is to show that the promise made to Abraham was by no means made void by the giving of the law. The law had another design, which did not interfere with the promise made to Abraham. That stood on its own merits, irrespective of the demands and the design of the law. It is possible, as Rosenmüller suggests, that Paul may have had his eye on an objection to his view. The objection may have been that there were important acts of legislation which succeeded the promise made to Abraham, and that that promise must have been superseded by the giving of the law. To this he replies that the Mosaic law given at a late period could not take away or nullify a solemn promise made to Abraham, but that it was intended for a different object. ¶ *Though* it be *but a man's covenant.* A compact or agreement between man and man. Even in such a case no one can add to it or take from it. The *argument* here is, that such a covenant or agreement must be much less important than a promise made by God. But even that could not be annulled. How much less, therefore, could a covenant made by God be treated as if it were vain. The word covenant here (διαθήκη) is in the margin rendered "Testament;" *i. e.* will. So Tindal renders it. Its proper classical signification is will or testament, though in the Septuagint and in the New Testament it is the word which is used to denote a covenant or compact; see Note, Acts iii. 25. Here it is used in the proper sense of the word covenant, or compact; a mutual agreement between man and man. The idea is, that where such a covenant exists; where the faith of a man is solemnly pledged in this manner, no change can be made in the agreement. It is ratified, and firm, and final. ¶ *If it be confirmed.* By a seal or otherwise. ¶ *No man disannulleth,* &c. It must stand. No one can change it. No new conditions can be annexed; nor can there be any drawing back from its terms. It binds the parties to a faithful fulfilment of all the conditions. This is well understood among men; and the apostle says that the same thing must take place in regard to God.

16. *Now to Abraham and his seed.* To him and his posterity. ¶ *Were the promises made.* The promise here referred to was that which is recorded in Gen. xxii. 17, 18. "In blessing I will bless thee, and in multiplying I will multiply thy seed as the stars of heaven, and as the sand which is upon the sea-shore; and in thy seed shall all the nations of the earth be blessed." ¶ *He saith not, And to seeds, as of many, but as of one,* &c. He does not use the plural term, as if the promise extended to many persons, but he speaks in the singular number, as if but one was intended; and that one must be the Messiah. Such is Paul's interpretation; such is evidently the sentiment which he intends to convey, and the argument which he intends to urge. He designs evidently to be understood as affirming that in the use of the *singular* number σπέρμα (seed), instead of the plural σπέρματα (seeds), there is a fair ground of argument to demonstrate that the promise related to Christ or the Messiah, and to him primarily if not exclusively. Now no one ever probably read this passage without feeling a difficulty, and without asking himself whether this argument is sound, and is worthy a man of candour, and especially of an inspired man. Some of the difficulties in the

16 Now to Abraham [a] and his seed were the promises made. He saith not, And to seeds, as of many; but as of one, And to thy seed which is Christ.

a Ge.12.3,7; 17.7.

passage are these. (1.) The promise referred to in Genesis seems to have related to the posterity of Abraham at large, without *any* particular reference to an individual. It is to his seed; his descendants; to all his seed or posterity. Such would be the fair and natural interpretation should it be read by hundreds or thousands of persons who had never heard of the interpretation here put upon it by Paul. (2.) The argument of the apostle seems to proceed on the supposition that the word "seed" (σπέρμα), *i. e.* posterity, here cannot refer to more than one person. If it had, says he, it would be in the plural number. But the fact is, that the word *is* often used to denote posterity at large; to refer to descendants without limitation, just as the word posterity is with us; and it is a fact, moreover, that the word is not used in the plural at all to denote a posterity, the singular form being constantly employed for that purpose. Any one who will open Tromm's Concordance to the Septuagint, or Schmids' on the New Testament, will see the most ample confirmation of this remark. Indeed the *plural* form of the word is never used except in this place in Galatians. The difficulty, therefore, is, that the remark here of Paul appears to be a *trick* of argument, or a *quibble* more worthy of a trifling Jewish Rabbi, than of a grave reasoner or an inspired man. I have stated this difficulty freely, just as I suppose it has struck hundreds of minds, because I do not wish to shrink from any real difficulty in examining the Bible, but to see whether it can be fairly met. In meeting it, expositors have resorted to various explanations, most of them, as it seems to me, unsatisfactory, and it is not necessary to detail them. Bishop Burnet, Doddridge, and some others suppose that the apostle means to say that the promises made to Abraham were *not only* appropriated to one class of his descendants, that is, to those by Isaac, but that they centred in *one illustrious* person, through whom all the rest are made partakers of the blessings of the Abrahamic covenant. This Doddridge admits the apostle says in "*bad Greek,*" but still he supposes that this is the true exposition. Noessett and Rosenmüller suppose that by the word σπέρμα (*seed*) here, is not meant the Messiah, but Christians in general; the body of believers. But this is evidently in contradiction of the apostle, who expressly affirms that Christ was intended. It is also liable to another objection that is fatal to the opinion. The very point of the argument of the apostle is, that the singular and not the plural form of the word is used, and that therefore an *individual*, and not a *collective body* or a number of individuals, is intended. But according to this interpretation the reference *is*, in fact, to a numerous body of individuals, to the whole body of Christians. Jerome affirms that the apostle made use of a false argument, which, although it might appear well enough to the stupid Galatians, would not be approved by wise or learned men. —*Chandler*. Borger endeavours to show that this was in accordance with the mode of speaking and writing among the Hebrews, and especially that the Jewish Rabbis were accustomed to draw an argument like this from *the singular number*, and that the Hebrew word (זרע) *seed* is often used by them in this manner; see his remarks as quoted by Bloomfield *in loc*. But the objection to this is, that though this might be common, yet it is not the less a quibble on the word, for certainly the very puerile reasoning of the Jewish Rabbis is no good authority on which to vindicate the authority of an apostle. Locke and Clarke suppose that this refers to Christ as the spiritual head of the mystical body, and to all believers in him. Le Clerc supposes that it is an allegorical kind of argument, that was fitted to convince the Jews only, who were accustomed to this kind of reasoning. I do not know but this solution may be satisfactory to many minds, and that it is capable of vindication, since it is not easy to say how far it is proper to make use of methods of argument used by an adversary in order to convince them. The *argumentum ad hominem* is certainly allowable to a certain extent, when designed to show the legitimate tendency of the principles advanced by an opponent. But here there is no evidence that Paul was reasoning with an adversary. He was showing the Galatians, not the Jews, what was the truth, and justice to the character of the apostle requires us to suppose that he would make use of only such arguments as are in accordance with the eternal principles of truth, and such as may be seen to be true in all countries and at all times. The question then is, whether the argument of the apostle here drawn from the use of the singular word *σπέρμα* (*seed*), is one that can be seen to be sound? or is it a mere quibble, as Jerome and Le Clerc suppose? or is it to be left to be *presumed* to have had a force which we cannot now trace? for *this* is possible. Socrates and Plato may have used arguments of a subtile nature, based on some nice distinctions of words which were perfectly sound, but which we, from our necessary ignorance of the delicate shades of meaning in the language, cannot now understand. Perhaps the following remarks may show that there is *real* force and propriety in the position which the apostle takes here. If not, then I confess my inability to explain the passage. (1.) There can be no reasonable objection to the opinion that the promise originally made to Abraham *included* the Messiah, and the promised blessings were to descend through him. This is so often affirmed in the New Testament, that to deny it would be to deny the repeated declarations of the sacred writers, and to make war on the whole structure of the Bible; see particularly Rom. iv.; comp. John viii. 56. If this general principle be admitted, it will remove much perplexity from the controversy. (2.) The promise made to Abraham (Gen. xxii 18), "and in thy seed (בזרעך, Sept. ἐ *τῷ σπέρματί σου*, where the words both in Heb. and in Gr. are in the singular number) shall all the nations of the earth be blessed," cannot refer to *all* the seed or the posterity of Abraham taken collectively. He had two sons, Isaac by Rebecca, and Ishmael by Hagar, besides numerous descendants by Keturah; Gen. xxv. 1, seq. Through a large part of these no particular blessings descended on the human family, and there is no sense in which all the families of the earth are particularly blessed in them. On any supposition, therefore, there must have been *some* limitation of the promise; or the word "seed" was intended to include only *some* portion of his descendants, whether a particular branch or an individual, does not yet appear. It must have referred to *a part* only of the posterity of Abraham, but to what part is to be learned only by subsequent revelations. (3.) It was the *intention* of God to confine the blessing to one branch of the family, to *Isaac* and his descendants. The *peculiar* promised blessing was to be through him, and not through the family of Ishmael. This intention is often expressed, Gen. xvii. 19—21; xxi. 12; xxv. 11; comp. Rom. ix. 7; Heb. xi. 18. Thus the original promise of a blessing through the posterity of Abraham became somewhat *narrowed down*, so as to show that there was to be a limitation of the promise to a particular portion of his posterity. (4.) If the promise had referred to the two branches of the family; if it had been intended to include Ishmael as well as Isaac, then some term would have been used that would have expressed this. So unlike were Isaac and Ishmael; so different in the circumstances of their birth and their future life; so dissimilar were the prophecies respecting them, that it might be said that their descendants were two races of men; and in scripture the race of Ishmael ceased to be spoken of as the descendants or the posterity of Abraham. There was a sense in which the posterity of Isaac was regarded as the seed or posterity of Abraham in which the descendants of Ishmael were not; and the term σπέρμα or "seed" therefore properly designated the posterity of Isaac. It might be said, then, that the promise "to thy seed" did not refer to the *two* races, as if he had said σπέρματα, "seeds," but to *one* (σπέρμα), "the seed" of Abraham, by way of eminence. (5.) This promise was subsequently *narrowed down* still more, so as to include only one portion of the descendants of Isaac. Thus it was limited to the posterity of *Jacob*, Esau being excluded; subsequently the peculiar blessing was promised to the family of *Judah*, one of the twelve sons of Jacob (Gen. xlix. 10); in subsequent times it was still further narrowed down or limited to the family of Jesse; then to that of David; then to that of Solomon, until it terminated in the Messiah. The original intention of the promise was that there *should be* a limitation, and that limitation was made from age to age, until it terminated in the Messiah, the Lord Jesus Christ. By being thus narrowed down from age to age, and limited by successive revelations, it was shown that the Messiah was eminently intended,—which is what Paul says here. The promise was indeed at first general, and the term used was of the most general nature; but it was shown from time to time that God *intended* that it should be applied only to one branch or portion of the family of Abraham; and that limitation was finally so made as to terminate in the Messiah. This I take to be the meaning of this very difficult passage of scripture; and though it may not be thought that *all* the perplexities are removed by these remarks, yet I trust they will be seen to be so far removed as that it will appear that there is real force in the argument of the apostle, and that it is not a mere trick of argument, or a quibble unworthy of him as an apostle and a man.

[Whatever may be thought of this solution of the difficulty, the author has certainly given more than due prominence to the objections that are supposed to lie against the apostle's argument. Whatever license a writer in the American Biblical Repository, or such like work, might take, it certainly is not wise in a commentary intended for Sabbath Schools to affirm, that the great difficulty of the passage is "that the remark here of Paul appears to be a trick of argument, or a quibble more worthy of a trifling Jewish Rabbi than of a grave reasoner and an inspired man," and then to exhibit such a formidable array of objection, and behind it a defence comparatively feeble, accompanied with the acknowledgment that if that be not sufficient the author can do no more! These objections, moreover, are not only stated "fairly" but strongly, and something more than strongly; so that while in the end the authority of the apostle is apparently vindicated, the effect is such, that the reader, unaccustomed to such treatment of inspired men, is tempted to exclaim, "non tali auxilio, nec defensoribus istis, tempus eget." Indeed we are surprised that, with Bloomfield and Borger before him, the author should ever have made some of the assertions which are set down under this text. As to objection *first*, it does not matter what interpretation hundreds and thousands of persons would naturally put on the passage in Genesis, since the authority of an inspired apostle must be allowed to settle its meaning against them all. The *second* objection affirms, that "the word σπερμα is not used in the plural at all to denote a posterity," on which Bloomfield thus remarks, "it has been denied that the word זרע is ever used in the plural, except to denote the seeds of vegetables. And the same assertion has been made respecting σπερμα. But the former position merely extends to the Old Testament, which only contains a fragment and small part of the Hebrew language. So that it cannot be proved that זרע was *never* used in the *plural* to denote *sons, races*. As to the latter assertion it is unfounded; for though σπερμα is used in the singular as a noun of multitude, to denote several children, yet it is sometimes used in the plural to signify several sons of the same family; as in Soph. Œd. Col. 599, γῆς ἐμῆς ἀπηλάθην Πρὸς τῶν ἐμαυτοῦ σπερμάτων."

The elaborate Latin Note of Borger, part of which is quoted in Bloomfield, will give complete satisfaction to the student who may wish thoroughly to examine this place. He maintains, 1st. That though the argument of the apostle may not be founded exactly on the use of the singular number, yet the absurdity of his application of the passage in Genesis to the Messiah, would have been obvious if, instead of the singular the plural had been used, "si non σπερματος sed σπερματων mentio fuisset facta;" from which he justly concludes, that at all events "numerum cum hac explicatione non pugnare." 2nd. The word זרע is in certain places understood of one man only (de uno homine) and therefore may be so here. 3rd. The apostle, arguing with Jews, employs an argu-

17 And this I say, *That* the covenant that was confirmed before of God in Christ, the law which [a] was four hundred and thirty years after, cannot disannul, that it should make the promise of none effect.

a Ex.12.40,41.

---

ment to which they were accustomed to attach importance; for they laid great stress on the respective use of the singular and plural number; which argument, indeed, would be liable to the objections stated against it by Mr. Barnes, if the thing to be proven rested entirely on this ground, and had not, besides, its foundation in the actual truth of the case. If the singular number in this place *really had that force attached to it* which the apostle declares, and if the Jews were influenced in other matters by arguments of this kind, it was certainly both lawful and wise to reason with them after their own fashion. 4th. What is still more to the point, the Jewish writers themselves frequently use the word זרע, *not only of one man*, but especially of the *Messiah*, "non tantum *de uno homine*, sed imprimis etiam de *Messia* exponere solent."

On the whole, the objections against the reasoning on this passage, are raised in defiance of apostolical interpretation. But, as has been well observed, "the apostle, to say nothing of his inspiration, might be supposed to be better qualified to decide on a point of this kind, than any modern philologist."—*Bloomfield in loco.*

17. *The covenant which was confirmed before of God.* By God, in his promise to Abraham. It was confirmed *before* the giving of the law. The confirmation was the solemn promise which God made to him. ¶ *In Christ.* With respect to the Messiah; a covenant relating to him, and which promised that he should descend from Abraham. The word "in," in the phrase "in Christ," does not quite express the meaning of the Greek εἰς Χριστὸν. That means rather "*unto* Christ;" or *unto* the Messiah; that is, the covenant had respect to him. This is a common signification of the preposition εἰς. ¶ *The law.* The law given by God to Moses on mount Sinai. ¶ *Which was four hundred and thirty years after.* In regard to the difficulties which have been felt respecting the chronology referred to here; see the Note on Acts vii. 6. The exact time here referred to was probably when Abraham was called, and when the promise was first made to him. Assuming that as the time referred to, it is not difficult to make out the period of four hundred and thirty years. That promise was made when Abraham was seventy-five years old; Gen. xii. 3, 4. From that time to the birth of Isaac, when Abraham was a hundred years old, was twenty-five years; Gen. xxi. 5. Isaac was sixty when Jacob was born; Gen. xxv. 26. Jacob went into Egypt when he was one hundred and thirty years old; Gen. xlvii. 9. And the Israelites sojourned there, according to the Septuagint (Ex. xii. 40), two hundred and fifteen years, which completes the number; see Doddridge, Whitby, and Bloomfield. This was doubtless the *common* computation in the time of Paul; and as his argument did not depend at all on the *exactness* of the reckoning, he took the estimate which was in common use, without pausing or embarrassing himself by an inquiry whether it was strictly accurate or not. His argument was the same, whether the law was given four hundred and thirty years after the promise, or only two hundred years. The argument is, that a law given *after* the solemn promise which had been made and confirmed, could not make that promise void. It would still be binding according to the original intention; and the law must have been given for some purpose entirely different from that of the promise. No one can doubt the soundness of this argument. The promise to Abraham was of the nature of a compact. But no law given by one of the parties to a treaty or compact can disannul it. Two nations make a treaty of peace, involving solemn prom es, pledges, and obligations. No *law* made afterwards by one of the nations can disannul or change that treaty. Two men make a contract with solemn pledges and promises. No act of *one* of the parties can change that, or alter the conditions. So it was with the covenant between God and Abraham. God made to him solemn promises which *could* not be affected by

18 For if [a] the inheritance *be* of
the law, *it is* no more of promise:
but God gave *it* to Abraham by
promise.
19 Wherefore then *serveth* the
law? [b] It was added because of
transgressions, till the seed [c] should
come to whom the promise was
made; *and it was* ordained by
angels [d] in the hand [e] of a Mediator.

a Rom.4.14. *b* Ro.5.20. *c* ver.16. *d* Ac.7.53; He.2.2. *e* Ex.20.19—22; De. 5.22—31.

a future giving of a law. God would feel himself to be under the most solemn obligation to fulfil *all* the promises which he had made to him.

18. *For if the inheritance.* The inheritance promised to Abraham. The sum of the promise was, that "he should be the heir of the world;" see Rom. iv. 13, and the Note on that verse. To that heirship or inheritance Paul refers here, and says that it was an essential part of it that it was to be in virtue of the promise made to him, and not by fulfilling the law. ¶ Be *of the law.* If it be by observing the law of Moses; or if it come in any way by the fulfilling of law. This is plain. Yet the Jews contended that the blessings of justification and salvation were to be in virtue of the observance of the law of Moses. But if so, says Paul, then it could not be by the promise made to Abraham, since there could not be two ways of obtaining the same blessing. ¶ *But God gave* it *to Abraham by promise.* That, says Paul, is a settled point. It is perfectly clear; and that is to be held as an indisputable fact, that the blessing was given to Abraham by a promise. That promise was confirmed and ratified hundreds of years before the law was given, and the giving of the law could not affect it. But that promise was, that he would be the ancestor of the Messiah, and that in him all the nations of the earth should be blessed. Of course, if they were to be blessed in this way, then it was not to be by the observance of the law, and the law must have been given for a different purpose. What that was, he states in the following verses.

19. *Wherefore then* serveth *the law?* This is obviously an objection which might be urged to the reasoning which the apostle had pursued. It was very obvious to ask, if the principles which he had laid down were correct, of what use was the law? Why was it given at all? Why were there so many wonderful exhibitions of the Divine power at its promulgation? Why were there so many commendations of it in the Scriptures? And why were there so many injunctions to obey it? Are all these to be regarded as nothing; and is the law to be esteemed as worthless? To all this, the apostle replies that the law was not useless, but that it was given by God for great and important purposes, and especially for purposes closely connected with the fulfilment of the promise made to Abraham and the work of the Mediator. ¶ *It was added* (προσετέθη). It was *appended* to all the previous institutions and promises. It was an *additional* arrangement on the part of God for great and important purposes. It was an arrangement *subsequent* to the giving of the promise, and was intended to secure important advantages until the superior arrangement under the Messiah should be introduced, and was with reference to that. ¶ *Because of transgressions.* On account of transgressions, or with reference to them. The meaning is, that the law was given to show the true nature of transgressions, or to show what was sin. It was not to reveal a way of justification, but it was to disclose the true nature of sin; to deter men from committing it; to declare its penalty; to convince men of it, and thus to be "ancillary" to, and preparatory to the work of redemption through the Redeemer. This is the true account of the law of God as given to apostate man, and this use of the law still exists. This effect of the law is accomplished, (1.) By showing us what God requires, and what is duty. It is the straight rule of what is right; and to depart from that is the measure of wrong. (2.) It

shows us the nature and extent of transgression by showing us how far we have departed from it. (3.) It shows what is the just penalty of transgression, and is thus fitted to reveal its true nature. (4.) It is fitted to produce *conviction* for sin, and thus shows how evil and bitter a thing transgression is; see Notes on Rom. iv. 15; vii. 7—11. (5.) It thus shows its own inability to justify and save men, and is a preparatory arrangement to lead men to the cross of the Redeemer; see Note on ver. 24. At the same time, (6.) The law was given with reference to transgressions in order to keep men from transgression. It was designed to restrain and control them by its denunciations, and by the fear of its threatened penalties. When Paul says that the law was given on account of transgressions, we are not to suppose that this was the *sole* use of the law; but that this was a main or leading purpose. It may accomplish many other important purposes (*Calvin*), but this is one leading design. And this design it still accomplishes. It shows men their duty. It reminds them of their guilt. It teaches them how far they have wandered from God. It reveals to them the penalty of disobedience. It shows them that justification by the law is impossible, and that there *must be* some other way by which men must be saved. And since these advantages are derived from it, it is of importance that that law should be still proclaimed, and that its high demands and its penalties should be constantly held up to the view of men. ¶ *Till the seed should come,* &c. The Messiah, to whom the promise particularly applied; see ver. 16. It is not implied here that the law would be of no use *after* that, but that it would accomplish important purposes *before* that. A large portion of the laws of Moses would then indeed cease to be binding. They were given to accomplish important purposes among the Jews until the Messiah should come, and then they would give way to the more important institutions of the gospel. But the moral law would continue to accomplish valuable objects *after* his advent, in showing men the nature of transgression and leading them to the cross of Christ. The essential idea of Paul here is, that the whole arrangement of the Mosaic economy, including all his laws, was with reference to the Messiah. It was a part of a great and glorious whole. It was not an independent thing. It did not stand by itself. It was incomplete and in many respects unintelligible until he came—as one part of a tally is unmeaning and useless until the other is found. In itself it did not justify or save men, but it served to introduce a system by which they could be saved. It contained no provisions for justifying men, but it was in the design of God an essential part of a system by which they could be saved. It was not a whole in itself, but it was a part of a glorious whole, and led to the completion and fulfilment of the entire scheme by which the race could be justified and brought to heaven. ¶ And it was *ordained by angels.* That is, the law was ordained by angels. The word ordained here (διαταγεὶς) usually means to arrange; to dispose in order; and is commonly used with reference to the marshalling of an army. In regard to the sentiment here that the law was ordained by angels, see the Note on Acts vii. 53. The Old Testament makes no mention of the presence of angels at the giving of the law, but it was a common opinion among the Jews that the law was given by the instrumentality of angels, and arranged by them; and Paul speaks in accordance with this opinion; comp. Heb. ii. 2. The sentiment here is that the law was prescribed, ordered, or arranged by the instrumentality of the angels; an opinion, certainly, which none can prove *not* to be true. In itself considered, there is no more absurdity in the opinion that the law of God should be given by the agency of angels, than there is that it should be done by the instrumentality of man. In the Septuagint (Deut. xxxiii. 2) there is an allusion of the same kind. The Hebrew is, "From his right hand went a fiery law for them." The LXX. render this, "His angels with him on his right hand;" comp. Joseph. Ant. xv. 5, 3. That angels were present at the giving of the law is more than implied, it is believed, in two passages of the Old Testament. The one is that which is referred to above, and a part of which the translators of the Septuagint expressly apply to angels; Deut. xxxiii. 2. The Hebrew is, "Jehovah came from Sinai, and rose up from Seir unto them; he shined forth from mount Paran, and he came [literally] with ten thousands of holiness;" that is, with his holy ten thousands, or with his holy myriads (מרבבת קדש). By the holy myriads here mentioned what can be meant but *the angels?* The word "holy" in the Scriptures is not given to storms and winds and tempests; and the natural interpretation is, that he was attended with vast hosts of intelligent beings. The same sentiment is found in Ps. lxviii. 17: "The chariots of God are myriads, thousands repeated; the Lord is in the midst of them, as in Sinai, as in his sanctuary." Does not this evidently imply that when he gave the law on Mount Sinai he was surrounded by a multitude of angels? see Stuart on the Hebrews, Excursus viii. pp. 565—567. It may be added, that in the fact itself there is no improbability. What is more natural than to suppose that when the law of God was promulgated in such a solemn manner on mount Sinai *to a world,* that the angels should be present? If any occasion on earth has ever occurred where their presence was allowable and proper, assuredly that was one. And yet the Scriptures abound with assurances that the angels are interested in human affairs, and that they have had an important agency in the concerns of man. ¶ *In the hand.* That is, under the direction, or control of. To be in the hand of one is to be under his control; and the idea is, that while this was done by the ordering of the angels or by their disposition, it was under the control of a Mediator Rosenmüller, however, and others suppose that this means simply *by* (*per*); that is, that it was done by the instrumentality of a Mediator. But it seems to me to imply more than this; that the Mediator here referred to had some jurisdiction or control over the law thus given; or that it was subject to him, or with reference to him. The interpretation however will be affected by the view which is taken of the meaning of the word Mediator. ¶ *Of a Mediator.* The word Mediator (Μεσίτης) means properly one who intervenes between two parties, either as an interpreter or *internuncius,* or as an intercessor or reconciler. In the New Testament, in all the places where it occurs, unless the passage before us be an exception, it is applied to the Lord Jesus, the great Mediator between God and man; 1 Tim. ii. 5; Heb. viii. 6; ix. 15; xii. 24. There has been some difference of opinion as to the reference of the word here. Rosenmüller, Grotius, Doddridge, Bloomfield, Robinson (*Lex.*), Chandler, and many others suppose that it refers to Moses. Calvin and many others suppose that the reference is to Christ. The common sentiment among expositors undoubtedly is, that the reference is to Moses; and it is by no means easy to show that that is not the correct opinion. But to me it seems that there are reasons why it should be regarded as having reference to the great Mediator between God and man. Some of the reasons which incline me to this opinion are, (1.) That the name Mediator is not, so far as I know, applied to Moses elsewhere in the Scriptures. (2.) The name is appropriated to the Lord Jesus. This is certainly the case in the New Testament, unless the passage before us be an exception; and the name is not found in the Old Testament. (3.) It is difficult to see the pertinency of the remark here, or the bearing on the argument, on the supposition that it refers to Moses. How would it affect the drift and purport of the apostle's reasoning? How would it bear on the case? But on the supposition that it refers to the Lord Jesus, that would be a material fact in the argument. It would show that the law was subordinate to the Messiah, and was with reference to him. It was not only subservient by

20 Now a mediator is not *a mediator* of one, but God[a] is one.

a De.6.4.

being ordained by angels, but as being under the Mediator, and with reference to him until he, the "promised seed," should come. (4.) It is only by such an interpretation that the following "vexed" verse can be understood. If that be applied to Moses, I see not that *any* sense can be affixed to it that shall be pertinent or intelligible. These reasons may not appear satisfactory to others; and I admit they are not as clear as would be desirable that reasons should be in the exposition of the Bible, but they may be allowed perhaps to have *some* weight. If they *are* of weight, then the sentiment of the passage is, that the law was wholly subordinate, and could not make the promise of no effect. For, (1.) It was given hundreds of years after the promise. (2.) It was under the direction of angels, who must themselves be inferior to, and subordinate to the Messiah, the Mediator between God and man. If given by their agency and instrumentality, however important it might be, it could not interfere with a direct promise made by God himself, but must be subordinate to that promise. (3.) It was under the Mediator, the promised Messiah. It was in his hand, and subject to him. It was a part of the great plan which was contemplated in the promise, and was tributary to that, and must be so regarded. It was not an independent scheme; not a thing that stood by itself; but a scheme subordinate and tributary, and wholly under the control of the Mediator, and a part of the plan of redemption, and of course to be modified or abrogated just as that plan should require, and to be regarded as wholly tributary to it. This view will accord certainly with the argument of Paul, and with his design in showing that the law could by no means, and in no way, interfere with the promise made to Abraham, but must be regarded as wholly subordinate to the plan of redemption.

20. *Now a mediator is not* a mediator *of one,* &c. This verse has given great perplexity to commentators. "There is, unquestionably," says Bloomfield, "no passage in the New Testament that has so much, and to so little purpose, exercised the learning and ingenuity of commentators as the present, which seems to defy all attempts to elicit any satisfactory sense, except by methods so violent as to be almost the same thing as writing the passage afresh." In regard, however, to the truth of the declarations here—that "a mediator is not a mediator of one," and that "God is one"—there can be no doubt, and no difficulty. The very idea of a mediator supposes that there are two parties or persons between whom the mediator comes either to reconcile them or to bear some message from the one to the other; and it is abundantly affirmed also in the Old Testament that there is but one God; see Deut. vi. 4. But the difficulty is, to see the pertinency or the bearing of the remark on the argument of the apostle. What does he intend to illustrate by the declaration? and how do the truths which he states, illustrate the point before him? It is not consistent with the design of these Notes to detail the numerous opinions which have been entertained of the passage. They may be found in the larger commentaries, and particularly may be seen in Koppe, Excursus vii. on the Galatians. After referring to a number of works on the passage, Rosenmüller adopts the following interpretation, proposed by Noessett, as expressing the true sense. But he (*i. e.* Moses) is not a mediator of one race (to wit, the Abrahamic), but God is the same God of them and of the Gentiles. The sense according to this is, that Moses had not reference in his office as mediator or as *internuncius* to the descendants of Abraham, or to that *one seed* or race, referred to in the promise. He added the hard conditions of the law; required its stern and severe observances; his institutions pertained to the Jews mainly. They indeed might obtain the favour of

God, but by compliance with the severe laws which he had ordained. But to the *one seed*, the whole posterity of Abraham, they concerning whom the promise was made, the Gentiles as well as the Jews, he had no reference in his institutions: all their favours, therefore, must depend on the fulfilment of the *promise* made to Abraham. But God is one and the same in reference to all. His promise pertains to all. He is the common God to the Jews and the Gentiles. There is great difficulty in embracing this view of the passage, but it is not necessary for me to state the difficulty or to attempt to show that the view here proposed cannot be defended. Whitby has expressed substantially the same interpretation of this passage. "But this mediator (namely, Moses) was only the mediator of the Jews, and so was only the mediator of one party, to whom belonged the blessing of Abraham, ver. 8, 14. But God, who made the promise, 'That in one should all the families of the earth be blessed,' is one; the God of the other party, the Gentiles as well as the Jews, and so as ready to justify the one as the other." According to this interpretation, the sense is, that Moses was mediator of *one part* of Abraham's seed, the Israelites; but was not the mediator of the *other part* of that seed, the Gentiles; yet there was the same God to both parties, who was equally ready to justify both. Locke has expressed a view of the passage which differs somewhat from this, but which has quite as much plausibility. According to his exposition it means, that God was but one of the parties to the promise. The Jews and the Gentiles made up the other. But at the giving of the law Moses was a mediator only between God and *the Israelites*, and, therefore, could not transact any thing which would tend to the disannulling of the promise which was between God and *the Jews and Gentiles together*, the other party to the promise. Or in other words, at the covenant made on mount Sinai, there was really present but one of the parties, and consequently nothing could be done that would affect the other. Moses did not appear in behalf of the Gentiles. They had no representative there. He was engaged only for the Jews, for *a part* only of the one party, and that part could not transact any thing for the whole. The giving of the law, therefore, could not affect the promise which was made to Abraham, and which related to the Jews and the Gentiles as together constituting one party. This view is plausible. It has been adopted by Doddridge, and perhaps *may* be the true interpretation. No one can deny, however, that it is forced, and that it is far from being obvious. It seems to be *making a meaning* for the apostle, or furnishing him with an argument, rather than *explaining* the one which he has chosen to use; and it may be doubted whether Paul would have used an argument that *required* so much explanation as this before it could be understood. All these expositions proceed on the supposition that the word "mediator" here refers to Moses, and that the transaction here referred to was that on mount Sinai. I would suggest a sense of the passage which I have found in none of the commentaries which I have consulted, and which I would, therefore, propose with diffidence. All that I can claim for it is, that it *may* possibly be the meaning. According to the view which I shall submit, the *words* here are to be regarded as used in their usual signification; and the simplest interpretation possible is to be given to the propositions in the verse. One proposition is, that a mediator is not appointed with reference to one party, but to two. This proposition is universal. Wherever there is a mediator there are *always* two parties. The other proposition is, that God is one; that is, that he is *the same one God*, in whatever form his will may be made known to men, whether by a promise as to Abraham, or by the law as to Moses. The interpretation which I would propose embraces the following particulars (1.) The *design* of the apostle is, to show that the giving of the law could not abrogate or affect the promise made to Abraham; and to show at the same time what *is* its true object. It could not *annul* the promises, says Paul. It was given long after, and could not affect them, ver. 17. It was an *addition*, an *appendage*, a subsequent enactment for a specific purpose, yet a part of the same general plan, and subordinate to the Mediator, ver. 19. It was to be shown also that the law was not *against* the promises of God. It was a good law (ver. 21); and was not designed to be an *opposing* system, or intended to *counteract* the promise, or the scheme of salvation *by* promise, but was a part of the *same* great plan. (2.) A mediator *always* supposes two parties. In *all* the transactions, therefore, where a mediator is employed, there is supposed to be two parties. When, therefore, the promise was made to Abraham with reference to the Messiah, the great Mediator; and when the law was given in the hand of the Mediator, and under his control, there is *always* supposed to be two parties. (3.) The *whole* arrangement here referred to is under the Mediator, and with reference to him. The promise made to Abraham had reference to him and to those who should believe on him; and the law given by Moses was also under him, and with reference to him. He was the grand object and agent of all. He was the Mediator with reference to both. Each transaction had reference to him, though in different ways; the transaction with Abraham relating to him in connection with a promise; the transaction at the giving of the law being under his control *as* Mediator, and being a part of the one great plan. There was an *identity* of plan; and the plan had reference to the Messiah, the great Mediator. (4.) God is one and the same. He is throughout one of the parties; *and he does not change.* However the arrangements may vary, whether in giving the law or imparting a promise, he is the same. There is but one God in all the transaction; and he, throughout, constitutes one of the parties. The other party is man, at first receiving the promise from this one God with reference to the Mediator through Abraham, and then receiving the law through the same Mediator on mount Sinai. He is still the one party unchanged; and there is the same Mediator; implying all along that there are two parties. (5.) It follows, therefore, agreeably to the argument of the apostle, that the law given so long after the promise, could not abrogate it, because they pertained to the same plan, were under the same one God, who was one unchanging party in all this transaction, and had reference to the same Mediator and were alike under his control. It followed, also, that the law was temporary (ver. 19); *interposed* for important purposes until the "seed should come," because it was a part of the same general arrangement, and was under the control of the same Mediator, and directed by the same one God, the unchanging one party in all these transactions. It followed, further, that the one could not be against the other (ver. 21), because they were a part of the same plan, under the control of the same Mediator, and where the same God remained unchanged as the one party. All that is assumed in this interpretation is, (*a*) That there was but *one* plan or arrangement; or that the transaction with Abraham and with Moses were parts of one great scheme; and, (*b*) That the Mediator here referred to was not Moses, but the Messiah, the Son of God. The following paraphrase will express the sense which I have endeavoured to convey. "The giving of the law could not annul or abrogate the promise made to Abraham. It was long after that, and it was itself subservient to that. It was given by the instrumentality of angels, and it was entirely under the control of the Mediator, the Messiah. The plan was one; and all the parts of it, in the promise made to Abraham and in the giving of the law, were subordinate to him. A mediator always supposes two parties, and the reference to the Mediator, alike in the promise to Abraham and in the giving of the law, supposes that there *were* two parties. God is one party, the same unchanging God in all the forms

21 *Is* the law then against[a] the
promises of God? God forbid: for
if[b] there had been a law given
which could have given life, verily
righteousness should have been by
the law.
22 But the Scripture hath concluded all[c] under sin, that the

a Mat.5.17. b chap.2.21. c Ro.4.11,12,16.

of the promise and of the law. In this state of things, it is impossible that the law should clash with the promise, or that it should supersede or modify it. It was *a part* of the one great plan; appointed with reference to the work which the Mediator came to do; and in accordance with the promise made to Abraham; and therefore they could not be contradictory and inconsistent." It is assumed in all this that the Messiah was contemplated in the whole arrangement, and that it was entered into with reference to him. That this *may* be assumed no one can deny who believes the scriptures. The whole arrangement in the Old Testament, it is supposed, was designed to be ancillary to redemption; and the interpretation which has been submitted above is based on that supposition.

21. Is *the law then against the promises of God?* Is the law of Moses to be regarded as opposed to the promises made to Abraham? Does this follow from any view which can be taken of the subject? The object of the apostle in asking this question is, evidently, to take an opportunity to deny in the most positive manner that there can be any such clashing or contradiction. He shows, therefore, what was the design of the law, and declares that the object was to further the plan contemplated in the promise made to Abraham. It was an auxiliary to that. It was as good as a law could be; and it was designed to prepare the way for the fulfilment of the promise made to Abraham. ¶ *God forbid.* It cannot be. It is impossible. I do not hold such an opinion. Such a sentiment by no means follows from what has been advanced; comp. Note, Rom. iii. 4. ¶ *For if there had been a law given which could have given life.* The law of Moses is as good as a law can be. It is pure, and holy, and good. It is not the design to insinuate any thing against the law in itself, or to say that as a law it is defective. But law *could not* give life. It is not its nature; and man cannot be justified by obedience to it. No man ever has yielded perfect compliance with it, and no man, therefore, can be justified by it; comp. Notes on chap. ii. 16; iii. 10. ¶ *Verily righteousness should have been by the law.* Or justification would have been secured by the law. The law of Moses was as well adapted to this as a law could be. No better law could have been originated for this purpose, and if men were to *attempt* to justify themselves before God by their own works, the law of Moses would be *as* favourable for such an undertaking as any law which could be revealed. It is as reasonable, and equal, and pure. Its demands are as just, and its terms as favourable as could be any of the terms of mere law. And *such* a law has been given in part in order to show that justification by the law is out of the question. If men could not be justified by a law so pure, and equal, and just; so reasonable in all its requirements and so perfect, how could they expect to be justified by conformity to any *inferior* or *less perfect* rule of life? The fact, therefore, that no one can be justified by the pure law revealed on mount Sinai, for ever settles the question about the possibility of being justified by law.

22. *But the Scripture.* The Old Testament (Note, John v. 39), containing the law of Moses. ¶ *Hath concluded all under sin.* Has *shut up* (συνέκλεισεν) all under the condemnation of sin; that is, has declared all men, no matter what their rank and external character, to be sinners. Of course, they cannot be justified by that law which declares them to be guilty, and which condemns them, any more than the law of the land will acquit a murderer, and pronounce him innocent, at the same time that it holds him to be guilty. In regard to

promise *a* by faith of Jesus Christ
might be given to them that believe.
23 But before faith came, we
were kept under the law, shut up
unto the faith which should afterwards be revealed.
24 Wherefore the law *b* was our

a Ro.3.9,19,23.

b Col.2.17; He.9.9,10.

the meaning of the expression here used; see Note on Rom. xi. 32; comp. Rom. iii. 9, 19. *That the promise by faith of Jesus Christ,* &c. That the promise referred to in the transaction with Abraham, the promise of justification and life by faith in the Messiah. Here we see *one* design of the law. It was to show that they could not be justified by their own works, to *hedge up their way* in regard to justification by their own righteousness, and to show them their need of a better righteousness. The law accomplishes the same end now. It shows men that they are guilty; and it does it in order that they may be brought under the influence of the pure system of the gospel, and become interested in the promises which are connected with eternal salvation.

23. *But before faith came.* That is, the system of salvation by faith in the Lord Jesus. Faith here denotes the Christian religion, because faith is its distinguishing characteristic. ¶ *We were kept under the law.* We, who were sinners; we, who have violated the law. It is a general truth, that before the gospel was introduced, men were under the condemning sentence of the law. ¶ *Shut up unto the faith.* Enclosed by the law with reference to the full and glorious revelation of a system of salvation by faith. The design and tendency of the law was to shut us up to that as the only method of salvation. All other means failed. The law condemned every other mode, and the law condemned all who attempted to be justified in any other way. Man, therefore, was shut up to that as his last hope; and could look only to that for any possible prospect of salvation. The word which in this verse is rendered "were kept" (ἐφρουρούμεθα), usually means to guard or watch, as in a castle, or as prisoners are guarded; and though the word should not be pressed too far in the interpretation, yet it implies that there was *a rigid scrutiny* observed; that the law guarded them; that there was no way of escape; and that they were shut up, as prisoners under sentence of death, to the only hope, which was that of *pardon.* ¶ *Unto the faith,* &c. That was the only hope. The law condemned them, and offered no hope of escape. Their only hope was in that system which was to be revealed through the Messiah, the system which extended forgiveness on the ground of faith in his atoning blood.

24. *Wherefore the law was our schoolmaster.* The word rendered *schoolmaster* (παιδαγωγὸς, whence the word *pedagogue*), referred originally to a slave or freedman, to whose care boys were committed, and who accompanied them to the public schools. The idea here is not that of *instructor,* but there is reference to the office and duty of the *pædagogus* among the ancients. The office was usually intrusted to slaves or freedmen. It is true, that when the *pædagogus* was properly qualified, he assisted the children committed to his care in preparing their lessons. But still his main duty was not *instruction,* but it was to watch over the boys; to restrain them from evil and temptation; and to conduct them to the schools, where they might receive instruction. See, for illustrations of this, Wetstein, Bloomfield, &c. In the passage before us, the proper notion of *pedagogue* is retained. In our sense of the word *schoolmaster,* Christ is the schoolmaster, and not the law. The law performs the office of the ancient pedagogue, to *lead us to* the teacher or the instructor. That teacher or instructor is Christ. The ways in which the law does this may be the following:—(1.) It *restrains* us and rebukes us, and keeps us as the ancient pedagogue did his boys. (2.) The whole law was designed to be introductory to Christ. The sacrifices and

schoolmaster *to bring us* unto Christ, that we might be justified by faith.

25 But after that faith is come, we are no longer under a schoolmaster.

26 For ye are all the children [a] of God by faith in Christ Jesus.

27 For [b] as many of you as have been baptized into Christ, have put on Christ.

28 There is [c] neither Jew nor

a John 1.12; 1 John 3.1,2. *b* Ro.6.3. *c* Col.3.11.

offerings were designed to shadow forth the Messiah, and to introduce him to the world. (3.) The moral law—the law of God—shows men their sin and danger, and thus leads them to the Saviour. It condemns them, and thus prepares them to welcome the offer of pardon through a Redeemer. (4.) It *still* does this. The whole economy of the Jews was designed to do this; and under the preaching of the gospel it is still done. Men see that they are condemned; they are convinced by the law that they cannot save themselves, and thus they are led to the Redeemer. The effect of the preached gospel is to show men their sins, and thus to be preparatory to the embracing of the offer of pardon. Hence the importance of preaching the law still; and hence it is needful that men should be made to feel that they are sinners, in order that they may be prepared to embrace the offers of mercy; comp. Note on Rom. x. 4.

25. *But after that faith is come.* The scheme of salvation by faith. After that is revealed; see Note on ver. 23. ¶ *We are no longer under a schoolmaster.* Under the *pædagogus*, or pedagogue. We are not kept in restraint, and under bondage, and led along *to* another to receive instruction. We are directly under the great Teacher, the Instructor himself; and have a kind of freedom which we were not allowed before. The bondage and servitude have passed away; and we are free from the burdensome ceremonies and expensive rites (comp Note on Acts xv. 10) of the Jewish law, and from the sense of condemnation which it imposes. This was true of the converts from Judaism to Christianity—that they became free from the burdensome rites of the law; and it is true of all converts to the faith of Christ, that, having been made to see their sin by the law, and having been conducted by it to the cross of the Redeemer, they are now made free.

26. *For ye are all the children of God,* &c. All who bear the Christian name—the converts from among the Jews and Gentiles alike; see Note on John i. 12. The idea here is, that they are no longer under tutors and governors; they are no longer subject to the direction and will of the *pædagogus;* they are arrived *at age,* and are admitted to the privileges of sons; see Note on chap. iv. 1. The language here is derived from the fact, that until the son arrived at age, he was in many respects not different from a servant. He was under laws and restraints; and subject to the will of another. When of age, he entered on the privileges of heirship, and was free to act for himself. Thus, under the law, men were under restraints, and subject to heavy exactions. Under the gospel, they are free, and admitted to the privileges of the sons of God.

27. *For as many of you.* Whether by nature Jews or Gentiles. ¶ *As have been baptized into Christ.* Or *unto* (εἰς—the same preposition which in ver. 24 is rendered *unto*) Christ. That is, they were baptized *with reference* to him, or receiving him as the Saviour; see this explained in the Note on Rom. vi. 3. ¶ *Have put on Christ.* That is, they have *put on* his sentiments, opinions, characteristic traits, &c., as a man clothes himself. This language was common among the ancient writers; see it explained in the Note on Rom. xiii. 14.

28. *There is neither Jew nor Greek.* All are on a level; all are saved in the same way; all are entitled to the same privileges. There is no favouritism on account of birth, beauty, or blood All confess that they are sinners; all are saved by the merits of the same Saviour; all are admitted to

Greek, there is neither bond nor free, there is neither male nor female: for ye are all one in Christ Jesus.

the same privileges as children of God. The word "Greek" here is used to denote the Gentiles generally; since the whole world was divided by the Jews into "Jews and Greeks"—the Greeks being the foreign nation best known to them. The Syriac renders it here "*Aramean*,"—using the word to denote the Gentiles generally. The meaning is, that whatever was the birth, or rank, or nation, or colour, or complexion, all under the gospel were on a level. They were admitted to the same privileges, and endowed with the same hopes of eternal life. This does not mean that all the civil distinctions among men are to be disregarded. It does not mean that no respect is to be shown to those in office, or to men in elevated rank. It does not mean that all are on a level in regard to talents, comforts, or wealth; but it means *only* that all men are on a level *in regard to religion.* This is the sole point under discussion; and the interpretation should be limited to this. It is not a fact that men are on a level in all things, nor is it a fact that the gospel designs to break down all the distinctions of society. Paul means to teach that no man has any preference or advantage in the kingdom of God because he is a rich man, or because he is of elevated rank; no one is under any disadvantage because he is poor, or because he is ignorant, or a slave. All at the foot of the cross are sinners; all at the communion table are saved by the same grace; all who enter into heaven, will enter clothed in the same robes of salvation, and arranged, not as princes and nobles, and rich men and poor men, in separate orders and ranks, but mingling together as redeemed by the same blood, and arranged in ranks according to their eminence in holiness; comp. my Notes on Isa. lvi. 8. ¶ *There is neither bond nor free.* The condition of a free man does not give him any peculiar claims or advantages in regard to religion; and the condition of a slave does not exclude him from the hope of heaven, or from being regarded as a child of God, on the same terms, and entitled to the same privileges as his master. In regard to religion, they are on the same level. They are alike sinners, and are alike saved by grace. They sit down at the same communion table; and they look forward to the same heaven. Christianity does not admit the one to favour because he is free, or exclude the other because he is a slave. Nor, when they are admitted to favour, does it give the one a right to lord it over the other, or to feel that he is of any more value in the eye of the Redeemer, or any nearer to his heart. The essential idea is, that they are on a level, and that they are admitted to the favour of God without respect to their external condition in society. I do not see any evidence in *this* passage that the Christian religion designed to abolish slavery, any more than I do in the following phrase, "there is neither male nor female," that it was intended to abolish the distinction of the sexes; nor do I see in this passage any evidence that there should not be proper respect shown by the servant to his master, though both of them are Christians, any more than there is in the following phrase, that suitable respect should not be shown in the intercourse with the sexes; comp. 1 Tim. vi. 1—5. But the proof is explicit, that masters and slaves may alike become Christians on the same terms, and are, in regard to their religious privileges and hopes, on a level. No peculiar favour is shown to the one, in the matter of salvation, because he is free, nor is the other excluded because he is a slave. And from this it follows:—(1.) That they should sit down to the same communion table. There should be no invidious and odious distinctions there. (2.) They should be regarded alike as Christian brethren in the house of God, and should be addressed and treated accordingly. (3.) The slave should excite the interest, and receive the watchful care of the pastor, as well as his master. Indeed, he may need it more; and from his ignorance, and the fewness of his opportunities, it may be proper that special attention should be bestowed on him. In regard to this doctrine of Christianity, that there is neither "bond nor free" among those who are saved, or that all are on a level in regard to salvation, we may remark further, (1.) That it is peculiar to Christianity. All other systems of religion and philosophy *make* different ranks, and endeavour to promote the distinctions of *caste* among men. They teach that certain men are the favourites of heaven, in virtue of their birth or their rank in life, or that they have peculiar facilities for salvation. Thus, in India the Brahmin is regarded as, by his birth, the favourite of heaven, and all others are supposed to be of a degraded rank. The great effort of men, in their systems of religion and philosophy, has been to show that there are favoured ranks and classes, and to make permanent distinctions on account of birth and blood. Christianity regards all men as made of one blood to dwell on all the face of the earth (see Note, Acts xvii. 26), and esteems them all to be equal in the matter of salvation; and whatever notions of *equality* prevail in the world are to be traced to the influence of the Christian religion. (2.) If men are regarded as equal before God, and as entitled to the same privileges of salvation; if there is in the great work of redemption "neither bond nor free," and those who are in the church are on a level, then such a view will induce a master to treat his slave with kindness, when that relation exists. The master who has any right feelings, will regard his servant as a Christian brother, redeemed by the same blood as himself, and destined to the same heaven. He will esteem him not as "a chattel" or "a thing," or as a piece "of property," but he will regard him as an immortal being, destined with himself to the same heaven, and about to sit down with him in the realms of glory. How can he treat such a brother with unkindness or severity? How can he rise from the same communion table with him, and give way to violent feelings against him, and regard him and treat him as if he were a brute? And Christianity, by the same principle that "the slave is a brother in the Lord," will do more to mitigate the horrors of slavery, than all the enactments that men can make, and all the other views and doctrines which can be made to prevail in society; see Philem. 16. (3.) This doctrine would lead to universal emancipation. All are on a level before God. In the kingdom of Jesus there is neither bond nor free. One is as much an object of favour as another. With this feeling, how can a Christian hold his fellow Christian in bondage? How can he regard as "a chattel" or "a thing," one who, like himself, is an heir of glory? How can he *sell* him on whom the blood of Jesus has been sprinkled? Let him feel that his slave is his equal in the sight of God; that with himself he is an heir of glory; that together they are soon to stand on Mount Zion above; that the slave is an immortal being, and has been redeemed by the blood of Calvary, and how *can* he hold such a being in bondage, and how *can* he transfer him from place to place and from hand to hand for gold? If all masters and all slaves were to become Christians, slavery would at once cease; and the prevalence of the single principle before us would put an end to all the ways in which man oppresses his fellow-man. Accordingly, it is well known that in about three centuries the influence of Christianity banished slavery from the Roman empire. ¶ *There is neither male nor female.* Neither the male nor the female have any peculiar advantages for salvation. There are no favours shown on account of sex. Both sexes are, in this respect, on a level. This does not mean, of course, that the sexes are to be regarded as in all respects equal; nor can it mean that the two sexes may not have peculiar duties and privileges in other respects. It does not prove that one of the sexes may not perform important offices in the church, which would not

29 And if ye *be* Christ's, then [a] are ye Abraham's seed, and heirs [b] according to the promise.

[a] ver.7. [b] Ro.8.17.

CHAPTER IV.

NOW I say, *That* the heir, as long as he is a child, differeth

be proper for the other. It does not prove that the duties of the ministry are to be performed by the female sex, nor that the various duties of domestic life, nor the various offices of society, should be performed without any reference to the distinction of sex. The interpretation should be confined to the matter under consideration; and the passage proves only that *in regard to salvation* they are on a level. One sex is not to be regarded as peculiarly the favourite of heaven, and the other to be excluded. Christianity thus elevates the female sex to an equality with the male, on the most important of all interests; and it has in this way made most important changes in the world wherever it has prevailed. Everywhere but in connection with the Christian religion, woman has been degraded. She has been kept in ignorance. She has been treated as an inferior in all respects. She has been doomed to unpitied drudgery, and ignorance, and toil. So she was among the ancient Greeks and Romans; so she is among the savages of America; so she is in China, and India, and in the islands of the sea; so she is regarded in the Koran, and in all Mohammedan countries. It is Christianity alone which has elevated her; and nowhere on earth does man regard the mother of his children as an intelligent companion and friend, except where the influence of the Christian religion has been felt. At the communion table, at the foot of the cross, and in the hopes of heaven, she is on a level with man; and this fact diffuses a mild, and purifying, and elevating influence over all the relations of life. Woman has been raised from deep degradation by the influence of Christianity; and, let me add, she has everywhere acknowledged the debt of gratitude, and devoted herself, as under a deep sense of obligation, to lessening the burdens of humanity, and to the work of elevating the degraded, instructing the ignorant, and comforting the afflicted, all over the world. Never has a debt been better repaid, or the advantages of elevating one portion of the race been more apparent. ¶ *For ye are all one in Christ Jesus.* You are all equally accepted through the Lord Jesus Christ; or you are all on the same level, and entitled to the same privileges in your Christian profession. Bond and free, male and female, Jew and Greek, are admitted to equal privileges, and are equally acceptable before God. And the church of God, no matter what may be the complexion, the country, the habits, or the rank of its members, IS ONE. Every man on whom is the image and the blood of Christ, is A BROTHER to every other one who bears that image, and should be treated accordingly. What an influence would be excited in the breaking up of the distinctions of rank and *caste* among men; what an effect in abolishing the prejudice on account of colour and country, if this were universally believed and felt!

29. *And if ye* be *Christ's.* If you belong to the Messiah, and are interested in his work. ¶ *Then are ye Abraham's seed.* The promise made to Abraham related to the Messiah. It was a promise that in him all should be blessed. Abraham believed in that Messiah, and was distinguished for his faith in him who was to come. If they believed in Christ, therefore, they showed that they were the spiritual descendants of Abraham. No matter whether they were Jews or Gentiles; whether they had been circumcised or not, they had the same spirit which he evinced, and were interested in the promises made to him. ¶ *And heirs according to the promise;* see Rom. viii. 17. Are heirs of God. You inherit the blessings promised to Abraham, and partake of the felicity to which he looked forward. You have become truly heirs of God, and this is in accordance with the promise

nothing from a servant, though he be lord of all;

2 But is under tutors and governors until the time appointed of the father.

made to Abraham. It is not by the obedience of the law ; it is by faith—in the same way that Abraham possessed the blessing ;—an arrangement *before* the giving of the law, and therefore one that may include *all*, whether Jews or Gentiles. All are on a level ; and all are alike the children of God, and in the same manner, and on the same terms that Abraham was.

CHAPTER IV.

ANALYSIS.

THE design of this chapter is, to show the effect of being under the law, and the inconsistency of that kind of bondage or servitude with the freedom which is vouchsafed to the true children of God by the gospel. It is, in accordance with the whole drift of the epistle, to recall the Galatians to just views of the gospel ; and to convince them of their error in returning to the practice of the Mosaic rites and customs. In the previous chapter he had shown them that believers in the gospel were the true children of Abraham ; that they had been delivered from the curse of the law ; that the law was a schoolmaster to lead them to Christ, and that they were all the children of God. To illustrate this further, and to show them the true nature of the freedom which they had as the children of God, is the design of the argument in this chapter. He therefore states :

(1.) That it was under the gospel only that they received the full advantages of freedom; ver. 1—5. Before Christ came, indeed, there were true children of God, and heirs of life. But they were in the condition of *minors;* they had not the privileges of *sons.* An heir to a great estate, says the apostle (ver. 1, 2), is treated substantially as if he were a servant. He is under tutors and governors ; he is not permitted to enter on his inheritance ; he is kept under the restraint of law. So it was with the people of God under the law of Moses. They were under restraints, and were admitted to comparatively few of the privileges of the children of God. But Christ came to redeem those who were under the law, and to place them in the elevated condition of adopted sons; ver. 4, 5. They were no longer servants ; and it was as unreasonable that they should conform again to the Mosaic rites and customs, as it would be for the heir of full age, and who has entered on his inheritance, to return to the condition of minorship, and to be placed again under tutors and governors, and to be treated as a servant.

(2.) As sons of God, God had sent forth the Spirit of his Son into their hearts, and they were enabled to cry Abba, Father. They were no longer servants, but heirs of God, and should avail themselves of the privileges of heirs; ver. 6, 7.

(3.) Sustaining this relation, and being admitted to these privileges, the apostle remonstrates with them for returning again to the "weak and beggarly elements" of the former dispensation—the condition of servitude to rites and customs in which they were before they embraced the gospel; ver. 8—11. When they were ignorant of God, they served those who were no gods, and there was some excuse for that; ver. 8. But now they had known God, they were acquainted with his laws ; they were admitted to the privileges of his children ; they were made free, and there could be *no* excuse for returning again to the bondage of those who had no true knowledge of the liberty which the gospel gave. Yet they observed days and times as though these were binding, and they had never been freed from them (ver. 10) ; and the apostle says, that he is afraid that his labours bestowed on them, to make them acquainted with the plan of redemption, had been in vain.

(4.) To bring them to a just sense of their error, he reminds them of their former attachment to him, ver 12—20. He had indeed preached to them amidst much infirmity, and much that was fitted to prejudice them against him (ver. 13); but they had disregarded that, and had evinced towards him the highest proofs of attachment—so, much so, that they had received him as an angel of God (ver. 14), and had been ready to pluck out their own eyes to give them to him, ver. 15. With great force, therefore, he asks them why they had changed their views towards him so far as to forsake his doctrines? Had he become their enemy by telling the truth? ver. 16. He tenderly addresses them, therefore, as little children, and says, that he has the deepest solicitude for their welfare, and the deepest anxiety on account of their danger—a solicitude which he compares (ver. 19,) with the pains of child-birth.

(5.) In order to enforce the whole subject, and to show the true nature of the conformity to the law compared with the liberty of the gospel, he allegorizes an interesting part of the Mosaic history—the history of the two children of Abraham; ver. 21—31. The condition of Hagar—a slave—under the command of a master—harshly treated—cast out and disowned, was an apt illustration of the condition of those who were under the servitude of the law. It would strikingly represent Mount Sinai, and the law that was promulgated there, and the condition of those who were under the law. That, too, was a condition of servitude. The law was stern,and showed no mercy. It was like a master of a slave, and would treat those who were under it with a rigidness that might be compared with the condition of Hagar and her son; ver. 24, 25. That same Mount Sinai also was a fair representation of Jerusalem as it was then—a city full of rites and ceremonies, where the law reigned with rigour, where there was a burdensome system of religion, and where there was none of the freedom which the gospel would furnish; ver. 25. On the other hand, the children of the free woman were an apt illustration of those who were made free from the opprescive ceremonies of the law by the gospel; ver. 22. *That* Jerusalem was free. The new system from heaven was one of liberty and rejoicing; ver. 26, 27. Christians were, like Isaac, the children of promise, and were not slaves to the law; ver. 28, 31. And as there was a command (ver. 30) to cast out the bondwoman and her son, so the command now was to reject all that would bring the mind into ignoble servitude, and prevent its enjoying the full freedom of the gospel. The whole argument is, that it would be as unreasonable for those who were Christians to submit again to the Jewish rites and ceremonies, as it would be for a freeman to sell himself into slavery. And the design of the whole is, to recall them from the conformity to Jewish rites and customs, and from their regarding them as now binding on Christians.

1. *Now I say.* He had before said (ch. iii. 24, 25) that while they were under the law they were in a state of minority. This sentiment he proceeds further to illustrate by showing the true condition of one who was a minor. ¶ That *the heir.* Any heir to an estate, or one who has a prospect of an inheritance. No matter how great is the estate; no matter how wealthy his father; no matter to how elevated a rank he may be raised on the moment that he enters on his inheritance, yet till that time he is in the condition of a servant. ¶ *As long as he is a child.* Until he arrives at the age. The word rendered "child" (νήπιος) properly means *an infant;* literally, *one not speaking* (νη insep. *un,* ἔπος), and hence a child or babe, but without any definite limitation.—*Rob.* It is used as the word infant is with us in law, to denote *a minor.* ¶ *Differeth nothing from a servant,* That is, he has no more control of his property; he has it not at his command. This does not mean that he does not differ *in any respect,* but only that *in the matter under consideration* he does not differ. He differs in his prospects of *inheriting* the property, and in the affections of the father, and usually in the advantages of education, and in the respect and attention shown him. but in regard to property, he does not differ, and he is like a servant, under the control and direction of others. ¶ *Though he be lord*

3 Even so we, when we were children, were in bondage under the [1] elements of the world:

1 *rudiments.* Col.2.8.20.

of all. That is, in prospect. He has a prospective right to all the property, which no one else has. The word "lord" here (κύριος), is used in the same sense in which it is often in the Scriptures, to denote master or owner. The idea which this is designed to illustrate is, that the condition of the Jews before the coming of the Messiah was inferior in many respects to what the condition of the friends of God would be under him—as inferior as the condition of an heir was before he was of age, to what it would be when he should enter on his inheritance. The Jews claimed, indeed, that they were the children or the sons of God, a title which the apostle would not withhold from the pious part of the nation; but it was a condition in which they had not entered on the full inheritance, and which was far inferior to that of those who had embraced the Messiah, and who were admitted to the full privileges of sonship. They were indeed heirs. They were interested in the promises. But still they were in a condition of comparative servitude, and could be made free only by the gospel.

2. *But is under.* Is subject to their control and direction. ¶ *Tutors.* The word *tutor* with us properly means *instructor*. But this is not quite the sense of the original. The word ἐπίτροπος properly means a steward, manager, agent; Matt. xx. 8; Luke viii. 3. As used here, it refers to one—usually a slave or a freedman—to whose care the boys of a family were committed, who trained them up, accompanied them to school, or sometimes instructed them at home; comp. Note on ch. iii. 24. Such a one would have the control of them. ¶ *And governors.* This word (οἰκόνομος; means a house-manager, an overseer, a steward. It properly refers to one who had authority over the slaves or servants of a family, to assign them their tasks and portions. They generally, also, had the management of the affairs of the household, and of the accounts. They were commonly slaves, who were intrusted with this office as a reward for fidelity; though sometimes free persons were employed; Luke xvi. 1, 3, 8. These persons had also charge of the sons of a family, probably in respect to their *pecuniary* matters, and thus differed from those called *tutors*. It is not necessary, however, to mark the difference in the words with great accuracy. The general meaning of the apostle is, that the heir was under government and restraint. ¶ *Until the time appointed of the father.* The time fixed for his entering on the inheritance. The time when he chose to give him his portion of the property. The law with us fixes the age at twenty-one when a son shall be at liberty to manage for himself. Other countries have affixed other times. But still, the time when the son shall inherit the father's property must be fixed by the father himself if he is living, or may be fixed by his will if he is deceased. The son cannot *claim* the property when he comes of age.

3. *Even so we.* We who were Jews—for so I think the word here is to be limited, and not extended to the heathen, as Bloomfield supposes. The reasons for limiting it are, (1). That the heathens in no sense sustained such a relation to the law and promises of God as is here supposed; (2.) Such an interpretation would not be pertinent to the design of Paul. He is stating reasons why there should not be subjection to the laws of Moses, and his argument is, that that condition was like that of bondage or minorship. ¶ *When we were children* (νήπιοι). Minors; see Note on ver. 1. The word is not υἱοι, *sons*; but the idea is, that they were in a state of nonage; and though heirs, yet were under severe discipline and regimen. They were under a kind of government that was fitted to that state, and not to the condition of those who had entered on their inheritance. ¶ *Were in bondage.* In a state of servitude. Treated as servants or slaves. ¶ *Under the ele-*

4 But when the fulness of the time was come, God sent forth his Son, made of a woman, made under the law,

ments of the world. Marg. *Rudiments.* The word rendered *elements* (sing. στοιχεῖον), properly means a row or series; a little step; a pin or peg, as the gnomon of a dial; and then any thing *elementary*, as a sound, a letter. It then denotes the elements or rudiments of any kind of instruction, and in the New Testament is applied to the first lessons or principles of religion; Heb. v. 15. It is applied to the elements or component parts of the physical world; 2 Pet. iii. 10, 12. Here the figure is kept up of the reference to the infant (ver. 1, 3); and the idea is, that lessons were taught under the Jewish system adapted to their nonage—to a state of childhood. They were treated as children under tutors and governors. The phrase "the elements of the world," occurs also in Col. ii. 8, 20. In ver. 9 of this chapter, Paul speaks of these lessons as "beggarly elements," referring to the same thing as here. Different opinions have been held as to the reason why the Jewish institutions are here called "the elements *of the world.*" Rosenmüller supposes it was because many of those rites were common to the Jews and to the heathen—as they also had altars, sacrifices, temples, libations, &c. Doddridge supposes it was because those rites were adapted to the low conceptions of children, who were most affected with sensible objects, and have no taste for spiritual and heavenly things. Locke supposes it was because those institutions led them not beyond this world, or into the possession and taste of their heavenly inheritance. It is probable that there is allusion to the Jewish manner of speakiug, so common in the Scriptures, where this world is opposed to the kingdom of God, and where it is spoken of as transient and worthless compared with the future glory. The world is fading, unsatisfactory, temporary. In allusion to this common use of the word, the Jewish institutions are called the *worldly rudiments.* It is not that they were in themselves evil—for that is not true; it is not that they were adapted to foster a worldly spirit—for that is not true; it is not that they had their origin from this world—for that is not true; nor is it from the fact that they resembled the institutions of the heathen world—for that is as little true; but it is, that, like the things of the world, they were transient, temporary, and of little value. They were unsatisfactory in their nature, and were soon to pass away, and to give place to a better system—as the things of this world are soon to give place to heaven.

4. *But when the fulness of the time was come.* The full time appointed by the Father; the completion (*filling up*, πλήρωμα,) of the designated period for the coming of the Messiah; see Notes on Isa. xlix. 7, 8; 2 Cor. vi. 2. The sense is, that the time which had been predicted, and when it was proper that he should come, was complete. The exact period had arrived when all things were ready for his coming. It is often asked why he did not come sooner, and why mankind did not have the benefit of his incarnation and atonement immediately after the fall? Why were four thousand dark and gloomy years allowed to roll on, and the world suffered to sink deeper and deeper in ignorance and sin? To these questions perhaps no answer entirely satisfactory can be given. God undoubtedly saw reasons which we cannot see, and reasons which we shall approve if they are disclosed to us. It may be observed, however, that this delay of redemption was in entire accordance with the whole system of divine arrangements, and with all the divine interpositions in favour of men. Men are suffered long to pine in want, to suffer from disease, to encounter the evils of ignorance, before interposition is granted. On all the subjects connected with human comfort and improvement, the same questions may be asked as on the subject of redemption. Why was the invention of the art of printing so long delayed,

and men suffered to remain in ignorance? Why was the discovery of vaccination delayed so long, and millions suffered to die who might have been saved? Why was not the bark of Peru sooner known, and why did so many millions die who might have been saved by its use? So of most of the medicines, and of the arts and inventions that go to ward off disease, and to promote the intelligence, the comfort, and the salvation of man. In respect to *all* of these, it may be true that they are made known *at the very best time*, the time that will on the whole most advance the welfare of the race. And so of the incarnation and work of the Saviour. It was seen by God to be the *best* time, the time when on the whole the race would be most benefited by his coming. Even with our limited and imperfect vision, *we* can see the following things in regard to its being the most fit and proper time. (1.) It was just the time when all the prophecies centred in him, and when there could be no doubt about their fulfilment. It was important that such an event should be predicted in order that there might be full evidence that he came from heaven; and yet in order that prophecy may be seen to have been uttered by God, it must be so far before the event as to make it impossible to have been the result of mere human conjecture. (2.) It was proper that the world should be brought to see its need of a Saviour, and that a fair and satisfactory opportunity should be given to men to try all other schemes of salvation that they might be prepared to welcome this. This had been done. Four thousand years were sufficient to show to man his own powers, and to give him an opportunity to devise some scheme of salvation. The opportunity had been furnished under every circumstance that could be deemed favourable. The most profound and splendid talent of the world had been brought to bear on it, especially in Greece and Rome; and ample opportunity had been given to make a fair trial of the various systems of religion devised on national happiness and individual welfare; their power to meet and arrest crime; to purify the heart; to promote public morals, and to support man in his trials; their power to conduct him to the true God, and to give him a well-founded hope of immortality. All had failed; and then it was a proper time for the Son of God to come and to reveal a better system. (3.) It was a time when the world was at peace. The temple of Janus, closed only in times of peace, was then shut, though it had been but once closed before during the Roman history. What an appropriate time for the "Prince of Peace" to come! The world was, to a great extent, under the Roman sceptre. Communications between different parts of the world were then more rapid and secure than they had been at any former period, and the gospel could be more easily propagated. Further, the Jews were scattered in almost all lands, acquainted with the promises, looking for the Messiah, furnishing facilities to their own countrymen the apostles to preach the gospel in numerous synagogues, and qualified, if they embraced the Messiah, to become most zealous and devoted missionaries. The same language, the Greek, was, moreover, after the time of Alexander the Great, the common language of no small part of the world, or at least was spoken and understood among a considerable portion of the nations of the earth. At no period before had there been so extensive a use of the same language. (4.) It was a proper period to make the new system known. It accorded with the benevolence of God, that it should be delayed no longer than that the world should be in a suitable state for receiving the Redeemer. When that period, therefore, had arrived, God did not delay, but sent his Son on the great work of the world's redemption. ¶ *God sent forth his Son.* This implies that the Son of God had an existence before his incarnation; see John xvi. 28. The Saviour is often represented as *sent* into the world, and as *coming forth* from God. ¶ *Made of a woman*, In human nature; born of a woman, This also implies that he had another

5 To redeem them that were
under the law, that we might receive the adoption of sons.
6 And because ye are sons, God
hath sent forth the Spirit [a] of his
Son into your hearts, crying, Abba,
Father.
7 Wherefore thou art no more
a servant, but a son; and if a
son, then an heir of God through
Christ.

a Ro.8.15,17.

---

nature than that which was derived from the woman. On the supposition that he was a mere man, how unmeaning would this assertion be! How natural to ask, in what other way could he appear than to be born of a woman? Why was *he* particularly designated as coming into the world in this manner? How strange would it sound if it were said, "In the sixteenth century came Faustus Socinus preaching Unitarianism, *made of a woman!*" or, "In the eighteenth century came Dr. Joseph Priestley, *born of a woman*, preaching the doctrines of Socinus!" How else could they appear? would be the natural inquiry. What was there peculiar in their birth and origin that rendered such language necessary? The *language* implies that there were other ways in which the Saviour might have come; that there was something peculiar in the fact that *he* was born of a woman; and that there was some special reason why that fact should be made prominently a matter of record. The promise was (Gen. iii. 15) that the Messiah should be the "seed" or the descendant of woman; and Paul probably here alludes to the fulfilment of that promise. ¶ *Made under the law.* As one of the human race, partaking of human nature, he was subject to the law of God. As a man he was bound by its requirements, and subject to its control. He took his place under the law that he might accomplish an important purpose for those who were under it. He made himself subject to it that he might become one of them, and secure their redemption.

5. *To redeem them.* By his death as an atoning sacrifice; see Note on chap. iii. 13. ¶ *Them that were under the law.* Sinners, who had violated the law, and who were exposed to its dread penalty. ¶ *That we might receive the adoption of sons* Be adopted as the sons or the children of God; see Notes, John i. 12; Rom. viii. 15.

6. *And because ye are sons.* As a consequence of your being adopted into the family of God, and being regarded as his sons. It follows as a part of his purpose of adoption that his children shall have the spirit of the Lord Jesus. ¶ *The Spirit of his Son.* The spirit of the Lord Jesus; the spirit which animated him, or which he evinced. The idea is, that as the Lord Jesus was enabled to approach God with the language of endearment and love, so they would be. He, being the true and exalted Son of God, had the spirit appropriate to such a relation; they being adopted, and made like him, have the same spirit. The "spirit" here referred to does not mean, as I suppose, the Holy Spirit as such; nor the miraculous endowments of the Holy Spirit, but the spirit which made them like the Lord Jesus; the spirit by which they were enabled to approach God as his children, and use the reverent, and tender, and affectionate language of a child addressing a father. It is that language used by Christians when they have evidence of adoption; the expression of the warm, and elevated, and glowing emotions which they have when they can approach God as their God, and address him as *their* Father. ¶ *Crying.* That is, the spirit thus cries, Πνεῦμα—κρᾶζον. Comp. Notes, Rom. viii. 26, 27. In Rom. viii. 15 it is, "wherewith we cry." ¶ *Abba, Father;* see Note, Rom. viii. 15. It is said in the Babylonian Gemara, a Jewish work, that it was not permitted slaves to use the title of *Abba* in addressing the master of the family to which they belonged. If so, then the language which Christians are

8 Howbeit then, when ye knew not God, ye did service unto them which by nature are no gods.

9 But now, after that ye have known God, or rather are known of God, how turn ye [1] again to the weak and beggarly [2] elements,

1 or, *back*. 2 *rudiments*.

---

here represented as using is the language of freemen, and denotes that they are not under the servitude of sin.

7. *Wherefore.* In consequence of this privilege of addressing God as your Father. ¶ *Thou art no more.* You who are Christians. ¶ *A servant.* In the servitude of sin; or treated as a servant by being bound under the oppressive rites and ceremonies of the law; comp. Note on ver. 3. ¶ *But a son.* A child of God, adopted into his family, and to be treated as a son. ¶ *And if a son,* &c. Entitled to all the privileges of a son, and of course to be regarded as an heir through the Redeemer, and with him. See the sentiment here expressed explained in the Note on Rom. viii. 17.

8. *Howbeit.* But, Ἀλλὰ. The address in this verse and the following is evidently to the portion of the Galatians who had been heathen. This is probably indicated by the particle ἀλλὰ, *but* denoting a transition. In the previous verses Paul had evidently had the Jewish converts more particularly in his eye, and had described their former condition as one of servitude to the Mosaic rites and customs, and had shown the inconveniences of that condition, compared with the freedom imparted by the gospel. To complete the description, he refers also to the Gentiles, as a condition of worse servitude still, and shows (ver. 9) the absurdity of *their* turning back to a state of bondage of any kind, after the glorious deliverance which they had obtained from the degrading servitude of pagan rites. The sense is, "If the Jews were in such a state of servitude, how much more galling and severe was that of those who had been heathens. Yet from *that* servitude the gospel had delivered them, and made them freemen. How absurd now to go back to a state of vassalage, and to become servants under the oppressive rites of the Jewish law!" ¶ *When ye knew not God.* In your state of heathenism, when you had no knowledge of the true God and of his service. The object is not to apologize for what they did, because they did not know God; it is to state the fact that they were in a state of gross and galling *servitude.* ¶ *Ye did service.* This does not express the force of the original. The meaning is, "Ye were *slaves* to (ἐδουλεύσατε); you were in a condition of *servitude,* as opposed to the freedom of the gospel;" comp. ver. 3, where the same word is used to describe the state of the Jews. The drift of the apostle is, to show that the Jews and Gentiles, before their conversion to Christianity, were in a state of vassalage or servitude, and that it was absurd in the highest degree to return to that condition again. ¶ *Unto them which by nature are no gods.* Idols, or false gods. The expression "by nature," φύσει, according to Grotius, means, *in fact re ipsa.* The sense is, that they *really* had no pretensions to divinity. Many of them were imaginary beings; many were the objects of creation, as the sun, and winds, and streams; and many were departed heroes that had been exalted to be objects of worship. Yet the *servitude* was real. It fettered their faculties; controlled their powers; bound their imagination, and commanded their time and property, and made them slaves. Idolatry is always slavery; and the servitude of sinners to their passions and appetites, to lust and gold, and ambition, is not less galling and severe than was the servitude to the pagan gods or the Jewish rites, or than is the servitude of the African now to a harsh and cruel master. Of all Christians it may be said that before their conversion they "did service," or were *slaves* to harsh and cruel masters; and nothing but the gospel has made them free. It may be added, that the chains of idolatry all over the world are as

whereunto ye desire again to be in bondage?

10 Ye observe days, and months, and times, and years.

---

fast riveted and as galling as they were in Galatia, and that nothing but the same gospel which Paul preached there can break those chains and restore man to freedom.

9. *But now,* &c. The sense is, that since they had been made free from their ignoble servitude in the worship of false gods, and had been admitted to the freedom found in the worship of the true God, it was absurd that they should return again to that which was truly slavery or bondage, the observance of the rites of the Jewish law. ¶ *That ye have known God.* The true God, and the ease and freedom of his service in the gospel. ¶ *Or rather are known of God* The sense is, "Or, to speak more accurately or precisely, are known by God." The *object* of this correction is to avoid the impression which might be derived from the former phrase that their acquaintance with God was owing *to themselves.* He therefore states, that it was rather that they were known of God; that it was all owing to him that they had been brought to an acquaintance with himself. Perhaps, also, he means to bring into view the idea that it was a favour and privilege to be known by God, and that therefore it was the more absurd to turn back to the weak and beggarly elements. ¶ *How turn ye again.* Marg. *Back.* "How is it that you are returning to such a bondage?" The question implies surprise and indignation that they should do it. ¶ *To the weak and beggarly elements.* To the rites and ceremonies of the Jewish law, imposing a servitude really not less severe than the customs of paganism. On the word *elements,* see Note on ver. 3. They are called "weak" because they had no power to save the soul; no power to justify the sinner before God. They are called "beggarly" (Gr. πτωχὰ, *poor*), because they could not impart spiritual riches. They really could confer few benefits on man. Or it may be, as Locke supposes, because the law kept men in the poor estate of pupils from the full enjoyment of the inheritance: ver. 1—3. ¶ *Whereunto ye desire again to be in bondage. As if* you had a wish to be under servitude. The absurdity is as great as it would be for a man who had been freed from slavery to desire again his chains. They had been freed by the gospel from the galling servitude of heathenism, and they now again had sunk into the Jewish observances, *as if they preferred slavery to freedom,* and were willing to go from one form of it to another. The main idea is, that it is absurd for men who have been made free by the gospel to go back again into any kind of servitude or bondage. We may apply it to Christians now. Many sink into a kind of servitude not less galling than was that to sin before their conversion. Some become the slaves of mere ceremonies and forms in religion. Some are slaves to fashion, and the world yet rules them with the hand of a tyrant. They have escaped, it may be, from the galling chains of ambition, and degrading vice, and low sensuality; but they became slaves to the love of money, or of dress, or of the fashions of the world, *as if they loved slavery and chains;* and they seem no more able to break loose than the slave is to break the bonds which bind him. And some are slaves to some expensive and foolish habit. Professed Christians, *and Christian ministers too,* become *slaves* to the disgusting and loathsome habit of using *tobacco,* bound by a servitude as galling and as firm as that which ever shackled the limbs of an African. I grieve to add also that many professed Christians are slaves to the habit of "sitting long at the wine" and indulging in it freely. O that such knew the liberty of Christian freedom, and would break away from all such shackles, and *show* how the gospel frees men from *all* foolish and absurd customs!

10. *Ye observe.* The object of this verse is to *specify* some of the things to which they had become enslaved. ¶ *Days.* The days here referred to

11 I am afraid of you, lest I have bestowed upon you labour in vain.

12 Brethren, I beseech you, be as I *am;* for I *am* as *ye are;* ye have not injured me at all.

are doubtless the days of the Jewish festivals. They had numerous days of such observances, and in addition to those specified in the Old Testament, the Jews had added many others as days commemorative of the destruction and rebuilding of the temple, and of other important events in their history. It is not a fair interpretation of this to suppose that the apostle refers to the *Sabbath,* properly so called, for this was a part of the Decalogue; and was observed by the Saviour himself, and by the apostles also. It *is* a fair interpretation to apply it to all those days which are not commanded to be kept holy in the Scriptures; and hence the passage is as applicable to the observance of saints' days, and days in honour of particular events in sacred history, as to the days observed by the Galatians. There is as real *servitude* in the observance of the numerous festivals, and fasts in the Papal communion and in some Protestant churches, as there was in the observance of the days in the Jewish ecclesiastical calendar, and for any thing that I can see, such observances are as inconsistent now with the freedom of the gospel as they were in the time of Paul. We should observe as seasons of holy time what it can be proved God has commanded us, and no more. ¶ *And months.* The festivals of the new moon, kept by the Jews. Num. x. 10; xxviii. 11—14. On this festival, in addition to the daily sacrifice, two bullocks, a ram, and seven sheep of a year old were offered in sacrifice. The appearance of the new-moon was announced by the sound of trumpets. See Jahn, Archae. § 352. ¶ *And times.* Stated times; festivals returning periodically, as the Passover, the feast of Pentecost, and the feast of Tabernacles. See Jahn, Archae. chap. 3. § 346—350. ¶ *And years.* The sabbatical year, or the year of jubilee. See Jahn as above.

11. *I am afraid of you,* &c. I have fears respecting you. His fears were that they had no genuine Christian principle. They had been so easily perverted and turned back to the servitude of ceremonies and rites, that he was apprehensive that there could be no real Christian principle in the case. What pastor has not often had such fears of his people, when he sees them turn to the weak and beggarly elements of the world, or when, after having "run well," he sees them become the slaves of fashion, or of some habit inconsistent with the simplicity of the gospel?

12. *Brethren, I beseech you, be as I* am, &c. There is great brevity in this passage, and no little obscurity, and a great many different interpretations have been given of it by commentators. The various views expressed may be seen in Bloomfield's Crit. Dig. Locke renders it, "Let you and I be as if we were all one, Think yourselves to be very me; as I in my own mind put no difference at all between you and myself." Koppe explains it thus: Imitate my example; for I, though a Jew by birth, care no more for Jewish rites than you." Rosenmüller explains it, "Imitate my manner of life in rejecting the Jewish rites; as I, having renounced the Jewish rites, was much like you when I preached the gospel to you." Other interpretations may be seen in Chandler, Doddridge, Calvin, &c. In our version there seems to be an impropriety of expression; for if he was as they were it would seem to be a matter of course that they would be like him, or would resemble him. The sense of the passage, however, it seems to me cannot be difficult. The reference is doubtless to the Jewish rites and customs, and to the question whether they were binding on Christians. Paul's object is to persuade them to abandon them. He appeals to them, therefore, by his own example. And it means evidently, "Imitate me in this thing. Follow my example, and yield no conformity to those rites and customs." The *ground* on which he

13 Ye know how, through [a] infirmity of the flesh I preached the gospel unto you at the first:
14 And my temptation which was in my flesh ye despised not nor rejected; but received me as an angel [b] of God, *even* as Christ [c] Jesus.

a 1 Co.2.3. b 2 Sa.19.27; Mal.2.7. c Mat 10.40

asks them to imitate him may be either, (1.) That *he* had abandoned them or, (2.) Because he asks them *to yield a point* to him. He had done so in many instances for their welfare, and had made many sacrifices for their salvation, and he now aks them to yield this *one* point, and to become as he was, and to cease these Jewish observances, as he had done. ¶ *For I am as ye* are. Gr. "For I as ye." This means, I suppose, "For I have conformed to your customs in many things. I have abandoned my own peculiarities; given up my customs as far as possible; conformed to you as Gentiles as far as I could do, in order to benefit and save you. I have laid aside the peculiarity of the Jew on the principle of becoming all things to all men (Notes, 1 Cor. ix. 20—22), in order that I might save you. I ask in return only the slight sacrifice that you will now become like me in the matter under consideration." ¶ *Ye have not injured me at all.* "It is not a personal matter. I have no cause of complaint. You have done me no personal wrong. There is no variance between us; no unkind feeling; no injury done as individuals. I may, therefore, with the more freedom, ask you to yield this point, when I assure you that I do not feel personally injured. I have no wrong to complain of, and I ask it on higher grounds than would be an individual request: it is for your good, and the good of the great cause." When Christians turn away from the truth, and disregard the instructions and exhortations of pastors, and become conformed to the world, it is not a personal matter, or a matter of personal offence to them, painful as it may be to them. They have no peculiar reason to say that they are personally injured. It is a higher matter. The cause suffers. The interests of religion are injured. The church at large is offended, and the Saviour is "wounded in the house of his friends." Conformity to the world, or a lapse into some sin, is a public offence, and should be regarded as an injury done to the cause of the Redeemer. It shows the magnanimity of Paul, that though they had abandoned his doctrines, and forgotten his love and his toils in their welfare, he did not regard it as a *personal* offence, and did not consider himself personally injured. An ambitious man or an impostor would have made that the main, if not the only thing.

13. *Ye know how.* To show them the folly of their embracing the new views which they had adopted, he reminds them of past times, and particularly of the strength of the attachment which they had evinced for him in former days. ¶ *Through infirmity of the flesh.* Gr. *Weakness* (ἀσθένειαν); comp. Notes on 1 Cor. ii. 3; 2 Cor. x. 10; xii. 7.

14. *And my temptation. My trial*, the thing which was to me a trial and calamity. The meaning is, that he was afflicted with various calamities and infirmities, but that this did not hinder their receiving him as an angel from heaven. There is, however, a considerable variety in the MSS. on this verse. Many MSS., instead of "*my* temptation," read "*your* temptation;" and Mill maintains that this is the true reading. Griesbach hesitates between the two. But it is not very important to determine which is the true reading. If it should be "*your*," then it means that they were tempted by his infirmities to reject him; and so it amounts to about the same thing. The general sense is, that he had some bodily infirmity, perhaps some periodically returning disease, that was a great trial to him, which they bore with, with great patience and affection. What that was, he has not informed us, and conjecture is vain. ¶ *But received me as an angel of God.* With the utmost respect, as if I had been an angel sent from God. ¶ Even

15 Where [1] is then the blessedness ye spake of? for I bear you record, that, if *it had been* possible, ye would have plucked out your own eyes, and have given them to me.

16 Am I therefore become your enemy, because I tell you the truth?

1 or, *what was.*

as Christ Jesus. As you would have done the Redeemer himself. Learn hence, (1.) That the Lord Jesus is superior to an angel of God. (2.) That the highest proof of attachment to a minister, is to receive him as the Saviour would be received. (3.) It showed their attachment to the Lord Jesus, that they received his apostle as they would have received the Saviour himself; comp. Mat. x. 40.

15. *Where is then the blessedness.* Marg. "What was"—in accordance with the Greek. The words "ye spake of" are not in the Greek, and should have been printed in Italic. But they obscure the sense at any rate. This is not to be regarded as a question, asking what had become of the blessedness, implying that it had departed; but it is rather to be regarded as an *exclamation,* referring to the happiness of that moment, and their affection and joy when they thus received him. "What blessedness you had then! How happy was that moment! What tenderness of affection! What overflowing joy!" It was a time full of joy, and love, and affectionate confidence. So Tindal well renders it, "How happy were ye then!" In this interpretation, Doddridge, Rosenmüller, Bloomfield, Koppe, Chandler, and others concur. Locke renders it, "What benedictions did you then pour out on me!" ¶ *For I bear you record.* I testify. ¶ *Ye would have plucked out your own eyes,* &c. No higher proof of attachment could have been given. They loved him so much, that they would have given to him *any* thing, however dear; they would have done any thing to contribute to his welfare. How changed, now that they had abandoned his doctrines, and yielded themselves to the guidance of those who taught a wholly different doctrine!

16. *Am I therefore become your enemy,* &c. Is my telling you the truth in regard to the tendency of the doctrines which you have embraced, and the character of those who have led you astray, and your own error, a proof that I have ceased to be your friend? How apt are we to feel that the man who tells us of our faults is our enemy! How apt are we to treat him coldly, and to "cut his acquaintance," and to regard him with dislike! The *reason* is, he gives us pain; and we cannot have pain given us, even by the stone against which we stumble, or by any of the brute creation, without momentary indignation, or regarding them for a time as our enemies. Besides, we do not like to have another person acquainted with our faults and our follies; and we naturally avoid the society of those who are thus acquainted with us. Such is human nature; and it requires no little grace for us to overcome this, and to regard the man who tells us of our faults, or the faults of our families, as our friend. We love to be flattered, and to have our friends flattered; and we shrink with pain from any exposure, or any necessity for repentance. Hence we become alienated from him who is faithful in reproving us for our faults. Hence men become offended with their ministers when they reprove them for their sins. Hence they become offended at the truth. Hence they resist the influences of the Holy Spirit, whose office it is to bring the truth to the heart, and to reprove men for their sins. There is nothing more difficult than to regard with steady and unwavering affection the man who faithfully tells us the truth at all times, when that truth is painful. Yet he is our best friend. "Faithful are the wounds of a friend, but the kisses of an enemy are deceitful." Prov. xxvii. 6. If I am in danger of falling down a precipice, he shows to me the purest friendship who tells me of it; if I am in danger of breathing the air of the pestilence, and it can be avoided, he shows to me pure kind-

17 They zealously affect you, *but* [a] not well; yea, they would exclude [1] you, that ye might affect them.

18 But *it is* good to be zealously affected always [b] in *a* good *thing*, and not only when I am present with you.

a Ro.10.2. 1 or, *us*. b 1 Co.15.58.

ness who tells me of it. So still more, if I am indulging in a course of conduct that may ruin me, or cherishing error that may endanger my salvation, he shows me the purest friendship who is most faithful in warning me, and apprising me of what must be the termination of my course.

17. *They zealously affect you;* see 1 Cor. xii. 31 (Gr.); xiv. 39. The word here used (Ζηλόω), means to be zealous towards, *i. e.*, for or against any person or thing; usually, in a good sense, to be eager for. Here it means, that the false teachers made a show of zeal towards the Galatians, or professed affection for them in order to gain them as their followers. They were full of ardour, and professed an extraordinary concern for their welfare—as men always do who are demagogues, or who seek to gain proselytes. The object of the apostle in this is, probably, to say, that it was not wholly owing to themselves that they had become alienated from the doctrines which he had taught. Great pains had been taken to do it; and there had been a show of zeal which would be likely to endanger any person. ¶ *But not well.* Not with good motives, or with good designs. ¶ *Yea, they would exclude you.* Marg. *Us.* A few printed editions of the New Testament have ἡμᾶς, *us*, instead of ὑμᾶς, *you.—Mill.* The word *exclude* here probably means, that they endeavoured to exclude the Galatians from the love and affection of Paul. They would shut them out from that, in order that they might secure them for their own purposes. If the reading in the margin, however, should be retained, the sense would be clearer. "They wish to exclude *us, i. e.*, me, the apostle, in order that they may have you wholly to themselves. If they can once get rid of your attachment to me, then they will have no difficulty in securing you for themselves." This reading, says Rosenmüller, is found "in many of the best codices, and versions, and fathers." It is adopted by Doddridge, Locke, and others. The main idea is clear: Paul stood in the way of their designs. The Galatians were truly attached to him, and it was necessary, in order to accomplish their ends, to withdraw their affections from him. When false teachers have designs on a people, they begin by alienating their confidence and affections from their pastors and teachers. They can hope for no success until this is done; and hence the efforts of errorists, and of infidels, and of scorners, is to undermine the confidence of a people in the ministry, and when this is done there is little difficulty in drawing them over to their own purposes. ¶ *That ye might affect them.* The same word as in the former part of the verse,—"that ye might zealously affect them"—*i. e.*, that ye might show ardent attachment to them. Their *first* work is to manifest *special interest* for your welfare; their *second*, to alienate you from him who had first preached the gospel to you; their *object*, not your salvation, or your real good, but to secure your zealous love for themselves.

18. *But* it is *good to be zealously affected.* The meaning of this is, "Understand me: I do not speak against zeal. I have not a word to say in its disparagement. In itself, it is good; and *their* zeal would be good if it were in a good cause." Probably, they relied much on their zeal; perhaps they maintained, as errorists and deceivers are very apt to do, that *zeal* was sufficient evidence of the goodness of their cause, and that persons who are *so very zealous* could not possibly be bad men. How often is this plea set up by the friends of errorists and deceivers! ¶ *And not only when I am present with you.* It seems to me that there is great adroitness and great delicacy of irony in

19 My[a] little children, of whom I travail in birth again until Christ be formed in you,

20 I desire to be present with you now, and to change my voice; for [1] I stand in doubt of you.

21 Tell me, ye that desire to be under the law, do ye not hear the law?

a 1 Co.4.15.

1 or, *I am perplexed for you.*

this remark; and that the apostle intends to remind them as gently as possible, that it would have been as well for them to have shown their zeal in a *good* cause when he was absent, as well as when he was with them. The sense may be, "You *were* exceedingly zealous in a good cause when I was with you. You loved the truth; you loved me. Since I left you, and as soon almost as I was out of your sight, your zeal died away, and your ardent love for me was transferred to others. Suffer me to remind you, that it would be well to be zealous of good when I am away, as well as when I am with you. There is not much true affection in that which dies away as soon as a man's back is turned." The *doctrine* is, that true zeal or love will live alike when the object is near and when it is removed; when our friends are present with us, and when they leave us; when their eye is upon us, and when it is turned away.

19. *My little children.* The language of tender affection, such as a parent would use towards his own offspring; see Note, 1 Cor. iv. 15; comp. Mat. xviii. 3; John xiii. 33; 1 John ii. 1, 12, 13; iv. 4; v. 21. The idea here is, that Paul felt that he sustained towards them the relation of a father, and he had for them the deep and tender feelings of a parent. ¶ *Of whom I travail in birth again.* For whose welfare I am deeply anxious: and for whom I endure deep anguish; comp. 1 Cor. iv. 15. His anxiety for them he compares to the deepest sufferings which human nature endures; and his language here is a striking illustration of what ministers of the gospel should feel, and do sometimes feel, in regard to their people. ¶ *Until Christ be formed in you.* The name *Christ* is often used to denote his religion, or the principles of his gospel; see Note on Rom. xiii. 14. Here it means, until Christ reigns wholly in your hearts; till you wholly and entirely embrace his doctrines; and till you become wholly imbued with his spirit; see Col. i. 27.

20. *I desire to be present with you now.* They had lost much by his absence; they had changed their views; they had in some measure become alienated from him; and he wishes that he might be again with them, as he was before. He would hope to accomplish much more by his personal presence than he could by letter. ¶ *And to change my voice.* That is, from complaint and censure, to tones of entire confidence. ¶ *For I stand in doubt of you.* Marg. "*I am perplexed for you.*" On the meaning of the word here used, see Note on 2 Cor. iv. 8. The sense is plain. Paul had much reason to doubt the sincerity and the solidity of their Christian principles, and he was deeply anxious on that account.

21. *Tell me, &c.* In order to show fully the nature and the effect of the law, Paul here introduces an illustration from an important fact in the Jewish history. This *allegory* has given great perplexity to expositors. and, in some respects, it is attended with real difficulty. An examination of the difficulties will be found in the larger commentaries. My object, without examining the expositions which have been proposed, will be to state, in as few words as possible, the simple meaning and design of the allegory. The *design* it is not difficult to understand. It is *to show the effect of being under the bondage or servitude of the Jewish law, compared with the freedom which the gospel imparts.* Paul had addressed the Galatians as having a real desire to be under bondage, or to be servants; Note on ver. 9. He had represented Christianity as a state of freedom, and Christians as the sons of God—not servants, but freemen. To show the difference of the two conditions, he appeals to two

22 For it is written, That Abraham had two sons; the one [a] by a bond-maid, the other [b] by a free woman.

23 But he *who was* of the [c] bondwoman was born after the flesh; but he of the free woman *was* by promise.

a Ge.16.15. b Ge.21.1,2. c Ro.9.7,8.

cases which would furnish a striking illustration of them. The one was the case of Hagar and her son. The effect of *bondage* was well illustrated there. She and her son were treated with severity, and were cast out and persecuted. This was *a fair illustration* of bondage under the law; of the servitude to the laws of Moses; and was a fit representation of Jerusalem as it was in the time of Paul. The other case was that of Isaac. He was the son of a free woman, and was treated accordingly. He was regarded as a son, not as a servant. And he was *a fair illustration* of the case of those who were made free by the gospel. They enjoyed a similar freedom and sonship, and should not seek a state of servitude or bondage. The condition of Isaac was a fit illustration of the New Jerusalem; the heavenly city; the true kingdom of God. But Paul does not mean to say, as I suppose, that the history of the son of Hagar and of the son of Rebecca was *mere* allegory, or that the narrative by Moses was *designed* to represent the different condition of those who were under the law and under the gospel. He uses it simply, *as showing the difference between servitude and freedom, and as a striking* ILLUSTRATION *of the nature of the bondage to the Jewish law, and of the freedom of the gospel*, just as any one may use a striking historical fact to illustrate a principle. These general remarks will constitute the *basis* of my interpretation of this celebrated allegory. The expression "tell me," is one of affectionate remonstrance and reasoning; see Luke vii. 42, "Tell me, therefore, which of these will love him most?" Comp. Isa. i. 18, "Come, now, and let us reason together, saith the Lord." ¶ *Ye that desire to be under the law;* Note, ver. 9. You who wish to yield obedience to the laws of Moses. You who maintain that conformity to those laws is necessary to justification. ¶ *Do ye not hear the law?* Do you not understand what the law says? Will you not listen to its own admonitions, and the instruction which may be derived from the law on the subject? The word "law" here refers not to the commands that were uttered on mount Sinai, but to the *book* of the law. The passage to which reference is made is in the Book of Genesis; but all the five books of Moses were by the Jews classed under the general name of the law; see Note on Luke xxiv. 44. The sense is, "Will you not listen to a narrative found in one of the books of the law itself, fully illustrating the nature of that servitude which you wish?"

22. *For it is written;* Gen. xvi. xxi. ¶ *Abraham had two sons.* Ishmael and Isaac. Abraham subsequently had several sons by Keturah after the death of Sarah; Gen. xxvi. 1—6. But the two sons by Hagar and Sarah were the most prominent, and the events of their lives furnished the particular illustration which Paul desired. ¶ *The one by a bond-maid.* Ishmael, the son of Hagar. Hagar was an Egyptian slave, whom Sarah gave to Abraham in order that he might not be wholly without posterity; Gen. xvi. 3. ¶ *The other by a free woman.* Isaac, the son of Sarah; Gen. xxi. 1, 2.

23. *But he* who was *of the bondwoman was born after the flesh.* In the ordinary course of nature, without any special promise, or any unusual divine interposition, as in the case of Isaac. ¶ *But he of the free woman,* &c. The birth of Isaac was in accordance with a special promise, and by a remarkable divine interposition; see Gen. xviii. 10; xxi. 1, 2; Heb. xi. 11, 12; comp. Notes on Rom. iv. 19—21. The idea here of Paul is, that the son of the slave was in a humble and inferior condition from his very birth. There was no special promise

24 Which things are an allegory: [a] for these are the two [1] covenants; the one from the mount [2] Sinai, [b] which gendereth to bondage, which is Agar.

a 1 Co.10.11. 1 or, *testaments*. 2 *Sina*. b De.33.2.

attending him. He was *born* into a state of inferiority and servitude which attended him through his whole life. Isaac, however, was met with promises as soon as he was born, and was under the benefit of those promises as long as he lived. The *object* of Paul is, to state the truth in regard to a condition of servitude and slavery. It is attended with evils from beginning to end; from the birth to the grave. By this illustration he means to show them the folly of becoming the voluntary slaves of the law after they had once been made free.

24. *Which things*. The different accounts of Ishmael and Isaac. ¶ *Are an allegory*. May be regarded allegorically, or as illustrating great principles in regard to the condition of slaves and freemen; and may therefore be used to illustrate the effect of servitude to the law of Moses compared with the freedom of the gospel. He does not mean to say that the historical record of Moses was not true, or was merely allegorical; nor does he mean to say that Moses *meant* this to be an allegory, or that he *intended* that it should be applied to the exact purpose to which Paul applied it. No such design is apparent in the narrative of Moses, and it is evident that he had no such intention. Nor can it be shown that Paul means to be understood as saying that Moses had any such design, or that his account was not a record of a plain historical fact. Paul uses it as he would any other historical fact that would illustrate the same principle, and he makes no more use of it than the Saviour did in his parables of real or fictitious narratives to illustrate an important truth, or than we always do of real history to illustrate an important principle. The word which is here used by Paul (ἀλληγορέω) is derived from ἄλλος, another, and ἀγορεύω, to speak, to speak openly or in public.—*Passow*. It properly means to speak any thing otherwise than it is understood (*Passow*); to speak allegorically; to allegorize. The word does not occur elsewhere in the New Testament, nor is it found in the Septuagint, though it occurs often in the classic writers. An allegory is a continued metaphor; see Blair's Lectures, xv. It is a figurative sentence or discourse, in which the principal object is described by another subject resembling it in its properties and circumstances.—*Webster*. Allegories are in words what hieroglyphics are in painting. The distinction between a *parable* and an *allegory* is said to be, that a parable is a *supposed* history to illustrate some important truth, as the parable of the good Samaritan, &c.; an allegory is based on *real facts*. It is not probable, however, that this distinction is always carefully observed. Sometimes the allegory is based on the resemblance to some inanimate object, as in the beautiful allegory in the eightieth psalm. Allegories, parables, and metaphors abound in the writings of the East. Truth was more easily treasured up in this way, and could be better preserved and transmitted when it was connected with an interesting story. The lively fancy of the people of the East also led them to this mode of communicating truth; though a love for it is probably founded in human nature. The best sustained allegory of any considerable length in the world is, doubtless, Bunyan's Pilgrim's Progress; and yet this is among the most popular of all books. The ancient Jews were exceedingly fond of allegories, and even turned a considerable part of the Old Testament into allegory. The ancient Greek philosophers also were fond of this mode of teaching. Pythagoras instructed his followers in this manner, and this was common among the Greeks, and was imitated much by the early Christians.—*Calmet*. Many of the Christian fathers, of the school of Origen, made the Old Testament almost wholly allegorical, and found mysteries in the plainest narratives. The Bible became thus with them a

25 For this Agar is mount Sinai in Arabia, and [1] answereth to Jerusalem which now is, and is in bondage with her children.

1 or, *is in the same rank with.*

book of enigmas, and exegesis consisted in an ingenious and fanciful accommodation of all the narratives in the scriptures to events in subsequent times. The most fanciful, and the most ingenious man, on this principle, was the best interpreter; and as any man might attach any hidden mystery which he chose to the scriptures, they became wholly useless as an infallible guide. Better principles of interpretation now prevail; and the great truth has gone forth, never more to be recalled, that the Bible is to be interpreted on the same principle as all other books; that its language is to be investigated by the same laws as language in all other books; and that no more liberty is to be taken in allegorizing the scriptures than may be taken with Herodotus or Livy. It is lawful to use narratives of real events to illustrate important principles always. Such a use is often made of history; and such a use, I suppose, the apostle Paul makes here of an important fact in the history of the Old Testament. ¶ *For these are.* These may be used to represent the two covenants. The apostle *could not* mean that the sons of Sarah and Hagar *were literally the two covenants;* for this could not be true, and the declaration would be unintelligible. In what sense could Ishmael be called *a covenant?* The meaning, therefore, must be, that they furnished an apt illustration or representation of the two covenants; they would show what the nature of the two covenants was. The words "are" and "is" are often used in this sense in the Bible, to denote that one thing *represents* another. Thus in the institution of the Lord's supper; "Take, eat, this is my body" (Matt. xxvi. 26); *i. e.*, this *represents* my body. The bread was not the living body that was then before them. So in ver. 28. "This is my blood of the new covenant;" *i. e.*, this represents my blood. The wine in the cup *could not* be the living blood of the Redeemer that was then flowing in his veins; see Note on that place; comp Gen. xli. 26. ¶ *The two covenants* Marg. *Testaments.* The word means here, covenants or compacts; see Note on 1 Cor. xi. 25. The two covenants here referred to, are the one on mount Sinai made with the Jews, and the other that which is made with the people of God in the gospel. The one resembles the condition of bondage in which Hagar and her son were; the other the condition of freedom in which Sarah and Isaac were. ¶ *The one from the mount Sinai.* Marg. *Sina.* The Greek is *Sina*, though the word may be written either way. ¶ *Which gendereth to bondage.* Which tends to produce bondage or servitude. That is, the laws are stern and severe; and the observance of them costly, and onerous like a state of bondage; see Note on Acts xv. 10. ¶ *Which is Agar.* Which Hagar would appropriately represent. The condition of servitude produced by the law had a strong resemblance to her condition as a slave.

25. *For this Agar is mount Sinai.* This Hagar well represents the law given on mount Sinai. No one can believe that Paul meant to say that Hagar was *literally* mount Sinai. A great deal of perplexity has been felt in regard to this passage, and Bentley proposed to cancel it altogether as an interpolation. But there is no good authority for this. Several MSS. and versions read it, "For this Sinai is a mountain in Arabia;" others, "to this Hagar Jerusalem answereth," &c. Griesbach has placed these readings in the margin, and has marked them as not to be rejected as certainly false, but as worthy of a more attentive examination; as sustained by some plausible arguments, though not in the whole satisfactory. The word Hagar in Arabic is said to signify *a rock;* and it has been supposed that the name was appropriately given to mount Sinai, because it was a pile of rocks, and that Paul had allusion to this meaning of the word here. So

26 But Jerusalem [a] which is above is free, which is the mother of us all.

27 For it is written, [b] Rejoice *thou* barren that bearest not; break forth and cry, thou that travailest

a He.12.22; Re.21.2,10.

b Isa.54.1.

Chandler, Rosenmüller, and others interpret it. But I cannot find in Castell or Gesenius that the word Hagar in Arabic has this signification; still less is there evidence that the name was ever given to mount Sinai by the Arabs, or that such a signification was known to Paul. The plainest and most obvious sense of a passage is generally the true sense; and the obvious sense here is, that Hagar was *a fair representation* of mount Sinai, and of the law given there. ¶ *In Arabia.* Mount Sinai is situated in Arabia Petræa, or the Rocky. Rosenmüller says that this means "in the Arabic language;" but probably in this interpretation he stands alone. ¶ *And answereth to Jerusalem.* Marg. *Is in the same rank with.* The margin is the better translation. The meaning is, it is just like it, or corresponds with it. Jerusalem as it is now (*i. e.*, in the days of Paul), is like mount Sinai. It is subject to laws, and rites, and customs; bound by a state of servitude, and fear, and trembling, such as existed when the law was given on mount Sinai. There is no freedom; there are no great and liberal views; there is none of the liberty which the gospel imparts to men. The word συστοιχεῖ, *answereth to*, means properly to advance in order together; to go together with, as soldiers march along in the same rank; and then to correspond to. It means here that mount Sinai and Jerusalem as it then was would be fitted *to march together* in the same platoon or rank. In marshalling an army, care is taken to place soldiers of the same height, and size, and skill, and courage, if possible, together. So here it means that they were *alike*. Both were connected with bondage, like Hagar. On the one, a law was given that led to bondage; and the other was in fact under a miserable servitude of rites and forms. ¶ *Which now is.* As it exists now; that is, *a slave* to rites and forms, as it was in fact in the time of Paul. ¶ *And is in bondage.* To laws and customs. She was under hard and oppressive rites, like slavery. She was also in bondage to sin (John viii. 33, 34); but this does not seem to be the idea here. ¶ *With her children.* Her inhabitants. She is represented as a mother, and her inhabitants, the Jews, are in the condition of the son of Hagar. On this passage comp. Notes on 1 Cor. x. 4, for a more full illustration of the principles involved here.

26. *But Jerusalem which is above.* The spiritual Jerusalem; the true church of God. Jerusalem was the place where God was worshipped, and hence it became synonymous with the word *church*, or is used to represent the people of God. The word rendered "above," (ἄνω) means properly *up above*, that which is above; and hence heavenly, celestial; Col. iii. 1, 2; John viii. 23. Here it means the heavenly or celestial Jerusalem; Rev. xxi. 2, "And I John saw the holy city, new Jerusalem, coming down from God, out of heaven." Heb. xii. 22, "Ye are come unto mount Zion, and unto the city of the living God, the heavenly Jerusalem." Here it is used to denote the church, as being of heavenly origin. ¶ *Is free.* The spirit of the gospel is that of freedom. It is freedom from sin, freedom from the bondage of rites and customs, and it tends to promote universal freedom; see Note on ver. 7; comp. John viii. 32, 36; Note, 2 Cor. iii. 17. ¶ *Which is the mother of us all.* Of all who are true Christians, whether we are by birth Jews or Gentiles. We should not, therefore, yield ourselves to any degrading and debasing servitude of any kind; comp. Note, 1 Cor. vi. 12.

27. *For it is written.* This passage is found in Isa. liv. 1. For an exposition of its meaning as it occurs there, see my Notes on Isaiah. The *object* of the apostle in introducing it here seems to be to prove that the

not; for the desolate hath many more children than she which hath an husband.

28 Now we, [a] brethren, as Isaac was, are the children of promise.

29 But as then he [b] that was

a Ac.3.25, chap.3.29.

b Ge.21.9.

Gentiles as well as the Jews would partake of the privileges connected with the heavenly Jerusalem. He had in the previous verse spoken of the Jerusalem from above as the common mother of ALL true Christians, whether by birth Jews or Gentiles. This might be disputed or doubted by the Jews; and he therefore adduces this proof from the Old Testament. Or if it was not doubted, still the quotation was pertinent, and would illustrate the sentiment which he had just uttered. The mention of Jerusalem as *a mother* seems to have suggested this text. Isaiah had spoken of Jerusalem as a female that had been long desolate and childless, now rejoicing by a large accession from the Gentile world, and increased in numbers like a female who should have more children than one who had been long married. To this Paul appropriately refers when he says that the whole church, Jews and Gentiles, were the children of the heavenly Jerusalem, represented here as a rejoicing mother. He has not quoted literally from the Hebrew, but he has used the Septuagint version, and has retained the sense. The sense is, that the accession from the Gentile world would be far more numerous than the Jewish people had ever been; a prophecy that has been already fulfilled. ¶ *Rejoice* thou *barren that bearest not*. As a woman who has had no children would rejoice. This represents probably the heathen world as having been apparently forsaken and abandoned, and with whom there had been none of the true children of God. ¶ *Break forth and cry*. Or "break forth and exclaim;" *i. e.* break out into loud and glad exclamations at the remarkable accession. The *cry* here referred to was to be a *joyful* cry or shout; the language of exultation. So the Hebrew word in Isa. liv. 1 (צהל) means. ¶ *For the desolate*. She who was desolate and apparently forsaken. It literally refers to a woman who had seemed to be desolate and forsaken, who was unmarried. In Isaiah it may refer to Jerusalem, long forsaken and desolate, or as some suppose to the Gentile world; see my Note on Isa. liv. 1. ¶ *Than she which hath an husband*. Perhaps referring to the Jewish people as in covenant with God, and often spoken of as *married* to him; Isa. lxii. 4, 5; liv. 5.

28. *Now we, brethren*. We who are Christians. ¶ *Are the children of the promise*. We so far resemble Isaac, that there are great and precious promises made to us. We are not in the condition of Ishmael, to whom no promise was made.

29. *But as then he that was born after the flesh*. Ishmael; see ver. 23. ¶ *Persecuted him* that was born *after the Spirit*. That is, Isaac. The phrase, "after the Spirit," here, is synonymous with "according to the promise" in the previous verse. It stands opposed to the phrase "after the flesh," and means that his birth was by the special or miraculous agency of God; see Rom. iv. It was not in the ordinary course of events. The *persecution* here referred to, was the injurious treatment which Isaac received from Ishmael, or the opposition which subsisted between them. The *particular* reference of Paul is doubtless to Gen. xxi. 9, where it is said that "Sarah saw the son of Hagar the Egyptian, which she had born unto Abraham, mocking." It was on account of this, and at the special request of Sarah, that Hagar and her son were expelled from the house of Abraham; Gen. xxi. 10. ¶ *Even so* it is *now*. That is, Christians, the children of the promise, are persecuted by the Jews, the inhabitants of Jerusalem, "as it now is," and who are uninterested in the promises, as Ishmael was. For an illustration of this, see Paley's *Horæ Paulinæ*, on this Epistle, No. V. Dr. Paley has remarked that it does not appear that

born after the flesh, persecuted him *that was born* after the Spirit, even so, [a] *it is* now.

30 Nevertheless, what saith [b] the Scripture? Cast out the bond-woman and her son: for the son of the bond-woman shall not be heir with the son of the free woman.

31 So then, brethren, we are not children of the bond-woman, but of the free.

a John 15.19. b Ge.21.10,12.

the apostle Paul was ever set upon by the Gentiles, unless they were first stirred up by the Jews, except in two instances. One of these was at Philippi, after the cure of the Pythoness (Acts xvi. 19); and the other at Ephesus, at the instance of Demetrius; Acts xix. 24. The persecutions of the Christians arose, therefore, mainly from the Jews, from those who were in bondage to the law, and to rites and customs; and Paul's allusion here to the case of the persecution which Isaac the free-born son endured, is exceedingly pertinent and happy.

30. *Nevertheless.* But (Ἀλλὰ). ¶ *What saith the Scripture?* What does the Scripture teach on the subject? What lesson does it convey in regard to the bondman? ¶ *Cast out the bondwoman and her son.* This was the language of Sarah, in an address to Abraham, requesting him to cast out Hagar and Ishmael; Gen. xxi. 10. That was done. Paul uses it here as applicable to the case before him. As used by him the meaning is, that every thing like servitude in the gospel is to be rejected, as Hagar and Ishmael were driven away. It does not mean, as it seems to me, that they were to expel the Jewish *teachers* in Galatia, but that they were to reject every thing like servitude and bondage; they were to adhere only to that which was free. Paul cannot here mean that the passage in Gen. xxi. 10, originally had reference to the gospel, for nothing evidently was farther from the mind of Sarah than any such reference; nor can it be shown that he meant to approve of or vindicate the conduct of Sarah; but he finds a passage applicable to his purpose, and he conveys his ideas in that language as exactly expressing his meaning. We all use language in that way wherever we find it.

[Yet God *confirmed* the sentence of Sarah; Gen. xxi. 12. Hence Mr. Scott thus paraphrases, "But as the Galatians might read in the Scriptures that *God himself* had *commanded* Hagar and Ishmael to be sent away from Abraham's family, that the son of the bondwoman might not share the inheritance with Isaac; even so the Jewish nation would soon be cast out of the church, and all who continued under the legal covenant excluded from heaven."]

31. *So then, brethren.* It follows from all this. Not from the allegory regarded as *an argument*—for Paul does not use it thus—but from the considerations suggested on the whole subject. Since the Christian religion is so superior to the Jewish; since we are by it freed from degrading servitude, and are not in bondage to rites and ceremonies; since it was designed to make us truly free, and since by that religion we are admitted to the privileges of sons, and are no longer under laws, and tutors, and governors, as if we were minors; from all this it follows, that we should feel and act, not as if we were children of a bondwoman, and born in slavery, but as if we were children of a free-woman, and born to liberty. It is the birthright of Christians to think, and feel, and act like freemen, and they should not allow themselves to become the slaves of customs, and rites, and ceremonies, but should feel that they are the adopted children of God.

Thus closes this celebrated allegory—an allegory that has greatly perplexed most expositors, and most readers of the Bible. In view of it, and of the exposition above, there are a few remarks which may not inappropriately be made.

(1.) It is by no means affirmed, that the history of Hagar and Sarah in Genesis, had any original reference to the gospel. The account there is a plain historical narrative, not *designed* to have any such reference.

(2.) The narrative contains important *principles,* that may be used as illustrating truth, and is so used by the apostle Paul. There are parallel points between the history and the truths of religion, where the one may be *illustrated* by the other.

(3.) The apostle does not use it at all in the way of *argument*, or as if that *proved* that the Galatians were not to submit to the Jewish rites and customs. It is an illustration of the comparative nature of servitude and freedom, and would, therefore, illustrate the difference between a servile compliance with Jewish rites, and the freedom of the gospel.

(4.) This use of an historical fact by the apostle does not make it proper for *us* to turn the Old Testament into allegory, or even to make a very free use of this mode of illustrating truth. That an allegory may be used sometimes with advantage, no one can doubt while the "Pilgrim's Progress" shall exist. Nor can any one doubt that Paul has here derived, in this manner, an important and striking illustration of truth from the Old Testament. But no one acquainted with the history of interpretation can doubt that vast injury has been done by a fanciful mode of explaining the Old Testament; by making every fact in its history an allegory; and every pin and pillar of the tabernacle and the temple a *type*. Nothing is better fitted to bring the whole science of interpretation into contempt; nothing more dishonours the Bible, than to make it a book of enigmas, and religion to consist in puerile conceits. The Bible is a book of sense; and all the doctrines essential to salvation are plainly revealed. It should be interpreted, not by mere conceit and by fancy, but by the sober laws according to which are interpreted other books. It should be explained, not under the influence of a vivid imagination, but under the influence of a heart imbued with a love of truth, and by an understanding disciplined to investigate the meaning of words and phrases, and capable of rendering *a reason* for the interpretation which is proposed. Men may abundantly use the facts in the Old Testament to illustrate human nature, as Paul did; but far distant be the day, when the principles of Origen and of Cocceius shall again prevail, and when it shall be assumed, that "the Bible means every thing that it can be made to mean."

[These are excellent remarks, and the caution which the author gives against extravagant and imaginative systems of interpreting scripture cannot be too often repeated. It is allowed, however, nearly on all hands, that this allegory is brought forward by way of *illustration* only, and not of argument. This being the case, the question, as to whether the history in Genesis were *originally* intended to represent the matter, to which Paul here applies it, is certainly not of very great importance, notwithstanding the learned labour that has been expended on it, and to such an extent as to justify the critic's remark, "vexavit interpretes vehementer vexatus ab iis et ipse." Whatever be the original design of the passage, the apostle *has* employed it as an illustration of his subject, and was guided by the Spirit of inspiration in so doing. But certainly we should not be very far wrong, if since an apostle has *affirmed* such spiritual representation, we should suppose it originally intended by the Spirit; nor are we in great danger of making types of every pin and pillar, *so long as we strictly confine ourselves to the admission of such only as rest upon apostolic authority.* "This transaction," says the eminently judicious Thomas Scott, "was so remarkable, the coincidence so exact, and the illustration so instructive, that we cannot doubt it *originally was intended*, by the Holy Spirit, as an allegory and type of those things to which the inspired apostle referred it."]

CHAPTER V.

ANALYSIS.

This chapter is properly a continuation of the argument in the previous chapter, and is designed to induce the Galatians to renounce their conformity to the Jewish law, and to become entirely conformed to the gospel. In particular, it seems to be designed to meet a charge that had been brought against him, that he had preached the necessity of circumcision, or that he had so practised it as to show that he believed that it was obligatory on others. Under his example, or pleading his authority, it seems the false teachers there had urged the necessity of its observance; see ver. 11. The argument and the exhortation consist of the following parts.

I. He exhorts them to stand firm in the liberty of Christianity, and not to be brought again under bondage; ver. 1.

II. He solemnly assures them, that if they depended on circumcision for salvation, they could derive no benefit from Christ. They put themselves into a perfect legal state, and must

CHAPTER V.

STAND [a] fast therefore in the [b] liberty wherewith Christ hath made us free, and be not entangled again with the yoke of bondage.

2 Behold, I Paul say unto you,

a Ep.6.14.
b John 8.32,36; Ro.6.18; Ac.15.10.

depend on that alone; and that was equivalent to renouncing Christ altogether, or to falling from grace; ver. 2—6.

III. He assures them that their present belief could not have come from him by whom they were originally brought to the knowledge of the truth; but must have been from some foreign influence, operating like leaven; ver. 7—9.

IV. He says he had confidence in them, on the whole, that they would obey the truth, and that they would suffer him who had troubled them to bear his proper judgment, gently insinuating that he should be disowned or cut off; ver. 10, 12.

V. He vindicates himself from the charge that he preached the necessity of circumcision. His vindication was, that if he had done that, he would have escaped persecution, for then the offence of the cross would have ceased; ver. 11.

VI. He assures them that they had been called unto liberty; that the gospel had made them free. Yet Paul felt how easy it was to abuse this doctrine, and to pretend that Christ had freed them from *all* restraint, and from the bondage of *all* law. Against this he cautions them. Their liberty was not licentiousness. It was not freedom from all the restraints of the law. It was not that they might give indulgence to the passions of the flesh. It was designed that they should serve one another; and not fall into the indulgence of raging passions, producing strife and mutual hatred; ver. 13—15.

VII. To illustrate this, and to show them the evils of giving indulgence to their appetites under the pretence that they were *free*, he proceeds to show what *were* the passions to which carnal indulgence would give rise, or what were the works of the flesh; ver. 16—21.

VIII. On the other hand, the Spirit produces a train of most lovely virtues, feelings, and affections, against which there could be no law; v. 22, 23.

IX. They who were Christians had in fact crucified the flesh. They were bound to live after the teachings of the Spirit, and Paul, therefore, exhorts them to lay aside all vain-glory and envy, and to live in peace; ver. 24—26.

1. *Stand fast, therefore.* Be firm and unwavering. This verse properly belongs to the previous chapter, and should not have been separated from it. The sense is, that they were to be firm and unyielding in maintaining the great principles of Christian liberty. They had been freed from the bondage of rites and ceremonies; and they should by no means, and in no form, yield to them again. ¶ *In the liberty,* &c.; comp. John viii. 32, 36; Rom. vi. 18; Notes, chap. iv. 3—5. ¶ *And be not entangled again.* Tindal renders this, "And wrap not yourselves again." The sense is, do not again allow such a yoke to be put on you; do not again become slaves to any rites, and customs, and habits. ¶ *The yoke of bondage.* Of servitude to the Jewish laws; see Note, Acts xv. 10.

2. *Behold, I Paul say unto you.* I, who at first preached the gospel to you; I, too, who have been circumcised, and who was formerly a strenuous assertor of the necessity of observing the laws of Moses; and I, too, who am charged (see ver. 11) with still preaching the necessity of circumcision, now solemnly say to you, that if you are circumcised with a view to being justified by that in whole or in part, it amounts to a rejection of the doctrine of justification by Christ, and an entire apostacy from him. He is to be "a whole Saviour." No one is to share with him in the honour of saving men; and no rite, no custom, no observance of law, is to divide the honour with his death. The design of Paul is to give them the most solemn assurance on this point; and

that if ye be circumcised, Christ shall profit you nothing.

3 For I testify again to every man that is circumcised, that he is a debtor to do the whole law

4 Christ is become of no ef-

by his own authority and experience to guard them from the danger, and to put the matter to rest. ¶ *That if ye be circumcised.* This must be understood with reference to the subject under consideration. If you are circumcised with such a view as is maintained by the false teachers that have come among you; that is, with an idea that it is necessary in order to your justification. He evidently did not mean that if any of them *had* been circumcised before their conversion to Christianity; nor could he mean to say, that circumcision in all cases amounted to a rejection of Christianity, for he had himself procured the circumcision of Timothy, Acts xvi. 3. If it was done, as it was then, for prudential considerations, and with a wish not necessarily to irritate the Jews, and to give one a more ready access to them, it was not to be regarded as wrong. But if, as the false teachers in Galatia claimed, as a thing *essential* to salvation, as *indispensable* to justification and acceptance with God, then the matter assumed a different aspect; and then it became in fact a renouncing of Christ as *himself sufficient* to save us. So with any thing else. Rites and ceremonies in religion may be in themselves well enough, if they are *held* to be matters not essential; but the moment they are regarded as vital and essential, that moment they begin to infringe on the doctrine of justification by faith alone, and that moment they are to be rejected; and it is because of the danger that this *will* be the case, that they are to be used sparingly in the Christian church. Who does not know the danger of depending upon prayers, and alms, and the sacraments, and extreme unction, and penance, and empty forms for salvation? And who does not know how much in the papal communion the great doctrine of justification has been obscured by numberless such rites and forms? ¶ *Christ shall profit you nothing.* Will be of no advantage to you. Your dependence on circumcision, in these circumstances, will in fact amount to a rejection of the Saviour, and of the doctrine of justification by him.

3. *For I testify again.* Probably he had stated this when he had preached the gospel to them first, and he now solemnly bears witness to the same thing *again.* Bloomfield, however, supposes that the word *again* here (πάλιν) means, on the other hand, or, *furthermore,* or, as we would say, "and again." ¶ *That he is a debtor to do the whole law.* He binds himself to obey all the law of Moses. Circumcision was the distinguishing badge of the Jews, as baptism is of Christians. A man, therefore, who became circumcised became *a professor of the Jewish religion,* and bound himself to obey all its peculiar laws. This must be understood, of course, with reference to the point under discussion; and means, if he did it with a view to justification, or as a thing that was neces sary and binding. It would not apply to such a case as that of Timothy, where it was a matter of mere expediency or prudence; see Note on ver. 2.

4. *Christ is become of no effect unto you.* You will derive no advantage from Christ. His work in regard to you is needless and vain. If you can be justified in any other way than by him, then of course you do not need him, and your adoption of the other mode is in fact a renunciation of him. Tindal renders this, "Ye are gone quite from Christ." The word here used (καταργέω), means properly, to render inactive, idle, useless; to do away, to put an end to; and here it means that they had withdrawn from Christ, if they attempted to be justified by the law. They would not need him if they could be thus justified; and they could derive no benefit from him. A man who can be justified by his own obedience, does not need the aid or the merit of another; and if it was true, as they seemed to suppose,

fect [a] unto you, whosoever of you are justified by the law: ye are fallen [b] from grace.

5 For we through the Spirit wait [c] for the hope of righteousness [d] by faith.

6 For in Jesus Christ neither

a Ro.9.31.32. b He.12.15. c Ro.8.25 d 2Ti.4.8.

that they could be justified by the law, it followed that the work of Christ was in vain so far as they were concerned. ¶ *Whosoever of you are justified by the law.* On the supposition that any of you are justified by the law; or if, as you seem to suppose, any are justified by the law. The apostle does not say that this had in fact ever occurred; but he merely makes a supposition. If such a thing should or could occur, it would follow that you had fallen from grace. ¶ *Ye are fallen from grace.* That is, this would amount to apostasy from the religion of the Redeemer, and would be in fact a rejection of the grace of the gospel. That this had ever in fact occurred among true Christians the apostle does not affirm *unless* he affirmed that men can in fact be justified by the law, since he makes the falling from grace a consequence of that. But did Paul mean to teach that? Did he mean to affirm that any man in fact had been, or could be justified by his own obedience to the law? Let his own writings answer; see, especially, Rom. iii. 20. But unless he held that, then this passage does not prove that any one who has ever been a true Christian has fallen away. The fair interpretation of the passage does not demand that. Its simple and obvious meaning is, that if a man who has been a professed Christian *should be* justified by his own conformity to the law, and adopt that mode of justification, then that would amount to a rejection of the mode of salvation by Christ, and would be a renouncing of the plan of justification by grace. The two systems cannot be united. The adoption of the one is, in fact, a rejection of the other. Christ will be "a whole Saviour," or none. This passage, therefore, *cannot* be adduced to prove that any true Christian has in fact fallen away from grace, unless it proves also that man may be justified by the deeds of the law, contrary to the repeated declarations of Paul himself. The word "grace" here, does not mean grace in the sense of *personal religion,* it means the *system* of salvation by grace, in contradistinction from that by merit or by works—the system of the gospel.

5. *For we.* We who are Christians. It is a characteristic of the true Christian. ¶ *Through the Spirit.* The Holy Spirit. We expect salvation only by his aid. ¶ *Wait for.* That is, we *expect* salvation in this way. The main idea is, not that of *waiting* as if the thing were *delayed;* it is that of *expecting.* The sense is, that true Christians have no other hope of salvation than by faith in the Lord Jesus. It is not by their own works, nor is it by any conformity to the law. The object of Paul is, to show them the true nature of the Christian hope of eternal life, and to recall them from dependence on their conformity to the law. ¶ *The hope of righteousness.* The hope of justification. They had no other hope of justification than by faith in the Redeemer; see Note on Rom. i. 17.

6. *For in Jesus Christ.* In the religion which Christ came to establish. ¶ *Neither circumcision,* &c. It makes no difference whether a man is circumcised or not. He is not saved *because* he is circumcised, nor is he condemned *because* he is not. The design of Christianity is to abolish these rites and ceremonies, and to introduce a way of salvation that shall be applicable to all mankind alike; see Notes on ch. iii. 28; 1 Cor. vii. 19; comp. Rom. ii. 29. ¶ *But faith which worketh by love.* Faith that evinces its existence by love to God, and benevolence to men. It is not a mere *intellectual* belief, but it is that which reaches the heart, and controls the affections. It is not a *dead* faith, but it is that which is operative, and which is seen in Christian kindness and affection. It is not mere belief of the truth, or mere *orthodoxy,* but it is that which produces true at-

[a] circumcision availeth any thing,
nor uncircumcision; but faith
which [b] worketh by love.
7 Ye did run well; who did
hinder you, that ye should not
obey the truth?
8 This persuasion *cometh* not of
him that calleth you.
9 A little [c] leaven leaveneth the
whole lump.
10 I have confidence in you
through the Lord, that ye will

a 1 Co.7.19. *b* 1 Ti.1,3; Ja.2.18—22.
1 or, *drive you back.* *c* Mat.13.33; 1 Co.5.6.

tachment to others. A mere intellectual assent to the truth may leave the heart cold and unaffected; mere orthodoxy, however bold and self-confident, and "sound," may not be inconsistent with contentions, and strifes, and logomachies, and divisions. The true faith is that which is seen in benevolence, in love to God, in love to all who bear the Christian name; in a readiness to do good to all mankind. This shows that the *heart* is affected by the faith that is held; and this is the nature and design of all genuine religion. Tindal renders this, "faith, which by love is mighty in operation."

7. *Ye did run well.* The Christian life is often represented as a race; see Notes on 1 Cor. ix. 24—26. Paul means here, that they began the Christian life with ardour and zeal; comp. chap. iv. 15. ¶ *Who did hinder you.* Marg. *Drive you back.* The word used here (ἀνακόπτω) means properly to beat or drive back. Hence it means to hinder, check, or retard. Dr. Doddridge remarks that this is "an Olympic expression, and properly signifies *coming across the course* while a person is running in it, in such a manner as to *jostle*, and throw him out of the way." Paul asks, with emphasis, who it could have been that retarded them in their Christian course, implying that it could have been done only by their own consent, or that there was really no cause why they should not have continued as they began. ¶ *That ye should not obey the truth.* The true system of justification by faith in the Redeemer. That you should have turned aside, and embraced the dangerous errors in regard to the necessity of obeying the laws of Moses.

8. *This persuasion.* This belief that it is necessary to obey the laws of Moses, and to intermingle the observance of Jewish rites with the belief of the Christian doctrines in order to be saved. ¶ *Not of him that calleth you.* That is, of God, who had called them into his kingdom. That it refers to God and not to Paul is plain. They knew well enough that Paul had not persuaded them to it, and it was important now to show them that it could not be traced to God, though they who taught it pretended to be commissioned by him.

9. *A little leaven*, &c. This is evidently a proverbial expression; see it explained in the Notes on 1 Cor. v. 6. Its meaning here is, that the embracing of the errors which they had adopted was to be traced to some influence existing among themselves, and acting like leaven. It may either mean that there was existing among them from the first a slight *tendency* to conform to rites and customs, and that this had now like leaven pervaded the mass; or it may mean that the false teachers there might be compared to leaven, whose doctrines, though *they* were few in number, had pervaded the mass of Christians; or it may mean, as many have supposed, that *any* conformity to the Jewish law was like leaven. If they practised circumcision, it would not stop there. The tendency to conform to Jewish rites would spread from that until it would infect all the doctrines of religion, and they would fall into the observance of *all* the rites of the Jewish law. It seems to me that the *second* interpretation referred to above is the correct one; and that the apostle means to say, that the influence which had brought this change about was at first small and unimportant; that there might have been but a few teachers of that kind, and it might have not been deemed worthy of particular attention or alarm; but that the doctrines thus infused into the churches,

be none otherwise minded: but he that troubleth you shall bear his [a] judgment, whosoever he be.

11 And I, brethren, if I yet preach circumcision, why do I yet suffer persecution? [b] then is the offence [c] of the cross ceased.

a 2 Co.10.6. b chap.6.12. c 1 Co.1.23.

had spread like leaven, until the whole mass had become affected.

10. *I have confidence in you,* &c. Though they had been led astray, and had embraced many false opinions, yet, on the whole, Paul had confidence in their piety, and believed they would yet return and embrace the truth. ¶ *That ye will be none otherwise minded.* That is, than you have been taught by me; or than I think and teach on the subject. Paul doubtless means to say, that he had full confidence that they would embrace the views which he was inculcating on the subject of justification, and he makes this remark in order to modify the severity of his tone of reprehension, and to show that, notwithstanding all he had said, he had confidence still in their piety. He believed that they would concide with him in his opinion, alike on the general subject of justification, and in regard to the cause of their alienation from the truth. He, therefore, gently insinuates that it was not to be traced to themselves that they had departed from the truth, but to the "little leaven" that had leavened the mass; and he adds, that whoever had done this, should be held to be responsible for it ¶ *But he that troubleth you.* By leading you into error. ¶ *Shall bear his judgment.* Shall be responsible for it, and will receive proper treatment from you. He gently states this general principle, which is so obvious; states that he does not believe that the defection is to be traced to themselves; and designs to prepare their minds for a proposition which he intends to submit (ver. 12), that the offending person or persons should be disowned and cut off. ¶ *Whosoever he be.* "I do not know who he is. I mention no names; accuse no one by name; and advise no severe measures against any particular individual. I state only the obvious principle that every man should bear his own burden, and be held responsible for what he has done—no matter who he is."

11. *And I, brethren.* Paul here proceeds to vindicate himself from giving countenance to the doctrines which they had advanced there. It is evident that the false teachers in Galatia appealed to Paul himself, and alleged that *he* insisted on the necessity of circumcision, and that they were teaching no more than he taught. On what they founded this is unknown. It *may* have been mere slander; or it may have arisen from the fact that he had circumcised Timothy (Acts xvi. 3), and, possibly, that he may have encouraged circumcision in some other similar cases. Or it may have been inferred from the fact (which was undoubtedly true) that Paul in general complied with the customs of the Jews when he was with them. But his conduct and example had been greatly perverted. He had *never* enjoined circumcision as necessary to salvation; and had never complied with Jewish customs where there was danger that it would be understood that he regarded them as at all indispensable, or as furnishing a ground of acceptance with God. ¶ *If I yet preach circumcision.* If I preach it as necessary to salvation; or if I enjoin it on those who are converted to Christianity. ¶ *Why do I yet suffer persecution?* That is, from the Jews. "Why do they oppose me? Circumcision is the peculiar badge of the Jewish religion; it implies all the rest (see ver. 2); and if I preach the necessity of that, it would satisfy the Jews, and save me from persecution. They would never persecute one who did that as they do me; and the fact that I *am* thus persecuted by them is full demonstration that I am not regarded as preaching the necessity of circumcision." It is remarkable that Paul does not expressly deny the charge. The reason may be, that his own word would be called in question,

12 I would they were even cut off which trouble you.

13 For, brethren, ye have been called unto liberty; only *use* not

or that it might require much explanation to show *why* he had recommended circumcision in any case, as in the case of Timothy; Acts xvi. 3. But the fact that he was persecuted by the Jews settled the question, and showed that he did not preach the necessity of circumcision in any such sense as to satisfy them, or in any such sense as was claimed by the false teachers in Galatia. In regard to the fact that Paul was persecuted by the Jews; see Acts xiv. 1, 2, 19; xvii. 4, 5, 13; comp. Paley, *Horæ Paulinæ*, Galat. No. V. ¶ *Then is the offence of the cross ceased.* "For if I should preach the necessity of circumcision, as is alleged, the offence of the cross of Christ would be removed. The necessity of depending on the merits of the sacrifice made on the cross would be taken away, since then men could be saved by conformity to the laws of Moses. The very thing that I have so much insisted on, and that has been such a stumbling-block to the Jews (Note, 1 Cor. i. 23), that conformity to their rites was of no avail, and that they must be saved only by the merits of a crucified Saviour, would be done away with." Paul means that if this had been done, he would have saved himself from giving offence, and from the evils of persecution. He would have preached that men could be saved by conformity to Jewish rites, and that would have saved him from all the persecutions which he had endured in consequence of preaching the necessity of salvation by the cross.

12. *I would they were even cut off.* That is, as I understand it, from the communion of the church. So far am I, says Paul, from agreeing with them, and preaching the necessity of circumcision as they do, that I sincerely wish they were excluded from the church as unworthy a place among the children of God. For a very singular and monstrous interpretation of this passage, though adopted by Chrysostom, Theodoret, Theophylact, Jerome, Grotius, Rosenmüller, Koppe, and others, the learned reader may consult Koppe on this verse. To my amazement, I find that this interpretation has also been adopted by Robinson in his Lexicon, on the word ἀποκόπτω. I will state the opinion in the words of Koppe. *Non modo circumcidant se, sed, si velint, etiam mutilant se—ipsa genitalia resecent.* The simple meaning is, I think, that Paul wished that the authors of these errors and disturbances were excluded from the church. ¶ *Which trouble you.* Who pervert the true doctrines of salvation, and who thus introduce error into the church. Error always sooner or later causes trouble; comp. Note, 1 Cor. v. 7.

13. *For, brethren, ye have been called unto liberty.* Freedom from Jewish rites and ceremonies; see the Notes on chap. iii. 28; iv. 9, 21—31. The meaning here is, that Paul wished the false teachers removed *because* true Christians had been called unto liberty, and they were abridging and destroying that liberty. They were not in subjection to the law of Moses, or to any thing else that savoured of bondage. They were free; free from the servitude of sin, and free from subjection to expensive and burdensome rites and customs. They were to remember this as a great and settled principle; and so vital a truth was this, and so important that it should be maintained, and so great the evil of forgetting it, that Paul says he earnestly wishes (ver. 12) that all who would reduce them to that state of servitude were cut off from the Christian church. ¶ *Only use not liberty*, &c. The word *use* here introduced by our translators, obscures the sense. The idea is, "You are called to liberty, but it is not liberty for an occasion to the flesh. It is not freedom from virtuous restraints, and from the laws of God. It is liberty from the servitude of sin, and religious rites and ceremonies, not freedom from the necessary restraints of virtue." It was necessary to give this caution, because, (1.) There was

[a] liberty for an occasion to the flesh, but by love serve [b] one another.

14 For all the law is fulfilled in one word, *even* in this, [c] Thou shalt love thy neighbour as thyself.

15 But if ye bite and devour one another, take heed that ye be not consumed one of another.

a 1 Co.8.9; 1 Pe.2.16. b 1 John 3.18. c Le.19.18; Mat.22.39,40; James 2.8.

a strong tendency in all converts from heathenism to relapse again into their former habits. Licentiousness abounded, and where they had been addicted to it before their conversion, and where they were surrounded by it on every hand, they were in constant danger of falling into it again. A bare and naked declaration, therefore, that they had been called to *liberty*, to freedom from restraint, might have been misunderstood, and some might have supposed that they were free from *all* restraints. (2.) It is needful to guard the doctrine from abuse at all times. There has been a strong tendency, as the history of the church has shown, to abuse the doctrine of grace. The doctrine that Christians are "free;" that there is liberty to them from restraint, has been perverted always by Antinomians, and been made the occasion of their indulging freely in sin. And the result has shown that nothing was more important than to guard the doctrine of *Christian liberty*, and to show exactly what Christians are *freed from*, and what laws are still binding on them. Paul is, therefore, at great pains to show that the doctrines which he had maintained did not lead to licentiousness, and did not allow the indulgence of sinful and corrupt passions. ¶ *An occasion.* As allowing indulgence to the flesh, or as a furtherance or help to corrupt passions; see the word explained in the Notes on Rom. vii. 8. ¶ *To the flesh.* The word flesh is often used in the writings of Paul to denote corrupt and gross passions and affections; see Notes on Rom. vii. 18; viii. 1. ¶ *But by love serve one another.* By the proper manifestation of love one to another strive to promote each other's welfare. To do this will not be inconsistent with the freedom of the gospel. When there is *love* there is no servitude. Duty is pleasant, and offices of kindness agreeable. Paul does not consider them as freed from *all* law and *all* restraint; but they are to be governed by the law of love. They were not to feel that they were *so* free that they might lawfully give indulgence to the desires of the flesh, but they were to regard themselves as under the law to love one another; and thus they would fulfil the law of Christian freedom.

14. *For all the law is fulfilled*, &c. That is, this expresses the substance of the whole law; it embraces and comprises all. The apostle of course here alludes to the law in regard to our duty to our fellow-men, since that was the point which he particularly enforces. He is saying that this law would counteract all the evil workings of the flesh, and if this were fulfilled, all our duty to others would be discharged. A similar sentiment he has expressed in Rom. xiii. 8—10; see Notes on that passage. The *turn* here in the discussion is worthy of particular notice. With great skill he changes the subject from a doctrinal argument to a strain of practical remark, and furnishes most important lessons for the right mode of overcoming our corrupt and sensual passions, and discharging our duty to others. ¶ *Thou shalt love thy neighbour*, &c; see this explained in the Note on Mat. xix. 19.

15. *But if ye bite.* The word here used (δάκνω), means, properly, to bite, to sting; and here seems to be used in the sense of contending and striving—a metaphor not improbably taken from dogs and wild beasts. ¶ *And devour one another.* As wild beasts do. The sense is, "if you contend with each other;" and the reference is, probably, to the strifes which would arise between the two parties in the churches—the Jewish and the Gentile converts. ¶ *Take heed that ye be not consumed*, &c. As wild beasts contend sometimes until both are

16 *This* I say then, Walk [a] in
the Spirit, and [1] ye shall not fulfil the lust of the flesh.
17 For [b] the flesh lusteth against
the Spirit, and the Spirit against the flesh: and these are contrary [c] the one to the other; so that [d] ye cannot do the things that ye would.

a Ro.8.1,4,13. 1 or, *fulfil not.* *b* Ro.7.21—23. *c* Ro.8.6,7. *d* Ro.7.15,19.

slain. Thus, the idea is, in their contentions they would destroy the spirituality and happiness of each other; their characters would be ruined; and the church be overthrown. The readiest way to destroy the spirituality of a church, and to annihilate the influence of religion, is to excite a spirit of contention.

16 This *I say then.* This is the true rule about overcoming the propensities of your carnal natures, and of avoiding the evils of strife and contention. ¶ *Walk.* The Christian life is often represented as a journey, and the word *walk,* in the scripture, is often equivalent to *live;* Mark vii. 5; Notes, Rom. iv. 12; vi. 4; viii. 1. ¶ *In the Spirit.* Live under the influences of the Holy Spirit; admit those influences fully into your hearts. Do not resist him, but yield to all his suggestions; see Note, Rom. viii. 1. What the Holy Spirit would produce, Paul states in ver. 22, 23. If a man would yield his heart to those influences, he would be able to overcome all his carnal propensities; and it is because he resists that Spirit, that he is ever overcome by the corrupt passions of his nature. Never was a better, a safer, or a more easy rule given to overcome our corrupt and sensual desires than that here furnished; comp. Notes, Rom. viii. 1—13. *And ye shall not fulfil,* &c. Marg. *Fulfil not*—as if it were a command. So Tindal renders it. But the more common interpretation, as it is the more significant, is that adopted by our translators. Thus it is not merely a command, it is the statement of an important and deeply interesting truth—that the only way to overcome the corrupt desires and propensities of our nature, is by submitting to the influences of the Holy Spirit. It is not by philosophy; it is not by mere resolutions to resist them; it is not by the force of education and laws; it is only by admitting into our souls the influence of religion, and yielding ourselves to the guidance of the Holy Spirit of God. If we live under the influences of that Spirit, we need not fear the power of the sensual and corrupt propensities of our nature.

17. *For the flesh lusteth against the Spirit.* The inclinations and desires of the flesh are contrary to those of the Spirit. They draw us away in an opposite direction, and while the Spirit of God would lead us one way, our carnal nature would lead us another, and thus produce the painful controversy which exists in our minds. The word "Spirit" here refers to the Spirit of God, and to his influences on the heart. ¶ *And these are contrary,* &c. They are opposite in their nature. They never can harmonize; see Rom. viii. 6, 7; comp. below ver. 19—23. The *contrariety* Paul has illustrated by showing what each produces; and they are as opposite as adultery, wrath, strife, murders, drunkenness, &c., are to love, joy, goodness, gentleness, and temperance. ¶ *So that ye cannot do the things that ye would;* see this sentiment illustrated in the Notes on Rom. vii. 15—19. The expression "cannot do" is stronger by far than the original, and it is doubted whether the original will bear this interpretation. The literal translation would be, "Lest what ye will, those things ye should do" (ἵνα μὴ ἃ ἂν θέλητε, ταῦτα ποιῆτε). It is rendered by Doddridge, "So that ye do not the things that ye would." By Locke, "You do not the things that you propose to yourselves;" and Locke remarks on the passage, "Ours is the only translation that I know which renders it cannot." The Vulgate and the Syriac give a literal translation of the Greek, "So that you do not what you would." This is undoubtedly the true rendering; and, in the original, there is no declaration about the possibility or

the impossibility, the ability or the inability to do these things. It is simply a statement *of a fact*, as it is in Rom. vii. 15, 19. That statement is, that in the mind of a renewed man there is a contrariety in the two influences which bear on his soul—the Spirit of God inclining him in one direction, and the lusts of the flesh in another; that one of these influences is so great as in fact to restrain and control the mind, and prevent its doing what it would otherwise do; that when there is an inclination in one direction, there is a controlling and overpowering influence in another, producing a conflict, which prevents it, and which finally checks and restrains the mind. There is no reason for interpreting this, moreover, as seems always to be the case, of the overpowering tendency in the mind to evil, as if it taught that the Christian was desirous of doing good, but *could not*, on account of his indwelling corruption. So far as the language of Paul or the fact is concerned, it may be understood of just the opposite, and may mean, that such are the restraints and influences of the Holy Spirit on the heart, that the Christian *does not* the evil which he otherwise would, and to which his corrupt nature inclines him. He (Paul) is exhorting them (ver. 16) to walk in the Spirit, and assures them that thus they would not fulfil the lusts of the flesh. To encourage them to this, he reminds them that there were contrary principles in their minds, the influences of the Spirit of God, and a carnal and downward tendency of the flesh. These are contrary one to the other; and such are, in fact, the influences of the Spirit on the mind, that the Christian does not do the things which he otherwise would. So understood, or understood in any fair interpretation of the original, it makes no assertion about the ability or inability of man to do right or wrong. It affirms *as a fact*, that where these opposite principles exist, a man does not do the things which otherwise he would do. If a man *could* not do otherwise than he actually does, he would not be to blame. Whether a Christian *could* not resist the influences of the Holy Spirit, and yield to the corrupt desires of the flesh; or whether he *could* not overcome these evil propensities and do right always, are points on which the apostle here makes no affirmation. His is the statement of *a mere fact*, that where these counteracting propensities exist in the mind, there is a conflict, and that the man does not do what he otherwise would do.

[The translation of this clause which the author has given, may be allowed. It is certainly adopted by many Calvinists, and by Mr. Scott among the number. Yet Bloomfield, who cannot be suspected of any great leaning towards that class of theologians, defends the common translation. "I am surprised," says he, "that Mr. Locke should think our common version is singular in the sense it assigns. The Latin versions are indeed dubious, but most of the early commentators were inclined to adopt the sense 'cannot do,' and so almost all eminent Biblical critics for the last century." Nor would we object to the meaning which the author has attached to the clause, viz. that such are the restraints and influences of the Holy Spirit on the heart, that the Christian *does not* the evil which he otherwise would. This sense is ably advocated by Dr. Wardlaw, in his Discourses on the Socinian controversy. He contends, that in this view, the connection is simple and obvious; and affirms "that the Spirit's opposition to the flesh, for the purpose of preventing the indulgence of its inclinations, is either assigned as a reason for the statement, that if they 'walked in the Spirit,' the lust of the flesh would not be fulfilled, or is presented as an encouragement to compliance with the admonition, so to walk;" otherwise, he thinks no legitimate sequence can be found in the apostle's exhortation; 5th edit. p. 398. Yet, were we disposed to insist on the other sense, might not the terrible contest between the fleshly and the spiritual nature be alleged as the apostle's reason for the exhortation, continually to abide, to *walk* in the Spirit as the only remedy for this perpetual malady? And, in this way, the sequence is just as natural and obvious as in the other view. Mr. Scott and many other commentators combine both senses. "Believers do not the things which they would. They are not so holy as they long to be; nor yet do they indulge those corrupt inclinations which still rise up in their hearts, and cause them much trouble."—Comment in loco. Our author's assertion, therefore, that this passage "seems *always* to be interpreted of the overpowering tendency in the mind to evil," admits of many exceptions, even on the Calvinistic side; and the implied censure, that passages are violently strained to support opinion, on the subject of human inability, different from his own, falls to the ground. The *new* sense, which, by implication, he affirms *never* to be mentioned by those of opposite views, is by them frequently asserted and vindicated!

But apart altogether from the proposed translation of the clause, and the meaning attached to it in its amended form—admitting both; it may, notwithstanding, be observed, on

18 But if [a] ye be led of the Spirit, ye are not under the law.
19 Now the works of the flesh [b] are manifest; which are *these*, Adultery, fornication, uncleanness, lasciviousness,

a Ro.6.14; 8.2. *b* Mat.15.19; Ep.5.3—6; Col.3.5,6; Re.22.15.

the whole passage, that if it contains nothing *directly* on the subject of human ability, yet the struggle it asserts between two opposite principles, the flesh and the spirit, in the renewed mind, is not over-favourable to *great* views as to what man *can* do, or *could* do. If in the renewed mind this can least prevail, and prevail to such an extent, as the passage intimates, what must be the state of the unrenewed mind? The answer is too obvious. Allow, that the apostle states no more than the *fact*, that, in consequence of this struggle, the Christian "does not do the things which otherwise he would do," and *even* take this in the sense of not doing the *evil* he otherwise would have done, still it follows, and with all the conviction of direct assertion, that, independently of spiritual aid, the man or the Christian *could not* or *would not* have acted rightly.

Mr. Barnes has expressed himself somewhat plainly on this subject under Rom. viii. 7, where the reader will find, in a supplementary Note on that passage, much that is applicable to what occurs here. "Whether," he there says, "the *man himself* might not obey the law, whether *he* has, or has not ability to do it, is a question which the apostle does not touch." He is careful, however, not directly to assert the affirmative, but leaves the reader to draw the inference in regard to the author's opinion. And in this place, especially, have we reason to complain of disingenuous ambiguity. The phraseology connected with this dispute, *can, could*, &c., should have been explained. If it had been affirmed that God requires nothing of us which is *physically* or *naturally* impossible for us to do; *e. g.*, He does not require us to transport ourselves from earth to heaven, and from heaven to earth, as angels do at his bidding, *because* for such service we have no *natural* powers—there could have been no disputing of this position. But if it be *natural* or *physical* power to which the author alludes, under the term *can* and *could*, why not say so, and by a brief explanation relieve his unthinking readers from their perplexity? If men can and could discharge duty only in so far as natural ability is concerned, but *morally* are allowed to be unable to think a good thought, all that sound Calvinists desire on this subject is conceded. Nor, remains there the slightest force in the objection. that "if a man *could not* do otherwise than he actually does, he would not be to blame." Men will not be taken to account for natural inabilities, for certainly they are not to blame that they have not the faculties of angels. But *moral* inability is *sin*, and for *it* we must answer. It is *rooted aversion* to that which is good. Meantime, statements, such as that quoted above, without explanation, have done unmeasureable mischief to certain classes of readers; and furnishing them with an argument against the doctrine of accountability, are fitted to harden them in sin.

There seems too much truth in the censure passed on the New School Divines of America, that even when they "retain the term *natural* in connection with ability, and thus *appear* to accord with those who are in the habit of making the distinction (of natural and moral ability) in reality, they occupy very different ground. Though when they speak of ability, they frequently annex to it the word "natural," they seldom speak of inability at all; *but produce the impression, that the ability which they preach is fully adequate to enable the sinner, independently of divine grace, to do all that God requires.*"—Old and New Views by James Wood, Philadelphia, p. 162. The same author asserts, and with some appearance of reason, that "though Mr. Barnes expresses himself with much more caution than Messrs. Finney and Duffield, it is apparent that he favours their sentiments." Ibid. page 168

18. *But if ye be led of the Spirit.* If you submit to the teachings and guidance of the Holy Spirit. ¶ *Ye are not under the law.* You are under a different dispensation—the dispensation of the Spirit. You are free from the restraints and control of the Mosaic law, and are under the control of the Spirit of God.

19. *Now the works of the flesh.* What the flesh, or what corrupt and unrenewed human nature produces. ¶ *Are manifest.* Plain, well-known. The world is full of illustrations of what corrupt human nature produces, and as to the existence and nature of those works, no one can be ignorant. It is evident here that the word σὰρξ, *flesh*, is used to denote *corrupt human nature*, and not merely the *body;* since many of the vices here enumerated are the passions of the *mind* or the *soul*, rather than of the body. Such are "wrath," "strife," "heresies," "envyings," &c., which cannot be said to have their seat in the body. If the word, therefore, is used to denote *human nature*, the passage furnishes a sad commentary on its tendency, and on the character of man. It is closely parallel to the declaration of the Saviour in Matt xv. 19. Of the *nature* of most of these sins, or works of the flesh, it is unnecessary to offer any comment. They are not so rare as not to be well known, and the meaning of the words requires little exposition. In regard to the *existence* of these vices as the result

20 Idolatry, witchcraft, hatred, variance, emulations, wrath, strife, seditions, heresies,

21 Envyings, murders, drunkenness, revellings, and such like: of the which I tell you before, as I have also told *you* in time past, that they which do such things shall not inherit the kingdom of God.

---

of human nature, the Notes on Rom. i. may be examined; or a single glance at the history of the past, or at the present condition of the heathen and a large part of the Christian world, would furnish an ample and a painful demonstration.

20. *Witchcraft.* Pretending to witchcraft. The apostle does not vouch for the actual existence of witchcraft; but he says that what was known as such was a proof of the corrupt nature of man, and was one of the fruits of it. No one can doubt it. It was a system of imposture and falsehood throughout; and nothing is a better demonstration of the depravity of the human heart than an extended and systematized attempt to impose on mankind. The word which is here used (φαρμακεία, whence our word *pharmacy*, from φάρμακον, a medicine, poison, magic potion) means, properly, the preparing and giving of medicine. Then it means also poisoning, and also magic art, or enchantment; because in savage nations pharmacy or medicine consisted much in magical incantations. Thence it means sorcery or enchantment, and it is so used uniformly in the New Testament. It is used only in Gal. v. 20; Rev. ix. 21; xviii. 23; xxi. 8. Some have supposed that it means here *poisoning*, a crime often practised; but the more correct interpretation is, to refer it to the black art, or to pretensions to witchcraft, and the numerous delusions which have grown out of it, as a striking illustration of the corrupt and depraved nature of man. ¶ *Hatred.* Gr. *Hatreds*, in the plural. Antipathies, and want of love, producing contentions and strifes. ¶ *Variance.* Contentions; see Note, Rom. i. 29. ¶ *Emulations* (ζῆλοι). In a bad sense, meaning heart-burning, or jealousy, or perhaps inordinate ambition. The sense is ardour or zeal *in a bad cause*, leading to strife, &c. ¶ *Wrath.* This also is plural in the Greek (θυμοὶ), meaning passions, *bursts of anger;* Note, 2 Cor. xii. 20. ¶ *Strife.* Also plural in the Greek; see Note, 2 Cor. xii. 20 ¶ *Seditions;* see Note, Rom. xvi. 17. ¶ *Heresies;* see Note, Acts v. 17; 1 Cor. xi. 19.

21. *Envyings;* Note, 2 Cor. xii. 20. ¶ *Revellings;* Notes, 2 Cor. xii. 20; Rom. xiii. 13. ¶ *And such like.* This class of evils, without attempting to specify all. ¶ *Of which I tell you before.* In regard to which I forewarn you. ¶ *As I have also told* you *in time past.* When he was with them. ¶ *Shall not inherit the kingdom of God.* Cannot possibly be saved; see Notes on 1 Cor. vi. 9—11. In regard to this passage, we may remark; (1.) That it furnishes the most striking and unanswerable proof of human depravity. Paul represents these things as "the works of the flesh," the works of the unrenewed nature of man. They are such as human nature, when left to itself, everywhere produces. The world shows that such is the fact; and we cannot but ask, is a nature producing this to be regarded as pure? Is man an unfallen being? Can he save himself? Does he need no Saviour? (2.) This passage is full of fearful admonition to those who indulge in any or all of these vices. Paul, inspired of God, has solemnly declared, that such cannot be saved. They *cannot* enter into the kingdom of heaven as they are. Nor is it *desirable* that they should. What would heaven be if filled up with adulterers, and fornicators, and idolaters, with the proud and envious, and with murderers, and drunkards? To call such a place *heaven*, would be an abuse of the word. No one could wish to dwell there; and such men *cannot* enter into heaven. (3.) The human heart must be changed, or man cannot be saved. This follows of course. If such is its tendency, then there is a

22 But the fruit [a] of the Spirit is love, joy, peace, long-suffering gentleness, goodness, faith,

a John 15.5; Ep.5.9.

necessity for such a change as that in regeneration, in order that man may be happy and be saved. (4.) We should rejoice that such men *cannot*, with their present characters, be admitted to heaven. We should rejoice that there *is* one world where these vices are unknown, a world of perfect and eternal purity. When we look at the earth; when we see how these vices prevail; when we reflect that every land is polluted, and that we cannot traverse a continent or an island, visit a nook or corner of the earth, dwell in any city or town, where these vices do not exist, O how refreshing and invigorating is it to look forward to a pure heaven! How cheering the thought that there is one world where these vices are unknown; one world, all whose ample plains may be traversed, and the note of blasphemy shall never fall on the ear; one world, where virtue shall be safe from the arts of the seducer; one world where we may for ever dwell, and not one reeling and staggering drunkard shall ever be seen; where there shall be not one family in want and tears from the vice of its unfaithful head! With what joy should we look forward to that world! With what ardour should we pant that it may be our own!

22. *But the fruit of the Spirit.* That which the Holy Spirit produces. It is not without design, evidently, that the apostle uses the word "Spirit" here, as denoting that these things do not flow from our own nature. The vices above enumerated are the proper "works" or result of the operations of the human heart; the virtues which he enumerates are produced by a foreign influence—the agency of the Holy Spirit. Hence Paul does not trace them to our own hearts, *even when renewed.* He says that they are to be regarded as the proper result of the Spirit's operations on the soul. ¶ *Is love.* To God and to men. Probably the latter here is particularly intended, as the fruits of the Spirit are placed in contradistinction from those vices which lead to strifes among men. On the meaning of the word *love,* see Notes on 1 Cor. xiii. 1; and for an illustration of its operations and effects, see the Notes on that whole chapter. ¶ *Joy.* In the love of God; in the evidences of pardon; in communion with the Redeemer, and in his service; in the duties of religion, in trial, and in the hope of heaven; see Notes, Rom. v. 2; comp. 1 Pet. i. 8. ¶ *Peace.* As the result of reconciliation with God; see Notes, Rom. v. 1. ¶ *Long-suffering.* In affliction and trial, and when injured by others; see Note, 1 Cor. xiii. 4. ¶ *Gentleness.* The same word which is translated *kindness* in 2 Cor. vi. 6; see Note on that place. The word means goodness, kindness, benignity; and is opposed to a harsh, crabbed, crooked temper. It is a disposition to be pleased; it is mildness of temper, calmness of spirit, an unruffled disposition, and a disposition to treat all with urbanity and politeness. This is one of the regular effects of the Spirit's operations on the heart. Religion makes no one crabbed, and morose, and sour. It sweetens the temper; corrects an irritable disposition; makes the heart kind; disposes us to make all around us as happy as possible. This is true politeness; a kind of politeness which can far better be learned in the school of Christ than in that of Chesterfield; by the study of the New Testament than under the direction of the dancing-master. ¶ *Goodness;* see Note on Rom. xv. 14. Here the word seems to be used in the sense of *beneficence,* or a disposition to do good to others. The sense is, that a Christian must be a good man. ¶ *Faith.* On the meaning of the word faith, see Note on Mark xvi. 16. The word here may be used in the sense of *fidelity,* and may denote that the Christian will be a *faithful man,* a man faithful to his word and promises; a man who can be trusted or confided in. It is probable that the word is used in this sense because the object

23 Meekness, temperance: against
[a] such there is no law.
24 And they that are Christ's
have crucified the flesh with the
affections and lusts.
25 If [b] we live in the Spirit, let
us also walk in the Spirit.

a 1 Ti.1.9. 1 or, *passions*. b Ro.8.4,5.

of the apostle is not to speak of the feelings which we have towards God so much as to illustrate the influences of the Spirit in directing and controlling our feelings towards men. True religion makes a man *faithful*. The Christian is faithful as a man; faithful as a neighbour, friend, father, husband, son. He is faithful to his contracts; faithful to his promises. No man can be a Christian who is not thus faithful, and all pretensions to being under the influences of the Spirit when such fidelity does not exist, are deceitful and vain.

23. *Meekness;* see Note, Mat. v. 5. ¶ *Temperance.* The word here used, (ἐγκράτεια), means properly *self-control, continence.* It is derived from ἐν and κράτος, *strength,* and has reference to the *power* or ascendancy which we have over exciting and evil passions of all kinds. It denotes the self-rule which a man has over the evil propensities of his nature. Our word *temperance* we use now in a much more limited sense, as referring mainly to abstinence from intoxicating drinks. But the word here used is employed in a much more extended signification. It includes the dominion over all evil propensities, and may denote continence, chastity, self-government, moderation in regard to all indulgences as well as abstinence from intoxicating drinks. See the word explained in the Notes on Acts xxiv. 25. The sense here is, that the influences of the Holy Spirit on the heart make a man *moderate* in all indulgences; teach him to restrain his passions, and to govern himself; to control his evil propensities, and to subdue all inordinate affection. The Christian will not only abstain from intoxicating drinks, but from all exciting passions; he will be temperate in his manner of living, and in the government of his temper. This *may* be applied to temperance properly so called with us; but it should not be limited to that. A Christian *must be* a temperate man; and if the effect of his religion is not to produce this, it is false and vain. Abstinence from intoxicating drinks, as well as from all improper excitement, is demanded by the very genius of his religion, and on this subject there is no danger of drawing the cords too close. No man was ever injured by the strictest temperance, by total abstinence from ardent spirits, and from wine as a beverage; no man is certainly safe who does not abstain; no man, it is believed, can be in a proper frame of mind for religious duties who indulges in the habitual use of intoxicating drinks. Nothing does more scandal to religion than such indulgences; and, other things being equal, he is the most under the influence of the Spirit of God who is the most thoroughly a man of temperance. ¶ *Against such there is no law.* That is, there is no law to condemn such persons. These are not the things which the law denounces. These, therefore, are the true freemen; free from the condemning sentence of the law, and free in the service of God. Law condemns sin; and they who evince the spirit here referred to are free from its denunciations.

24. *And they that are Christ's.* All who are true Christians. ¶ *Have crucified the flesh.* The corrupt passions of the soul have been put to death; *i. e.*, destroyed. They are as though they were dead, and have no power over us; see Note, chap. ii. 20. ¶ *With the affections.* Marg. *Passions.* All corrupt desires. ¶ *And lusts;* see Note, Rom. i. 24.

25. *If we live in the Spirit.* Note, ver. 16. The sense of this verse probably is, "We who are Christians profess to be under the influences of the Holy Spirit. By his influences and agency is our spiritual life. We profess not to be under the dominion of the flesh; not to be controlled by its appetites and desires. Let us then act in this manner, and as if we be-

26 Let [a] us not be desirous of vainglory, provoking one another, envying one another.

a Ph.2.3.

lieved this. Let us yield ourselves to his influences, and show that we are controlled by that Spirit." It is an earnest exhortation to Christians to yield wholly to the agency of the Holy Spirit on their hearts, and to submit to his guidance; see Notes, Rom. viii. 5, 9.

26. *Let us not be desirous of vainglory.* The word here used (κενόδοξοι) means proud or vain of empty advantages, as of birth, property, eloquence, or learning. The reference here is probably to the paltry competitions which arose on account of these supposed advantages. It is possible that this might have been one cause of the difficulties existing in the churches of Galatia, and the apostle is anxious wholly to check and remove it. The Jews prided themselves on their birth, and men are everywhere prone to overvalue the supposed advantages of birth and blood. The doctrines of Paul are, that on great and most vital respects men are on a level; that these things contribute nothing to salvation (Notes, chap. iii. 28); and that Christians should esteem them of little importance, and that they should not be suffered to interfere with their fellowship, or to mar their harmony and peace. ¶ *Provoking one another.* The sense is, that they who *are* desirous of vainglory, *do* provoke one another. They provoke those whom they regard as inferiors by a haughty carriage and a contemptuous manner towards them. They look upon them often with contempt; pass them by with disdain; treat them as beneath their notice; and this *provokes* on the other hand hard feeling, and hatred, and a disposition to take revenge. When men regard themselves as equal in their great and vital interests; when they feel that they are fellow-heirs of the grace of life; when they feel that they belong to one great family, and are in their great interests on a level; deriving no advantage from birth and blood; on a level as descendants of the same apostate father; as being themselves sinners; on a level at the foot of the cross, at the communion table, on beds of sickness, in the grave, and at the bar of God; when they feel this, then the consequences here referred to will be avoided. There will be no haughty carriage such as to provoke opposition; and on the other hand there will be no envy on account of the superior rank of others. ¶ *Envying one another.* On account of their superior wealth, rank, talent, learning. The true way to cure envy is to make men feel that in their great and important interests they are on a level. Their great interests are beyond the grave. The distinctions of this life are temporary, and are comparative trifles. Soon all will be on a level in the grave, and at the bar of God and in heaven. Wealth, and honour, and rank do not avail there. The poorest man will wear as bright a crown as the rich; the man of most humble birth will be admitted as near the throne as he who can boast the longest line of illustrious ancestors. Why should a man who is soon to wear a "crown incorruptible and undefiled and that fadeth not away," envy him who has a ducal coronet here, or a royal diadem—baubles that are soon to be laid aside for ever? Why should he, though poor here, who is soon to inherit the treasures of heaven where "moth and rust do not corrupt," envy him who can walk over a few acres as his own, or who has accumulated a glittering pile of dust, soon to be left for ever? Why should he who is soon to wear the robes of salvation, made "white in the blood of the Lamb," envy him who is "clothed in purple and fine linen," or who can adorn himself and his family in the most gorgeous attire which art and skill can make, soon to give place to the winding-sheet; soon to be succeeded by the simple garb which the most humble wears in the grave? If men feel that their great interests are beyond the tomb; that in the important matter of salvation they are on a level; that soon they are to be undistinguish-

CHAPTER VI.

BRETHREN, [1] if a man be overtaken in a fault, ye which are spiritual restore [a] such an one in the spirit of meekness; con-

1 or, *although*. a Ja.5.19,20.

ed beneath the clods of the valley, how unimportant comparatively would it seem to adorn their bodies, to advance their name and rank and to improve their estates! The rich and the great would cease to look down with contempt on those of more humble rank, and the poor would cease to envy those above them, for they are soon to be their equals in the grave; their equals, perhaps their superiors in heaven!

CHAPTER VI.

ANALYSIS.

THIS chapter is composed entirely of affectionate exhortation, and the expression of the apostle's earnest solicitude in the behalf of the Christians in Galatia. He exhorts them (ver. 1) to bring back to the ways of virtue any one who through the strength of strong temptation had been led astray. He entreats them (ver. 2) to bear one another's burdens, and thus to show that they were true friends of Christ, and governed by his laws. He entreats them not to be lifted up with pride, and not to affix an inordinate estimate to any thing that they possessed, assuring them that their true estimate was to be formed from the character of their own works; ver. 3—5. He exhorts them to minister to the wants of their public teachers, the preachers of the gospel; ver. 6. In ver. 7—10, he reminds them of the solemn day of judgment, when all will be tried; assures them that men will be judged and rewarded according to their works; and entreats them not to be weary in well-doing, but to labour on patiently in doing good, with the assurance that they should reap in due season. In ver. 11, he shows them the interest which he felt in them by his having done what was unusual for him, and what perhaps he had done in no other instance—writing an entire letter in his own hand. He then states the true reason why others wished them to be circumcised. It was the dread of persecution, and not any real love to the cause of religion. They did not themselves keep the law, and they only desired to glory in the number of converts to their views; ver. 12, 13. But Paul says that *he* would glory in nothing but in the cross of Christ. By that he had been crucified to the world, and the world had been crucified to him (ver. 14); and he repeats the solemn assurance that in the Christian religion neither circumcision nor uncircumcision was of any importance whatever; ver. 15. This was the true rule of life, and on as many as walked according to this principle, he invokes the blessing of God; ver. 16. He closes the epistle by entreating them to give him no more trouble. He bore in his body already the marks or sufferings which he had received in the cause of the Lord Jesus. His trials already were sufficient; and he entreats them to spare him from future molestation (ver. 17), and closes with the benediction; ver. 18.

1. *Brethren, if a man be overtaken.* Marg. *Although.* It is a case which the apostle supposes might happen. Christians were not perfect; and it was possible that they who were true Christians might be surprised by temptation, and fall into sin. The word rendered *be overtaken* (προληφθῇ from προλαμβάνω), means properly to take before another, to anticipate (1 Cor. xi. 21); then to be before taken or caught; and may here mean either that one had been *formerly* guilty of sin or had been recently *hurried on* by his passions or by temptations to commit a fault. It is probable that the latter here is the true sense, and that it means, if a man is found to be overtaken by any sin; if his passions, or if temptation get the better of him. Tindal renders it, "If any man be fallen by chance into any fault." It refers to cases of surprise, or of sudden temptation. Christians do not commit sin deliberately, and as a part of the plan of life; but they may be surprised by sudden temptation, or urged on by impetuous or head-strong pas-

sidering thyself, lest thou also be tempted.

2 Bear [a] ye one another's burdens, and so fulfil the law of Christ.

a Ro.15.1.

sion, as David and Peter were. Paul does not speak of the possibility of restoring one who deliberately forms the plan of sinning; he does not suppose that such a man could be a Christian, and that it would be proper to speak of *restoring* such a man. ¶ *Ye which are spiritual.* Who are under the influences of the Holy Spirit; see Note on chap. v. 22, 23. The apostle, in this verse, refers evidently to those who have fallen into some sensual indulgence (chap. v. 19—21), and says that they who have escaped these temptations, and who are under the influences of the Spirit, should recover such persons. It is a very important qualification for those who would recover others from sin, that they should not be guilty of the same sin themselves. Reformers should be holy men; men who exercise discipline in the church should be "spiritual" men—men in whom implicit confidence may be properly reposed. ¶ *Restore such an one.* On the meaning of the word here used, see Note on 2 Cor. xiii. 11. Here it means, not to restore him to the church after he has been excluded, but *set him right,* bring him back, recover him from his errors and his faults. The apostle does not say in what manner this is to be done; but it is usually to be done doubtless by affectionate admonition, by faithful instruction, and by prayer. Discipline or punishment should not be resorted to until the other methods are tried in vain; Mat. xviii. 15—17. ¶ *In the spirit of meekness.* With a kind, forbearing, and forgiving spirit; Note, Mat. v. 5. Not with anger; not with a lordly and overbearing mind; not with a love of finding others in fault, and with a desire for inflicting the discipline of the church; not with a harsh and unforgiving temper, but with love, and gentleness, and humility, and patience, and with a readiness to forgive when wrong has been done. This is an essential qualification for restoring and recovering an offending brother. No man should attempt to rebuke or admonish another who cannot do it in the spirit of meekness; no man should engage in any way in the work of reform who has not such a temper of mind. ¶ *Considering thyself,* &c. Remembering how liable you are yourself to err; and how much kindness and indulgence should therefore be shown to others. You are to act as if you felt it possible that you might also be overtaken with a fault; and you should act as you would wish that others should do towards you. Pliny (Epis. viii. 22) has expressed a similar sentiment in the following beautiful language. "Atque ego optimum et emendatissimum existimo, qui cæteris ita ignoscit, tanquam ipse quotidie peccet; ita peccatis abstinet, tanquam nemini ignoscat. Proinde hoc domi, hoc foris, hoc in omni vitæ genere teneamus, ut nobis implacabiles simus, exorabiles istis etiam, qui dare veniam nisi sibi nesciunt." The doctrine taught by Paul is, that such is human infirmity, and such the strength of human depravity, that no one knows into what sins he may himself fall. He may be tempted to commit the same sins which he endeavours to amend in others; he may be left to commit even worse sins. If this is the case, we should be tender while we are firm; forgiving while we set our faces against evil; prayerful while we rebuke; and compassionate when we are compelled to inflict on others the discipline of the church. Every man who has any proper feelings, when he attempts to recover an erring brother should pray for him and for himself also; and will regard his duty as only half done, and that very imperfectly, if he does not "consider also that he himself may be tempted."

2. *Bear ye one another's burdens;* see Note, Rom. xv. 1. Bear with each other; help each other in the divine life. The sense is, that every man has peculiar temptations and easily besetting

3 For if a man think himself to be something, when he is nothing, he deceiveth himself.

4 But let every man prove [a] his own work, and then shall he have rejoicing in himself [b] alone, and not in another:

a 2 Co.13.5. b Pr.14.14.

sins, which constitute a heavy burden. We should aid each other in regard to these, and help one another to overcome them. ¶ *And so fulfil the law of Christ.* The peculiar law of Christ, requiring us to love one another; see Note on John xiii 34. This was the distinguishing law of the Redeemer; and they could in no way better fulfil it than by aiding each other in the divine life. The law of Christ would not allow us to reproach the offender, or to taunt him, or to rejoice in his fall. We should help him to take up his load of infirmities, and sustain him by our counsels, our exhortations, and our prayers. Christians, conscious of their infirmities, have *a right* to the sympathy and the prayers of their brethren. They should not be cast off to a cold and heartless world; a world rejoicing over their fall, and ready to brand them as hypocrites. They should be pressed to the warm bosom of brotherly kindness; and prayer should be made to ascend without ceasing around an erring and a fallen brother. Is this the case in regard to all who bear the Christian name?

3. *For if a man think himself to be something,* &c.; see chap. v. 26. This is designed, evidently, to be another reason why we should be kind and tender to those who have erred. It is, that even those who are most confident may fall. They who feel secure, and think it impossible that they should sin, are not safe. They may be wholly deceived, and may be nothing, when they have the highest estimate of themselves. They may themselves fall into sin, and have need of all the sympathy and kindness of their brethren. ¶ *When he is nothing.* When he has no strength, and no moral worth. When he is not such as he apprehends, but is lifted up with vain self-conceit. ¶ *He deceiveth himself.* He understands not his own character. " The worst part of the fraud falls on his own head."—*Doddridge.* He does not accomplish what he expected to do; and instead of acquiring reputation from others, as he expected, he renders himself contemptible in their sight.

4. *But let every man prove.* That is, try or examine in a proper manner. Let him form a proper estimate of what is due to himself, according to his real character. Let him compare himself with the word of God, and the infallible rule which he has given, and by which we are to be judged in the last great day; comp. Note, Rom. xii. 3; 1 Cor. xi. 28; 2 Cor. xiii. 5. ¶ *His own work.* What he does. Let him form a fair and impartial estimate of his own character. ¶ *And then shall he have rejoicing.* That is, he will be appropriately rewarded, and will meet with no disappointment. The man who forms an improper estimate of his own character will be sure to be disappointed. The man who examines himself, and who forms no extravagant expectation in regard to what is due to himself, will be appropriately rewarded, and will be made happy. If, by the careful examination of himself, he finds his life to be virtuous, and his course of conduct pure; if he has done no wrong to others, and if he finds evidence that he is a child of God, then he will have cause of rejoicing. ¶ *In himself alone;* comp. Prov. xiv. 14: " A good man shall be satisfied from himself." The sentiment is, that he will find in himself a source of pure joy. He will not be dependent on the applause of others for happiness. In an approving conscience; in the evidence of the favour of God; in an honest effort to lead a pure and holy life, he will have happiness. The source of his joys will be within; and he will not be dependent, as the man of ambition, and the man who thinks of himself more highly than he ought, will, on the favours of a capricious multitude, and on the breath of popular applause. ¶ *And not in another.* He will not be dependent

5 For every man shall bear his own burden.
6 Let [a] him that is taught in the word communicate unto him that teacheth in all good things.
7 Be not deceived; God is not

a 1 Co.9.11—14.

on others for happiness. Here is the true secret of happiness. It consists, (1.) In not forming an improper estimate of ourselves; in knowing just what we are, and what is due to us; in not thinking ourselves to be something, when we are nothing. (2.) In leading such a life that it may be examined *to the core*, that we may know exactly what we are without being distressed or pained. That is, in having a good conscience, and in the honest and faithful discharge of our duty to God and man. (3.) In not being dependent on the fickle applause of the world for our comfort. The man who has no internal resources, and who has no approving conscience; who is happy only when others smile, and miserable when they frown, is a man who can have no security for enjoyment. The man who has a good conscience, and who enjoys the favour of God, and the hope of heaven, carries with him the source of perpetual joy. He cannot be deprived of it. His purse may be taken, and his house robbed, but the highwayman cannot rob him of his comforts. He carries with him an unfailing source of happiness when abroad, and the same source of happiness abides with him at home; he bears it into society, and it remains with him in solitude; it is his companion when in health, and when surrounded by his friends, and it is no less his companion when his friends leave him, and when he lies upon a bed of death.

5. *For every man shall bear his own burden.* This seems to be a kind of proverbial saying; and it means here, every man shall have his proper reward. If he is a virtuous man, he will be happy; if a vicious man, he will be miserable. If a virtuous man, he will have the source of happiness in himself; if a sinner, he must bear the proper penalty of his sin. In the great day every man shall be properly rewarded. Knowing this, we should be little anxious about the sentiments of others, and should seek to maintain a good conscience towards God and man. The design of this passage is, to prevent men from forming an improper estimate of themselves, and of the opinions of others. Let a man feel that he is soon to stand at the judgment-seat, and it will do much to keep him from an improper estimate of his own importance; let him feel that he must give an account to God, and that his great interests are to be determined by the estimate which *God* will affix to his character, and it will teach him that the opinion of the world is of little value. This will restrain his vanity and ambition. This will show him that the great business of life is to secure the favour of God, and to be prepared to give up his account; and there is no way so effectual of checking ambition, and subduing vanity and the love of applause, as to feel that we are soon to stand at the awful bar of God.

6. *Let him that is taught in the word.* In the word of God; *i. e.* the gospel. ¶ *Communicate unto him.* Let him *share* with him who teaches; let there be a *common* participation of all good things. ¶ *In all good things.* In every thing that is needful for their comfortable subsistence. On the duty here enjoined, see Notes on 1 Cor. ix. 11—13.

7. *Be not deceived.* That is, in regard to your character, and your hopes for eternity. This is a formula of introduction to some admonition that is peculiarly weighty and important. It implies that there was *danger* that they would be deceived in reference to their character. The *sources* of the danger were the corruption of their own hearts, the difficulty of knowing their true character, the instructions of false teachers, &c.; see Note on 1 Cor. vi. 9. ¶ *God is not mocked.* He cannot be imposed on, or mocked. He knows what our real character is, and he will judge us accordingly. The word rendered *mocked*

mocked: for whatsoever a man soweth, that shall he also reap.

8 For he that soweth to his[a] flesh shall of the flesh reap corrup-

a Job 4.8; Pr.22.8; Ho.8.7.

(μυκτηρίζω), means, properly, to turn up the nose in scorn; hence to mock, or deride, or insult. The sense is, that God could not be imposed on, or could not be insulted with impunity, or successfully. To *mock* is, properly, (1.) To imitate, to mimic; to imitate in contempt or derision. (2.) To deride, to laugh at, to ridicule. (3.) To defeat, or to illude, or to disappoint. (4.) To fool, to tantalize.—*Webster*. Here it cannot mean to *imitate*, or to *mimic*, but it refers to the principles of the divine administration, and must mean that they could not be treated with contempt, or successfully evaded. They could not hope to illude or impose on God. His principles of government were settled, and they could not impose on him. To what the reference is here, is not perfectly plain. In the connection in which it stands, it seems to refer to the support of the ministers of the gospel; and Paul introduces the general principle, that as a man sows he will reap, to show them what will be the effect of a liberal and proper use of their property. If they made a proper use of it; if they employed it for benevolent purposes; if they appropriated what they should to the support of religion, they would reap accordingly. God could not be imposed on in regard to this. They could not make him think that they had true religion when they were sowing to the flesh, and when they were spending their money in purchasing pleasure, and in luxury and vanity. No zeal, however ardent; no prayers, however fervent or long, no professions, however loud, would impose on God. And to make such prayers, and to manifest such zeal and such strong professions, while the heart was with the world, and they were spending their money for every thing else but religion, was mocking God. Alas, how much mockery of God like this still prevails! How much, when men *seem* disposed to make God believe that they are exceedingly zealous and devoted, while their heart is truly with the world! How many long prayers are offered; how much zeal is shown; how many warm professions are made, *as if* to make God and man believe that the heart was truly engaged in the cause of religion, while little or nothing is given in the cause of benevolence; while the ministers of religion are suffered to starve; and while the "loud professor" rolls in wealth, and is distinguished for luxury of living, for gayety of apparel, for splendour of equipage, and for extravagance in parties of pleasure! Such professors attempt to mock God. They are really sowing to the flesh; and of the flesh they must reap corruption. ¶ *For whatsoever a man soweth*, &c.; see Note, 2 Cor. ix. 6. This figure is taken from agriculture. A man who sows wheat, shall reap wheat; he who sows barley, shall reap barley; he who sows cockle, shall reap cockle. Every kind of grain will produce grain like itself. So it is in regard to our works. He who is liberal, shall be dealt with liberally; he who is righteous, shall be rewarded; he who is a sinner, shall reap according to his deeds.

8. *For he that soweth to his flesh* That makes provision for the indulgence of fleshly appetites and passions, see Notes on chap. v. 19—21. He who makes use of his property to give indulgence to licentiousness, intemperance, and vanity. ¶ *Shall of the flesh*. From the flesh, or as that which indulgence in fleshly appetites properly produces. Punishment, under the divine government, is commonly in the line of offences. The punishment of licentiousness and intemperance in this life is commonly loathsome and offensive disease; and when long indulged, the sensualist becomes haggard, and bloated, and corrupted, and sinks into the grave. Such, also, is often the punishment of luxurious living, of a pampered appetite, of gluttony, as well as of intemperate drinking. But if the punishment does not follow in this life, it will be sure to overtake the sensualist in the world

tion; but he that soweth to the Spirit, [a] shall of the Spirit reap life everlasting.

9 And let [b] us not be weary in well-doing; for in due season we shall reap, if [c] we faint not.

10 As we have therefore opportunity, [d] let us do good unto all [e]

a Pr.11.18; Ja.3.18. b 1 Co.15.58. c He.10.36; Re.2.10. d Ec.9.10. e Mat.5.43; Tit.3.8.

to come. There he shall reap ruin final and everlasting. ¶ *Corruption.* (1.) By disease. (2.) In the grave—the home to which the sensualist rapidly travels. (3.) In the world of woe. There all shall be corrupt. His virtue—even the semblance of virtue, shall all be gone. His understanding, will, fancy—his whole soul shall be debased and corrupt. No virtue will linger and live on the plains of ruin, but all shall be depravity and woe. Every thing in hell is debased and corrupt; and the whole harvest of sensuality in this world and the world to come, is degradation and defilement. ¶ *But he that soweth to the Spirit.* He who follows the leadings and cultivates the affections which the Holy Spirit would produce; see Notes on chap. v. 22, 23. ¶ *Shall of the Spirit.* As the result of following the leadings of the Spirit. ¶ *Reap life everlasting;* see Note on Rom. ii. 7.

9. *And let us not be weary in well-doing;* see Note on 1 Cor. xv. 58. The reference here is particularly to the support of the ministers of religion (ver. 6), but the apostle makes the exhortation general. Christians sometimes become weary. There is so much opposition to the best plans for doing good; there is so much to be done; there are so many calls on their time and their charities; and there is often so much ingratitude among those whom they endeavour to benefit, that they become disheartened. Such Paul addresses, and exhorts them not to give over, but to persevere. ¶ *For in due season.* At the day of judgment. Then we shall receive the full reward of all our self-denials and charities. ¶ *We shall reap, if we faint not.* If we do not give over, exhausted and disheartened. It is *implied* here, that unless a man perseveres in doing good to the end of life, he can hope for no reward. He who becomes disheartened, and who gives over his efforts; he that is appalled by obstacles, and that faints on account of the embarrassments thrown in his way; he that pines for ease, and withdraws from the field of benevolence, shows that he has no true attachment to the cause, and that his heart has never been truly in the work of religion. He who becomes a true Christian, becomes such FOR ETERNITY. He has enlisted, never to withdraw. He becomes pledged to do good and to serve God *always.* No obstacles are to deter, no embarrassments are to drive him from the field. With the vigour of his youth, and the wisdom and influence of his riper years; with his remaining powers when enfeebled by age; with the last pulsation of life here, and with his immortal energies in a higher world, he is to do good. For that he is to live. In that he is to die; and when he awakes in the resurrection with renovated powers, he is to awake to an everlasting service of doing good, as far as he may have opportunity, in the kingdom of God.

10. *As we have therefore opportunity, let us do good unto all men.* This is the true rule about doing good. "The opportunity to do good," says Cotton Mather, "imposes the obligation to do it." The simple rule is, that we are favoured with the opportunity, and that we have the power. It is not that we are to do it when it is convenient; or when it will advance the interest of a party; or when it may contribute to our fame; the rule is, that we are to do it when we have the opportunity. No matter how often that occurs; no matter how many objects of benevolence are presented—the more the better; no matter how much self-denial it may cost us; no matter how little *fame* we may get by it; still, if we have the *opportunity* to do good, we are to do it, and should be thankful for the privilege. And it is to be done *to all men.* Not

men, especially to them [a] who are
of the household of faith.
11 Ye see how large a letter I

a 1 John 3.14.

have written unto you with mine
own hand.
12 As many as desire to make

to our family only; not to our party; not to our neighbours; not to those of our own colour; not to those who live in the same land with us, but to all mankind. If we can reach and benefit a man who lives on the other side of the globe, whom we have never seen, and *shall* never see in this world or in the world to come, still we are to do him good. Such is Christianity. And in this, as in all other respects, it differs from the narrow and selfish spirit of *clanship* which prevails all over the world. ¶ *Especially*. On the same principle that a man is bound particularly to benefit his own family and friends. In his large and expansive zeal for the world at large, he is not to forget or neglect them. He is to feel that they have peculiar claims on him. They are near him. They are bound to him by tender ties. They may be particularly dependent on him. Christianity does not relax the ties which bind us to our country, our family, and our friends. It makes them more close and tender, and excites us more faithfully to discharge the duties which grow out of these relations. But, in addition to that, it excites us to do good to all men, and to bless the stranger as well as the friend; the man who has a different colour from our own, as well as he who has the same; the man who lives in another clime, as well as he who was born in the same country in which *we* live. ¶ *Of the household of faith*. Christians are distinguished from other men primarily by their *believing* the gospel, and by its influence on their lives.

11. *Ye see*. This might be rendered *see*, in the imperative. So Tindal renders it, "Behold." But it is more commonly supposed that it should be rendered in the indicative. The sense is not materially different whichever translation is adopted. The *object* of the apostle is, to direct their attention to the special proof of his love, which he had manifested in writing such a letter. ¶ *How large a letter*. Considerable variety has existed in regard to the interpretation of this phrase. The word here used and translated *how large* (πηλίκοις), means, properly, *how great*. Some have supposed that it refers to the *size of the letters* which Paul made in writing the epistle—the length and crudeness of the characters which he used. Such interpreters suppose that he was not well versed in writing Greek, and that he used large letters, and those somewhat rudely made, like the Hebrew. So Doddridge and Whitby interpret it; and so Theodoret, Jerome, Theophylact, and some others. He might not, says Doddridge, have been well versed in the Greek characters; or "this inaccuracy of his writings might have been owing to the infirmity or weakness of his nerves, which he had hinted at before." Jerome says, that Paul was a Hebrew, and that he was unacquainted with the mode of writing Greek letters; and that because necessity demanded that he should write a letter in his own hand, contrary to his usual custom, he was obliged to form his characters in this crude manner. According to this interpretation, it was, (1.) A pledge to the Galatians that the epistle was genuine, since it bore the marks of his own handwriting; and, (2.) It was proof of special affection for them that he was willing to undergo this labour on their account. Others suppose that he means to refer to the size *of the epistle* which he had written. Such is the interpretation of Grotius, Koppe, Bloomfield, Clarke, Locke, Chandler, and is, indeed, the common interpretation, as it is the obvious one. According to this, it was proof of special interest in them, and regard for them, that he had written to them a whole letter with his own hand. Usually he employed an amanuensis, and added his name, with a brief benediction or remark at the close; see Notes, Rom. xvi. 22; 1 Cor. xvi. 21. What *induced* him to depart from his

a fair show in the flesh, they constrain you to be circumcised; only lest they should suffer persecution for the cross of Christ.

13 For neither they themselves

usual custom here is unknown. Jerome supposes that he refers here to *what follows* from this verse to the end of the epistle, as that which he had written with his own hand, but the word ἔγραψα, says Rosenmüller, refers rather to what he *had* written, than to that which he intended to write. On this verse, the reader may consult with advantage, Tholuck on the Life and Writings of Paul: German Selections, by Edwards and Park, Andover, 1839, pp. 35, 64, 65.

12. *As many as desire to make a fair show in the flesh* To be distinguished for their conformity to external rites and customs. To be known for their zeal in this cause. They sought to show their zeal by making converts, and by inducing others also to conform to those customs. Paul here refers, doubtless, to the Jewish teachers, and he says that their main object was to evince their zeal in the observance of rites and ceremonies. ¶ *They constrain you.* You who are Gentiles. They insist on circumcision as indispensable to salvation. ¶ *Only lest they should suffer persecution.* It is not from any true love for the cause of religion. It is, that they may avoid persecution from the Jews. If they should renounce the doctrine which taught that circumcision was indispensable, they would be exposed to the rage of the Jews, and would suffer persecution. Rather than do this, they make a show of great zeal in inducing others to be circumcised. ¶ *For the cross of Christ.* From attachment to the cause of a crucified Saviour. If they insisted on entire dependence on the merits of his blood, and renounced all dependence on rites and ceremonies, they would suffer persecution. This verse shows the true cause of the zeal which the Judaizing teachers evinced. It was the fear of persecution. It was the want of independence and boldness in maintaining the doctrine that men were to be saved only by the merits of the Lord Jesus. By attempting to blend together the doctrines of Judaism and Christianity; by maintaining that the observance of the Jewish rites was necessary, and yet that Jesus was the Messiah, they endeavoured to keep in with both parties; and thus to escape the opposition of the Jews. It was an unhallowed compromise It was an attempt to blend things together which could not be united. One *must* really displace the other. If men depended on the rites of Moses, they had no need of dependence on the Messiah; if they professed to depend on him, then to rely on any thing else was in fact to disown and reject him. Embracing the one system was in fact renouncing the other. Such is the argument of Paul; and such his solemn remonstrance against embracing any doctrine which would obscure the glory of simple dependence on the cross of Christ.

13. *For neither they themselves who are circumcised.* The Jewish teachers, or perhaps *all* Jews. It was true in general that the Jews did not wholly and entirely obey the law of Moses, but it is probable that the apostle refers particularly here to the judaizing teachers in Galatia. ¶ *Keep the law.* The law of Moses, or the law of God. Paul's idea is, that if they were circumcised they brought themselves under obligation to keep the *whole* law of God; see Note, ch. v. 3. But *they* did not do it. (1.) No man *perfectly* observes the whole law of God. (2.) The Jewish nation as such were very far from doing it. (3.) It is probable that these persons did not *pretend* even to keep the whole law of Moses. Paul insists on it that if they were circumcised, and depended on that for salvation, they were under obligation to keep the whole law. But *they* did not. Probably they did not offer sacrifice, or join in any of the numerous observances of the Jewish nation, except some of the more prominent, such as circumcision. This, says Paul, is inconsistent in the highest degree; and they thus

who are circumcised keep the law; but desire to have you circumcised, that they may glory in your flesh.

14 But [a] God forbid that I should glory, save in the cross of our Lord Jesus Christ, [1] by

a Ph.3.3,7,8. 1 or, *whereby*.

show their insincerity and hypocrisy. ¶ *That they may glory in your flesh.* In having you as converts, and in persuading you to be circumcised, that they may show their zeal for the law, and thus escape persecution. The phrase "in your flesh" here, is equivalent to "in your circumcision;" making use of your circumcision to promote their own importance, and to save themselves from persecution.

14. *But God forbid.* Note, Rom. iii. 4. "For me it is not to glory except in the cross of Christ." The *object* of Paul here is evidently to place himself in contrast with the judaizing teachers, and to show his determined purpose to glory in nothing else but the cross of Christ. Well they knew that he had as much occasion for glorying in the things pertaining to the flesh, or in the observance of external rites and customs, as any of them. He had been circumcised. He had had all the advantages of accurate training in the knowledge of the Jewish law. He had entered on life with uncommon advantages. He had evinced a zeal that was not surpassed by any of them; and his life, so far as conformity to the religion in which he had been trained was concerned, was blameless; Phil. iii. 4—8. This must have been to a great extent known to the Galatians; and by placing his own conduct in strong contrast with that of the judaizing teachers, and showing that *he* had no ground of confidence in himself, he designed to bring back the minds of the Galatians to simple dependence on the cross. ¶ *That I should glory.* That I should boast; or that I should rely on any thing else. Others glory in their conformity to the laws of Moses; others in their zeal, or their talents, or their learning, or their orthodoxy; others in their wealth, or their accomplishments; others in their family alliances, and their birth; but the supreme boast and glorying of a Christian is in the cross of Christ. ¶ *In the cross of our Lord Jesus Christ.* In Jesus the crucified Messiah. It is a subject of rejoicing and glorying that we have *such* a Saviour. The world looked upon him with contempt; and the cross was a stumblingblock to the Jew, and folly to the Greek. Notes, 1 Cor. i. 23. But to the Christian, that cross is the subject of glorying. It is so because, (1.) Of the love of him who suffered there; (2.) Of the purity and holiness of his character, for the innocent died there for the guilty; (3.) Of the honour there put on the law of God by his dying to maintain it unsullied; (4.) Of the reconciliation there made for sin, accomplishing what could be done by no other oblation, and by no power of man; (5.) Of the pardon there procured for the guilty; (6.) Of the fact that through it we become dead to the world, and are made alive to God, (7.) Of the support and consolation which goes from that cross to sustain us in trial; and, (8.) Of the fact that it procured for us admission into heaven, a title to the world of glory. All is glory around the cross. It was a glorious Saviour who died; it was glorious love that led him to die; it was a glorious object to redeem a world; and it is unspeakable glory to which he will raise lost and ruined sinners by his death. O who would not glory in such a Saviour! Compared with this, what trifles are all the objects in which men usually boast! And what a lesson is here furnished to the true Christian! Let us not boast of our wealth. It will soon leave us, or we shall be taken from it, and it can aid us little in the great matters that are before us. It will not ward off disease; it will not enable us to bear pain; it will not smooth the couch of death; it will not save the soul. Let us not glory in our strength, for it will soon fail; in our beauty, for we shall soon be undistinguished in the corruptions of the tomb; in our accomplishments, for they will not save

Good

whom the world is crucified [a]
unto me, and I unto the world.
15 For [b] in Christ Jesus neither circumcision availeth any thing, nor uncircumcision, but a [c] new creature.
16 And as many as walk according to this rule, peace [d] be on them, and mercy, and upon the Israel of God.
17 From henceforth let no man trouble me: for [e] I bear in my body the marks of the Lord Jesus.

a ch.2.20. b ch.5.6. c 2 Co.5.17. d Ps.125.5. e Col.1.24.

us; in our learning, for it is not that by which we can be brought to heaven. But *let* us glory that we have for a Saviour the eternal Son of God—that glorious Being who was adored by the inhabitants of heaven; who made the worlds; who is pure, and lovely, and most holy; and who has undertaken our cause and died to save us. I desire no higher honour than to be saved by the Son of God. It is the exaltation of my nature, and shows me more than any thing else its true dignity, that one so great and glorious sought my redemption. That cannot be an object of temporary value which he sought by coming from heaven, and if there is any object of real magnitude in this world, it is the soul which the eternal Son of God died to redeem. ¶ *By whom the world is crucified unto me, &c.*; see Notes on ch. ii. 20.

15. *For in Christ Jesus.* In his religion; see Note on ch. v. 6. ¶ *But a new creature.* The fact that a man is created anew, or born again, constitutes the real difference between him and other men. This is what Christ requires; this is the distinction which he designs to make. It is not by conformity to certain rites and customs that a man is to be accepted; it is not by elevated rank, or by wealth, or beauty, or blood; it is not by the colour of the complexion; but the grand inquiry is, whether a man is born again, and is in fact a new creature in Christ Jesus; see Note on 2 Cor. v. 17, for an explanation of the phrase "a new creature."

16. *And as many as walk.* As many as *live*, for so the word *walk* is used in the Scriptures. *According to this rule.* Gr. This *canon*; see the word explained in the Notes on 2 Cor. x. 13. ¶ *Peace* be *on them*; see Note, Rom. xv. 33. ¶ *And upon the Israel of God.* The true church of God; all who are his true worshippers; see Notes on Rom. ii. 28, 29; ix. 6.

17. *From henceforth.* For the remaining time; that is, during the remainder of my life. ¶ *Let no man trouble me.* This implies that he had had trouble of some kind, and he earnestly desires that he may have no more. What particular trouble he here refers to, is not certainly known, and commentators have not been agreed. It seems to me that the connection requires us to understand it of the molestation which he had in regard to his call to the apostolic office, and his authority to explain and defend the religion of the Redeemer. This had been one principal subject of this epistle. His authority had been called in question. He had felt it necessary to go into a vindication of it. His instructions had been departed from on the ground that he was not one of the original apostles, and that he differed from others; see ch. i. 11. Hence all the anxiety and trouble which he had had in regard to their departure from the doctrines which he had taught them. He closes the whole subject of the epistle by this tender and affecting language, the sense of which has been well expressed by Crellius: "I have shown my apostolic authority, and proved that I am commisioned by the Lord Jesus. I have stated and vindicated the great doctrine of justification by faith, and shown that the Mosaic law is not necessarily binding. On these points may I have no more trouble. I have enough for my nature to bear of other kinds. I bear in my body the impressive proofs that I am an apostle, and the sufferings that require all my fortitude to sustain them. These marks, received in the service of the Lord Jesus, and so strongly resembling those which *he* himself received, prove

18 Brethren, the [a] grace of our Lord Jesus Christ *be* with your spirit. Amen.

Unto the Galatians, written from Rome.

a 2 Ti.4.22; Phil.8.25.

that I am truly engaged in his cause, and am commissioned by him. These wounds and sorrows are so many, that I have need of the kindness and prayers of Christians rather than to be compelled to vindicate myself, and to rebuke them for their own wanderings." ¶ *For I bear in my body the marks of the Lord Jesus.* The word here rendered "marks" (στίγματα), means properly the marks or brands which are pricked or burnt in upon the body. So slaves were sometimes branded by their masters to prevent their escape; and so devotees to an idol god sometimes caused to be impressed on themselves the name or image of the divinity which they adored. Herodotus (ii. 113) mentions a temple of Hercules in Egypt, in which if any slave took refuge, and had the sacred *brands* or marks impressed on him (στίγματα), he thereby devoted himself to the god, and it was not lawful for any one to injure him. Many have supposed that Paul here says, in allusion to such a custom, that he had the name of the Redeemer impressed on his body, and that he regarded himself as devoted to him and his cause. It seems to me that by these *marks* or brands he refers to the *weals* which he had received in his body; the marks of stripes and sufferings which he endured in the service of the Redeemer. Comp. 2 Cor. xi. 24, 25. He had repeatedly been scourged. He bore the marks of that on his person now. They were the evidences that he was devoted to the Saviour. He had received them in his cause; and they were the proofs that he belonged to the Lord Jesus. He had suffered for him, and had suffered much. Having thus suffered, and having thus the evidence that he belonged to the Saviour, and having by his sufferings given ample proof of that to others, he asks to be freed from further molestation. Some had in their body the marks of circumcision, the evidence that they were disciples of the law of Moses; others had perhaps in their persons the image and name of an idol to which they were devoted; but the marks which *he* bore were the *weals* which he had received by being again and again whipped publicly in the cause of the Redeemer. To that Redeemer, therefore, he felt himself united, and from that attachment he would not allow himself to be diverted. How often has an old soldier shown his *scars* with pride and exultation as a proof of his attachment to his country! Numerous scars; the loss of an arm, an eye, or a leg, are thus the much valued and vaunted pledges of attachment to liberty, and a passport to the confidence of every man who loves his country. "I prize this wound," said Lafayette, when struck in the foot by a musket ball at Germantown, "as among the most valued of my honours." So Paul felt in regard to the scourges which he had received in the cause of the Lord Jesus. They were his boast and his glory; the pledge that he had been engaged in the cause of the Saviour, and a passport to all who loved the Son of God. Christians now are not subjected to such stripes and scourgings. But let us have *some* marks of our attachment to the Lord Jesus. By a holy life; by self-denial; by subdued animal affections; by zeal in the cause of truth; by an imitation of the Lord Jesus; and by the marks of suffering in our body, if we should be called to it, let us have *some* evidence that we are his, and be able to say, when we look on death and eternity, "we bear with us the evidence that we belong to the Son of God." To us that will be of more value than any ribbon or star indicating elevated rank; more valuable than a ducal coronet; more valuable than the brightest jewel that ever sparkled on the brow of royalty.

18. *Brethren, the grace,* &c.; see Note, Rom. xvi. 20.

W. G. BLACKIE AND CO., PRINTERS, VILLAFIELD, GLASGOW.